Focus on Environmental Geology

There is one ocean, with coves having many names;
a single sea of atmosphere with no coves at all;
a thin miracle of soil, alive and giving life;
a last planet; and there is no spare.

David R. Brower

Focus on Environmental Geology

*A Collection of Case Histories
and Readings from Original Sources*

Selected and Edited by
Ronald Tank

New York
OXFORD UNIVERSITY PRESS
London 1973 Toronto

Second printing, 1973

Copyright © 1973 by Oxford University Press, Inc.
Library of Congress Catalogue Card Number: 72-92300
Printed in the United States of America

Foreword

For all intents and purposes, the dam on environmental geology burst on January 28, 1969. That was the day of the Santa Barbara oil blowout, a catastrophe that threatened the coast of California and the Santa Barbara Channel with between one and three million barrels of "black tide" and awakened all Americans to the environmental crisis. In fact, from the perspective of one who has toiled in the area of environmental policy since the 1950's, there is no question that this was the *one* event that triggered the increased public concern and made possible the tougher environmental laws that were written on the federal and state levels in the last few years.

Since the Santa Barbara disaster, geologists have found themselves more and more immersed in issues of acute public concern. Controversies over the Trans Alaska Pipeline, the underground nuclear test at Amchitka, and the development of a sound energy policy have made geological debates more public—and more important—than ever before. Laymen increasingly depend on geologists to help them understand the physical environment and to solve the problems we have created through the abuse of our natural resources. Thus, it is not only important for the geologist to understand the environmental aspects of his science, it is also vital that he or she communicate that understanding to the rest of us.

One of the alarming discoveries of the last several years of increased environmental concern and legislation has been how *little* we really know about what we have done to the earth—about what can be repaired and what cannot, and about what we must stop doing before it is too late. I hope that this useful anthology will encourage more students of geology to participate in the formation of public policy so that we can correct our errors before they overtake us.

Washington, D.C.   Edmund S. Muskie
November 1972

Preface

Even though we are in the midst of an environmental crisis, there is only a small collection of books dealing with environmental geology. This is somewhat ironical, since geology is intimately concerned with the environment. Geology includes investigations of earth materials, earth processes, and the landforms that result from the interaction of natural materials and natural processes. Geological investigations also go beyond surficial phenomena to include subsurface phenomena. The geologist should therefore be well equipped to contribute much toward the solution of a variety of problems concerning the physical environment. He is experienced in evaluating the earth's capacity for providing water, mineral resources, building sites, and waste disposal sites. A knowledge of earth processes and earth structure has enhanced his appreciation of pristine environments, and the historical viewpoint inherent in much of geologic thought provides him with a unique perspective.

A higher standard of living, spectacular increases in population in recent decades, and the gradual shift of population to urban centers has led to more intensive use of the land and its resources. Under these conditions Man's relationship with his environment is brought into sharper focus, and environmental problems take on a greater significance. This has led to the development of a new branch of geology, which is commonly called environmental geology. It deals with the interrelationships of geologic processes, earth materials, and Man. It anticipates conflicts between Man and his environment, attempts to evaluate the earth's potential for providing Man with vital resources, and provides the necessary tools for planning a more harmonious relationship between Man and his environment. It relies heavily upon the traditional branches of geology but takes on a more intradisciplinary and interdisciplinary orientation. As environmental geology grows we are witnessing a broader and more obvious involvement of geology with Man's social concerns.

The readings included in this collection are intended to give the student a sense of contact with environmental geology. The readings are arranged under three major categories. The first category includes those aspects of earth processes and geologic settings that are hazardous to

Man. As Man intensifies his use of the land it is obvious that he must recognize geologic hazards and develop plans to minimize their impact. The second category of readings deals with mineral resources—prospects for the future and the impact of mineral exploitation on the environment. This is a highly controversial subject, and the readings reflect opposing points of view. The third category deals with contemporary environmental problems peculiar to urbanization.

An anthology of readings has proven to be an asset in a variety of teaching situations. "Outside reading" has been a traditional supplement to the textbook and has occasionally been used in lieu of a textbook. This has certainly been true in the area of environmental studies. A major problem has been the fact that these readings are scattered in a wide variety of professional journals, trade journals, and geological survey reports. Even the larger libraries are finding it increasingly difficult to provide the student with all of the published literature.

The selection of a limited number of readings from the vast amount of material available was difficult. A number of general papers are included to introduce each topic, while more specific and technical papers are included to illustrate applications and case histories. Some background in geology would be helpful but most of the papers should be comprehensible, informative, and stimulating to a diverse audience. Some editing has been necessary, in view of the purpose of this book, but the editing has been accomplished without detracting from the style and goals of the original source.

Each section includes introductory comments that alert the reader to the general content of the articles and their relation to each other and to environmental geology. Original references are included with each article, and a supplementary reading list is included in each section. A glossary is provided for technical terms.

The field of environmental geology is undergoing rapid development and there are bound to be differences of opinion as to what should be included in an introduction to this field. Suggestions for changes in future editions of this anthology are invited. If this book is successful, the reader will come to appreciate the vital role of geology in a broad range of environmental concerns.

I wish to express my sincere appreciation to those students at Lawrence University who offered comments on the collection of readings included in a course in Environmental Geology. These comments were most helpful in selecting the readings which appear in this anthology. I also wish to thank the authors and publishers who have permitted the inclusion of their materials.

Contents

III   Urban Geology

Earthquake Damage, Anchorage, Alaska. Courtesy of U. S. Army.

I. Geologic Hazards and Hostile Environments

"More than ever before, local communities are seeking guidance concerning environmental hazards of all types that should be taken into account in planning for the use of land to be developed."

National Academy of Sciences

It seems appropriate to begin our analysis of the geological aspects of environmental problems by reviewing the impact of geologic processes on the environment and the activities of Man. These processes can be highly beneficial. They may, for example, produce valuable ore deposits, provide rich soil, and create spectacular scenery. The growth of economies and cultures can be directly related to many of these geologic processes. On the other hand, these same geologic processes can produce natural hazards or hostile environments that result in catastrophes. Given the highly sophisticated nature of modern technology, it would appear that Man could simply exploit the benefits and control the hazards, thereby exercising a high degree of control over his own destiny. Man's control of his own destiny is far from complete, however, because he has not understood or has frequently failed to make allowances for a variety of geologic hazards.

Part One deals with the hazards associated with six geologic agents. There are other potential geologic hazards, but the examples cited serve to illustrate the dynamic aspects of geologic agents and their impact on Man. Most of the problems associated with these hostile forces can be avoided or minimized by utilizing adequate geologic data.

Volcanism

All mountains, islands, and level lands have been raised up out of the bosom of the earth into the position they now occupy by the action of subterranean fires.

Lazzaro Moro

Volcanism is one of the most dynamic of all earth processes and one of the most terrifying hazards. Many volcanologists consider the prediction and control of volcanic activity the ultimate goal of their discipline. As magmas begin to rise toward the surface one can anticipate earth tremors, a swelling and tilting of the local topography, increases in ground temperatures, and local changes in the earth's magnetic field and in its electrical currents. All of these phenomena can be detected by sensitive instruments.

Forewarning of an eruption might therefore come from several sources, and one must keep in mind that there are significant differences among volcanoes and their patterns of eruption. For nine days, increasing numbers of earthquakes were felt near the town of San Juan de Parangaricutiro in Mexico. On the tenth day the volcano El Parícutin was born. The people in the vicinity of Taal Volcano in the Philippines received a much more subtle warning. A gradual increase in the water temperature of a crater lake was the only indication of the impending eruption. The events associated with the eruption of these volcanoes are vividly described in Readings 1 and 2. Although both volcanoes are part of the Circum-Pacific Belt of volcanoes they are quite different in their style of eruption and one must be alert to these differences when engaged in forecasting activities.

The Taal Volcano was inactive for

Photo on page 3. Parícutin, Feb. 20, 1948 (5 years old). View from upper Casita. Only one "island" is left of pre-lava topography between Casita and cone. Courtesy of U. S. Geological Survey.

fifty-four years and then suddenly erupted and killed scores of people. Parícutin lies within a region in which no volcanic activity had been known for two centuries; yet within a period of ten weeks a volcanic cone over 1100 feet high was constructed. These and other examples should alert us to the hazards represented by "extinct" volcanoes and the entire Circum-Pacific Belt.

In Reading 3 Dwight Crandell and Howard Waldron warn us of the hazards in the Cascade Range. Their concern is based on the past behavior of the volcanoes in this region as interpreted from postglacial strata. Their approach illustrates how one must use stratigraphic data in those instances in which the length of historical time is not sufficient to reveal the pattern of activity in dormant volcanoes. Man often complicates natural hazards through his activities, and nature, by presenting multiple hazards, frequently offers additional problems. Man's role is evident in the Cascade Range, where he has constructed numerous reservoirs and settled in valleys and lowlands well within the range of floods, mudflows, lava flows, and ash falls. It is obviously imperative to monitor the volcanoes of the Cascade Range, to recognize phenomena which might warn of an impending disaster, and to plan future developments so as to minimize the potential danger. (One cannot help wondering how many people in this area are aware of the hazardous setting and what preparations have been made to cope with a potential eruption.)

Although Man has the option to migrate to a less hazardous environment, he frequently chooses to remain in a hostile setting. Historically, there has been a tendency to view a catastrophe, such as a volcanic eruption, as the act of a vengeful god and with resignation to a fate that is beyond comprehension and control. Even with the vast amount of scientific information available today, Man's reaction to catastrophe and prediction of catastrophe frequently differs very little from that of his ancestors. Vesuvius has been intermittently active since A.D. 79, and, although thousands of people have been victims of this activity, nearby Naples today is a thriving city of 1.25 million people. The 1911 eruption of the Taal Volcano obliterated most life on the island and caused extensive property damage. It was the twenty-sixth explosive eruption since 1572, but it did not discourage resettlement. Although it is usually difficult to change human settlement patterns, steps can be taken to reduce the possible tragic consequences. Arnold Mason and Helen Foster describe some techniques for diverting lava streams from inhabited areas in Reading 4.

1   The Mexican Volcano Parícutin*
Dr. Parker D. Trask

The new volcano in Mexico, El Parícutin (pronounced Pah-*ree*-koo-teen) is a unique geological phenomenon; for, before our very eyes, it has sprung into existence and has grown to a very respectable height of 1,500 feet, all within a period of 8 months. It lies within a region in which no previous volcanic activity has been known within the memory of man, though in 1759 the

* Address presented before the Geologic Section of the New York Academy of Sciences in New York, October 4, 1943. Published by permission of The Director, Geological Survey, U. S. Department of the Interior.

Trask, P. D., 1943, "The Mexican Volcano Parícutin," *Science*, vol. 98, n. 2554, pp. 501–5. Reprinted with light editing by permission of the American Association for the Advancement of Science. Copyright 1943 by the A.A.A.S.
The late Dr. Trask was on the staff of the United States Geological Survey when he made his observations of El Parícutin.

volcano El Jorullo, some 50 miles to the southeast, likewise suddenly was born, grew to a height of more than 1,000 feet within 5 months, and then quieted down, never more to erupt violently. Will Parícutin do likewise? That remains to be seen, for at present it is still going strong.

For the first time in their lives geologists have been able to observe in a single volcano all stages of its history. Parícutin exhibits many of the features of other volcanoes; but other volcanoes have been encountered by geologists after they have been in existence for some time, and their early history is unknown. The early history of Parícutin therefore fills important gaps in our understanding of volcanism.

To me the most outstanding aspect of this volcano is the incredible rapidity with which it grew. Within one week it was 550 feet high and within 10 weeks it was 1,100 feet in altitude.

Up to this time, all the material in its cone had come from fragments that had been blown into the air from the volcano. No lava came from the cone until nearly four months after the eruption started; and then, contrary to some popular reports, it did not flow over the lip of the crater. Instead, it broke through the sides of the cone, undermining the overlying fragmental material. Lava appeared within two days of the first explosion, but it issued quietly from a fissure about 1,000 feet north of the explosive vent.

Geologists have been observing Parícutin practically from its inception. Dr. Ezéquiel Ordoñez, the grand old man of Mexican geology, despite some eight decades of age, reached the volcano, together with some associates from the Instituto Geológico de Mexico, within two days of its birth; and he has actively been watching its development ever since. Senor Téodor Flores, director of the Instituto Geológico, has devoted all available facilities of his institution to the study of Parícutin, and the passionate interest he has shown in this volcano would gladden the heart of any scientist.

Dr. William F. Foshag, of the U. S. National Museum, in charge of the war-minerals work of the U. S. Geological Survey in Mexico, has been making a systematic study of Parícutin, and I am indebted to him for practically all statements in this paper not based on my own observations. In addition, many other geologists have visited the volcano. Therefore eventually a rather complete record of its history will be available. I saw Parícutin three times: first, a week after its birth; a second time when it was nearly three months old; and once again, a month later, when I flew over it in an airplane during one of the stages when lava was pouring from the cone.

Parícutin is located in the state of Michoacan, 200 miles in airline due west of Mexico City in the Sierra Madre Occidental, which forms the west boundary of the high plateau that occupies the central part of Mexico. The volcano is situated in an area of forested hills and cultivated lowlands, and the base of the cone lies about 7,500 feet above sea level.

Parícutin is located in a region of volcanic rocks consisting of essentially the same andesitic basalt as its own lava. Several hundred volcanic cones lie within a radius of 75 miles of the volcano. These are of all ages; some are so fresh that they can hardly be more than a few hundred or a few thousand years old; others are so dissected by erosion that they must be many tens of thousands of years in age. Most of them are cinder cones— that is, cones composed of debris blown from a vent in the ground; others are composite cones consisting of both lava and fragmental material. They range in height mainly from 200 to 800 feet. The highest rises some 4,000 feet above the surrounding country. The soil is rich and is derived from volcanic ash and interbedded lava. Most of the cones are conical and have small craters, but a few consist of rings of fragmental material, 200 feet or less in height and some hundreds of feet in diameter. One such abortive cone is situated about one mile northwest of Parícutin; another lies some miles to the east. From the air this latter cone seems to be some 3,000 feet in diameter and less than 200 feet in height. It contains within it, but somewhat off center, a similar ring-like ridge about 1,500 feet in diameter.

The first intimation that something was about to happen was an account in the newspapers about February 12, 1943, that 25 to 30 earthquakes had been felt the previous day near the town of San Juan de Parangaricútiro. Each day thereafter increasingly more tremors were reported, and on February 19 some 300 earthquakes occurred. The next day the eruptions started.

Stories of the beginning of the volcano are legion, and as time goes on they probably will become more varied. One of the most colorful is that a farmer while plowing his field turned over a stone, whereupon lava gushed forth and, like the headless horseman in the Legend of Sleepy Hollow, raced down the furrows behind him as he fled. This story of course is fantastic; in the first place, no Mexican would plow a furrow down hill, and in the second place, the Parícutin lava was too viscous to flow rapidly.

The most reliable story is that a farmer, Dionisio Pulido, while plowing noticed a column of smoke about three inches in diameter spiralling upward from a small hole in the middle of the field. Thinking that he had inadvertently started a fire he went over to the smoke and put it out by placing a stone over the hole. He continued plowing and sometime later looked around and saw smoke emerging from the ground in greater force. He went forthwith to inform the Presidente of the town of San Juan, who sent a group to see what was happening. Upon arriving at the spot three hours later these people found a hole some 30 feet in depth from which dense clouds of dark smoke were issuing. About ten that night, February 20, the first explosion occurred, and since that time the volcano has been erupting steadily.

When I first visited the volcano, on February 28, a little over one week after its inception, the explosions were coming at fairly regular intervals of 4 seconds. At times two explosions would come in quick succession; at other times the interval between outbursts was 6 or 8 seconds. In general the explosions were of about equal force, though occasional loud outbursts occurred. One was strong enough to knock me off balance while walking some 3,000 feet from the crater.

The sound from the explosions seemed to originate within the crater at about the level of the ground, though occasional explosions took place in the ash cloud 500 feet above the top of the cone. Each explosion from the crater acted like a giant gun-burst. The material was ejected from the throat of the volcano in a cylindrical column to a height of 400 to 800 feet above the top of the volcano, and at this point, like water in hydraulic jump, suddenly formed dark expanding cumulus clouds of ash that billowed upward to a height of 6,000 to 8,000 feet above the ground, where steam would begin to condense. With increasing altitude the ash cloud became progressively whiter with water vapor until some 10,000 to 12,000 feet above the ground, where it was nearly pure white. The column of vapor continued upward to about 15,000 feet and was carried eastward in a horizontal cloud bank from which columns or large puffs of vapor curled upward for another 2,000 or 3,000 feet, like ostrich plumes sewed tandem on an ermine scarf.

At this time the material ejected from the crater was thrown upward at an angle deviating from the vertical by 10°, much as if it were coming from a sharply defined conduit. As a result of this inclined direction of outburst, more material fell on the west side of the cone than on the east, thus causing the top of the cone to be lopsided. In the course of four hours the angle of ejection changed gradually back to vertical and two hours later was deviating 5 degrees to the east, thus causing the east side of the cone to build up faster than the west side.

The column of ash ascended nearly vertically but was deflected slightly eastward by the wind. Trains of cinders, one-eighth to one-half inch in diameter, rained down from the ash clouds on the lee side of the cone. They were cool, light and very porous, and they sounded like sleet as they fell on one's hat. Few cinders were falling more than two miles from the volcano. At this distance the ground was just barely covered by them. Fine particles of ash were transported greater distances than cinders, and covered the country side in delicate films for as much as 15 miles away on the leeward side. The ash and cinders were 18 inches thick 500 feet from the edge of the cone, which was the closest to the volcano my courage permitted me to approach.

At this point the ground was pockmarked with pits three to five feet in diameter where large fragments or bombs had buried themselves in the ground. The average distance between bomb-pits at this point was about 20 feet. During some 30 minutes while I was standing there, two bombs fell within 300 feet. One bomb more than four feet in diameter landed 25 feet away. For awhile as it was coming down it looked as though it might make a direct hit, and the problem was which way to run, but eventually it veered slightly and the next moment it came down with a large whoosh and whistle, and buried itself. The top was about one foot beneath the surface of the ground. A piece broken from it was hot enough to light cigarettes. Another bomb two feet in diameter, landed 50 feet to the rear, breaking an oak limb eight inches in diameter, much as if it were a cleaver cutting a bone. This bomb buried itself three feet in the ground. It came down five feet from some girls, who immediately retired to a more discreet distance.

Most of the fragmental material ejected from the volcano in this stage of its history consisted of bombs, rather than of ash or cinders. With each explosion the bombs were blown 2,000 to 3,000 feet into the air. Most of them landed on the cone; the greatest distance at which I found a bomb was 3,500 feet from the center of the volcano. The bombs went so high that it took from 10 to 15 seconds for most of them to fall, after they had reached their greatest height. They were roughly spherical and ranged in size from a walnut to a big house. Most of them were between three and five feet in diameter. The largest I saw was a block 50 feet in diameter, which was blown 300 feet above the top of the crater; that is, 850 feet above the ground. Nearly all the bombs when they landed were so thoroughly solidified as not to change in shape, though many when they struck the sides of the cone, broke into pieces. A few were still liquid when they landed and splattered out like pancakes on the ground. Bombs of this type did not penetrate the earth for more than three inches. Others rotated slowly in the air, gradually thinning in the middle, and before they fell separated into two tear-shaped bodies. Some, after coming to rest on the cone, smoked for a considerable time, certainly for as long as 15 minutes. Most of the bombs consisted of highly vesicular basalt, but a very small proportion were composed of a light medium-grained granitic rock that looked like diorite. These granitic rocks were angular, and not vesicular. They evidently were blown from the conduit through which the lava was coming.

Most of the bombs landed upon the sides of the cone, ricocheting down the side until they came to rest. The sides of the cone were remarkably even and were at an angle of 33° with the horizontal. The volcano at this time was 550 feet high and 1,700 feet in diameter at the base. The diameter of the crater at the top of the cone was 250 feet, and the orifice from which the material was ejected seemingly was about 75 feet in diameter.

The volcano at night is a magnificent, never-to-be-forgotten sight. Nearly all the bombs that are blown from the crater are red hot, and they shower up like a gigantic Fourth-of-July flower-pot. The floral effect is complicated by the fact that four or five subsequent explosions have taken place before the bombs from any one explosion have all landed. Thus some bombs are going up, some are just arching over at their highest point, and others are falling. After the bombs strike the sides of the

cone they cascade down in great fiery arcs. Some come to rest on the sides; others roll to the bottom. The glow from the cone comes and goes, depending upon the number of bombs that fall and the interval between explosions. Big outbursts cover the whole volcano, and the cone progressively lightens up in an ever larger descending curtain of fiery red, as the fragments land progressively down the sides of the cone. Then, as the bombs cool, the red gradually darkens. Yet before the color finally vanishes another crop of bombs falls and the scene is repeated. Even though parts of the cone may fade into darkness before a succeeding increment of glowing bombs descends, a ring of red always remains around the edge of the cone where the rocks that roll completely down the sides come to rest.

A flow of lava first appeared in a plowed field about 1,000 feet north of the crater about two days after the birth of the volcano. In five days it had attained a length of 2,000 feet, a width of 600 feet and a thickness of 20 feet at the sides and front. It continued to grow for about 6 weeks until it was about 6,000 feet long, 3,000 feet wide and more than 100 feet high. The front and sides were steeply inclined; the top was nearly flat and consisted of blocks of congealed scraggly aa lava 3 to 15 feet in diameter.

At the time I saw the lava, five days after it first appeared, it was flowing westward down a gently sloping field at a rate of about three feet an hour in front and one foot an hour on the sides. Like a glacier the lava moved most rapidly in direction of greatest slope, and like a glacier it also developed pressure ridges as it flowed. It advanced by pushing large blocks of solidified lava, three to five feet in diameter, off the front and sides. These blocks fell down the edges of the flow, and in turn were covered by other blocks similarly spalled by the advancing lava. Gradually the molten rock inside the flow passed over the fallen blocks and incorporated them within itself, forming a volcanic flow breccia. At all times the surface of the lava was congealed, except for places from which blocks had broken off at the edges of the flow as the lava advanced. These freshly exposed places consisted of red, pasty, dense lava that solidified within a few minutes to hard rock.

Fumaroles came out of vents 6 inches to a foot in diameter and gave off dense clouds of white smoke, which, according to Foshag, is largely ammonium chloride. The ammonium chloride also condenses in a white powder around the orifices of the fumaroles, and in places a fringe of bright-orange iron chloride is also formed. Few poisonous gases seemingly are given off.

When I visited Parícutin the second time, about the middle of May, nearly three months after its birth, it was still erupting at about the same rate, but the explosions were less forceful and a much larger proportion of ash was coming out. The cone had doubled in height and the orifice from which the material was being ejected seemed to be about 150 feet in diameter. Ash was everywhere, and most of the trees within 5 miles of the volcano had been killed. The lava flow had stopped moving and was covered by 6 to 8 feet of ash. Even at Uruapan, 15 miles east of the volcano, the ash was 6 to 8 inches thick, and at San Juan, four miles to the west, it was 15 inches thick. A large part of this ash fell in one period of 36 hours early in April. Electrical discharges or lightning strokes were flashing at irregular intervals, sometimes as frequently as 30 an hour. These flashes were vertical in the cloud of ash, and generally started within a few hundred feet of the top of the cone. They ranged in length mainly from 500 to 1,500 feet, and produced sharp cracks but no loud thunder.

About four weeks after this visit, a phase of lava actively ensued. In the course of a week, 8 flows appeared, all from within the cone. Prior to this time, that is, for almost four months, no lava had come from the cone itself and there had been just the one flow. According to Foshag, each flow was preceded by a period of violent explosive activity, which terminated shortly before the lava came. While the lava was issuing from the volcano relatively few explosions took place. All these flows ruptured the sides of the cone, and those that came from the upper part of the volcano undermined the fragmental material above, leaving a large gap in the side of the cone. These gaps were rapidly filled by material blown from the crater after the lava ceased to move. One flow advanced in three days as far as the town of Parícutin, three miles to the west. When it approached Parícutin it was moving at a rate of about 100 feet an hour. Another flow on the east side of the cone spread out like a large fan at the base of the volcano. According to Foshag, this one went 1,500 feet in 15 minutes.

While one of these flows was in progress, I had the good fortune to fly over the volcano. At this time the crater was nearly full; lava extending to within 50 feet of the lip. The top of the lava in the crater was congealed, and was broken in large blocks. Ashes were issuing from a vent estimated to be 75 to 100 feet in diameter in the northwest part of the lava field within the crater, but relatively few explosions were seen. Lava was flowing from an opening on the east side of the cone. This vent was 50 to 75 feet in width and 200 to 300 feet in height. The upper limit was 100 to 150 feet beneath the lip of the crater. The lava coming through the opening was red hot, but it soon cooled and congealed while flowing down the sides of the volcano. The cone was intact above the point of escape of lava, but according to Foshag it subsequently was undermined by the flow.

At this time, June 19th, Parícutin was 1,200 feet in altitude. By late September it had reached a height of 1,500 feet. At that time it was still exploding at about the same rate as when it started, and was showing no signs of dying. In the meantime several other flows of lava had appeared, mostly from within the cone. Parícutin truly is now a full-fledged volcano.

2   The 1965 Eruption of Taal Volcano

James G. Moore, Kazuaki Nakamura, Arturo Alcaraz

From 28 to 30 September 1965 there occurred a moderately violent phreatomagmatic explosive eruption of Taal Volcano in southwest Luzon, Philippines, about 60 kilometers south of the city of Manila (Fig. 1). The eruption covered an area of approximately 60 square kilometers with a blanket of ash more than 25 centimeters thick. Present records of casualties show that

Moore, J. G., Nakamura, K., and Alcaraz, A., 1966, "The 1965 Eruption of Taal Volcano," *Science*, vol. 151, no. 3713, pp. 955–60. Lightly edited by permission of the senior author and reprinted by permission of the American Association for the Advancement of Science. Copyright 1966 by the A.A.A.S. Dr. Moore is on the staff of the U. S. Geological Survey, Menlo Park, California; Dr. Nakamura is affiliated with the Earthquake Research Institute, University of Tokyo, Japan; Dr. Alcaraz is a member of the Commission on Volcanology, Quezon City, Philippines.

51 bodies have been recovered and 138 persons are missing. The center of the eruption was on the southwest side of Volcano Island, an irregularly shaped island about 5 kilometers in diameter, in Lake Taal. Lake Taal is approximately 20 kilometers in diameter. Some authors consider it a caldera lake that occupies a depression formed by collapse of a former volcanic edifice of unknown height.[1]

Since the year 1572 there have been 26 explosive eruptions of Taal Volcano. All have occurred on, or very close to, Volcano Island. Before 1749 most of the eruptions took place on the northwest or southwest part of the island. The 12 eruptions that occurred from 1749 to 1911 were centered in the large crater in the middle of the island. The 1965 eruption is the first since 1749 to be located on the flanks of the island.

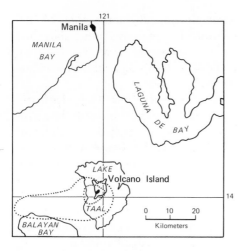

FIG. 1. Index map showing location of Lake Taal and Volcano Island, site of the recent eruption of Taal Volcano. Outer and inner dotted lines enclose, respectively, areas of ash thickness greater than 1 centimeter and greater than 50 centimeters.

The last previous eruption, that of 1911, was far more violent. It not only obliterated most life on the island but caused extensive damage to life and property on the shores of Lake Taal, except south and southeast of Volcano Island.[2] Approximately 1335 persons lost their lives.

This article is based on field investigations made by us during and after the eruption, until 13 October. Because of the limited time, and because of the logistics problems resulting from the eruption, the data gathered are incomplete, and this report must be considered preliminary.

Chronological Summary

Before the eruption there was no noticeable change in seismic or tilt activity. However, water temperature in the central crater lake on Volcano Is-

land showed a marked increase during early July 1965 from its 1964 average of 30° to 33° to 45°C on 21 July. By 25 September, when the last measurement prior to the eruption was made, the temperature had fallen to 43°C. On 5 October, after the eruption, the temperature was still 43°C.

Shortly after 0200 hours on 28 September 1965, residents of Volcano Island in Lake Taal were awakened by a rumbling, roaring, and hissing noise. People on the west-central coast of the island saw incandescent material shooting high in the air from the general vicinity of the newly formed cinder cone. This initial fountaining of basaltic spatter, cinders, and pumice was described as appearing like an enormous Roman candle. The color was distinctly red, not red-orange or orange. Some describe the fountaining as vertical, others describe it as directed toward the lake (toward the west) at perhaps 45 degrees from the vertical.

The observer with the Philippine Volcanological Commission, who was stationed at the seismograph station on the west-central coast of Volcano Island, was awakened a few minutes past 0200 hours. He felt earthquakes, heard rumbling noises, and immediately went to the seismograph, which had been recording earthquakes for several minutes. He noted that the double amplitude of the earthquakes was about 5 centimeters on the drums of the three-component Akashi seismometer system, which has a magnification of about 250. This smoked-paper record will probably not be seen again because the station was subsequently covered with 3 meters of ash. Other seismometers on the north shore of Lake Taal and in Manila show continuous strong seismic activity from 0220 to 0920 on 28 September.

The observer left the station about 0213, with 20 other persons from the nearby area, aboard the Commission's 14-foot (4.2-meter) boat, which has a normal capacity of six people. At the time they left, the explosive jetting of incandescent material continued, but as yet only very small, sand-sized particles were falling.

The observer returned by boat to the station at about 0325 but did not land. Explosions were continuing and ash was falling, but there were no noticeable air currents from the center of the activity, which was slightly more than 1 kilometer to the southeast. The observer was protected by a wet blanket, but he noticed that the falling ash was warm, not hot.

Between 0240 and 0330, a person on the northwest tip of Volcano Island observed a continuous display of lightning in the eruption cloud. The lightning and its accompanying thunder caused confusion in the reports regarding the presence of incandescent volcanic material and the time of the explosions.

The major explosive phase, apparently caused by lake water gaining access to the volcanic conduit, lasted from 0325 to about 0920 on 28 September. During this time enormous eruption clouds developed which were clearly visible from Manila, 60 kilometers to the north. These clouds reportedly rose to heights of 15 to 20 kilometers and were continually laced with lightning. At the base of the main cloud column a flat turbulent cloud spread out, radially transporting ejected material with hurricane velocity. Residents in the zone of ash fall on the west coast of Lake Taal reported that warm, wet ash fell very heavily slightly before daybreak, at about 0500. At about the same time, high waves swept that coast.

Aerial observation at 0830 showed many explosions occurring along the southwest-trending line of the present explosion crater, but the most intense activity was near the northeast end of the crater. The explosions migrated irregularly back and forth along this line. The present explosion crater formed during this major explosive phase; this crater, which is occupied by a new inlet of Lake Taal, was first noticed from the air at about 1100.

From 0920 on 28 September to 0600 on 30 September the explosion crater area was continually racked by explosions of somewhat reduced intensity. Explosion clouds were not nearly as high as those reported earlier and did not have their characteristic tiered shape.

From 0600 to 1550 on 30 September smaller explosions occurred during the waning period of activity. The new cinder cone within the explosion crater was apparently built during this phase. Small explosions every 5 to 10 minutes hurled up steam and black ejecta, much of which fell back into the vent area. After the last explosion, at 1550 on 30 September, steam puffs were observed above the new cinder cone, and these continued for several hours. About one-fourth of the surface of the new lake within this cinder cone was covered by a drifting, orange scum containing sulfur, arsenic, and iron, as determined by preliminary chemical analyses.

The temperature near the surface of the new lake within the cinder cone was 77°C on the morning of 3 October, and a thin steam cloud hovered over the lake. On 5 October the temperature was 76°C, and on 8 October it was 72°C. On 3 October the water temperature at the surface in the new inlet filling the explosion crater was 32° to 33°C, except within about 0.2 kilometer of the new cinder cone, where the temperature increased gradually to about 36°C.

During the evening of 9 October, the continual landsliding at the head of the new inlet caused disturbances that eroded the northeast side of the new cinder cone and breached it, forming a horseshoe-shaped rim. It is possible that a single large landslide from the cliff swept across the lake floor and struck the side of the cone. This is suggested by the fact that talus debris (similar to that occurring on the wall of the explosion crater, and foreign to the cinder cone) was noticed on the crest of the cinder cone adjacent to the new breach after the night of 9 October.

On 12 October, when a boat was taken inside the horseshoe-shaped cinder cone, the maximum water temperature was 46°C, the average water depth was 3 meters, and the maximum water depth was 11 meters. The temperature at the water surface of Lake Taal was 29°C on 12 October. Several areas of bubbling water were present within the new cinder cone and south and west of it, but the temperature was not higher in these areas than elsewhere, and the gas had no color or odor.

Explosion Crater

The explosion crater formed during the period 0325 to 0920 on 28 September is about 1.5 kilometers long and 0.3 kilometer wide. The crater is open to the lake on the southwest and is occupied by an arm of Lake Taal. Cliffs at the northeast end of the crater are about 150 meters high, and concentric fault scarps bounding landslide blocks are forming around the crater, particularly on its northwest side.

A preliminary estimate of the volume of the explosion crater above lake level is about 25 million cubic meters. Preliminary soundings show that the deepest part of the bay is about 50 meters deep. Hence the total volume of material removed from the explosion crater is probably about 40 million cubic meters.

The small breached cinder cone at the northeast end of the explosion crater is about 250 meters in diameter. The highest point on the rim of the cone is 18.5 meters above the level of Lake Taal.

Ejecta

Approximately 90 million cubic meters of ejecta were thrown out of the explosion crater and spread over Volcano Island, the bottom of Lake Taal, and the area to the west. Deposits thrown out by the volcanic explosions are of two major types: (i) juvenile magmatic material from depth, and (ii) shattered and pulverized old lava, ash, and lake sediments that filled the space now occupied by the explosion crater. Both types of ejecta were distributed in three ways: (i) by direct projection from explosion vent, (ii) by transport in horizontally directed dense, turbulent clouds laden with mud, steam, and coarse ejecta, and (iii) by fallout of fine material blasted to high elevations, blown by the winds, and carried to earth commonly by mud rains.

Apparently in the early stages of the eruption, magmatic material reached the surface and was ejected high in the air. The bottom 1 centimeter of the ash section at the old seismograph station (on the coast 1½ kilometers north of the new inlet) contains basaltic spatter up to 8 centimeters in diameter. Mixed through this ash section are layers of fresh pumice lapilli, apparently rounded by abrasion in the turbulent cloud.

Magmatic material was common also during the waning stages of activity. The new cone is made almost entirely of fresh, vesicular basaltic glass in the form of lapilli, ash, and volcanic bombs. The glassy, ellipsoidal bombs commonly have poorly developed bread-crust surface texture and some are more than 40 centimeters long. Some of the more vesicular blocks floated. The basalt is porphyritic, containing phenocrysts of plagioclase, augite, and olivine.

The shattered and pulverized old material thrown out of the explosion crater is intimately mixed with juvenile material, and the relative proportions of each are difficult to determine. Comparison of the volumes of the crater and of the ejecta suggests that the proportion of juvenile material is small, when the attendant decrease in specific gravity is considered.

Ash, lapilli, and blocks transported by horizontally moving eruption clouds compose the dominant part of the ejecta within the blast area shown in Fig. 2. Within 1 kilometer of the explosion crater, blocks up to 50 centimeters in diameter are common, and one block about 3 meters in diameter was noted 150 meters north of the explosion crater. At a distance of 2.5

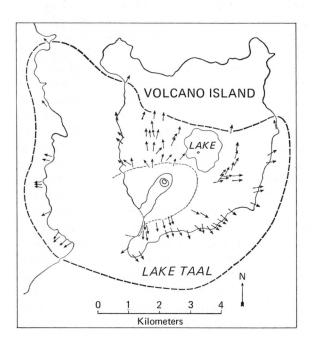

FIG. 2. Map showing the area affected by horizontally moving mud-laden eruptive clouds. (Arrows) Direction of horizontal blasts; (thick dashed line) outer limit of effect of directed blasts; (thin dashed line) outer limit of complete destruction of tree stumps;
new explosion crater occupied by the lake inlet and the new cinder cone.

kilometers from the crater the maximum diameter of the ejecta particles is about 1 centimeter.

Those blocks that landed on the surface produced typical impact craters, and buried craters or bomb sags are exposed in stream gullies. Much of this material is a chaotic mixture of fragments of all sizes, from silt-sized ash to blocks as much as 50 centimeters in diameter. The material commonly is crudely stratified, with dune-type bedding.

Within the area of blast effects, airfall material is dominant in the top and bottom of the section, and the explosively transported material occupies the middle. Outside the area of blast effects, air-fall material is the dominant ejecta. Much of the air-fall material is composed of accretionary lapilli in well-defined layers, generally with smaller and broken lapilli on the bottom of the bed and larger lapilli, as much as 10 millimeters in diameter, near the top. In some places the accretionary lapilli are as much as 20 millimeters in diameter. These lapilli were formed by accretion of fine ash to a wet nucleus as a result of the abundant moisture in the eruptive clouds. In one section 80 centimeters thick, on the west shore of Lake Taal, four distinct layers of accretionary lapilli are present. Between the lapilli layers are beds of fine ash, some of which contain layers of pumice or accidental fragments up to 3 or 4 millimeters in diameter.

Because of prevailing east and east-northeast winds, the zone of ash fall from the high eruption clouds extends for a great distance to the west. Ash more than 1 centimeter thick extends 33 kilometers to the west and only 6 kilometers to the east of the explosion crater (Fig. 1) and a deposit of fine volcanic ash was reported on Lubang Island 80 kilometers to the west.

Blast Effects

Effects of a series of tremendous blasts and their resultant horizontally moving eruptive clouds are evident within an area (Fig. 2) extending 2 to 6 kilometers from the explosion crater. In a ½- to 1-kilometer zone ringing the crater, all trees and stumps have been removed above the present level of new ejecta, which averages several meters in thickness. In the next zone, about ¼ kilometer wide, the trees remain but are strongly sandblasted and have little or no coating of mud. The sandblasting has abraded them to as little as half their former thickness, but the abrasion has been only on the crater side of the trees; although as much as 15 centimeters of wood has been removed from the crater side, the other side is usually still bark-covered. In the next zone all the trees show the effects of sandblasting and many have thick coatings of mud. The mud forms aerodynamic, parabolic coatings as much as 40 centimeters thick which point toward the crater. Generally when the mud coatings (now dry ash) are carefully sectioned they are seen to consist of several layers, each grading from coarse sand-size material closest to the tree to fine silt-size ash at the outer boundary. On several trees three well-defined blasts can be identified, but some trees have five or more distinct layers of ash. Many of the mud coatings show slight changes in azimuth of the blast from one layer to the next.

Outward from the crater toward the outer limit of the area of blast effects, the blast direction is recorded not only by the mud coatings but, successively, by stripping of the bark of trees, the breakage direction of stands of bamboo, tilting and deroofing of houses, stripping of palm tree fronds on the blast side and faint scarring of the bark of small bushes.

Cattle that were grazing inside the old crater survived the eruption. However, one large calf found there had been blinded and had had the hair sandblasted off the back of its ears and off its rump. After being blinded, the calf apparently faced away from the direction of the blasts.

In the entire area affected by the blast, there is no evidence of charring or burning. In the zone of mud plastering, it appears, the temperature of the debris-laden cloud was below 100°C, because the mud must have been mixed with water, not steam, to have been so sticky. The narrow inner zone of sandblasted trees not covered by mud may have been blasted by steam clouds slightly above 100°C.

In the inner half of the area of blast effects, giant ripple marks or sand dunes are common. They are oriented roughly at right angles to the direction of blast and have a wavelength of 3 to 15 meters and a height of about 1 meter. They can be clearly seen in section where gullies cut the ash, and they are present at depth in many horizons. They are steeper on the blast side and show evidence of scouring on that side. Migration of the crest away from the blast as the deposit was built up by deposition from each successive horizontal eruptive cloud.

Although trees in deep gullies and on the lee side of hills are less damaged by the blast effects than trees in more exposed sites, it is evident that the eruptive clouds followed the contours of the ground, passing up, over, and down the ridges. Scouring is evident even within the old central crater, which is surrounded by a cliff more than 100 meters high. The thickness of the ash-laden part of the horizontally moving eruptive cloud is not known, but mud is plastered on the blast side of the highest trees, 5 meters tall.

Other effects

Outside the zone of blast action, extensive damage was done to houses and vegetation by the heavy fall of ash. Where the ash blanket is thicker than about 10 centimeters the fronds of palm trees are broken down, and banana trees are damaged where the ash thickness is more than 5 centimeters.

The explosions within the crater area produced shock waves that generated water waves, which probably reached maximum height between Volcano Island and the west shore of Lake Taal. These waves capsized some of the boats filled with the fleeing residents of the island and accounted for many of the fatalities. The maximum height of the waves is not known, because evidence of wave height during the early, most violent phase of the eruption is now covered by layers of ash. However, on the west shore of Lake Taal, directly west of the mouth of the explosion crater, there is clear evidence that waves reached 4.7 meters above lake level and swept inshore as much as 80 meters. The debris left by these waves is on top of the air-fall ash, hence the waves must have occurred very late in the eruption. Undoubtedly much larger waves swept that coast earlier.

A streamflow gage 1.5 kilometers downstream from the outlet of Lake Taal shows an increase of flow from an average of 20,500 liters per second for several days before the eruption to a maximum of 28,400 liters per second on 28 September, followed by decreases to 23,800 liters per second on 29 September, and 22,800 liters per second on 30 September. Such an increase is probably due to excessive wave action and to seiches produced by the explosion shock waves, as well as to displacement of water by the ash fall and to the inordinately heavy rain that accompanied the eruption.

Immediately after the eruption, extensive slumping occurred at the site of stream deltas on the south shore of Volcano Island and the west shore of Lake Taal. The slumping, which produced notches up to several hundred meters wide in the previous shoreline, generally occurred where the ash thickness was greater than 1 meter. Such downslope slumping was presumably the result of rapid overloading of the deltaic deposits below lake level by swollen, ash-laden streams.

Summary

A moderately violent phreatomagmatic explosive eruption of Taal Volcano, in the Philippines, occurred from 28 to 30 September 1965. The main phreatic explosions, which were preceded by ejection of basaltic spatter, opened a new crater 1.5 kilometers long and 0.3 kilometer wide on the southwest side of Volcano Island in Lake Taal. The eruption covered an area of about 60 square kilometers with a blanket of ash more than 25 centimeters thick and killed approximately 190 persons.

The clouds that formed during the explosive eruption rose to heights of 15 to 20 kilometers and deposited fine ash as far as 80 kilometers west of the vent. At the base of the main explosion column, flat, turbulent clouds spread radially, with hurricane velocity, transporting ash, mud, lapilli, and blocks. The horizontally moving, debris-laden clouds sandblasted trees, coated the blast side of trees and houses with mud, and deposited coarse ejecta with dune-type bedding in a zone roughly 4 kilometers in all directions from the explosion crater.

Notes

[1] M. N. Van Padang, *Catalogue of the Active Volcanoes of the World: Part II, Philippine Islands and Cochin China* (International Volcanology Society, Naples, 1953), p. 34.

[2] W. E. Pratt, *Philippine J. Sci.* **6**, 63 (1911); D. C. Worcester, *Nat. Geograph. Mag.* **23**, 313 (1912).

3   Volcanic Hazards in the Cascade Range*

Dwight R. Crandell and Howard H. Waldron

Newspapers recently carried the story that the Vatican had just demoted 90 saints, including St. Januarius. You may recall that his blood is kept in vials in a cathedral in Naples and that it liquifies several times each year. One of these times is on December 16, which is the anniversary of the 1631 eruption of Mount Vesuvius. According to the newspaper article, St. Januarius has stopped the lava flows from Mount Vesuvius many times, and has repeatedly saved the Neapolitans from countless other catastrophes. Perhaps we should invoke the spirit of St. Januarius, as we discuss geologic hazards, and perhaps he should also be our patron saint.

We are pleased to report that the human casualty rate has been very low, probably nil, from volcanic eruptions in the Cascade Range (Fig. 1) within historic time. There is a report of an Indian who burned his leg against a lava flow from Mount St. Helens in 1844, and in 1914 a man who stood too close to the erupting crater of Lassen Peak was rather badly injured by

* Publication authorized by the Director, U. S. Geological Survey.

Crandell, D. R. and Waldron, H. H., 1969, "Volcanic Hazards in the Cascade Range," in *Geologic Hazards and Public Problems*, *Conf. Proceedings*, R. Olson and M. Wallace, eds., U. S. Govt. Printing Office, pp. 5–18. Lightly edited by permission of the senior author.
D. Crandell and H. Waldron are research geologists on the staff of the United States Geological Survey in Denver, Colorado.

a rock that flew out of the crater. But even he is still alive today.

So, we really cannot evaluate the dimension of volcanic hazards in the Cascade Range by the past casualty rate or by the amount of past property damage, as we can with some other geologic hazards. I think we will all agree that it's our good fortune to have volcanoes that are pretty tame. At least they are today!

This very lack of repeated eruptions in the Cascade Range is a problem in itself, for it is very difficult to predict the behavior of a volcano that has never been observed to erupt. For example, Arenal volcano in Costa Rica had been dormant for hundreds of years; in fact, it was thought to be extinct. But it erupted violently on July 29, 1968 with very little warning and killed more than 70 people in nearby villages. A year ago, if someone had asked which Costa Rican volcano might erupt next, Arenal probably would not have even been on the list; and, naturally, nothing was known about what kind of eruption could be expected.

Likewise, we don't know which of the Cascade volcanoes will be the next to erupt, but by means of a hazards evaluation study at a given volcano, we can predict some of the effects if that volcano *were* to erupt. We do this by finding the deposits of past eruptions, by dating these deposits, and by inferring what they mean in terms of kind, extent, and frequency of volcanic activity. We then assume that future eruptions most likely will follow the same pattern.

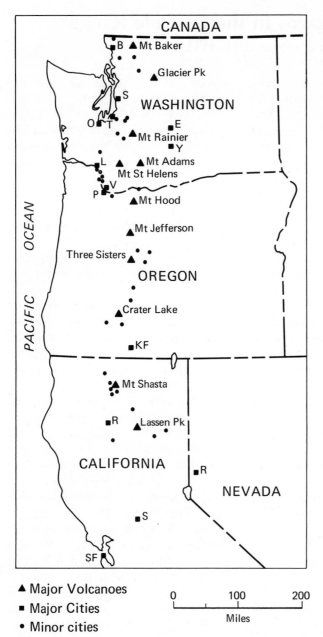

FIG. 1. Index map of Cascade Range, showing locations of major volcanoes, and major and minor cities in their vicinity.

CANADA

B ▲ Mt Baker

▲ Glacier Pk

S

WASHINGTON

O T ■ E

▲ Mt Rainier

■ Y

L ▲ ▲ Mt Adams

Mt St Helens

P ■ V

▲ Mt Hood

▲ Mt Jefferson

Three Sisters ▲

OREGON

▲ Crater Lake

■ KF

▲ Mt Shasta

■ R ▲ Lassen Pk

CALIFORNIA

■ R

NEVADA

■ S

SF ■

PACIFIC OCEAN

▲ Major Volcanoes
■ Major Cities
• Minor cities

0   100   200

Miles

Before going any farther, however, we need to go into a little background on volcanoes so that you'll understand some of the terminology we will use later on. The best way to start is by mentioning some of the kinds of eruptions, or other processes caused by volcanism, that might be dangerous. These are lava flows, eruptions of volcanic ash, eruptions of hot avalanches of volcanic ash and rock debris, and the formation of mudflows and floods due to an eruption. There are other volcanic processes, but we will limit our discussion to these four types.

Lava flows are the streams of molten rock that come from volcanoes. They are confined chiefly to valleys and other low areas. They may move at greatly different speeds, but most are so slow that people can easily get out of their way as they approach. The indirect effects of lava flows might be very dangerous. In fact, they may be much more dangerous than the direct effects. For example, lava flows might start forest fires or if the lava moves out onto snow and ice, it might cause very rapid melting and produce floods or mudflows.

In a *volcanic ash eruption*, great quantities of rock fragments and dust are blown high into the air by repeated explosions. And then the wind takes over. The fragments may be solid rock or pumice. Pumice is a volcanic rock full of bubbles and so light in weight that it can be transported great distances by wind for hundreds, even thousands, of miles.

Hot avalanches of ash and rock debris are a little harder to visualize. Sometimes a large volume of hot, dry fragments is blown from a crater by a volcanic explosion. The mass then avalanches down the side of the volcano, trapping air and heating it and becoming very mobile; gaining speed, it may move several miles beyond the base of the volcano. The rock fragments themselves may be giving off hot gas, which cushions and lubricates the debris so it acts just like a flow of fluid material. Such avalanches may move at speeds of 35 to more than 70

miles an hour. The temperature in the avalanche, and in the cloud of smoke and dust that rises above and accompanies it, may be hundreds of degrees centigrade, so that everything in its path is incinerated. The initial eruption of Arenal volcano in Costa Rica in July, 1968 produced one of these hot avalanches and clouds, which swept down into nearby villages. Two days later, another hot avalanche and cloud erupted just as a rescue party was moving in jeeps into the devastated area, and eight more people were killed.

The last process we'll consider is that of *floods and mudflows*. You all know what a flood is. A mudflow is simply a flood of wet mud and rock debris—it looks very much like wet concrete carrying boulders. Mudflows very commonly form on the sides of active volcanoes, chiefly because these steep slopes are frequently mantled with loose rock debris that is very unstable. When this material becomes mixed with water from rain or melting snow, or from the spillover of a crater lake, it may form a mudflow which will move many miles downstream at speeds of several tens of miles an hour.

Now, which of these volcanic events might present the greatest danger to the most people, if one of the Cascade volcanoes were to erupt? We believe that ash eruptions and mudflows are the two greatest hazards.

The degree of hazard from an ash eruption depends on the amount of material blown out, the rate and duration of the eruption, the strength and direction of the winds blowing at the time of the eruption, and also the distance people are from the volcano. On May 22, 1915, the most violent of a long series of eruptions of Lassen Peak in northern California sent a column of volcanic ash at least six miles into the air. Ash was deposited from this cloud as it drifted eastward into Nevada, and some fell as far east as Winnemucca, 100 miles downwind. But, fortunately it was a very brief eruption and only a relatively small amount of material was blown out.

Figure 2 shows an area covered by a pumice eruption at Crater Lake about 7,000 years ago. This was a catastrophic eruption. The pumice blanketed an area of several hundreds of thousands of square miles in the northwestern United States. The patterned area was covered by six inches or more of pumice, and the outer line shows the total area of the ash fall. The 6-inch fallout area has been superimposed on other volcanoes to give an idea of the area that might be most seriously affected if a similar type and scale of eruption should occur at any of them.

What are the actual hazards from volcanic ash? Breathing ash is like breathing in a duststorm; it's hard on the respiratory system as well as the eyes. Close to the volcano there may be also toxic fumes such as sulphur dioxide. Ash will destroy vegetation, including crops. It will reduce visibility for both highway and air travel, and aircraft could be damaged by flying through clouds of volcanic ash. Surface water supplies will be contaminated, both by sediment and by a temporary increase in acidity, although this acidity may go away within a few hours after the ash eruption stops. Roofs may be overloaded. A 1-inch ash fall, for example, will load a roof by about an additional ten pounds per square foot. This means perhaps a 7-ton load on a roof with a surface area of 1,500 square feet. Rainfall will increase the load, because the rain will soak into and saturate the ash. If rainfall is heavy, ash might be carried by running water into gutters, storm drains, and sewers, and it could also block streets; it may also run as mudflows if enough of the ash becomes saturated.

The U. S. Geological Survey Bulletin 1028-N, by Ray E. Wilcox, discusses the effects of volcanic ash falls; it will be a very useful reference when we have the next volcanic ash eruption here in the United States.

The other volcanic event of high potential hazard is that of mudflows and floods. The volcanoes in the Cascade Range are especially dangerous in this respect because most have a perennial snow cover, which can be melted readily by a lava flow or by a hot avalanche or by some other volcanic process. Mudflows are especially dangerous because they move at very high speeds. Generally speaking, they can move faster than water floods, and they can travel tens of miles down valley floors if they have enough volume.

Consider the unfortunate Indian who was standing at the townsite of Enumclaw in western Washington (Fig. 3) about 5,000 years ago. He was probably looking in wonder at the clouds of steam and ash rising from mighty Tahoma, the mountain he called God, and which we call Mount Rainier. Although he probably felt safe at his distance of 25 airline miles from the volcano, he didn't realize that a wall of mud hundreds of feet deep was rushing down the White River valley to-

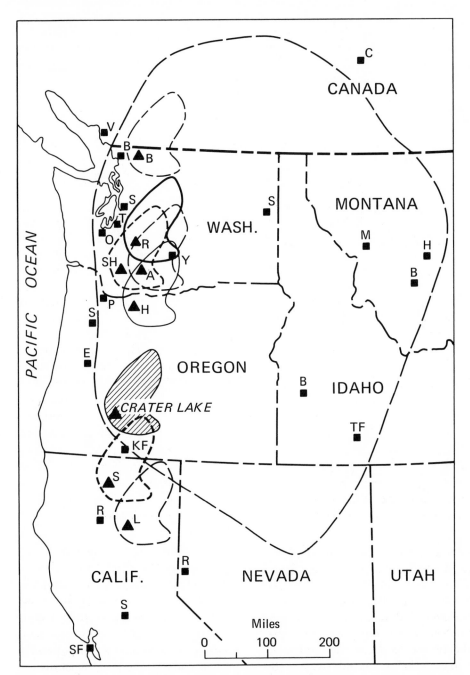

FIG. 2. Map of Cascade Range, showing area covered by pumice eruption at site of Crater Lake about 7,000 years ago. The outer line shows maximum limits of ash fall; inner line (pattern) shows area covered by 6 inches or more of pumice. The same 6-inch thickness line is shown superimposed on the other major volcanoes of the range. Data from reports by Howel Williams and H. A. Powers and R. E. Wilcox.

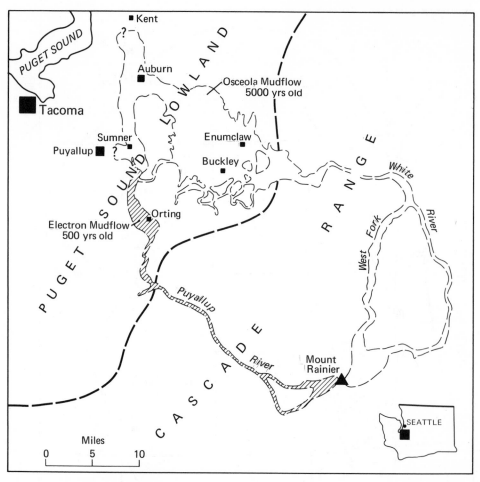

FIG. 3. Map of Mount Rainier and vicinity, showing extent of the Osceola Mudflow in the White River valley and the Electron Mudflow (pattern) in the Puyallup River Valley.

ward him. When he first saw the mudflow, it was still a mile away, but it was moving about 20 miles an hour.

What do you suppose the reaction would be today of the present citizens of Enumclaw in a similar circumstance? Probably the same as the Indian's—run like hell! But the only way to get out of the way of a mudflow as large as this would be by a car headed in the right direction. The right direction would be toward high ground, and this

is not necessarily the direction that highways go.

We wish to point out an important difference between mudflows and floods. Floods are generally preceded by heavy rain and by gradually rising rivers. People normally can get out of the way, unless the flood is caused by a dam failure or some other sudden event. When the flood recedes, the water drains away and the danger is over, whereas, in the case of a mudflow, the mud remains forever. For example, the mudflow beneath the townsite of Enumclaw (Fig. 3) is still there, tens of feet deep. The town of Herculaneum, in Italy, five miles from the foot of Vesuvius, now lies beneath a volcanic mudflow, or rather a succession of three volcanic mudflows that total 80 feet deep, formed during the eruptions of 79 AD.

Volcanic mudflows, especially the really big ones, can occur with little or no warning. Most are likely to start during an eruption, when the volcano is hidden by clouds of smoke, steam, and ash. The upper parts of valleys heading on volcanoes, therefore, should be watched very carefully during an eruption in order to take advantage of what little warning there might be, before a mudflow comes down into a populated area.

Now, we wish to appraise briefly four potentially dangerous volcanoes in the Cascade Range, which are, from north to south (Fig. 1), Mount Baker, Mount Rainier, Mount St. Helens, and Mount Shasta. These are not necessarily the only volcanoes that are potentially dangerous, or even the ones most likely to erupt next, but possibly they would threaten the largest number of people if they did erupt violently.

Very little is known about the frequency of volcanic activity at Mount Baker within the last 10,000 years, but we do know that it has erupted lava flows and volcanic ash several times. Minor eruptions of smoke or ash were reported by observers in 1843, several times between 1853 and 1859, and again in 1870. Unfortunately we know so little about Baker's behavior that we can't yet realistically assess the potential hazards there. We do suggest,

however, that the chief hazard might be related to a pair of reservoirs at the southeast base of the volcano. These reservoirs are Lake Shannon and Baker Lake, which have a combined length of 18 miles. Downstream from these hydroelectric reservoirs are communities on the floor of the Skagit River valley that have more than 15,000 inhabitants. A large flood or mudflow down the east side of Mount Baker seemingly would threaten the lakes and the downstream communities as well. If a mudflow or flood raised the reservoir level very rapidly, faster than the spillways could accommodate the overflow, spillover across the dam itself could occur, with disastrous results.

Going south, we come to Mount Rainier. We know quite a lot about the past behavior of this volcano. Our studies there are described in Geological Survey Bulletin 1238, entitled Volcanic Hazards at Mount Rainier, Washington. These studies show that within the last 10,000 years there have been at least 55 large mudflows, several hot avalanches of rock debris, at least one period of lava flows, and at least 12 eruptions of volcanic ash. The last major eruption was about 2,000 years ago; it involved an eruption of lava and of pumice, and there were also several large mudflows. This extensive eruptive record doesn't necessarily mean that Rainier has been more active than Baker, but only that we have a lot more information about it. Within historic time, many eruptions on a minor scale were recorded in the 1800's, but only one produced pumice. This eruption occurred between about 1820 and 1855—we can't date it any more closely than that. The last reported eruption of steam and smoke was in 1894.

If we assume that Rainier will continue to behave as it has during the last 10,000 years, the principal hazard will be from mudflows down valley floors. These might consist of a few million cubic yards of mud and be confined to the valley floors very close to the volcano, but there is also a possibility of a huge mudflow, like the Osceola, which covered the present site of Enumclaw. This would be a major catastrophe, comparable to or worse than the great 1902 eruption of Mount Pelée in the West Indies, which killed nearly 30,000 people. The most hazardous areas in the region around Mount Rainier, with respect to mudflows, are the low areas—the valley floors. Just how far down valley the hazard may extend depends on the size or volume of future mudflows.

To give you some idea of volume, we'll consider a few mudflows that have occurred in the past. One mudflow, which occurred about 6,000 years ago, contained about 800,000,000 cubic yards of material; it flowed down the White River valley for about 30 miles. Eight hundred million cubic yards is the equivalent of a square mile piled to a depth of 775 feet. The Osceola Mudflow (Fig. 3) occurred about 5,000 years ago. It contained a little more than 2½ billion cubic yards, that is, just a little more than half a cubic mile of material. The Osceola Mudflow covered an area of about 125 square miles in the Puget Sound Lowland in an area where at least 30,000 people now live. The Electron Mudflow (Fig. 3) occurred only about 500 years ago. It involved a little more than 200 million cubic yards and reached about 35 miles from

the volcano; between 2,000 and 3,000 people live on the surface of this mudflow today.

Two of the valleys that head on Mount Rainier are now blocked by dams. The White River valley, northwest of the volcano, is blocked by Mud Mountain Dam, built by the Corps of Engineers for flood control. It is generally kept empty and has a capacity of about 170 million cubic yards. In the Nisqually River valley, 20 miles west of Mount Rainier, Alder Dam impounds a hydroelectric reservoir with a capacity of about 375 million cubic yards, or 332,000 acre feet. Either dam or reservoir could contain most or all of a mudflow like the Electron, if the reservoir were empty, but neither would have much effect on a mudflow as large as the Osceola.

Fifty miles southwest of Mount Rainier is Mount St. Helens. This is a relatively young volcano which may have been formed entirely within the last 10,000 years. About 2,000 years ago a series of big mudflows, lava flows, and hot avalanches moved south from the volcano into the Lewis River valley. Mudflows also went down the Toutle River valley, west of the volcano, probably at least as far as Longview and Kelso. Mount St. Helens erupted frequently during the 1800's; many of these eruptions were actually observed in the period 1843 to 1857. Jack H. Hyde, of Tacoma Community College and the U. S. Geological Survey, recently has started a hazard-evaluation study of Mount St. Helens.

Our main cause for concern with Mount St. Helens is the presence of three large lakes—hydroelectric reservoirs—which occupy 25 linear miles of the Lewis River valley. Imagine the effect if an 800 million cubic yard mudflow were to move into the upper reservoir in a period of a few hours. This could set up a chain reaction that could cause half a million acre feet of water to spill over each successive dam. Downstream, below the mouth of the Lewis, more than 40,000 people live on the flood plain of the Columbia River. The city of Portland is just 20 miles upstream from the mouth of the Lewis River and essentially at tidewater. We feel that Mount St. Helens, therefore, is a possible threat to Portland and many smaller communities, especially if the volcano should erupt and send a very large mudflow, avalanche, or lava flow into these reservoirs.

Mount St. Helens seems to have been the biggest pumice producer of the Washington volcanoes. The biggest eruptions occurred about 3,500 and about 450 years ago. The one 3,500 years ago left two feet of pumice at a distance of 50 miles from the volcano, and the winds spread some of it northward into Canada. The eruption 450 years ago also deposited pumice to the north-northeast, but it was only about five inches thick at a distance of about 50 miles. During both of these eruptions winds were blowing toward the north-northeast, and the sites of the present large towns were missed by the pumice falls. This is a coincidence that wouldn't be counted on in any future eruption.

The Geological Survey is now working on the volcanic hazards at Lassen Peak in Lassen Volcanic National Park. The hazards there seem to be chiefly a local problem, for we see very little effect of the eruptions of Lassen beyond the limits of the park or a zone very close to the park. So, if future

eruptions follow the same pattern, we anticipate that their effects will also be limited in extent.

The Geological Survey also plans to start an appraisal of the volcanic hazards of Mount Shasta very soon. We know very little about the nature or frequency of volcanism at Shasta within the last 10,000 years, although we know there have been lava flows and ash eruptions within that period of time, and a hot avalanche may have extended down into the townsites of Weed and Mount Shasta. Much of the volcano is bordered by aprons of mudflow deposits, but we do not know how extensive they are. Although it is premature to predict future hazards from Mount Shasta, we're concerned with the possibility that a very large mudflow might extend 35 to 40 miles down the Sacramento River valley to Lake Shasta. Lake Shasta covers an area that is smaller than that now covered by the Osceola Mudflow. We can only speculate about the effects of an extremely large volcanic mudflow moving into Lake Shasta and causing the lake to spill over.

In this brief discussion of some typical volcanoes in the Cascade Range, you may have noticed a possible hazard common to each—large reservoirs within the reach of volcanic mudflows. We have read the geologists' reports on some of the damsites. The fact that there was a volcano upstream was recognized and was considered, but it was also noted that volcanic activity had been on a minor scale in historic time, and the geologists concluded that there seemed to be little or no cause for concern. Perhaps not, but we wish to suggest that the length of historic time in the case of Cascade volcanoes may not be long enough a sample. In order to reach a meaningful conclusion, one must sample at least the last few thousand years of a volcano's history to decide whether it does or does not constitute a hazard to a reservoir.

We will conclude by mentioning a few problems and making a few suggestions. One problem when the next eruption occurs will be that of moving people out of the danger zones. People who are camping near the volcano can usually leave easily, unless roads and bridges are destroyed by mudflows and floods. We might note in passing that very few bridges near any of these volcanoes could accommodate a very large flood, and none of them could accommodate a catastrophic mudflow.

If an eruption occurred without any warning, and there were casualties, it might be dangerous to rush in with a massive rescue operation, because an even bigger eruption might follow. We suggest that the initial rescue operations be kept to an absolute minimum —just large enough for the immediate job.

Water supplies downwind are very vulnerable from an ash eruption. People should be advised to store water as soon as possible, and, if they don't leave the area, to remain indoors during falls of ash.

There is the danger of forest fires caused by volcanism. They might be much more difficult to fight during an eruption because of the reduced visibility, and roads might be impassable.

We believe that some volcanoes should be monitored, especially those that are potentially dangerous—monitored with seismographs, tiltmeters, and by periodic aerial infrared sensing to detect temperature changes on the volcanoes.

We suggest that reservoir drawdown should be considered immediately if an eruption should start at an upstream volcano. We take some satisfaction in noting that the presence of a dam is not all bad. The reservoir could accommodate a flood, if drawdown had been accomplished in time, and a dam could also impound a mudflow permanently even thought this might not have been the purpose for which the dam was constructed. But this is one way in which a mudflow could be kept out of a populated area. It is better to trap the mudflow than to chance overtopping, or perhaps destroying, the dam.

We also wish to emphasize that comprehensive studies are desirable before other dams are built in the Cascade Range—studies in which volcanic hazards are appraised in terms of the life-time expectancy for the reservoir.

Finally, when an eruption does occur, and we think it is inevitable, we hope that the news media will work with geologists and the Office of Emergency Preparedness in informing the public of what could occur and what the hazards might be, so that if people refuse to leave a potential danger zone, at least they will know enough to leave their cars parked headed in the right direction.

4 Diversion of Lava Flows at O Shima, Japan*

Arnold C. Mason and Helen L. Foster

Introduction

Mihara Yama is the active central cone of O Shima Volcano on O Shima, an island 110 kilometers south-southwest of Tokyo, Japan. It has been active repeatedly in historic times, and major eruptions occurred in 1950 and 1951. During 1951 a flow reached a concrete and stone building and was partly blocked by it. Observations made on the characteristics of the flows and the effect of this obstruction suggest principles that might be applied in planning structures to divert lava streams from inhabited areas downslope.

Description of O Shima Volcano

O Shima Volcano composes all except a very small part of the island for which it is named. The wooded outer slopes of the volcano rise from the sea and steepen to about 25° near the caldera rim, or somma. The somma is a circular ridge with a gap on the northeast side. It has a diameter of about 3 kilometers and an altitude of about 580 meters (Fig. 1). The barren floor of the caldera within it is about 50

* Publication authorized by the Director, U. S. Geological Survey.

Mason, A. C. and Foster, H. L., 1953, "Diversion of Lava Flows at O Shima, Japan," *Amer. Jour. Sci.*, vol. 251, pp. 249–58. Lightly edited by permission of the junior author and reprinted by permission of *Amer. Jour. Sci.* Copyright 1953.
Helen Foster is on the staff of the U. S. Geological Survey, Menlo Park, California. The late Arnold Mason was also on the staff of the U. S. Geological Survey.

meters lower. Mihara Yama rises in the south part of the caldera and has the shape of a truncated cone, the upper slopes of which reach 33° in inclination. Its crest is a crater rim, which has a diameter of 800 meters and ranges in altitude from 675 meters on the north and west sides to 755 meters on the east, the highest point on the island. The enclosed crater has been the locus of all eruptions during historic times. In 1778 a great flow reached the sea and formed a lava delta, but despite the numerous periods of eruption in the interim, no lava overflowed the crater rim again until 1950. The material erupted is basalt.

Eruption of 1950

After 10 years of quiescence, Mihara Yama erupted on July 16, 1950, and was active for more than 2 months. Several cinder cones were built and lava filled the crater and overflowed the rim at four points on the low north and west sides (Fig. 2).

Eruption of 1951

Eruption commenced again on February 4, 1951 and continued intermittently for 5 months. Lava overflowed the crater rim in three places. A pond of highly fluid lava, with a temperature above 1200° C. formed in the crater area. When the surface of the pond welled up, the overflow became a torrent of lava 50 meters wide that descended the slopes of Mihara Yama at an estimated speed of 50 kilometers

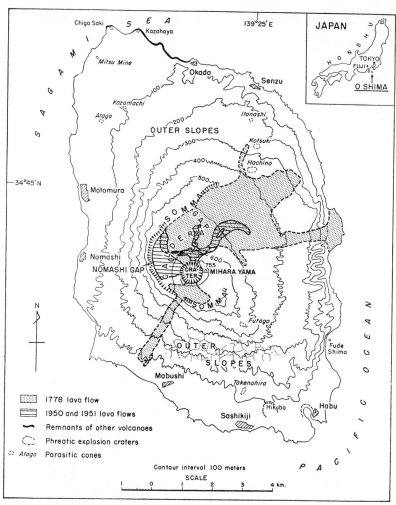

FIG. 1. O Shima and O Shima Volcano. The 1778, 1950, and 1951 lava flows issued from the crater of the central cone, Mihara Yama.

per hour and spread over the caldera floor. The rough surface of the earlier flows that it overran caused the fresh flow to have eddy and other turbulent currents comparable to those in flood waters. Eventually 1.5 square kilometers of the caldera floor became covered with the flows, which were composed largely of jagged, cindery aa lava.

Highly fluid lava was observed to advance rapidly downslope as thin sheets; it had a depth of more than 3 meters only where it accumulated in pools. Cooling, more viscous lava pushed forward more slowly, with aa fronts occasionally as high as 4 meters where the gradient lessened. Continuous flows caused little building up of the total thickness of lava except where the material accumulated in areas of little or no gradient, but pulsating and

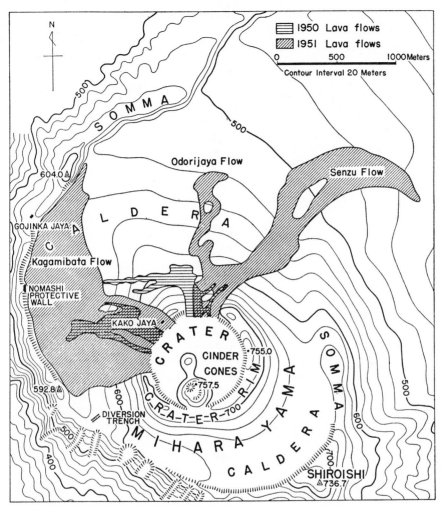

FIG. 2. Mihara Yama on April 20, 1951. The 1951 cinder cone was at its maximum altitude, 757.5 meters, but its height was reduced a few days later by partial collapse. The lava flows advanced no further, although eruption continued intermittently until June 28.

successive flows caused thickening of the deposits because during the period of lessened flow the lava stream cooled and solidified along the channels of flow.

Blocking of Lava by Kako Jaya

A building known as Kako Jaya (Crater Teahouse) was located on the north-

west side of the crater rim. It consisted of a rectangular room about 12 by 8 meters, with its long dimension paralleling the crest on which it stood. It had a concrete foundation and was constructed of concrete walls about 25 centimeters thick and 3 meters high, faced with mortared lava stone. There were doors on all sides and windows on the long sides. The walls were well constructed and in good condition. The gable roof was supported by wood rafters.

During the 1950 eruption, lava overflowed the crater rim both northeast and southwest of Kako Jaya but not at the building, which was on slightly higher ground. However, on March 9 about one month after the 1951 eruption began, new flows advanced and reached Kako Jaya. The lava ignited the timbers, and the roof and other combustible parts were destroyed. The walls resisted the pressure of the lava. The lava entered the building through windows and doors on the long southeast side, nearly filled the interior, and streamed out in small amounts through the doors and windows on the northwest side, hardening in lobate, ropy, pahoehoe form. The quantity which passed out through the openings was insufficient to flow more than about 10 meters down the slope. In contrast, the slope not in the lee of the building had long flows of lava extending down to the caldera floor. When the flow temporarily ceased, the surface of the lava collapsed slightly on the crater side of the teahouse, while the lava held within the room solidified in pahoehoe form. This mass acted as a block to the rise and advance of the next flow, the front of which was broken up in aa form.

During the later eruptions in 1951, lava again poured over the crater rim at this location, and eventually the walls of the building became almost completely buried by lava. It could be seen, however, that at least part of them were still standing and had not been pushed over by the lava.

Examples Elsewhere

Blocking or containing of lava by walls has been observed elsewhere. A wall of rubble masonry bounding the three sides of a cemetery adjacent to a destroyed church in Bosco Tre Case on the south slope of Vesuvius confined a tongue of lava which entered from the church side and covered and nearly filled the rectangular area. A similar occurrence was observed about 1911 at Matavanu on Savaii, Samoa.

On Hawaii, a loosely laid stone wall only a few feet high withstood the tip of the Mauna Iki flow of 1920 and diverted the flow at an angle of about 60° so that it ran parallel to the wall for a distance of 40 feet to a point where the wall was overtopped. Heavy but uncemented stone walls in 1935 confined a lava pool at Humuula, on the northeast side of Mauna Loa, until it rose sufficiently to overflow the walls. In 1950 the second flow of Mauna Loa to reach the sea advanced rapidly down a steep slope but was temporarily stopped by a 4-foot loose stone wall across its course until the lava piled up and spilled over the wall without pushing it over. In similar manner, on the slope of Mauna Iki, southwest of Kilauea crater, a lava flow was diverted by a small tongue of an older aa flow.

Types of Lava Pressure

Observation of the lava movement against the walls of Kako Jaya demonstrated that the pressure of the flow was not great. Two types of pressure may be exerted on a wall: hydrostatic pressure and pressure from the momentum of a flow. Only the first type affected Kako Jaya. This type of pressure is not great because it consists of little more than the vertical height of the lava column up to some point of relief, which, except in the case of some lava tubes, usually occurs nearby. This pressure may be decreased by diverting the flow, which has the effect of maintaining the point of relief to one side and at a low height.

On a steep slope the second type of pressure can be quite large, especially the momentum of first impact of a fluid material with the specific gravity of lava. This force can be decreased by locating a wall where it does not face a steep slope, by locating it below a forest or below rocky obstructions, by creating obstructions such as rock cairns, and by excavating a moat on the uphill side of the wall to break up the lineal downhill flow. A large, swift stream of lava might not be stopped by a weak wall, but it probably would be stopped by a wall of moderate strength, especially one protected by uphill obstructions. As mentioned above, even a rapidly advancing flow was temporarily stopped by a loose wall on the slope of Mauna Loa in 1950.

Overriding of Walls

The accumulation of flows so that walls are eventually overridden by later flows constitutes a difficult problem. For most situations, walls should be designed to divert and not to stop a flow, as lava would soon overtop a wall acting as a dam. To cause diversion, walls need to equal the height of very fluid lava flows, but can be slightly less than the height of cooler flows. Continuous flows cause little accumulation once they become channeled within their own chilled sides and there is some place for the material to move on down a gradient. Pulsating and successive flows permit cooling during periods of lessened flow, and solidification of the lava causes accumulation along the channels of flow. At first this causes succeeding flows to go to one side or the other, but if flows continue, later ones will overrun earlier ones and the general level of the surface will be raised, similar to the growth of an alluvial fan. To provide against this, either higher walls or a series of walls are needed.

Design of Walls

Observations made during the eruptions of Mihara Yama indicate that engineering structures can be made that will withstand and divert lava flows. Just as with flood water, the higher and more substantial these structures are, the greater the protection, but even small structures provide some protection.

Walls about 3 meters high should provide protection against most types of flow, but higher walls may be preferable in some places as determined by the cross section of a probable flow. Both sides may be sloped to obtain strength, but the upslope side should be steep enough to prevent overriding of the wall by the momentum of the lava. To enable a wall to divert a flow, and to minimize the likelihood of its being overtopped by an accumulation of lava, a wall should be located in a topographically strategic position and set diagonally to the slope in order to direct the flow into a selected channel wherein little damage will be done. To conduct the flow toward the safe channel, it may also be appropriate to excavate guide channels. Walls should be located below likely vents, but as far upslope as is topographically feasible. In some situations it might be advisable additionally to locate a wall downslope just above the area to be protected, in case of an outbreak at an unusually low point or failure or overtopping of the upslope protection.

Walls with ordinary triangular cross section require approximately four times as much material to build when the height is doubled. Two walls each 1.5 meters high, for example, would require roughly only half the material needed for one wall 3 meters high. If more than one wall is utilized, each should have a topographic position to permit diversion of lava. If the material for the walls were being field-gathered, much less carrying would be required to build two walls. In some cases, as a recourse, two or three inexpensive low walls might be loose-piled to provide partial protection, where an adequate single wall could not be afforded. However, two low walls are not equivalent for the purpose of diversion to one wall twice their height. Chilling of the lava in contact with the ground may raise the level of the bottom of a flow. Because of frictional drag at the bottom, usually the greater part of the movement of material is in the upper half of a flow. Hence, the two low walls might both be overtopped by a flow that the high wall would stop.

Construction of Walls Elsewhere

Walls to provide protection against lava flows have been built on the slopes of Vesuvius. In 1881 a wall was built to try to protect the Waiakea mill near Hilo, but the lava did not quite reach the wall.

Geologists early advocated the construction of walls to protect Hilo, and in 1937 made an estimate that a wall just outside the city would cost $400,000, an additional wall at Red Hill to divert lava at a point high up on the slope of Mauna Loa would cost $300,000, and a wall at Humuula Pass to protect the water supply of the city would cost another $100,000. In their plan submitted the same year, they made an estimate of $1,126,000. In the official report of the District Engineer completed in 1940, an estimate of $2,613,800 was made to construct a wall with a minimum height of 20 feet and a maximum of 68 feet to satisfy the requirements for assured protection.

The Nomashi Protective Wall

One wall was built on O Shima to provide protection against lava flows. The village of Nomashi is located below a narrow gap in the west side of the caldera rim. As successive flows from Mihara Yama accumulated in 1951, the lava reached the far side of the caldera and partly ascended the short rise on the inside of the caldera rim. The inhabitants of Nomashi, fearing the advance of the lava, built across the gap a stone wall 15 meters long, 2 to 4 meters high, and 3 meters thick.

As the wall was situated across a gap and not on a slope, it was designed to block the advance of the lava and prevent it from flowing through the gap. The lava would accumulate on the caldera floor, or, before reaching the wall, a part might be diverted by a trench about 8 meters wide which the villagers excavated in the caldera rim at a point 1200 meters to the south-southeast, and nearer Mihara Yama. The trench led to the head of a ravine, which would provide a safe channel down the outer slope of O Shima Volcano.

The lava reached a point within 75 meters of the wall and only 6 meters below it, before eruption ceased. Although the wall was not tested, it is believed that it would have withstood any flow reaching it. Only if an extremely large volume of lava accumulated in the caldera would the wall have been overtopped. If this became imminent, it might have been possible meanwhile to construct the wall higher. Ironically, the village was nearly totally destroyed by fire 6 months later.

Bombing of Lava Flows

Bombing has been utilized in attempts to stop the advance of lava flows. Bombing can be utilized effectively only against lava rivers or tubes, in which the lava has become confined in a channel formed by lava congealing on the margin of the flow. The channel acts as a feeder to an advancing tongue of lava. By bombing, the channel may be partly blocked and a breach formed through which the flow may escape. The recommended procedure is to bomb at the lowest effective point, and successively bomb at higher points if the threat of danger continues. In 1935 in the first attempt on Mauna Loa, bombing was directed on the main tubes of a lava flow. In 1942 the practicability of breaking down the levee of an open lava stream by aerial bombing was demonstrated on a flow heading toward Hilo.

Bombing has the advantage that the effort is directed to the point of danger and no expenditure is made unless danger threatens. However, a resort to bombing at such a time might be impossible because of weather conditions or poor visibility. Bombing is not effective, but a wall is, against large sheet flows, which often are associated with the beginning or renewal of activity and which may occur suddenly. Bombing can be utilized in some situations, but it provides no safeguard that is not provided by a wall, and it cannot take the place of diversion walls.

Summary

Lava flows during the 1951 eruption of Mihara Yama on O Shima, Japan, were partly blocked by a concrete building on the crater rim. Highly fluid lava filled the interior and poured out through the doors and windows on the opposite side. Observations made on the characteristics of the flows and the effect of this obstruction indicate that it is feasible to construct walls of sufficient strength to divert lava streams from inhabited areas. The pressure from the hydrostatic head of the flow in most cases is small, as it consists of the vertical height of the lava column up to a point of relief which usually is nearby. The impact from momentum may be large, but it can be decreased by locating the wall where it does not face a steep slope, and where there are obstructions above it. Diversion walls should be diagonal to the slope and located topographically to divert the flow to a safe channel.

Earthquake Activity

The earth is utterly broken, it is rent asunder and is violently shaken.
Isaiah 24:19

Earthquakes appear to be more common than volcanism. Each year several large earthquakes cause catastrophic damage while numerous others are destructive locally. In Reading 5 Gordon Oakeshott describes the San Andreas fault system and its attendant earthquakes. He reviews some of the unsolved problems associated with our understanding of the fault and offers the intriguing suggestion that although the solution of these problems might enable us to predict earthquake activity, this ability to predict activity might in itself create a completely new set of problems.

The March 1964 Alaska earthquake did much to call attention of the American public to the hazards of earthquakes. Reading 6 describes the setting of this earthquake and its effects on man and his physical environment. This is one of the few accounts that adequately describes the environmental impact of a large earthquake. The Alaskan earthquake occurred in a sparsely populated area and the loss of life and property damage were minor for a large quake. The San Fernando earthquake of February 1971 was a moderate earthquake but on the fringe of a densely populated area. Reading 7 elaborates on the lessons learned from early investigations of this disaster. This report is one of several recent reports written by a variety of committees, task forces, and panels gathered by the National Academy of Sciences, the Office of Science and Technology, and the Federal Council on Science and

Photo on page 36. Aerial view of the Daly City, California, area showing the trace of the San Andreas fault. Courtesy of U. S. Geological Survey.

Technology. There is a need for a concerted program to expand basic and applied seismic research and to assist "high-risk" cities in reducing earthquake hazards.

The role of Man as a geologic agent is a popular subject among environmentalists. Although Man is a relative newcomer to the environment, his technological skills have enabled him literally to move mountains. In those situations where Man has ignored geological hazards he has, on occasion, inadvertently triggered earthquakes. In 1962 a deep well at the Rocky Mountain Arsenal near Denver was used for disposing of waste water. Soon afterward, earthquakes began—the first in the area since 1882. In November 1965 David M. Evans, a consulting geologist, presented data which strongly indicated that the Denver earthquakes were being triggered by the fluid-waste disposal program. His disclosure (Reading 8) reveals a strong sense of responsibility to the citizens of Denver who were becoming anxious about the sudden occurrence of earthquake activity. It hastened official action which led to a more detailed monitoring of waste disposal and tremor activity. These studies supported Evans' contention that waste disposal appears to be a significant cause of the Denver area earthquakes. With subsequent suspension of the disposal program the area appears to have regained its former stability. This Reading demonstrates the urgent need for full use of geologic knowledge before we interfere with an environment which is in equilibrium.

Reading 9 illustrates the correlation between underground nuclear explosions and earthquake activity. The cause and effect relationship is convincing, but there are some uncertainties about magnitude, areal extent, and timing. The suggestion that nuclear tests, such as the Amchitka test, be used as feasibility studies for the control of earthquakes is a bold one.

It is fortunate that some earthquakes have occurred at times when many people were not in the vicinity. The Alaskan earthquake occurred on Good Friday. Many stores and schools were closed, thus averting a higher death toll. The San Fernando earthquake occurred at 6 a.m. when highways were relatively free of traffic and before most office and public buildings were occupied. The realization that the timing may not always be this fortuitous and that densely populated areas may be involved in the next large earthquake has stimulated research in the areas of earthquake prediction, control, and engineering. Reading 10 deals with the

question of prediction, and Reading 11 looks beyond prediction and discusses the controlled release of stored strain energy in active fault zones. The International Geophysical Year and Project Vela have contributed to advances in seismology that bring the prediction and control of earthquakes within the realm of possibility. It is, however, a sobering fact that the San Fernando earthquake and several other California earthquakes occurred in areas of low seismicity and were associated with portions of a fault not previously mapped. It is obvious that, like the recent volcanic history of the Cascade Range (Reading 3), the short-term local history of the San Andreas fault system is not an adequate base for estimating risks. These readings indicate the need for additional mapping, more comprehensive information on the accumulation of strain, and reconsideration of building codes and seismic zoning.

5   San Andreas Fault: Geologic and Earthquake History*

Gordon B. Oakeshott

The San Andreas fault is California's most spectacular and widely known structural feature. Few specific geologic features on earth have received more public attention. Sound reasons for this are found in the series of historic earth-

* Adapted largely from Oakeshott, Gordon B., 1966, San Andreas fault in the California Coast Ranges province: California Division of Mines and Geology Bulletin 190, pp. 357–373.

quakes which have originated in movements in the San Andreas fault zone, and in continuing surface displace-

Oakeshott, G. B., 1966, "San Andreas Fault: Geologic and Earthquake History," *Mineral Information Service*, vol. 19, no. 10, pp. 159–66. Abridged by permission of the author and reprinted by permission of California Division of Mines and Geology, Sacramento, California.
Dr. Oakeshott is Deputy Director of the California Division of Mines and Geology.

ments, both accompanied and unaccompanied by earthquakes. This active fault is of tremendous engineering significance, for no engineering structure can cross it without jeopardy and all major structures within its potential area of seismicity must incorporate earthquake-resistant design features. Recently a proposal for a great nuclear power plant installation on Bodega Head, north of San Francisco, was abandoned because of public controversy over the dangers of renewed movements and earthquakes on the nearby fault. Expensive design features are being incorporated into the State's plan to transport some of northern California's excess of water to water-deficient southern California in order to ensure uninterrupted service across the fault in the event of fault movements and earthquakes in the Tehachapi area.

Geologists and seismologists the world over have directed their attention to the San Andreas fault because of: (1) the great (Richter magnitude 8.25)[1] San Francisco earthquake of 1906 and many lesser shocks which have originated in the fault zone; (2) development of the "elastic rebound" theory of earthquakes by H. F. Reid; (3) striking geologic effects of former movements and continuing surface movements in the fault zone; and (4) postulated horizontal displacements of hundreds of miles—east block moving south.

The San Andreas has been frequently and widely cited in the scientific and popular literature as a classic example of a strike-slip fault with cumulative horizontal displacement of several hundred miles; however, the geologic evidence that can be documented is highly controversial.

Location and Extent

The San Andreas fault strikes (bears) approximately N. 35° W. in a nearly straight line in the Coast Ranges province and extends southward for a total length of about 650 miles from Shelter Cove on the coast of Humboldt County to the Salton Sea. This takes it completely across geologic structures and lineation of the Coast Ranges at a low angle, then south across the Transverse Ranges and into the Salton Trough. Latest movement in the fault zone, as noted by the late Professor A. C. Lawson who named and traced it, has thus been clearly later than all major structural features of those provinces. This recent movement may, however, be an expression of renewed activity along an older fault zone that antedated differentiation of the geologic provinces now in existence. If so, we need to distinguish between such an older, or "ancestral," San Andreas fault zone and latest movements on the modern, or Quaternary, San Andreas fault proper.

The long northwesterly trend of the fault zone is interrupted in three places (see Fig. 1): (1) At Cape Mendocino, where it turns abruptly westward to enter the Mendocino fault zone, as reflected in the Mendocino Escarpment; (2) at the south end where the Coast Ranges adjoin the Transverse Ranges and the fault turns to strike east into the complex knot of major faults in the Frazier Mountain area and on emerging splits into the 50-mile-wide system of related faults, including the San Andreas fault proper, in southern California; and (3) in the San Gorgonio Pass area where the San Andreas fault proper appears to change direction again and butt into the Mission Creek-Banning fault zone which continues into the Salton Trough.

Earthquake History

Earthquake history of California is extremely short. The earliest earthquake in written records was felt by explorer Gaspar de Portola and his party in 1769 while camped on the Santa Ana River about 30 miles southeast of Los Angeles. The earliest seismographs in use in California, and also the earliest in the United States, were installed by the University of California at Lick Observatory on Mount Hamilton, and

at the University at Berkeley in 1887. The earliest seismograms of a major California earthquake are those of the San Francisco earthquake of 1906, which was recorded at seven California stations as well as elsewhere throughout the world.

One of the Bay area's largest earthquakes centered on the Hayward fault (within the San Andreas fault *zone*) in the East Bay on June 10, 1836. Surface faulting (ground ruptures) took place at the base of the Berkeley Hills from Mission San Jose to San Pablo. On October 21, 1868 another large earthquake centered on the Hayward fault with surface faulting for about 20 miles from Warm Springs to San Leandro. Maximum right-lateral (east block moving south) offset was about 3 feet.

FIG. 1. San Andreas fault zone.

In June of 1838 a strong earthquake originating on the San Andreas fault was accompanied by surface rupturing from Santa Clara almost to San Francisco. This damaged the Presidio at San Francisco and the missions at San Jose, Santa Clara, and San Francisco. Another strong earthquake centered on the San Andreas fault in the Santa Cruz Mountains on October 8, 1865. This was accompanied by ground cracks, land-slides, and dust clouds; buildings were damaged in San Francisco and at the New Almaden mercury mine, which was only a few miles east of the active part of the fault.

On April 24, 1890, a strong earthquake damaged Watsonville, Hollister, and Gilroy. Joe Anzar, who was a young boy living in the San Andreas rift valley in the nearby Chittenden Pass area at the time of that earthquake, was interviewed in 1963 by Olaf P. Jenkins and the writer. Mr. Anzar clearly remembered ground breakage, which caused Anzar Lake to drain, and landslides, which closed the railroad and highway where the fault trace crosses Chittenden Pass. He judged the motion to be stronger (at his home) than during the San Francisco earthquake of 1906.

The famous San Francisco earthquake, 5:12 a.m. local time, April 18, 1906, was probably California's greatest. Visible surface faulting occurred from San Juan Bautista to Point Arena, where the San Andreas fault enters the ocean. At the same time surface faulting also occurred 75 miles north of Point Arena at Shelter Cove in Humboldt County, probably along an extension of the San Andreas fault. The 1906 scarp viewed at Shelter Cove in 1963 clearly shows upthrow of 6 to 8 feet on the east side; there was no evidence of a horizontal component of displacement. However, offset of a line of old trees and an old fence viewed east of Point Arena in 1963 gave clear evidence of right-lateral displacement on the order of about 14 feet. The epicenter of the earthquake was near Olema, at the south end of Tomales Bay, near where a road was offset 20 feet in a right-lateral sense. Richter magnitude is generally computed at about 8.25. Damage has been estimated at from $350 million to $1 billion. An estimated 700 people were killed. A large part of the loss was due to the tremendous fires in San Francisco, which resulted from broken gas mains and lack of water owing to numerous ruptures in the lines. Most extensive ground breaking in the city was near the waterfront in areas of natural Bay mud and artificial fill.

Another of California's great earthquakes, comparable in magnitude to the San Francisco 1906 earthquake, was caused by displacement on a segment of the San Andreas fault extending through the southern part of the Coast Ranges province and on beyond across the Transverse Ranges. This Fort Tejon earthquake of January 9, 1857, probably centered in the region between Fort Tejon in the Tehachapi Mountains and the Carrizo Plain in the southern Coast Ranges. Surface faulting extended for 200 to 275 miles from Cholame Valley along the northeast side of the Carrizo Plain through Tejon Pass, Elizabeth Lake, Cajon Pass, and along the south side of the San Bernardino Mountains. Accounts of this earthquake are unsatisfactory and inconclusive, but horizontal surface displacement almost certainly amounted to several feet in a right-lateral sense.

Perhaps among California's three greatest earthquakes was that in Owens Valley on March 26, 1872. At Lone Pine, 23 out of 250 people were killed and 52 out of 59 adobe houses were destroyed. The shock was felt from Shasta to San Diego. Surface faulting at the eastern foot of the Sierra Nevada produced scarps with a maximum net vertical displacement of about 13 feet and horizontal right-lateral offset of about 16 feet. Surface faulting extended for perhaps 100 miles. This fault, of course, has no direct relation to the San Andreas.

There have been in historic times two great earthquakes (Fort Tejon and San Francisco) originating on the San Andreas fault, each accompanied by more than 200 miles of surface ruptures: one at the southern end of the Coast Ranges and one in the north. Between is left a segment, roughly 90 miles long, in the southern Coast Ranges, which has not been disrupted by surface faulting in historic time. It is interesting to note that the two ends of this segment—the Hollister area and the Parkfield area—are now the most seismically active in the southern Coast Ranges. The extreme southern segment —south of the Tehachapi Mountains— is quiet on the San Andreas fault proper, but very active on the closely related San Jacinto, Elsinore, Inglewood, and Imperial faults. In the segment marked by surface rupture in 1906, many earthquakes have originated in the central and southern part on the San Andreas fault and its auxiliary faults in the East Bay—the Hayward and Calaveras faults. However,

since 1906 there have been no earthquakes on the most northerly segment from Marin to Humboldt Counties. The strongest earthquake in the Bay area since 1906 was the San Francisco earthquake of March 22, 1957, of magnitude 5.3. It originated at shallow depth near Mussel Rock, off the coast a few miles south of San Francisco; there was no surface faulting. No lives were lost, but minor damage to many homes in the Westlake-Daly City district totalled about a million dollars.

Land Forms in the Fault Zone

Extensive activity along the San Andreas fault zone in Quaternary time (last one million years of geologic time) has developed a linear depression, marked by all the features of a classic rift valley, extending the entire length of the fault and encompassing a width from a few hundred feet to over a mile and a half. Rift-valley features are particularly well expressed in the San Francisco Bay area, in the arid Carrizo Plain, and along the north side of the San Gabriel Mountains in southern California. Within the rift zone fault gouge and breccia always occur as well as a disorganized jumble of fault-brecciated rocks from both the eastern and western blocks, the result of hundreds of repeated ruptures on different fault planes in late Pleistocene and Recent time. Features of the rift valleys have resulted from: (1) Repeated, discontinuous fault ruptures on the surface, often with the development of minor graben, horsts, and pressure ridges; (2) land-sliding, triggered by earthquake waves and surface faulting; and (3) erosion of brecciated, readily weathered rock. Within the rift-valley troughs, it is common to find late Pliocene to Recent sediments.

Many of the observations made after the earthquake of 1906 are of great significance in understanding the origin and development of rift valleys and the nature of movement on the San Andreas fault: (1) open ruptures were mapped along the fault trace from San Juan Bautista to Point Arena, and at Telegraph Hill north of Shelter Cove in Humboldt County; (2) individual fault ruptures were not continuous, but extended for a few feet to a mile or a little more, with the continuations of the displacements being picked up along *en echelon* breaks; (3) the ruptures were often complex, with small grabens (downdropped blocks) and horsts (uplifted blocks) developed between breaks; (4) apparent movements were dominantly right lateral, with lesser vertical displacements; and (5) the amount of displacement varied irregularly along the fault trace, but in a gross way decreased in both directions from the maximum at the south end of Tomales Bay.

North of San Francisco, across Marin County, the fault follows a remarkably straight course approximately N. 35° W. The most prominent features are Bolinas Bay and the long, linear Tomales Bay which lie in portions of the rift valley drowned by rising sea waters following the Pleistocene glacial epoch. Between these bays, the rift zone is a steep-sided trough, in places as deep as 1,500 feet, with its lower levels characterized by a remarkable succession of minor, alternating ridges and gullies parallel to the general trend of the fault zone. Surfaces of the ridges and gullies are spotted by irregular

hummocks and hollows; many of the hollows are undrained and have developed sag ponds, which are common along the San Andreas rift. Geologically Recent adjustment of the drainage in the rift zone leaves little positive evidence of the amount and direction of Recent displacement, except for that which took place in 1906. Offset lines of trees in this area still show the 13- to 14-foot horizontal right slip of 1906, and just south of Point Arena trees also serve to show the 1906 offset. In the long stretch northward from Fort Ross to a point a few miles south of Point Arena, the broad expression of the rift zone is clear, but minor features within the zone have been obscured by erosion of the Gualala and Garcia Rivers and by the dense forest cover of the area.

South of San Francisco across San Mateo County the San Andreas fault zone follows the same trend as to the north but is less straight and is complicated by several subparallel faults. Near Mussel Rock, where the fault enters the land south of San Francisco, are great landslides which obscure the trace, and for a few miles to the southeast is a succession of sag ponds, notched ridges, and rift-valley lakes within a deeply trenched valley. The long, narrow San Andreas Lake and Crystal Springs Lakes are natural lakes which were enlarged many years ago by the artificial dams built to impound San Francisco's water supply. Similar rift-valley features mark the fault southward to the Tehachapi Mountains; because of the local aridity, they are particularly clear and striking in the Temblor Range area, in the Cholame Valley, and in the Carrizo Plain. As the fault enters its eastward bend in the San Emigdio Mountains area, the rift-valley features become less striking, perhaps because the contrast between the basement rocks in the east and west blocks disappears where the fault lies wholly within granitic rocks and older schists.

South of the Tehachapi the striking rift-valley land forms continue, through sag ponds like Elizabeth Lake and Palmdale Reservoir, along the northern margin of the San Gabriel Mountains through the Cajon Pass, and along the south side of the San Bernardino Mountains. None of the offsets and other rift-valley features in this southern segment of the great fault appears to be younger than 1857.

Displacement on the Fault

In 1953, geologists Mason L. Hill and T. W. Dibblee, Jr., advanced the possibility of cumulative horizontal right-lateral displacement of possibly 350 miles since Jurassic time (135,000,000 years ago) on the San Andreas fault. This hypothesis has received very wide acceptance among earth scientists, has intrigued geologists, and has been an important factor in stimulating work on the fault. Hill and Dibblee compared rock types, fossils, and gradational changes in rock characteristics in attempting to match units across the fault. By these methods they developed suggestions for horizontal displacement (east block moving south) of 10 miles since the Pleistocene (few thousand years), 65 miles since upper Miocene (about 12 million years), 225 miles since late Eocene (about 40 million years), and 350 miles since the Jurassic. At the opposite extreme, the late Professor N. L. Taliaferro of the

University of California felt less confident about this "matching" of rock units and stated unequivocally that horizontal movement on the northern segment of the San Andreas fault has been less than 1 mile! Taliaferro believed that the principal movements on this great fault have been vertical.

Thus, geologic evidence is so varied that geologists have drawn conflicting interpretations of the geologic history and characteristics of the fault; at one extreme are those who believe that there has been several hundred miles of right slip since Late Jurassic time, and at the other are those who consider that there has been large vertical displacement on an ancient San Andreas fault and relatively small horizontal displacements in late Pliocene and Quaternary time.

Some of the latest work by geologists and engineers on the San Andreas fault in the San Francisco Bay area, and the closely related Hayward fault in the East Bay, shows that these faults are still active. In several places surface "creep," or slippage, is taking place. At the Almaden Winery a few miles south of Hollister, for example, creep occurs in spasms of movement of small fractions of an inch, separated by intervals of weeks or months. Average displacement, east block moving relatively south, is a half-inch a year. Several cases of well-substantiated right-lateral creep on the order of an eighth to a quarter of an inch per year have now been recognized along the 1868 trace of the Hayward fault from Irvington (Fremont) to the University of California stadium. Frequent earthquakes, with epicenters on these faults, also show that present-day movements are taking place.

Unsolved Problems

In spite of the interests of geologists, and the very considerable amount of time and attention given by geologists and seismologists to study of the San Andreas fault, it remains very incompletely known and understood. There is no agreement on answers to such interesting and fundamental questions as: When did the fault originate? Should the late Quaternary and "ancestral" San Andreas be regarded as different faults, developed by different stresses, and with entirely different characteristics and displacements? Have the sense and direction of displacement (presently, right slip—east block moving south) always been the same, or has great vertical movement taken place? If the latter, which is the upthrown block? (Or has this changed from one side to the other in some segments during geologic time?) If dominantly right-lateral strike slip, has the present rate of displacement or strain been about the same for the last 100 million years? Is the cumulative displacement on the fault a few thousand feet or several hundred miles? To what depth does the faulting extend—5 or 6 miles, as suggested by the depth of earthquake foci, or several times this? Is the San Andreas fault becoming more, or less, active? Are earthquakes, which center in the San Andreas fault zone, relieving stresses and thus lessening the chances of future earthquakes, or do the continuing earthquakes merely indicate a high level of seismic activity portending many future earthquakes? When may the next earthquake be expected?

Answers to these problems, so vital to our generation and generations of Californians to come, await the intensive work of geologists, seismologists, and other scientists of many disciplines. At present, fault movements and earthquakes are unpredictable; perhaps, however, our problems will become even more acute when we reach the state of knowledge which will allow prediction of earthquakes in time and place!

Notes

[1] Dr. Charles F. Richter, in 1935, devised a means of comparing the total energy of earthquakes expressed in terms of a figure now called the "Richter magnitude." The logarithm of the maximum trace amplitude in thousandths of a millimeter is taken from the measurement of earthquake waves on the seismogram of a certain standard seismometer at a standard distance from the epicenter. Constants have been worked out to make the figures comparable for other seismometers at other distances. On this scale magnitude M = 2 is the smallest earthquake felt. Earthquakes of M = 4½ to 5 cause small local damage, and 5½–6 may cause an acceleration of one-tenth gravity and cause considerable damage. Earthquakes of 7 or more are called "major" earthquakes, and those of 7¾ and over are "great" earthquakes. Long Beach, 1933, with M = 6.3, was a "moderate" earthquake (but a very damaging one), Arvin-Tehachapi, 1952, at M = 7.7, was a major earthquake, and San Francisco, at 8.25 in 1906, was a great earthquake. Local size or strength has long been measured by an *intensity* scale based on how the earthquake is felt and its apparent damage. The commonest intensity scale in use is the Modified Mercalli.

References

Allen, C. R., St. Amand, P., Richter, C. F., and Nordquist, J. M., 1965, Relationship between seismicity and geologic structure in the southern California region: Seismological Society of American Bull., v. 55, no. 4, p. 753–797.

Bateman, Paul C., 1961, Willard D. Johnson and the strike-slip component of fault movement in the Owens Valley, California, earthquake of 1872: Seismological Society of America Bull., v. 51, p. 483–493.

Blanchard, F. B., and Laverty, C. L., 1966, Displacements in the Claremont Water Tunnel at the intersection with the Hayward fault: Seismological Society of America Bull., v. 56, no. 2, p. 291–294.

Bolt, Bruce A., and Marion, Walter C., 1966, Instrumental measurement of slippage on the Hayward fault: Seismological Society of America Bull., v. 56, no. 2, p. 305–316.

Bonilla, M. G., 1966, Deformation of railroad tracks by slippage on the Hayward fault in the Niles district of Fremont, California: Seismological Society of America Bull., v. 56, no. 2, p. 281–289.

Byerly, Perry, 1951, History of earthquakes in the San Francisco Bay area: California Division of Mines Bull. 154, p. 151–160.

California Division of Mines and Geology, 1958–1965, Geologic map of California, Olaf P. Jenkins edition, published sheets: California Division of Mines and Geology, scale 1:250,000.

California Resources Agency, 1964, Earthquake and geologic hazards conference, December 7 and 8, 1964, San Francisco, California, 154 p.

California Resources Agency, 1966, Landslide and subsidence conference, Los Angeles, California.

Cluff, Lloyd, 1965, Evidence of creep along the Hayward fault: Association of Engineering Geologists, First Ann. Joint Meeting San Francisco-Sacramento Section, paper delivered at Berkeley, Sept. 25, 1965.

Cluff, Lloyd S., and Steinbrugge, Karl V., 1966, Hayward fault slippage in the Irvington-Niles districts of Fremont, California: Seismological Society of America Bull., v. 56, no. 2, p. 257–279.

Hill, M. L., and Dibblee, T. W., Jr., 1953, San Andreas, Garlock, and Big Pine faults, California—a study of the character, history, and tectonic significance of their displacements: Geological Society of America Bull., v. 64, no. 4, p. 443–458.

Lawson, A. C., and others, 1908, The California earthquake of April 18, 1906, Report of the State Earthquake Investigation Committee: Carnegie Inst. Washington Pub. 87, v. 1, pts. 1–2, 451 p.

6 The Alaska Earthquake, March 27, 1964: Field Investigations and Reconstruction Effort

A Summary Description of the Alaska Earthquake— Its Setting and Effects

Wallace R. Hansen and Edwin B. Eckel

Introduction

One of the greatest geotectonic events of our time occurred in southern Alaska late in the afternoon of March 27, 1964. Beneath a leaden sky, the chill of evening was just settling over the Alaskan countryside. Light snow was falling on some communities. It was Good Friday, schools were closed, and

the business day was ending. Suddenly without warning half of Alaska was

Hansen, W. R. and Eckel, E. B., 1966, "A Summary Description of the Alaska Earthquake—Its Setting and Effects," U. S. Geol. Survey Professional Paper 541, pp. 1–37. Abridged by permission of the senior author. The authors are affiliated with the U. S. Geological Survey.

rocked and jarred by the most violent earthquake to occur in North America this century.

The descriptive summary that follows is based on the work of many investigators. A large and still-growing scientific literature has accumulated since the earthquake, and this literature has been freely drawn upon here. In particular, the writers have relied upon the findings of their colleagues in the Geological Survey. Some of these findings have been published, but some are still being prepared for publication. Moreover, some field investigations are still in progress.

Time and Magnitude

Seismologic events such as earthquakes are normally recorded in the scientific literature in Greenwich mean time. Greenwich time provides a worldwide standard of reference that obviates the difficulties of converting one local time to another. The Alaskan earthquake of 1964 thus began at about 5:36 p.m., Friday, March 27, 1964, Alaska standard time, but its onset is officially recorded in the seismological literature as 03:36:11.9 to 12.4, Saturday, March 28, 1964, Greenwich mean time.

This earthquake has become renowned for its savage destructiveness, for its long duration, and for the great breadth of its damage zone. Its magnitude has been computed by the U. S. Coast and Geodetic Survey as 8.3–8.4 on the Richter scale. Other observatories have calculated its magnitude as 8.4 (Pasadena) and 8.5–8.75 (Berkeley). These computations indicate something of the great size of the earthquake. Few earthquakes in history have been as large. In minutes, thousands of people were made homeless, 114 lives were lost, and the economy of an entire State was disrupted. Seismic sea waves swept the Pacific Ocean from the Gulf of Alaska to Antarctica; they caused extensive damage in British Columbia and California and took 12 lives in Crescent City, Calif., and 4 in Oregon. Unusually large waves, probably seiches, were recorded in the Gulf of Mexico. The entire earth vibrated like a tuning fork.

Epicenter

The epicenter of this great earthquake has been located in a forlorn wilderness of craggy peaks, glaciers, and fjords at the head of Prince William Sound, on the south flank of the rugged Chugach Mountains, about 80 miles east-southeast of Anchorage (Fig. 1). Computations by the Coast and Geodetic Survey fix the epicenter at lat. 61.1° N., long. 147.7° W.± 15 km. The hypocenter, or point of origin, was at a depth of 20–50 km. However, it is not meant to imply that the earthquake had a point source. During the quake, energy was released from a broad area south and southwest of the epicenter underlying and adjacent to Prince William Sound and the Gulf of Alaska. Epicenters of most aftershocks were dispersed throughout an area of about 100,000 square miles, mainly along the continental margin of the Aleutian Trench between Prince William Sound and the seaward side of Kodiak Island. This area coincides with a zone of tectonic uplift.

Duration and Extent

The total effect of the earthquake was intensified by the long duration of

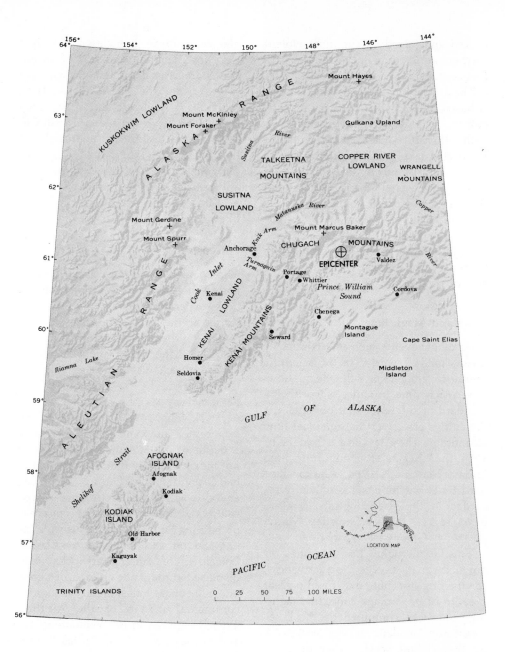

FIG. 1. Physiographic setting of south-central Alaska, including the area principally involved in the Alaska earthquake of 1964. The epicenter of the main shock is near the north end of Prince William Sound.

strong ground motion. The elapsed time can only be surmised from the estimates of eyewitnesses, inasmuch as no recording instruments capable of measuring the duration of the shock were in the affected area at the time. Several such instruments have since been installed. Some witnesses timed the quake by wrist or pocket watch, and their timings ranged from 1½ to 7 minutes or more. Most such timings ranged from 3 to 4 minutes, whether measured at Anchorage, Seward, Valdez, or elsewhere. By comparison, the great San Francisco earthquake of 1906 is said to have lasted about 1 minute.

Several factors besides the human element may influence the variation from place to place of the estimated duration of the shock. Shocks are more intense in some geologic settings than in others; the character and amplitude of seismic waves passing through one medium are unlike those passing through another of different elastic properties. Ground motion is more intense and sometimes more prolonged over thick unconsolidated fills as at Anchorage or Valdez than over firm bedrock, as in the Chugach Mountains. Under certain ground conditions the intensity of ground motion may be amplified by resonance. Motions are stronger in high buildings than in low ones, so an observer in a tall building is likely to record a longer duration than an observer in a low building. And under certain conditions, shaking may be prolonged locally after direct seismic motion has stopped: for example, if landslides or avalanches, triggered by the earthquake, are in progress in the vicinity. At any rate, even the shortest estimates indicated an earthquake of unusual duration, a du-

ration that had marked effects on the behavior of earth materials and man-made structures and on their susceptibility to damage.

The main shock was reportedly felt throughout most of Alaska, including such remote points as Cape Lisburne, Point Hope, Barrow, and Umiat on the Arctic slope of Alaska and at Unimak Island beyond the tip of the Alaska Peninsula—points 600–800 miles distant from the epicenter. The earthquake was recorded by seismographs throughout the world. It caused significant damage to ground and structures throughout a land area of about 50,000 square miles and it cracked ice on rivers and lakes throughout an area of about 100,000 square miles. Marked fluctuations of water levels in recording wells were noted at places as far distant as Georgia, Florida, and Puerto Rico.

Effects of so great an earthquake hold the utmost interest of scientists and engineers. Few earthquakes have had such marked effects on the crust of the earth and its mantle of soil. Perhaps the effects of no earthquake have been better documented. Early investigation has provided a clear picture of much that happened, but years will pass before all the effects are understood. In fact, secondary effects are still in progress. In the fjords and along the shores at tectonically disturbed tidal zones, wholesale extermination of sessile organisms has been followed by a slow restoration of the biotic balance. Marine shellfish are now seen attaching themselves to the branches of drowned spruce trees. Rivers are regrading their channels to new base levels. Long-term effects on glaciers, shorelines, and the ground-water regimen will bear further watching.

But despite its magnitude and its impressive related tectonic effects, the earthquake ranks far below many other great natural disasters in terms of property damaged and lives lost. Less violent earthquakes have killed many more people. The reasons are many: The damage zone of the Alaskan quake has a very low population density; much of it is uninhabited. In Anchorage, the one really populous area in the damage zone, many modern buildings had been designed and constructed with the danger of earthquakes in mind.

The generative area of the earthquake was also sparsely inhabited, and the long-period seismic vibrations that reached the relatively distant inhabited areas wreaked heavy damage on tall and wide-area buildings but caused mostly light damage to small one-family dwellings of the type prevalent in Alaska. Attenuation of sinusoidal seismic waves at low frequencies should vary as the square of the frequency. Thus, destructive short-period vibrations presumably were attenuated to feeble amplitudes not far from their points of origin. Most residential buildings moreover, were cross-braced wood-frame construction, and such buildings usually fare well in earthquakes.

The timing of the earthquake undoubtedly contributed to the low casualty rate. It was a holiday; many people who would otherwise have been at work or returning from work were at home. Schools were closed for the holiday. In coastal areas the tide was low; had tides been high, inundation and destruction by sea waves would have been much more severe. Nevertheless, sea waves caused more deaths than all other factors combined.

Hill (1965, p. 50) has compiled a chronological list of severe earthquakes dating back more than 1,100 years. Her list, Table 1, places the Alaskan earthquake of 1964 in a proper perspective so far as deaths are concerned.

Table 1 Severe earthquakes during last 1100 years, and resulting casualties [After Hill, 1965, p. 50]

Year	Place	Deaths
856	Corinth, Greece	45,000
1038	Shansi, China	23,000
1057	Chihli, China	25,000
1170	Sicily	15,000
1268	Silicia, Asia Minor	60,000
1290	Chihli, China	100,000
1293	Kamakura, Japan	30,000
1456	Naples, Italy	60,000
1531	Lisbon, Portugal	30,000
1556	Shenshi, China	830,000
1667	Shemaka, Caucasia	80,000
1693	Catania, Italy	60,000
1693	Naples, Italy	93,000
1731	Peking, China	100,000
1737	Calcutta, India	300,000
1755	Northern Persia	40,000

Table 1 (continued)

Year	Place	Deaths
1755	Lisbon, Portugal	30,000–60,000
1783	Calabria, Italy	50,000
1797	Quito, Ecuador	41,000
1811–12	New Madrid, Missouri, U. S. A.	
1819	Cutch, India	1,500
1822	Aleppo, Asia Minor	22,000
1828	Echigo (Honshu) Japan	30,000
1847	Zenkoji, Japan	34,000
1868	Peru and Ecuador	25,000
1875	Venezuela and Colombia	16,000
1896	Sanriku, Japan	27,000
1897	Assam, India	1,500
1898	Japan	[1] 22,000
1906	Valparaiso, Chile	1,500
1906	San Francisco, U. S. A.	500
1907	Kingston, Jamaica	1,400
1908	Messina, Italy	160,000
1915	Avezzano, Italy	30,000
1920	Kansu, China	180,000
1923	Tokyo, Japan	143,000
1930	Apennine Mountains, Italy	1,500
1932	Kansu, China	70,000
1935	Quetta, Baluchistan	60,000
1939	Chile	30,000
1939	Erzincan, Turkey	40,000
1946	Alaska-Hawaii, U. S. A.	[1] 150
1948	Fukui, Japan	5,000
1949	Ecuador	6,000
1950	Assam, India	1,500
1953	Northwestern Turkey	1,200
1954	Northern Algeria	1,600
1956	Kabul, Afghanistan	2,000
1957	Northern Iran	2,500
1957	Western Iran	1,400
1957	Outer Mongolia	1,200
1960	Southern Chile	5,700
1960	Agadir, Morocco	12,000
1962	Northwestern Iran	12,000
1963	Taiwan, Formosa	100
1963	Skopje, Yugoslavia	1,000
1964	Southern Alaska, U. S. A.	[2] 114

[1] Principally from seismic sea wave.
[2] Does not include 12 deaths in California and 4 deaths in Oregon, by drowning.

Throughout history, earthquakes have ranked high among the causes of sudden disaster and death, but many other causes have added as much or more to the misfortunes of mankind. Some of these, such as dam failures, for example, man has brought on himself. Others he has not. The great epidemics of the past are not likely to recur, but disease, famine, floods, and landslides all still take huge tolls. Single tornadoes in the American mid-continent have taken more lives than the Alaska earthquake of 1964; so have mine explosions. In East Pakistan, thousands of lives were lost in 1965 to floods and hurricanes ("cyclones"). It would be irrelevant to enlarge here on natural and manmade disasters. Hill, however, has compiled another table that sheds pertinent further light on some of the causes of human misery in the past 600 years, other than earthquakes. Wars have been omitted.

Some of the tolls listed in Hill's tables differ substantially from those reported by other authorities for the same disasters. Perhaps this difference is not surprising in view of the chaos and lack of communication that generally accompany great natural disasters and the varying casualty estimates, therefore, that appear in the subsequent literature. Nevertheless, used with caution, Hill's tables help to equate the magnitudes of past tragedies, and they provide some basis for comparing one disaster with another. Compared with the eruption of Mount Pelee in 1902, for example, or the sinking of the Titanic in 1912, the Alaska earthquake of 1964 took a small toll of lives. In view of the magnitude of the event, the relatively small size of the toll is in some ways remarkable.

Table 2 Deaths (rounded) from some of the world's worst manmade accidents and natural disasters [After Hill, 1965, p. 57]

Date	What and where	Deaths
1347–51	Bubonic plague in Europe and Asia.	75,000,000
1918	Influenza throughout the world.	22,000,000
1878	Famine in China	9,500,000
1887	Flood in China	900,000
1556	Earthquake in China	830,000
1881	Typhoon in Indochina	300,000
1902	Eruption of Mount Pelee, West Indies.	40,000
1883	Eruption of Krakatoa, near Sumatra.	36,000
1941	Snow avalanche in Peru	5,000
1963	Overflow of Vaiont Dam in Italy.	2,000
1942	Mine explosion Manchuria	[1] 1,500
1912	Sinking of the Titanic	[2] 1,500
1871	Forest fire, Wisconsin	1,000
1925	Tornado in south-central United States.	700
1944	Train stalled in Italy	[3] 500
1928	Collapse of St. Francis Dam, California.	500
1960	Airliners collided over New York City.	[4] 134

[1] Actual count 1,549.

[2] Known dead 1,513.

[3] Passengers suffocated when the train was caught in a tunnel; actual count 521.

[4] Including casualties on the ground.

Aftershocks

The long series of aftershocks that followed the main Alaska earthquake gradually diminished in frequency and intensity over a period of several months. Within 24 hours the initial shock was followed by 28 aftershocks, 10 of which exceeded Richter magnitude 6. The epicenters of these shocks were disposed in a zone 50–60 miles wide reaching from Prince William Sound southwest to the Trinity Islands area south of Kodiak. Fifty-five aftershocks with magnitudes greater than 4 were recorded within 48 hours after the main earthquake, including a shock of magnitude 6.7 on March 29 at 4:18 p.m. (March 30, 02:18:05.6 Gmt). Within a week 75 shocks with magnitudes greater than 4 had been recorded by the U. S. Coast and Geodetic Survey (1964, Table 2). In the 45 days following the earthquake, 728 aftershocks were recorded. About 12,000 aftershocks with magnitudes equal to or greater than 3.5 probably occurred in the 69-day period after the main shock, and several thousand more were recorded in the next year and a half.

Previous Alaskan Earthquakes

Southern Alaska and the adjoining Aleutian Island chain together constitute one of the world's most active seismic zones. Extending from Fairbanks on the north to the Gulf of Alaska on the south, the Alaskan seismic zone is but a part of the vast, near-continuous seismically active belt that circumscribes the entire Pacific Ocean basin. Figure 2 shows the distribution of earthquake epicenters of magnitude

FIG. 2. Epicenters of major Alaskan earthquakes, 1898–1961.

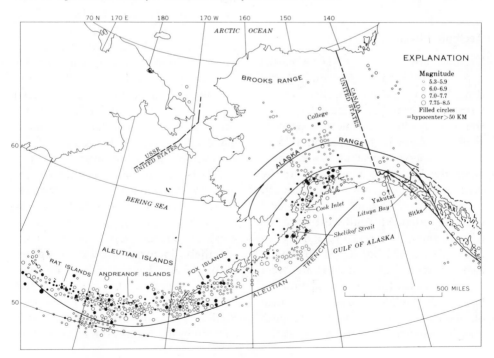

5.3 and greater recorded in Alaska since instrumental measurements began, through 1961. Between 1899 and May 1965, seven Alaska earthquakes have equaled or exceeded Richter magnitude 8, and more than 60 have equaled or exceeded magnitude 7. According to Gutenberg and Richter (1949, Table 7) about 7 percent of the seismic energy released annually on the globe originates in the Alaskan seismic zone.

This highly active zone is circumferential to the Gulf of Alaska and parallel to the Aleutian Trench. It embraces the rugged mountainous region of southern Alaska, Kodiak and the Aleutian Islands, the continental shelf, and the continental slope of the Aleutian Trench. Most of the earthquakes originate at shallow to intermediate depths—mostly less than 50 km—between the Aleutian Trench and the Aleutian Volcanic Arc.

Tectonic Effects

Tectonic effects of the Alaska earthquake of 1964 have been studied and described in detail by Plafker (1965). Crustal deformation associated with the earthquake was more extensive than any known deformation related to any known previous earthquake. From the Wrangell Mountains at the northeast to the Trinity Islands south of Kodiak, the zone of land-level changes extended southwest through the epicenter, a distance of more than 500 miles. From northwest to southeast it extended at least from the west shore of Cook Inlet to Middleton Island in the Gulf of Alaska, a distance of about 200 miles. Crustal warping may have extended inland as far as the

Alaska Range and seaward out onto the continental slope of the Aleutian Trench. East along the Alaska coast, deformation died out somewhere between the Bering Glacier and Yakataga. An area of at least 70,000 square miles and possibly 110,000 square miles or more was tectonically elevated or depressed during the earthquake. Tectonic changes, both up and down, caused extensive damage to the biota in such areas as coastal forests, migratory-bird nesting grounds, salmon spawning waters, and shellfish habitats. Land-level changes at Alaskan coastal communities are shown in Table 3.

Effects on Communities

Earthquake damage to the cities, towns, and villages of southern Alaska was caused by direct seismic vibration, ground breakage, mud or sand emission from cracks, ground lurching, subaerial and submarine landslides, fires, sea waves, and land-level changes. Not all these factors caused damage in every community. Some communities were devasted by only one; the village of Chenega, for example, was destroyed by a sea wave. Overall, landslides probably caused the most damage to manmade structures and property, but sea waves took the most lives.

Effects of one factor cannot always be separated from effects of another. Thus, at Seward the waterfront was racked by vibration, slides, sea waves, fires, subsidence, and ground cracks. All these factors contributed significantly to the havoc, and all in combination wiped out the economic base of the town. Comparable damage at Valdez, plus the threat of recurrent damage in the future, forced relocation of the village and abandonment of the present townsite (Coulter and Migliaccio, 1966).

Most of the small coastal villages in the earthquake zone were damaged chiefly by sea waves, subsidence, or both. Among the larger towns, only Cordova was significantly damaged by uplift, but the native village of Tatitlek and several canneries and residences at Sawmill Bay on Evans Island were also adversely affected by uplift.

Direct vibratory damage was significant chiefly in Anchorage and Whittier, although minor vibratory damage was widespread through the area of intense shaking. At Anchorage several buildings were destroyed by vibration, and nearly all multistory buildings were damaged. At Seward, Valdez, and Whittier, ground vibrations ruptured oil storage tanks, and the spilled petroleum quickly caught fire.

Ground breakage caused extensive damage in Anchorage, Seward, Whittier, and Valdez, not only to buildings but also to buried utilities such as water, sewer, gas, electric, and telephone lines. Cracked ground resulted from the passage of sinusoidal seismic waves through the soil, from lurching, from lateral spreading of soils under gravity, especially near the heads of landslides, and from differential settlement of alluvial and artificial fills.

Mud and sand were pumped from ground cracks throughout the damage zone where water tables were shallow in saturated granular soil. At Valdez, and to a lesser extent at Seward (Forest Acres), large volumes of sediment were ejected from cracks into cellars and crawl spaces.

Submarine and subaerial landslides triggered by the earthquake caused spectacular damage in Anchorage, Seward, Valdez, Whittier, and Homer. Four large slides in built-up parts of Anchorage were caused by failures along bluff lines in soft, sensitive silty clay whose water content at critical depths exceeded its liquid limit. Failure at Anchorage was mostly subaerial, although the large Turnagain Heights slide failed partly below sea level and slipped part way down the mudflat into Knik Arm of Cook Inlet. At Valdez and Seward, violent shaking spontaneously liquified granular deltaic materials; slumping which initiated well below sea level carried away the waterfronts of both towns. The seaward slopes of the deltas, moreover, were left less stable after the earthquake than they were before.

Estimates by the Federal Reconstruction and Development Planning Commission for Alaska, as of August 12, 1964, indicated that total property damage to Alaska by the earthquake exceeded $311 million (Fig. 3). This figure does not include loss of personal property or income. Not only was the economic base of entire communities destroyed, but the resultant loss of income severely crippled the economy of the whole State and deprived Alaska of a major share of its tax base at the time when funds were most needed to aid in restoration.

As also pointed out by the Federal Reconstruction and Development Planning Commission, the disaster struck at the heart of the State's economy, inasmuch as nearly half the people of the State reside in the stricken area. About 100,000 of the State's estimated 265,000 people live in the greater Anchorage area alone. Anchorage, because of its size, bore the brunt of

Table 3 Summary of earthquake damages to Alaskan communities

Place	Population 1960[1]	Deaths (total, 114)	Subsidence	Uplift	Land	Submarine	Ground cracks	Vibration	Waves	Fire
Afognak	190	0	×						×	
Anchorage	[2] 44,237	9			×		×	×		
Cape St. Elias	4	1			×				×	
Chenega	80	23	×						×	
Chugiak	51	0								
Cordova	1,128	0	×				×		×	
Cordova F A A airport	40	0					×	×		
Eagle River	130	0								
Ellemar	1	0		×						
Girdwood	63	0	×				×			
Homer	1,247	0	×			×		×		
Hope	44	0	×							
Kadiak Fisheries Cannery	2		×					×	×	
Kaguyak	36	3							×	
Kodiak	[3] 2,628	15	×						×	
McCord	8							×	×	
Old Harbor	193	0							×	
Ouzinkie	214	0	×						×	
Point Nowell	1	1							×	
Point Whitshed		1			×				×	
Portage	71	0	×				×			
Port Ashton		1							×	
Port Nellie Juan	3	3							×	
Seldovia	460	0	×							
Seward	1,891	13	×			×	×		×	×
Tatitlek				×						
Valdez	1,000	31	×			×	×		×	×
Whittier	70	13	×			×		×	×	×

Principal causes of damage — Landslides (Land, Submarine)

[1] Alaska Depart. Health and Welfare (1964).
[2] 82,833 including military personnel.
[3] 4,788 including personnel at Kodiak Naval Station.

property damage, but the per capita damage and the actual death toll were much greater in many smaller towns.

Although the combined population of Chenega, Kodiak, Seward, Valdez, and Whittier is less than 9,000 people, each

Place	Townsite acreage (estimated)			Premises (estimated)		Type of structures damaged							
	Total	Damaged	Percent	Total	Damaged	Homes	Business and public	Military	Harbor	Water supply	Other utilities	Highways	Airports
Afognak	20	2	10	38	23	X	X		X	X	0	X	
Anchorage	4,500	700	14	15,000	750	X	X	X	X	X	X	X	X
Cape St. Elias													
Chenega	20	20	100	20	20	X							
Chugiak				0	0					X			
Cordova	200	20	10	400	40	X	X		X	X	X		
Cordova F A A airport						X	X			X	X	X	X
Eagle River	20	1	5	0	0					X			
Kemar							X						
Girdwood						X	X						
Homer							X		X			X	
Hope	10	3	30		10	X				X			
Kodiak Fisheries Cannery				15	15	X	X		X	X	X		
Kaguyak	15			15	15	X	X						
Kodiak	285	31	11	1,100	130	X	X	X	X	X	X	X	X
McCord						X	X						
Old Harbor	30			38	35	X	X		X	X	0		
Ouzinkie	50		10	38	6	X	X		X				
Point Nowell				1	1	X							
Point Whitshed					10	X							
Portage			20			X	X				0	X	
Port Ashton					0								
Port Nellie Juan					0			X	X				
Seldovia						X	X		X				X
Seward	400	400	100	700	200	X	X	X	X	X	X	X	X
Tatitlek										X			
Valdez	300	300	100	200	40	X	X		X	X	X	X	X
Whittier	30	10	35	10	8	X	X	X	X	X	X	X	X

of these communities lost more lives than Anchorage.

Despite the extensive damage at Anchorage to residence and business properties, utilities, and transportation, a large segment of the economy was intact, and recovery was relatively rapid. But at many small towns and villages, where virtually entire populations were dependent on one or two industrial enterprises—fisheries, for example—the effects of the earthquake were staggering. Whole fishing fleets, harbor facilities, and canneries were destroyed.

The native villages of Chenega, Kaguyak, Old Harbor, and Afognak, all remote waterfront fishing villages, were nearly or completely destroyed by waves, especially Chenega, population 80 before the earthquake. There, 23 lives were lost, and only the schoolhouse remained of the village's buildings. Six homes were left standing at Old Harbor, where there had been about 35. There were nine homes in Kaguyak and a Russian Orthodox Church; all were carried away or destroyed. At Afognak, four homes, the community hall, and the grocery store were carried away by waves; several other homes were moved partly off their foundations (Alaska Depart. Health and Welfare, 1964b); and subsidence made the townsite uninhabitable. The sites of Chenega, Kaguyak,

and Afognak have been abandoned in favor of new townsites.

Earthquake damages to communities of Alaska are summarized in Table 3.

Damage to Transportation Facilities

The Alaska Railroad

Damage to The Alaska Railroad, totaled about $27 million. Most of the damage was along the 150 miles of trackage between the terminal at Seward and Anchorage. Damage to the terminal and marshaling yards at Seward, was caused by submarine slumping and waves. Two railroad docks valued at $4 million were completely destroyed, together with $2 million of freight and 50 freight cars. Between Seward and Anchorage, damage was caused by direct seismic shaking, landslides, subsidence, ground cracks and lurching, and inundation by high tides. Seventeen bridges were damaged or destroyed. Ground slumping along the right-of-way was severe at Kenai Lake and at Potter. Inundation and current scour were severe near Portage. Snow avalanches covered trackage along Turnagain Arm. At Anchorage shops and rolling stock were damaged by vibration and landslides. North of Anchorage light damage was reported as far as Hurricane. Trackage just south of Matanuska was inundated by high tides.

The spur line from Portage to Whittier was also severely damaged. The port facility at Whittier was destroyed.

Highways

Highway damage resulted chiefly from destruction of bridges and cracking, collapse, or differential compaction of fills that rested on unconsolidated de-

FIG. 3. Earthquake damages in Alaska. From estimates by the Office of Emergency Planning (1964a).

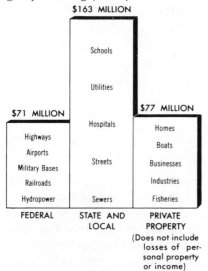

posits. Estimates for repairs alone came to about $21 million. Repairs plus upgrading to higher standards may come to $55–$65 million. The Seward Highway was severely damaged between Ingram Creek and Potter, where 22 bridges were destroyed. Between Potter and Anchorage there were many pavement breaks caused by differential subsidence of fills. Lurching displaced the alignment laterally at mile 69, and just outside Valdez there were many pavement breaks where large ground cracks crossed the highway.

The partly completed Copper River Highway was severely damaged from Allen glacier to Cordova. Nearly every bridge along the route was seriously damaged or destroyed, including the famous Million Dollar Bridge. Near Kodiak, highways were severely damaged by sea waves and by tectonic subsidence.

Airports

Damage to airports was relatively minor, although loss estimates totaled about $3.3 million. Greatest damage was at Anchorage International Airport, where a life was lost when the control tower collapsed under sustained seismic vibration and where minor damage was sustained by other buildings. Also, 20,000 barrels of aviation fuel was lost from a ruptured storage tank. Runways and taxi strips were only slightly damaged.

At Elmendorf Air Force Base just north of Anchorage, the control tower was damaged by cracks from its base to a height of about 15 feet. In Cordova, Homer, Kodiak Naval Station, Seldovia, Seward, and Valdez, damage to runways and taxi strips was mostly light.

Ports and Harbors

Water transportation is one of Alaska's vital links with the outside world and is the base for one of her major industries, commercial fishing. Many Alaska communities can be reached only by water or air. The severe damage to port and harbor facilities, therefore, was a staggering blow to the State's economy and health. Moreover, destruction of The Alaska Railroad terminal and port facilities at Seward and Whittier, coupled with the destruction of the highway port at Valdez, deprived Alaska of any ice-free, all-weather ship terminals.

Ports and harbors sustained heavy damage from several different causes. Damage by direct seismic vibration generally was subordinate to other secondary causes. Submarine slides, sea waves, ground cracks, fires, subsidence, and uplift all took large tolls. Hardest hit in terms of port and harbor facilities damaged or destroyed were Seward, Valdez, Kodiak, Whittier, Cordova, and Homer.

Submarine sliding at Seward, Valdez, and Whittier generated large local waves that added to the destruction already caused by the slides and shaking. Except at Whittier, subsequent damage was then caused by seismic sea waves generated in the Gulf of Alaska or possibly by seiches. When seismic vibration sundered petroleum storage tanks in Seward, Valdez, and Whittier, the contents quickly caught fire and added to the devastation. At Seward and Valdez,ʼ burning oil that was swept into the bay by submarine sliding was carried back across the waterfront by the returning surge of water; docks, piers, and small-boat harbors were thus destroyed by water and fire. At Seward, tugs, fishing boats, and a tanker were washed ashore. At Valdez, more than 40 boats were smashed. At Whittier, the railroad port facilities were swept away.

At Kodiak, damage was caused mostly by a succession of huge seismic sea waves, intensified by tectonic subsidence of 5–6 feet. Forty percent of the business district and many homes were destroyed, as well as 30 percent of the fishing industry facilities and most of the fishing fleet. Some vessels were washed several city blocks inland where they collided with buildings and houses like great battering rams. At Kodiak Naval Station more than $11 million damage was inflicted on buildings, materials, and equipment by 30-foot sea waves and by subsidence. Piers were covered by 10 feet of water, and the buoyed-up superstructure of the cargo pier shifted off its pilings. Boat-repair shops, gear-storage buildings, and warehouses were damaged or swept out to sea.

Port and harbor facilities at Cordova were damaged chiefly by tectonic uplift of about 6 feet and subordinately by sea waves. Although the immediate effect of uplift was to minimize wave damage, it placed docks and piers beyond reach of shipping during low tides. Boats were grounded in the small boat harbor, Orea Inlet shoaled, and passages through the adjacent islands became unnavigable.

Facilities at Homer were damaged by subsidence and submarine landsliding. Wave damage was minimal. The small-boat harbor disappeared into a "funnel-shaped" pool, and a lighthouse that had been on the harbor breakwater subsided into 40–50 feet of wa-

ter. Homer Spit, a gravel bar that extends 5 miles into Kachemak Bay and on which various commercial buildings and storage tanks were placed subsided 4–6 feet, partly by local compaction and lateral spreading and partly by regional tectonic lowering. During subsequent high tides, facilities on the bar were inundated.

Facilities at Seldovia sustained damage chiefly from subsidence. At Woody Island FAA facility outside Kodiak, docks and storage tanks were damaged by seismic sea waves and subsidence. A cannery at Shearwater Bay was thrown off its foundations by the earthquake and later destroyed by waves. At Cape St. Elias lighthouse, about 135 miles southeast of the epicenter, a coastguardsman was injured by a rockslide and later drowned by seismic sea waves.

The Port of Anchorage was damaged by ground displacements along fractures and by direct seismic shaking. The main pier lurched laterally 5–19 inches. It sustained large longitudinal and transverse cracks, and several buildings were cracked. Gantry cranes on the pier were damaged when they jumped their tracks. Approach roads settled as much as 18 inches. Cement-storage tanks were toppled. Bulk petroleum tanks were ruptured, and large quantities of fuel were lost.

Throughout coastal areas of the damage zone many fishing vessels and other small craft were destroyed by direct wave action or by being battered against docks or the shore. Boats in harbors or tied to docks were hit hardest; vessels underway in deep water were generally undamaged; one fishing boat was sunk with all hands while underway in shallow waters near Kodiak.

Atmospheric Effects

Widespread atmospheric effects are sometimes associated with large earthquakes; some have been documented (Richter, 1958, p. 128; Benioff and Gutenberg, 1939, p. 421; Van Dorn, 1964, p. 174). An atmospheric pressure wave attributed to the Alaskan earthquake was recorded by microbarographs at Scripps Institute of Oceanography at La Jolla, Calif., more than 2,000 miles from the epicenter, and at the University of California at Berkeley. The wave traveled at acoustical velocity, reaching La Jolla 3 hours and 19 minutes after the onset of the earthquake (at 06:55 Gmt., March 28, 1964); it was, therefore, the atmospheric counterpart of the seismic sea waves generated in the Gulf of Alaska. Like the seismic sea waves, the air wave must have been caused by the tectonic uplift of the sea floor and the overlying water column. To displace the atmosphere in the form of a pressure wave, uplift must have been very rapid over a very large area, and must have coincided with the time of the most violent earth tremors.

The earthquake also generated ordinary sound waves of very low subaudible frequencies in the atmosphere. These sound waves were recorded by the National Bureau of Standards at microphone stations in Washington, D. C., Boulder, Colo., and Boston, Mass. Sound waves were radiated by the earthquake at the epicenter and by seismic waves passing through the earth remote from the epicenter, exciting the atmosphere with their passage.

Thus, the Rocky Mountains and the Mississippi delta were local sources of sound as they vibrated with the passage of the shock. In addition, Rayleigh waves (surface seismic waves) crossing the continent displaced the ground surface about 2 inches in the conterminous United States and produced strong subaudible sound waves that traveled vertically upward to the ionosphere, amplifying greatly as they ascended. The ionosphere, in turn, oscillated up and down at a rate of several hundred yards per second in motions that were detected by means of reflected radio waves broadcast from one ground station to another.

Atmospheric waves coupled to surface seismic waves were also recorded by a barograph at Berkeley. These waves started at Berkeley about 14 minutes after the onset of the quake and lasted about 4 hours.

Possible Magnetic Effects

Magnetic disturbances that began 1 hour 4 minutes before the earthquake momentarily increased the magnetic field at Kodiak by as much as 100 gammas. (Moore, 1964, p. 508). Moore has inferred a possible casual relationship between the magnetic disturbances and the earthquake, and a possible means, therefore, of predicting major earthquakes by magnetic monitoring. Why abrupt magnetic disturbances should precede an earthquake is unknown, but "one possibility is that the magnetic events which preceded the Alaska earthquake resulted from piezomagnetic effects of rocks undergoing a change in stress" (Moore, 1964, p. 509).

Biologic Effects

Probably few earthquakes have so strongly affected the fauna and flora of a region as did the Alaska earthquake of 1964. Moreover, because of the complex interrelations of one organism to another, the total biologic effects will not be known for a long time. In the littoral zones of the Prince William Sound region, of the Kenai Peninsula, Kodiak and elsewhere, large communities of organisms were adversely affected when pronounced crustal changes completely altered the ecologic setting of the shore. Broad expanses of shore and sea bottom were elevated above tide water in Prince William Sound, and innumerable marine organisms were exterminated. Effects were equally marked in the subsided upper end of Turnagain Arm near Girdwood and Portage, where coastal marshlands and forest were inundated by salt water—areas that formerly had provided winter forage for moose and nesting grounds for migratory birds. Extensive forested and grassland areas of Kodiak and Afognak Islands were drowned, also.

Hanna (1964, p. 24) has summarized the biologic effects of the earthquake in the littoral zone of Prince William Sound, and he portrays the extent of the depopulation in the following passage:

"The exposed areas spread out before the observer are many hundreds of square miles, once densely populated by a varied fauna and flora, now completely desolated. Many of the great array of marine animals that you read about when you study zoology are dead. There is now no littoral zone anywhere that the land went up 10 feet or more. Most of the soft-bodied creatures had decomposed or had become food for birds by the time of our visit, 2 months after the earthquake, so the odor was not overpowering. The great array of living marine plants, so conspicuous along most coastlines, was gone. The *Fucus* had turned black from thirst; the calcareous algae were bleached white and so were the many species of green algae. The great fields of big brown kelp were gone, but the individual stalks left their stems and holdfasts, black and bent over, a menace to the unwary footman.

"In many places there were great accumulations of dried starfish; and in one, the dried necks of clams formed a solid mass covering about a square yard. We left to speculation the manner in which these objects came to congregate. In some places a shovel could have been used to collect almost pure concentrations of small shells. Bleached remains of Bryozoa and calcareous algae were so white that the rocky beaches rivalled the snow covered adjacent mountains in brightness."

During studies that are still in progress, G. D. Hanna and George Plafker jointly examined the distribution of tectonically disturbed zones of sessile organisms. Some of these organisms, such as barnacles and various algae, grow in response to rigorous water-depth controls, and their postearthquake vertical distribution above or below mean high-tide level provides a reliable measure of land displacement where geodetic control is unavailable.

Other deleterious effects on organisms were caused by sea waves. In addition to the enormous direct destruction caused by the waves themselves, salt water invaded many coastal lakes and destroyed, at least temporarily, the fresh-water habitat. Spawning beds for salmon in some instances were destroyed by siltation in river deltas. Direct kills of eggs and fry were caused by disturbance of the gravel beds of streams.

Fish populations were also destroyed when streams and lakes temporarily lost water into ground cracks, or when streams were dammed by landslides.

On the other hand, subsidence in some areas opened miles of new spawning habitat by inundating previously impassable falls and velocity barriers in coastal streams.

The salmon fishery is one of Alaska's foremost resources, and the full impact of the quake on this fishery will not be realized until the matured 1964 hatch returns from the sea to spawn. Spawning areas for pink and chum salmon, which are intertidal spawners, received major damage in nearly all coastal sections affected by sea waves, uplift, or subsidence. On Kodiak and Afognak Island, moreover, the waves struck at a critical time when pink salmon fry were just moving from the spawning beds into the stream estuaries. Spawning areas for red and silver salmon were little affected by the earthquake.

Mortalities of dungeness crab were noted in the Copper River delta area after the earthquake, but the commercial catch appears to have been unaffected. King Crab, a deeper water species, apparently was not significantly affected by the earthquake. Although the total crab population itself was not markedly affected by the earthquake the crab industry was severely damaged by the loss of boats, gear, harbor facilities, and canneries. The loss of fishing vessels amounted to about $7 million and of related facilities to about $13 million. To some extent the loss was offset on the market by unusually heavy catches of crab during the 1964 season, so that the crab harvest was actually larger than usual.

Much of the commercial clam habitat in Prince William Sound and in the Copper River delta was damaged or destroyed.

The effects of the earthquake on terrestrial wildlife are mixed, and some short-term effects have even been beneficial. Again, only time will disclose the long-term effects. In the mountains, some mountain goats are reported to have been killed by avalanches, and there probably was some mortality among mountain sheep, deer, and moose. Although uplift adversely affected shellfish habitats, it favorably altered nesting habitats of ducks, geese, and trumpeter swans by eliminating flood dangers. The long-term ecology may be less favorable—a new balance will be established as brush gradually invades upland areas and emergent vegetation spreads over former mudflats; nesting places will shift accordingly. In tectonically subsided areas where extensive fresh-water marshlands and meadows have been invaded by salt water, populations of moose and other grazing animals will have to readjust downward to the new restricted food supply.

Damage Outside Alaska

Secondary damage effects of the earthquake reached far beyond Alaska as seismic sea waves generated on the continental shelf in the Gulf of Alaska spread rapidly across the Pacific Ocean to Hawaii, Japan, and Antarctica. The source mechanism of the waves has been investigated by Van Dorn (1964), who concluded that the waves were caused by the sudden displacement of water in the Gulf of Alaska, accompanying the uplift of thousands of square miles of sea floor. A maximum wave height of 4 feet was reported in the Antarctic Peninsula (Palmer Peninsula), but heights in Japan were only a foot or so (Van Dorn, 1964, p. 187). Hilo, Hawaii, had a 7-foot wave, but received only minor damage. Apparently the source was directional, the waves radiating preferentially southeastward. Wave heights thus were greater along the North coast than they were in the Aleutian Islands at comparable distances from the source.

As the train of sea waves advanced southward it spread damage in British Columbia, Washington, Oregon, and California. Heavy damage was localized in Alberni and Port Alberni, B. C., in Hot Springs Cove, B. C., and in Crescent City, Calif. At Alberni and Port Alberni, damage to houses and a forest-industries complex totaled several million dollars; 260 houses were damaged, 60 heavily. Of the 17 homes at Hot Springs Cove, 5 were washed away and 10 were heavily damaged.

The coast of Washington was damaged lightly. In Grays Harbor County, the waves destroyed a bridge across the Copalis River and overturned several trailer houses.

The Oregon coast was struck by 10- to 14-foot waves. Damage was concentrated in estuaries; a family of four was drowned at De Poe Bay. At Seaside, where a trailer park was flooded as water backed up the Necanicum River, damage totaled about $250,000. At Cannon Beach, damages totaled $250,000; power and telephone services were cut off and several houses were toppled off their foundations. At Gold Coast, docks and small boats were smashed in the Rogue River.

At Coos Bay, an initial wave 10 feet above mean high water was attenuated by crossing wide tidal flats before it reached Poney Point 7 miles up the channel, but at Florence an 8-foot wave traveling up a narrow channel was negligibly dissipated.

In California, minor harbor damage was sustained as far south as San Diego where small craft were destroyed and dock installations were damaged. In San Francisco Bay, water surging through the Golden Gate set adrift a ferry boat and a house boat, and caused about $1 million damage to small boats and berthing facilities at San Rafael. At Santa Cruz, a 35-foot floating dredge was set adrift and a 38-foot power cruiser was crushed.

At Crescent City, which bore the brunt of wave damage in California, 12 lives were lost despite a 1-hour tsunami warning. Eight boats were sunk, 3 are unaccounted for, and 15 capsized. Docks, harbor facilities, and the seawall were heavily damaged. Fifty-four homes were destroyed, 13 were heavily damaged, and 24 were slightly damaged. Forty-two small business buildings were destroyed, 118 were heavily damaged, and 29 were slightly damaged. Fires were started by the rupture and explosion of 5 bulk-storage oil tanks.

The fifth seismic sea wave to arrive at Crescent City caused most of the damage and took all 12 lives. After the first wave crested at 14.5 feet above mean low low water (MLLW), a second wave slacked off at 12 feet, followed by two much smaller waves. The townspeople, thinking that the tsunami was over, had begun to return to the flooded area when the fifth wave—coming in on a high tide—crested at 20.5 feet above MLLW.

Seiches were generated in various places remote from Alaska by amplification of direct seismic vibrations. In the Gulf of Mexico off Texas—completely separated physically from any possible effects of tsunamis—waves as much as 6 feet high damaged small craft. In addition, water was agitated in many swimming pools in Texas and Louisiana. Surface-water gauges recorded fluctuations in Texas, Louisiana, Arkansas, Missouri, Kentucky, Tennessee, Alabama, Georgia, and Pennsylvania.

The ground-water regimen was affected throughout much of North America. Water-level fluctuations were noted in wells throughout the coterminous United States and at points as distant as Puerto Rico, the Virgin Islands, and Denmark. Fluctuations of as much as 6 cm were recorded in wells in Denmark. The maximum reported fluctuation was 23 feet in a well at Belle Fourche, S. D. Fluctuations apparently were greatest in a broad belt extending southeast from South Dakota and Wisconsin, through Missouri and Illinois and on through Georgia and Florida to Puerto Rico. Most level changes in wells were temporary, but some were permanent. The water in some wells was temporarily muddied.

References

Alaska Department of Health and Welfare, 1964a, Good Friday earthquake called on resources of all in State: *Alaska's Health and Welfare*, v. 21, June 1964, p. 5–7.

————, 1964b, Preliminary report of earthquake damage to environmental health facilities and services in Alaska: Juneau, Alaska Dept. Health and Welfare, Environmental Health Br., 46 p.

Benioff, Hugo, and Gutenberg, Beno, 1939, Waves and currents recorded by electromagnetic barographs: *Bull. Am. Meterorol. Soc.*, v. 20, p. 421–426.

Coulter, H. W., and Migliaccio, R. R., 1966 Effects of the March 27, 1964, earthquake at Valdez, Alaska: *U. S. Geol. Survey Prof. Paper 542–C*, 36 p.

Gutenberg, Beno, and Richter, C. F., 1949, *Seismicity of the earth and associated phenomena*: Princeton, N. J., Princeton Univ. Press, 273 p.

Hanna, G. D., 1964, Biological effects of an earthquake: *Pacific Discovery*, v. 17, no. 6, p. 24–26.

Hill, M. R., 1965, Earth hazards—an editorial: *California Div. Mines and Geology Mineral Inf. Service*, v. 18, no. 4, p. 57–59.

Moore, G. W., 1964, Magnetic disturbances preceding the Alaska earthquake: *Nature*, v. 203, no. 4944, p. 508–509.

Plafker, George, 1965, Tectonic deformation associated with the 1964 Alaska earthquake: *Science*, v. 148, no. 3678, p. 1675–1687.

Richter, C. F., 1958, *Elementary seismology*: San Francisco, W. H. Freeman and Co., 768 p.

U. S. Coast and Geodetic Survey, 1964, Prince William Sound, Alaskan earthquakes, March–April 1964: *U. S. Coast and Geod. Survey, Seismology Div., prelim. rept.*, 83 p.

Van Dorn, W. G., 1964, Source mechanism of the tsunami of March 28, 1964, in Alaska: *Coastal Eng. Conf., 9th, Lisbon, 1964, Proc.*, p. 166–190.

7   The San Fernando Earthquake of February 9, 1971

Lessons from a Moderate Earthquake on the Fringe of a Densely Populated Region

Prepared by The Joint Panel on the San Fernando Earthquake: Division of Earth Sciences, National Research Council, National Academy of Sciences, National Academy of Engineering

Introduction

The Los Angeles region, which was hard hit on its northern fringes by the moderate earthquake of February 9, 1971 (Richter magnitude 6.6), is a region in which much attention has been given to the earthquake hazard. Even then, this natural violence of the earth directly affected more than 400,000 people in the city of San Fernando and surroundings by damaging or destroying homes and public facilities and utilities—with a cost of 64 lives and perhaps as much as a billion dollars (see Fig. 1). Collapse of a portion of the Van Norman Dam led to the evacuation of 80,000 inhabitants living below the dam for several days while water was drained from the reservoir to avert imminent rupture of the dam and a catastrophe unprecedented in this country.

The ground quaked early in the morning (about six a.m. local time) while highways were relatively free of traffic and before most workers had

The San Fernando Earthquake of February 9, 1971, Lessons from a Moderate Earthquake on the Fringe of a Densely Populated Region, 1971, National Academy of Sciences. Reprinted by permission of the National Academy of Sciences and the National Academy of Engineering.

occupied offices in public buildings, and this minimized loss of life. Some of the earthquake losses can and will be restored in the near future; others, such as transportation disruption, severe damage to public utilities and facilities, and serious lowering of water-storage capacity, will take longer; and some losses can never be regained. These effects will force stricter earthquake preparedness measures in the Los Angeles area—and, we may hope, in other areas as well—as it is now clear that better preparation could have been made.

The particular location of this shock was not previously suspect any more than the heart of Los Angeles, where the damage would have been more catastrophic. Earthquakes of this size are not uncommon: More than 100 occur yearly around the world, but this one struck the edge of a great metropolis. It is certain that earthquakes of this size—and larger—will rock other places in the United States, rural and urban, in the future.

Earth scientists and earthquake engineers have been deeply concerned about their generally limited understanding of the hazards of earthquakes and by the consequent limited understanding by public officials responsible for the safety of millions. During the past few years, several reports have been written that both provide background knowledge and recommend action toward the mitigation of earthquake effects. The recommendations made in the reports listed in the references are as valid today as when they were written. What seems needed now is to learn from the San Fernando Earthquake how best to prepare for and cope with the effects of future disasters of this kind.

Lessons Learned

1. Significance of Permanent Ground Displacement

Disruptions of the ground surface by faulting and other closely associated permanent deformations of rock and soil were much more important causes of structural failure during this earthquake than in any previous United States earthquake. This emphasizes once again the hazards associated with urbanization of active fault zones. On the other hand, many of the faults that broke during this earthquake were not generally shown on geologic maps published prior to the event, and none had been considered particularly active. The need for making structures safe is obvious. At the same time, more intensive geological, geophysical, and geodetic studies of earthquake-prone regions of the country must be made. Were there unrecognized geological clues that might have revealed that this area, and these faults, were particularly hazardous? Are there other geologically similar areas in which comparable earthquakes might occur? Merely ask-

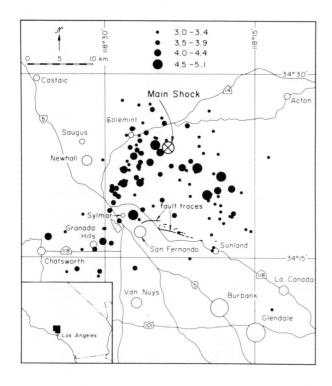

FIG. 1. The San Fernando Earthquake of February 9, 1971. The map shows the location of the epicenter of the main shock (magnitude 6.6) and of representative aftershocks (magnitudes greater than 3) through March 1, 1971. Approximate traces of some of the faulting activated during this earthquake are also shown. (Prepared by the Seismological Laboratory, California Institute of Technology.)

ing such questions points up the necessity for interdisciplinary effort by engineers, seismologists, and geologists in land-use planning for earthquake-prone regions.

2. Measurement of Strong Ground Shaking

An unprecedented description of the ground motions and resulting building responses was provided by more than 200 strong-motion accelerographs. This National Oceanic and Atmospheric Administration network operated well during the earthquake. Among the records were several obtained on dams. One instrument, in the epicentral region, showed the highest acceleration ever measured during an earthquake; it indicated in detail the time sequence of the main shock and many of the major aftershocks (see Fig. 2). These measurements will form the basis for a re-evaluation of earthquake-resistant design. The accelerograph records obtained in about 30 large modern buildings will permit many significant studies of the design of earthquake-resistant structures. The success of this network, and the potential value of such data for the protection of the public, leads us to recommend strongly that the currently very inadequate strong-motion-accelerograph coverage should include numerous building structures and ground sites in all urban areas in seismic regions and important engineering structures such as dams and nuclear power plants.

In addition, greater effort and appropriate instrumentation should be devoted to studies of the effects of topography and the character of geologic material on the distribution and amplitude of strong ground motion.

3. Significance of the Striking Local Ground Motions

This earthquake demonstrated that local ground motion is not a simple function of the size of the shock. This magnitude 6.6 earthquake was associated (mainly in a restricted region some ten miles long and five miles wide along the Valley edge) with a severity of ground motion that was probably close to the maximum generated by any earthquake. An earthquake of greater magnitude would involve strong ground motion over a greater area, consistent with longer fault breakage, and a greater duration of shaking.

The surface expression of the faulting and its character at depth as determined by seismological studies showed that the crustal materials beneath the San Gabriel Mountains were uplifted and thrust toward the northern margin of the Valley by six feet or more. In the Upper San Fernando Valley and in Sylmar, buildings were called upon to withstand extremely strong ground motions. In this local region, the motion consisted of both severe shaking and a heave upward and toward the south (perhaps in several episodes). The strong-motion accelerometer at

FIG. 2. Strong-motion accelerograph record of the main shock of the San Fernando Earthquake of February 9, 1971, in the epicentral region on a mountain ridge at Pacoima Dam of the Los Angeles County Flood Control District. This station is part of the NOAA accelerograph network. (Record processed by the Jet Propulsion Laboratory, Pasadena; made available by the Earthquake Engineering Research Laboratory, California Institute of Technology, which is supported by the National Science Foundation.)

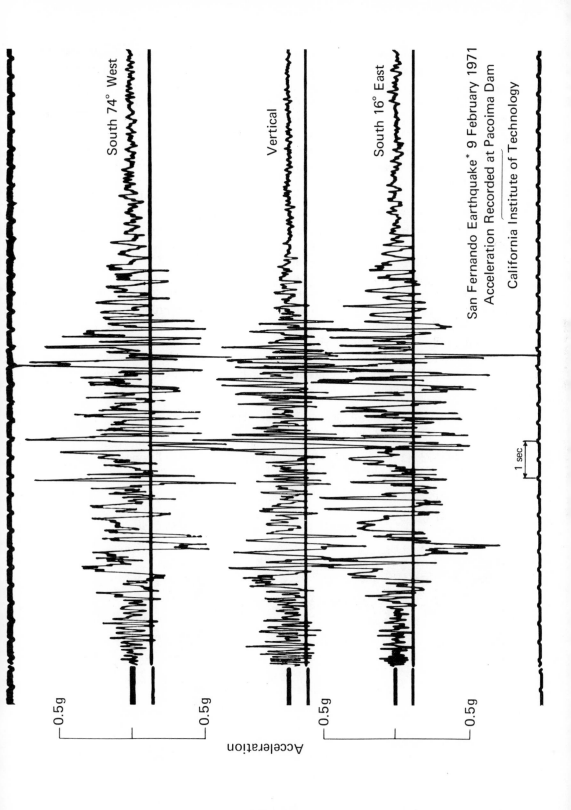

Acceleration

0.5g   0.5g   0.5g   0.5g

South 74° West

Vertical

South 16° East

San Fernando Earthquake* 9 February 1971
Acceleration Recorded at Pacoima Dam

California Institute of Technology

1 sec

Pacoima Dam, on solid rock, showed ground motions 50 to 75 percent of the earth's natural gravitational acceleration (with a few peaks equal to gravity) lasting approximately 12 seconds overall. The dam is less than two miles from the Sylmar Veterans Hospital, which sustained severe damage and loss of life (see Fig. 3).

4. Building Code Revision

This earthquake has provided the first really comprehensive practical test of United States earthquake codes in and close to an epicentral region. Modern structures designed according to the earthquake requirements of the building code performed well in the regions of moderately strong ground shaking (peak accelerations of 10 to 20 percent g). In the region of very strong ground motion, however, some modern buildings were severely damaged (see Fig. 4). A few that collapsed would have caused many additional deaths had they been occupied at this early hour. If the duration of strong ground shaking had been appreciably longer than ten seconds, as it would be in a great earthquake, some of the severely damaged structures would almost certainly have collapsed. It is clear that existing building codes do not provide adequate damage-control features. Such codes should be revised.

5. Back-up Emergency Services

In earthquake-prone regions, service organizations such as the police and fire departments, and medical services, will be put under heavy stress following an earthquake of significant size.

FIG. 3. Collapsed portion of Sylmar Veterans Hospital being removed in search for survivors. The last of 14 survivors was found shortly after this photograph was taken. In this Hospital, built before the current building codes were established, 42 people were killed. (Courtesy of Earthquake Engineering Research Laboratory, California Institute of Technology.)

The San Fernando Earthquake affected an area of only moderate size. It is necessary, therefore, to examine the organization and distribution of emergency services in the light of the fact that a major earthquake would affect a much larger area. Moreover, much of the loss of life and damage to property associated with an earthquake are attributable to aftereffects such as fire, flood, or seismic sea waves.

The opportunity should be seized to make a careful evaluation of the performance of emergency services following the San Fernando Earthquake and to determine the kinds and extent of back-up required to prepare for a much larger event. Such a study, preferably involving federal, state, and other organizations, would provide guidelines for other earthquake-prone regions of high population density as well.

6. Rapid Reconnaissance Studies

The vital need for rapid reconnaissance studies immediately following a damaging earthquake is once again emphasized by the experience of the San Fernando Earthquake. For example, the entire northern part of the San Fernando Valley should have been systematically photographed from the air at very large scale (one inch equal to several hundred feet) on the morning of the earthquake in order, as quickly as possible, to locate sites of severe damage and to delimit the overall extent of such damage, as well as to identify visible surface expression of

FIG. 4. Two-story Olive View Hospital psychiatric building, constructed in accordance with current building codes, collapsed so that the second floor is now at ground level. The first floor contained administrative offices and examination rooms that were, fortunately, unoccupied at the early hour of the earthquake. (Courtesy of Earthquake Engineering Research Laboratory, California Institute of Technology.)

the faulting. But apparently no agency had the responsibility to initiate such an effort. It is clear, therefore, that an agency should be designated to assume the responsibility to initiate rapid reconnaissance studies of this type following future major earthquakes, and that adequate funding should be provided.

7. Protection of Critical Public Buildings

A striking consequence of the earthquake was the fact that four hospitals in the San Fernando area were damaged so severely that they were no longer operational just when they were most needed. Certain critical structures should be designed so that they will remain functional even after experiencing the most severe ground shaking.

Included are hospitals, schools, and other high-occupancy buildings, as well as buildings housing police and fire departments and other agencies relied upon to cope with disasters. Basic utilities that must be depended upon to mitigate a disaster must also receive an extra measure of protection. Ordinary building codes cannot be depended upon to provide this extra protection, and special damage-control provisions should be mandatory to ensure such additional safety in high-risk areas.

8. Earthquake Safety of Dams

The near failure of the lower Van Norman Dam (see Fig. 5) endangered the lives of tens of thousands of people. Such risks are clearly unacceptable. An improved program for bringing older dams in earthquake-prone areas up to

FIG. 5. The Van Norman Dam, which was so severely damaged by the earthquake that 80,000 people living in the Valley below were evacuated because complete failure appeared imminent. They returned to their homes four days later, after the reservoir had been lowered to a safe level. (Courtesy of Earthquake Engineering Research Laboratory, California Institute of Technology.)

the best modern safety standards is imperative, and these best standards should themselves be constantly reviewed. Many existing dams in all parts of the country have not been designed to resist significant earthquake forces; these structures should be thoroughly examined and measures should be taken to reduce such hazards. Additional basic research into the behavior of dams and soil structures during earthquakes will be required for the implementation of such a program. The fact that the Van Norman Dam did not quite fail totally should not be a source of comfort.

9. Earthquake Hazard of Old Structures

During the San Fernando Earthquake, many old, weak buildings in the regions of strong and moderately strong shaking suffered severe damage, and the major loss of life occurred in one old building, the Sylmar Veterans Hospital, designed before the adoption of modern building codes. There are many thousands of such old buildings in California that will collapse if subjected to strong ground shaking. Programs should be undertaken to render such buildings safe, or to raze them, over a reasonable period of time.

A successful effort to improve or eliminate old structures has been underway for some time in the city of Long Beach, and in the city of Los Angeles especially hazardous parapet walls have been removed from several thousand buildings or have been strengthened. This earthquake dramatically demonstrated the value of such procedures. A much more extensive program to eliminate the major hazard of old buildings is strongly recommended. Urban renewal programs can provide a suitable opportunity for such improvements in California and in other earthquake-prone areas.

10. Safety of Bridges and Freeway Overpasses

A number of freeway overpass bridges collapsed during the San Fernando Earthquake, causing some deaths and resulting in significant local disruption of traffic. In an earthquake of greater extent, such interruption of transportation could greatly magnify the disastrous effects of the earthquake. Freeway bridges and important highway bridges should be designed for adequate safety against collapse. Present standard code requirements for earthquake design of highway bridges in high-risk areas are grossly inadequate and should be revised.

11. Safeness of School Buildings

It is noteworthy that school buildings in the region of strong shaking designed and constructed since enactment of the Field Act of the California State Legislature did not suffer structural damage that would have been dangerous to the occupants had the schools been in session. This demonstrated that one- and two-story school buildings can indeed be made safe by practicable code requirements, permitting them to withstand very strong shaking combined with appreciable ground deformation beneath the structure.

Older school buildings, which did not meet the requirements of the Field Act, suffered potentially hazardous damage as a result of moderately strong ground shaking. The lesson is clear that such hazardous school buildings must be eliminated or strengthened. Appropriate authorities in all seismic regions of the country should take this lesson to heart.

12. Study of Damaged Urban Dwellings

This earthquake throws an almost unique light on seismic hazard in a modern urban environment. Extensive damage to small homes and small-business structures occurred in zones where severe shaking was accompanied by permanent ground displacement associated with the faulting. Therefore, much crucial information can be gained by an immediate dwelling-by-dwelling study of earthquake damage. Such a study should be conducted by appropriate federal, state, and local agencies, with a view toward developing sounder guidelines for building construction, particularly of one- and two-story buildings.

13. Earthquake Insurance for Houses and Small Businesses

Because recognized geological evidence of active faulting was lacking in this particular area, the people who lost their homes and businesses in the Sylmar-San Fernando areas could have had no warning of the special hazards to which they were exposed. Permanent displacement of the ground caused by surface faulting, landslides, and consolidation and slumping of soils were responsible for much damage to structures. In many places, deformation of the ground beneath a structure greatly magnified the damaging effect of the ground shaking.

Such innocent victims of earthquakes should be protected by insurance, or the authorities must be pre-pared to consider better relief measures than those now used. The cost of repairing such unforeseeable damage should be shared by all who live in disaster-prone regions. A form of earthquake insurance that will be much more widely used should be developed, with Federal Government back-up if necessary.

14. Preservation of Vital Support Systems

Damage to the Sylmar Converter Station, a key link in a system for transmission of electric power into the Los Angeles area, will keep this system inoperable for about a year while replacement parts are manufactured. This demonstrates in a dramatic way the increasing vulnerability to earthquakes of our society's vital support systems. Networks for the distribution of electrical power, water, and gas, for disposal of sewage, and for transportation of food and other essentials continue to grow in size and complexity as the numbers of people dependent upon them reach into the multimillions.

The collapse of several highway overpasses during the earthquake had a limited effect on transportation, but such destruction could be more widespread in a larger earthquake, perhaps compounding transportation difficulties to disaster proportions.

A major unit of the water supply system, the Van Norman reservoir, was virtually eliminated without seriously disrupting distribution of water. Compounding of such effects in a larger earthquake is clear cause for concern.

For the crucial systems vital to millions of people, design of individual components is not adequate in the face of the known earthquake hazard. Continuing efforts must be exerted to build into the system sufficient redundancy to ensure against complete failure in the event of a major earthquake.

15. The Problem of Seismic Zoning

The unexpected occurrence of an earthquake in this location and the concentration of the most severe damage in zones of ground breakage forcefully illustrate both the importance and the difficulty of responsible and practicable seismic zoning. No evidence from previously completed geological or seismological studies had been generally interpreted as indicating that the region affected was a more likely place for a damaging earthquake than many other parts of the southern California seismic region.

This experience points out once again that the short-term local seismic history is not in itself an adequate base for estimating earthquake risk. Until we gain a better understanding of earthquake processes and probabilities, due regard for public safety demands that seismic hazard be considered high throughout wide areas, and seismic zoning maps must reflect this. Many agencies and groups are working constructively on the problem of recognizing seismic hazards, but this effort is so important that it deserves more support.

16. Land Use and Geologic Hazards

More than ever before, local communities are seeking guidance concerning environmental hazards of all types that should be taken into account in planning for the use of land to be developed. Permits for construction of residential and commercial buildings in areas subject to earthquakes, land-slides, and flooding, for example, should only be issued on the basis of a meaningful evaluation of the potential risks and only after the purchaser is aware of all the known facts.

State and local government needs support in the form of well-conceived regulations in order to resist political and economic pressures to develop land in ways that are unwise in terms of environmental hazards.

17. Study of the Southern Sector of the San Andreas Fault

The redistribution of crustal stresses caused by the San Fernando Earthquake cannot help but have some effect on the nearby segments of the San Andreas Fault, which has long been considered a source for much larger earthquakes. Because of this changed situation, the San Andreas Fault in this temporarily "locked" segment is a particularly critical area to study and to monitor, especially in view of its proximity to the largest metropolitan center in the Western United States. (The closest point on the San Andreas Fault to the center of Los Angeles is less than half again as far as was the epicenter of the San Fernando Earthquake.) It is strongly recommended that additional research programs be started at once to study the southern sector of the fault.

18. Seismological Studies

The San Fernando Earthquake was the best monitored earthquake in United States history because of the high level of scientific preparedness in this area and the immediate response of earthquake researchers. Immediately available seismic data were important in delineating the scope of the disaster, aided repair and reconstruction, and facilitated further scientific studies.

In the Los Angeles area, a telemetry-equipped seismic network that was in operation prior to the earthquake provided excellent records of pre- and post-earthquake seismicity, but even this network could have been markedly improved in effectiveness by a greater number of telemetry-equipped stations and a more comprehensive seismic monitoring program. It is clear that, prior to the earthquake, seismological information even for this region was not as complete as it could have been, and indeed should have been, given the capabilities of present technology. Pre- and post-earthquake geodetic observations should be an intrinsic part of such monitoring systems. Both seismologic and geodetic capabilities are urgently in need of upgrading in all earthquake-prone regions of the country.

The seismic data gathered during and following the earthquake provided the basis for locating the sources and determining the mechanics of the faulting at depth. Such studies, together with geologic and geodetic studies, will also yield important information about the earth deformation that occurred in association with this earthquake and its aftershocks. This will be important in assessing the seismic hazard elsewhere. The San Fernando Earthquake is a reminder that a vastly improved understanding of earth movements at all scales is needed.

References

Report of the Task Force on Earthquake Hazard Reduction, Program Priorities. Office of Science and Technology, Executive Office of the President, 1970.

Seismology: Responsibilities and Requirements of a Growing Science. Part I, *Summary and Recommendations;* Part II, *Problems and Prospects.* NRC Committee on Seismology, National Academy of Sciences, Washington, D. C., 1969.

Toward Reduction of Losses from Earthquakes. NRC Committee on the Alaska Earthquake, National Academy of Sciences, Washington, D. C., 1969.

Earthquake Engineering Research, NAE Committee on Earthquake Engineering Research, National Academy of Sciences, Washington, D. C., 1969.

Proposal for a Ten-Year National Earthquake Hazards Program. Report of the Ad Hoc Interagency Working Group for Earthquake Research of the Federal Council for Science and Technology, Interior—U. S. Geological Survey, Washington, D. C., 1968.

Earthquake Prediction. Report of the Ad Hoc Panel on Earthquake Prediction of the Office of Science and Technology, Executive Office of the President, 1965.

8 Man-made Earthquakes in Denver

David M. Evans

Evans, D. M., 1966, "Man-made Earthquakes in Denver," *Geotimes,* vol. 10, no. 9, pp. 11–18. Lightly edited by permission of the author and reprinted by permission of the American Geological Institute. Copyright 1966 by A. G. I.

Mr. Evans is a consulting geologist in Denver, Colorado.

From April 1962 to November 1965, Denver experienced more than 700 earthquakes. They were not damaging —the greatest magnitude was 4.3 on the Richter scale—but the community became increasingly concerned. More and more people took out earthquake insurance. There was talk in the press that Denver might be removed from the list of possible sites for a $375 million accelerator to be built by the Atomic Energy Commission because it was becoming known as an earthquake area.

In November 1962, I publicly suggested that there was a direct relationship between the earthquakes and contaminated waste-water being injected into a 12,045-foot disposal well at the Rocky Mountain Arsenal, northeast of Denver.[1] Representative Roy McVicker of Colorado immediately called for a full scientific investigation of the tremors, and on March 19, 1966, the U. S. Geological Survey released the results of its studies in coöperation with the Colorado School of Mines, Regis College in Denver, and the University of Colorado.[2] The USGS concluded that "The pumping of waste fluids into a deep disposal well at the Rocky Mountain Arsenal near Denver appears to be a significant cause of a series of minor earthquakes that have occurred just north of Denver since the spring of 1962."

Since 1942, the Rocky Mountain Arsenal has manufactured products on a large scale for chemical warfare and industrial use, under direction of the Chemical Corps of the U. S. Army. One by-product of this operation is contaminated waste-water and, until 1961, the water was disposed of by evaporation from earthen reservoirs.

When it was found that the waste-water was contaminating the ground water and endangering crops, the Chemical Corps tried evaporating the water from water-tight reservoirs. That failed, so the Corps decided to drill an injection disposal well.

It commissioned E. A. Polumbus Jr. & Associates Inc. to design the well, supervise drilling and completion, provide the necessary engineering-geology services, and manage the project. Louis J. Scopel, as an associate, was the project geologist. Another associate, George R. Downs, contributed to the initial design and acted as an adviser.

The well was drilled in NW¼ NE¼ sec. 26, T2S, R67W, Adams County, Colorado. It was completed in September 1961 at a total depth of 12,045 feet.[3]

Regional Geology

The Rocky Mountain Arsenal disposal well is on the gently dipping east flank of the Denver-Julesburg Basin, just a few miles east of the basin axis. As indicated in Fig. 1, it is in a region of the subcrop of Cambro-Ordovician rocks near the area where those rocks are truncated and overlain by Pennsylvanian sediments.[4] Figure 2 is a cross-section that shows the subsurface geology from the Arsenal well to the outcrop of Precambrian granite gneiss west of Denver.[5]

About 13,000 feet of structural relief exists between the top of the Precambrian in the Arsenal well and the Precambrian outcrops.

Injection in Precambrian Rocks

According to Scopel,[3] Precambrian rocks were penetrated in the Arsenal well from 11,950 feet to the total depth

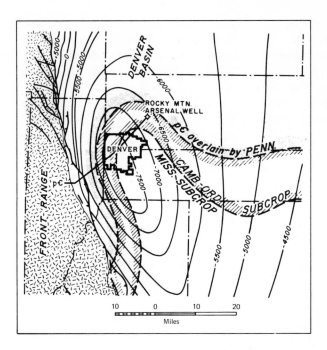

FIG. 1. Structural map of a part of the Denver-Julesburg Basin shows the location of the Rocky Mountain Arsenal Well. (After Anderman and Ackman[4])

of 12,045. He described the rocks as bright green weathered schist from 11,950 to 11,970 and as highly fractured hornblende granite gneiss containing pegmatite intrusions from 11,970 to the bottom of the hole.

As a part of the USGS study, Sheridan, Wrucke, and Wilcox[2] analyzed the core and cuttings from the lower part of the well, and concluded that the top of the Precambrian is at 11,935. They describe the section from 11,970 to 12,045 as "migmatitic gneiss: rock containing fine-to-medium-grained hornblendic biotite-quartz-feldspar rock, containing steeply dipping open fractures, and thin calcite and ankerite-filled veinlets and microbreccias." They point out the striking similarity between the fractured Precambrian gneiss of the Arsenal well and the breccia-reef faults and fracture zones in the

Precambrian outcrop of the Front Range west of Denver.

In the Arsenal well, a 5½-inch liner was cemented 5 feet into the Precambrian gneiss at 11,975 feet, and 5½-inch tubing was run to a depth of 9,011 feet, to complete the well for injection into the almost vertically fractured gneiss from 11,975 feet to 12,045.

Pumping and pressure-injection tests were made from November 1961 to February 1962 to obtain reservoir fluid samples and to determine rates and injection pressures at which the reservoir would take fluid.

A conventional oil-field pump was run in the well, and pumping tests were made. After pumping out 1,100 barrels of salt water more than the fluid lost in the hole during drilling, the well pumped down and recovery became negligible. It was concluded at the time of testing that fluid recovery was from fractures. It was believed further that as fluid was withdrawn from these fractures they were squeezed shut by compressive forces, which restricted fluid entry into the well bore.

When fluid injection tests were made, it was noticed that as fluid was injected the calculated drainage radius and formation capacity increased. That was interpreted as an indication that the reservoir consisted of fractures that expanded as additional fluid was injected.

In March 1962 the Arsenal disposal program began, and 4.2 million gallons of waste was injected. The Denver earthquakes started the next month.

The monthly volume of waste injected is shown in the lower half of Fig. 3. From March 1962 until September 1963, the maximum injection pressure is reported to have been about 550 pounds per square inch, with an injection rate of 200 gallons a minute.

At the end of September 1963 the injection well was shut down, and no fluid was injected until September 17, 1964. During the shut-down, surface evaporation from the settling basin was sufficient to handle the plant output.

From September 17, 1964, until the end of March 1965, injection was resumed by gravity discharge into the well. No well-head pressure was needed to inject the maximum of 2.4 million gallons of waste per month into the well. Beginning in April 1965 larger quantities of fluid were injected. During April and May a maximum pressure of 1,050 pounds was required to inject 300 gallons a minute.

The Denver Earthquakes

The U. S. Coast & Geodetic Survey reports that on November 7, 1882, an earthquake was felt in Denver and nearby Louisville and Georgetown, and in southeast Wyoming. According to Joseph V. Downey, director of the

FIG. 2. Cross-section shows subsurface geology from the Arsenal well to the outcrop of Precambrian granite gneiss west of Denver. (After M. F. and C. M. Boos and H. H. Odiorne) The line of cross-section is shown in Fig. 1.

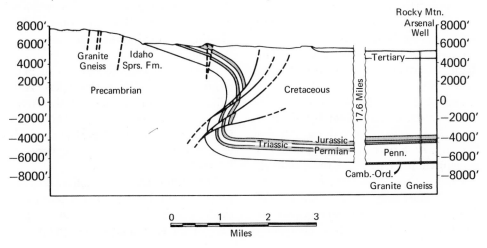

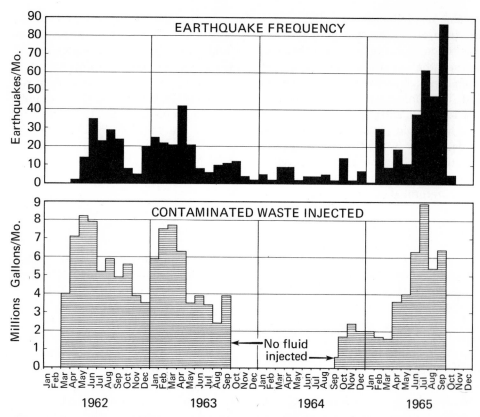

FIG. 3. Upper half: number of earthquakes per month recorded in the Denver area. Lower half: monthly volume of contaminated waste water injected into the Arsenal well.

Regis College Seismological Observatory, no earthquake epicenters were recorded in the Denver area by either the C&GS or Regis between 1882 and the first earthquake in April 1962. (The Regis Observatory has been operating since 1909.)

From 1954 to 1959 a seismic station was operated at the University of Colorado in Boulder, directed by Warren Longley. As a part of the recent USGS investigation, Harold L. Krivoy and M. P. Lane analyzed the records from that station.[2] They found a few small events that might have been earthquakes in the Derby area, but they concluded

that, since all those events occurred during weekday working hours, they were probably due to construction blasting or explosives disposal at the Arsenal.

From April 1962 to the end of September 1965, 710 earthquakes with epicenters in the vicinity of the Arsenal were recorded at the Cecil H. Green Observatory, Bergen Park, Colo., which is operated by Colorado School of Mines.[6]

The total number of earthquakes reported in the Denver area is plotted in the upper half of Fig. 3. The magnitude of the earthquakes reported range from 0.7 to 4.3 on the Richter scale. About 75 were intense enough to be felt. Yung-liang Wang[6] calculated the epicenters and hypocenters of the 1963–65 Denver earthquakes, and Fig. 4 shows the results of his calculations.

Most of the epicenters are within 5 miles of the well. All epicenters calculated from four or more recording stations are within 7 miles of the well.

Wang[6] calculated the best-fitting plane passing through the zone of hypocenters determined from four or more recording stations. He concluded that this plane might be a fault along which movement was taking place. The plane dips east and passes beneath the Arsenal well about 6.5 miles below the surface. (See Fig. 4.)

In the USGS study,[2] J. J. Healy, W. H. Jackson and J. R. Van Schaack report that Wang's data were compiled from records of available seismographs and that most of the earthquakes plotted were with fewer than four stations and that only a few were located with four stations. Also, the four stations available to Wang in his study were not optimally placed to locate earthquakes in the vicinity of the Arsenal. Therefore the USGS set up a seismic network around the Arsenal well that would greatly improve the accuracy of earthquake location. Up to eight seismic-refraction units were in operation at the same time, and during the study from one to 20 micro-earthquakes were recorded every day.

Healy, Jackson and Van Schaack concluded that the precise USGS work showed the epicenters clustered even more closely around the Arsenal well than Wang had reported. The epicenters located by the USGS outline a roughly ellipsoidal area (which includes the well) about six miles long and three miles wide, suggesting the presence of a fault or fracture zone trending about N 60° W. The epicenters of the events studied in detail were between 4.5 and 5.5 km deep.

Pressure Injection and Earthquake Frequency

Pressure injection began in March 1962. The first two earthquakes with epicenters in the Arsenal area were recorded in April 1962.

The lower half of Fig. 3 is a graph of the monthly volume of waste injected into the Arsenal well. The total number of earthquakes recorded in the Arsenal area is plotted for each month in the upper half of the graph.

During the initial injection period, from March 1962 to the end of September 1963, the injection program was often suspended for repairs to the filter plant. In this period there does not appear to be a direct month-by-month correlation. However, the high injection months of April, May and June 1962 seem to correlate with the high earthquake frequency months of June, July and August. The high injection months of February and March 1963 may correlate with the high earthquake month of April.

The period of no injection from September 1963 to September 1964 coincides with a period of minimum earthquake frequency. The period of low-volume injection by gravity flow, from September 1964 to April 1965, is characterized by two months (October and February) of greater earthquake frequency than experienced during the preceding year.

The most direct correlation of fluid

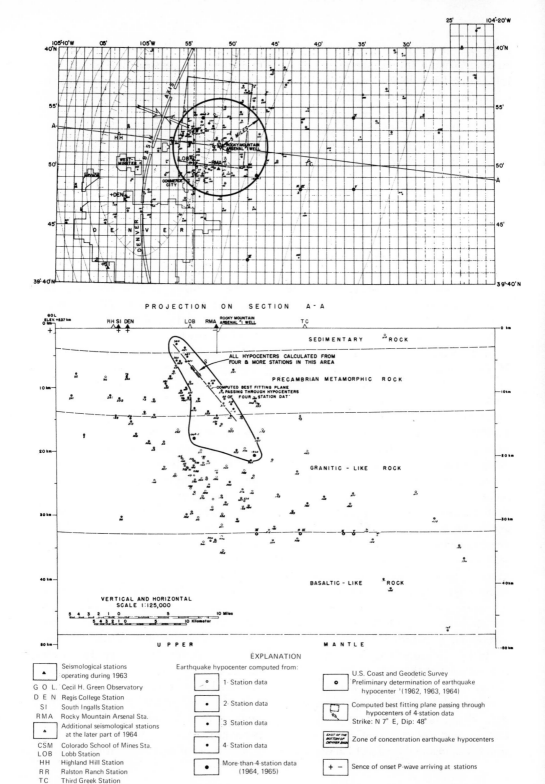

PROJECTION ON SECTION A-A

SEDIMENTARY ROCK

ALL HYPOCENTERS CALCULATED FROM
FOUR & MORE STATIONS IN THIS AREA

PRECAMBRIAN METAMORPHIC ROCK

COMPUTED BEST FITTING PLANE
PASSING THROUGH HYPOCENTERS
OF FOUR STATION DATA

GRANITIC - LIKE ROCK

BASALTIC - LIKE ROCK

VERTICAL AND HORIZONTAL
SCALE 1:125,000

UPPER MANTLE

EXPLANATION

Earthquake hypocenter computed from:

▲ Seismological stations
    operating during 1963
G O L. Cecil H. Green Observatory
D E N Regis College Station
S I South Ingalls Station
R M A Rocky Mountain Arsenal Sta.
▲ Additional seismological stations
    at the later part of 1964
CSM Colorado School of Mines Sta.
LOB Lobb Station
HH Highland Hill Station
R R Ralston Ranch Station
T C Third Greek Station

○ 1- Station data

● 2- Station data

● 3 Station data

● 4- Station data

● More-than-4-station data
    (1964, 1965)

○ U.S. Coast and Geodetic Survey
    Preliminary determination of earthquake
    hypocenter '(1962, 1963, 1964)

    Computed best fitting plane passing through
    hypocenters of 4-station data
    Strike: N 7° E, Dip: 48°

    Zone of concentration earthquake hypocenters

+ − Sence of onset P-wave arriving at stations

injection with earthquake frequency is during the months of June through September 1965. That period was characterized by the pumping of 300 gallons a minute, 16 to 24 hours a day, at a pressure of 800 to 1,050 pounds.

There have been five characteristic periods of injection (see Fig. 5):

April 1962–April 1963; high injection at medium pressure.

May 1963–September 1963; medium injection at medium pressure.

October 1963–September 1964; no injection.

September 1964–March 1965; low injection at no pressure (gravity feed).

April 1965–September 1965; high injection at high pressure.

The average numbers of earthquakes per month are shown in Fig. 5 above the average volumes of fluid injected per month for each of those five periods. The injection for March 1962 is not used in the averages because the exact day injection was started is unknown.

Figure 5 indicates that there is a direct correlation between average monthly injection and earthquake frequency when an injection program has been carried out for several months.

The period of October, November and December 1965 provided the first check period of the correlation between earthquakes and fluid injected. From October 1 to December 20 an average of 3.8 million gallons a month were injected at an average pressure of 1,000 pounds. On December 20 the pressure was reduced to 500 pounds. From Fig. 5, it can be seen that during May–September 1963 approximately the same amount of fluid was injected at roughly half the pressure and an average of 12 earthquakes a month were recorded. With an injection pressure of 1,000 pounds, about twice as many tremors (as recorded during April–September 1965) would be expected. Allowing for the 10 days in December when the pressure was reduced, an average of about 25 earthquakes a month would be predicted. Actually, 68 shocks were recorded, for an average of slightly less than 23 a month.

During January 1966, about 2.4 million gallons were injected, and 19 shocks were recorded. On January 20, 1966, pumping was stopped; during February, 200,000 gallons were injected by gravity flow. On February 20 the well was shut in. Ten earthquakes were recorded during February at the Cecil H. Green Observatory (whose earthquake count has been used in this report).

George Bardwell[7] has made a statistical analysis of the relationship between fluid injection at the Arsenal well and earthquake frequency in the area. Even though his study did not include the effect of injection pressure, he concluded that the probability of the injection-earthquake relationship being due to random fluctuation was about 1 in 1,000.

FIG. 4. Earthquake hypocenters are shown here for 1963–64 as computed by seismological stations in the Denver area. All epicenters calculated from four or more recording stations are within 7 miles of the Arsenal well. All hypocenters calculated from four or more recording stations are within the area indicated on section A-A. (After Wang[6])

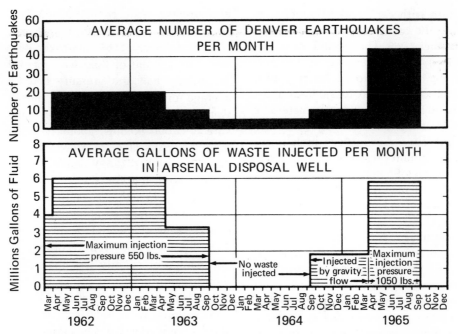

FIG. 5. Relationships of earthquake frequency and waste injection are shown here for five characteristic periods.

Fluid Pressure and the Arsenal Earthquakes

Evidence gained from drilling and testing the Arsenal disposal well indicates that the Precambrian reservoir is composed of a highly fractured gneiss that is substantially impermeable. It indicates that as fluid was pumped out of the reservoir the fractures closed, and as fluid was injected the fractures opened. In other words, the pumping and injection tests indicated that rock movement occurred as fluid was withdrawn or injected at relatively low pressures.

The pressure-depth relations of the Precambrian reservoir, showing hydrostatic and lithostatic pressure variations with depth, are shown in Fig. 6. Those data were determined from a drill-stem test. As shown on the chart, the observed pressure of the Precambrian reservoir is almost 900 pounds less than the hydrostatic pressure.

Hubbert and Rubey[8] have devised a simple and adequate way to reduce by the required amount the frictional resistance to the sliding of large overthrust blocks down very gentle slopes. It arises from the circumstance that the weight of such a block is jointly supported by solid stress and the pressure of interstitial fluids. As the fluid pressure approaches the lithostatic pressure, corresponding to flotation of the overburden, the shear stress required to move the block approaches zero.

If high fluid pressures reduce frictional resistance and permit rocks to slide down very gentle slopes, it follows that as fluid pressure is decreased frictional resistance between blocks of rock is increased, permitting them to come to rest on increasingly steep slopes. The steeper the slope on which a block of rock is at rest, the lower the required increase in fluid pressure necessary to produce movement.

In the case of the Precambrian reservoir beneath the Arsenal well, the rocks were at equilibrium on high-angle fracture planes with a fluid pressure of 900 pounds less than the hydrostatic pressure before injection began.

As fluid was injected into the Precambrian reservoir, the fluid pressure adjacent to the well bore rose, and the frictional resistance along the fracture planes was thereby reduced. When, finally, enough fluid pressure was exerted over enough area, movement occurred. The elastic energy released was recorded as an earthquake.

Since the formation fluid pressure is 900 pounds subhydrostatic, merely filling the hole with contaminated waste (mostly salt water) raises the formation pressure 900 pounds, or to the equivalent of hydrostatic pressure. Any applied injection pressure above that of gravity flow increases pressure to a total higher than hydrostatic pressure. For example, an injection pressure of 1,000 pounds would raise the reservoir pressure adjacent to the well bore to 1,900 pounds, or by the amount to bring the pressure to hydrostatic (by filling the hole) plus 1,000 pounds.

Apparently a rise in fluid pressure within the Precambrian reservoir of 900 to 1,900 pounds is enough to allow movement to occur.

Open Fractures

The hypocenters in the Arsenal area plotted from data derived from four or more recording stations indicate that movement takes place 1.5 to 12 miles below the well. If the Precambrian fracture system extends to a depth of 12 miles, then fluid pressure could be transmitted to that depth by moderate surface injection pressure as long as

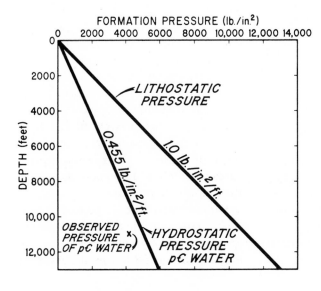

FIG. 6. Pressure-depth relations are shown here for the Precambrian reservoir at the Arsenal well.

the fracture system is open for transmission of that pressure.

Secor[9] concluded that open fractures can occur to great depths even with only moderately high fluid pressure-overburden weight ratios. It appears possible that high-angle open fractures may be present beneath the Arsenal well at great depths with much lower fluid pressure-overburden weight ratios than has formerly been considered possible.

Time Lag Between Fluid Injections and Earthquakes

The correlation of fluid injected with earthquake frequency (Fig. 3) suggests that the two are separated by a time lag. Bardwell[7] notes that the frequency of Denver earthquakes appears to lag waste injection by one to four months. This phenomenon is probably the same as that described by Serafim and Del Campo.[10] They describe the observed time lag between water levels in reservoirs and the pressures measured in the foundations of dams, and ascribe it to an unsteady rate of percolation through open joints in the rock mass, due to the opening and closing of the passages resulting from internal and externally applied pressures.

The time lag between waste injection in the Arsenal well and earthquake frequency is probably due to an unsteady rate of percolation through fractures in the Precambrian reservoir due to the opening and closing of these fractures resulting from the applied fluid pressure of the injected waste. The delayed application of this pressure at a distance from the well bore is believed to trigger the movement recorded as an earthquake.

Earthquakes During Shut-Down Period

In considering the earthquake frequency during the year the injection well was shut down, unfortunately neither periodic bottom-hole pressure tests nor checks of the fluid level in the hole were made. If these measurements had been made, we would know how long it took bottom-hole pressure to decline.

By the end of September 1963, about 102.3 million gallons of fluid had been injected into the well. It is believed that this injection had raised the fluid level pressure in the reservoir for some distance from the well bore. During shut-down, this elevated pressure was equalizing throughout the reservoir and at increasing distance from the well bore. As this fluid pressure reduced the frictional resistance in fractures farther from the well, movement occurred, and small earthquakes resulted.

Conclusion

The Precambrian reservoir receiving the Arsenal waste is highly fractured gneiss of very low permeability. The fractures are nearly vertical. The fracture porosity of the reservoir is filled with salt water. Reservoir pressure is 900 pounds subhydrostatic.

It appears that movement is taking place in this fractured reservoir as a result of the injection of water at pressures from 900 to 1,950 pounds greater than reservoir pressure.

Hubbert and Rubey[8] point out that rock masses in fluid-filled reservoirs are supported by solid stress and the pressure of interstitial fluids. As fluid pressure approaches lithostatic pressure, the shear stress required to move rock masses down very gently dipping slopes approaches zero.

These principles appear to explain the rock movement in the Arsenal reservoir. The highly fractured rocks of the reservoir are at rest on steep slopes under a condition of subhydrostatic fluid pressure. As the fluid pressure is raised within the reservoir, frictional resistance along fracture planes is reduced and, eventually, movement takes place. The elastic wave energy released is recorded as an earthquake.

In the present case, I believe that a stable situation in this Precambrian reservoir was made unstable by fluid pressure. It is interesting to speculate that the principle of increasing fluid pressure to release elastic wave energy could be applied to earthquake modification. That is, it might be possible to relieve the stresses along some fault zones in urban areas by increasing the fluid pressures along the zone, using a series of injection wells. The accumulated stress might thus be released at will in a series of non-damaging earthquakes instead of eventually resulting in one large event that might cause a major disaster.

Notes

[1] David M. Evans, 1966, The Denver area earthquakes and the Rocky Mountain Arsenal disposal well: *The mountain geologist*, v. 3, no. 1, p. 23–36.

[2] J. H. Healy and others, 1966, Geophysical and geological investigations relating to earthquakes in the Denver area, Colorado: U. S. Geological Survey open-file report.

[3] L. J. Scopel, 1964, Pressure injection disposal well, Rocky Mountain Arsenal, Denver, Colo.: *The mountain geologist*, v. 1, no. 1, p. 35–42.

[4] G. G. Anderman and E. J. Ackman, 1963, Structure of the Denver-Julesburg Basin and surrounding areas: in Rocky Mountain Association of Geologists' *Guidebook to the geology of the northern Denver Basin and adjacent uplifts.*

[5] C. M. Boos and M. F. Boos, 1957, Tectonics of the eastern flank and foothills of the Front Range, Colorado: American Assn. of Petroleum Geologists *Bulletin*, v. 41, p. 2,603-2,676.

[6] Yung-liang Wang, 1965, *Local hypocenter determination in linearly varying layers applied to earthquakes in the Denver area:* unpublished DSc dissertation, Colorado School of Mines.

[7] G. E. Bardwell, 1966, Some statistical features of the relationship between Rocky Mountain Arsenal waste disposal and frequency of earthquakes: *The mountain geologist*, v. 3, no. 1, p. 37–42.

[8] M. King Hubbert and W. W. Rubey, 1959, Role of fluid pressure in mechanics of overthrust faulting; part 1, Mechanics of fluid-filled porous solids and its application to overthrust faulting: Geological Society of America *Bulletin*, v. 70, p. 115–166.

[9] D. T. Secor Jr, 1965, Role of fluid pressure in jointing, *American journal of science*, v. 263, p. 633–646.

[10] J. L. Serafim and A. del Campo, 1965, Interstitial pressures of rock foundations of dams: *Journal of the Soil Mechanics & Foundations Division*, Proceedings of the American Society of Civil Engineers v. 91, no. SM5.

9 Underground Nuclear Explosions and the Control of Earthquakes

Cesare Emiliani, Christopher G. A. Harrison, and Mary Swanson

Among the numerous events recognized as trigger mechanisms for earthquakes, only two can be attributed to the activity of man—underground nuclear explosions and the injection of fluids into deep wells.[1-3] The association of earthquakes with underground nuclear explosions has been explored in some detail during the past 2 years.

In an examination of records from the University of Nevada's seismographic station network, Boucher et al.[2] found that large underground nuclear explosions produced a temporary but significant increase in the seismicity of the surrounding region to a degree dependent on the size of the blast. For explosions of magnitudes equal to or greater than 5.0, a substantial increase in activity occurred for at least 1 day following the test. This activity was confined to an area with a radius of about 20 km around the shot point, with a single exception possibly influencing activity to a distance of 40 km. The earthquakes related to nuclear tests were of small magnitude and always at least 1 magnitude unit less than that of the associated explosion. Attempts to ascertain distant effects of

Emiliani, C., Harrison, C., and Swanson, M., 1969, "Underground Nuclear Explosions and the Control of Earthquakes," *Science*, vol. 165, no. 3899, pp. 1255–56. Reprinted by permission of the senior author and the American Association for the Advancement of Science. Copyright 1969 by the A. A. A. S.
The authors are affiliated with The Institute of Marine Sciences, University of Miami, Florida.

these tests indicated that they are probably minor compared with normal variations in seismicity.

Ryall and Savage[3] studied the seismological effects of the 1.2-megaton Boxcar underground nuclear test of 26 April 1968. They recorded thousands of aftershocks within a 6-week period following the explosion, the aftershocks being restricted to an area 12 by 3 to 4 km and to a depth of 12 km. Most of the aftershock hypocenters were found to lie within 5.5 km of the surface, which is shallower than the hypocenters of natural earthquakes in the Nevada region.

We have compared the list of the Nevada underground explosions from 15 September 1961 to 29 September 1966 with a list of earthquakes occurring within 860 km of 37°04'N and 116°15'W, which is roughly at the center of the Nevada test site.[4] The explosions and earthquakes within the region and time interval considered totaled 171 and 1109, respectively.

The earthquake list was examined over thirteen 8-hour intervals after each explosion. The expected number of earthquakes in any 8-hour interval, assuming randomness, is 0.2062. The expected number of earthquakes in each 8-hour interval for all explosions, again assuming randomness, is 0.2062 × 171 or 35.26. The observed numbers for thirteen 8-hour intervals following each explosion are shown in Table 1. Under conditions of randomness, the numbers of Table 1 should be normally distributed around the mean of 35.26 with a standard deviation of $(35.26)^{1/2}$ or 5.94. Table 1 shows that this is not the case, the first four numbers averaging almost 4 standard deviations above the mean. It is clear, therefore, that underground explosions trigger earthquakes up to about 32 hours afterward. The data available to us show that in the 32-hour interval after the explosions there were 228 earthquakes, or an increase of about 62 percent over the expected number of 141.

By dividing the area under consideration into several annuli and by comparing, within each annulus, observed versus expected number of earthquakes, we have verified that the seismic effect of the explosions extends to the 860-km limit of our search. It may still be noticeable at greater distances.

While it is clear from the available evidence that man can affect earthquake activity, Carter[5] reports on conflicting views and feelings among scientists, engineers, and politicians regarding the proposed underground nuclear test at Amchitka Island, Alaska. There is some concern that this test may trigger an earthquake as disastrous as that of 1964 and some propose to limit underground nuclear tests to low-yield systems or to ban them altogether.

It would seem to us that properly spaced and properly timed deep underground nuclear tests could be used, possibly together with previous fluid injection in appropriate quantities, to release stresses in the lithosphere and therefore limit the severity of earthquakes. Stress in the lithosphere is built up by convection in the upper mantle, energized mainly by radioactive decay. It is to be expected that the longer the stress builds up, the more severe will be the earthquake activity releasing it. If so, it might be convenient to place a number of high-yield (1 to 10 megaton) nuclear devices in deep (3000 to 5000 m) wells appropriately spaced (20 to 50 km) along an active fault zone and release the accumulated stress by activating the devices. This procedure could then be repeated at appropriate time intervals (10 to 25 years), thus preventing large stress accumulation and disastrous earthquakes.

The proposed Amchitka test provides an excellent opportunity to evaluate our suggestion, if the nuclear device will be placed at sufficient depth and if the test were to be followed a few months later by a second identical test at the same location and depth. If nuclear devices have indeed a potential for earthquake activity control, the second test should trigger much less activity than the first one.

Table 1 Total number of earthquakes at 8-hour intervals after each explosion

Elapsed time (hr)	Earthquakes (No.)
0–8	67
8–16	42
16–24	56
24–32	63
32–40	38
40–48	36
48–56	42
56–64	43
64–72	26
72–80	27
80–88	35
88–96	32
96–104	37

While the western end of the Aleutian Island Arc appears to be an excellent laboratory to test the feasibility of using nuclear devices for earthquake control, actual application should exclude all inhabited seismic areas which have been free of major earthquakes for 25 years or more and should be initiated in areas recently (less than 10 years) affected by major seismic activity. It should then be continued at appropriate time intervals (10 to 25 years).

Notes

[1] J. H. Healy, W. W. Rubey, D. T. Griggs, C. B. Raleigh, Science 161, 1301 (1968); D. B. Hoover and J. A. Dietrich, U. S. Geol. Surv. Circ. 613 (1969).

[2] G. Boucher, A. Ryall, A. E. Jones, J. Geophy. Res. 74, 3808 (1969).

[3] A. Ryall and W. U. Savage, ibid., p. 4281.

[4] List of underground nuclear explosions obtained from U.S. Atomic Energy Commission; list of earthquakes obtained from Hypocenter Data File U. S. Coast and Geodetic Survey.

[5] L. J. Carter, Science 165, 773 (1969).

10 Earthquake Prediction

Frank Press and W. F. Brace

A few years ago the subject of earthquake prediction fell under the purview of astrologers, misguided amateurs, publicity seekers, and religious sects with doomsday philosophies. No wonder that the occasional scientist who ventured an opinion on the subject did so with trepidation and then with conservatism lest he be disowned by his colleagues.

The situation has changed dramatically in the past 3 years. Three of Japan's foremost earth scientists[1] proposed a program of research and concluded that "after ten years the amount of data should be fairly adequate for earthquake prediction." These experts were less certain about the prospects for organizing an efficient forecasting service and properly deferred consideration of this question until after the conclusion of the research program. In the United States an Ad Hoc Panel on Earthquake Prediction was appointed by the Office of Science and Technology. After some 15 months of deliberation the panel saw enough possibilities to justify a 10-year program of research, which they proposed to Donald Hornig, the director of OST.[2] Their report is now under consideration by several government agencies.

In examining why earthquake prediction is now not only respectable but highly recommended, we review some of the exciting recent developments in seismology. In the United States these advances stem primarily from the International Geophysical Year and Vela projects, which stimulated the design and deployment of advanced instruments and led to new interpretation

Press, F. and Brace, W. F., 1966, "Earthquake Prediction," Science, vol. 152, no. 3729, pp. 1575–84. Lightly edited by permission of the authors and reprinted by permission of the American Association for the Advancement of Science. Copyright 1966 by the A. A. A. S. The authors are Professor of Geophysics and Professor of Geology, respectively, at Massachusetts Institute of Technology, Cambridge, Massachusetts.

techniques based on extensive use of electronic computers. Systems procedures for large-scale field instrumentation were developed, and many new workers were brought into seismological research. In Japan the long history of observation of strains, tilts, displacements, and microseismicity in epicentral regions finally produced some evidence of changes in these parameters prior to and following earthquakes.

Seismology is an advanced science in Japan, and because of the severe earthquake hazard most workers in the field consider earthquake prediction the ultimate goal of their discipline. American seismologists are becoming increasingly concerned about the catastrophic effects of a major shock in one of the populous Pacific coast states.

Very few specialists doubt that California will eventually be visited by a major shock. Without going into an analysis here of the potential damage and casualties, one can appreciate the risk involved from Fig. 1, recently published by Allen et al.[3] It depicts the epicenters of the main shock, some 35 destructive aftershocks, and almost 100 damaging aftershocks of the 1960 Chilean earthquake, overlain to scale on a map of California.

The Earthquake Mechanism

Characteristics of the Hypocentral Region

The hypocentral region of an earthquake—the region where the earthquake is initiated—may never have been seen. Visible surface faulting

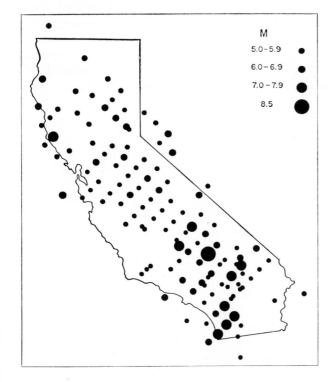

M
5.0 - 5.9
6.0 - 6.9
7.0 - 7.9
8.5

FIG. 1. Epicentral distribution of the major aftershocks (within 6 months) of the great Chilean earthquake of 1960, superimposed on a map of California at the same scale. (M) Magnitude. [From Allen et al.[3]]

sometimes occurs for large earthquakes. Deformation prior to and following the event has occasionally been documented, and strain jumps recorded at large distances have been reported. Precision locations of aftershocks and the radiation pattern of seismic waves are available for many large tremors. These diverse observations yield the following picture of the hypocentral region and fault zone.

Tocher's data on fault length as a function of magnitude, supplemented by additional data, are shown in Fig. 2.[5] It may be seen that the length of faulting associated with destructive earthquakes ranges from about 20 kilometers for events of magnitude 6 to about 1000 kilometers for shocks of magnitude 8¼. Rupture velocity has been measured for several large earthquakes, and values of 3 to 4 kilometers per second seem typical.

The vertical extent of faulting has been debated by seismologists. The best documented case for a great earthquake is that of the Alaskan shock of 1964, where it was found that faulting probably extended from near the surface to depths of 100 to 200 kilometers.[6] The strain and stress jumps in the source region can be inferred approximately from the displacements revealed by surveying or by sea-level changes. By representing the fault as a dislocation sheet, the stress (and strain) distributions needed to match the observed displacements may be obtained. When one assumes a finite rectangular sheet and strain change of 10^{-4} to 10^{-3}, surprisingly small stress jumps of 10 to 100 bars are obtained.[7] For the Alaskan earthquake, with magnitude of 8¼, numerical integration of the strain energy density yielded an energy release of 10^{25} ergs, a value which is roughly checked by the empirical conversion of magnitude to equivalent seismic energy. This value is equivalent in seismic energy to 100 nuclear explosions, each of 100 megatons.[8] Many seismologists accept Tsuboi's hypothesis that the strain energy density is independent of magnitude, the energy release and magnitude being determined by the source volume.

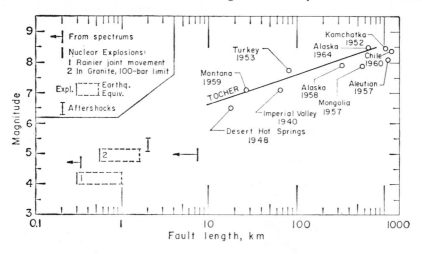

FIG. 2. Empirical data on fault length versus magnitude.

The seismic energy release generally decreases with depth, reaching zero at about 700 kilometers. Roughly 80 percent of the energy is released in the depth range 0 to 60 kilometers; the hydrostatic pressure range which corresponds to this depth range is 0 to 18 kilobars. A recent study[9] showed that, in southern California, most of the shocks occur at depths of about 5 kilometers. It is important to note that the main focal region of California is accessible by drilling! In Japan, most major shocks occur at depths of less than 60 kilometers; more than half occur at less than 30 kilometers.

The Earthquake Mechanism

The focal region of earthquakes has remained inaccessible to direct observation, so theories of the earthquake mechanism are based on indirect observation on—(i) the movements of surface rocks above the actual focal region, (ii) the behavior of samples of rock stressed in the laboratory under the high-pressure and high-temperature conditions found in the earth, and (iii) the radiation pattern of seismic waves.

The great 1906 earthquake in California was accompanied by widespread surface movement of rocks. Study of these movements led to Reid's elastic rebound theory for the earthquake source mechanism.[10] According to this theory an earthquake is the result of strain release caused by sudden shearing motion along a fault. This view of the origin of earthquakes is supported by the nature of seismic signals which emanate from many earthquakes, and is also reasonable in terms of laboratory behavior of rocks. If a rock such

as diabase is stressed under the confining pressure appropriate to the shallow crust, it fails by faulting. The failure is sudden and usually explosive. Jaeger[11] and Byerlee[12] have studied the characteristics of sliding on faults and artificial surfaces under pressure. These studies give some insight into the probable shallow-earthquake mechanism.

Typical sliding behavior of a fine-grained granite[12] is shown in Fig. 3. A cylindrical sample 12.5 millimeters in

FIG. 3. Force-displacement during sliding on a ground surface in Westerly granite.[12] Confining pressure, P, was 2.1 kilobars, and the loading arrangement used is suggested by the small figure at upper right. The position of the ground surface is shown by the inclined line in the small figure. The dashed parts of the curve are sudden stress drops; the true form of the curve during these stress drops is not known. The vertical bar shows axial stress difference in the specimen.

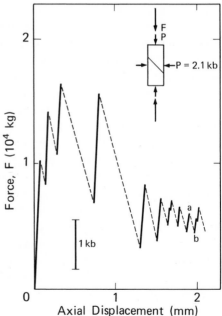

diameter and 31.7 millimeters long contained an artificial surface in an orientation close to the direction along which the rock would naturally fault. Compressive stress was applied to the ends of the sample, which was under confining pressure, until sliding occurred. A force-displacement curve (Fig. 3) shows that sliding was not smooth but was punctuated by sharp stress drops. Elastic shocks accompanied the stress drops, the magnitude of which ranged in this particular experiment from 50 bars to 2.5 kilobars.

The behavior of materials in experiments such as these recalls Bridgman's observations.[13] He found that jerky stick-slip accompanied the shearing of a great variety of materials, even when normal pressures were as high as 50 kilobars.

These observations suggest that, in terms of the Reid mechanism, earthquakes could be produced by sudden stress drops during sliding. The stress drop probably does not represent complete release of stress at the earthquake focus. In other words, the stress released during an earthquake is only a small fraction of the total stress supported by the rock around the fault.

The Reid mechanism will probably be enhanced in regions of abnormally high pore pressure. High pore pressure tends to lower the frictional resistance to sliding; in an extreme case, when pore pressure equals overburden pressure, resistance on a horizontal fault would drop to the very small value of the intrinsic strength. In regions of high pore pressure, then, faulting could be caused by relatively low tectonic stresses. Pore pressures have actually been measured which are within a few percent of overburden pressure; however, these are typically in nonseismic regions.

The influence of pore pressure may have been revealed in the recent seismic activity near Denver, Colorado. Many small earthquakes which occurred at depths of about 5 kilometers seem to be correlated with pumping of liquid wastes down a well 4 kilometers deep. Although the role of the injected fluids is not entirely clear, one hypothesis consistent with available information associates the earthquakes with increased pore pressure in the vicinity of a fault.[14]

It is also possible that, in regions of abnormally high pore pressure, the Reid mechanism may be important to considerably greater depths than the shallow crustal depths considered here. Faulting and other behavior which one expects at shallow depths may occur at considerably deeper levels when pore pressure is abnormally high. This was shown in a recent study, by Raleigh and Paterson,[15] of the effects of heating on rocks containing hydrous minerals. Embrittlement of serpentinite occurred at pressure of 5 kilobars and temperature of 700°C as water released during dehydration raised the pore pressure. Fractures formed in the course of these experiments and, therefore, might form in the earth, but it does not necessarily follow that jerky slip would also occur under these conditions. Nevertheless, it is tempting to consider the possibility, for breakdown of hydrous minerals must be a widespread phenomenon[16] throughout the deeper crust and even into the mantle. At these levels, however, the Reid mechanism would certainly be competing with some of the higher-temperature models which have been proposed.

Griggs and Blacic[17] have observed a drastic lowering of strength of silicate minerals which were deformed in the presence of water; the effect was attributed to the hydrolysis of the silicon-oxygen bonds. This weakening has been observed in a material as strong as quartz at temperatures as low as a few hundred degrees. In rocks under natural conditions, water weakening might so lower strength that sudden shearing failure would occur locally.

Orowan[18] has proposed an earthquake mechanism in which creep fracture plays an important role. According to his model, creep can occur through viscous grain-boundary sliding; at an advanced stage of creep, cavities form, a mechanical instability develops, and the rate of strain suddenly increases within certain narrow bands. This sudden increase in strain rate might produce an earthquake, much as the sudden frictional sliding in the Reid mechanism does. In the creep model, however, no actual frictional sliding takes place at the source. This model has not been tested experimentally for rocks.

Orowan[18] regards the Raleigh-Paterson effect[15] as due to lubrication by wet dehydrated serpentine and suggests that, throughout the region of 20 to 60 kilometers depth, strength could be lowered to a few hundred bars by decomposition of serpentine. Faulting might easily occur at these depths and cause earthquakes; stress drops would be of the correct magnitude. Only the largest faults which would originate at these depths would penetrate the upper 20 kilometers, where frictional resistance is high.

Premonitory Indications of An Earthquake

Forewarning of a large earthquake might come from three sources: from (i) tilts and strains in the epicentral region, (ii) the general increase in number of small seismic events, and (iii) changes in physical properties of rocks near the fault as they are strained. Some of these features have actually been observed prior to earthquakes, and others are suggested by consideration of possible source mechanisms.

Observed Deformation Before An Earthquake

Anomalous deformations preceding earthquakes in Japan have been reported.[1] These include anomalous changes in sea level (hours to days before the earthquakes), as reported by the public or as evidenced on tide gages. They include vertical and horizontal deformation, as revealed by precisely repeated surveys, the anomalous shifts being detected some months to years before the earthquake, depending on the frequency of the surveys.

Instrumental indications of anomalous tilt and strain changes preceding earthquakes by hours or days have also been reported.[19] Perhaps the most remarkable and best documented case occurred prior to the Niigata earthquake of 1964. This earthquake of magnitude $7\frac{1}{2}$ was not one of the great ones of recent years, but it was very destructive. An anomalous strain change was first detected some 9 hours before the earthquake. The sensing instruments were vertical strainmeters installed in shallow holes over a zone 10 kilometers long. This net was designed to measure subsidence associated with the withdrawal of natural gas. A vertical expansion of the ground of 0.3 to 0.4 millimeter was detected by 15 out of 20 instruments, corresponding to a strain change of 10^{-5} in the 9-hour period.[19] A sample record is shown in Fig. 4. The instruments were approximately 70 kilometers from the epicenter and 20 kilometers from one end of the after-shock zone.

An example of anomalous ground tilting is shown in Fig. 5. The station at Ikuno was 60 kilometers from the epicenter, in this case the Tottori earthquake of 1943, magnitude 7½. This record, obtained by Sassa, is famous in Japanese seismology and represents the first instrumental indication of possible deformation prior to an earthquake.[19] Both examples are suggestive but not uniquely indicative of the creep acceleration stage of creep fracture.[18]

Tantalizing as the few records indicative of prior deformation are, their validity and reliability must be tested. This calls for a much larger number of case histories, involving use of large numbers of sensors, each operating continuously over long periods of time under conditions of minimal interference from extraneous sources. Both the Japanese and the U. S. programs incorporate proposals to test these preliminary results. These tests range in scale and technique from precise surveying with modern electronic devices to measuring with arrays of sensitive strainmeters and tiltmeters, some of

FIG. 4. Trace motion of vertical extensometer located in a well 40 meters deep near Niigata, showing anomalous expansion (downward direction on the ordinate) beginning 9 hours before the earthquake. Each vertical space represents 0.1 millimeter. The abscissa gives the time in hours, beginning at 12 hours on 15 June 1964. The trace is interrupted by the earthquake.[19]

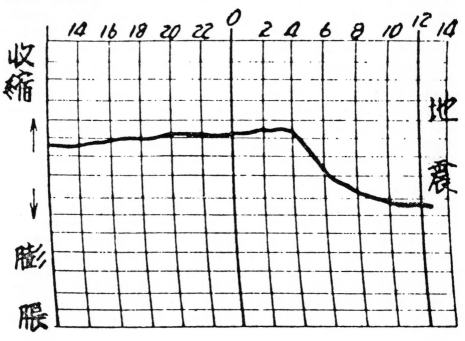

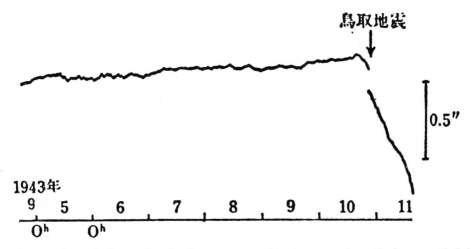

FIG. 5. Record, obtained at the Ikuno station, showing anomalous tilt that preceded the Tottori earthquake of September 1943. The abscissa represents days; the arrow indicates occurrence of the earthquake.[19]

them located in deep holes closer to, if not in, the possible focal region.

Seismic Activity

A program of monitoring small shocks in seismic belts can be useful in different ways. The radiation pattern of seismic waves leads to a definition of the regional stress pattern. The shocks themselves define seismic belts and sometimes specific faults. Some recent field studies show that regional microseismicity is not necessarily positively correlated with earthquake probability in a tectonically active region.[3] However, it is possible that the pattern of seismic release preceding an earthquake may be a forecasting element, as implied by the laboratory experiments described earlier.

As an example, we might cite Watanabe's study (see 20) in which he subjected rocks to uniaxial compression and used ultrasonic detectors to sense the small shocks associated with local brittle fractures. He measured strain

directly, and also the cumulative square root of the energy released by the shocks. The strain of the specimen and the strain release by the shocks both show anomalous change prior to rupture. This is a well-known characteristic of fracture of rocks in compression, particularly at low confining pressure.[20, 21]

A comparison of the release pattern of aftershocks and foreshocks, by Suyehiro *et al.*,[22] for a small, perceptible earthquake suggests the possibility that different regimes may occur. The foreshock activity has relatively fewer small shocks than the aftershock sequence—an observation which suggests a possible premonitory effect.

Physical Changes in Rock Which Precede Faulting

Although rocks in laboratory experiments frequently fault without much warning, a number of subtle premonitory changes do in fact occur. Many of these changes can be detected in the laboratory at stresses well below the maximum stress a rock can support. In the natural situation, these changes might warn of an impending earthquake.

The most obvious effect which precedes faulting in laboratory experiments is the increase in microseismic activity.[20, 21] This suggests either that the rock is cracking on a small scale or that surfaces within the rock are sliding on one another. Cracks have actually been observed to form on the surfaces of stressed samples,[23] and sensitive measurements of volume change suggest that the new cracks are open.[24]

Cracked rock has elastic and electric properties different from those of rock which is uncracked, particularly if the cracks are open. Moreover, the new cracks are apparently strongly aligned, in a direction parallel to the maximum compression. Thus, the changes in elastic and electrical properties ought to be markedly directional.

Compressional wave velocity was measured in two directions as a specimen of granite at 3.6 kilobars was stressed in compression.[25, 26] Not much change in the two velocities occurred at stresses up to about half the maximum stress; beyond that point the velocity in a direction perpendicular to the maximum compression began to decrease. At the maximum stress, when the rock faulted, the velocities parallel and perpendicular to the maximum compression differed by about 20 percent. Electrical properties of rock saturated with water changed a great deal more than this. Brace and Orange[27] found that resistivity in the direction of the maximum compression drops by a factor of 5 to 10.

Whether these results can be ex-tended to seismic regions of the earth is, of course, open to question. Although these phenomena are observed in the laboratory over a wide range of pressures, the temperatures and the physical character of rock in the natural environment may affect the changes in some unknown way. For example, the fissured, broken condition of rocks in the natural environment, particularly in seismic areas, may lower resistivity to such an extent that the changes that we observe in the laboratory for rock which is initially intact may not be detectable.

The small size of the stress drops associated with earthquakes may also make the task of detecting changes in physical properties quite difficult. Velocity and other elastic properties might change by perhaps a few percent; it is doubtful that changes this small could be detected. On the other hand, with a 100-bar stress change, changes of resistivity might amount to 50 percent; this should be detectable.

It is interesting to note that earth resistivity changes much smaller than these have apparently been detected;[28] the changes were associated with tidal deformation. Also, small velocity changes of the correct sign have been reported.[29] Statistical treatment of a number of scattered observations suggested a correlation of anomalous seismic velocities with time intervals preceding strong earthquakes. The anomalous P-wave velocities were about 12 percent lower than normal, and the anomalous V_p to V_s ratio was 6 percent lower than normal.

Earthquakes caused by creep fracture should, one would think, be preceded by a period of accelerated surface strain which might be detectable.

A severe and damaging earthquake due to a fault in a region of serpentinization might be preceded by a series of small shocks,[18] which would represent the deep faults that do not penetrate the surface. Experience may reveal a critical surface-strain accumulation associated with damaging faults of this kind.

Other Possible Indicators

If one takes the point of view that an earthquake-prediction research program should test all physical parameters which are responsive to changes in stress, or the physical-chemical state of rocks, or to the mechanism of failure, then a number of additional observations suggest themselves. There may be a critical stress, strain, or strain rate associated with earthquakes in a given area. Water-well levels are sensitive to dilational strains as small as 10^{-9} to 10^{-8}. Permanent changes were produced in the water levels of wells in the southeastern United States following the great Alaskan earthquake of 1964. Variations in the geomagnetic field (or in its gradient) may occur in response to changes in magnetic susceptibility or electrical conductivity, or they might occur if the Curie point were shifted. Earth currents, either natural or artificial, might be even more sensitive indicators since they directly respond to resistivity changes which, in turn, may indicate the buildup of stress, as described above.

Field Investigations

It is not our purpose, in this article, to design an earthquake prediction program. However, it seems obvious that a major feature of such a program would be the monitoring, with the greatest achievable sensitivity, of all possible indicators foretelling the occurrence of earthquakes. Networks of instruments would be deployed in seismic belts and would be operated continuously over long periods of time in such a way as to provide the greatest possible likelihood that many earthquakes would be "trapped" within the arrays. Although this is essentially an empirical and somewhat wasteful approach, the absence of a confirmed theory for the earthquake mechanism justifies it. All pre-earthquake activity predicted by the main theories of the earthquake mechanism would be tested, as would the phenomena reported, by reputable scientists, to have preceded earthquakes.

The New Generation of Instruments

Seismological observations are primarily concerned either with detecting propagating seismic waves or with sensing secular strains, tilts, and displacements associated with strain accumulation and release in seismic belts. For many years now the detection of seismic waves has been limited by background noise emanating from winds, sea waves, and industrial vibrations and not by instrumental sensitivity. At some frequencies of the seismic spectrum the noise can cause displacements as large as 10^5 angstroms. Seismometers are currently available which can detect ground motion as small as 1 to 10 angstroms. Advances in seismic wave detection have come through locating seismometers in deep wells at depths of several thousand meters, or through deploying arrays of large numbers of sensors. The instruments in deep wells gain in sensitivity because the "skin" effect associated with elastic surface waves (which comprise seismic noise) leads to rapid decrease in noise amplitude with depth. Array processing leads to an increase in the signal-to-noise ratio by a factor somewhat better than the square root of the number of sensors. Optimum frequency filtering and wave-number filtering techniques are employed—an adaption of methods developed in radar signal processing. The filters exploit differences in frequency and phase velocity between signal and noise. The signal is typically coherent over the array; this is not always the case for the noise.

A large-aperture seismic array (LASA) was recently placed in operation under the auspices of Project Vela.[30] This array, depicted in Fig. 6, consists of 21 clusters, each composed of 25 seismometers buried at depths of 30 meters. The array covers a circular area of about 200-kilometer diameter. The LASA contribution to the earthquake forecasting problem lies, perhaps even more than in the improved signal-to-noise ratio, in its systems approach to a large-scale multisensor field experiment. LASA demonstrates how hundreds of detectors distributed in a seismically active region can be tied together by microwave and telephone-line telemetry in which signal data are transmitted to on-line-monitoring computers. We discuss below how this systems concept can be modified to provide an essential tool in a prediction research program.

The tools for testing seismic activity as a forecasting element are arrays of

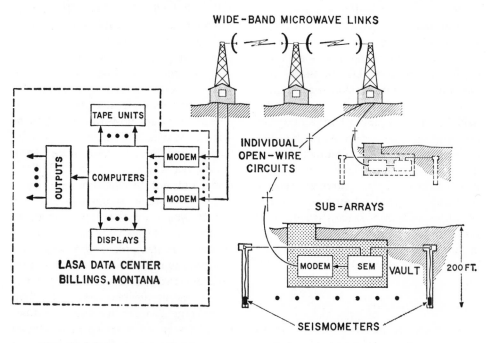

FIG. 6. The LASA system for acquiring and processing seismic data, for possible use in an earthquake prediction system.[30]

extremely sensitive seismographs located in seismic belts, monitoring microearthquakes on an on-line basis. Some of the sensors would be in deep holes, possibly as deep as 5 kilometers. The procedure of monitoring the microearthquakes and characterizing the pattern of release would, of necessity, be automated, since the system would be dealing with thousands, if not millions, of events.

Observations of strain and tilt are also limited by ground noise. In this case the noise derives from thermal stresses associated with diurnal and seasonal temperature changes in the rock, from loading of the earth by rainfall, from changes in sea level, from varying barometric pressure, and from wind. These noise sources can produce strain changes of as much as 10^{-16} over a period of weeks to months. Smaller, short-period fluctuations (hours to days) also occur. The semidiurnal tides contribute strains of the order of 10^{-8}. Compare these disturbances with secular strain rates of 10^{-6} to 10^{-5} per year which might be expected in tectonic belts, or with the strain drop of 10^{-4} inferred for the epicentral region following an earthquake. Premonitory strain changes could be smaller than 10^{-4} by several orders of magnitude.

A strainmeter of the type developed by Benioff[31] can detect short-term strains, associated with seismic waves, as small as 10^{-10}. Strain changes of 10^{-9} to 10^{-8} corresponding to strain jumps in the epicentral region of large, distant earthquakes have also been detected.[32] Whether this sensitivity is adequate for detecting premonitory strain changes is not yet known. If greater sensitivity is needed, noise re-duction methods must be devised. These would include miniaturizing of strain seismographs so that they could be placed in deep holes. Deployment of arrays of strain seismographs is another possibility for improving signal-to-noise ratios.

The use of laser interferometers, modulated light beams, and microwave phase measurements over distances of 1 to 10 kilometers has often been proposed. The advantages of long-range observations have never been demonstrated, but it is not unreasonable to suppose that local and extraneous strains which affect conventional strain seismographs would tend to be reduced, whereas regional strains associated with earthquakes would be emphasized. In a recent analysis, Gehrels[33] concluded that distances can be measured over 10 kilometers with a precision of 1 part in 10^7 by means of modulated-light-beam techniques which will soon be practicable. The effect of atmospheric temperatures is reduced by employing beams of different colors and by using the dispersion properties of the atmosphere. A strain of 10^{-7} is about 10^{-2} to 10^{-1} times the annual strain accumulation in a seismic belt and is 10^{-3} times the strain drop associated with major earthquakes.

Laser interferometers offer even greater sensitivity, but with certain restrictions. Long-term stability of the laser frequency of several parts in 10^{10} is currently attainable.[34] This would be the instrumental accuracy of a laser strain seismograph in which the light beam traverses a controlled atmosphere, as in a buried light pipe. Practical considerations limit the use of such a device to strain sensing over a distance of a kilometer, and this may be all that is needed in a monitoring system. However, if sensing over distances between 1 and 10 kilometers is needed, this may be achieved by building arrays of shorter strainmeters or by using long atmospheric paths. In the latter case multicolor dispersion methods could be used to correct for atmospheric temperature, pressure, and humidity, and strain changes as small as 10^{-9} to 10^{-8} might be observed, provided coherence could be maintained through the open atmosphere. The uncertainty here pertains to beam coherence and the earth noise for these long paths.

Strains and tilts are both derivatives of a displacement field. Mechanical and liquid tiltmeters have been constructed, the latter on the basis of Michelson's concept of liquid flowing between two reservoirs. These instruments are capable of monitoring tilts as small as 10^{-8} radian.[35] In seismically active regions like Japan, tilt rates of as much as 10^{-5} radian per year are observed. Tiltmeters are subject to the same limitations as strainmeters—namely, excessive ground noise which restricts instrumental sensitivity. Liquid tiltmeters varying in length from 1 meter to 1 kilometer are currently being constructed.

The only instruments currently available for measuring ground displacements over long periods of time are tide gages and gravimeters. Because of the large, erratic sea-level fluctuations associated with swell, tides, and seasonal effects, it is difficult to see how tide gages could be used in a forecasting system, though they would provide valuable data on regional deformation before and after earthquakes. Gravimeters with long-term stability of 1 part in $10^{-9}g$ (1 microgal) are now available. These instruments are subject to semidiurnal tidal accelerations larger than this by a factor of 200. They respond to motion of the ground in the manner of accelerometers and displacement meters. The displacement effect predominates for periods somewhat longer than half an hour and is due to an equivalent "free-air" or Bouguer gravity change. A sensitivity of 1 microgal corresponds to a change in elevation of a few millimeters when the displacement is due to the addition of mass in the section. Arrays of gravimeters could provide useful information on vertical motions by reducing extraneous effects, such as loading of the crust by sea-level and atmospheric-pressure changes and solid-earth tides. Instruments for sensing horizontal displacements are not yet available, although proposals have been advanced for constructing such a device with the precise accelerometers of inertial navigation instruments as its main component.

Magnetometers operating by atomic processes show long-term stability in the range of $\pm$ 0.01 gamma (0.1 micro-oersted). They may be operated in a gradient configuration; this cancels micropulsations and provides great sensitivity to local changes in the magnetic field. The relation between magnetic field changes and tectonic processes is not yet established. It may involve susceptibility or Curie point changes due to variations in temperature and stress.

Strain-, tilt-, and displacement meters, by their nature, monitor variations subsequent to the installation of the instrument. Thus, their role in an earthquake prediction scheme depends on an anomalous premonitory effect.

They could not sense critical values. Although some development is still needed, techniques exist for determining absolute stress *in situ*, a measurement which would be of great importance if critical stresses are involved in the earthquake mechanism. The methods were primarily developed to monitor stresses in mines and tunnels. One procedure involves isolating a specimen of rock (on which strain gages have been mounted) from the stress field in the surrounding rock by overdrilling. The stress relief sensed by strain gages is then related to the preexisting stress field.[36]

The measurement of temporal variations in seismic velocity and electrical conductivity in earthquake regions should be mentioned to complete the picture. The measurement of conductivity may be of special importance in view of the laboratory results described earlier. The field procedure consists of deploying current sources and detecting voltmeters, with an electrode spacing appropriate for penetration to the focal region.

Instrumenting Seismic Belts

The Ad Hoc Panel on Earthquake Prediction proposed that field observations be organized around permanently installed instrumental clusters, augmented by special surveying devices. The clusters primarily monitor local deformation, microseismicity, and gravitational, magnetic, and electric fields. The special surveying devices extend the point observations of the cluster element and also tie the cluster together by monitoring regional deformation. The clusters are sited along major earthquake belts, on the basis of

low background noise, auxiliary evidence of a high probability of earthquake occurrence, and consistency with the overall coverage of the seismic belt.

A cluster would consist of the following instruments distributed over an area of 100 to 1000 square kilometers.

1) Microseismicity array: ten sensitive seismographs each buried in a hole about 30 meters deep. The frequency response will be somewhere within the short-period range (1 to 100 cycles per second) and will be selected on the basis of local noise and spectrum of microearthquakes; sensitivity will be the maximum that ground noise permits.

2) Tiltmeter array: ten small two-component tiltmeters. Tiltmeters will be temperature-compensated, will have sensitivity of 10^{-9} radian or better, and will be installed in trenches to limit the effect of surface disturbances associated with atmospheric pressure and temperature changes.

3) Strainmeter array: ten small three-component strainmeters of strain sensitivity 10^{-9} or better will be installed in shallow holes or trenches. Background noise may make it difficult or impossible to achieve these goals for tilt and strain sensitivity.

4) Two magnetometers (rubidium-vapor or the equivalent); sensitivity, 0.1 gamma. The two horizontal components of the earth's natural telluric field will be measured at the same places. Artificially induced current will also be monitored as an indicator of resistivity changes.

5) Two recording gravimeters; sensitivity, 1 microgal; zero position must be recoverable after motion corresponding to $0.1g$. Two recording meters will permit measurement and comparison

of gravity differences of two nearby locations.

6) Meteorological instruments and tide gages to monitor noise sources and forcing functions.

7) Deep-hole seismometers, tiltmeters, and strainmeters located in a borehole at depths of 3 to 5 kilometers. Since background noise is primarily generated at the surface, the operation of deephole instruments at tenfold to 100-fold gains may be possible. Furthermore, this approach offers the possibility (in California, at least) of siting instruments close to the seismic focus, where effects preceding an earthquake would probably be enhanced.

All of the instruments described, except for the deep-hole strainmeter and tiltmeter, will soon be available.

The special surveying devices consist of laser strainmeters permanently installed in each cluster, designed to measure strain changes of the order of 10^{-9} over distances of about a kilometer. These devices, which will soon be available, will probably involve the use of light paths in buried pipes which are evacuated or filled with dry nitrogen. In addition, optical or electronic strainmeters capable of observing regional strains over distances of 10 to 20 kilometers are highly desirable for tying clusters together and for facilitating regional surveying. To develop them will require development of a surveying device designed to operate in air in such a way as to achieve strain sensitivity of 10^{-8} to 10^{-7} after correction—that is, after compensation for changes in air pressure, temperature, and humidity.

Since strainmeters and tiltmeters only measure changes that occur subsequent to installation, it is proposed that absolute stress determinations be made on a daily basis. These observations may reveal the status of a region in the stress-accumulation, stress-release cycle.

The Ad Hoc Panel recommended that these clusters be deployed in Alaska and in the California-Nevada region, the two most seismic areas of the United States. In California-Nevada, a Y-shaped zone is defined by the major earthquakes which have occurred in this region over the last 100 years (Fig. 7). This zone includes such major fault systems as the San Andreas, Garlock, and Owens Valley systems in California and the Dixie Valley in Nevada (east of Reno). Some 15 permanent clusters and one movable one would be spaced at intervals of 50 to 100 kilometers along the San Andreas system and the other faults, as shown in Fig. 7. A schematic view of a cluster is shown in Fig. 8. Also shown in Fig. 8 are the special surveying devices designed to monitor regional strain.

All told, some 1000 to 1500 sensors would be used in the California-Nevada experiment. A system similar to that devised for LASA would be used to automate the data acquisition and analysis. The elements of the clusters and the clusters themselves would be linked by open-wire digital telephone circuitry and by microwave links, all feeding into a central computing and analysis facility. The computers would monitor microseismicity statistics, deformation, and variations in the several internal fields. The sensors would be correlated, among themselves, with external forcing functions such as atmospheric pressure, sea-level changes, ti-

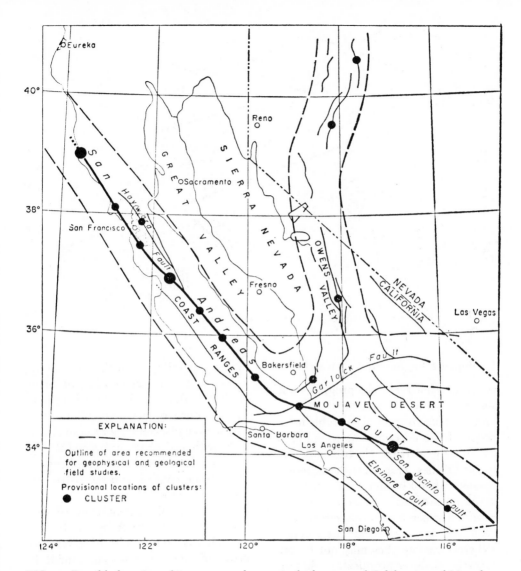

FIG. 7. Possible location of instrument clusters in fault zones of California and Nevada.

dal forces, diurnal heating and cooling, tectonic stress variations, and earthquakes. Numerical correlation and prediction techniques would be programmed into the computers.

The instrumental program proposed by the U.S. and Japanese panels covers regions which have experienced some of the most destructive earthquakes in recorded history. If these programs are fully implemented, it is reasonable to expect that many earthquakes will occur in localities where instruments to test for premonitory indications have been located. If earthquake forecasting elements occur in nature, these programs have a good chance of finding them.

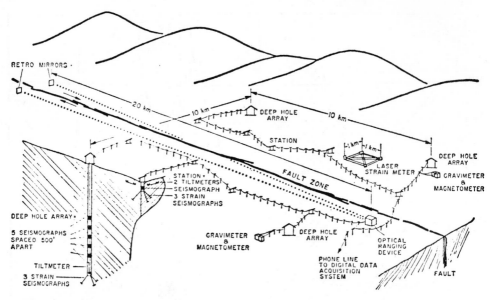

FIG. 8. Preliminary conception of an instrumental cluster.

Earthquake Engineering Research

A successful research program—one which leads to a forecasting system—would make the casualty problem less severe. It would reduce damage caused by fire by alerting electric, gas, and water utilities. However, the economic loss would still be significant, and only a special program of earthquake engineering research can be effective in reducing damage and destruction. Whereas earthquakes may not be predictable, there is no question that engineering research can reduce the vulnerability of urban areas to destruction by earthquakes. For this reason, the U. S. Ad Hoc Panel went beyond its guidelines and included a major program of earthquake engineering research in its proposal. In addition to basic engineering studies, expansion of the more practical aspects of antiseismic engineering would be needed.

In anticipation of advances in pre-diction capability or in the engineering aspects of the earthquake problem, studies evaluating the effectiveness of the response of urban populations to earthquake disasters are recommended. Even with a reasonably successful forecasting capability, the problems of evacuation, control, and reconstruction are severe ones.

In view of the public concern with earthquakes, it cannot be emphasized enough that the results of a research program such as this one cannot be anticipated. The goal is to go from the present capability of probabilistic prediction to specific forecasting. The problem is unquestionably a difficult one, yet specialists in Japan and the United States are anxious to attack it because they feel that significant contributions can be made. In joining earthquake prediction research with earthquake engineering research, they expect, as a minimum result, an increase in knowledge of fault tectonics and an improvement in construction practices in seismic belts, for reducing casualties and property damage.

Aside from forecasting, the instrumental development and field programs will contribute to some of the major unresolved problems of geology. The continental pattern of deformation, which will be monitored for the first time on a short-term basis, bears on such basic questions as orogeny and continental drift, and the stress sources which produce them.

Notes

[1] C. Tsuboi, K. Wadati, T. Hagiwara, "Report by the Earthquake Prediction Research Group in Japan" (Earthquake Research Institute, Tokyo University, Tokyo, 1962).

[2] The panel members were H. Benioff, R. A. Frosch, D. T. Griggs, J. Handin, R. E. Hanson, H. H. Hess, G. W. Housner, W. H. Munk, E. Orowan, L. C. Pakiser, Jr., G. Sutton, and F. Press, Chairman.

[3] C. R. Allen, P. St. Amand, C. F. Richter, S. M. Nordquist, Bull. Seismol. Soc. Amer. 55, 753 (1965).

[4] J. N. Brune, C. R. Allen, F. Press, paper presented before the Seismological Society of America, 1966 annual meeting.

[5] D. Tocher, Bull. Seismol. Soc. Amer. 48, 147 (1963); F. Press, "Vesiac Report on Source Mechanism of Shallow Seismic Events" (Univ. of Michigan, Ann Arbor, in press).

[6] F. Press, J. Geophys. Res. 70, 2395 (1965).

[7] M. A. Chinnery, ibid., 69, 2085 (1964).

[8] F. Press and D. Jackson, Science 147, 867 (1965).

[9] A. Cisternas, thesis, California Institute of Technology, 1964.

[10] H. F. Reid, Univ. Calif. Publ. Bull. Dept. Geol. 6, 413 (1911); H. Benioff, Science 143, 1399 (1964).

[11] J. C. Jaeger, Geofis. Pura Appl. 43, 148 (1959).

[12] J. D. Byerlee, thesis, Massachusetts Institute of Technology, 1966.

[13] P. W. Bridgman. Proc. Amer. Acad. Arts Sci. 71, 387 (1960).

[14] W. Sullivan, news report, New York Times (27 Mar. 1966).

[15] C. B. Raleigh and M. S. Paterson, J. Geophys. Res. 70, 3965 (1965).

[16] H. C. Heard and W. W. Rubey, Bull. Geol. Soc. Amer., in press.

[17] D. T. Griggs and J. D. Blacic, Science 147, 292 (1965); Trans. Amer. Geophys. Union 46, 163 (1965).

[18] E. Orowan, Geol. Soc. Amer. Mem. 79, 323 (1960); see also review in "Earthquake Prediction," U. S. Office Sci. Technol. Publ. (1965). Orowan's view of the Raleigh-Paterson effect was given in a personal communication, 15, Feb. 1965.

[19] Professor K. Aki discussed the two examples which follow at a symposium on earthquake prediction held at the California Institute of Technology in October 1965. He also brought to my attention a lecture by T. Kitamura before the Earthquake Research Institute of Tokyo University in September 1964, at which the Niigata data were presented. Also see introduction by E. Nishimura to Geophysical Papers Dedicated to Professor K. Sassa (Geophysical Institute, Kyoto University, Kyoto, 1963).

[20] H. Watanabe, in Geophysical Papers Dedicated to Professor K. Sassa (Geophysical Institute, Kyoto University, Kyoto), p. 653.

[21] K. Mogi, Bull. Earthquake Res. Inst. Tokyo Univ. 40, 125 (1962); ———, ibid., p. 815; L. Obert and W. T. Duvall, U. S. Bur. Mines Bull. 573 (1957).

[22] S. Suyehiro, T. Asada, M. Ohtake, Papers Meteorol. Geophys. Tokyo 15, 71 (1964).

[23] O. Y. Berg, Dokl. Akad. Nauk SSSR 70, 617 (1950).

[24] W. F. Brace, B. W. Paulding, C. Scholz, in preparation.

[25] D. Tocher, Trans. Amer. Geophys. Union 38, 89 (1957); R. Jones, Brit. J. Appl. Phys. 3, 229 (1952).

[26] S. Matsushima, Disaster Prevent. Res. Inst. Bull. No. 32 (1960), pt. 1.

[27] W. F. Brace and A. S. Orange, in preparation.

[28] T. Rikitake, U. S.-Japan Conference on Research Related to Earthquake Prediction Problems (1964), p. 87.

[29] A. M. Kondratenko and I. L. Nersesov, *Trudy. Inst. Fiz. Zemli Akad. Nauk SSSR* 25, 198 (1962).
[30] P. E. Green, Jr., R. A. Frosch, C. F. Romney, *Proc. I.E.E.E. (Inst. Elec. Electron. Engrs.)*, in press.
[31] H. Benioff, *Bull. Geol. Soc. Amer.* 70, 1019 (1959); a recent version is the work of L. Blayney and R. Gilman, *Bull, Seismol. Soc. Amer.* 55, 955 (1965).
[32] H. Benioff, *Bull. Seismol. Soc. Amer.* 53,

893 (1963); F. Press, *J. Geophys. Res.* 70, 2395 (1965).
[33] E. Gehrels, *Lincoln Lab., M.I.T. Tech. Note.* 1965–62 (1965).
[34] K. Shimoda and A. Javan, *J. Appl. Phys.* 36, 3 (1965).
[35] H. Benioff and W. Gile of the California Institute of Technology developed a modern version of Michelson's tiltmeter.
[36] W. R. Judd, Ed., *State of Stress in the Earth's Crust* (Elsevier, New York, 1964).

11   Earthquake Prediction and Control

L. C. Pakiser, J. P. Eaton, J. H. Healy, C. B. Raleigh

The great Alaska earthquake (Richter magnitude, 8.4 to 8.6) of 27 March 1964 awakened earth scientists and public officials to the need for intensified research on earthquakes, their effects on man and his works, and possible means of reducing their hazards. Although the loss of life in Alaska (115) and property damage ($300 million) were small for such a great earthquake, the realization that an earthquake of similar magnitude could occur in densely populated coastal California, where loss of life would almost certainly be in the thousands and property damage in the billions of dollars, dramatized the urgent need for remedial action.

Following the 1964 Alaska earthquake, an Ad Hoc Panel on Earthquake

Pakiser, L. C., Eaton, J. P., Healy, J. H., and Raleigh, C. B., 1969, "Earthquake Prediction and Control," *Science*, vol. 166, no. 3912, pp. 1467–74. Lightly edited by permission of the senior author and reprinted by permission of the American Association for the Advancement of Science. Copyright 1969 by the A. A. A. S.
The authors are affiliated with the U. S. Geological Survey.

Prediction was organized by Frank Press of the Massachusetts Institute of Technology at the request of the President's Science Advisor, Donald Hornig, to study the opportunities for research on earthquake prediction. The report of the panel[1] was completed in September 1965 and released by Hornig in October. The 10-year program recommended by the panel calls for a new generation of instruments for monitoring earthquake faults in California and Alaska, extensive geological and geophysical surveys of fault zones, laboratory and theoretical studies of mechanisms of rock failure, research in prediction theory, and strongly augmented research in earthquake engineering. The panel estimated the cost of the program at $137 million.

Although the Press Panel report has not been adopted as a national program, many of its recommendations are being carried out on a modest scale by government agencies and universities. The Ad Hoc Interagency Working Group for Earthquake Research[2] reported that six federal government agencies spent $7.4 million on earthquake research in fiscal year 1967. Both the Environmental Science Services Administration and the U. S. Geological Survey have established new earthquake-research laboratories in California. The research programs they have established are guided to a significant degree by the recommendations of the Press Panel, but they fall far short of providing the information needed for safe development of coastal California and other U. S. areas subject to earthquakes. The magnitude of the problem can be seen from the Urban Land Institute's estimate[2] that, by the year 2000, the population of California will have increased from one-tenth to one-seventh of the national total, or to about 40 million in a national population of 300 million.

In 1962, the Earthquake Prediction Research Group in Japan outlined a plan for research on the prediction of earthquakes.[3] In 1965, following the destructive Niigata earthquake of 1964, the Japanese government sponsored and provided financial support for a 5-year plan for research on earthquake prediction.[4] The program is now well advanced.[5]

Earthquakes are a cause of common concern to Japan and the United States. The National Science Foundation and the Japan Society for Promotion of Science have jointly sponsored three conferences on research related to earthquake prediction.[6] The most recent of these, held at the U. S. Geological Survey's National Center for Earthquake Research, in October and November 1968, reviewed the latest progress in Japan and the United States on studies of premonitory phenomena associated with earthquakes, and related problems.[7]

The discovery[8, 9] that injection of waste fluids in a well drilled into the Precambrian rocks beneath the Rocky Mountain Arsenal near Denver, Colorado, had triggered a series of earthquakes, and evidence that earthquakes are triggered by the impounding of water in reservoirs[10, 11] and by large underground nuclear explosions[12, 12a], have raised the possibility that earthquake hazards can be reduced by the controlled release of stored strain energy in active fault zones.

Earthquakes in California

There has been no major breakthrough in earthquake prediction since the reviews by Press[13] and Rikitake,[5] but steady progress has been made toward understanding the nature of earthquakes along the continental margins, including coastal California. An enormous amount of evidence has been marshaled in support of Hess's concept of sea-floor spreading, Wilson's transform faults, and the later ideas of Vine, Le Pichon, Isacks, Oliver, Sykes, and others, on the motions of large, rigid plates of the lithosphere that plunge downward under the island arcs and continental margins to form the major earthquake belts of the globe.[14, 15] These revolutionary new concepts provide a global tectonic framework in which we can envision, for the first time, the kinematic processes that operate to generate earthquakes at depths ranging from the shallow crust to 700 kilometers.

In this framework, the San Andreas fault system of California is seen as a transform fault associated with spreading from the East Pacific Rise and with northwestward motion of a large, rigid plate of oceanic lithosphere toward the Aleutian Islands, where it descends into the earth's mantle at a rate of about 5 centimeters per year.

Allen and others have identified areas of contrasting seismic behavior along different segments of the San Andreas fault zone in California.[16] The segments corresponding to the surface breaks of the great 1906 San Francisco and 1857 Fort Tejon earthquakes (Fig. 1) seem to be "locked" and characterized by infrequent but very severe earthquakes. At present, the seismic activity is extremely low in the locked zones, and no fault creep—the quiet, steady-to-episodic slippage along the fault—has been discovered in these segments. These segments are likely candidates for great earthquakes in the future, perhaps within the next few decades, because the crust there is capable of storing large amounts of strain energy which can be released suddenly and violently. The "active" areas between San Francisco and Parkfield, southeast of San Bernardino, and also probably northwest of Cape Mendocino seem to be characterized by fault creep, accompanied by frequent minor-to-severe (but not great) earthquakes; thus the accumulation of large amounts of stored strain energy is inhibited. In our judgment, the segment of the San Andreas fault on the San Francisco Peninsula northwest of Hollister should be considered locked, although the Hayward and Calaveras faults east of San Francisco Bay are active. The San Andreas may be locked over much of its length because of the pronounced curvature of the fault near the north

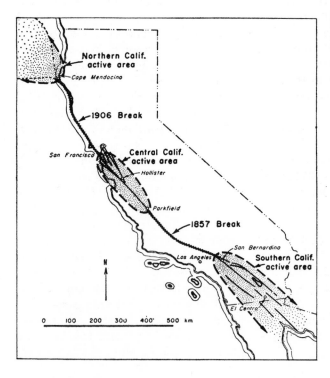

FIG. 1. Areas of contrasting seismic behavior along the San Andreas fault zone in California. [From C. R. Allen,[16] with permission]

end of the 1906 break at Cape Mendocino and near the center of the 1857 break (Fig. 1). If this pattern of contrasting seismic behavior is valid, it is clear that both Los Angeles and San Francisco are vulnerable to severe earthquake damage in the future.

The San Andreas fault zone also exhibits markedly differing patterns of seismic behavior when viewed in detail. Aftershocks of the June 1966 Parkfield-Cholame[17] earthquake lie along a narrow, near-vertical zone about 15 kilometers deep which nearly coincides at the surface with the mapped fault break. Cumulative fault creep of about 20 centimeters has been measured in this segment since 1966.

On the other hand, most of the aftershocks of a moderate earthquake that occurred southeast of Hollister at Bear Valley in 1967 were tightly clustered in a more or less spherical zone 3 kilometers in diameter and centered, just west of the San Andreas fault, at a depth of 3 kilometers. Bear Valley is near the inferred junction of the San Andreas and Calaveras faults. The center of the hypocentral zone at Bear Valley is within easy range of conventional drilling techniques and is thus available for direct observation and experimentation.

The results in the Parkfield-Cholame area and at Bear Valley were obtained from networks of portable seismographs. Seismic activity in California is also being continuously monitored by telemetered nets of short-period seismographs operated by the University of California at Berkeley, the California Institute of Technology, and the U. S. Geological Survey. In the vicinity of Hollister and Gilroy, micro-earthquakes recorded on the Geological Survey's telemetered net exhibit well-defined epicenter trends along, or near, the Sargent, San Andreas, and Calaveras faults.

In this area, as elsewhere in California, focal depths of micro-earthquakes do not exceed 15 kilometers. Crustal thickness averages about 25 kilometers. Thus, brittle behavior of the rocks in the San Andreas fault system seems to be confined to the upper crust; this implies some form of smooth slippage or flow along the faults in the lower crust and upper mantle.

Fault movements along the San Andreas system are being monitored by several federal, state, and local governmental agencies, and by universities. The most extensive fault-movement studies are the Geodimeter measurements of the State of California Department of Water Resources (now being continued by the State Division of Mines and Geology). These studies reveal a fault-movement rate that averages about 4 centimeters per year. The movement between Hollister and Cholame seems to be primarily in the form of fault creep.[18] North of Hollister, in the San Francisco Bay area, the movement is distributed primarily between the Calaveras and Hayward faults, and prominent creep has been noted at several places along the Hayward fault. No local fault movement was detected south of Cholame in the segment of the San Andreas fault that broke in 1857. These observations are compatible with the contrasting seismic behavior along different segments of the San Andreas fault zone.

Significantly, the Department of Water Resources found that earthquakes are often preceded by changes, and even reversals, in the rates of movement of the faults along which they occur.[18] Breiner and Kovach[19] have found evidence that fault-creep episodes are frequently preceded by local fluctuations in the earth's magnetic field.

Laboratory Investigations

Laboratory investigations related to the mechanism of earthquakes and the physical properties of rocks in earthquake source regions have been intensified recently in several governmental and university research institutions. Some results relevant to the problem of earthquake prediction were recently reviewed by Brace.[20] He particularly drew attention to the discovery by Raleigh and Paterson[21] that serpentine, under pressures at which it normally is ductile, becomes embrittled at high temperatures because of dehydration. Brittle fracture may, therefore, occur at depths extending into the upper mantle where hydrous phases in the mantle reach temperatures at which they dehydrate. This discovery seems to provide a mechanism for intermediate and perhaps deep-focus earthquakes as the rigid lithosphere descends into the mantle beneath island arcs and continental margins.

Byerlee and Brace[22] have shown that when two surfaces of granite or unaltered gabbro slide past one another under high confining pressure, the motion occurs through stick slip that is qualitatively similar to the shallow-focus earthquakes of the San Andreas fault system, but the confining pressures and stress drops are larger than those inferred for California. On the other hand, motion for gabbro and dunite in which olivine has been altered to serpentine occurs by stable sliding similar to the behavior of the San Andreas fault system in the deep crust and upper mantle.

It is well known that seismic velocity, electrical resistivity, and magnetic susceptibility of rocks are strongly dependent on stress. Brace and Orange[23] have shown in particular that rocks under confining pressure undergo large decreases in resistivity as they become dilatant at stresses near that for fracture. Resistivity decreased following an initial increase with stress for all rocks except marble as new cracks formed in water-saturated rocks; the decrease was accompanied by a small increase in volume. This observation suggests the possibility of monitoring stress variations in fault zones by resistivity measurements obtained with surface or in-hole electrode arrays.

Man-Made Earthquakes

Man-made earthquakes have been known since Carder[10] documented the occurrence of about 600 local tremors during the 10 years following the formation of Lake Mead, in Arizona and Nevada, by Hoover Dam in 1935. Most of these tremors were micro-earthquakes, but one had a magnitude of about 5, and two had magnitudes of about 4. Carder concluded that the seismic activity was caused by the load of water in Lake Mead that reactivated faults in the area.

Carder's discovery remained of academic interest until Evans[8] dramatically demonstrated a correlation between the rate of injection of waste fluids and the frequency of earthquakes in the vicinity of the Rocky Mountain Arsenal well near Denver, Colorado, following the first injection of fluids in March 1962. The U. S. Geological Survey recorded the seismic activity in the vicinity of the Rocky Mountain Arsenal well, and Healy and his co-workers demonstrated[9] that the epicenters of the earthquakes occurred in a narrow, nearly linear zone about 8 kilometers long and trending northwestward, with the well near the center of the zone. Focal depths of the earthquakes ranged from 4 to 6 kilometers, just below the bottom of the 3.8-kilometer-deep Arsenal well. Following termination of fluid injection in February 1966, the frequency of the earthquakes declined, as had been expected, but in late 1966 seismic activity began again, unexpectedly, and it continued through most of 1967. The largest earthquakes, of magnitudes up to 5.5, occurred during this period and caused minor damage. The seismic activity declined again in 1968 and has continued at a low level into 1969.

Seismic radiation patterns of the first motion on seismograms recorded at the Arsenal indicate right-lateral strike-slip movement along fractures oriented parallel to the trend of the seismic zone. This led Healy and his co-workers to conclude[9] that the earthquakes were triggered by reduction of frictional resistance to faulting with increasing pore pressure, a conclusion which was supported by an analysis, according to the theory of Hubbert and Rubey,[24] of the conditions in the hypocentral zone of the earthquakes.

Stimulated by the occurrence of the earthquakes near Denver, a search for similar phenomena elsewhere led to the recognition that the Unita Basin Seismological Observatory, in Utah, had recorded a series of minor earthquakes with epicenters near the Rangely oil field in northwestern Colorado. The Rangely oil field is the site of a secondary-recovery operation involving the injection of water under pressure. To verify the location of the earthquakes, four portable seismographs were installed by the U. S. Geological Survey near the oil field in 1967 and operated for 10 days. A high level of seismic activity was recorded. At all four stations, about 20 microearthquakes were recorded strongly enough to be located.[25] These earthquakes occurred near parts of the oil field where the fluid-injection operation has produced the largest recent increases in fluid pressures (Fig. 2).

Recently Rothé[11] reviewed the association of earthquakes with the filling of reservoirs. Several examples were found, the most significant being the Koyna, India, earthquake of 10 December 1967, which had a magnitude of about 6½ and resulted in the deaths of about 200 people and in widespread destruction. The epicenter was estimated to have been within 10 kilometers of the Koyna dam, about 150 kilometers southeast of Bombay, which created a reservoir of 2 billion cubic meters in 1962 and 1963. Minor tremors had been previously recorded in the Koyna reservoir area, beginning in 1963. These events led Indian scientists to convene a special meeting in New Delhi on 19 December 1967 to consider the Koyna earthquake and its implications; the proceedings were published in a special number of the *Journal of the Indian Geophysical Union.*[26] Lee and Raleigh[27] made a fault-plane solution of the 10 December earthquake; their solution indicates that the

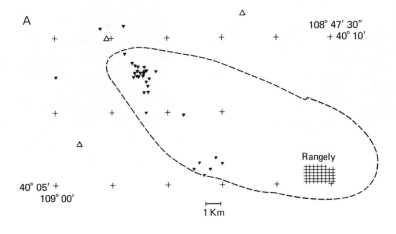

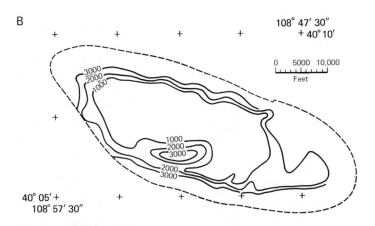

FIG. 2. Micro-earthquakes at the Rangely oil field, in Colorado. (a) Epicenters of 32 micro-earthquakes located by means of four stations. (Small inverted triangles) Epicenters; (larger triangles) stations. (b) Fluid pressures in the oil-producing horizon, the Weber sand, September 1967. Injection wells are near the perimeter of the field. Bottom hole pressure contour interval, 1000 pounds per square inch. [Pressure contours published with permission of the Chevron Oil Company]

mechanism was strike-slip faulting. From this study they concluded that tectonic strain stored in the rocks of the Koyna region was the source of the energy that released the earthquake.

Rothé[11] and Gough and Gough[28] have called attention to the earthquakes at Lake Kariba in the Kariba Gorge of the Zambezi River, Zambia. Thousands of earthquakes were recorded on a seismograph net installed after the lake was impounded by a hydroelectric dam in 1958. Gough and Gough concluded that normal faults in the area were reactivated by the reservoir load, by fault lubrication, or by both.[28] The largest of the earthquakes had a magnitude of 5.8.

Ryall and his co-workers[29] have noted numerous instances in which earthquakes were triggered by underground nuclear explosions at the Atomic Energy Commission's Nevada Test Site. In particular, they studied the Boxcar explosion of April 1968 and demonstrated that the blast triggered thousands of aftershocks in a northeast-trending zone 12 kilometers long and 4 kilometers wide.

Prior to the Benham underground nuclear explosion (yield, 1.1 megatons) of 19 December 1968, the U. S. Geological Survey installed a network of 27 seismographs in the vicinity of the Nevada Test Site.[12] Aftershocks of the explosion recorded by the network occurred as far as 13 kilometers from ground zero. Focal depths computed for the shocks ranged from the surface to a depth of about 7 kilometers. The magnitudes of the thousands of aftershocks recorded were generally small and did not exceed 5.0, as compared to the Benham magnitude of 6.3. The epicenters of the shocks migrated with time. Most were within 7 kilometers of ground zero during the first week following the explosion. After about 3 weeks the fracture zone was extended about 3 to 4 kilometers southward, and there was an accompanying increase in seismic activity. The aftershocks occurred west of ground zero, however, rather than along the zone of prominent surface fracturing to the east that developed after the Benham explosion and several earlier explosions. Analysis of the first motions of seismograms recorded from the Benham aftershocks suggest that they were triggered primarily by release of natural tectonic stress.

It is becoming increasingly evident that man can inadvertently trigger earthquakes by building dams, injecting fluids into the rocks of the earth's crust, and exploding nuclear devices underground. Earthquakes triggered by reservoirs and fluid injection have been destructive, some (as at Koyna) severely so, but, so far, seismic activity associated with explosions has occurred in the immediate vicinity of ground zero and has been less severe than the direct seismic effects of the explosions. It thus seems necessary for engineers of dams, and of fluid-injection projects in particular, to give heed to the possibility that their works may trigger destructive and even death-dealing earthquakes. These discoveries also suggest the possibility of using fluid injection and perhaps explosions beneficially to control the release of stored tectonic stress and thus reduce earthquake hazards.

Outlook for Prediction and Control

Since 1964, most earth scientists have concluded that earthquake prediction is a legitimate subject for research, but they differ widely in their estimates of the prospects for success. Several developments of the 1960's lead us to conclude that the prospects for success during the next 10 years are good.

In 1965, at Matsushiro in the Nagano prefecture of Japan, swarms of earthquakes began which were so intense that as many as 600 were felt on some days. Some of the earthquakes were destructive, with magnitudes of about 5. By the time the Matsushiro seismic activity declined, in 1967, Japanese scientists had issued the first warnings of future earthquake hazards, in the form of estimates of the location and probable maximum magnitude of potentially damaging earthquakes expected over a period of a few months.[5] The warnings were based on an intensive program of leveling and Geodimeter surveys, micro-earthquake recordings, tiltmeter measurements, and geomagnetic observations. The Japanese scientists found that, without exception, swarms of very small shocks occurred in the epicentral regions of shocks that came several months later. Ground tilt was found to correlate strongly with the growth and decay of the seismic activity, and anomalous tilt was observed shortly before the occurrence of some earthquakes of magnitude about 5. Anomalous magnetic fluctuations were also observed. By continuously correlating the various changes that were occurring, the Japanese scientists were able to forecast periods of danger and to issue their warnings.

Rikitake[5] considers the Matsushiro warnings to have been a scientific success and "helpful for local governments," but notes that "those engaged in the sightseeing and hotel business were not really pleased. . . . Great care must be taken to find an adequate way of issuing a warning. . . . It is also of importance to train people . . . to properly behave in case of an earthquake warning."

In our judgment, long-range forecasting (of the order of a year) of general locations and approximate magnitudes of earthquakes, based on observed changes in the rates of vertical and horizontal motions and on seismic activity in fault zones, is attainable

in the near future. In 1955, prior to the 1964 Niigata earthquake in Japan, the rate of uplift of bench marks north of the epicenter increased to about 5 times that of the preceding years. The rate of uplift began to decrease in 1959, and later there was a tendency toward subsidence. Considerable subsidence had been observed before the earthquake occurred.[5] This suggests that an earthquake-warning system might be provided in part by leveling surveys repeated every few months or so.

The rate of movement along different segments of the San Andreas fault in seismically active areas was observed to change before the occurrence of moderate earthquakes.[18] The change was manifested as changes in the length of Geodimeter lines crossing faults: the lines lengthen or shorten depending on their orientation with respect to the fault. If a fault in a zone characterized by creep becomes locally locked, we would expect the lengthening or shortening of lines crossing the fault to slow down or stop. If the movement should be transferred to an adjacent fault, we might expect the direction of movement even to reverse. Locking or transfer of fault movement would tend to create the conditions favoring a moderate earthquake. Such locking and transfer appear to have occurred repeatedly in California,[18] and this suggests that a partial earthquake-warning system might also be provided by Geodimeter surveys repeated every few months.

Combined leveling and Geodimeter surveying, accompanied by continuous monitoring of seismic activity, appears, therefore, to offer a promising basis for a long-range earthquake-warning system.

It seems reasonable to hope that short-range prediction of earthquakes (on the order of hours or days) may be achieved through *continuous* monitoring of ground tilt, strain, seismic activity, and possibly fluctuations in the earth's magnetic field. Such monitoring should be accompanied by periodic measurement of rock stress in drill holes and by periodic or continuous observation of physical properties (for example, electrical resistivity or seismic velocity) that are stress-dependent. Short-range prediction capability cannot be achieved, however, in the absence of accelerating research on earthquake prediction along the general lines of the Press[1] and Pecora[2] reports (see [30]).

It has been demonstrated that earthquakes can be artificially triggered by fluid injection, impounding of water in reservoirs, and explosion of nuclear devices underground, and also that many earthquakes in California and Nevada occur at depths accessible to the drill. We can soberly conclude from these observations that it may be possible to develop a practical method for artificially dislodging locked sections of a major fault and to induce steady creep or periodic release of accumulating elastic strain energy along the fault to inhibit the natural accumulation of sufficient energy to produce a disastrous earthquake.[31] It is also clear that our current knowledge of the processes involved in the generation of earthquakes is insufficient to guide an engineering program for earthquake control. We suggest that an intensified program of field, laboratory, and theoretical studies aimed at improving our understanding of earthquakes will not only advance the prospects for earthquake prediction but also provide an adequate basis for planning and implementing earthquake-control experiments that might ultimately provide the basis for a system of earthquake control.

Notes

[1] *Earthquake Prediction: a Proposal for a Ten-Year Program of Research* (Office of Science and Technology, Washington, D. C., 1965).

[2] *Proposal for a Ten-Year National Earthquake Hazards Program: a Partnership of Science and the Community* (Federal Council for Science and Technology, Washington, D. C., 1968). The members of the Working Group were L. Alldredge, W. E. Benson, W. Heitman, S. J. Lukasik, T. W. Mermel, L. C. Pakiser, A. J. Pressesky, W. A. Raney, H. B. Schechter, C. F. Scheffey, V. R. Willmarth, W. E. Hall (executive secretary), and W. T. Pecora (chairman). The report recommended implementation of a 10-year national earthquake hazards program along the general lines of the Press Panel report, but with less emphasis on earthquake prediction, greater emphasis on earthquake engineering, and estimated costs increased to $220 million.

[3] *Prediction of Earthquakes: Progress to Date and Plans for Further Development* (Earthquake Research Institute, University of Tokyo, Tokyo, 1962).

[4] T. Hagiwara and T. Rikitake, *Science* 157, 761 (1967).

[5] T. Rikitake, *Earth-Sci. Rev.* 4, 245 (1968).

[6] Proceedings of the 1st (1964) and 2nd (1966) United States-Japan Conferences on Research Related to Earthquake Prediction Problems, held, respectively, at the University of Tokyo and the Lamont Geological Observatory (available from the Earthquake Research Institute, University of Tokyo, or the Lamont Geological Observatory, Palisades, N. Y.)

[7] J. Oliver, *Science* 164, 92 (1969); see also a series of papers presented at the conference (L. Alsop and J. Oliver, Eds.), *Trans. Amer. Geophys. Union* 50, 376 (1969).

[8] D. Evans, *Mountain Geol.* 3, 23 (1966).

9 J. H. Healy, W. W. Rubey, D. T. Griggs, C. B. Raleigh, *Science* 161, 1301 (1968).

10 D. S. Carder, *Bull. Seismol. Soc. Amer.* 35, 175 (1945).

11 J. P. Rothé, *New Sci.* 39, 75 (1968).

12 *Trans. Amer. Geophys. Union* 50, 247 (1969) (abstracts of the symposium on Seismic Effects of Large Underground Nuclear Explosions, Golden Anniversary Meeting of the American Geophysical Union). See especially abstracts by J. H. Healy and R. M. Hamilton; A. Ryall, G. Boucher, W. V. Savage, and A. E. Jones; F. A. McKeown, D. D. Dickey, and G. E. Brethauer; S. W. Smith; J. Evernden; and E. R. Engdahl, W. V. Mickey, S. R. Brockman, and K. W. King.

12a R. M. Hamilton, F. A. McKeown, J. H. Healy, *Science* 166, 604 (1969).

13 F. Press and W. F. Brace, *Science* 152, 1575 (1966).

14 B. Isacks, J. Oliver, L. R. Sykes, *J. Geophys. Res.* 73, 5855 (1968).

15 H. H. Hess, in *Petrological Studies: A Volume in Honor of A. F. Buddington*, A. E. J. Engels, H. L. James, B. F. Leonard, Eds., (Geological Society of America, New York, 1962), p. 599; J. T. Wilson, *Science* 150, 482 (1965); F. J. Vine and J. T. Wilson, *ibid.*, p. 485; X. Le Pichon, *J. Geophys. Res.* 73, 3661 (1968); see also R. S. Dietz, *Nature* 190, 854 (1961).

16 C. R. Allen, in "Proceedings, Conference on the Geologic Problems of the San Andreas Fault System," *Stanford Univ. Pub. Univ. Ser. Geol. Sci. No. 11* (1968), p. 70.

17 J. P. Eaton, in "The Parkfield-Cholame, California, Earthquakes of June-August 1966: Surface Geologic Effects, Water-Resources Aspects, and Preliminary Seismic Data," *U. S. Geol. Surv. Prof. Pap. No. 579* (1967), p. 57.

18 "Geodimeter Fault Movement Investigations in California," *Calif. Dep. Water Resour. Bull. No. 116–6* (1968).

19 S. Breiner and R. L. Kovach, in "Proceedings, Conference on the Geologic Problems of the San Andreas Fault System, *Stanford Univ. Pub. Univ. Ser. Geol. Sci. No. 11* (1968), p. 70.

20 W. F. Brace, *Tectonophys.* 6, 75 (1968).

21 C. B. Raleigh and M. S. Paterson, *J. Geophys. Res.* 67, 4956 (1964).

22 J. D. Byerlee and W. F. Brace, *ibid.* 73, 6031 (1968).

23 W. F. Brace and A. S. Orange, *Science* 153, 1525 (1966).

24 M. K. Hubbert and W. W. Rubey, *Bull. Geol. Soc. Amer.* 70, 115 (1959).

25 J. H. Healy, C. B. Raleigh, J. M. Coakley, paper presented before the 64th Annual Meeting of the Cordilleran Section of the Geological Society of America, the Seismological Society of America, and the Paleontological Society of America, Tucson, Ariz., April 1968.

26 *J. Indian Geophys. Union* 5 (1968).

27 W. H. K. Lee and C. B. Raleigh, *Nature* 223, 172 (1969).

28 D. I. Gough and W. I. Gough, *Trans. Amer. Geophys. Union* 50, 236 (1969).

29 A. Ryall, G. Boncher, W. V. Savage, A. E. Jones, *ibid.*, p. 236.

30 A fairly comprehensive review of the status of research on earthquake prediction is contained in a special issue of *Tectonophysics* [6, No. 1 (1968)].

31 C. Y. King [*J. Geophys. Res.* 74, 1702 (1969)] has suggested that the fraction of stress energy released at the source of an earthquake radiated as seismic-wave energy decreases with decreasing magnitude, and is zero for fault creep. Therefore the number of small earthquakes needed to release dangerous crustal stresses should be much smaller than the number estimated on the basis of magnitude alone.

Tectonic Movements and Sea Level Changes

*What was solid earth has become sea,
and solid ground has issued from the
bosom of the waters.*
            Ovid, METAMORPHOSES

Even a casual examination of the rock record reveals a pattern of sea level changes throughout geological time. Sedimentary rocks of marine origin are found in the continental interiors and on mountain peaks, attesting to larger oceanic areas in prehistoric time. Exposed wave-cut terraces and drowned river valleys also attest to the changing relationships between land and sea. It is even possible that the deluge described in the Old Testament was produced by relatively recent sea level changes. Some of these changes are unequivocally related to the glacial cycles. Others are related to large-scale crustal warping or local subsidence. Temperature cycles deduced from the fossil record may help us to predict future changes, but the possible causes of sea level changes are complex and the direction and degree of change are therefore difficult to predict. Is it possible that Man will have to face another deluge, or are the long-term prospects in the direction of a lowering of sea level? Whatever the direction of change, there is little doubt that it will be significant and will have a profound effect on mankind.

Venice, Queen City of the Adriatic, is only one of the many coastal cities plagued by periodic flooding. In Venice, the impact of the worldwide rise in sea level due to melting of continental ice caps is compounded by local subsi-

Photo on page 119. Elevated Marine Terrace, Monterey County, California. Courtesy of B. Willis, U. S. Geological Survey.

dence. Trevor Christie calls our attention to this problem and the other environmental problems Venice is facing today. It is interesting to note the classic struggle between the traditionalists (environmentalists?) and the modernists as Venice attempts to come to terms with its changing physical, sociological, and economic environment.

Crustal warping, with the attendant sea level changes, is one aspect of tectonic activity. Movement along faults is another expression of tectonic activity. This movement may be slow and almost imperceptible (tectonic creep), but it can endanger structures and present costly repair problems. Readings 13 and 14 document the occurrence of tectonic creep in the San Andreas fault system. It is important to note that, although man-made structures are used to document and quantify the occurrence of tectonic creep, there are numerous topographic expressions of prehistoric tectonic activity which could alert the developer or planner to the hazardous setting. It is obvious, however, that in some cases the topographic indicators have either been ignored or have not been recognized. These readings illustrate the efforts of the geologic community to bring these hazards to the attention of persons concerned with building location, design, construction, and maintenance. Previous readings (Readings 7, 10, and 11) alerted us to the earthquake hazards associated with the "locked" portion of a fault system.

12   Is Venice Sinking?

Trevor L. Christie

Beautiful Venice, the Queen City of the Adriatic, rose out of the sea like Venus, and like Venus may be destined to return to the sea. Regardless of its past luster, it is facing a dubious future. It is either sinking slowly into its lagoon or the waters of the Adriatic are rising slowly to drown it—or both —according to how you view the evidence. Some surveys show that Venice as a whole has sunk about four inches in the past fifty years, but it varies from place to place. The ground beneath the Campanile of St. Mark's, which collapsed in 1902 and had to be rebuilt from the ruins, for instance, has sunk about seven inches in that time. Some engineers estimate that the city as a whole has been subsiding at an average rate of about one-tenth of an inch a year.

Every winter the tides of the Adriatic sweep higher and higher into Piazza San Marco, turning the marble expanse in front of the cathedral into a small lake two and one half feet deep and washing over its entrance steps. In the past seven years there have been twenty-five serious floods. Mellow old monuments such as the Forte Sant' Andrea at the entrance to the port have had their walls split open by the creeping waters and have begun to fall into the sea. (This is the fort from which

Christie, Trevor L., 1967, "Is Venice Sinking?" *Saturday Rev.*, March 25, 1967, pp. 40, 42. Reprinted by permission of Mrs. Trevor L. Christie and Saturday Review, Inc., Copyright 1967 by Saturday Review, Inc.
The article was originally adapted from Mr. Christie's book, *Antiquities in Peril*.

Casanova, the notorious adventurer, is supposed to have escaped after conviction for an infraction of the law.)

The assault on Venice comes not only from the sea. Whereas the original canals were carved out in conformity with the currents of the lagoon, new ones have been artificially plotted in a straight line and are exposed to a greater impact of the ebb and flow of the tides, eating away at the foundation and subfoundation of the city. The fleets of large motorboats (*vaporettas*) and small speedboats (*motoscafi*) which are rapidly replacing the traditional gondolas of romantic memory are also contributing to the decline. The wash of their powerful engines surges from one side of the canals to the other, gnawing away at the city's underpinnings. Every city has its traffic problems, but in a city which bans the motor car out of necessity, this problem is unique.

Venice is also under attack from other enemies: salt-water erosion, the ejection of motorboat fuel oil, industrial pollution from the air, and even the droppings of the beloved pigeons. All these combine to erode the city's foundation and crumble the facades of its monuments. As the movement of the tides carries sand from one part of the lagoon bed to another, the Lido Beach, once the most famous in Europe, has been shrunk to a narrow ribbon of sand. Of Venice's 200 palaces, it is calculated that about 50 per cent stand in need of repair, and of her 110 churches at least 10 per cent are almost beyond reconstruction.

In the face of these dangers a national city planning organization called *Italia Nostra* (Our Italy) was set up in 1958, and its first goal was to preserve and restore the historic heart of Venice with most of its monuments and to combat plans to commercialize it. The Municipal Council, supported by the city's business interests, had just approved a master plan of civic improvement to allow automobiles into the city for the first time by building a highway from the mainland, to erect skyscrapers which would overshadow the great palaces, and to create an administrative center on the islands. The two forces clashed head-on in a battle royal.

Both sides recognized that Venice, aside from its other afflictions, was in deep economic trouble, and neither wished to turn it into a "museum city," with all its citizens cast in the role of guides or gondoliers. Old Venice was losing residents at the rate of 2,500 to 3,000 a year and the population had been reduced to about 125,000 from a 1952 peak of around 175,000, while the industrial suburb of Mestre and the port of Marghera on the mainland were gaining in proportion. The modernists argued that the city was stagnating outside the tourist season and that it needed a transfusion of industrial blood. The traditionalists replied that the proposed changes would destroy the cultural atmosphere of the city and would drive away the lucrative tourist trade without bringing compensating revenue.

To hold back the sea, *Italia Nostra* countered with a proposal that locks be placed at the main entrance to the lagoon to control the water level and prevent high tides. To improve the economic health of the city, it proposed

that Venice be transformed into an international center on the order of Geneva to accommodate cultural conventions. To halt the outward flow of Venetians, it proposed that a new residential suburb be built between the city and nearby Mestre. To stop the deterioration of the city, it proposed a program of strict zoning and slum clearance which would raze nondescript structures of recent origin but would save genuine old villas. To block the advance of industry, it proposed that large factories be restricted to the mainland but that small, nonpolluting plants be permitted in certain sections. In general, it was proposing a Greater Venice with a careful balance between culture and commerce—each in its proper place.

Famous architects such as Frank Lloyd Wright and Le Corbusier, and writers such as Ernest Hemingway, sided with *Italia Nostra* for the most part, but real estate, shipping, and manufacturing interests fought the suggestions fang and claw. Their struggle stirred up a torrent of public debate in the press and generated many private maneuvers behind the scenes, cutting across political lines and even dividing prominent families over a period of several years. At length, the Municipal Council caved in and reversed itself, partially under pressure from the Ministry of Public Works in Rome. Most of *Italia Nostra's* ideas were accepted, but they have yet to be put into practice. The *Italia Nostra* recognizes that a conflict such as this is never finally settled and maintains constant vigilance to protect its victory.

As a supporter of *Italia Nostra*, Pietro Gazzola, State Inspector of Fine

Arts and Antiques, and one of the most respected authorities in Italy on the subject, lists five causes for the perilous condition of Venice: (1) the slow submergence of the bed of the lagoon due to unnatural hydraulic practices; (2) the erosion of the canals' underpinnings as a result of the motor-boats' operations and other causes; (3) lack of maintenance of the larger monuments; (4) the concentration of the populace in a restricted area, shutting out light and air; (5) the deterioration of the smaller structures to the extent that whole areas have been turned into near-slums. He contends:

"Venice, to survive, must have a complete and sane plan in which each of the separate problems is confronted and all the aspects of the situation are covered. The reclaiming of the lagoon calls for different measures according to the particular zone. The reform of the various means of transportation must be carefully studied and weighed against the characteristics of the canals and the houses and, above all, the vulnerability of the under-foundations.

"Every people—every man—has a long-standing and contingent debt to Venice. Civilization itself has a debt not easily put aside. It appears clear that only a supranational organization such as UNESCO is capable of representing all those who today, as well as yesterday and tomorrow, look to Venice as the most dramatic expression of the intelligence and spirit of mankind."

Under the stimulus of Professor Gazzola, *Italia Nostra*, and other civic-minded elements, the Italian government has set aside more than $1,000,-000 for the use of a commission to study methods of curing Venice of its ailments. While the commission argues and deliberates these days, the waters rise ever so slowly in the lagoon, the motorboats roar up and down the canals, the monuments crumble imperceptibly under erosion, and the pigeons wheel in the sky over St. Marks'; but no concrete steps have been taken to preserve the Queen City for posterity.

Editor's note: In October, 1972, the Italian Senate passed a long-delayed $400 million law to safeguard Venice. It is anticipated that the bill will be approved by the Chamber of Deputies in December. The bill provides funds for the restoration of paintings, frescoes, sculptures, Renaissance palaces, and unpalatial homes. There are also provisions for a sewerage system and laws against dumping noxious wastes into the surrounding water. Domestic heating units would be converted from sulphurous fuels to methane, and a $10 million aqueduct from the Sile River would replace artesian wells. An $80 million set of moveable dikes would be installed to hold back flood waters. Further filling of the Venetian Lagoon would be prohibited.

13 Tectonic Creep in the Hayward Fault Zone, California

Introduction

Dorothy H. Radbruch and M. G. Bonilla

Damage to Culvert Under Memorial Stadium University of California, Berkeley

Dorothy H. Radbruch and Ben J. Lennert, Lennert and Associates

Introduction

Tectonic creep has recently been recognized in the Hayward fault zone (Fig. 1). Tectonic creep is here considered to be slight apparently continuous movement along a fault, usually not accompanied by felt earthquakes; it has also been called slippage (Whitten and Claire, 1960). Much construction is going on in the areas of creep, and the probability of damage due to slow movement of faults, in addition to the possibility of sudden rupture, should be brought to the attention of persons concerned with design, construction, or maintenance of structures in the Hayward fault zone.

The Hayward fault zone is a northwest-trending zone of faults near the western front of the hills bordering the east side of San Francisco Bay (Fig. 2). It extends southeastward from San

Radbruch, D. H., Bonilla, M. G., and Lennert, B. J., Lennert and Associates, 1966, "Tectonic Creep in the Hayward Fault Zone, California," U. S. Geol. Survey Circ. 525, 13 p. Reprinted with light editing, pp. 1–6.
D. H. Radbruch and M. G. Bonilla are on the staff of the United States Geological Survey, Engineering Geology Branch, Menlo Park, California. B. J. Lennert is a civil engineer with Lennert and Associates, Oakland, California.

Pablo to Warm Springs, and possibly even farther both northwestward and southeastward. The zone in which recent movement has taken place ranges in width from approximately 500 feet south of Lake Temescal to about 1¾ miles near the Mission San Jose district. Many of the faults within the zone are actually bands of sheared rock, tens or possibly even hundreds of feet wide, in which are many anastomosing fault surfaces.

In places the surface expression of the many faults within the fault zone is very obvious. Near San Pablo the course of a fault is indicated by a short valley southeast of the Mira Vista Country Club; near the University of California in Berkeley and at Decoto the steep westward-facing front of the hills is probably a fault scarp. Lake Temescal in Oakland lies in a pronounced trench which shows the course of the fault zone, and between Niles and Irvington the main fault trace is marked by two conspicuous sag ponds. In general, the extent of the zone is indicated by such geomorphic features as shutter ridges, offset streams, lines of springs, scarps, and sag ponds.

In historic time, movements within the fault zone have caused two major earthquakes with accompanying sur-

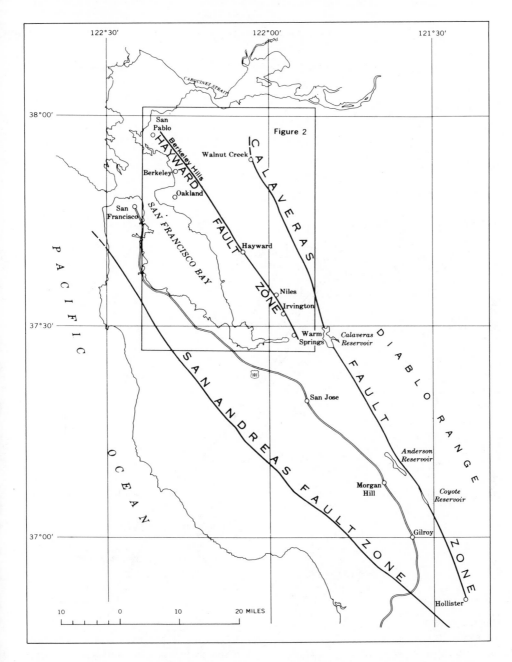

FIG. 1. Location of Hayward, San Andreas, and Calaveras fault zones, and approximate boundaries of Fig. 2. The towns of Niles, Irvington, and Warm Springs are now districts within the larger town of Fremont.

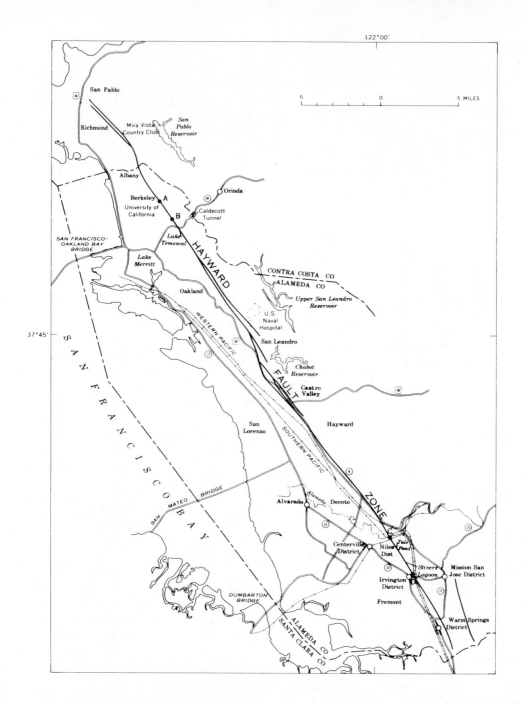

FIG. 2. Approximate location of fault traces of the Hayward fault zone and localities
(A–D) where evidence of creep has been found.

face rupture—one in 1836 and one in 1868 (Wood, 1916)—and numerous small shocks (Tocher, 1959). Both horizontal and vertical movement were reported at the time of the 1868 shock.

During the last few years evidence of tectonic creep along the Hayward fault zone has been found independently by several people from different organizations. In 1960, L. S. Cluff of Woodward-Clyde-Sherard and Associates noted distortion of a warehouse (loc. D, Fig. 2) in the Irvington district of Fremont. In December 1964 the East Bay Municipal Utility District found offsets in the Claremont water tunnel (loc. B, Fig. 2) in Berkeley while the tunnel was temporarily drained. In March 1965 M. G. Bonilla of the U. S. Geological Survey found distortion in railroad tracks (loc. C, Fig. 2) in the Niles district of Fremont. More recently, D. H. Radbruch of the U. S. Geological Survey and Ben J. Lennert, consulting engineer, confirmed a reported cracking of the culvert (loc. A, Fig. 2) under the University of California stadium in Berkeley. In each area the movement has been right lateral; that is, the northeast side of the fault has moved southeastward with respect to the southwest side of the fault.

As may be seen from Fig. 2, these four areas are near the ends of a 28-mile segment of the Hayward fault zone, but creep may be occurring in the intervening reaches. It is hoped that publicizing this phenomenon will encourage others to look for similar movements in other parts of the zone.

Faults do not suddenly change their habits, and therefore additional major earthquakes and tectonic creep along the Hayward fault zone can be ex-

pected. Future movement will probably take place within the fairly narrow band where historic movement and present creep are known. Direct injury to persons as a result of creep is not likely, but creep may progressively weaken structures which could fail and cause injuries.

The recognition, by geologic studies, of narrow bands of active movement permits (1) concentration of measurement for scientific and practical uses, and (2) precautions to minimize the destructive effects of the movement.

Damage to Culvert Under Memorial Stadium, University of California, Berkeley

The Hayward fault zone has long been known to extend northwestward across the campus of the University of California at Berkeley (Buwalda, 1929; G. D. Louderback, unpub. data). The University of California Memorial Stadium lies directly on the fault zone, its long axis being roughly parallel to it, at a spot where right-lateral movement along a sheared band or fault plane has offset the southwest-trending canyon of Strawberry Creek. The southwest side of the fault has moved northwest with respect to the northeast side, so that the downstream part of Strawberry Creek is now northwest of the upstream part. The two parts are connected by a northwest-trending section, about 1,200 feet, which flows in a culvert under the stadium. Part of the water of Strawberry Creek is carried by a bypass culvert which extends across the fault northwest of the stadium (Fig. 3).

On June 23, 1965, Dorothy H. Radbruch, of the U. S. Geological Survey, and Ben J. Lennert, of Lennert and Associates, soils engineers, consultants to the University of California, examined both of the Strawberry Creek drainage culverts.

The following description of damage to the culverts and their history of construction, damage, and repair is derived in part from field observation and in part from correspondence, reports, and drawings kindly furnished by the Division of Architecture and Engineering of the University of California and by Walter T. Steilberg, architect, consultant to the University of California. The assistance of Mr. Steilberg and

the University officials and their authorization to use the material furnished are gratefully acknowledged.

The part of the Strawberry Creek stadium culvert which lies under the Memorial Stadium was constructed in 1923, as part of the stadium contract. It is a cast-in-place concrete box culvert 4 feet wide that ranges from 3 feet 9 inches to 4 feet in height. The original culvert extended only from what is now the Corporation Yard to a point under the present Kleeberger Field. Other sections were added later.

Minor cracks in the culvert were noted when it was first inspected in

FIG. 3. Location of University of California Memorial Stadium, Berkeley, Calif.; fault or shear zone within the Hayward fault zone (stippled); two Strawberry Creek culverts, with station designations on culverts; and location of major cracking of stadium culvert.

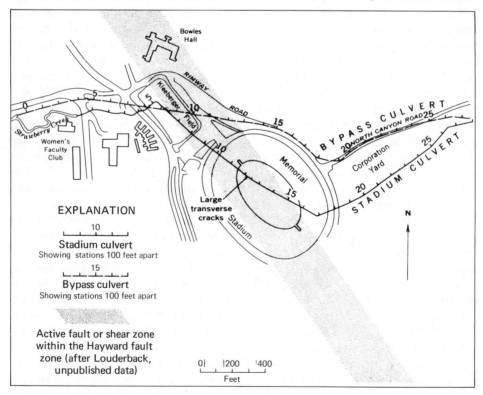

1932. Complete records of repair at that time are not available, but it is assumed that some repairs were made. In 1948 the culvert was again inspected and was found to be in very poor condition. In addition to leaky construction joints, holes in the floor (invert), and minor cracking, two large cracks were observed at stations 12+51.5 and 12+57 (Fig. 3). The large cracks were not those mentioned in the 1932 inspection report; they were described as being 1 inch wide completely around the culvert. A notation that the cracks might be due to movement along the Hayward fault zone was made by Walter T. Steilberg on a 1948 construction drawing. Repairs consisted primarily of grouting and installation of mine screwjacks as temporary shores in two parts of the culvert between stations 10+50 and 13+00, and between stations 16+50 and 17+50. The two large cracks were filled with mortar.

In 1954 the culvert was again inspected before making more permanent repairs. According to Walter T. Steilberg (oral commun., 1965), the cracks at stations 12+51.5 and 12+57 had widened between 1948 and 1954. At this time much of the floor of the culvert was paved, and 40 gunite rings, 41 inches long and 36 inches in inside diameter, were installed to replace the screwjacks. The large transverse cracks were repaired with gunite, but no details are available regarding their exact width at the time or the precise nature of the repairs.

When the culvert was inspected in 1965, the damage consisted of some leaky construction joints; erosion of the invert; hairline cracks on the northeast side of the culvert at approximately stations 8+45, 9+25, and 10+70 and between stations 14+27 and 15+80; and two major cracks at approximately stations 12+50 and 12+55. There is no doubt that the latter two cracks are the same as those previously recorded at stations 12+51.5 and 12+57.

The northwest (downstream) major crack, at about station 12+50, trends approximately at right angles to the culvert walls; in 1965 it had a maximum width of 1¼ inches in the floor and a maximum width of 3½ inches on the northeast side of the ceiling, between the centerline and the junction with the wall. The southeastern (upstream) crack, which has a sinuous trend across the floor, showed a maximum gap of a quarter of an inch in the floor and a maximum width of 2¾ inches on the southwest side of the wall. No lateral or vertical displacement of the cracks was apparent; the slight left-lateral offset reported in 1948 could not be confirmed. Water was pouring from the ceiling at both cracks, and the sides of the cracks and the walls near the cracks were coated with iron-stained calcium-carbonate, undoubtedly deposited by water entering the culvert through the cracks.

It can be assumed that the cracking of the floor has taken place since the floor was paved in 1954. The total average widening of the two cracks in the floor has been about 1.25 inches in 11 years, approximately 0.11 inch per year.

The main area of cracking and repair—stations 10+50 to 13+00—is thought to lie within an active sheared band or fault which is part of the Hayward fault zone (G. D. Louderback, unpub. data). The general trend of the fault probably crosses the culvert at an angle of about 20°. Right-lateral movement along this fault has taken place, as evidenced by the offsetting of Strawberry Creek. Right-lateral movement along the active zone would exert tension on the culvert, and tension cracks would be expected in the walls of the culvert. The formation and constant widening of the cracks that have been observed have probably resulted from such tensile stresses, and do not provide a direct measure of total movement on the fault since the culvert was installed.

No measurable lateral or vertical displacement of the cracks was observed, but the culvert appears to be slightly deflected laterally in the area of the two major cracks (Fig. 4).

The Strawberry Creek bypass culvert, which carries part of the waters of Strawberry Creek north of the stadium, was constructed in 1954. G. D. Louderback (unpub. data), who was a consulting geologist for the architect in charge of construction, was of the opinion that two main faults or branches of the Hayward fault zone extend northwest across the campus,

one lying under the stadium, and the other perhaps 400 to 500 feet farther west. He recommended that the section of the bypass culvert which would cross the easternmost fault be made of precast sections 4 feet in length, rather than the 8-foot sections used for the rest of the culvert. According to Walter T. Steilberg, architect (oral commun., 1965), weak mortar was used between the 4-foot sections, so that any failure in this area would take place along the joints rather than damaging the pipe sections. Construction plans show that the 4-foot sections were installed from station 7+96 to station 15+50, as given on Fig. 3, or a distance of 754 feet.

When the culvert was inspected in 1965, minor cracking was observed in many joints throughout the length of the culvert. The most pronounced and numerous cracks, some as much as one-eighth of an inch wide, were between stations 8+00 and 9+00, and between stations 10+80 and 12+80. The localities lie within the area thought to be crossing the active part of the fault. It is also in a place where

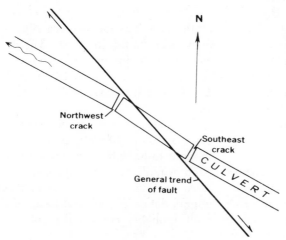

FIG. 4. General relationship of fault to damaged culvert under the University of California Memorial Stadium, relative direction of movement of opposite sides of fault, and nature of damage to culvert (not to scale).

the culvert slopes steeply, and all or part of the cracking in this area could be due to downslope movement of the pipe.

Maintenance personnel of the university report recurrent trouble with utilities, such as bending or breaking of conduit, on the rimway road near the playfield north of the stadium; the exact location is unknown at present.

Although the cracks in the stadium culvert could be due to a number of causes, such as weight of overlying fill or downslope creep of fill, it seems more probable that they are due to movement along a fault or belt of shearing within the Hayward fault zone. The major cracking of the stadium culvert, the most extensive cracking of joints of the by-pass culvert, and the location of reported difficulties with utilities all lie in a northwest-trending band that is coincident with the probable location of the fault.

Since the stadium culvert was installed, there has been one earthquake (in 1937) severe enough to crack walls and fell chimneys in the Berkeley area, as well as numerous lesser shocks (Byerly, 1951). None of them were accompanied by any visible surface rupture. Damage to the culverts is therefore probably due to slow movement or creep along the fault, with the possible exception of a small sudden movement in 1937. Records show that widening of the tension cracks in the stadium culvert has been constant, although we do not know whether it has been continuous or in small increments. Moreover, it is not possible to tell whether movement has been along one plane or distributed in a wide zone.

Preliminary observations indicate that the stadium culvert has been slightly offset in a right-lateral direction. This apparent right-lateral deflection is consistent with direction of creep noted elsewhere on the fault.

References

Buwalda, J. P., 1929, Nature of the late movements on the Haywards rift, central California: Seismol. Soc. America Bull., v. 19, no. 4, p. 187–199.

Byerly, Perry, 1951, History of earthquakes in the San Francisco Bay area: California Div. Mines Bull. 154, p. 151–160.

Tocher, Don, 1959, Seismic history of the San Francisco Bay region, *in* San Francisco earthquakes of March 1957: California Div. Mines Spec. Rept. 57, p. 39–48.

Whitten, C. A., and Claire, C. N., 1960, Creep on the San Andreas fault [California]—Analysis of geodetic measurements along the San Andreas fault: Seismol. Soc. America Bull., v. 50, no. 3, p. 404–415.

Wood, H. O., 1916, California earthquakes; a synthetic study of recorded shocks: Seismol. Soc. America Bull., v. 6, p. 55–180.

14   Creep on the San Andreas Fault
Fault Creep and Property Damage
Karl V. Steinbrugge and Edwin G. Zacher

Introduction

In the course of a building inspection of the W. A. Taylor Winery in April, 1956, Mr. Edwin G. Zacher noticed fractures in reinforced concrete walls and displacement of concrete slabs which could not be explained by landslide or attributed to other conventional causes. The winery is on the

Steinbrugge, K. V. and Zacher, E. G., 1960, "Creep on the San Andreas Fault," Article 1: "Fault Creep and Property Damage," *Bull. Seismol. Soc. Amer.*, vol. 50, no. 3, pp. 389–96. Reprinted with light editing by permission of the senior author and the publisher. Copyright 1960, S. S. A.
Mr. Steinbrugge is associated with Insurance Services Office, San Francisco, California.

Cienega Road about 7 miles south of Hollister, California.

An examination of geologic maps placed it in the San Andreas fault zone. On a relatively detailed geologic map Taliaferro (1949) shows the fault as a line going through the winery buildings. Since conventional explanations failed, a study was made of a possible connection between the damage and earthquakes and between the damage and possible fault movements.

Observed Damage

The observed building damage is found more or less along a straight line as may be seen in Fig. 2, and this line is

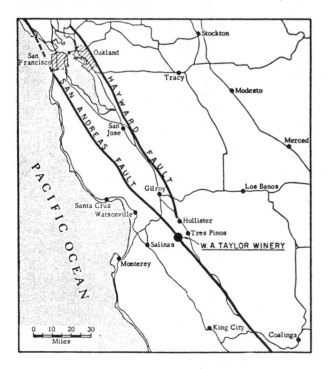

FIG. 1. Location map of W. A. Taylor Winery in California.

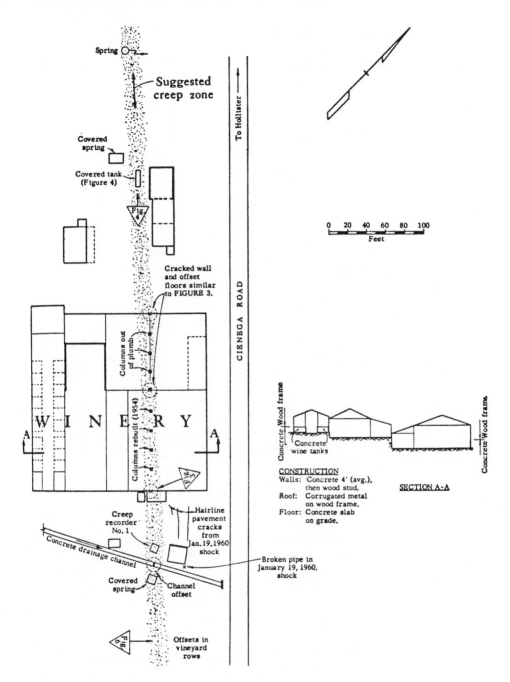

FIG. 2. W. A. Taylor Winery, showing locations of creep damage.

oriented in the direction of the San Andreas fault. Evidence at all damage locations indicates that the westerly portion of the main building is moving northward with respect to the easterly portion; in geologic terms, this is right-lateral movement. The total movement of one portion of the building with respect to the other between 1948, when the building was constructed, and December, 1959, is almost 6 inches.

Winery employees with many years' service have known of the damage and were aware of its growth. However, its growth was slow and gave no alarm.

This shearing movement has caused reinforced concrete walls to break at three places. Figure 3 shows an offset between wall and floor slab and is one indication of the total movement. Some columns along the line of creep were so badly affected that major reconstruction was required in 1954. Concrete floor slabs have moved along construction joints or have broken, again in a right-lateral sense.

Damage outside the main building is consistent with the linearity and type of motion taking place within the building. A concrete-lined drainage ditch south of the winery, constructed about 1943, has been ruptured. In the fall of 1957 two waterlines between the winery and the drainage ditch were broken. When subsequently they were under repair, it was observed that several ruptures had occurred here in previous years. Another pipeline break occurred in the January 19, 1960, earthquake (Fig. 2). A covered tank in the ground and adjacent to the office building north of the winery also shows distortion due to right-lateral movement. Vineyard rows just south of the main building have offsets.

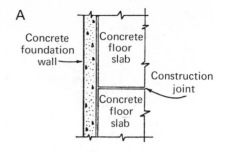

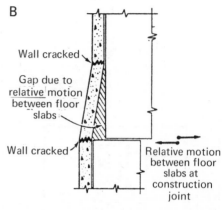

FIG. 3. Diagrammatic plans show the effects of creep, and may be considered as typical of all three broken walls. A: as originally built. B: effect of creep.

Measurements within the building have been made periodically by the authors since 1956, using as references the face of the walls, the edges of the floor slabs, and marks chiseled in the surface of the floor slabs. The data are plotted in Fig. 4, and indicate about one-half inch right-lateral movement per year.

Damage from Earthquakes

This area has had a number of felt shocks, probably more than the average for the Pacific coast region; however, the historic record makes no

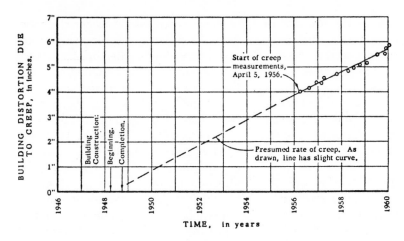

FIG. 4. San Andreas fault creep as measured by building distortions. The average creep is one-half inch per year.

mention of surface faulting at this location. Four felt shocks are of special interest.

The buildings at this winery (then known as Palmtag's Winery) were damaged in the April 18, 1906, San Francisco shock (Lawson et al., 1908): "At Palmtag's winery, in the hills southwest of Tres Pinos, the shock seems to have been more severe than elsewhere in the vicinity of that village. Furniture was moved, water was thrown from troughs, and an adobe building was badly cracked. One low brick winery was unharmed." A local resident who was in or near the buildings at the time, has stated to one author that "loose adobe brick" then fell from a wall. The 1906 surface faulting ended about 11 miles to the northwest.

On June 24, 1939, a local earthquake occurred which had a Modified Mercalli Intensity of VII, and its field epicenter was in the vicinity of this winery. Records of the U. S. Coast and Geodetic Survey (1939a, b) relate that an adobe wall pulled away from a side

wall; girders pulled away from brickwork and the brickwork was badly cracked; new cracks were formed and old ones opened 1 or 2 inches in width; many fresh ground cracks appeared in the neighborhood of the building, and their general trend appeared to be northwest-southeast and at right angles thereto. The observer did not comment further on the ground cracks.

The U. S. Coast and Geodetic Survey report (1939b) with its accompanying photographs has been reviewed by Mr. John Ohrwall, the present W. A. Taylor Company superintendent, who was present at the time of the 1939 shock. He says that the ground cracks were in the same location as the present movement. The parts of the winery which now lie across the creep zone have been built since 1939.

Another local earthquake, occurring on August 10, 1947, was also studied by the U. S. Coast and Geodetic Survey (1948). Their report regarding the winery states: "There was a small differential settlement at the junction of the old and new portions of one of the buildings, the older section having settled with respect to the newer. Furthermore, there was a transverse crack extending all the way across a concrete platform about 4 feet wide." Examination of the concrete-platform crack indicated local damage of no particular significance.

On January 19, 1960 (January 20, 1960, GCT), a strong local earthquake caused minor damage at the winery and also resulted in one-eighth inch of "instantaneous creep" in the building, a movement that was recorded at the time of the shock by University of California instruments at the winery. This movement caused cracks in the floors and walls to widen, and some concrete spalling occurred. Hairline ground cracks were noted in the paving to the south of the winery (Fig. 2), and an underground pipe was broken. The ground cracks and the pipe breakage were undoubtedly associated with the one-eighth inch movement. Typical other damage: some objects were thrown from shelves, a hollow concrete block chimney cracked, catwalks over large wooden wine tanks pulled apart, and some wine barrels worked loose from their chocks.

The published historic record, plus interviews with winery employees, ruled out the creep damage as the result of an earthquake or some other obvious event, except for the January 19, 1960, earthquake.

Fault Creep

Since the winery was in the San Andreas fault zone and since the damage had been progressive, the possibility

of fault creep was considered almost immediately and measurements were taken accordingly (Steinbrugge, 1957).

The winery is on a sloping site, and there are springs near and under the main building. There has been some conjecture that what is taking place may be somehow related to landslide. Springs beneath the building could facilitate the movement. However, the direction of the motion is essentially at right angles to the slope, and no noticeable downhill component of motion can be found. It would seem that landslide and other gravity effects cannot be present.

Practically all damage locations fall in a narrow straight zone as shown in Fig. 2. The bearing of this zone is essentially that of the strike of the San Andreas fault. Near-by springs, such as are often noted on a fault trace, also fall in the zone. Geologic mapping, which was done independently of the building damage, places the fault through the buildings (Taliaferro, 1949). The right-lateral movement is consistent with the right-lateral faulting known to have occurred on the San Andreas fault and is also consistent with possible creep resulting from the known regional strain pattern. The creep through the building appeared to be gradual as far as visual observation and the aforementioned crude measurements could determine, except for the earthquake of January 19, 1960.

All the foregoing is consistent with the theory of fault creep.

There is local opinion to the effect that the previous building at this site had been damaged in a similar manner. The description of the damage (skewed roof trusses), and wall offsets of about two feet in perhaps half a century, suggest that the rate of creep of one-half inch per year may have been fairly constant for many years.

Fences to the north and south of the winery show no damage or offsets which could be the result of fault creep. It is not known if the creep is markedly local, or if the fences are so situated as not to be indicative of creep.

References

Lawson, A. C., et al., 1908. *The California Earthquake of April 18, 1906; Report of the State Earthquake Investigation Commission* (Washington, D. C.: Carnegie Institution of Washington, 2 vols. plus atlas).

Steinbrugge, Karl V., 1957. *Building Damage on the San Andreas Fault*, report dated February 18, 1957, published by the Pacific Fire Rating Bureau for private circulation.

Taliaferro, N. L., 1949. "Geologic Map of the Hollister Quadrangle, California," Plate 1 of California Division of Mines *Bulletin 143* (text not published).

U. S. Coast and Geodetic Survey, 1939a. *Abstracts of Earthquake Reports from the Pacific Coast and the Western Mountain Region*, MSA-22, April 1, 1939, to June 30, 1939. 1939b. "Central California Earthquake of June 24, 1939" (unpublished manuscript prepared by Dean S. Carder). 1948. *Abstracts of Earthquake Reports from the Pacific Coast and the Western Mountain Region*, MSA-55, July, August, September, 1947.

Mass
Movement

Unstable sedimentary deposits represent a major hazard in many localities throughout the world. Quintin Aune (Reading 15) describes an unusual clay deposit which led to earthquake-triggered landslides 75 miles from the epicenter of the Good Friday Alaskan earthquake. Geologists had cited the hazardous nature of these clay deposits, but the area was nevertheless developed as a fashionable suburb of Anchorage. Similar deposits have plagued Scandinavia and other areas where marine clays composed essentially of glacial rock flour have been elevated above sea level as a result of postglacial rebound. These clays have experienced a natural leaching of their electrolytes and are highly unstable. Mr. Aune asks if the activities of man could also lead to the leaching of other clay deposits and set the stage for the generation of quick clays and major landslides. His suggestions should be carefully considered by those who are evaluating sites for new developments.

Not all landslides are related to the presence of quick clays. In Reading 16 William Alden describes a common landslide setting, that is, unfavorable geologic structures and heavy precipitation. Slope failure, a process unrelated to Man's activities in this case, led to the formation of a natural dam which later failed and created the hazards associated with natural flooding. The discussion portion of Alden's paper illustrates the broad concern about this problem and the similarity between the Gros Ventre slide and slides in other localities. Reading 17 is a case study of the disastrous landslide at the Vaiont Dam in northern Italy. Adverse geologic features were the major factors contributing to this slide, but man-made conditions upset the delicate balance and more than 2000 people lost their lives in less than six minutes.

The examples of mass movement cited in this section share notable similarities. The hazardous settings at Anchorage and Vaiont were well documented prior to mass movement. Development at Vaiont was a calculated risk. At Anchorage it appears that those in authority may not have been aware of the hazards involved. There were preliminary warnings of disaster at Gros Ventre and Vaiont. The warnings were, however, either unheeded or misinterpreted. Improved communications among geologists, engineers, government personnel, and the public are clearly needed to avoid similar disasters.

Photo on page 138. Aerial view of Turnagain Heights landslide, Anchorage, Alaska. Courtesy of U. S. Army.

15 Quick Clays and California's Clays: No Quick Solutions

Quintin A. Aune

The March 27 Good Friday earthquake of 1964 caused extensive damage at Anchorage, Alaska, 75 miles from the earthquake hinge belt and epicenter. Much of the damage can be related to earthquake-triggered landslides. What is there about the geologic setting of Anchorage which led to localized landslide activity? U. S. Geological Survey Water-Supply Paper 1773, Geology and Ground-water Resources of the Anchorage Area, Alaska (Cederstrom et al., 1964), although written before the Good Friday earthquake, contains several clues.

The accompanying map, (Fig. 1) adapted from the ground-water study, shows distribution of earthquake-triggered landslides relative to subsurface distribution of the Bootlegger Cove Clay. These landslides contributed to a substantial part of the damage at Anchorage; they are known to have been caused by local failure of the Bootlegger Cove Clay. Major landslide failure was not uniform over the entire area underlain by the clay, but was restricted to low escarpments paralleling Knik Arm and Ship Creek in the western part of the Anchorage area.

Aune, Q. A., 1966, "Quick Clays and California's Clays: No Quick Solutions," *Mineral Information Service*, vol. 19, no. 8, pp. 119–23. Lightly edited by permission of the author and reprinted by permission of California Division of Mines and Geology, Sacramento, California.

Quintin Aune is a geologist on the staff of the California Division of Mines and Geology.

What caused failure of the Bootlegger Cove Clay? Cederstrom et al. (1964, p. 32, and Table 4) indicate that sand in lenses in the Bootlegger Cove Clay "commonly becomes quicksand when penetrated by the (well) drill." Quicksand has the peculiar property of losing all its cohesive strength and acting as a liquid when disturbed, as by the sudden jar of a man's footsteps on the surface, or the sudden vibration of a drill—or an earthquake—beneath the surface. Some clays develop similar properties, and are called quick clays because of their analogous behavior. As we shall see below, there is reason to suspect that part of the clay fraction of the Bootlegger Cove Clay assumed the properties of a quick clay.

Quick clays are generally confined to the far north areas. They are known to have caused excessive damage in eastern Canada and Scandinavia in the past (Kerr, 1963; Liebling and Kerr, 1965). They result when a marine or brackish water clay composed essentially of glacial rock flour is elevated above sea level. Such post-Pleistocene elevation is common in the far north due to isostatic adjustment of the land surface resulting from the melting of the great overburden of glacial ice only a few thousands of years ago.

Clay derived from rock flour consists of the minutely ground up particles of many minerals, generally including several clay minerals. It is not excessively responsive to disturbance as long as the intermolecular water—

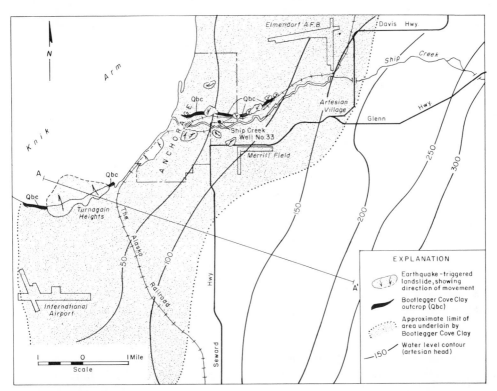

FIG. 1. Geologic map of the Anchorage area, Alaska, showing critical features of the geology pertaining to slope failures precipitated by the Good Friday Earthquake. *Adapted from text, maps, and data of the U. S. Geological Survey, Water-Supply Paper 1773, 1964.*

the formation water—contains dissolved salt (sodium chloride). The salt acts as an electrolytic "glue" which adheres to the clay particles and provides cohesiveness and structure to the clay (Kerr, 1963, p. 134). Once the clay is elevated above sea level the salts—this natural "glue"—may be progressively flushed out by fresh groundwater. Cederstrom et al. (1964, p. 72) cite evidence to show current loss of sodium electrolyte to well water (Well #33) that penetrates the Bootlegger Cove Clay in the Anchorage area. The sodium salt may be flushed out, reducing or destroying the clay's

cohesive properties, or its sodium may be replaced by calcium, greatly reducing the clay's cohesiveness. Because this process has gone on only in the past few thousand years, only portions of the clay have recently become extremely responsive to disturbance. There was, therefore, little obvious geological evidence of the clay's present instability—such as landslide scarps —until the major earthquake disturbance disrupted it at Anchorage.

As shown in the cross-section the Bootlegger Cove Clay, (Fig. 2) as defined in well-logs (Cederstrom et al., 1964), lies athwart the path of west-

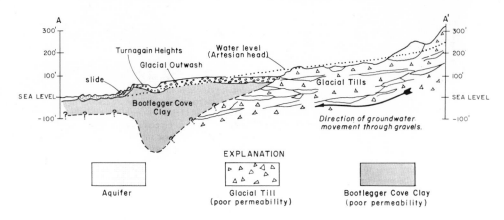

FIG. 2. Geologic cross section, A-A', from Fig. 1.

ward-flowing ground-water. It was indeed fortunate for Anchorage that the salt leaching or exchange process, sensitizing the Bootlegger Cove Clay, is a slow, incomplete one. Impermeability of the clay and position of much of the formation below sea level have significantly retarded the invasion of fresh water and "leaching" or exchange of the sodium ions.

Shown also on the cross-section and on the map is the artesian head, the level to which water from a well will rise when confined in a standing pipe. It may be seen from the cross-section that this level is well above the ground surface in the area along the eastern margin of the Bootlegger Cove Clay but drops off rapidly as one travels west across the area underlain by the clay.

In the Anchorage area, artesian water travels in a crudely interconnected system of gravels, confined from above by impermeable till (east half of the cross-section). The westward passage of the water is impeded by the Bootlegger Cove Clay. If the clay were absent, water in the underground channels or "pipe system" would pass unobstructed to the sea and no high confining pressure could be built up, but such is not the case.

Theoretically, this relationship can be very dangerous. Confined groundwater in a unified hydraulic system has much the effect of a hydraulic ram. Here, it exerts a constant pressure against the clay barrier—the Bootlegger Cove Clay—to the west. As long as that formation is coherent, and has shearing strength, it will hold together, and its molecules will not "collapse" into an unoriented liquid substance at the onset of a major shock, as an earthquake. If rendered incoherent, however, as it was in the disastrous quick-clay slides in eastern Canada and Scandinavia (Kerr, 1963), entire sections of the Bootlegger Cove Clay could break and glide laterally in translation movement, settling ultimately into a disheveled landslide "mush." Such a mass might flow seaward, carrying part or even all of Anchorage with it, because nearly all of Anchorage is underlain by the Bootlegger Cove Clay.

The slides at Anchorage were minor, compared to the above-inferred catastrophe, because the main earthquake shock was far distant, and because much of the Bootlegger Cove Clay is not yet a quick clay. As shown by Well #33 (Fig. 1), it is still "in the making." Perhaps the limited disaster was fortunate for Alaska. It will stimulate the residents, scientists, and engineers to recognize the problems they face, and to learn through industry and science how they can control or work around their problems at Anchorage and elsewhere in Alaska (*Time*, 1965).

Could a similar "Good Friday" earthquake-landslide disaster happen to California? Because of the Ice-Age genesis of known quick clay deposits, California probably has no quick clays as such. It has no geological environment in which natural forces are actively flushing out the electrolytic "glue" to create structural hazards. Then does the Alaskan example apply to California? Many poorly consolidated marine and evaporite clay-bearing formations in California contain electrolytes—in the form of saline formation waters—which add to their stability. It has often been demonstrated in California that this stability may readily be disrupted during the substitution of fresh water for saline waters by a drilling mud during the drilling of oil wells (Morris et al., 1959).

California's recent geologic history is one of frequent volcanism. Volcanoes produce ash which settles into the sea or becomes concentrated in saline evaporite lakes, and later becomes part of the soil or of underlying marine lake bed formations or terrace deposits. Eventually the ash alters into illite and montmorillonite clay minerals. Such clays, while not reaching the extremes of quick clays, are nevertheless potentially sensitive and may even approach quick clays in this respect. As with quick clays, the sensitivity of these clays to shock or disturbance may be greatly increased by the flushing out

FIG. 3. Cross-section of a hypothetical California landscape analogous to Anchorage. Schematic buildings represent what could be a major subdivision; irrigation losses may represent runoff from thousands of acres. Leaching of sodium ions from clay may reduce its coherence, set stage for major landslide.

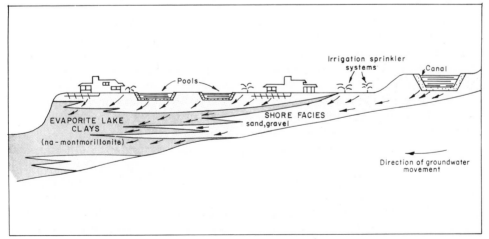

of saline formation water with its electrolytic "glue," and substitution of fresh, "unglued" solutions in its place.

Geological processes strive toward stability. Stability of a clay deposit is a relative state. It is relative to the nature of the formation water, the type and condition of the clay, and the nature of the slope. This stability may be affected by: (1) a change in the clay through the addition of abnormal amounts of water. Certain montmorillonites will adsorb water until the "rock"—it actually becomes a gel—contains as much as 20 parts of water to one part of clay; (2) a change in salinity of the formation water, as at Anchorage; (3) a change in the slope or load conditions, by the driving of a pile or the excavation for a building foundation.

All three of these possible means of clay stability change are active to some extent in California today, in the form of man-made building excavations; canal construction and subsequent leakage of fresh canal water into salt-bearing clays; and in related activities of man. A concrete structure may give off free calcium in solution, to substitute for sodium in a clay formation electrolyte, changing the sensitivity of the clay. The number of stability changes in potentially unstable clays may be expected to accelerate greatly in California in the immediate future, as a direct result of the transportation of vast quantities of fresh northern California water to the south to satisfy the needs of that rapidly expanding area.

This water will be delivered to areas of need, many of which are the loci of poorly consolidated clay-bearing formations, such as in the southern San Joaquin Valley, southern Coast Ranges, vast areas of the Mojave Desert, and in Los Angeles Basin region. Many of these areas contain saline clay-bearing sedimentary basins which may become vulnerable, through wastage, leakage, and plan, to fresh water invasion. This can be somewhat analogous to the Anchorage area. While disasters of the magnitude of Anchorage are unlikely, nevertheless substantial losses in life and property may result unless care is exercised.

What is our lesson from the Good Friday Alaskan earthquake? It is that change—even innocuous change, such as substitution of a fresh formation water for saline water—may breed instability in clay-bearing beds. A new residential property, and especially a "view" property which abuts against an escarpment or "free face" susceptible to landslide failure, invites disaster even without a "Good Friday" earthquake if the foundation conditions underlying the property are subjected to uncompensated stability changes. With the occurrence of a major earthquake —a potentiality in most populated areas of California—the stakes are indeed high.

Clay technology and clay mineralogy are new and dynamic branches of scientific study. Only in the past dozen years have up-to-date texts become available on these subjects. Few geologists are trained in clay problem studies and fewer laboratories are equipped to cope with them. Yet, there is a "need to know" these subjects. Great cities are growing. New ones will grow. The press is outward, to marginal development sites, to unproved development areas. Drill hole subsurface data, qualitative information on clay and pore water properties, and geologic know-how are lacking in many of these areas.

If expansion and development are to be judicious and safe, they must be accompanied by careful planning. Such planning must be based on geologic maps, which show locations of potential hazard due to past slides or presence of potentially sensitive clay formations. It must be based on complementary maps showing clay and groundwater properties of various geologic map units, so that appropriate care may be taken where potentially sensitive clays are encountered. Following such planning, competent development of an area will anticipate and prevent possible man-made "natural" disasters by utilization or preparation of foundation conditions that can resist them, and by avoiding construction of high population density developments in areas where foundation conditions are or may become too poor or unreliable to be remedied.

References

Cederstrom, D. J., Trainer, F. W., and Waller, R. M., 1964, Geology and ground-water resources of the Anchorage area, Alaska: U. S. Geological Survey Water-Supply Paper 1773.

Coulter, H. W., and Migliaccio, R. R., 1966, Effects of the earthquake of March 27, 1964, at Valdez, Alaska: U. S. Geological Survey Professional Paper 542-C, p. C1–C36.

Grim, Ralph E., 1962, Applied clay mineralogy: McGraw-Hill Book Co., Inc., New York, 422 p. Chapter 5, "Clay Mineralogy in relation to the engineering properties of clay materials," gives an excellent technical discussion of clays and foundation problems resulting from instability within clay-water systems.

Hansen, W. R., 1965, Effects of the earthquake of March 27, 1964, at Anchorage, Alaska: U. S. Geological Survey Professional Paper 542-A, p. A1–A64.

Kachadoorian, Reuben, 1965, Effects of the earthquake of March 27, at Whittier, Alaska: U. S. Geological Survey Professional Paper 542-B, p. B1–B21.

Kerr, Paul F., and Drew, Isabella M., 1965, Quick-clay movements, Anchorage, Alaska (Abstract): Geological Society of America Program, 1965 annual meetings, p. 86–87.

Kerr, Paul F., 1963, Quick clay: Scientific American, Vol. 209, no. 5 (November, 1963), p. 132–142.

Liebling, Richard S., and Kerr, Paul F., 1965, Observations on quick clay: Geological Society of America Bulletin, vol. 76, no. 8, p. 853–877.

Mielenz, Richard C., and King, Myrle E., 1955, Physical-chemical properties and engineering performance of clays: in Clays and clay technology.

Mitchell, James K., 1963, Engineering properties and problems of the San Francisco Bay mud: in California Division of Mines Special Report 82, p. 25–32.

Morris, F. C., Aune, Q. A., and Gates, G. L., 1959, Clays in petroleum reservoir rocks: U. S. Bureau of Mines Report of Investigations 5425, 65 p.

Oakeshott, Gordon B., 1964, The Alaskan earthquake: Mineral Information Service, July issue, p. 119–121, 124–125.

Schlocker, Julius, Bonilla, M. G. and Radbruch, Dorothy H., 1958, Geology of the San Francisco North quadrangle, California: U. S. Geological Survey Miscellaneous Geologic Investigations Map I-272.

Time Magazine, 1965. Anchorage's feet of clay: Time, vol. 86, no. 25, Dec. 17, 1965, p. 62.

16   Landslide and Flood at Gros Ventre, Wyoming*

William C. Alden†

A great landslide occurred on June 23, 1925, in the valley of Gros Ventre River, about 35 miles south of Yellowstone National Park (Fig. 1). The relations of the north-easterly dipping rock formations of the slide scarp and of the dam formed by the slide are

* Published by permission of the Director, U. S. Geological Survey.
† U. S. Geological Survey.

Alden, W. C., 1928, "Landslide and Flood at Gros Ventre, Wyoming," *American Institute of Mining and Metallurgical Engineers*, trans. vol. 76, pp. 347–58. Abridged and reprinted by permission of American Institute of Mining, Metallurgical and Petroleum Engineers.

shown in the diagrammatic cross-section of the valley (Fig. 2). This generalized section is based on unpublished maps and notes by Eliot Blackwelder, in the files of the U. S. Geological Survey.

Heavy rains and melting snow in the Gros Ventre Mountains had saturated clay layers in the Carboniferous strata, which dip toward the valley at angles of 18° to 21°, consequently an enormous mass of rock at the end of the north spur of Sheep Mountain became loosened and, on the afternoon of June 23, slid suddenly down into the valley. Within a few minutes this mass of debris—estimated as 50,000,000 cu.

FIG. 1. Map showing dam and lake formed by landslide blocking Gros Ventre River.

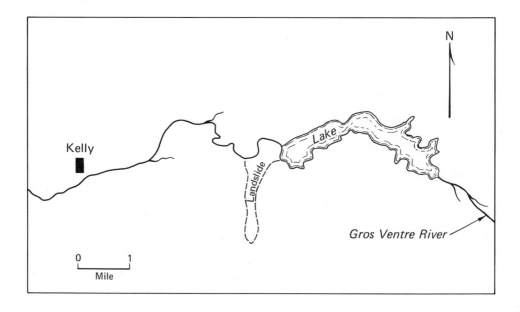

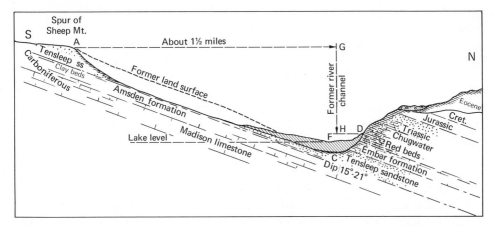

FIG. 2. Diagrammatic section (N. S.) illustrating damming of Gros Ventre River valley, Wyo., by landslide.

C-F = Height of dam (shaded) at river channel about 225 ft.

C-H = Height of dam north end of dump about 350 ft.

Geological section based on unpublished maps and notes by Eliot Blackwelder, in files of U. S. Geological Survey.

yd.—carrying on its surface a dense pine forest, rushed across the valley, piled up about 350 ft. high against the cliffs of red sandstone on the north and partly slumped back and spread so as to form a dam 225 to 250 ft. high above the lower toe of the dump. The path of the slide and the resulting dam are shown in Figs. 1 and 2. The river, which was in flood, was completely blocked and rapidly filled the basin behind the dam, so that within 18 hr. a ranch house standing 60 ft. above the river was floated off its foundation and in about three weeks the lake (shown in Fig. 1) reached a depth of about 200 ft. at the back of the dam, an average width of about ½ mile, a length of about 3 miles, and an estimated area of about 11,000 acres.

Soon after the slide, water began seeping through the dam. This took care of the inflow, which decreased as the summer came on. On Aug. 18, 1925, Depue Falck, of the U. S. Geological Survey, estimated the seepage as 500 sec.-ft. On account of this seepage the lake did not overtop the dam, and when I visited it about a month later the lake level had fallen about 9 ft. below the high-water mark.

There was considerable speculation by engineers and others as to what would occur when the snow melted in the spring of 1926. It happened that there was a light snowfall in the Gros Ventre Mountains in the winter of 1925–26, so no spring flood occurred, and conditions remained practically unchanged. In September, 1926, I crossed the dam just above the point of vigorous outflow and examined the crest of the dam from end to end. G. E. Manger, my assistant, and I climbed the mountain slope along the east margin of the scarp to its head, which my barometer indicated to be about 2100 ft. above the bed of the stream below the dam—that is, nearly four times as high as the Washington Monument.

The place where the break eventually occurred is about opposite the lowest point of the lake shore. Although there was such a mass of big blocks of rock on the outer front of the dam back of this belt of rocks, the top of this part of the dam appeared to be composed very largely of fine, loose, easily erodable material, greenish-white clay, reddish clay, and sand with fewer large stones. There was a narrow sag in the crest of the dam and the high-water mark showed that the lake had extended into this sag, but I saw no evidence at that time (September, 1926) that there had been any erosion of a channel or that water had gone over the top of the dam. I was told, however, that some water had gone over the dam, but I hardly understand how it could have done so without cutting a channel through the loose fine material.

On the steep slope adjacent to the upper half of the slide scarp we found old breaks indicating that at some time great masses of rock had started to slide, but lodged. Ranchers said, however, that no other slides are known to have occurred in this part of the valley since it was settled. There have been numerous slides farther up the valley. One of these was described by Blackwelder.[1]

Several hundred feet below the top of a scarp is a mass which started to slide, but lodged with the trees standing upon it. The declivity at the head of the scarp is 30° to 45°. Farther down it is about the same as the dip of the strata; i.e., 15° to 21°. A line of sight from the top of the scarp to the lowest point of the lake dips 17° and to the farthest high point of the dam is 13°. Limestone and sandstone are exposed in the scarp, also reddish and whitish clays such as were noted in the dam. Saturation of such clayey layers by water was doubtless the cause of the big slide.

The Flood of May, 1927

The prediction of some engineers, and the fact that there was no break in the dam for nearly two years after the slide occurred, had given rise to a feeling of security and a rather general belief that the dam would hold. In the winter of 1926–27 heavy snows fell in the Gros Ventre Mountains and a period of rapid melting, together with rain, in May, 1927, caused a rapid rise of the lake, which, on the morning of May 18, overtopped the lowest part of the dam and caused a disastrous flood. In July, 1927, in company with my assistant, Edward F. Richards, I revisited the place to see the effects of the flood and the condition of the dam and lake. From the forest ranger, C. E. Dibble, and other residents of the village of Kelly, I obtained information as to what occurred.

We found that the outflow had cut a channel nearly 100 yd. wide and about 100 ft. deep beneath the crest of the dam near its downstream face. The channel had a rather steep gradient and the head of the outlet was considerably back of the highest part of the dam, where a shallow, but a swift stream was flowing over the rocky debris. Measurement with a hand level showed the lake surface to be about 60 ft. below the high-water mark, so that there was yet probably a maximum depth of nearly 150 ft. of water in the lake.

In 1925, Herman Stabler, of the Geological Survey, estimated that, with the basin filled to the point of overflow, there would be 164,000 acre-feet impounded and that the cutting of a channel only 25 ft. deep would release about a quarter of this great amount of water, or 48,000 acre-feet. It was then predicted that sudden release of such a flood could scarcely result otherwise than disastrously. The dam did not fail as a whole, but the lake was lowered more than 50 ft. in a very short time, and disaster resulted.

The river had been slowly rising during the morning of May 18 at the village of Kelly, about 4 miles below the dam, and efforts were being made to prevent the highway bridge from being washed out. The stream had not overflowed its 10 to 15-ft. banks there up to 10 a.m. The appearance of some ranch utensils in the stream, however, warned Mr. Dibble that something was wrong at the dam. Rushing over the hills in his automobile, on the road leading up the valley, he witnessed the destruction of the buildings at Woodward's ranch about a mile below the dam and out of sight of it. He then sped back to the village and messages were sent down Gros Ventre and Snake River valleys to warn the inhabitants of the approaching flood. It is reported that about 11 a.m. there suddenly came from the mouth of the gorge above Kelly a great rush of water described as a wave 15 ft. or more in height, which caught some of the villagers as they were trying to save some of their effects. All the buildings were swept away with the rush excepting the schoolhouse and a small church and near-by cottage on a little higher level at the north edge of the village.

In 1925, Kelly had a population of 60 or 70 people, of whom a few were drowned. Besides the destruction of the buildings and their contents in this village, several ranches on Gros Ventre and Snake River were more or less damaged. Six or seven persons were drowned, some had very narrow escapes, bridges were washed out and effects of the flood were felt as far down Snake River as Idaho Falls, Idaho. It appears that there was time after the warning was given for all persons to have escaped with their lives if they had not stopped to save any of their effects. As is usually the case, however, some apparently did not appreciate the necessity for such haste. It is reported that water began to flow over the dam in three places on the afternoon before, but it does not appear that any definite watch was maintained at the dam even after flood conditions began to develop.

That which is of most interest to geologists and engineers is what actually happened at the dam. The great blocks of sandstone and limestone which it had been thought by some would retard the outflow in case of an actual break now lie on a low terrace over which the flood rushed as it swung against the north side of the gorge below the dam. Some of these blocks are 15 to 20 ft. in diameter. They are somewhat scratched and their edges are bruised. I do not know just how far down the valley such blocks were carried by the flood. The terrace on which these rocks lie corresponds to the remnant of a terrace in the cut through the dam.

The terrace along the south wall of the channel is 15 or 20 ft. above the stream. It was probably the bottom of the channel at the time the great rush of water passed through. From this the main current swung to the north side of the valley, dumping the big rocks on the inner side of the bend, and cutting into the base of the cliffs. The narrowed but still vigorous stream flow after the big rush probably cut the inner channel below the terrace. Loose and heterogeneous material formed the dam. This bluff is about 100 ft. in height and it is composed of a mixture of loose sliding sand, crushed rock, and large and small angular fragments of limestone and sandstone. Evidently such a jumble of loose porous material as composes the upper part of the dump would not form a permanent dam capable of withstanding overflow without controlling gates and adequate spillways. No trees or logs were seen buried in the rock debris. Evidently the forest trees rode down on top of the slide and were not mixed into the debris very much by rolling over. They form an almost impassable tangle of criss-crossed trees, some of them still alive, on top of the dam.

Apparently no person saw just what actually took place at the dam, but the composition of the upper part of the dam may explain why the main flood came so suddenly and with such great volume. Probably seepage increased rapidly as the lake rose and this tended to undermine at the same time as overflow at the lowest point cut the initial channel. There was an enormous quantity of water in the upper 50 ft. of the impounded body. Rapid deepening of the trench across the crest must have caused rapid slumping at the sides and

the loose material must have at once been swept out of the way, opening a broad outlet toward which the enormous body of water started moving with rapidly increasing velocity. Repeated slumpings of the sides may have caused the reported succession of wavelike crests of the flood. Driftwood was found 10 to 14 ft. above the ground in trees on the flat below Kelly, so that there was a considerable depth of water, though it is said to have spread out to a maximum width of about ¾ mile within a mile below the mouth of the gorge. From an instrumental survey made by L. C. Bishop, it has been estimated that there was in the upper 50 ft. of the lake body nearly 43,000 acre-feet of water, and apparently all of this went out. By 4 p.m. the flood had passed Kelly and the stream had receded within its banks.

So great is the width of the dam ¼ mile or more from front to back below the high-water level that after trenching the first 50 ft. the amount of material to be moved was enormously greater and the rate of deepening became very much slower. With the lowering of the lake level the sill of the outlet thus moved gradually back while the channel below the crest of the dam was further deepened another 40 ft. The lake was lowered only about 60 ft. before the rate of cutting became so slow as to end the flood.

Completed melting of the snow and cessation of rainfall also soon reduced the inflow so that on July 5, 1927, the lake had lowered only about 2 ft. farther below a fairly definite water mark. I have no information as to conditions since that date. Probably the lake slowly lowered through the summer of

1927 and through the past winter as the outlet channel deepened.

There was still an enormous amount of water impounded in July, 1927, for the lake extended 3 or 4 miles up the valley, nearly as far as before. It probably yet had a maximum depth of 100 ft. or more after the flood, for the tops of tall trees were emerging only near the borders of the lake.

What will happen in case there is another period of rapid melting of heavy snows in the mountains, together with much rainfall? Of course, one can not say definitely, but certainly the danger of such a flood as that of May, 1927, is greatly reduced. The outlet now provided may be deepened and broadened somewhat, but I see no reason to expect anything more than a normal high-water stage in the river below the dam. It may be that further deepening of the outlet may start renewed sliding on the south side of the valley. If this does not occur suddenly, it may simply retard the outflow by gradually encroaching on the stream, as has occurred in the case of an older slide about 15 miles farther up the valley. It would not, however, seem advisable to rebuild the village of Kelly on the same site on the low flat terrace directly below the mouth of the gorge.

Discussion

G. S. RICE, Washington, D. C.—Those who are interested in the question of landslides in connection with mining operations should read a very excellent paper by Professor Knox.[2] He classifies slides into "break-deformation slides" (such as those at the Panama Canal) and "gravity slides"; he also refers to mud flows. Professor Knox has gone into the question

quite thoroughly. He has cited some cases of landslides in various countries, both naturally induced and those produced by artificial agencies, such as excavations and waste piles.

W. C. ALDEN (written discussion).—On Sept. 22, 1928, I again visited the Gros Ventre valley and reexamined the landslide dam. In general, conditions were about the same as at the time of my visit in July, 1927. I was informed by John A. Evans, road overseer of Teton National Forest, that there was a good deal of snow in the mountains in the spring of 1928 and the usual spring flood occurred, but resulted in little damage. Repeated freezing retarded melting of the snows and held back some of the outflow. I made a measurement which showed the lake to be approximately 60 ft. below the high-water mark, or about the same as in July, 1927. Whence it appears that the outlet has not been deepened appreciably during the intervening 14 months.

G. KNOX, Treforest, South Wales (written discussion).—I read with great interest Mr. Alden's excellent paper on the great landslide and flood at Gros Ventre, Wyoming. This is an excellent example in confirmation of the theory that water is the chief agent in the causation of landslides. In the diagrammatic section (Fig. 2) the Tensleep sandstone is shown resting on clay beds having a dip of $15° 21'$ towards the valley. This sandstone is no doubt semiporous and well jointed, and receives a good supply of water from the gathering ground on Sheep Mountain. With melting snow a very large percentage of the water percolates into the strata, which probably produced a slow creep of the sandstones over the clay beds. The fissures resulting from this creep enable a still greater percentage of the rainfall or melting snow to percolate down to the impervious clays. This slow movement would upset the natural drainage of the area, resulting in the lubrication of the clay and supersaturation of the sandstone, which, combined, produced conditions so unstable that the whole mass of debris suddenly rushed into the valley forming the large dam.

The Gros Ventre landslide appears to have been similar in character to the great landslide which recently took place on Mount Arbino in Switzerland, the largest known to have occurred in that country famed for landslides. The debris displaced amounted to 30,000,000 cu. m., but thanks to the vigilance of the geologists of the Swiss Topographical Service the slow creep which usually precedes these great movements was noted and warning given to the inhabitants of the villages in the valley of Arbedo.

In this case the first movement was noted as far back as 1888, and during the following 40 years the total movement was only 5 ft. 9 in. The sliding debris finally rushed down from a height of 4000 ft. over a distance of 5000 ft., forming a dam 900 ft. high in the valley below. The holding power of this dam is exercising the minds of the Swiss engineers just as that of Gros Ventre did in your country, because should this be breached a terrible disaster is likely to result.

Further movements have recently taken place higher up the valley slope and it is expected that eventually it will reach the top of the mountain 6000 ft. high. The estimated amount of debris included in the total movement is 200,000,000 cubic meters.

In South Wales there are continual movements of the mantles on the valley slopes and although not so disastrous as the landslides referred to above are a continual source of trouble and expense to the community. Most of these valleys have been formed by the erosion of the Middle coal measures, which consists of hundreds of feet of hard sandstones known as the Pennant Series. Where the valleys are confined to this series they are steep and narrow but immediately the

Lower coal measures consisting of alternating beds of sandstone, shale and fireclay—with many workable coal seams—are reached, the valleys begin to widen rapidly.

In the Middle Series the eroding action of the rivers is accompanied by slides of the "rock-fall" type, but as soon as the Lower Series is reached the slides become composite in character, consisting of the mantles formed by the rock falls of the Middle Series together with the rocks resting on the clays.

The dividing line between the two series is the No. 2 Rhondda (Brithdir, Tillery or Ynysarwed) coal seam which forms a plane of saturation on the underclay below. Downhill of this saturation plane all the soil creep or "gravity" slides take place. They work backwards (uphill) towards the saturation plane forming a series of steep crags in the hard sandstones of the Middle coal measures above the saturation plane. This leads to "break deformation" slides in the hard sandstones providing fresh material for a new mantle which in turn slides into the valley.

In these cases the debris has to slide over the outcropping edges of the strata which are nearly horizontal and in this respect differ from the Gros Ventre landslide.

As the valleys provide the only suitable place for sinking the shafts from which the coal has to be worked, they have become densely populated. Apart from the necessary buildings for domestic and industrial purposes the valleys contain all the necessary public works such as railways, canals, roads, sewage, gas and water mains, etc., so that any movement in the mantle is the cause of considerable trouble.

The cause of these South Wales landslides has been somewhat obscured owing to the fact that large heaps of colliery refuse were deposited on the hillsides during the early stages of mining development. Whenever a landslide took place in which one of these masses of refuse was included the cause was attributed to the great weight of the colliery rubbish. Failing that it was attributed to mining subsidence, with the result that many colliery companies have had to pay considerable sums for damage attributed to mining operations although the real cause was landslide movement.

The natural dam formed by a landslide such as that described in Mr. Alden's paper is always a source of great danger to the district downhill of it. The debris from the "lubricating" clays while more or less mixed up in the rock boulder mess forming the dam, will usually contain a more or less definite stratum of clay near the base, as landslides move faster at the bottom than at the top of the mass. This will act as a sliding plane on which movement may ultimately be expected and the safest plan would be to gradually breach the dam during the dry season by artificial cuttings.

Notes

[1] E. Blackwelder: The Gros Ventre Slide an Active Earth Flow. *Bull*. Geol. Soc. Amer. (1912) 23, 487.
[2] G. Knox: Landslides in South Wales Valleys. *Proc*. South Wales Inst. Engrs. (1927) 43, 161.

17   The Vaiont Reservoir Disaster

George A. Kiersch

The worst dam disaster in history occurred on October 9, 1963, at the Vaiont Dam, in Italy, when some 2600 lives were lost. The greatest loss of life in any similar disaster was 2,209 in the Johnstown Flood in Pennsylvania in 1899. The Vaiont tragedy is unique in many respects because:

It involved the world's second highest dam, of 265.5 meters (875 ft.).

The dam, the world's highest thin arch, sustained no damage to the main shell or

Kiersch, G. A., 1965, "The Vaiont Reservoir Disaster," *Mineral Information Service*, vol. 18, no. 7, pp. 129–38. Abridged by permission of the author and reprinted by permission of California Division of Mines and Geology. The report was first published in *Civil Engineering* (vol. 34, no. 3, 1964) and the American Society of Civil Engineers has permitted its reprinting in a revised form.
Professor Kiersch is Professor of Engineering Geology at Cornell University, Ithaca, New York.

abutments, even though it was subjected to a force estimated at 4 million tons from the combined slide and overtopping wave, far in excess of design pressures.

The catastrophe was caused by subsurface forces, set up wholly within the area of the slide, 1.8 kilometers long and 1.6 km. wide.

The slide volume exceeded 240 million cu. m. (312 million cu. yd.), mostly rock.

The reservoir was completely filled with slide material for 1.8 km. and up to heights of 150 m. (488 ft.) above reservoir level, all within a period of 30 to 60 sec. (A point in the mass moved at a speed of 25 to 30 m. per sec.)

The slide created strong earth tremors, recorded as far away as Vienna and Brussels.

The quick sliding of the tremendous rock mass created an updraft of air accompanied by rocks and water that climbed up the right canyon wall a distance of 240 m. (780 ft.) above reser-

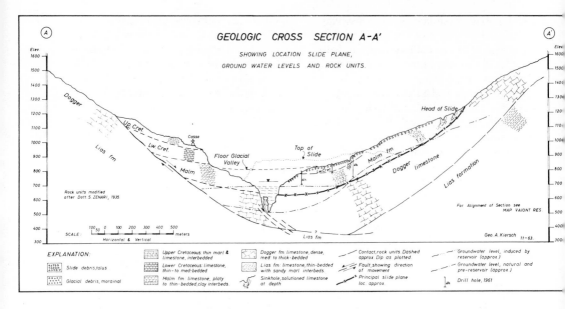

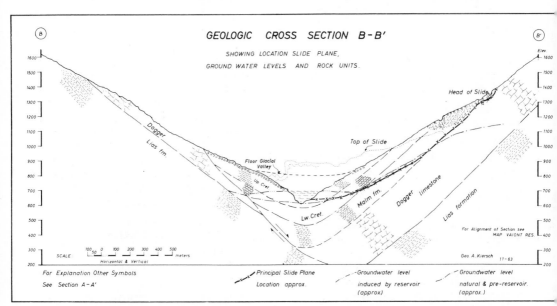

FIG. 1. On geologic cross-sections of slide and reservoir canyon, running from north to south, principal features of the slide plane, rock units and water levels are shown. For location of Sections A-A′ and B-B′, see Fig. 2.

voir level. (References to right and left assume that the observer is looking downstream.) Subsequent waves of water swept over both abutments to a height of some 100 m. (328 ft.) above the crest of the dam. It was over 70 m. (230 ft.) high at the confluence with the Piave Valley, one mile away. Everything in the path of the flood for miles downstream was destroyed.

A terrific, compressive air blast preceded the main volume of water. The overtopping jet of water penetrated all the galleries and interior works of the dam and abutments. Air currents then acted in decompression; this tensional phase opened the chamber-locked safety doors of all the galleries and works and completed destruction of the dam installations, from crest to canyon floor.

This catastrophe, from the slide to complete destruction downstream, occurred within the brief span of some 7 min. It was caused by a combination of: (1) adverse geologic features in the reservoir area; (2) man-made conditions imposed by impounded water

FIG. 2. Map of Vaiont Dam area and Piave River valley shows geographic features, limits of slide and of destructive flood waves.

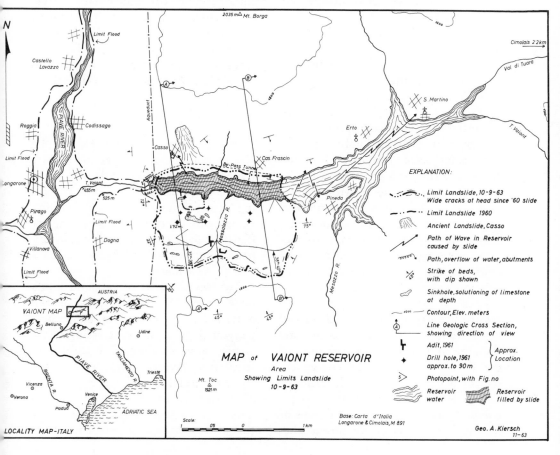

with bank storage, affecting the otherwise delicately balanced stability of a steep rock slope; and (3) the progressive weakening of the rock mass with time, accelerated by excessive groundwater recharge.

Design and Construction

Vaiont Dam is a double-curved, thinarch, concrete structure completed in the fall of 1960. The dam is 3.4 m. (11.2 ft.) wide at the top and 22.7 m. (74.5 ft.) wide at the plug in the bottom of the canyon. It has an overflow spillway, carried a two-lane highway on a deck over the crest, and had an underground powerhouse in the left abutment. Reservoir capacity was 150 million cu. m. (196 million cu. yd., or 316,000 acre-ft.).

The way in which the dam resisted the unexpected forces created by the slide is indeed a tribute to designer Carlo Semanza and the thoroughness of construction engineer Mario Pancini.

Design and construction had to overcome some disadvantages both of the site and of the proposed structure. The foundation was wholly within limestone beds, and a number of unusual geologic conditions were noted during the abutment excavation and construction. A strong set of rebound (relief) joints parallel to the canyon walls facilitated extensive scaling within the destressed, external rock "layer." Excessive stress relief within the disturbed outer zone caused rock bursts and slabbing in excavations and tunnels of the lower canyon. Strain energy released within the external, unstable "skin" of the abutment walls was recorded by seismograph as vibrations of the medium. This active strain phenomenon in the abutments was stabilized with a grout curtain to 150 m. (500 ft.) outward at the base—and the effects were verified by a seismograph record. Grouting was controlled through variations of the elastic modulus.

The potential for landslides was considered a major objection to the site by some early investigators; others believed that "the slide potential can be treated with modern technical methods."

The Geologic Setting

The Vaiont area is characterized by a thick section of sedimentary rocks, dominantly limestone with frequent clayey interbeds and a series of alternating limey and marl layers. The general subsurface distribution is shown in the geologic cross sections. (Fig. 1).

Retained Stress

The young folded mountains of the Vaiont region retain a part of the active tectonic stresses that deformed the rock sequence. Faulting and local folding accompanied the regional tilting along with abundant tectonic fracturing. This deformation, further aided by bedding planes and relief joints, created blocky rock masses.

The development of rebound joints beneath the floor and walls of the outer valley is shown in an accompanying (Fig. 3). This destressing effect creates a weak zone of highly fractured and "layered" rock, accentuated by the natural dip of the rock units. This weak zone is normally 100 to 150 m. (330 to 500 ft.) thick. Below this a stress balance is reached and the undisturbed rock has the natural stresses of mass.

Rapid carving of the inner valley resulted in the formation of a second set of rebound joints—in this case parallel to the walls of the present Vaiont canyon. The active, unstable "skin" of the inner canyon was fully confirmed during the construction of the dam.

The two sets of rebound joints, younger and older, intersect and coalesce within the upper part of the inner valley. This sector of the canyon walls, weakened by overlapping rebound joints, along with abundant tectonic fractures and inclined bedding planes, is a very unstable rock mass and prone to creep until it attains the proper slope.

Causes of Slide

Several adverse geologic features of the reservoir area contributed to the landslide on October 9:

Rock units that occur in a semicircular outcrop on the north slopes of Mt. Toc are steeply tilted. When deformed, some slipping and fault movement between the beds weakened frictional bond.

Steep dip of beds changes northward to Vaiont canyon, where rock units flatten along the synclinal axis; in three dimensions the area is bowl-shaped. The down-dip toe of the steep slopes is an escarpment offering no resistance to gravity sliding.

Rock units involved are inherently weak and possess low shearing resistance; they are of limestone with seams and clay partings alternating with thin beds of limestone and marl, and frequent interbeds of claystone.

Steep profile of the inner canyon walls offer a strong gravity force to produce visco-elastic, gravitational creep and sliding.

Semicircular dip pattern confined the tendency for gravitational deformation to the bowl-shaped area.

Active dissolving of limestone by ground-water circulation has occurred at intervals since early Tertiary time. The result has been subsurface development of extensive tubes, openings, cavities and widening of joints and bedding planes. Sinkholes formed in the floor of the outer valley, particularly along the strike of the Malm formation on the upper slopes; these served as catchment basins for runoff for recharge of the ground-water reservoir. The interconnected ground-water system weakened the physical bonding of the rocks and also increased the hydrostatic uplift. The buoyant flow reduced gravitational friction, thereby facilitating sliding in the rocks.

Two sets of strong rebound joints, combined with inclined bedding planes and tectonic and natural fracture planes, created a very unstable rock mass throughout the upper part of the inner canyon.

Heavy rains in August and September produced an excessive inflow of ground-water from the drainage area on the north slopes of Mt. Toc. This recharge raised the natural ground-water level through a critical section of the slide plane (headward part) and subsequently raised the level of the induced water table in the vicinity of their junction (critical area of tensional action). The approximate position of both water levels at the time of the slide is shown in the accompanying figure (Fig. 3).

Excessive ground-water inflow in

early October increased the bulk density of the rocks occurring above the initial water table; this added weight contributed to a reduction in the gross shear strength. Swelling of some clay minerals in the seams, partings and beds created additional uplift and contributed to sliding. The upstream sector is composed largely of marl and thin beds of limestone with clay partings—a rock sequence that is inherently less stable than the downstream sector.

The bowl-shaped configuration of the beds in the slide area increased the confinement of ground water within the mass; steeply inclined clay partings aided the containment on the east, south, and west.

Two exploratory adits driven in 1961 reportedly exposed clay seams and small-scale slide planes. Drill holes bored near the head of the 1960 slide were slowly closed and sheared off. This confirmed the view that a slow gravitational creep was in progress following the 1960 slide and probably even before that—caused by a combination of geologic causes. Creep and

Fig. 3. On sketch of inner Vaiont canyon and remnants of the outer glacial valley, are shown rebound joints—old and young set—from stress relief within the walls of the valley to depths of 100 to 150 m. (330 to 500 ft.).

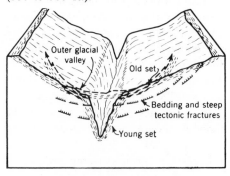

the accompanying vibrations due to stress relief were later described by Muller.

Effects of Man's Activities

Construction of Vaiont Reservoir created an induced ground-water level which increased the hydrostatic uplift pressure throughout a triangular subsurface mass aided by fractures and the interconnected system of solution openings in the limestone.

Before April 1963, the reservoir was maintained at El. 680 m. or lower, except for two months in 1962 when it was maintained at 690–700 m. In September, five months after the induced water table was raised 20 m. or higher (700–710 m.), the slide area increased its rate of creep. This action has three possible explanations: (1) a very delicate balance existed between the strength of the rock mass and the internal stresses (shear and tensile), which was destroyed by the 20-m. rise of bank storage and accompanying increase in hydrostatic pressure; (2) the same reaction resulted from the large subsurface inflow in early October due to rains; or (3) the induced ground-water level from the reservoir at El. 680 m. during 1961–1962 did not attain maximum lateral infiltration until September 1963, when creep accelerated. In any case, the rate of ground-water migration into bank storage is believed to have been critical.

Evidence indicates that the immediate cause of the slide was an increase in the internal stresses and a gross reduction in the strength of the rock mass, particularly the upstream sector where this mass consists largely of marl and alternating thin beds of limestone and marl. Actual collapse was triggered by an excess of ground water, which created a change in the mass density and increased the hydrostatic uplift and swelling pressures along planes of inherent weakness, combined with the numerous geologic features that enhanced and facilitated gravitional sliding.

The final movement was sudden—no causes from "outside" the affected area are thought to have been responsible.

Sequence of Slide Events

Large-scale landslides are common on the slopes of Vaiont Valley; witness the ancient slide at Casso and the prehistoric blocking of the valley at Pineda. Movement at new localities is to be expected periodically because of the adverse geologic setting of the valley. The principal events preceding the movement on October 9 were:

In 1960, a slide of some 700,000 cu. m. (one million cu. yd.) occurred on the left bank of the reservoir near the dam. This movement was accompanied by creep over a much larger area; a pattern of cracks developed upslope from the slide and continued eastward. These fractures ultimately marked the approximate limits of the October 9 slide. The slopes of Mt. Toc were observed to be creeping and the area showed many indications of instability.

In 1960–1961, a bypass tunnel 5 m. (16.4 ft.) in diameter was driven along the right wall of the reservoir for a distance of 2 km. (6,560 ft.), to assure that water could reach the outlet works of the dam in case of future slides.

As a precaution, after the 1960 slide the reservoir elevation was generally held at a maximum of 680 m. and a grid of geodetic stations on concrete pillars was installed throughout the potential slide area extending 4 km. (2.5 miles) upstream, to measure any movement.

The potential slide area was explored in 1961 both by drill holes and by man-sized adits (see map for depth). Reportedly, no confirmation of a major slide plane could be detected in either drill holes or adit. An analysis now indicates that the drill holes were too shallow to intercept the major slide plane of October 9, and what was in all probability the deepest plane of gravitational creep started by the 1960 slide and active thereafter.

Gravitational creep of the left reservoir slope was observed during the 1960–1961 period, and Muller reports "movement of 25 to 30 cm. (10 to 12 in.) per week (on occasion) which was followed in close succession by small, local earth tremors due to stress relief within the slope centered at depths of 50 to 500 m. (164 to 1,640 ft.). The total rock mass that was creeping was about 200 million cu. m. (260 million cu. yd.)."

During the spring and summer of 1963, the eventual slide area moved very slowly; scattered observations showed a creep distance of 1 cm. (3/8 in.) per week, an average rate since the 1960 slide.

Beginning about September 18, numerous geodetic stations were observed to be moving 1 cm. a day. However it was generally believed that only individual blocks were creeping; it was not suspected that the entire area was moving as a mass.

Heavy rains began about September 28 and continued steadily until after October 9. Excessive run-off increased ground-water recharge and surface inflow; the reservoir was at El. 700m. or higher, about 100 ft. below the crest.

About October 1, animals grazing on the north slopes of Mt. Toc and the reservoir bank sensed danger and moved away. The mayor of Casso ordered townspeople to evacuate the slopes, and posted notice of an expected 20-m. (65-ft.) wave in the reservoir from the anticipated landslide. (The 20 m. was also the estimate of engineers for the height of the wave that would follow such a slide, based on experience of the slide at nearby Pontesi Dam in 1959.)

Movements of geodetic stations throughout the slide area reported for about three weeks before the collapse showed a steady increase from about 1 centimeter per day in mid-September to between 20 and 30 centimeters to as much as 80 centimeters on the day of failure.

About October 8, engineers realized that all the observation stations were moving together as a "uniform" unstable mass; and furthermore the actual slide involved some five times the area thought to be moving and expected to collapse about mid-November.

On October 8, engineers began to lower the reservoir level from El. 700 m. in anticipation of a slide. Two outlet tunnels on the left abutment were discharging a total of 5,000 cfs. but heavy inflow from runoff reduced the actual lowering of the water. The reservoir contained about 120 million cu. m. of water at the time of the disaster.

On October 9, the accelerated rate of movement was reported by the engineer in charge. A five-member board of advisers were evaluating conditions, and authorities were assessing the situation on an around-the-clock basis. Although the bypass outlet gates were open, oral reports describe a rise in the reservoir level on October 9. This is logical if lateral movement of the left bank had progressed to a point where it was reducing the reservoir capacity. These reports also mention difficulty with the intake gates in the left abutment (El. 591 m.) a few hours before the fatal slide.

Movement, Flood and Destruction

Those who witnessed the collapse included 20 technical personnel stationed in the control building on the left abutment and some 40 people in the office and hotel building on the right abutment. But no one who witnessed the collapse survived the destructive flood wave that accompanied the sudden slide at 22 hours 41 min. 40 sec. (Central European Time). However, a resident of Casso living over 260 m. (850 ft.) above the reservoir, and on the opposite side from the slide, reported the following sequence of events:

About 10:15 p.m. he was awakened by a very loud and continuous sound of rolling rocks. He suspected nothing unusual as talus slides are very common.

The rolling of rocks continued and steadily grew louder. It was raining hard.

About 10:40 p.m. a very strong wind struck the house, breaking the window panes. Then the house shook violently; there was a very loud rumbling noise. Soon afterward the roof of the house was lifted up so that rain and rocks came hurtling into the room (on the second floor) for what seemed like half a minute.

He had jumped out of bed to open the door and leave when the roof collapsed onto the bed. The wind suddenly died down and everything in the valley was quiet.

Observers in Longarone reported that a wall of water came down the canyon about 10:43 p.m. and at the same time a strong wind broke windows, and houses shook from strong earth tremors. The flood wave was over 70 m. (230 ft.) high at the mouth of Vaiont canyon and hit Longarone head on. Everything in its path was destroyed. The flood moved upstream in the Piave Valley beyond Castello Lavazzo, where a 5-m. (16-ft.) wave wrecked the lower part of Codissago. The main volume swept downstream from Longarone, hitting Pirago and Villanova. By 10:55 p.m. the flood waters had receded and all was quiet in the valley.

The character and effect of the air blast that accompanied the main flood wave at the dam have been described in the introduction. The destruction wrought by the blast, the jet of water, and the decompression phase are difficult to imagine. For example, the steel I-beams in the underground powerhouse were twisted like a corkscrew and sheared; the steel doors of the safety chamber were torn from their hinges, bent, and carried 12 m. (43 ft.) away.

Seismic tremors caused by the rock slide were recorded over a wide area of Europe—at Rome, Trieste, Vienna, Basel, Stuttgart, and Brussels. The kinetic energy of the falling earth mass

was the sole cause of the seismic tremors recorded from Vaiont according to Toperczer. No deep-seated earthquake occurred to trigger the slide. The seismic record clearly demonstrates that surface waves ($L_1 = 3.26$ km. per sec., or about 730 mph.) were first to arrive at the regional seismic stations, followed by secondary surface waves ($L_2 = 2.55$ km. per sec. or 570 mph). There was no forewarning in the form of small shocks and no follow-up shocks—which are typical of earthquakes from subsurface sources. No P or S waves were recorded.

Pattern of Sliding

The actual release and unrestricted movement of the slide was extremely rapid. Seismological records show that the major sliding took place within less than 30 sec. (under 14 sec. for the full record of the L_1 wave) and thereafter sliding ceased. The speed of the mass movement (25 to 30 m. per sec.) and the depth of the principal slide are strikingly demonstrated by the preservation intact of the Masselezza River canyon and the grassy surface soil with distinctive "fracture" pattern.

Wave Action Due to Slide

Sketchy reports from observers at Erto described the first wave by stating that "the entire reservoir for 1.8 km. (1.1 miles) piled up as one vast curving wave" for a period of 10 sec. The strong updraft of air created by the rapid slide was confined in movement by the deep Vaiont Valley encircled by high peaks. The updraft within the confined outer valley sucked the water, accompanied by rocks, up to El. 960 m.

(885 ft. or more above the original reservoir level) and accounted for part of the force possessed by the initial wave.

At the dam, the initial wave split on hitting the right canyon wall, after demolishing the hotel building at El. 780 m. (300 ft. above the reservoir surface). Some of the water followed the canyon wall downstream and moved above and around the dam. The major volume, however, seems to have bounced off the right wall, swept back across the canyon to the left abutment and moved upslope and around the dam to at least El. 820 m. (460 ft. above the reservoir level).

The overflow waves from the right and left abutments were joined in the canyon by the main surge, which overtopped the dam, and together these constituted the flood wave that hit Longarone. Water overtopped the dam crest on the left side for some hours after the slide, strongly the next morning, and during this time also displaced water drained from pools scattered over the slide surface.

Upstream the wave generated by the slide moved first into the area opposite Pineda, where it demolished homes, bounced off the canyon wall and moved southward, hitting the Pineda peninsula. On receding from there, the wave moved northeastward across the full length of the lake and struck San Martino with full force, bypassing Erto, which went unharmed.

Conditions Since the Slide

The water level just behind the dam dropped at the rate of 50 to 80 cm. (20 to 32 in.) per day during the first two weeks after the slide. This loss is believed due in part to leakage through the intake gates for the bypass aqueduct and powerhouse conduits. Geologically, there was a substantial loss due to the new conditions of bank storage, subsurface circulation and saturation of material filling the canyon.

A pond that formed at the Massalezza River canyon, along the foot of the slide plane, dropped in level rapidly and was dry on October 24, confirming the idea of ground-water recharge to slide material and the establishment of a water table within the newly formed mass. Smaller ponds initially formed upstream from the dam along the zone of contact between the slide and the right reservoir bank. These likewise dried up by October 24 as a result of groundwater recharge and readjustment in the water table within the slide mass.

The lake level behind the slide dam rose steadily from the inflow of tributary streams. For example, two weeks after the slide, the reservoir was 13 m. (43 ft.) higher than the water level at the dam—a major problem in the future operation of Vaiont Dam.

Strong funneling craters developed during the first days after the slide in the soil and glacial debris concentrated near the toe of the slide. This cratering was of concern to some as indicating large-scale movement to come, but other conditions are the probable causes of the surface subsidence. Large blocks of rock, with some bridging action, fill the canyon and create much void space in the lower mass. Some of these spaces are filled by normal gravity shifting of fines, and ground-water circulation also distributes fines into these void spaces. Formation of craters is restricted to the section of the slide that fills the former canyon, and craters appear at intervals along its entire length. They are most extensive in the slope behind the dam.

Numerous small, step-like slide blocks occur at different levels on the main slip plane. These blocks were loosened by the movement on October 9 and have since moved slowly down the slip plane, some to the bottom of the escarpment. Talus runs are common from small V-notched canyons along the edge of the steep eastern sector of the slide.

Future of the Reservoir

The steeply dipping beds along the head of the slide will undoubtedly fail from time to time as a result of gravitational creep. Ultimately the upper most part of the slip plane will be flattened and thereby will attain a stable natural slope.

The Italian Ministry of Public Works has announced that Vaiont Dam will no longer be used as a power source. The cost of clearing the reservoir would be prohibitive because of the volume involved, the distance of 4 or 5 km. (3 miles) that waste material would have to be hauled to the Piave Valley, and the 300-m. (1,000-ft.) lift required to transport the waste over the divide west of the dam.

The bypass tunnel in the right wall of the reservoir could be ultimately used to pond water behind the dam for release through the existing outlet works. Another alternative would be to divert the reservoir water southeastward to the Cellina River drainage by a tunnel driven from the upper end of the lake. Such diversion would develop the upper catchment area of Cellina and utilize Vaiont storage, behind the slide dam, as a multi-seasonal storage astride the Piave and Cellina catchments.

Vaiont in Retrospect

Vaiont has tragically demonstrated the critical importance of geologic features within a reservoir and in its vicinity—even though the site may be otherwise satisfactory for a dam of outstanding design.

In future, preconstruction studies must give thorough consideration to the properties of a rock mass as such, in contrast to a substance, and particularly to its potential for deformation with the passage of time. An assessment that is theoretical only is inadequate. The soundest approach is a systematic appraisal that includes:

An investigation of the geologic setting and its critical features

An assessment of past events that have modified features and properties of the site rocks

A forecast of the effects of the engineering works on geologic features in the area and on the strength of the site rocks

The geologic reaction to changed conditions in the process of time.

Project plans should set forth a system for acquiring data on the interaction between geologic conditions and changes induced by project operation.

Time, in terms of the life of the project, is a key to safety and doubtless was a controlling factor at Vaiont. Since 1959, eight major dams around the world have failed in some manner. It seems imperative that the following factors be recognized:

1. Rock masses, under changed en-

vironmental conditions, can weaken within short periods of time—days, weeks, months.

2. The strength of a rock mass can decrease very rapidly once creep gets under way.

3. Evidence of active creep should be considered as a warning that warrants immediate technical assessment, since acceleration to collapse can occur quickly.

Engineering Implications

Speed of sliding movement. Rock masses are capable of translatory movement as fast as quick clays or at a liquid-like speed.

Strain energy: its influence on a rock mass, its release and associated movement are critical. The interplay between wetting of a rock mass, buoyancy effect, and the lightening of a rock mass (1.0 or less in density) allows an accelerated release of the inherent strain energy, thereby creating more release fractures and the cycle is repeated. The net result is the increase in amount of water and a stronger buoyancy effect—both aided by the energy release phenomenon.

Potential for landslides at reservoir sites that have been in operation for many years must be studied; new projects must be evaluated for landslide potential in a more critical manner.

The tremendous amount of potential energy that is stored in a rock mass undergoing creep on an incline (as at Vaiont). With the increasing displacements, gliding friction factor drops and the velocity of mass increases. This means that a sliding mass has a potential to increase from slow creep to a fantastically high rate of movement in a brief time of seconds or minutes. The energy goes into momentum and not into deforming the interior of the sliding mass as in the typical rotational slide.

Two techniques assist the engineer today in this connection. First, he has and can use the most improved methods for observing and measuring the changes of strain within a rock mass. And second, he can use a fore-warning system in case this phenomenon acts quickly and the failure of a rock is imminent.

References

Anon. 1958. Some SADE developments: *Water Power*, vol. 10, nos. 3-6, Mar.-June 1958.

Anon. 1961. Italy builds more dams: *Engineering News-Record*, vol. 167, no. 18, pp. 30-36.

Anon. 1963. Vaiont Dam survives immense overtopping: *Engineering News-Record*, vol. 171, no. 16, pp. 22–23, Oct. 17, 1963.

Boyer, G. R. 1913. Etude géologique des environs de Longarone (Alpes venitiennes): *Soc. Géologique de France, Bulletin*, vol. 13, no. 4, pp. 451–485.

Muller, L. 1963. Differences in the characteristic features of rocks and mountain masses: 5th Conference of the International Bureau of Rock Mechanics, *Proceedings*. Leipzig, Germany, Nov. 1963.

Muller, L. 1963. Rock mechanics considerations in the design of rock slopes, in *State of Stress in the Earth's Crust*, International Conference, Rand Corp., Santa Monica, Calif., June 1963.

Pancini, M. 1961. Observations and surveys on the abutments of Vaiont Dam. *Geologie und Bauwesen*, vol. 26, no. 1, pp. 122–141.

Pancini, M. 1962. Results of first series of tests performed on a model reproducing the actual structure of the abutment rock of the Vaiont Dam. *Geologie und Bauwesen*, vol. 27, no. 1, pp. 105–119.

Erosion, Sedimentation, and Floods

And the waters prevailed and were increased greatly upon the earth.
Genesis

The processes of erosion and sedimentation are less dramatic than volcanic eruptions, earthquakes, and landslides, but they affect the entire surface of the continents and have a significant impact on Man. What information is available concerning the erosion of continents? To what extent is the erosion of soils due to Man's activities? What portion is simply the result of natural phenomena? Is it possible to determine the rate of erosion? These questions are considered by Sheldon Judson in Reading 18.

Drainage basin size appears to be an important factor controlling the rate of erosion. Apparently the rates of erosion in small drainage basins that are intensively used are often considerably greater than expected. The resulting implications on the design and maintenance of reservoirs are impressively documented by Farris Dendy in Reading 19. The negative impact of sedimentation extends well beyond the loss of reservoir capacity. A. R. Robinson presents some insights on the role of sediment as a carrier or scavenger of other pollutants in Reading 20. It may be initially disturbing to note that federal and state water quality standards tend to ignore suspended sediments that may be a major pollutant of water. But is it possible to develop standards when we are uncertain about the exchange mechanism whereby a pollutant can be either taken up or released from the sediment phase?

Like erosion and sedimentation, floods are natural and recurrent events. They become a problem when Man attempts to compete with a river for the use of the flood-plain. There is no complete record of flood damages, but it is a sobering fact that despite numerous federal programs designed to alleviate flood-plain problems, property damage on the flood-plain continues to increase. This is in part because of urban pressures forcing increased development on flood-plains. In view of this trend it has become necessary to develop new techniques to reduce the hazards associated with flood-plain development. The concept and application of flood-hazard mapping are reviewed in Reading 21.

Although running water has always played a vital role in our lives, the knowledge required to manage it is far from complete. These readings clearly demonstrate the need to sharpen our abilities to predict and control erosion, sedimentation, and flooding. Although efforts in the general area of flood information appear to be better organized than those dealing with erosion and sedimentation, many aspects of flooding are not understood. Research should be intensified, and project design should recognize the close relationship between all phases of the hydrologic cycle and the dynamic nature of the cycle.

Photo on page 165. Flood of March 12, 1963, on North Fork Kentucky River at Hazard, Kentucky. A graphic example of man and nature competing for a river flood plain. Photograph by Billy Davis, "Courier-Journal and Louisville Times."

18 Erosion of the Land,
or What's Happening to Our Continents?
Sheldon Judson

Not quite two centuries ago James Hutton, Scottish medical man, agriculturalist, and natural scientist—now enshrined as the founder of modern geology—and Jean André de Luc, Swiss emigré, scientist, and reader to England's Queen Charlotte, carried on a spirited discussion concerning the nature and extent of erosion of the natural landscape. De Luc believed that once vegetation had spread its protective cloak across the land, erosion ceased. Not so, in Hutton's opinion. He argued (Hutton, 1795):

According to the doctrine of this author (de Luc) our mountains of Tweed-dale and Tiviotdale, being all covered with vegetation, are arrived at the period in the course of times when they should be permanent. But is it really so? Do they never waste? Look at rivers in a flood—if these run clear, this philosopher has reasoned right, and I have lost my argument. [But] our clearest streams run muddy in a flood. The great causes, therefore, for the degradation of mountains never stop as long as there is water to run; although as the heights of mountains diminish, the progress of their diminution may be more and more retarded.

Judson, S., 1968, "Erosion of the Land, or What's Happening to Our Continents?" Amer. Scientist, vol. 56, pp. 356–74. Lightly edited by permission of the author and reprinted by permission of The Society of Sigma Xi. Copyright 1969 by The Society of Sigma Xi.
Dr. Judson is Professor of Geology at Princeton University, Princeton, New Jersey.

We know today, of course, that vegetation plays an important role in the preparation of material for erosion. We know also that although vegetation may slow the removal of material from a slope it does not stop it completely. Hutton's view is overwhelmingly accepted today. Erosion continues in spite of the plant cover, which in fact is conducive to certain aspects of erosion. The discussion now centers on the factors determining erosion, the nature of the products of this process, how these products are moved from one place to another, and at what rates the products are being produced. Hutton, in his day, had no data upon which to make a quantitative estimate of the rates at which erosion progressed. Today we, unlike Hutton, measure rates of erosion for periods of a fraction of a man's lifetime, as well as for periods of a few hundreds or thousands of years of human history. In addition, radioactive dating and refined techniques of study in field and laboratory allow us to make some quantitative statements about the rates at which our solid lands are wasted and moved particle by particle, ion by ion, to the ocean basins.

This report sets forth some of what we know about these erosional rates. We will understand that erosion is the process by which earth materials are worn away and moved from one spot to another. As such, the action of water, wind, ice, frost-action, plants and animals, and gravity all play their roles.

The destination of material eroded is eventually the great world ocean, although there are pauses in the journey and, as we will see later, the material delivered to the ocean must be in some way reincorporated into the continents.

Some Modern Records

Let us now examine some modern records of erosion of various small areas on the earth's crust, essentially determinations of rates at specific points. There is a large amount of information to be gleaned from agricultural, forestry, and conservation studies as well as from some studies by geologists.[1]

Even a casual inspection of our cemeteries demonstrates that some rock goes to pieces at a measurable rate and that rocks have differing resistance to destruction. Four marble headstones photographed in 1968 in the Princeton, N. J., cemetery indicate what can happen to marble in the 172 years involved. The marker erected in 1898 was still easily legible 70 years later, but the crisp, sharp outline of the stone carver's chisel was gone. The headstone erected 70 years earlier was still partially legible in 1968, but the stone put up in 1796 was completely illegible. In this instance the calcite ($CaCO_3$), which makes up the marble, was attacked by a carbonic acid formed by rain water and the CO_2 of the atmosphere. In general, marble headstones become illegible in the humid northeastern states after 150 to 175 years of exposure.

In contrast to the marble headstones is a marker in the Cambridge, Massachusetts Burying Ground, that was erected in 1699 and photographed in 1968. It is made of slate, often used as a headstone material in many New England cemeteries until marble became fashionable at the turn of the nineteenth century. Unlike marble it is resistant to chemical erosion. Nearly 270 years after the stone was erected the inscription stands out clearly.

Graveyards do most certainly provide examples of the impermanence of rock material as well as of the relative resistance of different rock types. The earliest study in such an environment that I have seen was by Sir Archibald Geikie, in Edinburgh, published in 1880. More recent studies have been made of the rates at which erosion proceeds on tombstones. Thus, in an area near Middletown, Connecticut, it is estimated that tombstones of a local red sandstone are weathering at the rate of about 0.006 centimeters per year (Matthias, 1967). In general, however, a graveyard does not present the best conditions for the accumulation of quantitative data.

More reliable data seem to come from agricultural stations. Here is an example. A summary of measurements has been made at 17 different stations on plots measuring 6 by 72.6 ft and under differing conditions of rainfall, soil, slope, and vegetative cover (Musgrave, 1954). Periods of record in this instance vary between 4 and 11 years. On the average, erosion from plots with continuous grass cover annually lost 75 tons per square kilometer, a lowering of about 3 meters per 1000 years. This is a dramatic demonstration of the role of plants in affecting erosion. In this instance the rate of erosion increased 100 times between grass-covered plots and well-tilled row-crop plots.

Obviously climate will also affect the

rate of erosion. For example, recent studies by Washburn (1967) in eastern Greenland show that seasonal freeze and thaw in a nearly glacial climate produce erosion rates ranging between 9 and 37 meters per thousand years. This contrasts with the rates in more temperate climates cited previously. In semiarid lands, where vegetation is discontinuous and rainfall low (± 25 cm per year) and unpredictable, the erosion rates are high but not as high as those in the rigorous climate of northeastern Greenland. Studies of bristlecone pines in Utah and California have allowed an estimate of erosion rates on a time base of hundreds and even thousands of years (Eardley, 1967). Thus the pines, which may reach 4000 years in age, betray the amount of erosion during their lifetime by the amount of exposure of their root systems. The depth of exposed roots on living trees is a measure of the amount the land surface has been reduced since the tree began to grow. Rates of lowering in general vary with exposure (greater on north-facing slopes) and with declivity of slopes (greater on steeper slopes). On the average, the rate varies between about 2 cm per 1000 years on slopes of 5 degrees and 10 cm on slopes of 30 degrees. A total of 42 observations indicate a direct relation between the erosion rate and the sine of the slope.

A different sort of study, this one in the rain forest of New Guinea Mountains, has yielded the estimate that between 1 and 2 cm per 1000 years is lost from the area by landslides alone (Simonett, 1967). How much additional material is lost through the agency of other processes is not known.

Archaeological sites may yield information on erosional rates and have, as in the case of the bristlecone pines, a fairly long time base. Data collected in Italy show that for the sites studied the range in rates is 30 to 100 cm per 1000 years (Judson, 1968).

These are but a sample of the type of information that abounds in the literature on the rate of erosion. They are enough, however, to indicate how variable the rates can be when, as in the examples cited, the observation is for a single spot or limited area. Not only are they highly variable but they can hardly be representative of rates of erosion over large areas. It is apparent that the material eroded in one spot may be deposited nearby, at least temporarily, and thus the net loss to an area may be little or nothing. Erosion is more rapid at some spots than others for any one of many different reasons. Material removed from its position at any single spot on the landscape follows a slow, halting, devious course as natural processes transport it from the land to the ocean.

River Records

When we ask now how much material is being lost by the continents to the ocean, the spot measurements such as those reported above are of little help. We need some method of integrating these rates over larger areas. One way to do this is to measure material carried by a stream from its drainage basin at the point where the stream leaves the basin. Alternatively, the amount of sediment deposited in a reservoir or in a natural lake over a specific length of time is indicative of the rate at which the land has been worn away in the basin lying upstream. The mass of sediments accumulated in unit time can be averaged out over the area of the contributing drainage basin to produce an erosion rate. Of course the erosion rate is not uniform over the entire basin, but it is convenient for our purposes here to assume that it is.

If we examine the solid load of a stream carried in suspension past a gauging station we discover that the amount of material per unit area of the drainage basin varies considerably according to a number of factors. But, if we hold the size of the drainage basin relatively constant, we find pronounced correlation between erosion and precipitation. Figure 1 is based on data presented by Langbein and Schumm (1958) from about 100 sediment gauging stations in basins averaging 3900 sq km. It suggests that a maximum rate of erosion is reached in areas of limited rainfall ($\pm$ 25 cm per year) and decreases in more arid as well as in more humid lands.

Considering small drainage basins (averaging 78 km^2), Langbein and

Schumm also show a similar variation in erosion with rainfall, but at rates which are 2 to 3 times as rapid as for the larger basins. In still smaller basins erosion rates increase even more. A small drainage basin in the Loess Hills of Iowa, having an area of 3.4 km^2 provides an extreme example. Here sediments are being removed at a rate which produces a lowering for the basin of 12.8 m per 1000 years.

We have data based on river records for larger areas. Judson and Ritter (1964) have surveyed the regional erosion rates in the United States and have shown that, on the average, erosion is proceeding at about 6 cm^2 per 1000 years. Here too, as shown in Table 1, there are variations. These appear to be related to climate as in the smaller areas already discussed. Greatest erosion occurs in the dry Colorado River basin. In examining the rates of regional erosion we note that although erosion rates increase with decrease in discharge per unit area, they do not increase quite as rapidly as

Table 1 Rates of regional erosion in the United States (After Judson and Ritter, 1964)

Drainage Region	Drainage[1] Area Km^2 $\times 10^3 \times 10^3$	Runoff m^3/sec	Load tons Km^2/yr			Erosion cm/1000 yr	% Area sampled	Avg. years of record
			Dissolved	Solid	Total			
Colorado	629	0.6	23	417	440	17	56	32
Pacific Slopes, California	303	2.3	36	209	245	9	44	4
Western Gulf	829	1.6	41	101	142	5	9	9
Mississippi	3238	17.5	39	94	133	5	99	12
S. Atlantic & Eastern Gulf	736	9.2	61	48	109	4	19	7
N. Atlantic	383	5.9	57	69	126	5	10	5
Columbia	679	9.8	57	44	101	4	39	<2
Totals	6797	46.9	43	119	162	6		

[1] Great Basin, St. Lawrence, Hudson Bay drainage not considered.

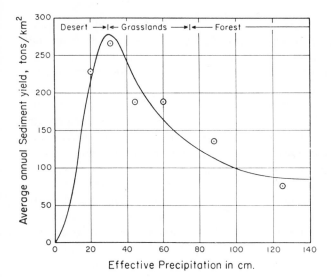

FIG. 1. Variation of the yield of sediments with precipitation. Effective precipitation is defined as precipitation necessary to produce a given amount of runoff. (After Langbein and Schumm, 1958.)

the major component, the detrital load, increases. This is so because the absolute dissolved load decreases with decreasing discharge per unit area. This inverse relation between solid and dissolved load is shown in Fig. 2.

These data suggest that on the average the United States is now being eroded at a rate which reduces the land surface by 6 cm each 1000 years. Actually the rate is somewhat less when we consider that the area of the Great Basin, with no discharge to the sea, is

not included in these figures—and that for all practical purposes the net loss from this area is presently close to zero.

Effect of Man

What effect does man's use of the land have on the rate at which it is destroyed by natural forces? Three examples are cited here:

Bonatti and Hutchinson have described cores from a small volcanic crater lake, Lago di Monterosi, 41 km

FIG. 2. Relation by regions in the United States between solid load and dissolved load in tons/km²/yr. (After Judson and Ritter, 1964.)

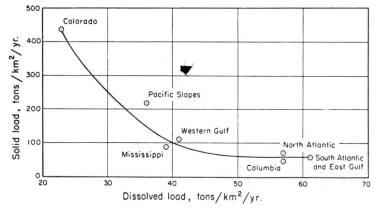

north of Rome. (See Judson, 1968, note 3.) An archaeological survey of the environs of the lake indicate that intense human activity dates from approximately the second century B.C. when the Via Cassia was constructed through the area. At this moment the cores indicate a sudden increase of sedimentation in the lake. The rate varies somewhat but continues high to the present. Extrapolation of the sedimentation rate in the lake to the surrounding watershed shows that prior to intensive occupation by man (that is, prior to the second century B.C.) the erosion rate was 2 to 3 cm per 1000 years. Thereafter it rose abruptly to an average of about 20 cm per 1000 years.

Ursic and Dendy (1965) have studied the annual sediment yields from individual watersheds in northern Mississippi. The results of their data are shown in Fig. 3. These indicate that, when the land is intensively cultivated, the rate of sediment production and hence the rate of erosion is three orders of magnitude or more above that experienced from areas with mature forest cover or from pine plantations.

Wolman (1967) has described the variation of sediment yield with land use for an area near Washington, D. C. These data are summarized in Fig. 4. They show that, under original forest conditions, erosion proceeded at the low rate of about 0.2 cm per 1000 years. With the rapid increase of farm-

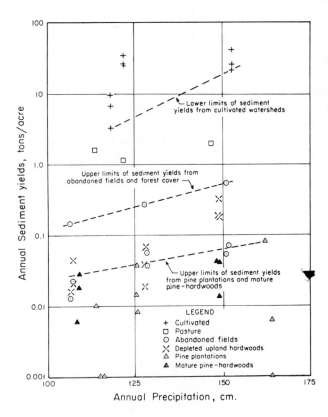

FIG. 3. Variation in sediment yields from individual watersheds in northern Mississippi under different types of land use and changing amounts of precipitation. One ton/acre equals 224 tons/km². (After Ursic and Dendy, 1965.)

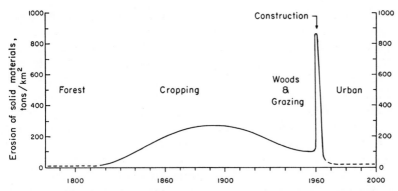

FIG. 4. A sequence of land use changes and sediment yield beginning prior to the advent of extensive farming and continuing through a period of construction and subsequent urban landscape. Based on experience in the Middle Atlantic region of the United States. (After Wolman, 1967.)

land in the early nineteenth century the rate increased to approximately 10 cm per 1000 years. With the return of some of this land to grazing and forest in the 1940's and 1950's this high rate of erosion was reduced perhaps by one-half. Areas undergoing construction during the 1960's show yields which exceed 100,000 tons per square kilometer for very small areas, which approximate a rate of lowering of 10 m per 1000 years. For completely urban areas the erosion rates are low, less than 1 cm per 1000 years.

There is no question that man's occupancy of the land increases the rate of erosion. Where that occupation is intense and is directed toward the use of land for cultivated crops the difference is one or more orders of magnitude greater than when the land is under a complete natural vegetative cover such as grass or forest. The intervention of man in the geologic processes raises questions when we begin to consider the rates of erosion for the earth as a whole and to apply modern rates to the processes of the past before man was a factor in promoting erosion.

Ian Douglas (1967) postulates that man's use of the landscape has so increased the rates of erosion that they far exceed those of the past before man became an important geologic agent. He presents persuasive data and arguments to suggest that any computation of present-day erosion rates on a world-wide basis are unrepresentative of those that pre-date man's tampering with the landscape. So, as we turn to the question of world-wide erosion, we will want to distinguish between present-day rates which are profoundly affected by man's activity and those of the immediate past before man introduced grazing, agriculture, and other activities.

Let us first attempt an estimate of erosion before man began to affect the process. It is estimated that approximately one fourth of the United States is in cropland. If this area is now undergoing a rate of erosion ten times that of its natural rate then, for the United States as a whole, the increase of rate of erosion because of man's use of the land increases the rate of the removal of solid particles from the earth's crust by a factor of a little over three times. Assuming that this is correct and that the dissolved load does not change appreciably, then, as a first approximation, the present rates of erosion listed in Table 1 for the United States would be decreased to approximately 3 cm per 1000 years, which is about 78 tons per square kilometer per year. This figure would apply then to the area of the United States before the intervention of man with intensive agricultural practices.

Rates for Entire Earth

What can we say now about the rate of erosion for the entire earth? Presented in Table 2 are data for approximately 10 per cent of the earth's surface. The table includes erosional data for the drainage basins for the Amazon, the world's largest river; the Congo; and for that part of United States covered in Table 1. Here, however, the data for the United States have been adjusted to account for the increased rates of erosion presumed to have occurred because of man's cultivation of the land. Neither the Congo nor the Amazon basins are significantly affected by man. For the 15 million square kilometers of these three areas the average rate of erosion is 3.6 cm per 1000 years, or 93 tons per square kilometer annually.

Let us accept the figures just given as representative of erosion rates prior to man's intervention in the process and use them to extrapolate to erosion rates for the whole area of the earth. The earth's land surface has approximately 151 million square kilometers, but much of this area has no streams which drain directly to the ocean. For example, a large area of western United States is without direct drainage to the sea, as is a large percentage, about 50 per cent, of Australia. Areas of little or no drainage to the sea are estimated to occupy approximately one third of the earth's surface. So for our purposes we estimate that 100 million kilometers of the earth's surface are

Table 2   Rates of erosion for the Amazon River Basin, United States and Congo River Basin

Drainage region	Drainage area Km² × 10⁶	Load, tons × 10⁶/yr			Tons Km²/yr	Erosion cm/1000 yr
		Dissolved	Solid	Total		
Amazon River[1]						
Basin	6.3	232	548[2]	780	124	4.7
United States[3]	6.8	292	248[3]	540	78	3.0
Congo River[4]						
Basin	2.5	99	34[2]	133	53	2.0
Totals	15.6	623	830	1453	93	3.6

[1] From Gibbs, 1967.

[2] Solid load increased by considering bed load as 10% of suspended load.

[3] From Judson and Ritter, 1964. Solid load reduced to adjust for increased erosion because of man's activity.

[4] From Spronck, 1941, quoted in Gibbs 1967.

contributing sediments directly to the sea by running water. In addition to this there is a certain amount of wind erosion, and part of the materials eroded by the wind are delivered to the sea. It is even more difficult to find data on the amounts of regional erosion by wind than it is by running water. We have some preliminary estimates for the amount of eolian material which has been dumped into the oceans. These lie between 1 and 0.25 mm per 1000 years.[2] Whatever the figure, wind erosion of the land is volumetrically unimportant when compared with the amount of material carried by the streams.

We can estimate, then, the amount of sediment carried as solids and as dissolved material from the continents each year to the ocean basins as 9.3×10^9 tons. This figure is based on the assumption that, on the average, 3.6

cm per 1000 years are eroded from the 100 million square kilometers of land which are estimated to drain into the oceans. Further, the figure attempts to eliminate the effect on the erosion rate of man's activity. If we include an estimate for the amount of erosion by wind action then this figure increases by an amount approximating 10^8 tons. Glacier ice may add a similar amount.

We can now compare this estimate of the tonnage of eroded materials with other estimates in the following paragraphs and Table 3.

Barth (1962) presents data on some geochemical cycles indicating that weathering of the land produces on the average of 2.5 kg per cm^2 per million years. From this figure we calculate that the average tonnage per year of all material, dissolved and solid, would be 3.8×10^9 tons which seems low. Strakhov (1967) quotes Lopatin

Table 3. Estimates of world-wide erosion rates by various authors. All material assumed to reach the oceans

	10^9 metric tons/yr
Carried by rivers	
Dissolved load	
Livingstone (1963)	3.9
Clarke (1924)	2.7
Solid load[1]	
Fournier (1960) as calculated by Holeman (1968)	58
Kuenen (1950)	32.5
Schumm (1963) as calculated by Holeman (1968)	20.5
Holeman 1968	18.3
MacKenzie and Garrels (1967)	8.3
Combined solid and dissolved loads	
Lopatin (1950)[1]	17.5
Judson (this paper)[2]	9.3
Barth (1962)[2]	3.8
Carried by wind from land	
Calculated from various sources	0.06–0.36
Carried by glacier ice	
Estimated	0.1

[1] Does not include bed load.

[2] Solid load includes both suspended and bed load.

(1950) to the effect that annual dissolved and solid loads of the rivers total 17.5×10^9 tons of which 4.9×10^9 tons are dissolved material. Two other estimates on dissolved loads should be quoted. Clarke (1924) estimates 2.7×10^9 tons per year and Livingstone (1963) 3.9×10^9 tons per year. This last figure can be duplicated by extrapolation of the data in Table 3. Livingstone indicates that the figure might be high. Indeed new figures on the salinity and discharge of the Amazon River by Gibbs (1967) indicate that Livingstone's figure should be adjusted downward by 5 per cent.

MacKenzie and Garrels (1966) estimate that the rivers of the world carry 8.3×10^9 tons of *solid material alone* to the oceans each year. In arriving at this figure they adopted from Livingstone an average annual world-wide runoff of 3.3×10^{16} liters and an average suspended sediment concentration equal to that of the Mississippi River. If man's occupancy has indeed increased erosion rates as we have suggested, then this figure is high. Kuenen (1950) gives an estimate for solid load of 32.5×10^9 tons per year, a high estimate, the basis for which is not clear.

Even higher is the estimate of 58×10^9 tons of suspended load calculated by Holeman (1968) from data in Fournier (1960). Douglas (1967) points out that the data presented by Fournier seem to be strongly influenced by man's activity. Holeman also extrapolates data of Schumm (1963), from selected drainage basins in central United States to obtain a figure of 18.3×10^9 tons of suspended sediment per year. These data, too, are affected by man. Holeman, himself (1968), presents suspended sediment data for rivers draining 39 million square kilometers of the earth's surface, and extrapolates this to the approximately 100 million square kilometers of land surface draining to the ocean. He obtains a figure of 18.3×10^9 tons per year of suspended sediments carried annually to the oceans. The figure is strongly affected by data from the Asiatic rivers, particularly those of China, India, and the Southeast. These provide 80 per cent of the total sediment from 25 per cent of the land area in Holeman's figures. These are the same areas where the world's greatest population is concentrated and where the largest areas of intensive agriculture are located.

Let us now estimate the present rate of erosion. In this the major component is the suspended load carried by rivers. Of the data available, Holeman's appear to be the most inclusive and reliable. Allowing the bed load to be 10 per cent of suspended load and adding these two figures to the dissolved load as calculated by Livingstone, then the total material delivered annually to the sea by rivers at the present is 24×10^9 metric tons. This is about two and one half times the rate that we estimated existed before man started tampering with the landscape on a large scale (See Table 4).

Returning now to our estimate of the material produced by erosion be-

Table 4 Mass of material estimated as moved annually by rivers to the ocean before and after the intervention of man

	10^9 **metric tons**
Before man's intervention	9.3
After man's intervention	24

fore the serious intervention by man, we should be able to check our figure by comparing it with the amount of material deposited annually in the oceans. Thus far our only way of determining annual sedimentation rates over large areas is to average them out over the last several thousand years. Because man has only recently become a world-wide influence on erosion, this averaging serves to curtail his impact on the rate of accumulation of the sedimentary record.

What figures do we have on sedimentation in the oceans? Large areas of the ocean floor and the rates at which sedimentation takes place there are but dimly known at the present. We have data from coring of the ocean bottom but our data are scanty at best. In considering the tonnage which settles annually to the ocean floors we should distinguish between the deep oceans and the shallower oceans. As far as sedimentation goes there is probably a difference between those ocean floors lying below 3000 m and those above 3000 m. For the deep seas —those below 3000 m—current figures suggest something like 4.2×10^{-4} gm per cm^2 per year.[3] Spread over the nearly 280,000,000 km^2 of area for the deep sea, this amounts to 1.17×10^9 tons of sediments per year. Estimates for the shallower waters are probably less reliable than for the deep waters. For those waters shallower than 3000 m, about 72,000,000 km^2, I have assumed that between 10 and 20 cm of sediment accumulates every thousand years. Given a density of 0.7, there would be approximately 7 to 14×10^{-3} gm deposited for each square centimeter per year. This is equivalent to a total tonnage of between 5 and 10 $\times$

10^9 tons per year. Totaling the tonnage for the deep and shallow waters, we have a range of 6.2 to 11.2×10^9 tons. Most of this is provided by the rivers. Wind provides an estimated 10^8 tons per year. The contribution of ice is also estimated as 10^8 tons. Extra-terrestrial material is estimated by various authors as between 3.5×10^4 to 1.4×10^8 tons per year (Barker and Anders, 1968). Table 5 compares the estimate of the amount of material deposited each year in the oceans with the estimate of the amount delivered by various agents annually to the oceans. In both estimates we have tried to eliminate the effect of man.

Whether we use the rate of erosion prevailing before or after man's advent, our figures pose the problem of why our continents have survived. If we accept the rate of sediment production as 10^{10} metric tons per year (the pre-human intervention figure) then the continents are being lowered at the rate of 2.4 cm per 1000 years. At this rate the ocean basins, with a volume of 1.37×10^{18} m^3, would be filled in 340 million years. The geologic record indicates that this has never happened in the past, and there is no reason to believe it will happen in the geologically foreseeable future. Furthermore, at the present rate of erosion, the continents, which now average 875 m in elevation, would be reduced to close to sea level in about 34 million years. But the geologic record shows a continuous sedimentary history, and hence a continuous source of sediments. So we reason that the continents have always been high enough to supply sediments to the oceans.

Geologists long ago concluded that the earth was a dynamic system, being

Table 5 Estimated mass of material deposited annually in the oceans compared with estimated mass of material delivered annually to the oceans by different agents[1]

	10^9 metric tons/year
Estimated mass of material deposited in ocean	
Oceans shallower than 3000 meters	5–10
Oceans deeper than 3000 meters	1.17
Total	6.2–11.2
Estimated mass of material delivered to oceans	
From continents	
By rivers	9.3
By wind	0.06–0.36
By glacier ice	0.1
From extraterrestrial sources	0.00035–0.14
Total	~9.6

[1] Man's influence on rates of erosion is excluded from estimates.

destroyed in some places and renewed in others. Such a state would help resolve the problem of what happens to the sediments and why continents persist. Thus, although the sediments are carried from continents to oceans to form sedimentary rocks, we know that these rocks may be brought again to the continental surface. There they are in turn eroded and the products of erosion returned to the ocean. These sedimentary rocks may also be subjected to pressures and temperatures which convert them from sedimentary rocks to metamorphic rocks. If this pressure and temperature is great enough, the metamorphic rocks in turn will melt and become the parent material of igneous rock. These relationships are the well known rock cycle which has been going on as long as we can read the earth's rock record.

Inasmuch as we have been talking about the sedimentary aspects of the rock cycle, we should ask how much time it takes to complete at least the

sedimentary route within the whole cycle. Poldervaart (1954) gives the total mass of sediments (including the sedimentary rocks) as 1.7×10^{18} tons. Taking the annual production of sediments as 10^{10} tons, then one turn in the sedimentary cycle approximates 1.7×10^8 years. At the present rates then we could fit in about 25 such cycles during the 4.5 billion years of earth history.

Accepting Poldervaart's figure of 2.4×10^{19} tons as the mass of the earth's crust then there has been time enough for a mass equivalent to the earth's crust to have moved two times through the sedimentary portion of the cycle.

We began this review with a brief examination of the homely process of erosion. As we continued we found that man has appeared on the scene as an important geologic agent, increasing the rates of erosion by a factor of two or three. We end the review face to face with larger problems. Regardless of the role of man, the reality of continental erosion raises anew the question of the nature and origin of the forces that drive our continents above sea level. In short, we now seek the mechanics of continental survival.

Notes

[1] Data on erosion are expressed in metric tons per square kilometer and as centimeters of lowering either per year or per thousand years. A specific gravity of 2.6 is assumed for material eroded from the land.

[2] Although data are very incomplete the interested reader will find some specific information in Bonatti and Arrhenius (1965); Delany, et al. (1967); Folger and Heezen (in press); Goldberg and Griffin (1964); Rex and Goldberg (1958, 1962); and Riseborough, et al. (1968).

[3] I use data from deep sea cores as reported by Ku, Broecker and Opdyke, 1968. In calculating weights of sediments from rates of sedimentation I have used a density of 0.7 per cm^3 (Ku, personal communication, 1968) and sedimentation rates which include original $CaCO_3$ content.

References

Barker, John L., Jr. and Edward Anders, 1968. Accretion rate of cosmic matter from iridium and osmium contents of deep-sea sediments. *Geochimica et Cosmochimica Acta*, 32, p. 627–645.

Barth, T. F. W., 1962. *Theoretical Petrology.* 2nd edition. John Wiley & Sons, Inc.: New York and London, 416 pp.

Bonatti, E. and G. Arrhenius, 1965. Eolian sedimentation in the Pacific off northern Mexico. *Marine Geology*, 3, p. 337–348.

Clarke, F. W., 1924. Data of geochemistry, 5th edition, *U. S. Geological Survey, Bulletin 770*, 841 p.

Delany, A. C. et al., 1967. Airborne dust collected at Barbados. *Geochimica et Cosmochimica Acta*, 31, p. 885–909.

Douglas, Ian, 1967. Man, vegetation and the sediment yields of rivers. *Nature, 215*, Pt. 2, p. 925–928.

Eardley, A. G., 1967. Rates of denudation as measured by bristlecone pines, Cedar Breaks, Utah. *Utah Geological and Mineralogical Survey, Special Studies, 21*, 13 p.

Folger, D. W. and B. C. Heezen. (in press), Trans Atlantic sediment transport by wind. (abstract) *Geological Society of America.* Special paper.

Fournier, F., 1960. *Climat et Erosion*, Presses Universitaires de France.

Geikie, Archibald, 1880. Rock-weathering as illustrated in Edinburgh church yards. *Proceedings, Royal Society, Edinburgh, 10*, p. 518–532.

Gibbs, R. J., 1967. The geochemistry of the Amazon River system: Part I, *Bulletin, Geological Society of America, 78*, p. 1203–1232.

Goldberg, E. D. and J. J. Griffin, 1964. Sedimentation rates and mineralogy in the South Atlantic. *Jour. of Geophysical Research, 69*, p. 4293–4309.

Holeman, John N., 1968. The Sediment Yield of Major Rivers of the World. *Water Resources Research, 4*, No. 4, p. 737–747.

Hutton, James, 1795. *Theory of the earth.* Vol. 2, Edinburgh.

Judson, Sheldon, 1968. Erosion rates near Rome, Italy. *Science, 160*, p. 1444–1446.

Judson, Sheldon and D. F. Ritter, 1964. Rates of regional dunudation in the United States. *Journal of Geophysical Research, 69*, p. 3395–3401.

Ku, Teh-Lung, W. S. Broecker, and Neil Opdyke, 1968. Comparison of sedimentation rates measured by paleomagnetic and the ionium methods of age determinations. *Earth and Planetary Science Letters, 4*, p. 1–16.

Kuenen, Ph. H., 1950. *Marine Geology.* John Wiley and Sons: New York and London, 551 p.

Langbein, W. B. and S. A. Schumm, 1958. Yield of sediment in relation to mean annual precipitation. *Transactions, American Geophysical Union, 39*, p. 1076–1084.

Leet, L. Don and Sheldon Judson, 1965. *Physical Geology.* 3d edition. Prentice-Hall, Inc.: Englewood Cliffs, N. J., 406 p.

Livingstone, D. A., 1963. Chemical Composition of Rivers and Lakes. *U. S. Geological Survey Professional Paper 440-G.*, 64 p.

Lopatin, G. V., 1950. Erosion and detrital discharge. *Priroda*, No. 7. (Quoted by Strakhov, 1967.)

MacKenzie, F. T. and R. M. Garrels, 1966. Chemical mass balance between rivers and oceans. *American Journal of Science*, *264*, p. 507–525.

Matthias, George F., 1967. Weathering rates of Portland arkose tombstones. *Journal of Geological Education*, *15*, p. 140–144.

Musgrave, G. W., 1954. Estimating land erosion-sheet erosion. *Association Internationale d' Hydrologie Scientifique*, *Assemblée Générale de Rome*, *1*, p. 207–215.

Poldervaart, Arie, 1954. Chemistry of the earth's crust, in *Crust of the earth*. Edited by A. Poldervaart. Geological Society of America Special Paper 62, p. 119–144.

Rex, R. W. and E. D. Goldberg, 1958. Quartz content of pelagic sediments of the Pacific Ocean. *Tellus*, *10*, p. 153–159.

——, 1962. Insolubles. *in* M. Hill, ed. *The Sea*, Interscience: New York, vol. 1, p. 295–312.

Riseborough, R. W., R. J. Huggett, J. J. Griffin, and E. D. Goldberg, 1968. Pesticides: Transatlantic movements in the northeast trades. *Science*, *159*, p. 1233–1236.

Schumm, S. A., 1963. The disparity between present rates of denudation and orogeny, *U. S. Geological Survey*, Prof. Paper 454H, p. 1–13.

Simonett, David S., 1967. Landslide distribution and earthquakes in the Bewani and Torricelli Mountains, New Guinea, in *Landscape Studies from Australia and New Guinea*, Edited by J. N. Jennings and J. A. Mabbutt, Australian National University Press: Canberra, p. 64–84.

Spronck, R. 1941. Measures hydrographique effectuées dans la region divagante du Bief Maritime du Fleuve Congo. *Brussels, Institute Royale Colonial Belge Memoire*, 156 p. (quoted by Gibbs, 1967).

Strakhov, N. M. 1967, *Principles of Lithogenesis*, vol. 1. Translated from the 1962 Russian edition by J. P. Fitzsimmons. Oliver and Boyd: Edinburgh and London, 245 p.

Ursic, S. J. and F. E. Dendy, 1965. Sediment yields from small watersheds under various land uses and forest covers. *Proceedings of the Federal Inter-Agency Sedimentation Conference, 1963, U. S. Department of Agriculture*, Miscellaneous Publications 970, p. 47–52.

Washburn, A. L., 1967. Instrumental observations of mass-wasting in the Mesters Vig district, northeast Greenland. *Meddeleser om Gronland*, *166*, No. 4, p. 1–296.

Wolman, M. G., 1967. A cycle of sedimentation and erosion in urban river channels. *Geografiska Annaler*, *49-A*, p. 385–395.

19   Sedimentation in the Nation's Reservoirs

Farris E. Dendy

Dendy, F. E., 1968, "Sedimentation in the Nation's Reservoirs," *Jour. Soil and Water Conservation*, vol. 23, no. 4, pp. 135–37. Reprinted by permission of the author and the Soil Conservation Society of America. Copyright 1968 by S. C. S. A.
Farris Dendy is a Research Hydraulic Engineer at the U. S. Department of Agriculture Sedimentation Laboratory, Oxford, Mississippi.

Awareness of reservoir sedimentation as a national problem has been greatly extended in recent years, largely in concert with increasing activities under watershed protection and flood prevention programs. Expansion of such programs to attain national soil and water conservation objectives has increased the need for information on expected sedimentation rates in small floodwater-retarding, multiple-use and other structures. Although much information has been accumulated, the need is still critical in many parts of the country. With increased emphasis on clean water in streams and lakes for wildlife and recreation, the need for improved sediment prediction and control methods is expected to be even greater.

Extent of Sedimentation Damages

Glymph[8] recently indicated that 1 million acre-feet of sediment is deposited in the Nation's reservoirs each year. As early as 1948, Brown[3] estimated the value of reservoir storage lost to sediment at $50 million annually.

Reservoir sedimentation data, compiled at the U. S. Department of Agriculture Sedimentation Laboratory under the auspices of the Subcommittee on Sedimentation of the Inter-Agency Committee on Water Resources, afford further insight into the siltation problem.[13] These data, which represent virtually every section of the coterminous United States, were obtained from various federal, state, and local agencies.

The geographic distribution of the 968 reservoirs used in this study is shown, by river basins, in Fig. 1. River basin boundaries were established by the Subcommittee on Hydrology of the Inter-Agency Committee on Water Resources.[15] Although the areal distribution is generally good, many river basins are not adequately represented. Best represented are the midwestern states, Texas and California.

The reservoirs range in size from small pond-type structures to those with capacities exceeding 1 million acre-feet. Storage capacity and storage depletion data for all of the reservoirs are summarized in Table 1. Storage capacity is the capacity below the crest

FIG. 1. Geographic distribution of reservoirs.

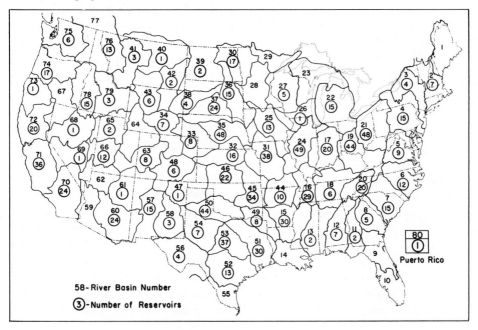

58 - River Basin Number

③ - Number of Reservoirs

Table 1 Summary of reservoir capacity and storage depletion data

Reservoir Capacity (a.-ft.)	Number of Reservoirs	Total Initial Storage Capacity (a.-ft.)	Total Storage Depletion (a.-ft.)	Total Storage Depletion (pct.)	Individual Reservoir Storage Depletion Average (pct./yr.)	Individual Reservoir Storage Depletion Median (pct./yr.)	Average Period of Record (yrs.)
0-10	161	685	180	26.3	3.41	2.20	11.0
10-100	228	8,199	1,711	20.9	3.17	1.32	14.7
100-1,000	251	97,044	16,224	16.7	1.02	.61	23.6
1,000-10,000	155	488,374	51,096	10.5	.78	.50	20.5
10,000-100,000	99	4,213,330	368,786	8.8	.45	.26	21.4
100,000-1,000,000	56	18,269,832	634,247	3.5	.26	.13	16.9
Over 1,000,000	18	38,161,556	1,338,222	3.5	.16	.10	17.1
Total or average	968	61,239,020	2,410,466	3.9	1.77	.72	18.2[1]

[1] The capacity-weighted period of record for all reservoirs was 16.1 years.

elevation of ungated spillways or the top of the gates for gated spillways when construction was completed or at the time of the original sedimentation survey. Storage depletion is the loss of capacity due to sediment deposition. For most of the reservoirs the period of record is also the reservoir age at the time of the last survey. Additional information on storage depletion and sediment accumulation rates by river basins is given in a recent U. S. Department of Agriculture publication.[5]

Average annual storage loss in the study reservoirs was about 150,000 acre-feet, slightly more than 0.2 percent of the total initial capacity. This is well within the design requirements of most reservoirs. However, average depletion rates were much higher in reservoirs with original capacities of 100 acre-feet or less (Table 1). These reservoirs account for a small percentage of the total storage capacity, but they represent 40 percent of the total number of reservoirs.

Generally, storage depletion rates decreased as reservoir capacity and drainage area increased. Individual res-

ervoir rates varied widely, particularly among the smaller reservoirs. Depletion rates ranged from 0 to 100 percent annually for those with less than 100 acre-feet capacity. On the other hand, annual depletion rates were less than 1 percent for all reservoirs, except two, with capacities of 100,000 acre-feet or more. Further analysis of the data revealed that 58 percent of the reservoirs had annual storage depletion rates of less than 1 percent; 15 percent had rates in excess of 3 percent; and 2 percent had rates in excess of 10 percent (Fig. 2).

Sediment accumulation rates per square mile of net sediment contributing drainage area (acre-feet per square mile per year) followed a similar distribution pattern (Fig. 3). (Areas above upstream reservoirs, which serve as effective sediment traps, were considered non-contributing.) Nearly 65 percent of the reservoirs had sediment accumulation rates of less than 1 acre-foot per square mile per year. Only 4 percent had rates exceeding 5 acre-feet per square mile per year. The maxi-

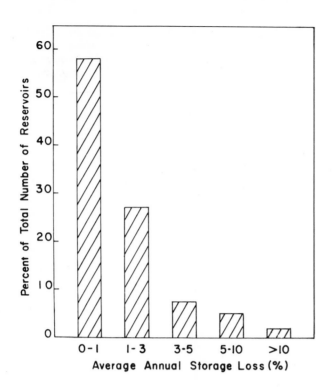

FIG. 2. Reservoir storage depletion rates.

mum rate reported was 61 acre-feet per square mile per year for a small reservoir in Iowa. Generally, average sediment accumulation rates decreased as drainage area increased.

Variation in Depletion Rates

The amount of trapped sediment is usually less than the amount of sediment delivered to a reservoir. The ratio of trapped to delivered sediment is called the trap efficiency. Although the two are interrelated, the quantity of sediment delivered (watershed sediment yield) is normally the predominant factor and the most difficult to predict.

Many watershed and reservoir parameters are known to influence reservoir sedimentation rates. Some of the more important are reservoir size and shape; reservoir capacity-watershed area ratio; reservoir capacity-annual inflow ratio; watershed topography, land use and vegetative cover; slope and density of the watershed channel network; and physical and chemical characteristics of the inflowing sediment.

As previously indicated, storage depletion rates for the smaller reservoirs varied greatly, even within a given river basin or land resource area. This is to be expected because the contrast in watershed factors affecting sediment yield is greater among the smaller watersheds. For example, the entire drainage area above a small upland reservoir might be in clean-tilled crops, whereas the drainage area for a companion reservoir might be totally in forest or

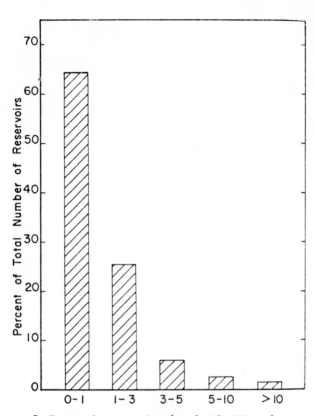

FIG. 3. Average annual sediment accumulations per square mile of net sediment contributing drainage area.

pasture. Such a contrast in land use and sediment production potential would hardly be expected in a watershed containing several hundred square miles.

Studies of selected groups of reservoirs, usually concentrated in a given land resource area, have shown a reasonably good correlation between sediment accumulation rates and various reservoir and watershed parameters.[4, 6, 7, 9, 11, 12, 14] Generally, however, the investigators pointed out that their findings were applicable only in the areas where developed.

In a study of 24 small reservoirs Beer and his co-workers[1] found four empirically developed prediction methods to be unreliable for the loess soils of western Iowa and Missouri. The predicted sediment deposits were within ± 50 percent of measured values in only about 40 percent of the reservoirs.

Multiple use of reservoirs requires more precise estimates of sedimentation rates. With the current impetus on recreational, wildlife and esthetic aspects of reservoir development, the horizontal and vertical distribution of sediment becomes more important. Sediment in and around lakeside recreational and swimming areas is undesirable. Although some work has been done in this area, there is a dearth of information on sediment distribution in small reservoirs.[2, 10]

Summary and Conclusions

The wide variation in sedimentation rates in small reservoirs with comparable capacity-watershed area ratios, even within a given physiographic province, illustrates the complexity of predicting sediment accumulation rates. Many processes are involved, and the relative importance of controlling factors varies from region to region and within a region. Although some success has been achieved, existing prediction techniques for small reservoirs are inadequate for many sections of the country. Most are based on empirical relationships and are applicable only for the land resource area and conditions for which they were developed.

If one assumes the data summarized in this report to represent a fair cross section of the Nation's reservoirs, some general conclusions can be drawn: (a) The overall storage depletion rate of about 0.2 percent annually is not alarming; (b) the relatively high average storage depletion rate of 3 percent in small upland reservoirs seems excessive; (c) if present siltation rates continue, about 20 percent of the Nation's small reservoirs will be half filled with sediment and, in many instances, their utility seriously impaired in about 30 years.

Notes

[1] Beer, C. E., C. W. Farnham and H. G. Heinemann. 1966. *Evaluating sediment prediction techniques in western Iowa*. ASAE Trans. 9(6):828–831.

[2] Borland, Whitney M., and Carl R. Miller. 1958. *Distribution of sediment in large reservoirs*. J. Hydr. Div., ASCE Proc. 84(HY2): 166–180.

[3] Brown, Carl B. 1948. *Perspective on sedimentation*. In *Proceedings, Federal Inter-Agency Sedimentation Conference*. U. S. Bur. Rec., Washington, D. C.

[4] Brune, Gunnar M. 1953. *Trap efficiency of reservoirs*. AGU Trans. 34(3):407–418.

[5] Dendy, F. E., J. A. Spraberry and W. A. Champion. 1967. *Sediment deposition in reservoirs in the United States*. ARS 41–137. U. S. Dept. Agr., Washington, D. C.

[6] Farnham, C. W., C. E. Beer and H. G. Heinemann. 1966. *Evaluation of factors affecting reservoir sediment deposition*. IASH Pub. No. 71, Symposium of Garda, 747–758.

[7] Flaxman, Elliott M. 1966. *Some variables which influence rates of reservoir sedimentation in western United States*. IASH Pub. No. 71, Symposium of Garda, 824–838.

[8] Glymph, L. M., and H. C. Storey. 1967. *Sediment—Its consequences and control*. In *Agriculture and the Quality of Our Environment*. Pub. 85. Am. Assoc. Adv. Sci., Washington, D. C. pp. 205–220.

[9] Gottschalk, L. C., and Gunnar M. Brune. 1950. *Sediment design criteria for the Missouri basin loess hills*. U. S. TP-97. Soil Cons. Ser., Washington, D. C. 34 pp.

[10] Heinemann, H. G., D. L. Rausch and R. S. Campbell. 1966. *Sedimentation in a small channel-type reservoir*. IASH Pub. No. 71, Symposium of Garda, 769–779.

[11] Maner, Sam B. 1958. *Factors affecting sediment delivery rates in the Red Hills physiographic area*. AGU Trans. 39(4): 669–675.

[12] Roehl, John W. 1962. *Sediment source areas, delivery ratios and influencing morphological factors*. IASH Pub. No. 59, Commission of Land Erosion, 202–213.

[13] Spraberry, J. A. 1960. *Summary of reservoir sediment deposition surveys made in the United States through 1960*. Misc. Pub. 964. U. S. Dept. Agr., Washington, D. C.

[14] Stall, J. B., and L. J. Bartelli. 1959. *Correlation of reservoir sedimentation and watershed factors*. Rept. of Invest. 37, Ill. State Water Survey, Urbana.

[15] U. S. Inter-Agency Committee on Water Resources. 1961, *River basin maps showing hydrologic stations*. Notes on Hydrol. Activities Bul. 11. U. S. Weather Bureau, Washington, D. C.

20 Sediment, Our Greatest Pollutant?*

A. R. Robinson

Introduction

The statement is being made with great regularity that sediment is our *greatest* pollutant. The term pollution carries a connotation of something bad and undesirable. Sediment is said to be a perfect example of the definition of a pollutant, which is a resource out of place. Sediment has a two-fold effect: it depletes the land resource from which it is delivered, and it impairs the quality of the water resource in which it is entrained and deposited.[6]

President Nixon noted the seriousness of water pollution from the land in his message on the environment during February 1970. He stated: "Water pollution has three principal sources: municipal, industrial and agricultural wastes. Of these three, the most troublesome to control are those from agricultural sources: animal wastes, *eroded soil*, fertilizers and pesticides."

Secretary of Agriculture, Clifford N. Hardin, said in a recent speech before

* Contribution from the USDA Sedimentation Laboratory, Soil and Water Conservation Research Division, Agricultural Research Service, United States Department of Agriculture in cooperation with the University of Mississippi and the Mississippi Agricultural Experiment Station.

Robinson, A. R., 1970, "Sediment, Our Greatest Pollutant?" Paper 70–701. Presented at the 1970 Winter Meeting, Amer. Soc. Agric. Engin. Reprinted by permission of the author and the A. S. A. E.

Mr. Robinson is the Director, U. S. D. A. Sedimentation Laboratory, Oxford, Mississippi.

the National Farm Institute, "*Siltation* is still the largest single pollutant of water." He stated: "Our responsibility is to manage the environment for the widest range of beneficial uses, without degrading it, without risk to health or safety, and without loss of future productivity."

In a recent revision on long-range water resources research needs by the Federal Council for Science and Technology,[10] "Controlling Sediment" was one of ten important problem areas identified. The statement is made that controlling pollution caused by sediment warrants immediate increased research support.

Many people are so accustomed to to seeing muddy water in streams, ponds and reservoirs that they look upon the situation as something necessary, like taxes. Some look upon the present emphasis on pollution as a passing fad. A recent statement said that there are actually "three types of pollution: actual pollution, political pollution and hysterical pollution."[2] One can be assured that pollution in all its forms is real and must be dealt with.

The Problem

Sediment is an economic liability and the monetary loss due to sediment is high. The total annual damage from sediment in streams, not including loss of agricultural productivity of farm land lost to erosion, was estimated to be 262 million dollars in 1966.[12] This amount can be broken down as follows: deposition on flood plains, 50 million dollars; storage space destroyed in reservoirs, 50 million dollars; dredging sediment from inland navigation channels and harbors, 83 million; removal of excess turbidity from public water supplies, 14 million; removal of sediments from drainage ditches and irrigation canals, 34 million; other damages including sediment removal, cleaning, and added maintenance, 31 million.

Sediment is composed primarily of clay, silt, sand, gravel, rock fragments and mineral particles. In terms of mass alone, sediment is by far the major water pollutant. The mass of sediment loading in our streams is from 500 to 700 times that from sewage delivery. Over 4 billion tons of sediment move from the land to water courses in the average year. The average annual sediment concentration for all rivers in the United States ranges from around 200 to 50,000 parts per million.[3] Sediment concentrations for individual runoff events and for small upstream watersheds are frequently much higher than these average values. As a general rule, sediment concentrations are lowest in the more humid parts of the country and tend to increase with diminishing precipitation.

The magnitude of the sediment problems has been evaluated largely in physical terms.

The storage capacity of man-made reservoirs is reduced about 1 million acre-feet each year by sediment.

The Mississippi River delivers about 500 million tons of sediment to the Gulf of Mexico each year.

Sediment yields in the Mississippi basin average about 390 tons per square mile annually.

The 12-year average annual yield for the Pigeon Roost Creek Watershed in northern Mississippi is 2860 tons per square mile.

Soil losses from cropland in the Missouri basin can exceed 100 tons per acre (0.69 inches) if proper management and erosion control measures are not followed.[16]

Sediment yields from agricultural lands along the lower Mississippi range from 5 to 13 tons per acre per year. In the Southeast, sediment yields average about 7 tons per acre per year. Some sources have suggested that about 1 ton per acre per year is an acceptable sediment yield rate from croplands.[12] Despite the successes achieved in controlling agricultural erosion through scientific farming methods such as contour farming, strip cropping and terracing, soil erosion from agricultural lands continues to be extensive.

Soil losses from fraction-acre test plots in northern Mississippi indicate the possible sediment production as a result of cultural practices. Soil loss on bare fallow plots amounted to 70–90 tons per acre per year. Plots with corn planted on contoured, graded rows yielded from 1–4 tons per acre; those with corn planted up and down slopes yielded as much as 11 tons per acre of soil loss. In the same year, plots under an established grass cover yielded only 1.1 tons of sediment per acre.[9]

The 500 million tons of sediment moving to the Gulf of Mexico in the Mississippi River carry an estimated 17 million tons of plant nutrients.[16] It is estimated that 750,000 tons of phosphate are included in these nutrients, but much of this is native to the soil itself and not the result of fertilization. About 14 million tons of primary plant nutrients were applied to soils in the United States during 1967. This consisted of 6 million tons of nitrogen, 4.3 million tons of phosphate and 3.6 million tons of potash.

Approximately 50 percent of the erosional sediment is attributed to agricultural endeavors.[15] The largest single contributor of the remaining 50 percent is streambank erosion. Recent surveys in the Intermountain area of the West indicate that 66 to 90 percent of the sediment contained in many of the streams in the area comes from streambank and streambed erosion.[4] Erosion from highway and roadway construction sites is a major contributor as well as that from construction sites in urban and suburban developments. The sediment yield from highway construction areas during an average storm has been found to be 10 times greater than that from cultivated land, 200 times greater than from grassed areas and 2,000 times greater than from forested areas.

Sediments may deposit in valleys, floodplains, on alluvial fans or in stream channels. Deposition in stream channels or on floodplains may cause channels to overflow more frequently and result in additional damage. Sediments deposited on fertile alluvial soils may reduce their productivity. However, the deposition of sediment on floodplain lands may also be beneficial. Before construction of the high Aswan Dam, the annual enrichment of the Nile Valley was a classic example of an area benefited by sediment deposi-

tion. On floodplains in Nebraska, corn yields increased as much as 45% over a 3-year period after floods depositing a layer of 4 to 6 inches of sediment over the area.[4] Sediment deposition may result in incidental benefits, but there is no question that the damage caused by this misplaced soil far outweighs the benefits.

Erosion is a selective process that removes finer soil particles more rapidly than coarser particles. Both the physical and chemical properties of fine grain sediments must be considered, whereas only the physical properties of the coarse grain sediments are usually significant. The fine grain sediments, consisting of clay minerals, amorphous and organic materials, have chemically active surfaces.[5] These sediments may either sorb ions from solution or release ions to solution depending on the chemical environment. Reactions between chemicals and colloidal sediments determine the relative concentration of pollutants in solution and suspension. This will determine the pollutant transportation and deposition for a given hydraulic condition. In general, the coarse sediments serve as a buffer, modifying the erosive potential of the streamflow, and the fine sediments tend to modify the dissolved and suspended chemical load.

Sediment's Role

Recently, increased attention has been given to the role of sediment as a carrier of plant nutrients, pesticides and toxic elements such as lead, mercury, cadmium, nickel and arsenic. Plant nutrients such as nitrogen, phosphorous, potassium and certain trace elements are sorbed on sediments and may have biological significance in the eutrophication of our ponds, reservoirs and lakes. Little information is available on this aspect of sedimentation. There is also little information available on the chemical trap efficiency of reservoirs, the contribution of chemicals adsorbed on sediment to the biological activity of the impoundment and the changes in water quality after impoundment.

Research indicates that the clays and organic fractions of sediments have active surfaces that can react with an array of chemicals. Unfortunately, this research is based on controlled laboratory studies that cannot be easily extrapolated to the field problems.

Pollutants that adhere to sediment particles are often transported at rates that are several orders of magnitude slower than dissolved pollutants. This may result in the buildup of a high concentration of pollutants in bed sediments even though the concentration dissolved in the water is well within permissible limits. If the sediment permanently assimilates the pollutant, this may be an acceptable means of waste disposal. However, in some cases, a relatively slight change in the chemical constituents of the water might cause the pollutants to be released into solution. Therefore, exchange mechanisms whereby the pollutant can be either taken up or released from the sediment phase should be considered, in addition to the transport properties of the sediment to which the pollutant is attached.

During natural sediment movement, polluted sediments may concentrate as channel deposits.[8] Subsequent transport of these polluted sediments by high-velocity flows may produce different bed sediment concentrations downstream. The pollution of bottom sediments of the lower Mississippi River by pesticides from manufacturing wastes originating near Memphis, Tennessee, is thought to be a result of this type of deposition, resuspension and transport. A recent survey of the Mississippi River sediments[1] showed no DDT at the 0.05 ppm level in the bed sediments of the lower Mississippi River. However, concentrations of up to 0.49 ppm of DDT were found in the sediments of some of the tributary streams draining from manufacturing plants. The most significant conclusion from these investigations was that the large amount of chlorinated hydrocarbons applied to crops in the Mississippi River Delta has not created widespread contamination of the streambed materials. This survey was made to determine the contribution of chlorinated hydrocarbons to massive fish kills which occurred in the river. The finding that the kill was not related to pesticides in runoff from agricultural lands has received very little attention.[16]

Federal Water Pollution Legislation has been enacted to deal with pollution problems.[7] Water quality standards, along with plans for implementing and enforcing them, are now established for all 50 states. In these standards as of 1969, not one state has set forth specific criteria on suspended solids pertaining to water quality. This is a disturbing situation since sediment has been named as the major pollutant of waters.

Besides filling stream channels, ponds and reservoirs, sediment in water increases the expense of clarification and treatment of the water used by humans. Sediment has other effects to change the environment, generally to the detriment of animal and plant life.[15] Suspended sediment impairs the dissolved oxygen balance in water and may slow the breakdown of other oxygen-demanding wastes. Reduced oxygen supply hurts fish life. If the dissolved oxygen content goes much below 4 parts per million, most fish will die from asphyxiation. Fish population is also reduced by sediment blanketing fish spawning grounds and fish food supplies.

Bottom sediments in ponds, lakes and streams have been reported to be a source of water-soluble nutrients available to algae and other microorganisms. In shallow water, the bottom sediments support aquatic plants that live, die and decay, contributing nutrients and organic matter to eutrophying lakes and ponds. Sediment-water equilibria should be evaluated to determine changes in nutrient solubility and availability from transported or deposited sediments.

The magnitude of the sediment pollution problem tends to obscure the benefits of proper sediment concentrations. Generally overlooked is the fact that a flowing stream is a dynamic body which has energy to transport sediment. Unless flowing in a channel that is nonerodible, such as concrete, the stream will attempt to transport sediment up to its energy ability, and may erode or degrade the bed or surface to obtain this material. If the load exceeds the available energy, then deposition occurs. Therefore, the flowing stream must be considered to be almost a living body and treated as such.[11] All the sediment moving in a natural stream cannot be eliminated.

Sediment pollution of nutrient-rich waters may help prevent eutrophication and the accompanying water quality deterioration. Sediment may receive chemicals from the solution phase and may serve as a trap or sink to remove the materials from the flowing stream.

Other Factors

Each ton of sediment carries about 1 pound of phosphorus fixed to its surface.[16] By contrast, the amount of phosphorus delivered in metropolitan sewage amounts to about 2 pounds per person per year. This phosphorus largely accrues from use of detergents. Thus, sewage effluent from a city of one million people will carry at least 1000 tons of phosphorus per year.

Phosphorus is attached to soil surfaces so tenaciously that only minute quantities are ever released to solution in the water. For each pound of phosphorus per ton of suspended sediment, not more than 10 percent of the phosphorus is available for plant nutrition.[15] Algae grows vigorously if the water contains only 0.1 ppm of phosphorus and growth is stimulated by only 0.05 ppm. To prevent algae growth, phosphorus content must be below 0.01 ppm.

Phosphorus from farmlands may be transported into streams and lakes in solution in the runoff and adsorbed on the sediment contained in the runoff. The total amount of phosphorus released from sediment is largely a function of the sediment concentration. Sediments can be expected to adsorb-desorb phosphorus from solution during transport. However, sediments deficient in phosphorus can adsorb significant amounts of phosphorus from solution. Research has shown that a Memphis soil, at sediment concentrations of 10,000 ppm, is capable of reducing the phosphorus concentration in solution from sewage effluent from 6.6 ppm to 4.3 ppm.[14]

Research has shown that the surface chemistry of sediments may vary appreciably during runoff events. The ratio of cations sorbed on suspended sediments to those in solution reaches a maximum of 0.8 in eastern streams and may be 3 or more in western streams. The maximum ratio for a stream in Mississippi was found to be 1.9 with a minimum near 1.0. Maximum ratios for the stream usually occur at the peak of suspended sediment concentration.[5] Concentration of agrichemicals in solution are frequently higher in the initial runoff from farmlands. The major portion of the dissolved chemical load is transported at or near the peak water discharge. Significant quantities of K, Ca and Mg were found to be transported in association with sediment.

Research has also shown that lake bottom sediments can effectively remove dissolved phosphates from solution.[13] Studies in Minnesota have indicated that sedimentation can effectively remove dissolved phosphate from lake waters. Apparently, sediments transported into the lake waters in this area are not a major source of soluble phosphates.

Summary

Sediment becomes a pollutant when it occupies water storage reservoirs, fills lakes and ponds, clogs stream channels, settles on productive lands, destroys aquatic habitat, creates turbidity that detracts from recreational use of water, as well as when it degrades water for consumptive or other uses, increases water treatment costs, or damages water distribution systems. Sediment is also the carrier of other pollutants such as plant nutrients, insecticides, herbicides and heavy metals. There is evidence that bacteria and virus are carried by sediments and this possibility should be investigated.

Because of erodible boundaries and the energy available in flowing streams, sediment will continue to be produced and carried by moving water and will carry with it available pollutants. It is primarily the larger sediment particles that are most readily controlled by available technology. However it is the fine particles that are the principal carriers, the more active chemically, and transported further before deposition. There are not yet adequate means for controlling the amount of clay and colloidal fractions which make up the bulk of the sediment problem. This is true both at the source and in the final deposition.

It is true that sediment is our greatest pollutant of waters in terms of volume. However, sediment may be a carrier of other pollutants and in some instances actually remove and deposit these pollutants from the solution. In this case, sediment acts as a scavenger.

If there is to be control of sediment pollution, there must also be control of other pollutants associated with the sediments. Sediment control practices, such as soil conservation measures, must be applied more thoroughly and effectively throughout the country.

Notes

[1] Barthel, W. F., J. C. Hawthorne, J. H. Ford, G. C. Bolton, L. L. McDowell, E. H. Grissinger and D. A. Parsons. 1969. Pesticide residue in sediments of the lower Mississippi river and its tributaries. Pesticide Monitoring Jour. 3(1): 8–66.

[2] Bellinger, E. H. 1969. Severity of Lake Erie's pollution debated. Chemical and Engineering News 47 (21): 43 p.

[3] Glymph, L. M. and C. W. Carlson. 1966. Cleaning up our rivers and lakes. ASAE Paper No. 66–711. 14 p.

[4] Glymph, L. M. and H. C. Storey. 1967. Sediment—its consequences and control. AAAS Pub. 85. p. 205–220.

[5] Grissinger, E. H. and L. L. McDowell. 1970. Sediment in relation to water quality. Water Resources Bull. 6(1): 7–14.

[6] Joint Task Force of the U. S. Dept. of Agriculture and the State Universities and Land Grant Colleges. 1968. A National program of research for environmental quality-pollution in relation to agriculture and forestry. 111 p.

[7] Klein, C. L. 1969. Sediment pollution and water quality standards. Proceedings of the National Conf. on Sediment Control, Washington, D. C. p. 26–30.

[8] McDowell, L. L. and E. H. Grissinger. 1966. Pollutant sources and routing in watershed programs. Proceedings of the 21st Annual Meeting, SCSA. p. 147–161.

[9] McGregor, K. C., J. D. Greer, G. E. Gurley and G. C. Bolton. 1969. Runoff and sediment production from north Mississippi loessial soils. Mississippi State University, Experiment Station Bull. 777. 30 p.

[10] Office of Science and Technology, Executive Office of the President. 1969. Federal Water Resources Research Program for FY 1970. Federal Council for Science and Technology. 47 p.

[11] Robinson, A. R. 1969. Technology for sediment control in urban areas. Proceedings of the National Conf. on Sediment Control. p. 41–47.

[12] Stall, J. B. 1966. Man's role in affecting the sedimentation of streams and reservoirs. Amer. Water Resources Assn. Proceedings of the 2nd Annual Amer. Water Resources Conf. (University of Chicago) p. 79–95.

[13] USDA North Central Soil Conservation Research Center, Morris, Minnesota, Annual Report. 1968.

[14] USDA Sedimentation Laboratory, Oxford, Mississippi, Annual Report. 1969.

[15] Wadleigh, C. H. 1968. Wastes in relation to agriculture and forestry. USDA Pub. 1065. 112 p.

[16] Walker, K. C. and C. H. Wadleigh. 1968. Water pollution from land runoff. Plant Food Review, No. 1. 4 p.

21 Flood-Hazard Mapping in Metropolitan Chicago

John R. Sheaffer, Davis W. Ellis, and Andrew M. Spieker

Introduction

The effective management of flood plains consists of more than building detention reservoirs and levees. As urban pressures are forcing more and more developments on flood plains, such devices as flood-plain regulations and flood proofing are coming into wider use. These devices, however, require information as to what areas are likely to be flooded. The need for flood-

Sheaffer, J. R., Ellis, D. W., and Spieker, A. M., 1969, "Flood-Hazard Mapping in Metropolitan Chicago" U. S. Geol. Survey Circ. 601-C, 14 pp.

Mr. Sheaffer is affiliated with the Center for Urban Studies, The University of Chicago. Davis Ellis and Andrew Spieker are on the staff of the U. S. Geological Survey.

plain information is further intensified by Federal legislation such as the National Flood Insurance Act of 1968 (Title XIII, Public Law 90–448) and recent Federal policies on use of flood plains (U. S. Congress, 1966; Executive Order 11296).

The present report describes how these needs are being met in the Chicago SMSA (Standard Metropolitan Statistical Area) by a cooperative program involving the six counties of the metropolitan area—Cook, Du Page, Kane, Lake, McHenry, and Will—the Northeastern Illinois Planning Commission, the State of Illinois, and the U. S. Geological Survey. This unique flood-mapping program, in progress since 1961, has resulted in coverage of nearly the entire six-county metropolitan area by maps showing the flood hazard. Figure 1 is a map of the area showing the extent of coverage in June 1969. Quadrangles showing an HA (U. S. Geological Survey Hydrologic Investigations Atlas) number are published and available for sale at the Northeastern Illinois Planning Commission, or the U. S. Geological Survey, Washington, D. C. Quadrangles without an HA designation are in progress or are scheduled for future mapping. At present this coverage is about 85 percent complete. Metropolitan Chicago is the only large metropolitan area in the United States for which this information is so widely available.

The purpose of this report is to describe how the program originated and is being carried out, the outlook for improving this program to meet the changing needs of the rapidly urbanizing metropolitan area, and the various ways flood maps can be used by individuals and public and private institutions.

Flooding in Metropolitan Chicago

Floodflows in the rivers and waterways of Metropolitan Chicago have periodically spilled from their channels and inundated the adjacent lowlands or flood plains. The earliest recorded flood in the Chicago area occurred on March 29, 1674, when the explorer priest Marquette and his companions were driven from their camp near Damen Avenue by high water coming through Mud Lake, from the Des Plaines River. However, such overflows did not become hazards, except possibly to navigation, until development of the flood plains gave the floods something to damage.

In retrospect, it is conceivable that if adequate land-use planning, based on sound hydrologic data in conjunction with regulatory and flood-proofing measures, had guided the development of our flood plains, there would be little, if any, improper use today and no major flood problems would exist.

Flood damages have been steadily increasing as urban sprawl has engulfed many flood plains and subdivisions have been located on sites subject to flooding. The absence of accurate information on these areas subject to flooding has been a limitation on efforts to formulate a comprehensive flood damage reduction program. The need for this information is particularly acute in Metropolitan Chicago and other topographically similar regions of flat terrain and poorly developed drainage, where the flood plains are not readily perceptible to the human eye.

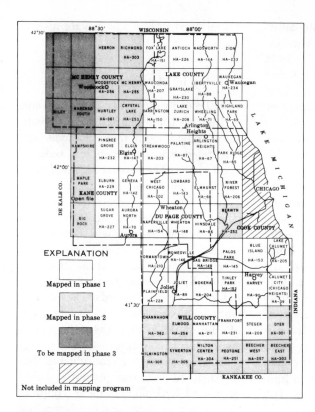

FIG. 1. The Chicago metropolitan area showing location of quadrangles included in flood-hazard mapping program.

The Concept of Flood-Hazard Mapping

Flood-hazard mapping is a means of providing flood-plain information for planning and management programs. Such information should be designed to assist officials and private interests in making decisions and alternative plans concerning the development of specific lands subject to flooding. Proper use of flood-hazard mapping will help to:

1. Prevent improper land development in flood-plain areas.

2. Restrict uses that would be hazardous to health and welfare and which would lead to undue claims upon public agencies for remedy.

3. Encourage adequate stream channel cross-section maintenance.

4. Protect prospective home buyers from locating in flood-prone areas.

5. Preserve potential for natural ground-water recharge during flood events.

6. Guide the purchase of public open space.

7. Avoid water pollution resulting from the flooding of sewage treatment plants and solid waste disposal sites that were located on flood plains.

What is a Flood-Hazard Map?

A flood-hazard map uses as its base a standard U. S. Geological Survey topographic quadrangle which includes contours that define the ground elevation at stated intervals. Each of the quadrangles covers an area 7½ minutes of longitude wide by 7½ minutes of latitude deep, or approximately 57 square miles. The scale of the flood maps is 1:24,000, or 1 inch equals 2,000 feet. The area inundated by a particular "flood of record" is superimposed in light blue on the map to designate the "flood-hazard area." Also marked on the flood-hazard map are distances (at ½-mile intervals) along and above the mouth of each stream and the locations of gaging stations, crest-stage gages, and drainage divides. Figure 2 shows part of the Elmhurst quadrangle, a typical flood map.

Profiles and Probabilities

Accompanying the flood-hazard map are explanatory texts, tables, and graphs, which facilitate their use. One set of graphs shows the linear flood profiles (see Fig. 3) of the major streams in the quadrangle; from them, the user can tell how high the water rose at any given point during one or more floods.

Another valuable tool (Fig. 4) is a set of graphs showing probable frequency of flooding at selected gaging stations. These charts indicate the average interval (in years) between floods that are expected to exceed a given elevation. Frequencies can also be expressed as probabilities which make it possible to express the flood risk or "flood hazard" for a particular property; for example, a given area may have a 5-percent chance of being inundated by flood waters in each year.

How to Use a Flood-Hazard Map

To illustrate the use of a flood-hazard map, assume that you own property along Salt Creek, near Elmhurst and about half a mile south of Lake Street.

Perhaps you plan to build there, and you want to know the risk of being flooded. You examine the Elmhurst quadrangle flood-hazard map (Fig. 2) and note that your property is located at a point 23.5 miles above the mouth of Salt Creek. (The river miles are shown on the map.)

One of the graphs accompanying the map is a flood-frequency curve for Salt Creek (Fig. 4). This curve, however, is for a particular point on Salt Creek—the Lake Street Bridge. To apply the flood-frequency relationship to your own property will require an adjustment for the water-surface slope between the two points. So you consult another graph, the one which shows profiles or high-water elevations, of floods along Salt Creek (Fig. 3). There, you find that at the Lake Street Bridge (river mile 24) the 1954 flood crested at 671.5 feet, while at the point you are interested in (river mile 23.5) the crest was at 671 feet.

Returning now to the flood-frequency curve, you find that the 1954 flood has an 8-year "recurrence interval," meaning that, over a long period of time, floods can be expected to reach or exceed that level on an average of once every 8 years. That level, you have already found, is 671.5 feet at Lake Street and 671 feet at your property. Another way of thinking of it is this: if you were to erect a building on your property at 671-foot elevation, the chances of a flood reaching the structure in any given year would be approximately one in eight. These are only odds—probabilities—and the actuality may be better or worse. But the odds are poorer than most property owners are willing to accept, so you

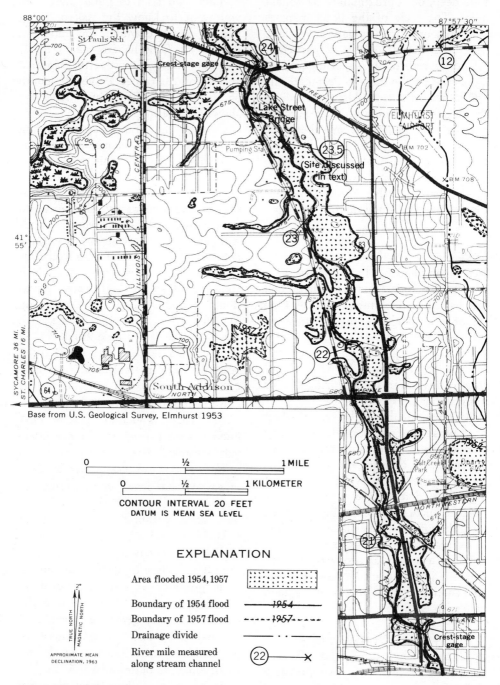

FIG. 2. Flood-hazard map of part of the Elmhurst quadrangle. Adapted from Ellis, Allen, and Noehre (1963).

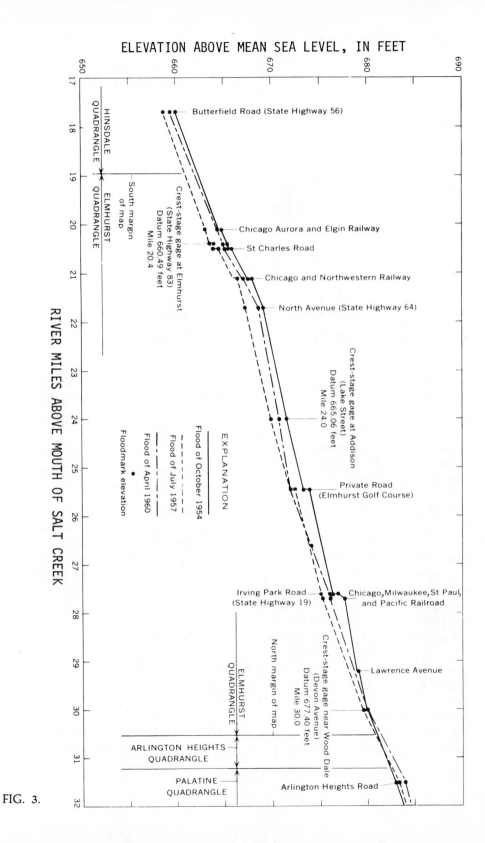

ELEVATION ABOVE MEAN SEA LEVEL, IN FEET

RIVER MILES ABOVE MOUTH OF SALT CREEK

Butterfield Road (State Highway 56)

HINSDALE QUADRANGLE

ELMHURST QUADRANGLE

South margin of map

Crest-stage gage at Elmhurst
(State Highway 83)
Datum 660.49 feet
Mile 20.4

Chicago Aurora and Elgin Railway

St Charles Road

Chicago and Northwestern Railway

North Avenue (State Highway 64)

Crest-stage gage at Addison
(Lake Street)
Datum 665.06 feet
Mile 24.0

EXPLANATION

Flood of October 1954

Flood of July 1957

Flood of April 1960

Floodmark elevation

Private Road
(Elmhurst Golf Course)

Irving Park Road
(State Highway 19)

Chicago, Milwaukee, St Paul,
and Pacific Railroad

ELMHURST QUADRANGLE

North margin of map

Crest-stage gage near Wood Dale
(Devon Avenue)
Datum 677.40 feet
Mile 30.0

Lawrence Avenue

ARLINGTON HEIGHTS QUADRANGLE

PALATINE QUADRANGLE

Arlington Heights Road

FIG. 3.

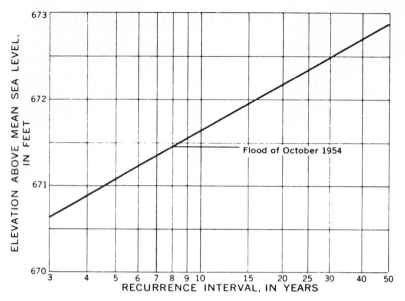

FIG. 4. Frequency of floods on Salt Creek at Addison (Lake Street).

will probably want to seek better odds at higher ground.

Suppose you were willing to accept a flood risk of one every 25 years: What is the ground elevation at which a building should be situated to enjoy that much security?

The flood-frequency curve indicates that, at the Lake Street Bridge, an elevation of 672.3 feet corresponds to the 25-year recurrence interval. You now plot this elevation at river mile 24 on the flood-profile chart and draw a straight line through the point you have plotted and parallel to the 1954 flood profile. You now have the profile for a flood with a 25-year recurrence interval, and it shows that the elevation reached by such a flood at your property would be 671.8 feet. Using the line you have drawn, you can determine corresponding elevations (for the same recurrence interval) at other points along Salt Creek. And, of course, you can use the method outlined to approximate the elevation at your property for other recurrence intervals—up to 50 years.

The Metropolitan Chicago Flood-Mapping Program

It was determined that flood-hazard mapping could meet some of the needs that had become evident in Metropolitan Chicago. However, it was also recognized that flood-hazard mapping of such a large area could not be accomplished overnight. It would require financing, time, careful planning, and data. The flood-mapping program is a cooperative effort, financed jointly by the six counties of Metropolitan Chicago, the Northeastern Illinois Planning Commission, the State of Illinois, and the U. S. Geological Survey. Funds offered by the six counties through the Planning Commission which serves in an administrative and coordinating role, are matched on a one-to-one basis with Federal funds. The actual mapping is done by personnel of the U. S. Geological Survey. In 1968 the State of Illinois entered into a separate, though similar, cooperative agreement with the U. S. Geological Survey to assist with part of the financing. The flood-mapping program was carried out in phases. The first phase extended from July 1, 1961 to June 30, 1966. Phase 2 extended from July 1, 1966 to June 30, 1969. The formulation of a phase 3 is currently (1969) being discussed among the principal agencies involved.

Phase 1

In phase 1 of the program, flood maps were prepared for 43 7½-minute quadrangles in the six-county area. One flood atlas, U. S. Geological Survey Hydrologic Investigations Atlas HA–39, "Floods in the Little Calumet River basin near Chicago Heights, Ill.," had been prepared previously by the Geological Survey as a prototype for the program. Each quadrangle is given the name of a principal city or prominent geographic feature located on the map. The location of these quadrangles is shown in Fig. 1.

The scope of phase 1 is shown in Table 1 and Fig. 1. The average cost of preparing a flood map initially was estimated as $6,250, or a cost to the local agencies of $3,125, and the initial agreements between local agencies and the Planning Commission were prepared on this basis. Early in the program, however, it was found that, for several quadrangles, particularly in Lake County, there was need for supplemental contours on the flood-plain

areas. These were provided under a supplemental agreement among the appropriate agencies. Partly because of this change, and partly because of steadily rising costs throughout the 5-year period of the program, the total expenditure for phase 1, including the supplemental contours, the preparation of inundation maps for 43 quadrangles, and the installation and operation to June 30, 1966, of the initial 229 crest-stage gages, was $299,860, or about $6,975 per quadrangle.

Another item of possible interest to those who may plan similar programs is the expenditure of manpower. All operations were conducted from the Survey subdistrict office at Oak Park, near the geographic center of the area. A total of 37,372 direct man-hours were required to complete phase 1; this indicates an average of 869 direct man-hours per quadrangle. There was, however, considerable variation for the individual quadrangles, ranging from a maximum of 1,455 man-hours to a minimum of 520 man-hours. Man-hours required for providing the supplemental contours are not included in these figures, as this part of the work

Table 1 Scope of phase I of flood-mapping program, July 1961 to June 1966

Counties	Quadrangles mapped
Cook	[1]13
Du Page	6
Kane	6
Lake	10
McHenry	1
Will	8
Total	44

[1] Includes Calumet City quadrangle. Chicago Heights, which was prepared as a pilot project, was not included as part of program.

was performed under a contractual arrangement with the Topographic Division of the Geological Survey.

Because of insufficient hydrologic data in much of the area, it was necessary to establish 229 crest-stage gages to record instantaneous flood peaks so that flood profiles and flood-plain limits could be better defined along the approximately 1,000 miles of streams located in the 43 quadrangles.

Preparation for phase 2 of the flood-mapping program involved the installation of an additional 165 crest-stage gages in McHenry, Kane, and Will Counties in 1963. The installation of these gages was necessary because the hydrologic events on many of the streams in southern Will County and western Kane and McHenry Counties had never been recorded. These gages are located in 19 quadrangles which were scheduled for mapping during phase 2. The costs were covered by supplementary cooperative agreements with the affected counties.

A flood-hazard mapping program can lead to other related hydrologic studies. A study of the role of flood-plain information and related water resource management concepts in comprehensive land-use planning (Spieker, 1969) was made by the Geological Survey, at the request of the Planning Commission, in 1965–67. This study used the Salt Creek basin in Cook and Du Page Counties as a demonstration area to illustrate principles which govern the effects of alternative land-use practices, particularly uses of the flood plains, on the overall water resources of the area. Emphasis was placed on the interrelationship of the various components of the hydrologic system,

particularly the interrelationship between surface water and ground water.

Phase 2

Phase 2 involved the preparation of 19 additional flood maps. (See Fig. 1.) In addition, the 394 crest-stage gages, including those located in areas already mapped, were kept in operation as part of phase 2 to extend the hydrologic records. The completion of phase 2 will make flood maps available for the entire metropolitan area with the exception of the western part of McHenry County and the completely urbanized area of Chicago and the close-in suburbs in Cook County. This area, which comprises four quadrangles, was not mapped because urbanization has obliterated nearly all the natural flood plains and overbank flooding is generally not a problem.

The scope of phase 2 is presented in Table 2. A proportionally larger share of the local cost was allocated to McHenry and Will Counties because a major part of the work was done in those two counties. In 1967, the State of Illinois, through the Division of Waterways of the Department of Public Works and Buildings entered into a separate cooperative agreement with the Geological Survey to assume part of Will County's share of phase 2 mapping. The cost of mapping in phase 2 was $174,600, of which $86,200 was provided by local agencies and $88,400, by the Geological Survey. (The difference of $2,200 was due to supplemental allotments of Survey funds, unmatched by local funds, to partially cover interim increases in Federal salary rates.) At the completion of phase 2, the total cost of flood mapping in the metropolitan area was

Table 2 Scope of phase 2 of flood-mapping program, July 1966 to June 1969

Counties	Quad-rangles mapped	Total number of gages	Gages having peak discharge data
Cook	2	70	8
Du Page		36	12
Kane	3	58	11
Lake		40	11
McHenry	6	52	8
Will	8	138	19
Total	19	394	69

$474,460. (This cost includes operation of the entire network of 394 crest-stage gages to June 30, 1969.)

The Formulation of Phase 3

Providing adequate flood information in an urban area is a continuing activity. Floods will continue to occur and will provide new and additional information. Spreading urbanization can alter both the frequency and the patterns of flooding. Paving and covering of the land tends to accelerate storm runoff and increase flood peaks. Manmade changes in the channel cross section can alter flooding patterns. Examples of such changes are bridges, culverts, fill on the flood plain, and building on the flood plain. These changes take place at a rapid pace in a fast growing area such as Metropolitan Chicago.

To keep up with these changes will require periodic revision of the flood-hazard maps. Many of the maps are based on information which is 8 years old. Additional flooding and a great deal of urbanization has taken place during these 8 years. The crest-stage gage network has provided a wealth of data to document these flood events and to help in analyzing the changes resulting from urbanization.

Phase 2 of the flood-mapping program terminated in 1969. In continuing the program into its third phase, the following four activities should be considered.

1. Continued operation of the existing network of crest-stage gages. The crest-stage gage network is believed to be the densest such network in the country. About 8 years of record will be available at the completion of phase 2 of the program. As urban development continues, the continued availability of flood-stage information will be increasingly important. Such data would be valuable in determining rates if a flood-insurance program became operational.

2. Evaluation of the crest-stage gage network for adequacy and relevance. Although the existing network is one of the most comprehensive in the country, there exists a need for its review to eliminate redundant gages and to add new ones where needed. The 8 years of record would be useful in this evaluation.

3. Extension of the program to unmapped areas. At the completion of phase 2 all of the six-county metropolitan areas except the completely urbanized central city and the western 40 percent of McHenry County will be mapped. The remainder of McHenry County is already planned for inclusion in phase 3. Before the metropolitan area expands into Kankakee and Kendall Counties, the flood-mapping program should be extended there to provide a part of the basis for orderly growth.

4. Periodic and systematic revision of the flood maps prepared in phases 1 and 2. All existing maps should be evaluated as to their adequacy and a systematic program should be planned for updating the maps where urbanization and additional flood data warrant it. This should be a continuing process. Examples of maps greatly in need of revision are the Calumet City (HA–39) and Arlington Heights (HA–67) quadrangles. In addition to mapping floods of record, consideration should be given to defining floods of given frequencies: for example, at 25-, 50-, and 100-year recurrence intervals. Even though the cost of such a mapping program would be considerably greater than that of mapping historical floods, the maps would provide a more sound and consistent basis for considering the element of risk in planning and decision making. Profiles at the selected frequencies also should be included in future mapping. This kind of flood information would be especially useful in determining premium rates under the National Flood Insurance Act of 1968. It has been agreed,[1] for example, that the area inundated by the 100-year flood should define the regulatory area under the Flood Insurance Act.

Continuation of the cooperative flood-hazard mapping program along these lines will assure that local governmental bodies, industries, utilities, developers, and citizens of Metropolitan Chicago will have more and better flood information which can be used in furthering the region's orderly development.

The Crest-Stage Gage Network

The Northeastern Illinois Planning Commission and the U. S. Geological Survey's cooperative flood-mapping program required the establishment of a network of crest-stage gaging stations.

A crest-stage gage is a rather simple device that records the maximum elevation of floods. These gages are mounted on wingwalls or piers of highway bridges and culverts or anchored in concrete along stream banks. After the gages are mounted, levels are run from nearby benchmarks to establish datum (zero) of the gages referred to mean sea level, datum of 1929. The base of these gages is set above normal water levels so that they record only flood elevations. The sketch in Fig. 5 illustrates how the gage functions. Water enters the gage through specially designed holes at the bottom of the pipe. Finely ground cork at the bottom of the gage floats on the water surface and comes in contact with the wooden staff located inside of the pipe. As the water recedes, the cork adheres to the staff and provides a record of the maximum stage of the flood.

After a flood, the crest-stage gage is serviced by opening the gage, withdrawing the staff, and measuring the

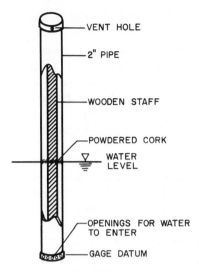

FIG. 5. Typical crest-stage gage.

distance from the base of the staff to the top of the cork line. After the measurements are made, the cork is removed from the staff, any debris that has collected is removed from the holes at the base of the gage, new cork is added, and the gage is reassembled. It is then ready to record the elevation of the next flood. By adding the depth of water recorded on the staff (gage height) to the gage datum, the elevation of the flood in feet above mean sea level is determined.

Usefulness of Flood-Hazard Maps in Urban Development

The main purpose of flood-hazard mapping, as stated previously, is to make available information which can be used to bring about the orderly and beneficial use of areas subject to flooding. A wide range of institutions and devices exists through which this information can be put to use. The following outline presents the general categories of flood-plain information use:

1. Regulation of private development:
   a. By public institutions:
      (1) Building, subdivision, and zoning regulations.
      (2) Sewer connection permits.
      (3) Public financial institutions (that is, Federal Housing Administration, Veterans Administration).
      (4) Land management and use criteria of the flood insurance program.
   b. By private institutions:
      (1) Financial institutions.
      (2) Private utilities (that is, gas, electric).
2. Purchase of property for public use:
   a. Forest preserve districts (county).
   b. Parks and recreation facilities.
   c. Municipal parking lots.
3. Development of public facilities:
   a. Highways and streets.
   b. Sewer extensions, treatment plant locations.
4. Guidelines (planning) for future development.

Following is a résumé of how the flood-hazard maps have actually been used to give direction to urban development in the Chicago metropolitan area.

Regulation of Private Development

One of the most frequently employed devices of flood-plain management is flood-plain zoning. The zoning authority is usually delegated to local governments, villages, and cities. County governments may exercise zoning powers in the unincorporated areas.

The Northeastern Illinois Planning Commission (1964) has prepared a model flood-plain zoning ordinance for the assistance of county and local governments. This model is the basis for many of the flood-plain zoning ordinances that have been adopted by Metropolitan Chicago communities.

Progress in the adoption of flood-plain zoning ordinances by county and municipal governments has been varied. As of late 1968 three of the six metropolitan counties—Cook, Du Page, and Lake—had adopted such ordinances. Kane County does not have a flood-plain zoning ordinance as such, although its zoning ordinance and subdivision regulations set forth conditions for subdivision development in flood-hazard areas. As of October 1968, 94 of the 117 Cook County municipalities located in the Metropolitan Sanitary District had adopted flood-plain zoning ordinances. There are 20 Cook County municipalities within the Sanitary District which do not have recognized flood hazards. An additional three are revising ordinances which have been rejected as unsatisfactory. Outside of Cook County, only a few municipalities have adopted flood-plain zoning ordinances.

One of the reasons for the large number of Cook County municipalities taking action is the policy adopted in 1967 by the Metropolitan Sanitary District regarding the issuance of sewer permits. The policy states that: "No permits shall be issued by the Metropolitan Sanitary District for sewers to be constructed within a flood-hazard area, as delineated on the maps prepared by the United States Geological Survey in cooperation with the Northeastern Illinois Planning Commission, until the local municipality has adopted a flood-plain zoning ordinance which

meets the approval of the Sanitary District."

"Permits in undeveloped areas will not be approved until Cook County adopts flood-plain zoning regulations."

"The ordinance shall include but not be limited to the following:

1. Restrictions on residential development.

2. Provisions for establishing permanent flood way channels through acquisition of rights-of-way, including easements for maintenance and improvements.

3. Requirements for flood proofing buildings within the flood-hazard areas. The ordinance shall be adopted before September 1, 1967."

This policy has proved highly effective in encouraging municipalities to adopt flood-plain zoning ordinances. In addition, Cook County has adopted a flood-plain ordinance which applies to all its unincorporated areas.

Financial institutions, public and private, can exert a powerful influence over the location of private urban development. Where flood-plain information is available, these institutions are generally reluctant to finance housing development in flood-hazard areas. The financing of housing in flood-prone areas is a risk that financial institutions would rather not assume, provided that there exists a knowledge of this risk. In the Chicago metropolitan area the Veterans Administration and the Federal Housing Administration routinely check the location on the U. S. Geological Survey's flood-hazard maps of new housing developments which they are considering financing. These agencies as a matter of policy will not finance developments in areas known to be subject to flooding. A large number of private financial institutions (banks, savings and loan companies) make similar use of the flood-hazard maps.

Private utility companies can influence urban development by where they choose to extend—or not to extend—gas and electric lines. By recognizing that development on flood plains is not wise, utility companies are in an excellent position to prevent their development by refusing to service them. Flood-hazard maps thus can be useful to utility companies by helping them to identify those areas where they might wish to discourage development.

Purchase of Property for Public Use

The public development of flood-hazard areas for recreation or aesthetic purposes has long been recognized as a technique of flood-plain management. Green belts, or undeveloped areas along streams, can provide breaks in the monotony of urban sprawl. The construction of municipal parking lots is another example of public use of flood plains. Identification on flood-hazard maps of those areas subject to flooding can assist public officials in acquiring these lands at a reasonable price.

The Du Page County Forest Preserve District is now engaged in a long-range program of land acquisition whose purpose is to develop a major green belt along the West Branch of the Du Page River. The U. S. Geological Survey's flood-hazard maps have been extremely useful in providing guidelines for land purchase. Also, they have been helpful in negotiations for public open space acquisition in Cook and Lake Counties.

Development of Public Facilities

Public facilities frequently lead urban development into flood-hazard areas. The State Division of Highways has made frequent use of the flood-plain maps in their highway planning process. Proper planning of access can tend to discourage improper flood-plain development.

The location of sewage treatment plants and sanitary landfills is also influenced by flood-plain information. An example of such use is found in "Rules and Regulations for Refuse Disposal Sites and Facilities" (Illinois Department of Public Health, 1966, p. 1). This document states that: "sites subject to flooding should be avoided . . . or protected by impervious dikes and pumping facilities provided." Thus, flood-plain information becomes involved in all decisions regarding the establishment of disposal sites and facilities and is cited by the State Geological Survey in their site-evaluation reports.

Guidelines (Planning) for Future Development

Planning, or the formulation of guidelines for future development, provides the overall framework in which the previously discussed uses of flood-hazard maps are implemented. It is in the planning process that the broad, long-range goals and objectives are set out. These objectives can be attained by alternate tactics.

The importance of wise management of the flood plains has been recognized by the Regional Planning Agency for Metropolitan Chicago, Northeastern Illinois Planning Commission, almost from its inception. Examples of how the flood-hazard maps are influencing long-range planning can be found in the two following policy statements taken from the Northeastern Illinois Planning Commission's comprehensive general plan for Metropolitan Chicago (Northeastern Illinois Planning Commission, 1968, p. 7): "Lands unsuited for intensive development due to flooding, unstable soil conditions, or where the provision of essential public services and facilities is difficult, should be maintained in suitable open space use." And on page 11: "Intensive urban development should be directed so as to avoid flood plains, protect ground water deposits, and preserve lands particularly suited for multi-purpose resources management programs."

Notes

[1] Consensus of Seminar on Flood Plain Management held at the Center for Urban Studies, University of Chicago, December 16-18, 1968, at the request of the U. S. Department of Housing and Urban Development.

References

Bue, C. D., 1967, Flood information for flood-plain planning: U. S. Geological Survey Circular 539, 10 p.

Ellis, D. W., Allen, H. E., and Noehre, A. W.,
1963, Floods in Elmhurst quadrangle, Illinois: U. S. Geol. Survey Hydrol. Inv. Atlas HA-68.

Illinois Department of Public Health, 1966, Rules and Regulations for Refuse Disposal Sites and Facilities: Illinois Dept. Public Health, Springfield, Ill., 7 p.

Mitchell, W. D., 1964, Some problems in flood mapping in Illinois: Natl. Acad. Sci.—Natl. Research Council Highway Research Board, Highway Research Rec. 58, p. 42–43.

Northeastern Illinois Planning Commission, 1964, Suggested flood damage prevention ordinance with commentary: Northeastern Illinois Planning Comm., Chicago, Ill., 28 p.

——— 1968, A regional armature for the future: The comprehensive general plan for the development of the northeastern Illinois counties: Northeastern Illinois Planning Comm., Chicago, Ill., 12 p.

Sheaffer, J. R., 1964, The use of flood maps in northeastern Illinois: Natl. Acad. Sci. —Natl. Research Council Highway Research Board, Highway Research Rec. 58, p. 44–46.

Sheaffer, J. R., Zeizel, A. J., and others, 1966, The water resources in northeastern Illinois—Planning its use: Northeastern Illinois Planning Comm. Tech. Rept. 4, 182 p.

Spieker, A. M., 1969, Water in metropolitan area planning: U. S. Geological Survey Water-Supply Paper 2002. (In press.)

U. S. Congress, 1965, A unified national program for managing flood losses: U. S. 89th Cong., 2d sess., House Doc. 465, 47 p.

Supplementary Readings

General

Flawn, P. T., 1970, Environmental Geology— Conservation, Land-Use Planning, and Resource Management, Harper and Row, New York, 313 pp.

Leet, L. D., 1948, Causes of Catastrophe, Mc-Graw-Hill Book Co., Inc.

Leet, L. D. and Judson, S., 1971, Physical Geology, 4th ed., Prentice-Hall Inc., New Jersey, 687 pp.

Olson, R. A. and Wallace, M. M., 1969, Geologic Hazards and Public Problems, Conference Proceedings (May 27–28, 1969), U. S. Office of Emergency Preparedness, 335 pp.

Putman, W. C., 1971, *Geology*, 2nd ed. revised by A. B. Bassett, Oxford Univ. Press, New York, 586 pp.

Volcanism

Bullard, F. M., 1962, *Volcanoes: in History, in Theory, in Eruption*, University of Texas Press, Austin, Texas.

Crandell, Dwight R. and Mullineaux, Donal R., 1967, Volcanic Hazards at Mount Rainier, *U. S. Geol. Survey Bull. 1238*, 26 pp.

Eaton, J. P., Richter, D. H., and Ault, W. V., 1961, The Tsunami of May 23, 1960, on the Island of Hawaii, *Seismological Soc. of Amer. Bull.* v. 51, pp. 135–57.

Jaggar, T. A., 1945, Protection of Harbors from Lava Flow, *Amer. Jour. Sci.*, v. 243-A, pp. 333–35.

Lear, J., 1966, The Volcano that Shaped the Western World, *Saturday Rev.*, v. 49 (Nov. 5, 1966), pp. 57–66.

Maiuri, A., Bianchi, P. V., and Battaglia, L. E., 1961, Last Moments of the Pompeians, *Natl. Geog.*, v. 120, pp. 651–69.

Tyrrell, George, W., 1931, *Volcanoes*, Oxford Univ. Press.

Wexler, Harry, 1952, Volcanoes and World Climates, *Sci. Amer.*, v. 186, n. 4, pp. 74–80.

Wilcox, Ray E., 1959, Some Effects of Recent Volcanic Ash Falls with Especial Reference to Alaska, *U. S. Geol. Survey Bull. 1028-N*, pp. 409–76.

Williams, Howell, 1951, Volcanoes, *Sci. Amer.*, v. 185, n. 5, pp. 45–53.

Earthquake Activity

Anderson, D. L., 1971, The San Andreas Fault, *Sci. Amer.*, v. 225, n. 5, pp. 52–67.

Bernstein, J., 1954, Tsunamis, *Sci. Amer.*, v. 191, n. 2, pp. 60–63.

Eckel, E., 1970, The Alaska Earthquake March 27, 1964: Lessons and Conclusions, *U. S. Geol. Survey Prof. Paper 546*, 57 pp.

Fuller, M. L., 1914, The New Madrid Earthquake, *U. S. Geol. Survey Bull. 494*.

Hagiwara, T. and Rikitake, T., 1967, Japanese

Program on Earthquake Prediction and Control, *Science*, v. 166, no. 3912, pp. 1467–74.

Hodgson, J. H., 1964, *Earthquakes and Earth Structure*, Prentice-Hall, Inc., New Jersey, 166 pp.

Palmer, D. and Henyey, T., 1971, San Fernando Earthquake of 9 February 1971: Pattern of Faulting, *Science*, v. 172, p. 712–15.

Reid, H. F., 1914, The Lisbon Earthquake of November 1, 1755, *Seismol. Soc. of Amer. Bull.*, v. 4, pp. 53–80.

Tectonic Movements and Sea Level Changes

Dickinson, W. R. and Grantz, A., eds., 1968, Proceedings of Conference on Geologic Problems of San Andreas Fault System, *Stanford Univ. Pubs. Geol. Sci.*, v. 11 pp. 70–82.

Fairbridge, R., 1958, Dating the Latest Movements of the Quaternary Sea Level, *Trans. N. Y. Acad. Sci., Ser. II.* v. 20, n. 6, pp. 471–82.

Fairbridge, R., 1960, The Changing Level of the Sea, *Sci. Amer.* v. 202 n. 5, pp. 70–79.

Flint, R. F., 1971, *Glacial and Quaternary Geology* (chap. 12, Fluctuation of Sea-level, and chap. 13, Glacial-Isostatic Deformation), John Wiley & Sons, Inc., New York, 892 pp.

Gutenburg, B., 1941, Changes in Sea Level, Postglacial Uplift and Mobility of the Earth's Interior. *Bull. Geol. Soc. Amer.*, v. 52, n. 5, pp. 721–72.

Hess, H. H., 1946, Drowned Ancient Islands of the Pacific Basin. *Amer. Jour. Sci.*, v. 244, pp. 772–91.

Parkin, E. J., 1948, Vertical Movement in the Los Angeles Region, 1906–1946, *Trans. Amer. Geophys. Union*, v. 29, n. 1, pp. 17–26.

Rogers, T. H., 1969, A Trip to An Active Fault in the City of Hollister, *Mineral Information Service*, v. 22, n. 10, pp. 159–64.

Ryall, A., Slemmons, D. B., and Gedney, L. D., 1966, Seismicity, Tectonism, and Surface Faulting in the Western United States During Historic Time, *Seismol.*

Soc. Amer. Bull. v. 61, n. 12, pt. 2, pp. 1529–30.

Mass Movements

Black, R. F., 1954, Permafrost—a Review, *Geol. Soc. Amer. Bull.*, v. 65, pp. 839–56.

Kerr, Paul F., 1963, Quick Clay, *Sci. Amer.*, v. 209, n. 5, pp. 132–42.

McDowell, B. and Fletcher, J., 1962. Avalanche! 3,500 Peruvians Perish in Seven Minutes, *Natl. Geog.*, v. 121, pp. 855–80.

Sharpe, C. F. S., 1938, *Landslides and Related Phenomena*, Columbia Univ. Press, New York.

Shreve, R. L., 1968, The Blackhawk Landslide; *Geol. Soc. Amer., Spec. Paper No. 108.*

Terzaghi, K., 1950, Mechanism of Landslides, *Geol. Soc. Amer., Berkey Volume*, pp. 83–123.

Varnes, D. J., 1958, Landslide Types and Processes, chap. 3 in *Landslides and Engineering Practice, Highway Research Board, Spec. Rept. 29.*

Erosion, Sedimentation and Floods

Bue, C. D., 1967, Flood Information for Flood-Plain Planning, *U. S. Geol. Survey Circ. 539*, 10 pp.

Emerson, J. W., 1971, Channelization: A Case Study, *Science*, v. 173, pp. 325–26.

Fisk, N. H., 1952, Geological Investigations of the Atchafalaya Basin and the Problem of Mississippi River Diversion, *Corps of Engineers, U. S. Army Waterways Exp. Station, Vicksburg, Miss.*

Hinson, H. G., 1965, Floods on Small Streams in North Carolina, Probable Magnitude and Frequency, *U. S. Geol. Survey Circ. 517*, 7 pp.

Hoyt, W. G. and Langbein, W. B., 1955, *Floods*, Princeton Univ. Press, Princeton, N. J.

Judge, J., 1967, Florence Rises from the Flood, *Natl. Geog.*, v. 132, pp. 1–43.

Leopold, L. B., 1962, Rivers, *Amer. Scientist*, v. 50, pp. 511–37.

Stall, J. B., 1966. Man's Role in Affecting Sedimentation of Streams and Reservoirs, pp. 79–95, in Bowder, K. L., ed., *Proceedings, 2nd Ann. Amer. Water Resources Cong.* 465 pp.

II. Mineral Resources and the Environment

The readings in Part One dealt with the geologic hazards that limit Man's use of the physical environment. They illustrate that there are environmental limits that function, or should function, as constraints on the activities of Man. Part Two deals with natural resources. Readings 22 to 26 focus on the limits of these resources. Readings 27 to 32 consider the environmental impact of Man's intensive exploitation of these resources.

Photo on page 210. Courtesy of John Ward. Illustration on page 212. Artist's rendering of sea production stations. Courtesy of Mobil Oil Corporation.

Outlook for
the Future

"All the water in the world is all the water there is."

Pliny the Elder described the earth as "gentle and indulgent, ever subservient to the wants of man." Today, however, we often express concern about the ability of the earth to provide sufficient materials, energy, and food. In Reading 22 Alvin Weinberg presents an optimistic view of the future but one that implies a drastically altered, energy-intensive world. Cheap nuclear power as an almost limitless energy source is the basis for his optimism. The cheap and almost limitless energy is applied to the desalination of sea water, the electrolytic reduction of metaliferous ores, and the development of a highly rationalized agro-industrial complex. While Weinberg recognizes the need for population control —a difficult social problem—he attempts to demonstrate how technology can be used to expand our resources.

Thomas S. Lovering challenges the concept of unlimited raw materials in Reading 23. While acknowledging the role of economics and technology in evaluating current and potential resources, he is careful to demonstrate that these are not the sole factors governing the availability of nonfuel mineral resources, noting that many economic-technologic assumptions are simply unwarranted. For example, the availability of inexhaustible cheap energy is debatable; the record also indicates that price increases do not always expand the base of our reserves and, finally, the theory of continuous variation from ore to the average crustal rock cannot be applied to many critical metals. He expresses grave concern over potential mineral shortages and lack of preparations to cope with diminished supplies and increasing demands.

T. S. Lovering and others have noted the need for more realistic inventories of our natural resources. Attempts at inventorying our water resources, offshore petroleum reserves, and organic-rich shales are presented in Readings 24, 25, and 26. These readings represent "credible first approximations" and are instructive in indicating how to deal with limited data in the development of an inventory. The reader should question the adequacy of the data, their application to larger areas, and other fundamental assumptions presented in the readings. It is important to keep in mind that an inventory is dynamic; the process of information-gathering never ends.

A. M. Piper (Reading 24) includes estimates and projections— to the year 2000—of the water supplies and demands of the major drainage basins of the United States. Geographic variations in hydrology are great and frequently match neither present nor prospective patterns of water use. Some basins obviously face a gloomy future while others have supplies which exceed projected demands. Piper stresses the need for more sophisticated data and prudent and rational management of the nation's water resources if we are to avoid disruptions to the economic and social development of many areas. Time in which to accomplish efficient management is all too short and no single course of action is seen as a panacea for all water-supply problems.

The U. S. Bureau of Mines estimates that energy consumption in the United States reached 6.9×10^{16} British thermal units in 1971—a record high and a 2.3 per cent increase over 1970. Petroleum supplied 44 per cent of all domestic energy needs, natural gas (33 per cent), followed by coal (18.3 per cent), water power (4.1 per cent), and nuclear power (0.6 per cent). The rate of energy consumption seems destined to accelerate. If hydrocarbons are to continue to supply the bulk of our energy needs in the near future, we will have to exploit every conceivable occurrence.

In 1947 Keer-McGee brought in the first major offshore oil strike. Since then, offshore petroleum production has increased to the point where it now accounts for 18 per cent of the world's total production. It is estimated that offshore production will account for one-third of the world's total by 1980, and will rise to one-half of the world's total during the 1980's.

Lewis Weeks examines the potential hydrocarbon resources under the seas and concludes that 57 per cent of the acreage included in the continental shelf and outer slope (10,763,000 square miles) is potentially productive. The estimated petroleum reserves in this acreage amount to approximately 700 billion barrels of oil. His assessment of the subsea hydrocarbon resources is based on the geologic factors that control the accumulation of oil and on the exploration and exploitation experience of the petroleum industry under similar geologic conditions. This experience is worldwide and includes thousands of instances. Until Man begins to desalinate sea water on an expanded scale, the hydrocarbon resources will be the most important of the seas' mineral resources.

Although organic-rich shale has been used as a solid fuel and a source of oil for more than 125 years, total world production has been about only 400 million barrels of oil. The small production has not been due to a lack of adequate resources. In Reading 26 Donald Duncan and Vernon Swanson estimate that the world's organic-rich shales hold an equivalent of 2 quadrillion barrels of oil—an energy potential of 24,000 Q (10^{18} Btu)! Of the total resources, 190 billion barrels of oil equivalent are recoverable under approximately present conditions. World resources are estimated statistically; in some cases the estimates are based on a number of critical assumptions. The largest single deposit is the Green River Formation of Colorado, Utah, and Wyoming. Though the reserves are staggering, they have not attracted large-scale exploration and exploitation in the face of competition from conventional sources of fossil fuels.

22   Raw Materials Unlimited
Alvin M. Weinberg

Weinberg, A. M., 1968, "Raw Materials Unlimited," *Texas Quarterly*, vol. 11, no. 2. Reprinted with light editing by permission of the author and the publisher.
Mr. Weinberg is the director of the Oak Ridge National Laboratory, Oak Ridge, Tennessee.

A technologist like me is confused by the difference in attitude toward the world's resources displayed on the one hand by economists, and on the other hand by many demographers and geologists. One would expect the economists to be pessimists since their distinguished predecessor David Ricardo was such a pessimist. It was he who predicted that we would always have to extract raw materials from ever-poorer natural resources; even if we controlled our population, we would have to pay more and more for our basic raw materials and therefore our economic situation would inevitably decline. Yet economists, when asked about the future, tend to be very jaunty: technology will more than keep pace with the depletion of natural resources. This view is best summarized by Harold Barnett, professor of economics from Washington University, in an article "The Myth of Our Vanishing Resources" (*Trans-Action* 4, 6–10. June 1967). Barnett starts by quoting Keynes, "The ideas of economists and political philosophers, both when they are right and when they are wrong, are more powerful than is commonly understood." He then goes on to say that the idea that our natural resources are vanishing is just a myth. For example, although the demand for minerals between 1870 and 1957 increased about fortyfold, the cost of a unit of minerals decreased to a level only one-fifth as large as it was in 1870. The yearly decline in the unit cost of minerals up to World War I was about 1 per cent per year and in the period from 1919 to 1957 about 3 per cent per year.

The key to Professor Barnett's optimism is energy. This is asserted by the geologist Dean F. Frasché in a National Academy report on natural resources where he speaks of the connection between energy and minerals: "The extraction of mineral raw materials from low-grade rock is a problem in the application of energy—at a price." (*Mineral Resources*, A Report to the Committee on Natural Resources, National Academy of Sciences, Publication 1000-C, p. 18. December 1962.) "Total exhaustion of any mineral resource will never occur: Minerals and rocks that are unexploited will always remain in the earth's crust. The basic problem is how to avoid reaching a point where the cost of exploiting those mineral deposits which remain will be so costly, because of depth, size, or grade, that we cannot produce what we need without completely disrupting our social and economic structures." This is indeed the problem: we can always get iron at a cost; we can always get aluminum at a cost. What we really are concerned with is that the costs of these basic raw materials do not rise so precipitously that a segment of the economy which now represents say 2 per cent of our total expenditure jumps to 20 or 30 per cent. If jumps of that order occur, the living standard of the society will deteriorate seriously. And, according to Frasché, the key to maintaining our mineral and other resources at a reasonable price is cheap, inexhaustible energy. As long as we can get energy at a very low price, we can get other natural resources economically: in short, cheap energy ultimately would provide the technological basis for Professor Barnett's lack of concern about the future.

In sharp contrast to this view is the alarmingly pessimistic view held, by and large, by demographers. Their argument is simple: if you don't finally limit the population, then Malthus will finally be proved right. With this view, again, one cannot quarrel. Of course, the population eventually will have to level off if we are not to sink to an animal-like existence.

How many people can the earth ultimately support at a level of comfort that would be considered acceptable? Is the present population already too large as some insist; or is seven billion, the figure suggested by others, too large; or the extraordinary estimate of Professor Richard Meier, University of California, Berkeley, of between thirty-five and fifty billion by the twenty-second century? With fifty billion people the entire world will be one vast city. Could we survive in a totally urbanized world? Obviously life would be very different from what it is today, and, to our mind, very much less worth living.

I shall present a rather optimistic point of view about these huge questions. Yet I want to make clear that nothing I say implies opposition to attempts to keep the population of the earth at some manageable level. The burden of my remarks is that technology may prove the optimists—that is the economists and the technologists —right in the short run; but of course, the demographers and the geologists— in short, the pessimists—are right in the long run unless we act most urgently to control population.

Why does an old-time nuclear scientist like me find ground for optimism in the face of the unmitigated pessimism expressed by the Paddocks in their book *Famine—1975!* (William and Paul Paddock, *Famine—1975!*, Little, Brown and Co., Boston 1967)? It is because of four major technological advances: cheap nuclear energy, cheap desalination, high-yielding grains, and cheap electrolytic hydrogen which, when taken together, provide the means for forestalling the Malthusian catastrophe at least for a while. I shall describe where we stand in each of these technologies, and shall show how they can be used, in principle, to expand our resources of minerals and of foods. Whether in fact they will be used is a difficult social question that I am unable to deal with.

Nuclear Energy

First, I mention the major breakthrough in the cost of nuclear power. The dimensions of this breakthrough are so massive as to have caught the nuclear power people themselves by surprise. For the past twenty years people said that nuclear power was going to be competitive ten years from today (and it really didn't make any difference when today was, it was always ten years hence). Then, in 1962, the General Electric Company executed a firm price bid with the Jersey Central Power & Light Company for a 515 megawatt boiling water reactor, the famous Oyster Creek reactor, at a capital cost of around $130 per kilowatt—lower than the capital cost for conventional plants of the same size. This was the signal for the rush to nuclear power, and in the past year rather better than half of all of the new central generating plants that have been ordered by the utilities, are nuclear. There are now fifty million kilowatts of electrical capacity in operation, on order, or under construction in the United States, and with an additional ten million kilowatts planned it seems that there is little sign of this activity abating. The costs are a little hard to judge at the moment; the most detailed analysis of the cost of nuclear power was given by TVA, in connection with its Browns Ferry Plant. The estimated energy generating costs for the Browns Ferry reactors is about 2.37 mills per kilowatt hour. This is lower than would be the corresponding costs for a privately owned utility, since the fixed charges in the TVA system are around 6 per cent as compared to the 12 per cent charges for a private utility. If the TVA fixed charges were at 12 per cent, their costs would go up to perhaps 3.3 mills per kilowatt hour.

Since Browns Ferry the price of nuclear reactors has gone up. But it seems very likely that very large boiling or pressurized water reactors will be available for about $125.00 to $135.00 per kilowatt; though this is somewhat higher than the price of coal-fired plants, the over-all cost of energy from the current generation of water reactors should still be competitive with energy from fossil fuel costing around 22¢ per million British thermal units. This would mean that nuclear reactors will probably be used for at least 60 per cent of all new steam capacity in the United States during the next decade.

The reactors now being sold in the United States burn the rare isotope of uranium, U^{235}. The cost of the fuel cycle includes the cost of the U^{235} which is burned, the cost of refabricating unspent fuel, the fixed charges on the fuel held in inventory, and the insurance on fuel. These fuel cycle costs now total about 1.5 mills per kilowatt hour, with an expectation that for the first twelve years of operation of reactors like Browns Ferry the fuel cycle might average only 1.2 mills per kilowatt hour. This corresponds to fossil fuel at about 15¢ per million British

thermal units. Of course the higher capital cost of the nuclear plant diminishes the advantage nuclear fuel enjoys over fossil fuel.

There are many of us who believe that the cost of nuclear energy ought to fall significantly below the figure that I have quoted. First, with respect to capital costs, one might ask why was it that despite all the very gloomy predictions which became quite fashionable about nuclear energy in the late forties and early fifties the General Electric Company offered a reactor at a capital cost that was quite competitive with the capital cost for a fossil fuel plant? The main reason really was that the early thinkers about the nuclear energy business were thinking about much smaller reactors than the ones that are now being built. For example, in 1947 the economists Walter Isard and Vincent Whitney ("Atomic Power and the Location of Industry," *Harvard Business Review 28*, 45–54 [March 1950]; see also Isard and Whitney, "Atomic Power and Economic Development," *Bulletin of the Atomic Scientists 5*, 73–78 [March 1949]) made the flat statement that nuclear energy would never become competitive with fossil fuel, and particularly the capital costs of nuclear plants would always exceed those of fossile fueled plants. Their error was in thinking too small. To these economists, 75 megawatts was a very big plant, and 200 megawatts was about as large as their imagination could visualize. Yet now we are constructing many reactors with capacities of more than a million kilowatts. There is no basic reason, at least for some types of reactors, why individual reactors should not produce 2,000 megawatts or even

3,000 megawatts of electricity. Now devices of this sort scale rather favorably; the larger the reactor, the smaller the price per kilowatt. Moreover, as the energy demands of society increase, the unit size of each energy producing device can also be expected to increase.

There are several other reasons why some experts believe that the costs of very large nuclear power plants ought eventually to be less than a hundred dollars per kilowatt. For example, I mention the possibility of generating electricity at 400 cycles rather than at 60 cycles. A 400 cycle generator is only about a sixth as large as a 60 cycle generator, and therefore the higher frequency generator should be much cheaper. Of course, higher frequency is unusable if the reactor is tied in with a 60 cycle system; however, if the energy is used on the spot, say for chemical processing, or is transmitted by direct current, the frequency of generation is unimportant.

But we cannot achieve really cheap energy, unless we can significantly lower the fuel cycle cost, which in the present generation of reactors is rather higher than 1 mill per kilowatt hour. The reason it is this high is because the U^{235} burned in the reactors is a rather expensive fuel. One gram of separated U^{235} costs about $10.00 and, when converted to electricity at 45 per cent thermal efficiency, contributes about 1 mill per kilowatt to the cost of the fuel cycle. But, in breeder reactors the fuel is the much cheaper and abundant U^{238} or Th^{232}. At $8.00 per pound, a gram of U^{238} or Th^{232} costs about 2¢. Thus the intrinsic cost of the fuel in a breeder reactor is only one five-hundredth the cost of the fuel in the current "burner" reactors.

Even if the cost of uranium or thorium increased tenfold, as would happen when we deplete our rich reserves, the intrinsic cost of the fuel is negligible—about .03 mill per kilowatt hour. And it is on this account that some of us believe we see the possibility of getting energy at extremely low cost, possibly as low as 1.5 mills or even 1 mill per kilowatt hour for the entire cost. Moreover, once we achieve reactors that burn sizeable parts of the uranium and thorium instead of just the rare U^{235}, we have an essentially inexhaustible energy source. I don't have to tell geologists that there is only a certain amount of uranium at $8.00 per pound; but if one goes to $80.00 or even $200.00 per pound then the amount of uranium that one can extract from the earth increases vastly. But the intrinsic cost of the fuel even at $100.00 per pound is still so small that we must consider rocks containing uranium and thorium at such low concentrations perfectly useable as fuel. At $80.00 per pound, there must be vast amounts of thorium and uranium in the earth's crust. For example, John Adams from Rice University, a few years ago showed that the Conway granites contain about thirty million tons of thorium available at around $40.00 per pound.

Even if we make rather extravagant estimates of how much energy we shall need in the future, the thorium in the Conway granite alone, the thirty million tons, is almost surely enough to keep society in adequate energy resources for something like a thousand years. If one goes to $120.00-per-pound granites, it is a little foolish to ask how long this energy resource would last. It will undoubtedly supply our energy for millions and millions of years, provided we develop a breeder reactor that burns the abundant isotope U^{238} and thorium.

Where do we stand in the development of breeder reactors? Several experimental "fast" breeder reactors based on the U^{238} plutonium cycle are now operating. There have been three such reactors in the United States; there is one in England; there is one in France; and there is one in the Soviet Union. These reactors represent a rather difficult technology because the reactors are very compact and they have to be cooled with sodium. The sort of difficulty that has been encountered is illustrated by the Fermi reactor near Detroit. An inadvertent blockage of one of the channels caused a fuel element to melt. As a result, the reactor has been sitting idle for the last year while technicians tried to fish out the damaged fuel element. Still, the Russians and the British are taking a very aggressive and optimistic attitude toward fast breeders: the British have started to build a 250 megawatt fast breeder reactor, and the Russians are planning two fast breeder reactors, one at 250 megawatts electric, another at 600 megawatts electric.

Although the fast breeder reactor represents the main line of breeder development, there is another, to my mind more attractive, possibility based on thorium. This reactor type uses molten fluoride salts as its fuel. In the molten salt breeder a mixture of molten uranium fluoride, thorium fluoride, lithium fluoride, and beryllium fluoride circulates through a graphite matrix. The salt enters the graphite at about 1150° F. and emerges at about 1300° F. It gives its heat up to raise steam that operates a turbine. The great advantage of the molten salt system is that the uranium and thorium are always in liquid form, and thus the newly bred uranium can be extracted from the reactor relatively simply. We have been running a small molten salt reactor very successfully at the Oak Ridge National Laboratory for more than two years. At the moment we are trying to get money to build a larger version of the reactor.

To summarize, then, with respect to nuclear power itself, I am highly optimistic, especially about the molten salt breeders. One must take seriously the probability that inexhaustible, and ubiquitous energy at between 1 and 2 mills per kilowatt hour will be available within, say, fifteen years.

Desalination

The situation with respect to desalting the sea, using nuclear or other energy sources, can be summarized about like this. The thermodynamic minimum amount of energy required to desalt a thousand gallons of sea water is about three kilowatt hours. At two mills per kilowatt hour the energy cost would be 6¢ per thousand gallons, and this, of course, is the theoretical minimum cost to get fresh water from the sea. Since all real desalting plants operate irreversibly, the actual cost of desalted water is greater than the theoretical minimum. To approach the thermodynamic minimum, the distillation plants require an infinite number of stages. An infinite number of stages would cost an infinite amount, so one in practice must use more energy to save on the number of stages. If nuclear energy costs as little as I have suggested, and in particular, if we combine the desalting plant with an electrical plant so that the steam to energize the still is merely waste from the exhaust of the turbine, then our economic optimum will be a very cheap still utilizing very few stages. Moreover, there are new advances in heat transfer technology which ought further to lower capital costs of large sea water stills. We now have designs on the drawing board which suggest that even with present day reactors, desalted water might cost as little as 15¢ per thousand gallons, as compared with the 22–25¢ per thousand gallons expected at the new Metropolitan Water District Plant in Los Angeles. Many of us believe that when advanced breeders become available this cost will go down to perhaps less than 10¢ per thousand gallons.

The New Grains

The third major development may possibly be the most important technological development of the century, but it is one that has received very little attention. I refer to the extraordinary development, largely under the aegis of the Rockefeller Foundation, of the new high-yielding grain crops. These new varieties of corn and wheat have converted Mexico from an importer of grain to an exporter of grain. The new wheats, developed jointly by Rockefeller and the Mexican government, are particularly important because they do so well in the environment of West Pakistan and in the Ganges basin of India. In West Pakistan just six or eight years ago the population was going up, and the food per capita was going down; now the two are coming very much closer together. And the

Rockefeller people are optimistic about what can be done in introducing these varieties into India. Last year a half million acres in India were planted in Mexican wheat; this year about six million acres are expected to be so planted. Since the yields of these varieties are three times that of the older types, the over-all increase in output should be very significant.

Can desalted sea water be used to raise these new grains at acceptable costs? Ordinarily about two thousand gallons of water are needed to supply the 2,400 calories for a man's daily food. Now if the water costs 15¢ per thousand gallons, then 2,000 gallons would cost 30¢ per day—obviously too much for an underdeveloped country. But, if one assumes that the average yield demonstrated with the Mexican-Rockefeller Foundation wheat can be achieved and if one assumes that fertilizer and water are available when needed and that agriculture is conducted scientifically, then it appears that only 200 gallons of water would be needed per person per day. This estimate was first put forward by Dr. R. Philip Hammond, originally from the Los Alamos Scientific Laboratory and now at Oak Ridge, and it has been verified by agricultural experts at the Rockefeller Foundation.

If one can achieve anything close to 200 gallons per day, then at 15¢ per 1000 gallons this comes to about 3¢ per day for the water needed to feed a person with a modest but adequate diet. This is in a range that is interesting for underdeveloped countries. The Rockefeller Foundation is sufficiently interested in this line of thinking that it is examining the possibility of trying out this new kind of highly rational desert agriculture based on distilled water. I hope that a pilot farm might be started within the next year or so in a coastal desert.

Cheap Electrolytic Hydrogen; Electrolytic Metals

The fourth development, a spin-off from space technology and from submarine technology, is to some extent still a gleam in peoples' eyes. I refer to the development of very high current electrodes for the electrolytic production of hydrogen. Ordinarily in electrolytic production of hydrogen, one assumes that the current density is 150 amperes per square foot. As a result of developments in fuel cell technology it is possible now to anticipate electrode densities of 1,500 amperes per square foot. If this technology is now scaled up to the large-scale production of hydrogen and if one then assumes that electrical energy is available at around 2 mills per kilowatt hour, one comes out with costs of hydrogen which are surprisingly interesting— about 21¢ per thousand standard cubic feet, assuming one sells the oxygen at $4.00 per ton. Now 21¢ per thousand standard cubic feet is not the cheapest hydrogen that one can get but neither is it the most expensive; some of our consultants tell us this is comparable to hydrogen from natural gas costing about 37¢ per million British thermal units. Moreover, since sea water is ubiquitous, we have in principle here a way of producing hydrogen, indefinitely, at a price that is quite acceptable even today.

Hydrogen is the universal reducing agent; insofar as much of extractive metallurgy requires reducing agents, the availability of cheap hydrogen extends our mineral resources. Thus hydrogen can be used instead of coke to produce iron. The Bethlehem Steel Company has a pilot plant near Los Angeles which produces about 40,000 tons per year of hydrogen iron. Professor Arthur Squires, a well-known chemical engineer, estimates if energy costs 2 mills per kilowatt hour, hydrogen iron competes with steel by the usual blast furnace process. Or to mention another possibility that involves electrolysis, magnesium can be used as a structural metal instead of aluminum. Can magnesium from sea water compete with aluminum? My impression is that it can: if, for example, we extract *anhydrous* magnesium chloride from sea water concentrates and then electrolyze the salt, the magnesium will be cheaper than aluminum; some estimates put the market for magnesium at perhaps 25 to 30 per cent of that for aluminum if anhydrous magnesium chloride can be won readily from sea water.

In my examples of electrolytic production of hydrogen, iron, and magnesium, I have given instances of how cheap electricity can be converted into basic materials. The elasticity of demand for electricity for energy-intensive processes ought to be very high: that is, with power available at, say, 2 mills per kilowatt hour, many more industrial processes will be performed electrically than when power costs 3 mills per kilowatt hour. If we were to plot the cumulative number of industrial processes performed electrically versus cost of electric power, we would get a curve such as Fig. 1 in which the number of industrial processes based on electricity increases sharply as the cost of energy decreases. If electricity delivered to the plant were really cost-less, we probably would reduce iron electrolytically, hydrogenate coal to make liquid fuel, gasify coal with electric heat, etc. etc. In other words, the incentive toward extremely low-cost power is not simply that we would thereby save on processes that already use electricity. It is rather that we would choose to perform many industrial processes in an energy-intensive manner: we would substitute energy for raw materials such as coke, or natural gas, or high quality ores whose geographic distribution is uneven and capricious.

It is for this reason that I consider the achievement of very low-cost energy through the molten salt breeder reactor to be a matter of the highest urgency. It is not merely that with the molten salt breeder reactor we shall have a practically infinite source of energy, nor that we believe it will be cheaper than the non-breeder. It is rather that, because of the aforementioned elasticity of demand for electrical energy, the very cheap nuclear energy source could become the basis for a new kind of industrial development in which energy-intensive processes replace raw material-intensive processes.

The Agro-Industrial Complex

Can we combine cheap energy, relatively cheap desalting, highly rationalized agriculture, and production of hydrogen and other energy-intensive industrial materials into economically viable agricultural and industrial complexes in which the basic raw material is electrical energy rather than coal or petro-chemicals? At Oak Ridge we have studied such nuclear powered agro-industrial complexes. An example is summarized in Table 1.

The complex centers around two reactors producing 2,000 megawatts of

Table 1 Agro-industrial complex, light water reactors

Electric capacity	2,000 Mwe
Water capacity	500,000,000 gals/day
Investment	
Reactor	$160,000,000
Turbogenerator	135,000,000
Water plant	240,000,000
Industrial complex	230,000,000
Food factory	110,000,000
Town	20,000,000
Electric grid	5,000,000
	$900,000,000
Number of Workers	8,200
Annual Value of Products	
Industrial Products	$230,000,000
Agriculture	100,000,000
	$330,000,000
Annual operating expense	$194,000,000
Income less expense	$136,000,000
Annual return on investment	15%

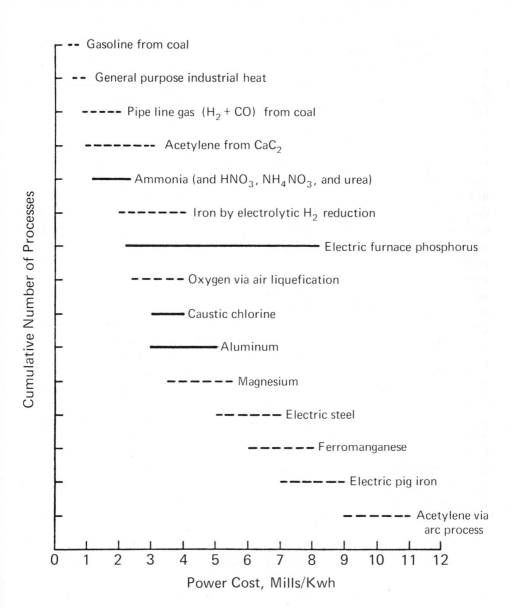

FIG. 1. Elasticity of the demand for power.

electricity and a distillation plant producing 500 million gallons of water per day. Included in this complex is land under intensive cultivation based on distilled water. The agriculture is so highly rationalized that we prefer to use the words "food factory" rather than farm. Fertilizer is applied exactly at the right time, the water requirements of the plants are continuously monitored, and so on. This particular complex produces ammonia, electro-refines phosphorus, produces caustic chlorine, and salt. We have looked at a variety of cases; the one summarized in the table costs perhaps $900,000,000 to build, and its annual income is about 15 percent of the investment. The food factory would occupy 180,000 acres and would produce enough food to feed perhaps two and one half to three million people.

The idea of a nuclear powered agro-industrial complex has received a good deal of attention. Recently a team of a half dozen people from Oak Ridge visited India to talk with their counterparts there and determine the extent to which massive technological packages of this sort might make some dent on the bitter problems facing India. I would like to close therefore by describing a variant of this scheme which I hope we shall hear a great deal more about in the next few years. The President's Science Advisory Commitee last year, in its report on world food problems (*The World Food Problem*, A Report of the President's Science Advisory Committee, U. S. Government Printing Office, Washington, D. C., May 1967), suggested that probably there are large amounts of ground water in the Gangetic Plains of India and that in the Indian climate this ground water can possibly be used to irrigate crops in the dry season. About the same time, a distinguished agricultural scientist, Professor Perry R. Stout of the University of California, Davis, while visiting Uttar Pradesh in India, was struck by the similarity between the topography, geology, and soil in this area and that in the San Joaquin Valley in California. The flourishing agriculture of the San Joaquin Valley is based on pumping ground

water for irrigation. At present the agriculture in Uttar Pradesh is confined to the monsoon season, which lasts about four months during the year. If, however, a hundred thousand tube wells, each about twenty feet deep and each powered by about a five horsepower motor, could be dug, then one would be able to irrigate something like five million acres, and the water would be available for two crops and, if one is lucky, three crops could be produced here, because the climate is so equable. Moreover, if the new varieties of wheat I mentioned earlier were now introduced and if there were available sufficient ammonia fertilizer, Stout estimates that within ten years of the onset of such a project the yield of wheat in this area could be increased not by 10 per cent, not by 30 per cent, but by factors between four and ten. Now what are the problems? Well, I will skip the social problems because I'm sure that these will come out in discussion, but the first problem is the hydrology of the area. The hydrology has not really been studied, and one does not really know that all that ground water is there. But most geologists think that there is probably plenty of ground water. At least there are right now in this area about nine thousand tube wells, generally run by oxen or by diesels. At any rate, the monsoon rainwater has to go somewhere, and it is Perry Stout's belief that the ground water is being replenished each year. The second problem is electrical energy to power the tube wells and to produce the ammonia. Stout, therefore, proposes that a million kilowatts of electricity be installed. It doesn't have to be nuclear; there is coal about six hundred miles away in this area. If the Uttar Pradesh project is successful here, Stout proposes extending the project to a million tube wells. The total cost of this entire one million tube well project with the required energy sources and distribution system would be ten billion dollars. But the return would be extraordinary. Stout estimates that the extended project could convert India from an importer of $800,000,000 worth of food each year to an exporter of food!

Let me close in the following vein: I don't want anybody to misunderstand; I am not saying that these technological gimmicks based on energy should substitute for aggressive direct attacks on the population problem. But, on the other hand, I reject the attitude expressed in the book *Famine—1975!*—an attitude that pre-empts the future by saying that nothing can be done about the future of India. Ten billion dollars for the Stout Plan spent over five years in India is not all that big a sum of money. Though one million tube wells seem excessive, in West Pakistan alone in the last two years, forty thousand tube wells have been drilled. These wells have been drilled not by people just saying we have to drill forty thousand tube wells, but rather, by the farmers themselves. The Paddocks and other soothsayers of doom to the contrary notwithstanding, these farmers are not dumb, they're smart; and when they see that they are going to get the fertilizer and that the irrigation is going to work, they will drill the tube wells. I leave you with this possibility. I stand accused of being an optimist, but if we were not to some extent optimistic, we would to this extent not be human.

23 Non-Fuel Mineral Resources in the Next Century

T. S. Lovering

The total volume of commercial mineral deposits is an insignificant fraction of 1 per cent of the earth's crust and each deposit represents some accident of geology in the remote past. It must be exploited where it occurs. Each has its limits, however, and if worked long enough must sooner or later be exhausted. No second crop will materialize; rich mineral deposits are a nation's

Lovering, T. S., 1968, "Non-Fuel Mineral Resources in the Next Century," *Texas Quarterly*, vol. 11, no. 2. Reprinted by permission of the author and the publisher.
Mr. Lovering is on the staff of the U. S. Geological Survey, Denver, Colorado.

most valuable but ephemeral possession—its quick assets. Continued extraction of ore leads to increasing costs as the material mined comes from greater and greater depths, but sometimes improved technology makes possible continuation or renewal of work in deposits that would otherwise have been shut down because of competition with deposits more favorably situated or where cost per unit of output was appreciably less.

Demand for mineral products comes chiefly from the chemical and manufacturing industries and from agriculture. The constant arrival of large quantities of raw materials is essential to maintaining output and continuing output is vital to a healthy industrial economy. An adequate supply is more easily assured if the mineral deposits are under domestic control and within the national boundaries of the country where they are to be consumed. The greater the dependence on foreign sources the greater the risk of industrial stress caused by foreign institutional action such as price rises due to cartel action, trade barriers set up by governments, or by adverse military action.

Satisfactory substitutes for most raw materials exist if the price of the substitute is not a consideration. Some minerals, however, have unique properties for which there is no satisfactory substitute and many others are essential to successful commercial competition in the world markets. The minerals that are currently most essential to civilization are probably coal, iron, copper, aluminum, petroleum, and the fertilizer minerals. Only a very few industrial countries have adequate internal sources of all these minerals to supply their current industrial needs and none have reserves adequate for the next century using foreseeable technology. Although it is possible in times of distress, when free access to world sources is cut off, to work deposits that otherwise are noncommercial, it must be remembered that low-grade deposits require much time and capital to develop. Economic chaos can result if foreign sources of supply are denied to a country that has allowed itself to become dependent on them. And dependent all industrial nations are, entirely or in large part, on foreign sources of supply for some or most of the essential metals demanded by their industries. This dependence grows ever greater with the years.

That sources of supply will inevitably shift is evident not only from the hard geological facts but also from a review of historical events. Three thousand years ago the Middle East was the center of the iron mining industry of the ancient world. For several hundred years ancient Greece was the center of lead and silver mining of the western civilized world. For a long time Germany was the leading producer of lead, zinc, and silver in medieval Europe, but Belgium became the chief producer of zinc at the beginning of the industrial era. In the nineteenth century Great Britain was successively the world's foremost producer of lead, of copper, of tin, of iron, of coal, and during that period she was the wealthiest nation in the world; from 1700 to 1850 the United Kingdom mined 50 per cent of the world's lead, from 1820 to 1840 she produced 45 per cent of the world's copper, from 1850 to 1890 she increased her iron production from one-third to one-half of the entire world output. At the turn of the century, Russia was the leading producer of petroleum in the world and during the latter part of the nineteenth century she was the foremost gold producer—until the discovery of the great Transvaal gold deposits in South Africa. Most of the manganese ore mined until after the second World War, came from a comparatively small area in southern Russia. Now large new deposits in Africa, Australia, and Brazil threaten the dominance of the U.S.S.R. and have cut deeply into the manganese market.

Hewett (1929) made a penetrating

analysis of the normal history of mineral exploitation in a nation and recognized five stages between discovery and exhaustion. In the forty years since his study, exploitation of mineral resources has strengthened his conclusions that discovery is followed successively by flush production, proliferation of smelters, decline in production, cessation of export metal, growing dependence on imports, and ultimately complete dependence on imported metals.

Between 1905 and 1938 more metal was produced than had been consumed in the entire history of the world prior to 1905; a similar amount of metal was produced and consumed in a far shorter interval after the start of World War II. In the meanwhile the world population has more than doubled so that per capita consumption has not increased appreciably even in industrial countries. The reserves of known and undiscovered ore deposits of commercial grade are finite and diminishing, whereas the demand for metals is growing at an exponential rate; it is clear that exhaustion of deposits of currently commercial grade is inevitable. The cost of mining deposits of lower grade involves increased costs for capital, labor, energy, and transportation; decreased costs of energy from the ultimate development of breeder reactors will only cut energy costs a relatively small amount because their major cost is that of invested capital.

It would seem that grave concern may be justified over mineral supplies during the lifetime of those now living. There is, however, an optimism among mineral economists now (1968) that may be shortsighted. Future mineral resources depend on the cost of

supplying market places, and this in turn is a function of relative locations, cost per unit of mine output, market price, the market location, and any institutional incentives or restrictions placed on operations. The current but questionable assumptions of the majority of mineral economists as given in The Paley Report, the book *Scarcity and Growth* (Barnett and Chandler, 1963) and *Natural Resources for U. S. Growth* (Landsberg, 1964) may be summarized as follows:

1. Technology for the past fifty years has steadily made increasing amounts of raw material available at lower costs per unit and, therefore, will continue to do so into the "foreseeable future";

2. As the grade of a mineral deposit decreases arithmetically the reserves increase geometrically;

3. Non-renewable resources are therefore inexhaustible;

4. Scarcity can always be prevented by a rise in price of the raw materials and

5. Since the cost of raw materials is only a fraction of the final cost, a material rise in price for any raw material will have an insignificant effect on the price of manufactured items and on the general economy;

6. Any industrial nation will have adequate access to deposits throughout the world;

7. There will be only insignificant institutional restraints on access;

8. The United States and other industrial nations must have an "ever-expanding economy"—the GNP (Gross National Product) increasing continuously at an annual rate of about 4 per cent because their economic well-being requires it;

9. The population of western industrial nations will continue to increase at a rate of about 1.5 per cent per year for several generations; and finally,

10. The under-developed nations will achieve a per capita income comparable to that currently enjoyed by the United States within one or two generations.

All these assumptions are debatable; some are based more on rhetoric than reason, some seem a sort of struthionic optimism unrelated to physical factors, some are simply wrong. If accepted as guides to future policy they may lead to a lethal complacency as to natural resources.

The basic assumptions underlying the current optimism concerning the adequacy of mineral resources stems in large part from Lasky's classic paper (Lasky, 1948, 1950) in which he analyzed the relations between grade and reserves of ore in eight copper porphyries of the Southwest. The optimism generated by the current interpretation of Lasky's work has been greatly increased by Barnett and Morris (1963) whose book *Scarcity and Growth* and summary article "The Myth of Our Vanishing Resources" (Barnett, 1967) formulate clearly, specifically, and persuasively the basic position and the happy philosophy of most mineral economists. They reformulate the Ricardian hypothesis of scarcity as follows (p. 249): "The character of the resource base presents man with a never ending stream of problems;—that man will face a series of particular scarcities as the result of growth, is a foregone conclusion; that these problems will impose general scarcity as shown by increasing costs per unit output is not a legitimate

corollary." According to them (p. 230), "technological progress is automatic and self-reproducing in modern economies." They state that "natural resource building blocks are now to a large extent atoms and molecules . . . units of mass and energy, and the problem thus is one of manipulating the available stores of iron, magnesium, aluminum, carbon, and oxygen atoms— even electrons—so that we obtain those resources required by industry." The exuberant optimism reflected in such a belief leads Barnett and Morris to conclude: "The progress of growth generates antidotes to a general increase in resource scarcity" (p. 290), and to believe also that the sea is a continually augmenting store of resource of all kinds, ready at hand to supply man bountifully for all future time. Barnett and Morris state (p. 249) that principles "that have clear relevance in a Ricardian world where today's depletion curtails tomorrow's production, have little if any relevance in a progressive world." This will be heartening news to all mine owners!

Barnett and Morris looked at the net decrease in unit costs for the mineral industry and certain specific mineral commodities over a period of some seventy-five years and concluded that the improvement in efficiency caused by improved technology had resulted in a continuing net decrease in the cost per unit of mineral extracted; furthermore, that this increased efficiency would continue into the indefinite future. Within the mineral industry, the increased mechanization that accompanied the increased production of coal and oil, resulted in current costs of one-third to one-fourth those of 1920; this Barnett interprets as showing the opposite of increased scarcity or the lessening of economic quality. The curves for lead and zinc, however, show no such change and rather an increase during this period. For copper and for iron, the trend towards lower unit cost flattens greatly between 1940 and 1960 and as shown in their graph for timber, the trend for many years has been the opposite of that which Barnett postulates for minerals. Conservationists, who are unduly belabored by Barnett (1967) might make something of this!

Changing costs in mineral extraction reflect the relative efficiency of operation as opposed to the increasing costs of capital, labor, and energy. The efficiency in operations must approach an irreducible minimum as maximum mechanization is achieved; it would require major innovations not yet in sight to start another marked downward slope in the curve representing price times grade. The present trend of the ratio of copper grade to price (in constant dollars) is not encouraging (Fig. 1) but the discovery rate is.

Lasky's analysis of the relation of reserves to tonnage and average grade of ore produced in copper porphyries (Lasky, 1950) resulted in his stating the principle that is now known as the "arithmetic-geometric ratio" (or simply

FIG. 1.

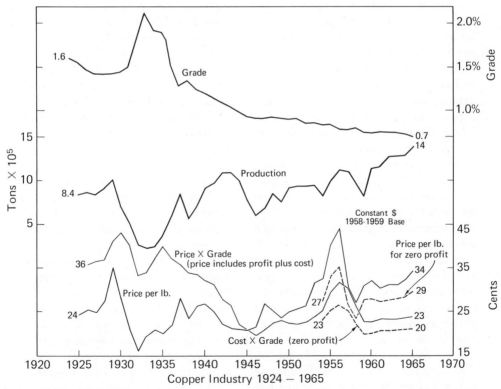

Copper Industry 1924 – 1965

Source: U.S. Bur. Mines Statistics

Outlook for the Future

the A/G ratio): The reserves of ore increase geometrically as the average grade mined decreases arithmetically, or as Lasky (1951) expressed it

Grade = $K_1 - K_2$ log tonnage.

The problem of exhaustibility thus need cause no concern according to current (1967–68) economic philosophy because over a long period of time the decreased grade that is now mined, shows that reserves have increased or at least been maintained. The past half century refutes the gloomy forecasts made in 1912 which indicated that the United States would run out of many major resources long before now. From this unequivocal fact, some very dubious deductions stem.

In referring to his equation and the curve it generates, Lasky (1948) said, "It fits the porphyry coppers . . . and apparently also other deposits of similar type in which small quantities of ore minerals are scattered through great volumes of shattered rock." According to Lasky then, "It may be stated as a general principle that in many mineral deposits in which there is a gradation from relatively rich to relatively lean material, the tonnage increases at a constant geometric rate as the grade decreases." A typical curve for a porphyry copper plots as a straight line on semi-logarithmic paper for which the decrements in grade are represented by the arithmetically spaced vertical lines and the increments in tonnage are scaled by logarithmic ordinate lines. The straight line plot represents the cumulative production or tonnage of a porphyry copper for decreasing average grade of the *total tonnage extracted* as ever leaner ore is mined. *This constraint is a very important one* —but has apparently been misunder-

stood by many economists who use this analysis as a springboard from which to leap into a sea of optimism.

Lasky averaged the characteristics of the eight major porphyry copper deposits in the United States (as of 1950) and notes that for such an average deposit, there would be somewhat more than 600 million tons of ore averaging about 0.6 per cent of copper when it had been *mined out—down to and including "zero cut-off grade."* In this average deposit, the tonnage increases at a rate of about 18 per cent for each unit decrease in grade of 0.1 per cent. Most of the copper is contained in the 175 million tons having a copper content between 0.5 and 0.9 per cent. Lasky's analysis is a major contribution to our concepts of grade and tonnage for the type of deposit that he considers. It should be noted, however, that the curves rigidly defined the situation over a range of grade of about 1.5 per cent, but that even for porphyry coppers they cannot express the relations for higher grades of ore and for the very lean rocks which should be represented by the extensions of the curve to the left and to the right respectively. For his average copper porphyry deposit which contains sixty million tons of ore averaging 2 per cent copper and six hundred million tons of ore averaging 0.6 per cent of copper, Lasky's mathematical expression is "Grade = $12.9 - 1.4$ log tonnage"; from this we deduce that Zero grade = $12.9 - 1.4 \times 9.2$ and as $9.2 =$ log (1.58×10^9) Zero grade is reached at 1.58×10^9 tons, *which is impossible!* The clarke (average abundance of an element) of many igneous rocks is 0.004 to 0.010 per cent copper; for Lasky's average porphyry copper deposit in question, an average grade of 0.3 per cent copper corresponds to a tonnage of one billion tons—not an unreasonable figure if the cut-off grade is held close to the average grade mined. Somewhere between a grade of a few tenths of a per cent and a hundredth of a per cent, the tonnage must increase astronomically but there is no geologic reason why the curve should maintain its slope or change smoothly from the one calculated by Lasky's formula into the curve that might express the change in copper content of the various rock units found in the crust of the earth. It is more than likely that the cumulative curve would first flatten and then rise precipitously. At the other end of the curve, consider what happens for ore minerals. The formula shows a "tonnage" of one milligram of ore having a grade of 24.5 per cent copper or one ton (out of sixty million tons averaging 2 per cent copper) having a grade of 12.8 per cent copper. It is obvious that the curve generated by the Lasky formula departs widely from reality between 0.01 per cent and 0.3 per cent on the one side and for any masses of ore containing substantial amounts of the common copper ore minerals.

Most ores are deposited over an appreciable time interval by complex processes. The large mass of mineralized intensely fractured rock that marks deposits of the porphyry copper type does have its limits, and beyond these limits the metal content drops off sharply. Most such bodies show a history of repeated fracturing and mineralization; in some several stages of metallization are present, in others only one stage of metallization but several stages of barren alteration may

be represented. Where the fractured rock has been enriched by successive waves of metallizing solutions, each wave is apt to be localized in somewhat restricted masses of refractured rock; these localized blocks of better ore result in a stepwise change in grade for the deposit as a whole, but such a change is not reflected in the product of mining which represents a predetermined mixture. Where a very low grade protore—less than 0.10 Cu —has been enriched by weathering processes, a shallow mass of ore may carry ten times as much metal as the protore. In such porphyry copper deposits there is an abrupt transition from ore grade to unmineable rock. Any attempt to use an A/G curve for them is obviously absurd. Lowering the grade by decrements of 0.10 per cent would increase the total tonnages of ore by only a small fraction until the grade of the protore was reached, when an enormous increase might take place in reserves of protore, though not necessarily in total tonnage of contained copper.

Even though the porphyry copper type deposits share many characteristics in common, each individual deposit is unique. It is clear that generalizations based on a few biased samples will not apply to the entire population; the extension of these generalizations to deposits of entirely different origin and geologic habitat is not only unwarranted, unscientific, and illogical, it is also downright dangerous in its psychological effects.

In his cautious first statement of the problem, Lasky says that the curve generated by his equation is meaningful for many types of deposits, but he adds the proviso "the geological evidence permitting." It is this reservation that has been neglected. There is absolutely no geological reason for concluding that the so-called arithmetic-geometric ratio holds for ore deposits in general. Most especially is it an error to believe there must be undiscovered low grade deposits of astronomical tonnage to bridge the gap between known commercial ore and the millions of cubic miles of crustal rocks that have measurable trace amounts of the various metals in them. The closer the mineable grade approaches the clarke of an element for major rocks, the more probable is the existence of an exponential ratio of tonnage to grades far below that of commercial ore.

The geologic processes that operate to give us mineable ores include huge tonnages provided by *sedimentation*; this process will cause dilution as well as concentration in detrital deposits and there are, of course, far larger volumes of sediments containing metals in the parts per million range—except for iron, aluminum, and magnesium—than there are that contain ore metals in per cent amounts. In sedimentary rocks, however, the A/G ratio may well hold far down towards the clarke of certain metals. The areas where the greatest concentrations of a mineral occur in sedimentary precipitates, whether by evaporation, inorganic chemical reactions, or biogenic activity, are much more limited in time and space than in precipitation areas of less intense chemical selectivity contaminated both by other precipitates and by detrital components. A special kind of mechanical precipitates would include some magmatic segregations where a desired mineral constituent

has concentrated in a liquid magma as an igneous sediment at high temperatures. Many ores of this type show abrupt gradations and others show gradual changes in concentration, especially when followed along the layers that contain the segregation itself. For some segregation deposits the A/G ratio will hold through a tenfold change in grade, but for many segregations, there is an abrupt change from ore deposit to barren rock.

Both for igneous segregations and for precipitates from aqueous solutions in fractured or chemically reactive rocks such as limestone and dolomite, there is no geologic reason to expect geometric increase in tonnage with decrease in grade beyond certain well defined limits which vary not only with type of deposits but with the individual deposit considered. Nearly all these deposits have an outer margin of mineralization controlled by igneous contacts or by fractures or by hostrock where the grade decreases sharply.

Fracture controlled deposits range from those with abrupt transitions between high and low grade ores such as are found in the typical "fissure" veins characteristic of the western United States to the disseminated ores of the porphyry copper type where the A/G ratios have been established for changes in grade of approximately one order of magnitude. Ore deposits the majority of which do not show the A/G ratio would include those of mercury, gold, silver, tungsten, lead, zinc, antimony, beryllium, tantalum, niobium, and the rare earth elements.

Weathering, the precursor of sedimentation, may result in widespread gradational deposits derived from rock protores of huge tonnage; both residual enrichment through leaching, and secondary enrichment through precipitation of elements at depth form important ore bodies having large tonnages. Some of these deposits show abrupt changes in grade from worthless material to valuable ore, as in the upper part of most sulfide deposits; others show a gradual enrichment, as with many lateritic nickel ores.

In many important types of mineral deposits, all available evidence indicates a paucity of the low-grade material essential to the concept of the arithmetic-geometric ratios. For lead-zinc replacement deposits in carbonate rocks, this zone is commonly but a few feet wide, and limestone carrying 20 or 30 ppm may be within arm's reach of a huge ore body having a grade ten thousand times that of the countryrock (Morris and Lovering, 1952). Lowering the grade of a typical large high-grade lead manta ore body from 20 per cent to 10 per cent would not increase the total quantity of reserves greatly and lowering the grade from 10 per cent to 1 per cent would increase the reserves only as barren rock was added to the ore to bring its average down to the proposed low cut-off value.

Many other geologic types of ore deposits scattered over the surface of our planet have characteristics in common. Bonanza epithermal silver and gold ores are characterized by rich ores that commonly bottom at shallow depths and have relatively sharp boundaries with their wallrocks. Most mercury deposits and antimony deposits fall in this epithermal class. For the vast majority of such deposits there is little hope of a geometric increase in tonnage with arithmetic decrease in grade, but we should expect to find an exceptional deposit occasionally somewhere in the world that shows promise of a geometric (but finite) increase in ore reserves with decreasing grade.

Production of several of the metal vitamins essential to the life of industrial giants is concentrated in a few major deposits contained in very small areas of the world, but minor production may come from a large number of small intermittently worked deposits. Mercury belongs in this class. It is worthy of note that the clarke of mercury is 0.000,04 per cent or 400 ppb; this is four orders of magnitude less than in ore, which commonly contains from 0.2 to 0.5 per cent mercury. A similar range exists for other important industrial elements such as tungsten (clarke less than 2 ppm), tantalum, silver, tin, vanadium, molybdenum, and others. Several metals fall in an intermediate class between the iron-aluminum group and the mercury-tungsten group; these would include copper (ore grade approximately 0.4 to 0.8 per cent and having a clarke in basic igneous rocks of 87 ppm, although in some igneous rock it averages several hundred ppm, only an order of magnitude below the present cut-off grade in some porphyry coppers. Cobalt, nickel, and vanadium have similar abundance ratios of clarke to ore grades. Both zinc and lead approach this group but currently the ratio of ore grade to clarke is distinctly higher than in this latter trio.

It has been optimistically said (Brown, Bonner, and Weir, p. 91, 1957) that with the advent of cheap nuclear energy, common rock—granite—would become "ore" and supply unlimited quantities of all the metals needed by industry but even the breeder reactor is not expected to make energy costs appreciably less than current costs of cheap hydroelectric or geothermal power (2.5 mills per kilowatt hour). Surprisingly enough, many men unfamiliar with the mineral industry believe that the beneficent gods of Technology are about to open the cornucopia of granite and sea, flooding industry with any and all metals desired. Unfortunately cheap energy little reduces the total costs—chiefly made up of capital and labor—required for mining and processing rock. The enormous quantities of unusable waste produced for each unit of metal also are more easily disposed of on a blueprint than in the field.

The difference in physical and chemical form of the compounds containing the metals in common rock would require development of a new and complex technology to extract them, and the unit costs of labor and capital (and even cheap energy!) could be orders of magnitude above those of the present. For at least another century or so metals will come from ores that have metal concentrations well above the clarkes of metals in rocks, with only few exceptions such as that represented by the magnetic black sands concentrated in the U.S.S.R.

Even where the arithmetic-geometric ratio holds, each deposit will approach zero grade at a very finite tonnage. This does not mean that large tonnages of very low grade currently noncommercial copper-bearing rock will not be developed ultimately in the porphyry type copper deposits. Indeed, with a moderate increase in price and substantial decrease in grade, there would seem to be ample copper within the Western Hemisphere to supply the

needs of North America for at least another fifty years. Currently the outlook for adequate supplies of molybdenum also invites cautious optimism.

Few if any mining geologists see any reason to expect semi-infinite volumes of copper-bearing rock containing about 0.1 per cent copper; most especially they do not by analogy with porphyry type deposits assume any A/G increase in tonnage for ore bodies of the many other metals that are totally different in their geologic habitat and genesis. In spite of the excellent start on a continuing inventory of United States and world ore reserves made by the Geological Survey under Lasky's guidance and by the U. S. Bureau of Mines in the early fifties, far too little has been done in this field with geologic guidance since, and we desperately need such studies of a wide variety of ore deposits, guided by geologic insight and much field study.

Technology and Mineral Resources

It may be true that in the future technology and science will always provide answers to our problems but it is also true that much time, money, and effort will be required as grade diminishes, mineralogy changes, and entirely different types of deposits are exploited. The widespread belief that technology is continually lowering the unit costs while allowing us to work lower grade deposits is belied by the trends revealed in the copper industry as shown in Fig. 1. Here the continuing change in average grade of copper as mined is shown, ranging from a high of 2.12 per cent to the current low of about 0.70 per cent; the tonnage produced yearly shows a general upward trend as would be expected. Assuming that the price of copper represents the summation of costs plus profit and that the costs of capital, labor and energy comprise the total costs, it then follows that the product of grade times price should give us an index representing the contribution of technology in lowering the cost per unit produced. The three-year moving average of this "grade times price" is shown in the same illustration and exhibits the expected sharp down slope from the early 1920s to the end of World War II; during the past twenty years, however, this type curve is nearly horizontal. Improving technology was almost compensating for the ever decreasing grade of ore mined and the increasing costs of capital and labor. Of especial interest is the plot for corrected price representing zero profit; the average price is reduced by the percentage of the total sales represented by net earnings of the major copper companies each year since 1954 to indicate the break-even price at which they might have operated. (Figures taken from annual review of 500 major U. S. corporations in *Fortune* Magazine.)

When this break-even price is used and multiplied by the current average grade of copper mined, the line plots with a perceptible upward trend showing that current technology is not quite keeping pace with the increased costs of extraction; contrary to the Barnett school of thought, *unit costs are not* declining. The major costs of extraction are those of labor and capital, so that a decline in the cost of energy from 3 to 2.5 mills per kilowatt hour will not greatly affect the cost of extraction. To maintain the current dividend rate the major porphyry copper

producers will need a continued price increase or will have to devise an entirely different and appreciably more efficient way of extracting copper from the ores. A rough approximation for zero profit is price times grade must equal 0.20. To maintain present production at the average grade of copper mined in the United States and to allow the net earnings comparable to those currently had by the major copper companies, price times grade (in constant dollars 1958–59 base) would have to be 0.24. To maintain present returns on investment, assuming average grade of copper ore mined times the price must be 0.24, an average grade of 0.5 per cent (average grade in 1966 was 0.7 per cent Cu) would require a price in constant dollars (1958–59 base) of forty-eight cents per pound in the United States. For this type of deposit, it seems probable that an increase in price, if guaranteed and maintained, would bring out a corresponding increase in production. This is not true, however, of some other metals. Some elements occur in minor amounts in ores exploited chiefly for some other metal; molybdenum is a valuable by-product of the concentrating processes used for getting copper from porphyry coppers. Tin and tungsten are worthwhile by-products from some molybdenum deposits that have all the characteristics of the copper porphyries except that copper is present in only trace amounts.

Most of the production of silver, gold, and antimony in the United States comes as by-products from the mining of other ores and such deposits can form a limited source of additional by-product metals for a sufficient increase in price of the by-product metal, but at the risk of flooding and depressing the market for the major constituents. When this happens, most such deposits would become uneconomic to operate.

It is often suggested that successful development of the breeder reactor will bring unlimited quantities of cheap (almost free!) power and revolutionize mining and other industries. The cost of nuclear fuel for the breeder reactor will indeed be negligible, but the cost of the large capital investment, of power transmission, of waste disposal, and of operation, combine to bring the price per kilowatt hour to essentially that of cheap steam-coal electric generating plants. Breeder reactors will be a wonderful asset to industrial nations not because they provide power at very low cost but because they may provide desperately needed power when fossil fuels are depleted.

Mining costs always increase with depth, and for those deposits which have an A/G ratio that extends down to low grades and huge tonnages, technology will inevitably cease to produce larger tonnages at lower unit costs; the trend that is currently evident in open pit copper mines manifests itself also in other types of deposits. To maintain production would require a gradually rising price for the domestic product, or increased dependence on foreign sources and new discoveries. For types of deposits other than those characterized by an A/G ratio, the increase in price may not be gradual, but instead may accelerate rapidly to where the metal will price itself out of the market except for the most unusual and essential uses. In other words, a real scarcity will develop as measured by the change in price.

If the change in grade with time is gradual as with copper, the change in price (in constant dollars) should also be gradual. The assumption that a similar slow change in price will hold for other mineral industries is not borne out by either geologic theory or current mineral statistics. A 20 per cent increase in the price of copper, if maintained, would certainly stimulate activity in the copper industry and increase the production more than 20 per cent within a year or so; for deposits that characteristically lack the Lasky grade/tonnage relation but instead show an abrupt transition between ore and country rock, no such increase in production will result.

Rise in price may well increase production temporarily, hastening producers toward exhaustion, stimulating marginal and submarginal mines into a flurry of activity, with the result that industrial nations increasingly are vulnerable to the vagaries of outside institutional action. For some commodities, however, a substantial rise in price does not bring about any commensurate production of a new material either at home or abroad though it may make available temporarily ore from marginal producers and sufficient secondary or hoarded metal (a stockpile may be regarded as a "hoard") to satisfy demand—as witness the supply-price behavior of mercury for the past few decades.

As a pointed illustration of the impropriety of generalizing about all mineral deposits from data on a special kind of deposit the two basic assumptions for copper are considered in relation to mercury: (1) geometric increase in tonnage accompanies an arithmetic decrease in grade; (2) a moderate increase in price brings a large increase in production. Bearing significantly on the A/G ratio as applied to mercury, we have the figures resulting from an intensive exploration effort by the Bureau of Mines and the Geological Survey during World War II. More than 330 examinations of mercury occurrences were made and forty-three deposits were explored. Commercial ore was developed on thirty-eight of them; 370,000 tons of ore averaging 0.8 per cent (16.2 pounds per ton); 1,220,000 tons averaging 0.125 per cent (2.5 pounds per ton), and only 285,000 tons averaging 0.08 per cent or 1.6 pounds per ton. This is equivalent to 2,960 tons of mercury in the 0.8 per cent ore, 1,525 tons of mercury in the 0.12 per cent ore, and only 228 tons of mercury in the 0.008 per cent ore. To sum up the relations, an arithmetic decrease in grade from 0.8 per cent to 0.125 per cent (and actually a sixfold change) resulted in a geometric increase in tonnage of three-fold *but the total mercury in the larger tonnage was only one-half* that in the smaller high-grade tonnage. A further decrease of 0.004 per cent in grade resulted in additional tonnage containing only one-tenth as much mercury as that in the high-grade ore.

The U. S. Bureau of Mines Yearbook figures for mercury show the lowest output in twenty-five years for the United States was 5,000 flasks (of seventy-six pounds each) in 1950 when the price was approximately $90 per flask, which was the average price from 1946 to 1950, during which time the output fell steadily from 25,000 to 5,000 flasks. From 1951 to 1953, the price rose rapidly to an average of $200 per flask and in 1954, the United

States government guaranteed a minimum price of $225 a flask for a three-year period—a 250 per cent increase in the 1946–50 price! United States production climbed to nearly 12,000 flasks by the end of 1953, about half the 1946 production. Although the price after 1956 fluctuated on both sides of $200 per flask, this is not far from the average that obtained until a few years ago. During this period the production from the United States mercury mines reached a high of 38,000 flasks in 1958 but from then on dropped steadily until it reached a low of 14,000 flasks in 1964. In that year, however, the price of mercury again more than doubled, reaching an all-time high of about $800 per flask in the latter part of 1965, resulting in an average price of over $500 a flask. The substantial increase in price—a sixfold increase in twenty-one years—resulted in another increase in domestic production which reached 22,000 flasks in 1965, somewhat less than was produced in 1947 when the average price of mercury was only $83 per flask. It is worthy of note that at $1,500 per flask the price of mercury would approximate the coinage value of silver at $1.35 per troy ounce.

Mercury resembles silver in many of its occurrences but most silver now produced comes as a by-product of mining complex lead ores. The high-grade silver mines are depleted just as most of the high-grade mercury mines have been depleted. Very little mercury is recovered as a by-product from complex ores so that this source will contribute only an insignificant amount of mercury in the future whereas silver will continue to increase as the production of the complex ores continues to increase. The average consumption of mercury in the United States has increased at a rate of 3 per cent per year for twenty years, equivalent to a doubling in consumption every twenty-three years. But in the same period *the price of mercury has increased more than 500 per cent!* Presumably a price of more than $1,000 per flask might maintain world production of mercury for fifty years or more but the source of this mercury would be increasingly concentrated in a few large deposits such as those of Spain and Italy where cartel action rather than costs per unit output determine market price.

Distribution of Future Demand and Supply

Hans Landsberg (1964, p. 6) in his scholarly study of the sources of natural resources for the United States during the next forty years, has based his projections on the following assumptions: "Three basic assumptions built in from the start were: continuing gains in technology, improvements in political and social arrangements, and a reasonably free flow of world trade . . . and that there will be neither a large scale war nor a widespread economic depression like that of the early 1930's." There is little evidence in the history of the past half century to justify such an optimistic outlook, but there is some encouragement if one believes, with the writer, that history does *not* repeat itself. Perhaps Landsberg's assumptions will be justified by the next few decades, but only if attention is given to their alternatives, and if policy is devised to prevent the unpleasant consequences of failure to achieve conditions implicit in the assumptions.

Before considering future supplies of the non-fuel minerals, it is necessary to consider potential future demands. The demand for products in a modern world is a function of culture and population, of the relation of the growth rates of GNP and specific populations as well as their particular type of culture (Blackett, 1967). At present cultures all over the world show a marked convergent trend toward a materialistic western way of life which demands an increasing standard of living for the average person; such an increased standard is quickly reflected in the per capita income of the population.

The average income in the United States in 1965 was something over $2,500 per capita. In India the average income then was about $80 per capita, and the average income from some underdeveloped countries was even less. For several years the GNP in the United States has grown at a rate of about 4 per cent per annum while the rate of population growth has been about 1.5 per cent per annum; this results in a per capita income growth rate of approximately 2.5 per cent per year. Projected into the future this would suggest a per capita income increase from $2,500 in 1965 to $5,000 in 1993 and to $10,000 in the year 2021. Meanwhile if the effective fertility rate of 2.5 per cent per year for India were maintained, its population would double every twenty-eight years. The per capita income increase in India, if governed by the present ratio of GNP to population increase, would be far slower; if the GNP were to increase at 4 per cent per annum but the population continued to increase at 2.5 per cent, the actual increase in per capita income would be at the rate of 1.5 per cent per annum. The current per capita income of about $80 would reach $160 in the year 2012 and $320 in the year 2060. Such figures cannot be dismissed as unrealistic unless we also dismiss the basic premise of an "ever expanding economy" at 4 per cent and a population increasing at a constant rate as also unrealistic. Even if population growth slows down substantially in the underdeveloped countries and their GNP is greatly increased, it may be many generations before per capita income can approximate that currently enjoyed by the United States. In the meantime the disparity between incomes will not only be maintained but greatly increased unless a drastic and dramatic change in current trends takes place.

During the early years of industrialization, however, the rate of increase of GNP in backward countries where outside financial assistance is available may be phenomenal. The investment of excess Japanese capital in Korea together with a campaign to control family size has resulted in a steady decline in the birth rate (about 0.1 per cent per year decrease) and an increase in the GNP of approximately 8 per cent per year from 1964–67.

A few demographers (Bogue, 1965) believe that the present population explosion will soon be regarded as an anachronism and that populations will stabilize themselves shortly. This hopeful attitude is not shared by the majority of demographers and is not even considered by economists. The dramatic decline in birth rate in Japan during the fifties following a year of intensive propaganda and appropriate legislation startled the western world. The steady but slow decline in birth rate in the United States since the introduction of modern (1963) contraceptives is also worthy of note. If the industrial and political leaders of a nation become convinced that it is helpful to the national economy and the strength of the nation as a whole to slow down the rate of effective fertility, this can happen within a surprisingly short time.

The demand for goods whether in small amounts per capita for rapidly increasing population or in large amounts per capita for a static population will strain industrial capacity and mineral productivity for the next century. Per capita consumption in the industrial nations first shows exponential growth, usually for a few decades, and then flattens to a merely arithmetic increase usually at a relatively low figure. A nearly static population in underdeveloped countries would certainly result in a tremendous surge in the demand for the nonrenewable resources of the world. For this reason it would seem the current estimates of the United States and world consumption during the rest of the twentieth century as given in Landsberg's study (1964) are too conservative. All available evidence indicates that demand for minerals will increase at an exponential rate for at least fifty or seventy-five years before it begins to level off—as it must do eventually if for no other reason than that the supply is finite.

If events in South Korea and Japan foreshadow those in other Asiatic nations, the demand for minerals and other resources clearly will increase far faster than the rate of 1.5 per cent per year suggested by projection of current fertility rates and an assumed 4 per cent per year increase in GNP.

The world's demand (i.e., production) for industrial metals has been growing at a rate of more than 6 per cent per annum for nearly a decade. It is most unlikely that all underdeveloped nations will want a completely western type culture, but enough of them have already indicated their desire to become industrialized to justify the conclusion that major demands will be made on mineral resources far into the twenty-first century.

Industry requires an increasing tonnage and variety of mineral raw materials. Many that are deemed essential to modern industry have understudies that can play their part adequately, but technology has found no satisfactory substitute for some. The locations of mineral raw materials are fixed by geologic accident in the remote past and many potential sources of supply lie far from the centers of consumption.

In considering future mineral resources certain factors stand out. Because all known individual deposits will be exhausted sooner or later if present patterns of use are maintained, future production depends on the continued discovery of new deposits. Currently discovery techniques seem to be developing rapidly and many new deposits have been found by the application of geology, geophysics and geochemistry. Future sources of ore will be of two types; many known noncommercial deposits will become ore through technical innovations, future availability of cheaper transportation, or a rise in price. The second and larger group includes future sources that are now unknown but will be discovered by exploitation. These deposits will be chiefly in remote or underdeveloped areas if they crop out at the surface, and will be found more and more by a combination of geology, geophysics and geochemistry. Such deposits are expensive to find and will require well financed companies or government supported groups because of the high cost of exploration and development far from supply centers. A second type of unknown ore bodies includes those that do not come to the surface—blind ore bodies. To search successfully for them is even more expensive than to find exposed ore bodies in remote areas. Much money will be spent in preliminary exploration and reconnaissance for every drill hole that zeros in on a commercial ore body. It might be said that the cost of discovery and the cost of development are proportional to the depth below the surface of the ore body.

The kind and locale of blind ore bodies can be guessed by a study of the metalogenetic provinces of the world and their geology. At present our geologic theories are inadequate to say with confidence where to drill for blind ore bodies and a substantial amount of adequately financed well planned research should be devoted to establishing sound theories of ore genesis.

Since the number of deposits is finite, the lead time necessary for successful search increases as the number of shallow deposits found grows larger. Both time and money must be allocated for an inventory of known resources and for planning programs and program revision.

The amount of metal consumed in one generation at the current rate of increase in consumption approximates all the metal that has been used previously. The entire metal production of the world prior to World War II is about that which has been consumed since the beginning of that unhappy event. Ore deposits have been sought most actively ever since the industrial era began and the major industrial powers have a similar history of mineral exploitation and exhaustion. The Middle East, Greece, Spain, England, Belgium, France, Germany, Sweden, Mexico, Peru, and the United States have all had their day as the world's foremost producer of one or several metals only to become plagued by either exhaustion or continuing decline.

As individual nations use up the cheap supplies in their own countries first, they inevitably become more and more dependent on foreign sources for most of their raw materials. At present all industrial nations except possibly the U.S.S.R. are net importers of most of the metals or the ores used by them. This dependence on foreign sources will almost certainly grow far greater for the United States during the next generation except possibly for molybdenum, magnesium, copper, and the fertilizer minerals potash, sulphur, and phosphate. Increasing dependence on foreign sources inevitably brings increased vulnerability to military, political, or economic action. Some of the metals most vital to the economic well-being of industrial nations are in areas of political instability or lie in the Communist countries with which many nations are currently at odds. Most of the known reserves of tungsten and antimony lie in Communist lands, as well as a large part of the world's manganese, nickel, chromium, and platinum. The future and present sources of manganese for Europe and North America are mostly in Africa;

of tin, in Southeast Asia; of aluminum ore, in various underdeveloped tropical countries. If the present dichotomy in the world economy persists, the non-Communist nations must develop a technology that will insure a viable economy which is independent of Communist control of vital resources, or else exploit Communist scarcities in those commodities of which they have an inexplorable surplus. It would seem profitable to further the policy of "co-existence."

Discovery is required that will develop reserves at an exponential rate until a static population is achieved together with a constant per capita demand for metals. The lead time from discovery to production of a major deposit averages three to five years or more and a similar time is usually required for the exploration involved in its discovery. It is apparent then that mineral reserves should be available for a minimum of ten years future production on the basis of present demand and that for those metals which show increasing demand, the reserves must increase even faster.

The resources ready to hand are those first mined, and hence future resources will come from less industrialized countries which, however, will be making maximum efforts to become industrialized. The increased vulnerability of industrial nations in both peace and war suggests that the assumption of equitable access will be affected in the future as it has in the past by institutional restraints and the counter measures which will seem in the best interests of the countries concerned. National attitude, economic advantages, military advantages, and current leaders, will all change with time. Their interplay will require constant vigilance on the part of the industrial nations if they are to maintain a healthy economy. In order to plan for the decades ahead which may be needed to give sufficient lead time for economic and technical adjustments, national and international watchdog groups of experts will be required to warn of impending critical resource situations and to recommend the most desirable remedies. For such groups industrial countries should begin at once to develop continuing national inventories of reserves both at home and abroad. Unfortunately the results of studies guided primarily by mineral economists have led to a "cornucopian" concept of mineral resources that allows policy makers to ignore potential mineral shortages. We are rapidly approaching a time when indifferences can be disastrous.

The main escape hatch for scarcity is technical advance along a broad front, as noted by Landsberg (p. 240), and this will depend on extensive and effective programs of research and development in science, engineering, economics, and management. The more immediate the promise of practical results the greater the willingness of private industry to finance the necessary research. Much of the required research, however, would be of the more exploratory kind, the results of which cannot be guaranteed, but from which eventually answers of crucial importance will come. Planning and prosecution of such research should be a continuing function of the government of major industrial nations. There is a desperate need for integrated national and international resources policies that harmonize or adjudicate the needs of the many special segments of an economy that utilizes natural resources. We especially need research on blind bodies and the factors that are critical to their implacement, research on the genesis of ore bodies. This should lead to new discovery techniques which must be tested by the drill. Exploration should emphasize metals in short supply or which have diminishing reserves. The over-all policy concerning mineral resources should be in the hands of a continuing group of legislative officers working in close cooperation with a full time watchdog group of experts from business, government and the educational field. With such a group functioning effectively, stresses caused by utilization of exhaustible foreign and domestic ore sources should be minimized; without it recurrent or persistent shortages will occur in the supply of some metals. Periods of needlessly high prices for some mineral products will alternate with prices so low that many potential sources of ore will be lost, and certain it is that many disastrous political errors will be made through lack of appreciation of the future importance of trade between areas of industry and potential mineral raw materials.

At present we are living in an epoch of localized affluence such as has recurred throughout historical time when new treasures of metal or mineral were discovered. In the past mineral deposits have led to invasion, conquest, and wealth, for a comparative few. Now, more happily, the utilization of mineral resources of not only the industrial countries but also of some of the underdeveloped countries has led to affluence for many people rather than a select few, but it is well to realize that mineral deposits are still the "quick assets" of the country that possesses them and that ultimately these resources will be exhausted or will decrease their contribution to a fraction of their flush protection. To insure a more equitable distribution of end results of the exploitation of mineral wealth, is one of the foremost but rarely stated objectives of successful, modern economic systems. During the next century this will not be achieved merely by recycling metal as scrap, nor by processing dozens of cubic kilometers of common rock to supply the metal needs of each major industrial nation. When the time comes for living in a society dependent on scrap for "high grade" and on common rocks for "commercial ore," the "affluent society" will be much overworked to maintain a standard of living equal to that of a century ago. The foreseeable exhaustion of ores of some metals and the continually decreasing grade of most ore deposits now used show that it is no small prudence to provide ample lead time for technology to work out such answers as it can and to allow the economy time to make the necessary adjustments to changing mineral supplies.

References

Barnett, H. J. and Morris, Chandler, 1963. Scarcity and Growth. Johns Hopkins Press, Baltimore, Maryland.

Barnett, H. J., 1967. The Myth of Our Vanishing Resources. Transactions Social Science and Modern Society, June, p. 7–10.

Blackett, P. M. S., 1967. The Ever Widening Gap. Science, Feb. Vol. 155, No. 3765, p. 959–964.

Bogue, D. J., 1965. The prospects for world population control. Community and Family Study Center, University of Chicago.

Brown, Harrison; Bonner, James; and Weir, John; 1957. The next hundred years. Viking Press, New York, 193 p.

Bureau of Mines Staff, 1965. Minerals Year Book, Vol. 1, Metals and Minerals. U. S. Government Printing Office, Washington.

———, 1965. Mercury potential of the United States. U. S. Bureau of Mines, I. C. 8252, U. S. Government Printing Office, 376 p.

———, 1956. Mineral Facts and Problems. U. S. Government Printing Office, Washington, D. C., 1042 p.

Landsberg, H. M., 1964. Natural Resources for U. S. Growth. The Johns Hopkins Press, Baltimore, Maryland, 260 p.

Lasky, S. G., 1948. Mineral Resources Appraisal by the U. S. Geological Survey. Colorado School of Mines Quarterly, Golden, Colorado, p. 1–27.

Lasky, S. G., 1950. How Tonnage Grade Relations Help Predict Ore Reserves. Engineering and Mining Journal, Vol. 151, No. 4, p. 81–86.

Lasky, S. G., 1951. Mineral Industry Futures. Engineering and Mining Journal, Vol. 152, No. 8, p. 60–63.

Lasky, S. G., 1955. Mineral Industry Futures Can Be Predicted II. Engineering and Mining Journal, Vol. 155, No. 9.

McMahon, A. D., 1965. Copper, a Material Survey. IC. Bureau of Mines Information Cir. 8225, U. S. Bureau of Mines.

Morris, H. T., and Lovering, T. S., 1952. Supergene and hydrothermal dispersion of heavy metals in wall rocks near ore bodies, Tintic district, Utah: Econ. Geol., v. 47, p. 685–716.

Staffs, Bureau of Mines and U. S. Geological Survey, 1948. Mineral Resources of the United States. Public Affairs Press, Washington, D. C. 212 p.

24   Has the United States Enough Water?

A. M. Piper

Perspective

The destiny of the Nation's water supply is currently a topic of frequent concern in the popular and quasi-technical press. Overly pessimistic writers imply or all but conclude that, within the foreseeable future, much of the United States will have dissipated its available water by consuming it or by grossly polluting it and that consequently industrial expansion must cease at one place or another, irrigated agriculture will wane or even vanish, and social evolution will retrograde. On the other hand, overly optimistic writers foresee no such stringencies within the next several centuries. In considerable part, such implications have come about by treating extreme situations as though they were average or usual, by projecting trends that are not wholly relevant or by assuming that a given volume of water can be "used" only once (the pessimistic view) or can be reused an infinite number of times (the optimistic view).

With an appreciation that he may be oversimplifying, the writer ventures that the United States can be assured of sufficient water of acceptable quality for essential needs within the early foreseeable future, provided that it (1) informs itself, much more searchingly than it has thus far, in preparation for

Piper, A. M., 1965, "Has the United States Enough Water?" *U. S. Geol. Survey Water Supply Paper 1797*, 27 pp. Figures 1-3 are from *River of Life*, U. S. Department of the Interior Conservation Yearbook Series, vol. 6. Mr. Piper is on the staff of the United States Geological Survey.

the decisions that can lead to prudent and rational management of all its natural water supplies; (2) is not deluded into expecting a simple panacea for water-supply stringencies that are emerging; (3) finds courage for compromise among potentially competitive uses for water; and (4) accepts and can absorb a considerable cost for new water-management works, of which a substantial part will need be bold in scale and novel in purpose.

Although this general appraisal is derived for the conterminous United States in particular, it is equally valid for Hawaii and Alaska. Components of this generalization now will be examined at some length.

Elements of Water Supply

Nearly all the fresh water naturally available to man is derived from precipitation. Over the United States, excluding Alaska and Hawaii, this ultimate source averages about 1.4 mgd per mi^2 (million gallons per day per square mile), or 30 inches a year. Of this, about 1.0 mgd per mi^2 (21½ inches a year) returns to the atmosphere as water vapor—by evaporation from water surfaces and wetlands and by evapotranspiration of vegetation (native and cultivated). The remainder, about 0.4 mgd per mi^2 (8½ inches a year), sustains the flow of streams and contributes to ground storage (Langbein, 1949). This remainder constitutes the water potentially available for withdrawal to serve man's uses; it is equivalent to constant flow of 1,200,000 mgd (million gallons per day) or 1,900,000 cfs (cubic feet per second).

In this paper, quantities of water are stated usually in millions of gallons per day. Common equivalents of this unit are shown in the following table.

Precipitation

Even in the "normal" year, precipitation on the conterminous United States ranges from more than 4 mgd per mi^2 (85 in. per year) locally in the Pacific Northwest to less than 0.2 mgd per mi^2 (4 in. per year) locally in the Pacific Southwest. (Fig. 1.) Between wet and dry years the range is even greater.

Precipitation is used immediately and directly by man to the extent that it sustains the soil water on which nonirrigated crop plants and native vegetation depend. On the basis of this relation to "use," three precipitation provinces can be discriminated:

1. Over about the eastern half of the United States—that is, over the Atlantic and Gulf Coastal Plains, Appalachian Highlands, Interior Low Plateaus, Interior Highlands, and most of the Central Lowland—aver-

age precipitation ranges about from 1 to 3 mgd per mi^2 (20–60 in. per year), changes only gradually from one place to another, and commonly reaches a seasonal maximum at or near the height of the growing season. Ordinarily it is ample for crop plants and for marketable native vegetation. In this province especially, to a certain extent man can manipulate soil-water storage to his advantage by land treatments and by water-retarding structures.

2. Over the western fringe of the Central Lowland and westward across the Great Plains, average precipitation diminishes from about 1 to about 0.5 mgd per mi^2 (20–10 in. per year). The seasonal peak commonly occurs early in the growing season. In most of the province, only water-thrifty crops such as wheat can be grown without irrigation, even in the wetter years.

3. Over the Rocky Mountains, Columbia and Colorado Plateaus, Basin and Range province, Sierra-Cascade Mountains, and most of the Pacific Border, average precipitation ranges

Hydraulic equivalents [Equivalent values are on the same horizontal line]

Million gallons per day (mgd)	Million gallons per year (mgy)	Gallons per minute (gpm)	Cubic feet per second (cfs)	Acre-feet per day (afd)	Acre-feet per year (afy)	Inches on 1 square mile per year (in per mi^2)
1.0	365.0	694.44	1.5472	3.0689	1,120.15	21.002
.0027397	1.0	1.9026	.0042390	.0084079	3.0689	.057541
.0014400	.52560	1.0	.0022280	.0044192	1.6129	.030244
.64632	235.91	448.83	1.0	1.9835	723.97	13.574
.32585	118.96	226.29	.50417	1.0	365.00	6.8433
.00089274	.32585	.61996	.0013813	.0027397	1.0	.018750
.047607	17.377	33.065	.073668	.14612	53.333	1.0

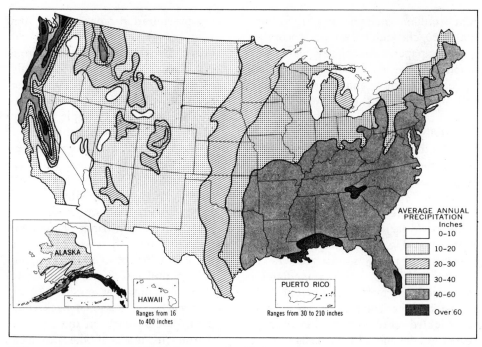

FIG. 1. Average annual precipitation in the U. S.

widely, from about 0.2 to about 4 mgd per mi^2 (4–85 or more in. per year), and the greater amounts fall on the higher parts of the rugged terrain. Seasonal maximum comes in midwinter; summer precipitation is nominal. Variation from month to month and from year to year is extreme. Here, softwood timber thrives on the better watered uplands and affords a profitable crop from lands not suited to most agricultural pursuits. On the lowlands, only the hardiest of forage and grain crops can be grown widely without irrigation. Here the geographic distribution of precipitation and that of arable land are mismatched. In this province, therefore, except in a very local sense, the overriding purpose of management must be so to conserve water that it

can be used at a remote place and a later time, in relation to place and time of precipitation.

It is owing to these and other disparities in precipitation, and in the water supplies which precipitation generates, that the necessities of water-supply management differ so greatly from one region to another.

Evaporation and Transpiration

In the sense that precipitation constitutes gross water supply, evaporation from open-water surfaces—from lakes, reservoirs, streams, ponds, and bogs—and transpiration through vegetation constitute a preemptive, and heavy, tax by Nature. Man can do relatively little to diminish the tax; he gains some advantage from it by substituting marketable vegetation for native species that are not marketable. Man increases the tax whenever he enlarges natural open-water areas or creates such areas artificially and whenever he irrigates land that naturally is "dry." Evapotranspiration that is, the sum of evaporation from wetted surfaces and of transpiration by vegetation—averages about 1.1 mgd per mi² (22 in. per year), nearly 75 percent of the precipitation; however, it varies greatly from one place to another.

Potential evaporation from openwater surface ranges about from 1 to nearly 5 mgd per mi² (20–90 in. per year). On the Atlantic Slope and Atlantic Coastal Plain, it ranges from 20 inches per year in northern Maine to 54 inches in southern Florida; over the Central Lowland and Great Plains, from 24 to nearly 40 inches per year on the north and 50 to 80 inches across Texas; over the Rocky Mountains, Intermountain Plateaus, and the Pacific Mountains, from 20 inches in northwestern Washington to a maximum of about 90 inches in Death Valley and the lower basin of the Colorado River. Details have been published by the U. S. Weather Bureau (1959).

At such rates, the aggregate loss from open-water surfaces is substantial. Meyers (1962) estimates that it averages 21,100 mgd (23,641,000 acre-feet per year) from the 17 Western States, distributed as follows: From 51 principal reservoirs and regulated lakes, 8,090 mgd or 38 percent of the aggregate; from 600-odd other principal reservoirs and regulated lakes, 2,890 mgd; from other lakes exceeding 500 acres in area, 1,770 mgd; from principal streams and canals, 3,950 mgd; from small ponds and reservoirs, 3,010 mgd;

and from small streams, 1,400 mgd. Per year, this loss from principal reservoirs, regulated lakes, small reservoirs, and ponds amounts to 8.1 percent of the total usable storage capacity.

Potential evapotranspiration—that which would occur under optimum soil-water conditions and optimum vegetal cover—generally is somewhat less than potential evaporation. As estimated by Thornthwaite (1952), potential evapotranspiration ranges about from 18 inches per year in the Rocky Mountain province to 60 inches per year in Death Valley and the lower basin of the Colorado River.

The crucial aspect of evapotranspiration is that it may, and over extensive areas commonly does, exceed precipitation. In oversimplified principle, if potential evapotranspiration exceeds precipitation, the potential moisture requirement of vegetation is not satisfied in full, and water is not available for overland flow to streams. In other words, the climate is arid. Conversely, if evapotranspiration is less than precipitation, runoff is generated perennially. These generalizations are acceptable only as first approximations. Actually, some runoff may occur even though concurrent potential evapotranspiration is not satisfied—perennially or intermittently in the arid regions and intermittently in the humid regions. This situation can occur if: (1) Some runoff is generated by effluent ground-water seepage and (2) if the rate of precipitation exceeds infiltration capacity of the soil so that, however great evapotranspiration may be, part of the precipitation is rejected at the land surface and becomes immediate overland flow.

Figure 2 shows mean potential for perennial yield of withdrawable water —that is, average precipitation minus average potential evapotranspiration. Notable is the relatively large area of water deficiency in the western regions—specifically, the area in which potential evaporation and potential transpiration exceed precipitation and which ordinarily does not contribute perennially to water yield. This area encompasses the westernmost part of the Central Lowland and virtually all the Great Plains; much of the Rocky Mountains, the Columbia and Colorado Plateaus, and the Basin and Range province; and a considerable part of the Pacific Border province in California. Conversely, essentially all the eastern half of the 48 States is an area of potential water surplus which con-tributes to perennial water yield; there, evaporation and transpiration are exceeded by precipitation.

In the western region of general water deficiency, areas of potential water surplus exist only over the higher and mountainous uplands and over inter-mountain lowlands northward from San Francisco Bay. These discontinuous and relatively inextensive areas generate nearly all the perennial stream-flow in the West.

Being based on average yearly precipitation and evapotranspiration, the areal pattern of Fig. 2 is itself an average. The areas of surplus or deficiency enlarge and diminish reciprocally from one season to another and from a wet year to a dry year. However, the major feature of the pattern persists—a water-plentiful or humid East and a water-deficient or arid West.

FIG. 2. Water supply and water deficiency in the U. S.

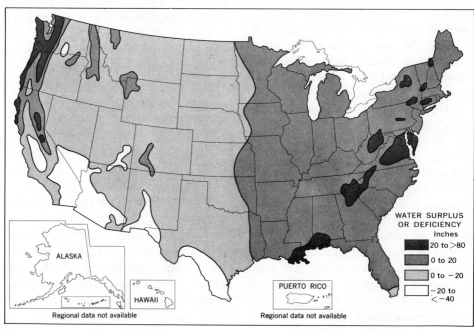

WATER SURPLUS
OR DEFICIENCY
Inches

20 to >80
0 to 20
0 to −20
−20 to
< −40

ALASKA
Regional data not available

HAWAII

PUERTO RICO
Regional data not available

Streamflow

The preemptive tax of evaporation and transpiration having been satisfied, the remainder of the gross water supply (precipitation) sustains the sources from which man can withdraw fresh water for his uses. These sources are the streams, natural lakes, manmade reservoirs, and bodies of ground water. Over any long term of years, neither lakes, reservoirs, nor ground-water bodies increase the fresh-water supply potentially available in the streams, except to the extent that they may be unwatered permanently (a ground-water body thus unwatered is said to be "mined"). Thus, for the purposes of this report, it suffices to measure use and prospective demand of water against streamflow alone.

On the average, aggregate flow of the streams is about 8½ inches a year or 0.4 mgd per mi². This flow is fivefold greater than present withdrawals of water for use and twentyfold greater than consumption in use. However, the comparison is meaningless because both use and supply of water (in this instance, streamflow) are neither uniform from place to place nor constant in time. Indeed, the variability of streamflow is a basic obstacle to full use of all streams; some principal facets of this obstacle are summarized below and are shown by Fig. 3.

Different regions yield greatly different quantities of streamflow: A minimum from the arid Southwest and a maximum from the Pacific Northwest. Among individual stream basins, maximum yield (per unit of area) is roughly 200-fold greater than the minimum. In contrast, in the humid East, maximum yield is less than tenfold greater than

FIG. 3. Average annual run-off in the U. S.

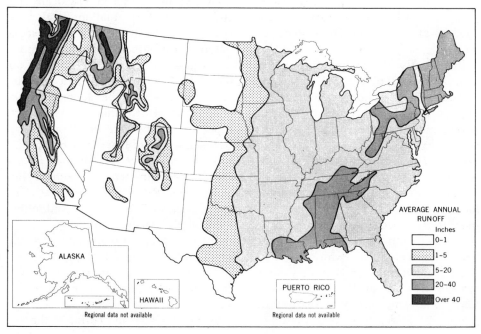

AVERAGE ANNUAL RUNOFF

Inches
- 0–1
- 1–5
- 5–20
- 20–40
- Over 40

ALASKA

HAWAII

Regional data not available

PUERTO RICO

Regional data not available

the minimum. There are other contrasts of interest: 66 percent of the streamflow occurs east of the Mississippi River (tributaries of the Mississippi from the west excluded); the relatively small Pacific Northwest, which includes the Columbia River and other Pacific slope streams in Washington and Oregon, yields 13 percent of the streamflow from all the 48 conterminous States, and 72 percent of that from all the Pacific slope; this yield of Pacific Northwest streams is 1.1-fold greater than that of all tributaries to the Mississippi from the west and 3.1-fold greater than that of western Gulf streams. These geographic variations in stream yield match neither present nor prospective patterns of water use.

As has been implied, most streamflow in the West is generated on uplands and but little is generated on lowlands. Yet man's occupancy is almost exclusively in the lowlands. Here, then, the water supply must be managed at places remote from points of use.

In virtually all streams, flow varies from one year to another, from one season to another, and even from one hour to another. This variability is of paramount consequence to use of the stream by man because, unless flows are regulated artificially, assured withdrawal can be no more than natural minimum flow and, if the variability is large, a major part of the total flow may pass unused. An example of a river having minimum variability is the St. Lawrence River, whose flow is regulated naturally by the very large storage capacity of the Great Lakes. On this stream, maximum yearly flow is only 1.5-fold greater than the mini-

mum; maximum monthly flow, 2.0-fold greater. In contrast, in numerous principal streams, maximum yearly flow is fivefold or more greater than the minimum, and maximum monthly flow is tenfold or more greater. Flows so variable occur in streams both large and small. They are notably common in streams of the Great Plains province, the western part of the Gulf Coastal Plain, and the southern part of the Basin and Range and Pacific Border provinces.

Variation of flow with the seasons may or may not be a disadvantage— a disadvantage when greatest flow and greatest use occur in different seasons but an advantage when they fall in the same season.

The extreme events of fluctuating streamflow are floods and droughts. Both recur at irregular intervals of time. Floods are of short duration, but commonly their volume is much greater than can be contained practically by reservoirs. In this situation, flood management aims at passing the excess volume downstream with a minimum of damage but, also, with little or no use. The water so passed and unavailable for use may be a considerable part of total streamflow. Floods are especially troublesome in Atlantic slope basins northward from the Chesapeake Bay; in the Ohio River, Missouri River, and lower main-stem segments of the Mississippi River basin; and also in the Columbia River basin and other parts of the Pacific slope.

By definition, drought is an event more prolonged or notably more severe than the ordinary dry season. Thus, even though it may occur infrequently, commonly it induces the greatest withdrawals of water and so limits the assured capability of water-supply systems. Drought has been most notable over parts of the Great Plains, Basin and Range, and southernmost Pacific Border provinces.

To the extent that his requirements exceed natural minimum streamflow, man must suppress these geographic and temporal variations of water yield. The principal and all but exclusive means to this end is detaining streamflow in reservoirs during intervals of surplus flow and releasing the stored water during intervals of deficient natural flow. (See Fig. 4.) Even so, however, all the natural streamflow never can be captured and withdrawn, because reservoirs inevitably increase the open-water area from which evaporation preempts its toll. In other words, the ultimate water-supply capability of a stream basin is something less than its average natural yield. (See also Langbein, 1959.) The difference between supply capability and average natural yield increases as the natural variability in streamflow increases, especially as the range widens between maximum and minimum yearly flows. (Present investigations indicate that, if a fatty-alcohol film can be maintained on the surface of a reservoir, evaporation will diminish moderately but will not be eliminated.)

Reservoirs cost money, and ordinarily the cost per unit volume of water they control increases as successive reservoirs are constructed in a given stream basin. Thus, limits of acceptable cost may also determine the extent to which man will suppress the natural variations of streamflow—that is, will "regulate" the flow—to increase usable water supply. At this economic limit, an appreciable fraction of streamflow ordinarily will remain unused in the wetter years or seasons.

The limit of practicable streamflow regulation to increase dependable yield of water depends upon a complex of conditions unique to each stream basin. For the purposes of this report, it will be assumed that the greatest regulated yield that can be sustained continuously would, under conditions of natural flow, have been exceeded 50 percent of the time—in other words, that the limit of continuous regulated yield is about equal to median natural flow, regionwide. For no major stream of the United States has the water yield yet been so fully regulated; in one basin, that of the Colorado River, works now authorized or under construction will increase aggregate regulating capability almost to the assumed limit.

With water yield at the assumed perennial limit, from one-fourth to three-fourths of natural streamflow may be considered perennially usable; nationwide, somewhat more than half. This degree of perennial yield probably will not be reached on all major streams, but on some it probably can be exceeded feasibly. For clarity, it is emphasized that the preceding discussion of streamflow regulation is wholly about achieving maximum perennial water yield. It should not be overlooked that regulation may be desirable for a purpose other than increased yield or may be justifiable for a purpose that sacrifices potential yield in some measure.

On most major streams, the assumed limit of continuous regulated yield cannot be achieved at a cost that currently is acceptable. However, acceptable cost of managing and regulating water sources will increase, inevitably

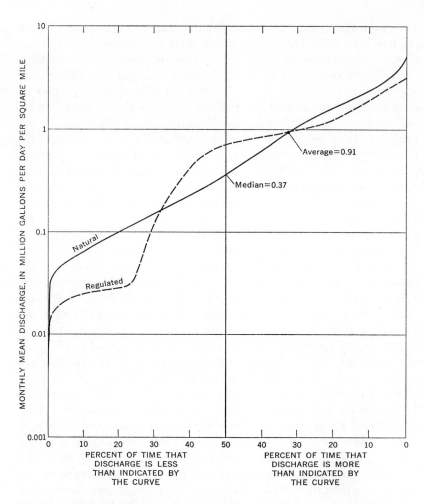

FIG. 4. Natural and regulated streamflow, Merced River at Exchequer, Calif. Usable capacity of the reservoir here is about 29 percent of the average yearly runoff. The streamflow is regulated for generating hydroelectric power in one plant of a wide-flung system; the particular plant operates intermittently to provide "peaking capacity."

Under regulation, both low flows and high flows of the natural regimen are diminished (60 percent of the time), but medium-range flows are increased (40 percent of the time). The regulated flow has been near the natural average 20 percent of the time and greater than the natural median about 60 percent of the time.

If this reservoir were operated to meet a continuous, steady demand (rather than an intermittent, fluctuating demand), the controlled flows would have been substantially less.

Table 1 Approximate mean water-supply elements, by regions

Region	Area (mi²) (1)	Precipitation (mgd per mi²) (2)	Potential evaporation (mgd per mi²) (3)	Natural depletion (mgd per mi²) (4)	Natural runoff mgd per mi² (5)	Natural runoff mgd (6)	Depleted runoff, as of 1960 Average (mgd) (7)	Depleted runoff, as of 1960 Median mgd (8)	Depleted runoff, as of 1960 Median Per cent (9)
New England	62,500	1.93	1.16	0.84	1.09	67,900	67,200	39,400	59
Delaware-Hudson	36,500	1.97	1.58	1.06	.91	33,300	31,700	18,700	59
Chesapeake	67,600	1.97	1.56	1.20	.77	52,000	51,600	31,700	61
South Atlantic-Eastern Gulf	274,300	2.55	2.07	1.77	.78	214,700	212,000	126,000	59
Eastern Great Lakes	48,300	1.71	1.26	.86	.85	40,900	40,300	19,400	48
Western Great Lakes	89,500	1.37	1.33	.89	.48	43,200	42,500	31,700	75
Ohio	143,400	2.02	1.52	1.24	.78	111,400	110,500	45,900	41
Cumberland-Tennessee	60,300	2.42	1.66	1.42	1.00	60,500	59,800	36,200	60
Upper Mississippi	184,800	1.45	1.58	1.11	.34	63,600	62,400	40,700	65
Lower Mississippi	61,900	2.48	2.12	1.67	.81	50,200	48,800	21,300	44
Upper Missouri-Hudson Bay	509,100	.81	1.86	.75	.058	29,700	18,500	9,050	49
Lower Missouri	54,100	1.67	1.88	1.24	.43	23,400	23,100	5,820	25
Upper Arkansas-Red	171,500	1.07	2.84	.98	.088	15,100	11,000	4,520	41
Lower Arkansas-Red-White	112,600	2.12	2.19	1.42	.70	78,600	76,900	20,000	26
Western Gulf-Rio Grande-Pecos	331,100	1.15	2.93	.98	.17	56,800	46,100	14,200	31
Colorado	255,300	.52	2.67	.48	.044	11,300	3,170	1,680	54
Great Basin	191,800	.48	2.20	.44	.042	8,100	3,750	2,130	57
Pacific Northwest	250,100	1.15	1.39	.54	.61	152,600	143,000	75,600	53
Central and South Pacific	122,000	1.11	2.24	.60	.51	62,300	48,200	15,700	33
Total or mean	3,026,700	1.33	2.05	.94	.39	1,175,600	1,100,500	559,700	51

Column:
1.—After U. S. Dept. of Agriculture (1960) but adjusted to the value given by Douglas (1932, p. 248) for aggregate area of land and water except "that part of the water area of the Great Lakes, the Atlantic Ocean, the Gulf of Mexico, the Pacific Ocean, and the Strait of Juan de Fuca that is under the jurisdiction of the United States."
2 and 3.—After U. S. Weather Bureau (1959, 1960), adjusted to distribute apparent discrepancies among columns 2 to 5.
4.—Column 2 minus column 5.
5 and 6.—Depleted runoff as of 1960 (after Oltman and others, 1960) plus water consumed in use as of 1960 (after MacKichan and Kammerer, 1961) plus depletion by reservoirs (from Table 2). "On-site" consumption of water here is excluded. Such consumption—that is, by land-treatment procedures and structures, by swamps and wetlands, and by fish hatcheries—has been estimated by Eliasberg (1960). As of

1960, however, this consumption is very largely from naturally wet areas and is therefore more a component of Nature's preemptive "take" of water than an effect of activities by man. In other words, current "on-site" use is not chargeable as a depletion or current runoff.

Here and elsewhere in this report, runoff and water yield credited to each of the several regions is that which originates in the particular region. Ten of the regions are parts of two major river basins, those of the St. Lawrence River and the Mississippi River. Thus, runoff credited to the western Great Lakes and eastern Great Lakes cannot be accumulated to show main-stem flow, because yield from the part of the basin in Canada is excluded. Main-stem flow of the Mississippi River may be determined by accumulating yields from the eight regions involved, in downstream sequence.

7 and 8.—After Oltman and others (1960).
9.—Per cent of average.

Table 2 Reservoirs and regulated lakes, existing and under construction as of 1954

Region	Usable capacity mg (1)	Days (2)	Surface area (acres) (3)	Effective depth (feet) (4)	Yearly net depletion Feet (5)	mg (6)	Per cent (7)
New England	2,898,000	43	840,000	10.6	0.55	149,000	5
Delaware-Hudson	992,400	30	903,000	3.4	.92	270,000	27
Chesapeake	309,100	6	50,500	18.8	.64	10,600	3
South Atlantic-Eastern Gulf	5,334,000	25	1,500,000	10.9	.54	262,000	5
Eastern Great Lakes	543,300	13	261,000	6.4	.71	60,000	11
Western Great Lakes	419,500	10	305,000	4.2	.78	77,400	18
Ohio	1,875,000	17	226,000	25.5	.47	34,900	2
Cumberland-Tennessee	6,957,000	115	895,000	23.9	.42	122,000	2
Upper Mississippi	1,138,000	18	808,000	4.3	.82	216,000	19
Lower Mississippi	1,455,000	29	208,000	21.4	.79	53,800	4
Upper Missouri-Hudson Bay	24,720,000	832	2,140,000	35.4	1.94	1,353,000	5
Lower Missouri	406,000	17	59,700	20.9	1.13	21,900	5
Upper Arkansas-Red	2,472,000	164	317,000	23.9	3.24	335,000	14
Lower Arkansas-Red-White	7,275,000	93	699,000	31.9	1.34	304,000	4
Western Gulf-Rio Grande-Pecos	4,667,000	82	483,000	29.7	3.42	538,000	12
Colorado	11,326,000	1,002	306,000	113.6	3.84	383,000	3
Great Basin	1,659,000	205	398,000	12.8	3.08	400,000	24
Pacific Northwest	9,082,000	60	982,000	28.4	1.50	480,000	5
Central and South Pacific	5,512,000	88	436,000	38.8	2.87	408,000	7
Total or mean	89,040,000	76	11,820,000	23.1	1.42	5,479,000	6

Column:

1.—Summarized from Thomas and Harbeck (1956); includes those reservoirs and regulated lakes whose capacity is 5,000 acre-feet or more, generally without flashboards.

2.—Column 1 divided by column 6 of Table 1. For any single reservoir, this capacity ratio indicates the time required to impound or release a volume of water equal to the usable capacity; it assumes a rate equal to that of mean runoff. Among the 19 regions, only in the upper Missouri-Hudson Bay and Colorado does usable capacity exceed average yearly runoff. In 9 of the 19 regions, usable capacity is less than 10 per cent of average yearly runoff—that is, only a minor part of the water supply is provided by reservoirs. These nine regions span 32 per cent of the Nation's area—all the Atlantic slope and eastern Gulf areas, except New England, and also the Ohio, Upper Mississippi, Lower Mississippi, and Lower Missouri regions.

3.—Summarized from Thomas and Harbeck (1956).

4.—Column 1 divided by column 3, each converted to appropriate units. Other factors being the same, the greater the effective depth, the smaller the proportion of stored water that evaporates.

5.—Potential evaporation minus the depletion that would have occurred naturally had the reservoir not existed. This column is derived from Table 1—specifically, column 3 minus column 4 of that table, or column 3 minus column 2 plus column 5, converted to yearly depth in feet.

and substantially. The writer believes that eventually construction of additional storage for greater regulated yield will be limited principally by major engineering complexities, competition with other potential uses for the land of reservoir sites, or competition with other objectives of stream management.

Water-Supply Elements by Regions

The preceding discussion emphasizes the considerable variation of each water-supply element from one region to another. More meaningful values for the several elements can be derived according to water-resource regions of which each is relatively homogeneous in respect to water yield. Figure 5 shows the water-resource regions that have been adopted for this report; in the main they are coextensive with the regions adopted by the Select Committee on National Water Resources. Tables 1, 2, and 3 summarize water-supply components by these regions.

Present and Prospective Use of Water

The Overall Situation

As of 1960, the aggregate of all water withdrawals in the 48 conterminous States was about 270,000 mgd, of which about 68,000 mgd was consumed by evaporation in the course of use (MacKichan and Kammerer, 1961). By categories of use, these amounts were distributed as shown in Table 4.

Thus, as of 1960, total consumption of water in the course of use (68,000 mgd) was about 25 percent of the aggregate withdrawn from all water sources (270,000 mgd) but somewhat less than 6 percent of aggregate streamflow (1,200,000 mgd). Among the several categories of use, consumption was about 2.3 percent of the withdrawal for self-supplied industry, 17 percent of that for public supplies, 55 percent of that for irrigation, and 78 percent of the small withdrawal for rural uses.

Like streamflow, these uses of water fluctuate. Use from public supplies may increase severalfold during summer, largely for watering grounds and for air conditioning; obviously this seasonal increase is greatest in the warmer and drier regions. As a whole, industrial use is relatively constant throughout the year, although locally and for certain industries—such as food processing—the water requirement is seasonal and fluctuates widely. Use for irrigation is almost wholly within the growing season and is virtually nil in 6 to 9 months of the year.

Seasonal fluctuation in water use is much greater in the West, where most of the irrigation use occurs, and is of small consequence in the industrial East. In both the West and the East, however, a large part of the aggregate water use is focused in relatively small but intensively developed areas—the

---

6.—Column 3 multiplied by column 5, and the product converted to million gallons a day.

7.—Per cent of usable capacity—that is, column 6 divided by column 1. As has been stated, the greater the effective depth, the less the percentage depletion, other factors being the same. Note in particular that percentage depletion is greatest in the Delaware-Hudson region even though potential evaporation is comparatively small, presumably because effective depth is least. In contrast, percentage depletion is small in the Colorado region even though potential evaporation is large; in this region, effective depth is severalfold greater than in any other of the regions.

metropolitan centers, major industrial complexes, and principal irrigated tracts.

Thus, water use varies both in time and in place, and commonly its variations do not match those of the water sources. Water demand commonly is large when yield of the water sources is small, and large demands commonly arise in areas remote from large water sources. This mismatch is an all-pervading problem of water-supply management.

Withdrawal use of water in the United States increases; at the current rate of increase, aggregate use would double in 25 to 30 years. Even greater rates of increase have been projected by Wollman (1960, p. 6, 79–121), who has estimated water withdrawn and water consumed as of 1980 and 2000. Table 5 summarizes his estimates.

The estimates of water withdrawn and water consumed as of 1980 and 2000 are based on medium-level projections of population, economic activity, and water use (Wollman, 1960, p. 5–6). They are accepted by the writer as credible first approximations for comparison with estimates of assured supply. From 1960 to 2000, they embody increases per decade of about 17 percent in population; 19 percent in water withdrawn for public supplies, but 12 percent in water consumed by such use; 47 percent in water withdrawn but 66 percent in water consumed by industry; and 14 percent in water withdrawn but 20 percent in water consumed in irrigation and rural uses.

Certain trends implied by these projections are noteworthy. Per-capita withdrawal for public supplies would

FIG. 5. Water-supply and water-use regions of the conterminous United States. Each of the regions outlined either is dominated by a single major source of water or encompasses several sources that are similar in magnitude and variability.

Table 3 Reservoirs required to assure flow equal to present median flow

Region	Additional capacity (mg) (1)	Total capacity mg (2)	Total capacity Days (3)	Surface area (acres) (4)	Total yearly net depletion mg (5)	Total yearly net depletion Per cent (6)
New England	8,500,000	11,400,000	170	1,700,000	305,000	3
Delaware-Hudson	3,600,000	4,600,000	140	950,000	285,000	6
Chesapeake	6,500,000	6,800,000	130	1,400,000	292,000	4
South Atlantic-Eastern Gulf	25,400,000	30,700,000	140	3,800,000	669,000	2
Eastern Great Lakes	3,600,000	4,100,000	100	840,000	194,000	5
Western Great Lakes	6,500,000	6,900,000	160	1,400,000	356,000	5
Ohio	9,400,000	11,300,000	100	1,400,000	214,000	2
Cumberland-Tennessee	4,100,000	11,000,000	180	1,400,000	192,000	2
Upper Mississippi	8,500,000	9,600,000	150	2,000,000	534,000	6
Lower Mississippi	4,600,000	6,100,000	120	750,000	193,000	3
Upper Missouri-Hudson Bay	1,900,000	26,600,000	900	2,300,000	1,450,000	5
Lower Missouri	1,700,000	2,100,000	90	320,000	118,000	6
Upper Arkansas-Red	1,100,000	3,600,000	240	440,000	465,000	13
Lower Arkansas-Red-White	7,200,000	14,500,000	180	1,500,000	655,000	5
Western Gulf-Rio Grande-Pecos	3,900,000	8,600,000	150	880,000	981,000	11
Colorado	390,000	11,700,000	1,040	360,000	450,000	4
Great Basin	320,000	2,000,000	250	410,000	411,000	20
Pacific Northwest	15,300,000	24,400,000	160	2,100,000	1,030,000	4
Central and South Pacific	3,600,000	9,100,000	150	700,000	655,000	7
Total or mean	116,000,000	205,000,000	170	24,650,000	9,449,000	5

Column:

1.—After Oltman and others (1960).

2.—Column 1 plus column 1 of Table 2.

3.—To nearest multiple of 10 days. See explanation of Table 2, column 2. Note that, to assure flow equal to present median flow, usable storage capacity must exceed 25 per cent of average natural yearly runoff in all regions, and exceed 50 per cent in 6 of the 19 regions. In two of the latter six—the Upper Missouri-Hudson Bay and Colorado regions—required usable capacity would be 2.5-fold and 2.8-fold greater than average yearly runoff, respectively. Thus, in dry years, most of the streams in most of the regions would need to be regulated continuously to assure flow not less than present median flow. As has been stated elsewhere natural median flow approaches the maximum perennial water supply that can be developed practically under ordinary environmental and economic circumstances.

4.—Order-of-magnitude estimate only. The estimates take into account the expectation that future reservoirs will have greater effective depth and smaller percentage depletion.

5.—Column 4 multiplied by column 5 of Table 2, and the product converted to million gallons a day.

6.—Column 5 divided by column 2.

Table 4 Water withdrawn and water consumed, 1960 [After MacKichan and Kammerer (1961), modified]

Use	Withdrawn		Consumed	
	mgd	Per cent	mgd	Per cent
Rural	3,600	1.3	2,800	4.1
Public supplies	21,000	7.8	3,500	5.2
Self-supplied industry	140,000	52	3,200	4.7
Irrigation:				
Conveyance losses	23,000	8.5	[1] 7,500	11
Delivered to farms	83,000	31	[2] 51,000	75
Totals (rounded)	[3] 270,000	100	68,000	100

[1] Commonly it is assumed that all the water lost in conveyance by irrigation canals returns ultimately to the streams. However, transpiration by canal-bank vegetation is appreciable in some areas. The writer postulates that, from this cause and others, about one-third of the gross conveyance loss is removed permanently from the stream system.
[2] Water consumed by nonirrigated crops is even greater in amount but is taken from soil water which, in the context of this paper, is not withdrawable.
[3] Includes 32,000 mgd of saline water.

increase slightly but per-capita consumption would diminish 15 per cent over the four decades. Such improvement in efficiency of water use is possible and desirable, but it is neither assured nor, in the writer's judgment, easily realized. Per capita withdrawal by industry would increase 2.6-fold, per capita consumption 7.5-fold. These per capita increases seem inordinately large, although industry likely will consume an increasing proportion of its water. Irrigation withdrawals would increase 1.7-fold, and irrigation consumption 2.1-fold. These projections imply that the efficiency of irrigation use will decrease, whereas it should increase under technologic improvements.

According to Wollman's projections, by the year 2000 aggregate withdrawal would be no more than 74 percent of present streamflow; consumption would be 29 percent of withdrawals and 21 percent of streamflow. Of course, these percentages do not indicate that all the projected demands for

water can be satisfied without depletion of any stream. Any such inference would be false on several points, including: (1) It would presume that either water or persons and their uses of water can be transported freely and completely in order to balance total water supply against total demand. Transportation so free is not practical. (2) It would presume that all the water yield that is surplus during the wetter seasons and years could be impounded and held for use during the drier seasons and years. As has been shown, the perennially dependable supply is substantially less than the theoretical average supply in all stream basins. (3) It presumes that all water withdrawn but not consumed remains usable for any purpose. Actually, any use of water depreciates the quality of the fraction not consumed; with repeated reuse, progressive depreciation in quality eventually makes some fraction of the supply unusable for many purposes. (4) It does not take into ac-

Table 5 Estimated water withdrawn and water consumed, 1980 and 2000 [After Wollman (1960); in millions of gallons per day]

Use	Withdrawn		Consumed	
	1980	2000	1980	2000
Municipal (public supplies)	29,000	42,000	3,500	5,500
Mining, manufacturing, and steam-electric (industry)	363,000	662,000	11,000	24,000
Agriculture (rural and irrigation)	167,000	184,000	104,000	126,000
"On site"[1]			71,000	97,000
Totals	559,000	888,000	190,000	253,000

[1] Water consumed by "on-site" uses comprises the effects of land treatment and structures, enlarged swamps and wetlands, and fish hatcheries. In large part, water consumed by such uses is intercepted before it has entered a perennial stream; in other words, streamflow is depleted even though water may not be withdrawn in the usual sense.

Owing to past and present depletion of this kind, accepted values of streamflow as measured and published by the U. S. Geological Survey presumably are smaller than natural flows. Thus, present on-site consumption is not charged as an encumbrance against measured water supply. However, the estimates of on-site consumption as of 1980 and 2000 are for expected increases in such consumption; these must be charged against available supply as now measured.

count necessary on-site and in-channel uses—for hydroelectric power, diluting and transporting fluid wastes, navigation, depletion by reservoirs, habitat for fish and waterfowl, and recreation —which, in the aggregate, may be severalfold greater than withdrawal uses.

Demand and Supply by Regions

Tables 6 and 7 present a reasonably realistic comparison of the projected demand and supply of water as of the year 2000, by types of use and by water-resources regions. (See Fig. 5.) Implicit in this comparison are certain generalizations and assumptions, as follows:

1. Assured water supply is equal to median natural streamflow; for all the 48 conterminous States this median would be about 54 percent of total streamflow.

Wollman (1960) and Eliasberg (1960) derive "maximum low flow(s) that can be sustained" which, for all the 48 conterminous States, aggregate 92 percent of total natural runoff and for certain regions are as much as 98 percent. In the writer's judgment, sustained yields so great would be virtually impossible to achieve regionwide.

2. The potential yield of ground-water bodies can be realized only at the expense of an equal diminution in streamflow, over the long haul. In other words, ground-water sources do not increase the aggregate potential supply of water. This fact would become literally true if total potential yield were being put to use.

3. As derived by Wollman (1960) and Eliasberg (1960) and accepted for this report, projected demands for water are not scaled to supplies.

Table 6 Projected demand and supply of water as of the year 2000, by types of demand and by regions [In millions of gallons per day. After Eliasberg (1960), except as indicated in notes]

| Region | Water consumed in off-channel use | | | | Water consumed on site | | | | Dominant in-channel flow | | Maximum projected commitment | Potential assured supply | Supply-to-commitment ratio |
	Municipalities (1)	Industry (2)	Agriculture (3)	Subtotal (4)	Land treatment (5)	Wetlands (6)	Reservoir depletion (7)	Subtotal (8)	Use (9)	Amount (10)	(11)	(12)	(13)
New England	200	1,100	300	1,600	500	400	840	1,740	Hp	26,800	30,100	40,000	1.3
Delaware-Hudson	500	1,000	500	2,000	-200	1,300	780	1,880	Fs	23,400	27,300	20,300	.74
Chesapeake	200	600	1,200	2,000	100	900	800	1,800	Fs	33,000	36,800	32,000	.87
South Atlantic-Eastern Gulf	300	3,400	8,100	11,800	900	19,900	1,830	22,630	Hp	67,000	101,400	128,700	1.3
Eastern Great Lakes	400	800	600	1,800	0	1,100	530	1,630	Hp	101,800	105,200	20,000	.19
Western Great Lakes	500	2,500	1,200	4,200	100	3,600	980	4,680	Wd	51,200	60,100	32,400	.54
Ohio	300	2,100	1,800	4,200	500	200	590	1,290	Hp	35,700	41,200	46,800	1.1
Cumberland-Tennessee	(1)	500	400	900	400	100	530	1,030	Hp	47,300	49,200	36,900	.75
Upper Mississippi	300	700	4,600	5,600	600	4,900	1,460	6,960	Nv	48,500	61,100	41,900	.69
Lower Mississippi	100	500	3,100	3,700	300	9,500	530	10,330	Nv	97,100	111,100	22,800	.21
Upper Missouri-													

	1	2	3	4	5	6	7	8	9	10	11	12	13
Lower Arkansas-Red-White	[1]	700	3,000	3,700	700	2,000	1,790	4,490	Hp	29,500	37,700	21,700	.58
Western Gulf-Rio Grande-Pecos	500	5,200	14,800	20,500	600	14,300		17,590	Wd	18,400	56,500	24,900	.44
Colorado	100	1,100	13,200	14,400	100	2,600	2,690	3,930	Fs	15,900	34,200	9,800	.29
Great Basin	100	300	6,100	6,500	[1]	5,300	1,230	6,430	Fs	4,000	16,900	6,500	.38
Pacific Northwest	500	900	13,600	15,000	200	1,200	2,820	4,220	Hp	133,900	153,100	85,200	.56
Central and South Pacific	1,200	1,600	27,500	30,300	100	3,800	1,790	5,690	Wd	36,000	72,000	29,800	.41
Total	5,500	24,300	126,500	156,300	6,900	89,900	25,880	122,680		821,700	1,100,600	634,700	.58

[1] Less than 50 mgd.

Column:

2.—Manufacturing, 20,900 mgd over all the United States; steam-electric power, 2,800 mgd; mining, 600 mgd.

3.—Chiefly irrigation.

5.—Water that naturally would reach a stream, but that is dissipated by land-treatment practices or structures. Quantities represent increases above those of 1954 and so are chargeable as depletions of runoff. (See note to Table 1, columns 5 and 6.) The negative quantity for the Delaware-Hudson region implies an increase in water yield owing to land-treatment measures.

6.—Water dissipated from manmade wetlands and by fish hatcheries, both constructed after 1954; accordingly, the quantities are chargeable as future depletions of streamflow.

7.—From Table 3, column 5.

9.—Only the largest of potential in-channel water requirements is listed on the assumption that in-channel flow will be sufficient for all if the largest is satisfied. This assumption may or may not be valid. Types of in-channel requirements include: Hp, hydroelectric power; Fs, sport fishing habitat; Wd, waste dilution; Nv, navigation.

11.—Sum of columns 4, 8, and 10. Such summation is valid as a first approximation, provided the column 10 quantity is severalfold greater than the sum of those in columns 4 and 8. If the column 10 component is not severalfold greater, the column 11 summation may be smaller than the flow required to satisfy both off-channel and in-channel uses.

12.—Potential assured supply is assumed equal to median natural flow. As an approximation of this median, the column 12 quantity is equal to column 8 from Table 1, plus water consumed in use as of 1960 (after MacKichan and Kammerer, 1961), plus depletion by reservoirs as of 1954 (Table 2, column 6). The note to Table 1, columns 5 and 6, also applies. In the Mississippi River basin, assured main-stem supply can be approximated by accumulating supplies of the several regions involved, less water consumed off-channel and on-site, in downstream sequence.

13.—Column 12 divided by column 11.

Rather, each potential use or commitment of water is projected independently, as though it is preemptive; it is also projected according to estimated nationwide or regionwide requirement for the products derivable from the use. This basis leads to certain incongruously large projections, to which further reference will be made.

4. Biological oxygen demand (BOD) of municipal sewage and of industrial waste will be largely removed by treatment, and effluents from treatment plants will be diluted sufficiently to maintain dissolved oxygen at regionwide averages of 4 milligrams per liter. (This amount of dissolved oxygen is about the minimum for a satisfactory fish and wildlife habitat.) In the projections by Wollman and Eliasberg, the degree of waste treatment is either that which involves the least cost for treatment plant plus water for dilution or, in certain water-deficient regions, that which requires the least dilution. By these criteria, percentage BOD removal from sewage would range between 80 and 97.5 percent among the several regions; that from industrial wastes, between 50 and 97.5 percent. This degree of BOD removal is far greater than is now achieved regionwide. The greater of these BOD removals may not be achievable at acceptable costs; if not, requirements of water for dilution would be increased commensurately.

5. (a) Water allocated for in-channel uses—for hydroelectric power, waste dilution, navigation, habitat for fish and wildlife, and recreation —also will satisfy all withdrawal uses. (b) The water allocated to the largest in-channel use will suffice for all such uses. (c) In consequence, maximum net commitment against potential supply is the sum of water consumed in off-channel and on-site uses plus that allocated to the largest, or dominant, in-channel use. Strictly, this latter generalization is not valid; as a first approximation, however, it is acceptable.

Table 8 and Fig. 6 summarize the preceding comparison.

Briefly, potential assured supply exceeds projected commitment in three regions: New England, South Atlantic-Eastern Gulf, and Ohio. Only in these three is it expectable that water requirements for the economic and social evolution projected by Wollman and Eliasberg could be realized easily. In the remaining 16 regions, projected commitments exceed assured supply as here defined.

In 7 of the 16 regions of seeming water deficiency, assured supply is greater than projected consumption (off-channel plus on-site) and total streamflow equals or exceeds total commitment. In these seven regions, therefore, most water requirements for the projected economic and social evolution can be realized if virtually complete regulation of streamflow proves feasible. The seven regions are the Delaware-Hudson, Chesapeake, Cumberland-Tennessee, Upper Mississippi, Upper Arkansas-Red, Lower Arkansas-Red-White, and Pacific Northwest.

In the remaining nine regions, total commitment exceeds total streamflow. Projected consumption exceeds assured supply in five of these nine, and exceeds total streamflow in three. Consequently, in these nine regions it is ex-

Table 7 Summary of projected demand and supply of water as of the year 2000, by regions [In million gallons a day per square mile]

Region	Demand						Supply	
	Consumed in use (1)	Consumed on site[1] (2)	Depletion by reservoirs (3)	Subtotal (4)	In-channel commitment (5)	Total (6)	Potentially assured (7)	Total streamflow (8)
New England	0.0256	0.0144	0.0134	0.0534	0.429	0.482	0.640	1.086
Delaware-Hudson	.0548	.0301	.0214	.1063	.641	.748	.556	.912
Chesapeake	.0296	.0148	.0118	.0562	.488	.544	.473	.769
South Atlantic-Eastern Gulf	.0430	.0758	.0067	.1255	.244	.370	.469	.783
Eastern Great Lakes	.0372	.0228	.0110	.0710	2.107	2.178	.414	.847
Western Great Lakes	.0469	.0413	.0109	.0992	.572	.671	.362	.483
Ohio	.0293	.0049	.0041	.0383	.249	.287	.326	.777
Cumberland-Tennessee	.0149	.0083	.0088	.0320	.784	.816	.612	1.003
Upper Mississippi	.0303	.0298	.0079	.0680	.262	.330	.227	.344
Lower Mississippi	.0598	.1584	.0085	.2267	1.569	1.795	.368	.811
Upper Missouri-Hudson Bay	.0412	.0375	.0078	.0865	.0491	.1356	.0399	.0583
Lower Missouri	.0277	.0055	.0059	.0391	.417	.456	.113	.433
Upper Arkansas-Red	.0326	.0082	.0074	.0482	.0268	.0750	.0501	.0880
Lower Arkansas-Red-White	.0328	.0240	.0159	.0727	.262	.335	.193	.698
Western Gulf-Rio Grande-Pecos	.0619	.0450	.0081	.1150	.0556	.1706	.0752	.172
Colorado	.0564	.0106	.0048	.0718	.0623	.1341	.0384	.0443
Great Basin	.0339	.0276	.0059	.0674	.0209	.0883	.0339	.0446
Pacific Northwest	.0600	.0056	.0113	.0768	.535	.612	.341	.610
Central and South Pacific	.2483	.0320	.0147	.2950	.295	.590	.244	.511
Mean	.0516	.0320	.0086	.0922	.271	.363	.210	.388

[1] Land-treatment measures and wetlands only.

Table 8 Projected water demand as of the year 2000 [In percent of potential assured supply]

Region	Consumed off channel	Consumed on site	Dominant in-channel flow	Total
New England	4	4	67	75
Delaware-Hudson	10	9	115	134
Chesapeake	6	6	103	115
South Atlantic-Eastern Gulf	9	18	52	79
Eastern Great Lakes	9	8	509	526
Western Great Lakes	13	14	158	185
Ohio	9	3	76	88
Cumberland-Tennessee	2	3	128	133
Upper Mississippi	13	17	116	146
Lower Mississippi	16	45	426	487
Upper Missouri-Hudson Bay	103	114	123	340
Lower Missouri	25	10	370	405
Upper Arkansas-Red	65	31	53	150
Lower Arkansas-Red-White	17	21	136	174
Western Gulf-Rio Grande-Pecos	82	71	74	227
Colorado	147	40	162	349
Great Basin	100	99	62	260
Pacific Northwest	18	5	157	180
Central and South Pacific	102	19	121	242
Mean	25	19	129	173

pectable that, even with streamflow regulated to the utmost, economic and social evolution will be handicapped moderately to severely. The nine regions in this category are the Eastern Great Lakes, Western Great Lakes, Lower Mississippi, Upper Missouri-Hudson Bay, Lower Missouri, Western Gulf-Rio Grande-Pecos, Colorado, Great Basin, and Central and South Pacific. Together, the nine span 55 percent of the 48 conterminous States.

Courses of Action

Obviously, pure water is becoming a critical commodity whose abundance is about to set an upper limit of economic evolution in a few parts of the Nation and inevitably will do so rather widely within half a century or less. Prudence requires that the Nation learn to manage its water supplies boldly, imaginatively, and with utmost efficiency. Time in which to develop such competence is all too short.

As the basis for water-management decisions that seem imminently necessary, the Nation has only a bare minimum of relevant information. Water facts of all kinds, in ever wider scope and ever greater detail, will be prerequisite to sound decisions. So also will plans for alternative schemes for comprehensive water control and management and for corresponding schedules of cost—in dollars, in economic opportunities created on the one hand and foreclosed on the other, and in "second-generation" problems that can be anticipated. Here the all-embracing plan, immutable for all time, rises as

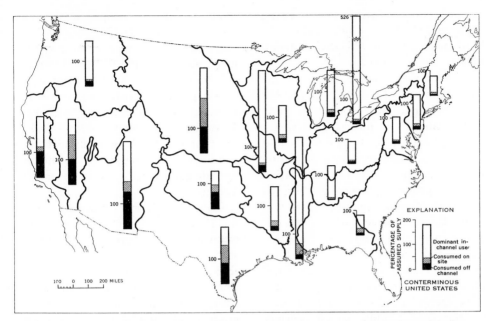

FIG. 6. Projected water demand as of the year 2000. The bar diagrams show, for the water-resources regions, water demand, as projected by Wollman (1960) and Eliasburg (1960), expressed as percentage of assured supply. Thus, in a crude way, the height of bar is proportional to expectable difficulty in satisfying the projected demand.

an enticing will-o'-the-wisp. In actuality, the process of information gathering, decision, and action will never end. Each such cycle inevitably will create the seed of an ensuing cycle, and successive cycles will deal with progressively more complex situations and will be less susceptible to "crash" procedures.

No single course of action can be a panacea for all water-supply ills. Thus, the objectives of water-supply management must be varied from one situation to another.

As one example, consider the case for desalting ocean water or other brines as a "new" source of fresh water, potentially in extremely large volume. Several effective techniques for desalting are established and are being

refined. On a pilot-plant scale, the cost approaches but has not yet reached the target of $1 per thousand gallons of fresh-water product. It is reasonable to expect that cost at point of production ultimately can be diminished to and below the target. However, considering the quantity of energy required for separating water from dissolved salts and, further, considering costs at which energy reasonably can be produced and applied to the separation, the writer considers it highly unlikely that the overall cost of desalting ocean water can, in the foreseeable future, be diminished by an order of magnitude below the target—that is, to as little as 10 cents per thousand gallons. Actual use of desalted ocean water will involve an additional increment of cost—

that of pumping from the desalting plant to the place of use against the head necessary for effective distribution.

In contrast, average costs in the United States in 1954 were about 18½ cents per thousand gallons for pure, fresh water from municipal systems, commonly as little as one-tenth that amount for industrial and irrigation water, and about 8 cents for treating sewage. From one place to another, the approximate range in local costs was from 50 to 200 percent of the average. These costs include operation, maintenance, and amortization of capital investment. Those for municipally supplied water and for treating sewage were derived by the writer from data by the U. S. Public Health Service (1960 and 1960a).

Thus, at current and prospective costs as cited above, fresh water obtained by desalting oceanic and other brines seems most unlikely to be universally advantageous. Desalting can, and probably will, compete economically as a source for municipal supply in areas along the immediate coast where water from streams and other conventional sources is unobtainable in adequate volume and where the salts that are removed can be returned to the ocean at little cost. Probably it will compete also in deriving usable supplies from inland brackish waters; at inland sites, however, disposal of the removed salts may be difficult and costly. Elsewhere, "rules of the market place" dictate that the principal course of future action be concerted management of the conventional surface-water and ground-water sources, including those now submarginal in cost.

Much water must be reclaimed from industrial and municipal wastes and reused several times. For such reclaiming, desalting may prove feasible (Oltman and others, 1960). Repeated reuse will become necessary throughout the East if projected consuming uses are to be satisfied from projected in-channel flows. Reuse diminishes withdrawal at the source but does not diminish consumption. Thus, reuse will not modify the demand-supply comparisons of Table 6.

Over most of the West, except only the Pacific Northwest, projected commitment—that is, off-channel and on-site consumption plus dominant in-channel flow—exceeds assured supply. There, the obvious alternatives are either less consumption per unit of product or diminished production. There a considerable part of the commitment, even a major part, is consumption in agriculture, largely in irrigation. There, substantially diminished consumption implies improved efficiency in irrigation. Such improvement must be sought diligently; it will not easily be realized in a large measure.

Of on-site consumption, 68 percent of that projected for improving fish-and-wildlife habitat occurs in four regions—South Atlantic-Eastern Gulf, Lower Mississippi, Upper Missouri-Hudson Bay, and Western Gulf-Rio Grande-Pecos. (See Table 6, column 6.) Only in the first of these regions can this particular projection be realized concurrently with other projected demands, each in full. In the remaining three regions, the respective projections are 42 percent, 87 percent, and 57 percent of potential assured supply (as defined by the writer). In these three, and to a smaller degree in five additional regions—Western Great

Lakes, Upper Mississippi, Lower Arkansas-Red-White, Colorado, and Great Basin—compromise seems ultimately inevitable between an ideal habitat for fish and wildlife on the one hand and the several potentially competing demands for water on the other hand. In this connection, it is emphasized that all the habitat here considered, and covered under Table 6, is that proposed to be created by man.

By the year 2000, estimated reservoir depletion will be only 4 percent of potential assured supply (Table 6, column 7). However, it would exceed 10 percent in five regions—Upper Missouri-Hudson Bay, Upper Arkansas-Red, Western Gulf-Rio Grande-Pecos, Colorado, and Great Basin. Particularly in these five, measures that substantially diminish evaporation would ease prospective deficiencies in water supply. Although results have been disappointing thus far, attempts to discover effective measures and materials should continue as long as there is hope for success.

Depletion by evaporation from water surfaces can, in principle, be diminished also to the extent that streamflow can be regulated in natural underground reservoirs in lieu of manmade reservoirs on the land surface. Capability of underground reservoirs for water-supply management seems potentially large. Field studies to evaluate such capability and to establish procedures are urged.

The potential for salvaging part of the water transpired by noneconomic native vegetation is in a sense analogous to suppression of evaporation from reservoirs, but differs in that a "new" water-supply component would be created. The quantity of this water is large; in the 17 Western States about 20,000 mgd is transpired by phreatophytes, plants withdrawing water that otherwise would reach a stream (Oltman and others, 1960). Methods for eradicating phreatophytes at acceptable cost are under test, principally by the U. S. Army Corps of Engineers and the U. S. Bureau of Reclamation. Field evaluation of the eradication in terms of increased water supply is pending.

A principal concern of the future will be with in-channel flows and, in particular, with flow for diluting wastes. It appears implicit in the projections by Wollman (1960) and by Reid (1960) that nearly all wastes would be commingled with all the available water and that, with certain pretreatment of the wastes, dilution could be sufficient that the mixture would be usable for substantially all purposes. According to the projections in Table 6, however, water for dilution would be insufficient in most regions—definitely in Western Great Lakes, Upper Arkansas-Red, Western Gulf-Rio Grande-Pecos, and Central and South Pacific—and also to a smaller and variable degree in all other regions except the three in which assured supply exceeds projected commitment.

Means must be found to diminish the dilution requirement. Relief will not lie in more inclusive pretreatment of wastes, because the projections already assume a very large percentage removal of BOD. Measures alternative to dilution, that can be considered where and when need arises, include the following:

1. In metropolitan areas, separate distribution of high-purity water for intake by humans and animals, and

of lower purity water for industrial purposes, fire protection, sanitary flushing, and the like. Native stream and ground waters would be conserved for the high-purity system; reclaimed waters could go to the lower purity system. Currently, somewhat less than 10 percent of all water used off-channel is in municipal-supply systems that require high purity.

2. Partial or complete removal of solutes from waste fluids, in effect diluting the waste sufficiently for general reuse. Practical means for so reclaiming waste waters should be sought with some sense of urgency.

3. Waste canals or pipelines, separated from stream channels and leading to off-channel disposal areas where feasible. Part of or all the wastes might be concentrated in some degree prior to disposal or they might even be desiccated.

4. Chemical disintegration or separate disposal, or both, of industrial wastes that do not oxidize under conventional treatment. These would include toxins and "exotic" wastes from the chemical and nuclear-energy industries, wastes that presumably will be produced in ever larger quantities.

Measures such as those just outlined would be simplified if sources of the most troublesome wastes were segregated by area, preferably downbasin. Zoning of this sort has been recommended to delineate and conserve opportunities for outdoor recreation (U. S. Geological Survey, 1962). It might best be realized through the local and State police powers, coupled with conservancy commissions of local, statewide, or even regionwide jurisdiction. Re-

gionwide jurisdictions would preforce rest on interstate negotiations. Whatever its purpose, however, zoning is distasteful; probably, therefore, it will prove to be a last-resort tool in managing water supplies.

Commonly the dominant in-channel projection is for a purpose other than dilution of wastes—for fish and wildfowl habitat, for hydroelectric power, or for navigation. Locally, it might be for recreation. Commonly, also, it exceeds assured supply—for example, the projections for hydroelectric power in the Eastern Great Lakes and Pacific Northwest regions, those for navigation in the Mississippi and Missouri River basins, and that for fish and wildfowl habitat in the Colorado River basin. (See Table 6.) These and other in-channel projections cannot be realized in full. Inevitably, realistic compromises must be reached among off-channel consumption, on-site consumption, and the several in-channel requirements and opportunities.

All these matters concern management of water supply in the engineering sense. Beyond them are related unresolved questions in the field of administrative management. What would be the most appropriate ultimate assignment of responsibility and authority over such unlike matters as inventory of uncommitted water resources, planning and construction for river regulation, allocation of the resource among potentially competitive and mutually exclusive uses, segregation and appropriate treatment or disposal of wastes? Responsibility and authority now rest in many agencies—municipal, State, and Federal, but commonly are either too fragmentary or too specialized to encompass all the necessary courses of action. Is there some reasonable, workable compromise between this presently fractionated concern and overall authority assigned to a single governmental colossus?

Cost of water-supply management as here outlined will be large obviously. How can this large cost be shared equitably among the individual user and taxpayer, the private entrepreneur of commerce or industry, and the many agencies of government?

Current legal rights of the individual to water or to its exclusive use could, if unmodified or unrestrained, greatly complicate water-management procedures of the year 2000. Should these rights, now absolute in most States, be relaxed to the end that a common advantage may be realized from a simpler, more effective procedure? In another context, the writer has concluded that they will be so relaxed, by evolution (Piper, 1959).

The title of this paper is a general question, "Has the United States enough water?" A comprehensive answer, binding as of the year 2000, is not possible from information at hand or in early prospect. However, this paper has served its purpose if it has broken down the general question into correlative aspects and courses of early action. Definitive answers to the numerous residual questions must be found.

References

Douglas, E. M., 1932, Boundaries, areas, geographic centers of the United States and the several States: U. S. Geological Survey Bull. 817, 265 p.

Eliasberg V. F., 1960, Regional water supply and projected uses. In Wollman, 1960 [see below].

Langbein, W. B., 1959, Water yield and reservoir storage in the United States: U. S. Geol. Survey Circ. 409, 5 p.

Langbein, W. B., and others, 1949, Annual runoff in the United States: U. S. Geol. Survey Circ. 52, p. 5.

MacKichan, K. A., and Kammerer, J. C., 1961. Estimated use of water in the United States, 1960: U. S. Geol. Survey Circ. 456, 44 p., 10 fig.

Meyers, J. S., 1962, Evaporation from the 17 Western States: U. S. Geol. Survey Prof. Paper 272-D, p. 93–95.

Oltman, R. E., and others, 1960, National water resources and problems: U. S. Senate, Select Comm. on National Water Resources, 86th Cong., 2d sess., Comm. Print 3, 42 p., 43 fig.

Piper, A. M., 1959, Requirements of a model water law: Am. Water Works Assoc. Jour., v. 51 p. 1211–1216.

Reid, G. W., 1960, Methods of approximating dilution water requirements as a supplemental measure for control of water quality in rivers: U. S. Senate, Select Comm. on National Water Resources, 86th Cong., 2d sess., Comm. Print 29, 28 p.

Thomas, N. O., and Harbeck, G. E., Jr., 1956, Reservoirs in the United States: U. S. Geol. Survey Water-Supply Paper 1360-A, 99 p., 1 pl., 3 fig.

Thornthwaite, C. W., 1952, Evapotranspiration in the hydrologic cycle, in The physical and economic foundation of natural resources: U. S. House of Representatives, Interior and Insular Affairs Comm., v. 2, p. 25–35.

U. S. Dept. Agriculture, 1960, Estimated water requirements for agricultural purposes, and their effects on water supplies: U. S. Senate, Select Comm. on National Water Resources, 86th Cong., 2d sess., Comm. Print 13, 24 p.

U. S. Geological Survey, 1962, Water for recreation—Values and opportunities: Outdoor Recreation Resources Review Comm. Study Rept. 10, 73 p.

U. S. Public Health Service, 1960, Future water requirements for municipal purposes: U. S. Senate, Select Comm. on

National Water Resources, 86th Cong., 2d sess., Comm. Print 7, 24 p.

——— 1960a, Pollution abatement: U. S. Senate, Select Comm. on National Water Resources, 86th Cong., 2d sess., Comm. Print 9, 38 p.

U. S. Weather Bureau, 1959, Evaporation maps for the United States: U. S. Weather Bureau Tech. Paper 37.

——— 1960, in U. S. Dept. Agriculture, 1960 [see above].

Wollman, Nathaniel, 1960, A preliminary report on the supply of and demand for water in the United States as estimated for 1980 and 2000: U. S. Senate, Select Comm. on National Water Resources, 86th Cong., 2d sess., Comm. Print 32, 131 p.

25   World Offshore Petroleum Resources

L. G. Weeks

Introductory Statement

Energy resources available to man today comprise two major classes. They are the forms of energy that are of inorganic nature and those that are of organic origin. Among the inorganic energy sources are those of atomic and of solar derivation. Included also are tidal energy, and the energy of geothermal (the internal heat of the earth) nature. The inorganic sources of energy are unlimited as far as man's use of them is concerned. Part of the inor-

Weeks, L. G., 1965, "World Offshore Petroleum Resources," Bull. Amer. Assoc. of Petroleum Geologists, vol. 49, no. 10, pp. 1680–93. Abridged and reprinted by permission of the author and the American Association of Petroleum Geologists. Copyright 1965 by A. A. P. G.

This is a revision of a paper presented orally by the writer at a Symposium on the Mineral Resources of the Seas organized by the Society of Mining Engineers of A. I. M. E. for the Annual Meeting in Chicago, 1965; modified, with permission, from the following paper: Lewis G. Weeks, 1965, Offshore Oil, Oil and Gas Jour., vol. 63, no. 25, pp. 127–48. Mr. Weeks, Westport, Connecticut, is a worldwide geological consultant. Prior to his retirement in 1958 he was chief geologist for Standard Oil Company of New Jersey.

ganic sources first named may be derivable from outer space.

The organic energy resources of the earth include the so-called "fossil fuels." Most familiar are the various types of coal, and the liquid, gaseous, and solid petroleums. They also include substances of petroleum or petroleum-like nature, such as can be derived from oil-sands, from bituminous accumulations, and from bituminous shales and limestones.

Energy from organic sources has come from the geologic past. Through the agency of photosynthesis, the sun's heat-energy was preserved originally in the fantastically large volumes of plant and animal matter in the seas, and thence in the sediments. And it was similarly incorporated in the coal, most of which accumulated on the lands. The organic sources of energy, though they are vast beyond any precise estimation, are in reality somewhat limited as far as man's very long-range future needs are concerned.

The hydrocarbon resources of the sea areas are probably the most immediately important of all minerals associated with the sea, unless man can learn soon to use the water economically.

Any worth-while assessment of the potential hydrocarbon resources under the seas must consider two basic factors: the first is the areal and volumetric distribution of sedimentary rocks underlying the present seas; the second and by far the most important factor is the degree of favorability of the sediments in each area. This is determined by the environment of deposition of the sediments and their subsequent history. The most critical factor, therefore, is purely geologic, but it involves many considerations.

Industry must look to the continental shelves and the closely adjoining deeper waters for most of the hydrocarbons to be obtained from beneath the sea. There are two reasons for this. The first is geologic. Subsea sedimentary rocks favorable for petroleum are confined very largely to these shelves and adjacent offshore areas. The second reason is economic. It is the least important of the two, because if petroleum existed in quantity at great water depths man would find a way to recover it.

World-Wide Inventory

It is evident that the first step in assessing the subsea hydrocarbon resources is to take an inventory worldwide, area by area, to determine the area and volume distribution of sedimentary rocks of interest offshore. Second, each of the sedimentary areas must be classified or rated according to its estimated degree of favorability for petroleum. The next and final step is to estimate the amount of petroleum commercially recoverable from each area by present and likely future techniques and economics. These estimates are based on the experience of the industry under similar geological conditions.

Sediment Distribution

The total offshore area in square miles out to 1,000 feet of water depth is given for each major world subdivision and for the world as a whole in Table 1. In each case the total area is subdivided into four rating categories —A, B, C, and D—in decreasing order of favorability for petroleum.

At the right of the number of square miles in each category is the percentage of total for the region or major subdivision of the world. Beneath each area figure is the percentage of the world total in that rating category.

This very general manner of rating is one that is commonly used, though too often not in a concise manner. As used here, areas placed in the A column are those which contain or are in continuity with an excellent producing area and which have like geology. Areas in the B column are those in continuity with a fair producing area, or whose geology is favorable for like commercial production. The C column contains areas whose prospects are judged to be submarginal or not commercially attractive on the basis of present information, but which in some cases can not be ruled out of a higher (or lower) category. Areas in column D are those whose geology indicates no prospects; usually there is inadequate or no sedimentary cover.

The figures in the *Total* column in Table 1 are those of the entire continental shelf and adjoining slope to a

Table 1 World continental shelf areas[1] (thousands of square miles) Rated according to estimated petroleum potential[2]

	A	%	B	%	C	%	D	%	Total	%
North America	40	1.9	315	14.7	875	40.9	910	42.5	2,140	100
	21.3%		19.0		20.2		19.8		19.9	
South America	20	2.2	150	16.5	425	46.7	315	34.6	910	100
	10.0%		9.1		9.8		6.9		8.5	
Europe	5	0.7	90	12.2	255	34.7	385	52.4	735	100
	2.7%		5.4		5.9		8.4		6.8	
Africa	8	1.4	82	13.9	245	41.5	255	43.2	590	100
	4.2%		4.9		5.7		5.6		5.5	
Middle East, Asia	40	20.0	65	32.5	67	33.5	28	14.0	200	100
	21.3%		3.9		1.5		0.6		1.8	
Far East, Asia (less Red China)	5	0.7	110	15.7	285	40.7	300	42.9	700	100
	2.7%		6.6		6.6		6.5		6.5	
East Indies Islands (incl. Philippines)	35	2.6	305	22.6	600	44.4	410	30.4	1,350	100
	18.6%		18.4		13.9		8.9		12.6	
Australia and New Zealand	—		130	14.9	405	46.6	335	38.5	870	100
			7.8		9.4		7.3		8.1	
Antarctica	—		25	4.6	125	22.7	400	72.7	550	100
			1.5		2.9		8.7		5.1	
Iron Curtain countries	35	1.3	385	14.2	1,043	38.4	1,255	46.1	2,718	100
	18.6%		23.2		24.1		27.3		25.2	
Totals	188	1.8	1,657	15.3	4,325	40.2	4,593	42.7	10,763	100
	100%		100		100		100		100	

[1] To 1000 feet of water depth.

[2] Basis of rating:

A. Contains or is in continuity with excellent producing area and with like geology.

B. Contains or is in continuity with a fair producing area, or whose geology is similarly favorable for commercial production.

C. Prospects are submarginal or not commercially attractive on the basis of present information, but in some cases can not be ruled out of higher classification.

D. Geology indicates no prospects, usually because of inadequate sedimentary cover.

water depth of 1,000 feet. These figures give a total world shelf and upper slope area of 10,763,000 square miles.

It is common practice to limit the area designated as shelf to that above the 100-fathom or 600-foot water-depth contour, or to the 200-meter (656-foot) isobath. Water depth in the present seas normally increases rapidly as the 600-foot depth is approached, and it increases more rapidly beyond. For this reason, the inclusion of the area between the 600- and the 1,000-foot depth contours scarcely adds 10 per cent to the total sea bottom area measured only to the 600-foot contour.

This fact is important because, on many of the world's very wide shelves, there is inadequate sedimentary fill, or there may be no sediments at all beneath the broad, flat, shallow, main areas of the shelf. Yet, in many places, sediments of Tertiary and even older age are known to occur under the deeper-water outer shelf and slope.

Degree of Favorability

Only the areas that are included in columns A, B, and C are important or possibly important parts of the sedimentary basins. Because only in these areas is there any appreciable thickness of sediments, Table 2 is presented in order to give a breakdown of the total shelf area of each of the world's major subdivisions into: (1) the total area that is possibly petroleum-bearing, and (2) the balance of the shelf area in which the presence of any significant quantity of hydrocarbons is impossible or unlikely.

The percentage of total shelf that is underlain by appreciable quantities of sediments, in which the existence of

petroleum pools is possible, ranges from as low as 47 per cent in Europe to 86 per cent in the Middle East. It is 57 per cent for the world as a whole.

Petroleum Potential

Any assessment of the potential petroleum resources offshore can be based only on the results of industry experience in exploring basin areas of like category onshore. Therefore, as far as possible, it is necessary to use area figures that mean the same thing in both cases.

To simplify the comparison, Table 3 was prepared to include only the sedimentary basin areas—the areas of A, B, and C categories. The non-sedimentary basins or impossible petroleum-bearing areas of the shelf (category D of the preceding tables) are eliminated.

The total area of world offshore basins is 6,170,000 square miles. This is about 57 per cent of the total shelf area.

Measured on the same basis, the total basin area underlying the lands of the world is about 18–18.5 million square miles. Thus, the world's offshore basins to 1,000 feet of water depth have a total area about one-third that of the basins on land. Expressed in another way, the world's offshore basin area constitutes about one-fourth that of the entire land- and water-basin area of the world.

The percentage distribution of the A, B, and C acreage in each of the 10 major regions are compared. These are the percentage figures at the right of the square-mile figures. In all of the regions except the Middle-East, basin acreage of A category is less than 4 per cent of the total offshore basin area,

Table 2 World continental shelf areas[1] (thousands of square miles) Rated according to estimated petroleum potential[2]

	1 Possible petroleum-bearing area A + B + C	%	2 Impossible or unlikely petroleum-bearing area D	%	Total area	%
North America	1,230 20.0%	57.5	910 19.8	42.5	2,140 19.9	100
South America	595 9.6%	65.4	315 6.9	34.6	910 8.5	100
Europe	350 5.7%	47.6	385 8.4	52.4	735 6.8	100
Africa	335 5.4%	56.8	255 5.6	43.2	590 5.5	100
Middle East, Asia	172 2.8%	86.0	28 6.6	14.0	200 1.8	100
Far East, Asia	400 6.5%	57.1	300 6.5	42.9	700 6.5	100
East Indies Islands (incl. Philippines)	940 15.2%	69.6	410 8.9	30.4	1,350 12.6	100
Australia and New Zealand	535 8.7%	61.5	335 7.3	38.5	870 8.1	100
Antarctica	150 2.4%	27.3	400 8.7	72.7	550 5.1	100
Iron Curtain countries	1,463 23.7%	53.9	1,255 27.3	46.1	2,718 25.2	100
Totals	6,170 100%	57.3	4,593 100%	42.7	10,763 100%	100

[1] To 1000 feet of water depth.
[2] Basis of rating is the same as for Table 1.

whereas it is about 23 per cent of the total offshore basin area in the Middle East. For the world as a whole, category A acreage comprises 3 per cent of the total offshore basin area out to 1,000 feet of water depth.

For most of the countries, acreage of B category comprises about one-fourth of the total offshore basin area. Again, it is the highest, at about 37.8 per cent, in the Middle East. It comprises about 27 per cent for the world.

The remaining offshore basin acreage, that of C category, is about 70–73 per cent of total basin area in most of the regions. The Middle East has the lowest percentage (about 39 per cent) of this least attractive basin acreage. For the world, the figure is about 70 per cent.

The percentage figures just cited tell nothing about the size of the total basin area in each region. For instance, the total offshore basin area ranges from as little as 172,000 square miles in the Middle East to 1,230,000 square

Table 3 World continental shelf sedimentary basin areas[1] (thousands of square miles) Rated according to estimated petroleum potential[2]

	A	%	B	%	C	%	Total	%
North America	40	3.3	315	25.6	875	71.1	1,230	100
	21.3%		19.0		20.2		20.0	
South America	20	3.4	150	25.2	425	71.4	595	100
	10.6%		9.1		9.8		9.6	
Europe	5	1.4	90	25.7	255	72.9	350	100
	2.7%		5.4		5.9		5.7	
Africa	8	2.4	82	24.5	245	73.1	335	100
	4.2%		4.9		5.7		5.4	
Middle East, Asia	40	23.3	65	37.8	67	38.9	172	100
	21.3%		3.9		1.5		2.8	
Far East, Asia (Less Red China)	5	1.3	110	27.5	285	70.1	400	100
	2.7%		6.6		6.6		6.5	
East Indies Islands (incl. Philippines)	35	3.7	305	32.4	600	63.9	940	100
	18.6%		18.4		13.9		15.2	
Australia and New Zealand	—		130	24.3	405	75.7	535	100
			7.8		9.4		8.7	
Antarctica	—		25	16.7	125	83.3	150	100
			1.5		2.9		2.4	
Iron Curtain countries	35	2.4	385	26.3	1,043	71.3	1,463	100
	18.6%		23.2		24.1		23.7	
Totals	188	3.0	1,657	26.9	4,325	70.1	6,170	100
	100%		100%		100%		100%	

[1] To 1000 feet of water depth.
[2] Basis of rating is the same as for Table 1.

miles for North America and 1,463,000 square miles for the Iron Curtain countries.

So, the relative standing of the 10 major world subdivisions in each of categories A, B, and C should be considered. This is shown on Table 3 by the percentage figures beneath the square-mile figures. In this case the percentages are directly representative of the size of the areas. North America and the Middle East are each shown with 21.3 per cent of the world's offshore Class A acreage, succeeded by the East Indies and the Iron Curtain countries with 18.6 per cent each, and South America with 10.6 per cent.

In the B category of offshore acreage, the Iron Curtain countries, North America, and the East Indies rank first in area, with 23.2, 19.0, and 18.4 per cent, respectively, of world total. South America ranks fourth with 9.1 per cent.

In the submarginal or C category, the Iron Curtain countries and North America have about 24 and 20 per cent, respectively, of the world total; the East Indies offshore have about 14 per cent, and South America, about 9.8 per cent.

Prospect Assessment

So much for the areal extent of the world's offshore basins and their classification or ratings based on prospects. It is now necessary to assess those prospects.

Such commonly applied ratings as A, B, C, D, *etc.*, or good, fair, poor, and so on, are subject to a wide range of interpretations. This is true even though they are carefully defined as in this paper.

The many ratings of basins or basin areas of the world that the writer has made over the past 25 years or more were expressed in terms of the amount of petroleum which he estimated that the basin, or part of a basin, would ultimately produce. The areas thus rated include many that are highly or partly developed, and others that are unexplored.

Every possible benefit is taken from industry exploration experience and the vast quantity of facts concerning oil occurrence in general. Ratings based on careful judgments of potential yields are quantitative expressions. They force analytical study and unequivocal representation. They permit making very advantageous checks by comparisons with any one or several, or even hundreds, of other areas.

Geology Controls

Because petroleum occurrence depends wholly on the geology, and on nothing else, the only sound basis of rating must be geologic understanding of the factors that control occurrence. These factors are very real and understandable, though they are not in all respects superficially evident. It is for these reasons that estimates need to be brought up-to-date as new facts require it.

Forty years of study of oil occurrence and the factors that control its incidence have produced a number of well-documented basic factors. These factors permit applying productivity numbers to the particular set of geological conditions present. These ultimate-yield numbers are, of course, estimates. They are based on sound study and analysis of industry experience in relation to the geology in many producing basins or basin areas of similar basic geology. However, there are various sources of error, of which the following are the principal ones: incomplete understanding of the geology; failure to recognize all of the various factors of major importance that determine the incidence of oil occurrence; and incomplete appreciation of the relative importance of each of the factors.

This is not the place to delve into what would need to be a lengthy discussion of basic considerations. It is pertinent for the purposes of this paper, however, to cite some basic figures for basins of different categories.

One of these is the average percentage of total area that is likely to prove productive. The other is the average yield per unit of productive area.

It should be recognized that the figures used here are averages of many widely differing figures, and that the division between the A and B areas, the only two here rated commercially productive, is an arbitrary one. Figures that are based on the widest possible number of examples, preferably worldwide, have the greatest value for use in broad regional estimates. They are particularly applicable in this case because the writer is concerned with averages to be applied world-wide, or to major subdivisions of the world.

Productive Averages

Once the basin areas are subdivided areally into the proper categories or subcategories, the indicated average percentages of area likely to prove productive may be applied. To this product the average number of barrels of recoverable oil determined to be ap-

plicable in each case may then be applied.

Reasonable gross average figures for the world as a whole are: 4 per cent of total class A acreage at 35,000 barrels per acre, and 2½ per cent of total class B acreage at 20,000 barrels per acre. The estimates thus derived are those of ultimate oil resources recoverable by conventional methods. It should be repeated that they are general averages of many widely variable figures. A high percentage of productive acres may be counterbalanced by a low yield per productive acre, and *vice versa*. In some cases, a better basis for rating may be the productivity per square mile, or per cubic mile of sediments.

On applying the foregoing world averages to the world total offshore basin areas of rating categories A and B, the following figures are derived.

	Barrels
Total A area	168,450,000,000
Total B area	530,240,000,000
Grand total	698,690,000,000

or, say 700 billion barrels of petroleum liquids.

There are other ways of arriving at the estimates, and these may be used to advantage to check their reasonableness. On the basis of the method actually used here, the estimates give a productivity per square mile as follows.

Total A area   896,000 barrels per square mile
Total B area   320,000 barrels per square mile

In three fairly recent papers by the writer (Weeks, 1961, 1962, 1963), an estimate of the potential ultimate petroleum resources of the world was given, including both onshore and offshore, by major world subdivisions. The figure used for oil for the United

States was 270 billion barrels, and 2,000 billion barrels was estimated for the world. The barrels-per-square-mile figure just cited as average for all A- and B-rated offshore areas of the world is comparable with that resulting from calculations for all of the world's basin areas.

All figures of this nature indicate an order of magnitude of resources. They are determined on the soundest possible basis. The greatest chance of error is believed to be on the side of conservatism. But regardless of the direction of error, the estimates have the virtue of being similarly based and comparable.

Because nothing can be considered to be a reserve or a resource unless it can be produced and used profitably, the higher costs of offshore operations will preclude from resource status some of the offshore accumulations that would be included if they occurred onshore. However, as the great bulk of the world's oil and gas reserves are accounted for by the major accumulations, the loss on this score will not be sizeable. Moreover, engineering developments are certain to effect economies; and perhaps certain forms of secondary recovery may be handled more economically offshore.

Young Sediments Predominate

Actually, several factors will probably more than offset any loss of reserves resulting from higher cost.

There is indeed one factor which, by itself, probably will more than offset any deductions from higher operating costs. This is based on the geologic fact that practically all of the world's offshore oil and gas accumulations will be found in young sediments, that is, in sediments of Tertiary or Mesozoic-Tertiary age. These young sediments have a record of much greater yield than older sediments. About 87–90 per cent of the world's proved reserves are in sediments of these young ages.

All of this oil comes from a geologic age span which represents only the last 40 per cent of the oil-bearing period of geological history. In fact, fully 30 per cent of present world oil reserves are in sediments of only the last 6 per cent of the earth's oil-bearing period.

More important from the standpoint of economics—and this affects the offshore particularly—the per-acre yields of the Mesozoic-Tertiary average much higher than those of the older sediments of the longer Paleozoic period.

One might add that most geological and geophysical costs are lower offshore than on land. Actual drilling rates in the less consolidated, soft sediments are among the highest. In areas where proration and high bonuses exist, these latter factors may affect profit margins more than any other, and thus present a quite unfair, or at least unrealistic, cost of producing comparison. Actually, some of the lowest-cost reserves in the United States today are being found off the Louisiana coast, and may be found off other coasts.

Incidentally, off the Louisiana coast, expenditures are running at the rate of about a million dollars per day, as operators are racing to meet their lease obligations, a task that is made very difficult by the difficult rig-supply situation. Interest is maintained by a discovery rate higher than for any other part of the United States, as well as by the finding of the largest fields in recent years. On the west coast of the United States, exploration for petroleum is getting under way off each of the three coastal States. The areas of interest extend into water depths of 250–1,000 feet and call for deep-water semi-submersible equipment.

Search Is World-Wide

There is a rapidly growing world-wide demand for offshore drilling equipment. Outside of the United States today there are about 35 offshore rigs operating. It now appears that the number will be increased by at least 15–20 in 1965. All existing rigs are in use, mostly on long-term contracts. A dozen or more operators were planning to start drilling campaigns in the North Sea in the spring of 1965. Shipyards in the United States, Britain, and elsewhere are besieged with orders for rigs.

From the world-wide scramble for offshore rigs a better understanding of rig requirements ultimately will evolve. The successful rig builders will be able to meet these requirements with a smaller number of more versatile rig types. So adaptable will the rigs become that five years from now offshore drilling in waters 1,000 feet deep or more will present no really serious problems. However, problems of completion and producing operations will be solved somewhat more slowly, but again necessity will father the solution.

That the subject of this paper is timely is shown by the almost explosive spread of interest in recent years in the search for petroleum to all parts of the world. Whereas, only 12 years ago there were but a very few, mostly major companies, looking for oil abroad, there are today literally hundreds of companies, large and small, carrying out exploration or producing operations, or both, in more than 100 countries.

Sixty Countries Exploring Offshore

With respect to all this, the one observation that stands out with greatest emphasis today is the rapid growth of interest in offshore exploration.

Eight years ago one could count the areas of the world with offshore activity on the fingers of one hand. Today, at least 60 countries, or more than half of those now interested in finding petroleum, are actively engaged in some degree of offshore exploration or development.

Already, about 4 million barrels per day, or 16 per cent of the Free World's daily production, comes from the offshore.

As of today, the Free World's offshore proved oil reserves total about 55 billion barrels, 17 per cent of the world's total reserve.

Seventeen countries are producing offshore oil today. World-wide, the rates of increase in oil reserves and in daily production offshore are much more rapid than onshore. Concern about depth of water has rapidly given way to the far more basically important questions of geology and the facts of oil occurrence. Engineering problems have a way of disappearing, as shown by the fantastic growth in development of offshore equipment. Ultimately, these facts, and particularly the results from exploration, become evident to managements as well as to geologists, even though they may not have foreseen the reasons for the successes.

Geologic History the Key

The question may arise in the minds of some geologists, as well as of those who are not geologists, why it is that the offshore basin sediments should be preponderantly of the late and best part of the oil-furnishing period of geologic history?

Without going into a lengthy technical explanation, the reason can be stated simply and briefly as follows: as a result of the manner in which the continental masses of the earth were built, throughout 4 billion years of geological history, the younger basins, and particularly those of the Tertiary, were developed near the continental margins. In fact, the attractive parts of some of these young basins actually lie under the shelves, rather than onshore. On the other hand, those parts of the older basins of the Paleozoic that still remain commercially oil-bearing are spread widely over the interior of the continents.

There are exceptions to most rules in geology (though many of these only appear to be exceptions because of inaccurate diagnosis). For example, with respect to the foregoing statement that the areas in which the youngest basins are best developed for petroleum lie at or near the continental margins, there are some young basins (as for example, the Caspian Sea area) where interior subsidence was of exceptional duration and prominence. (It is only fair to add, however, that the Caspian Sea basin is clearly related to an existing sea, whose surface is today below sea-level, and that the most petroliferous part may lie offshore.)

The estimate of 700 billion barrels of offshore potential petroleum resources includes natural gas liquids, that is, those liquids that are dissolved in the gas at the pressures existing in the reservoir, but which separate from solution at the lower pressures at the earth's surface. Natural gas liquids may represent as much as 10 per cent of the total in many places, depending on the occurrence and the recovery practices. The potential resource figures already given do not include petroleum which may be recovered by such secondary techniques as repressuring the oil reservoir by means of gas or water injection and other methods of stimulating the flow from the reservoir rock to the well bore.

The larger secondary recoveries today generally are from the older fields that were produced under primary-recovery practices less efficient than those of today. Secondary recovery in many older fields may add a volume of oil and gas equal to 50 per cent, and possibly 80 per cent or even double that recovered by the primary methods. As the term is used here, secondary recovery includes such improvements in primary recovery as will probably be developed beyond those now in general use.

On this basis, it is estimated that 300 billion barrels of additional oil will be recovered by secondary methods (Table 4).

Other Hydrocarbons

So far only the liquid hydrocarbons have been considered. There are other sources of hydrocarbon energy which should be included in an inventory of this sort. In an inventory of world energy made 4 years ago (Weeks, 1960), it was estimated that the equivalent of 1,100 billion barrels of oil energy would be derived from heavy oil-sands, or what are commonly and erroneously referred to as "tar"-sands. Most of this heavy oil will be recovered from the lands, because of the probable lesser occurrence offshore as well as the less favorable economics. The equivalent of 200 billion barrels of oil may be recovered from offshore heavy oil-sands by applicable methods.

Bituminous sediments, such as oil shales, from which the hydrocarbons need to be freed by heat distillation, occur under the offshore as well as under the land basin areas. The total amount of hydrocarbons that are thus locked in close association with the sediments is almost beyond calculation. However, the proportion of the total that ultimately will be reserves will depend on the extent to which man can economically delve.

In the inventory of world energy resources previously mentioned, the amount of such resources attributable to oil shales and kindred sediments was estimated to have the energy equivalent of 12,000 billion barrels of oil.

Because of various facts of geology, the relatively younger offshore sediments probably will be found to contain fewer oil shales than the older basin sediments of the land, or than the young basin sediments of the continental interior. For this reason, as well as the economics, the energy equivalent of only 1,000 billion barrels of oil is estimated to be possibly derivable from bituminous sediments beneath the sea by methods yet to be developed. That they will be satisfactorily developed as the need arises is confidently expected and is a basic premise of this estimate.

Gas Too

So much for the subsea hydrocarbon resources presently existing in liquid and solid form. Gaseous hydrocarbons occur also in vast amounts. They occur in association with liquid hydrocarbons in the reservoir, either in solution in the oil or as a gas cap above the oil, or both. They occur also in reservoirs by themselves as so-called "nonassociated" gas.

In the inventory of world energy resources previously mentioned, it was estimated that world hydrocarbon gas resources are adequate ultimately to supply the energy equivalent of 1,000 billion barrels of oil. After further study, and in comparison with other estimates, this figure is now considered to be too low. Correspondingly, it is raised to 1,200 billion. Of this world total, it is estimated that gas, equivalent in energy to 300 billion barrels of oil, is available from beneath the sea (Table 4).

A complete inventory of hydrocarbons derivable from sources beneath the sea might also be expected to include those which are extractable from the coals present there. The amount of such hydrocarbons will depend on the

Table 4

Source	Billions of barrels of oil or equivalent
Petroleum liquids by primary recovery	700
Petroleum liquids by secondary recovery	300
Oil ("tar")-sands	200
Bituminous rocks (oil shales, *etc.*)	1000
Petroleum gas	300
Total	2500

total volume of extractable coal, the economics of its extraction, and the use to which the coal is put, that is, what percentage, if any, will be converted into hydrocarbons by hydrogenation or other processes.

Perspective Look

No apology is made for the foregoing hydrocarbon resource estimates.

They were made on request to complete a symposium on the mineral resources of the seas. Their consideration must form a very important part of any general assessment of world sea and subsea mineral resources. Indeed, they must form a part of any assessment of world resources.

The figures given are only estimates. However, they are based on the only possible acceptable parameters for making such estimates, which are geological. Estimates of any value can be reached only through an understanding of the geological why and wherefore, the facts, of oil occurrence. Analysis of these facts in the light of industry exploration experience in thousands of instances world-wide provide an abundance of empirical support. Many of the basic data are measurable, and anyone can make his own analyses, interpretations, and estimates.

The figures here presented apply only to the offshore. To some students the figures may appear too conservative. A lesser number may think them too high.

Although the organic sources of energy are vast beyond any precise estimation they are in reality relatively limited as far as man's very long future needs are concerned. Though they may seem vast by today's yardsticks of energy needs, it must be remembered that the rate of energy consumption is accelerating, and this accelerating growth seems destined to continue.

Rather recently, in another connection, the writer estimated that by the end of this century the rate of energy use will be about six times that of today. Already, the annual increase in world daily demand just for oil alone is about 2,200,000 barrels per day.

To give a little perspective on the size of this annual increase in daily oil demand, it is 18 per cent greater than the present daily production of Iran, one of the world's largest suppliers of oil. The annual growth in daily consumption is 43 per cent greater than the entire daily production of Iraq, to mention another of the world's major producers.

References

Lewis G. Weeks, 1960, The next hundred years energy demand and sources of supply (abbrev. version): GeoTimes (July-August), Am. Geol. Inst., Washington, D. C. A revised and complete paper of this title was published in Alberta Soc. Petroleum Geologists Jour., Calgary, Alberta, Canada, v. 9, no. 5 (May, 1961).

—— 1962, World gas reserves, production, occurrence: presented to Southwestern Legal Foundation, Dallas, Texas, and published in the Foundation's "Economics of the Gas Industry," by Matthew Bender & Co., Inc., Albany, N. Y., 1962.

—— 1963, Worldwide review of petroleum exploration: Soc. Petroleum Engineers Paper 638, presented at 38th Ann. Fall Meeting of Soc. Petroleum Engineers of A. I. M. E. in New Orleans, La., October 6-9. Pub. by the Society, 6300 North Central Expressway, Dallas 6, Texas. Revision of paper presented in 6th World Petroleum Congr. Plenary Sess., Frankfurt, Germany, June, 1963.

26 Organic-Rich Shale of the United States and World Land Areas

Donald C. Duncan and Vernon E. Swanson

Introduction

Fine-grained sedimentary rocks containing substantial amounts of combustible organic matter constitute an enormous low-grade source of potential energy. Thus far, such deposits have been used as sources of synthetic oil and combustible gas or as solid fuel only on a small scale, but their use is expected to increase in the future as methods of mining and processing are developed and improved. The deposits included in this inventory vary widely in composition of organic matter and in mineral content. The group of deposits as a whole is herein designated "organic-rich shale," and selected parts of these deposits that yield oil in substantial amounts by conventional destructive distillation methods are designated "oil shale."

Previous Summaries

No published summary of the total energy potential of organic-rich shale is known to the authors. Previous summaries of world resources of oil shale include reports by the Great Britain Mineral Resource Bureau (1924), proceedings of two conferences on oil shale and cannel coal published by The Institute of Petroleum (1938, 1951),

Duncan, D. C. and Swanson, V. E., 1965, "Organic-Rich Shale of the United States and World Land Areas," U. S. Geol. Survey Circ. 523, 30 pp. Abridged.

Cadman (1948), Guthrie and Thorne (1954), Jaffé (1962), and Thorne, Stanfield, Dinneen, and Murphy (1962). Summaries covering parts of oil shale and black shale resources of the United States include reports by Winchester (1923, 1928), U. S. Bureau of Mines (1960), U. S. Geological Survey (1951), Rubel (1955), Duncan (1958), Swanson (1960), and Shultz (1962).

These summaries reflect an increasing knowledge of shale oil resources and contribute to a general increase in estimates of resources in known deposits. The estimates of the better known shale oil resources in the United States have increased from about 140 billion barrels in the 1920's to more than 2 trillion barrels in 1963, and the world known resource estimates from a few hundred billion barrels to more than 3 trillion barrels during the same period. Weeks (1960) estimated that "possible potential resources" of the higher grade organic-rich shale in the United States were about 2 trillion barrels oil equivalent and in the world about 12 trillion barrels.

Types of Deposits

Organic-rich shales were deposited in bodies of water that contained abundant aquatic plants (and animals), or debris from land plants, under conditions that prevented oxidation of much of the organic debris that accumulated on the bottom. The principal environments in which the known organic-rich shales were formed were (1) large lake basins, (2) large marine basins, and (3) smaller bodies of water such as lakes, stagnant streams, and lagoons near coal-forming swamps. Oil-shale deposits of various sizes and grade, and associated organic-rich shales, which have low or undetermined oil yields are widely distributed in deposits formed in each of these environments.

Potential Energy, Oil, or Gas Yield of the Organic Matter in Shale

The potential thermal energy of organic-rich shale deposits, which are considered in this report, is based mainly on correlation of the estimated energy content of organic matter with a few hundred actual calorimetric measurements of random shale samples reported in the literature.

The principal energy-producing materials of organic matter in shale are organic carbon, which by direct combustion yields about 14,500 Btu per lb, and chemically combined hydrogen, which yields 52,000–61,000 Btu per lb. Inorganic or oxidized carbon such as that contained in carbonate minerals and hydrogen combined with oxygen principally as water are excluded for purposes of estimating energy content. Ratios of organic carbon to combined hydrogen in the organic matter range from about 6:1 in some unmetamorphosed deposits (Smith, Smith, and Kommes, 1959) to about 50:1 in some metamorphosed deposits. A carbon-hydrogen ratio of 10:1 is assumed to be average for the moisture-free organic matter in the principal unmetamorphosed deposits that compose the resources considered in this report; thus, a pound of organic matter containing 67 percent carbon and 6.7 percent combined hydrogen yields on the average about 13,000 Btu, and a ton of moisture-free organic matter yields 26 million Btu. Most of the organic matter of different types of shale can be converted to light oil or to combustible gas products by one or more experimental extraction methods (Hubbard and Fester, 1959; Elliott and others, 1961; Shultz, 1962), as for example, the hydrogenolysis of shale under high confining pressures. For purposes of estimating potential resources it is assumed that about half the energy potential of any organic-rich shale can be converted by such methods to energy-producing light oil or gas products and that the remaining thermal energy of the organic matter can be used for the conversion process. Thus a ton of "average" organic-rich shale containing 10 percent organic matter is assumed to yield 2.6 million Btu by direct combustion, or 10 gallons of light-oil product, or 1,300 cubic feet of gas per ton by such methods.

Many oil-shale deposits have been examined and sampled systematically. The principal analytical data obtained, however, are analyses of oil that is extractable from the deposits by destructive distillation of the organic matter in a conventional retort. Data relating to gross energy content of the organic matter, the energy content of produced gas, or the residual char or coke after extraction of the oil are generally incompletely known except for the mined parts of some deposits. The energy extractable as heavier oil by normal destructive distillation from selected deposits ranges from about ¼ to ¾ of the gross potential energy of the shale. In addition some unspecified amounts of hydrocarbon gas and heat from residual char or coke not included in the estimates would be produced and would be available for use in processing the shale or for marketed energy.

Extraction methods other than the conventional retort process applied either to oil shale or other organic-rich shale perhaps yield substantially different amounts and quality of oil and gas products. For example, hydrogenolysis of numerous shales under high confining pressure allows almost complete conversion of the organic matter to oil or gas, but the process consumes substantial energy herein assumed to be half the contained energy of the organic matter. In situ processing by partial combustion underground or by extraction with catalysts or special solvents at high temperatures and pressures would doubtlessly yield products in different amounts. Many schemes to extract energy or products are patented, but few have been developed commercially.

Status of the Shale Industry

World Production

Although organic-rich shale has been used as a solid fuel and as a source of oil and combustible gas in fuel-short areas of the world during the past 125 years, the world production has been small, totaling by the close of 1961 an estimated 770 million tons of shale, which has an estimated energy content of about 4–4.5 quadrillion Btu. The energy recovered from the shale deposits was marketed mostly in the form of oil which probably contained about 2.3 quadrillion Btu.

Oil-shale deposits in Scotland, France, Russia, Estonia, Sweden, Germany, Spain, South Africa, Australia, and Manchuria have been mined at modest sustained commercial scale to produce a total of about 400 million barrels of oil to the end of 1961. The principal production had been from deposits in Scotland (about 100 million bbl), Estonia (possibly 100 million bbl), and Manchuria (probably more than 100 million bbl). Industries each producing about 500–750 thousand barrels of shale oil per year closed down in Scotland and Sweden in 1962, but a similar small industry at that time was in operation in Spain. Expanding oil-shale industries in Estonia and Manchuria were reported during the same period; the larger Manchurian industry was probably producing 40,000 barrels of oil per day or more.

Illuminating gas produced from cannel shale and other oil-shale deposits was used in small amounts during the 19th century in Europe, Eastern United States, and Australia. Shale gas, produced as a byproduct with shale oil, has been used locally for heating or power generation in connection with several European oil-shale industries. The only substantial modern commercial shale gas production, however, is reported in Estonia and in the Leningrad region of Russia where large quantities of low-heat-value gas have been produced since about 1950 for domestic and industrial purposes.

Shale has been used as solid fuel in a small way for domestic heat and for industrial purposes in parts of Europe. In addition, the residual carbonaceous matter left in some oil shale after distillation of oil and gas is used to produce process heat or steam for power generation.

Byproducts

Nitrogen compounds and sulfur, which normally occur in the organic matter of shale, but which are undesirable in fuels, are extracted as useful byproducts in some of the European oil-shale industries. Other materials such as vanadium, uranium, copper, trona, and phosphatic material are also present in some deposits of oil shale in sufficient amounts to be of commercial interest as coproducts. Other oil-shale industries produce lime, brick, or lightweight aggregate from the ash of the shale. Some oil-shale deposits associated with coal are mined as a byproduct with the coal.

Activities in the United States

In the Eastern United States minor high-grade cannel shale and lower grade black shale were mined to produce small amounts of oil and illuminating gas prior to the discovery of abundant petroleum in 1859. Several commercial experiments to produce shale oil in the United States have been conducted during the present century although no sustained production has been attained. Recent pilot-scale mining and extraction of one of the higher grade oil-shale deposits in western Colorado by the U. S. Bureau of Mines and by oil companies suggest that shale oil can be produced from the higher grade deposits with demonstrated mining and retorting methods at prices somewhat comparable to or a little above the present prices of similar petroleum or coal-tar products (about 5 cents per gallon). Some experiments to extract oil from shale in place also have been conducted by commercial concerns, but results have not been published.

Classification of Resources

As there is only minor use of oil shale or other organic-rich shale, under present conditions the deposits are generally considered uneconomic energy sources. In special situations, however, where other fuels are in short or uncertain supply and where shale industries are developed or contemplated, selected deposits are provisionally considered economically recoverable energy sources.

Known Resources

The known resources reported used in Tables 2 and 3 include parts of deposits for which knowledge of organic content and oil or gas yield is based on assays and for which knowledge of size is based on measurements and mapping. The known resources as recognized in this report include such categories used in literature as proven, measured, indicated, minimum, and some inferred, possible, and maximum "reserves" used in technical reports. The so-called "inferred reserves" and similar categories included here in the known resources generally are partly sampled and mapped, but the estimator has considered his estimate to be subject to large error.

Possible Extensions of Known Resources

Parts of deposits in areas remote from sampled and mapped parts are classed in a separate category as possible extensions of known resources. The estimates of these possible resources are mostly conjectural. They include some "inferred" resources of some reports.

Undiscovered and Unappraised Resources

Deposits that are inadequately sampled or mapped for detailed appraisal along with deposits that are inferred to exist but are truly undiscovered are classed as undiscovered and unappraised resources.

Total Resources

Total resources include all potential energy, oil, or gas resources of organic-rich shale including oil shale. Estimates of the order of magnitude of the total energy resources of shale containing more than 5 percent organic matter are shown separately in Table 1; their alternative potential oil yields are shown in Tables 2 and 3.

Recoverable Resources

Oil-shale deposits that are mined or that are in advanced stages of planned development and in areas where petroleum is in short or uncertain supply are considered usable at present for purposes of this report. The more accessible, higher grade parts of such deposits are classed as "recoverable resources." In the United States these resources are assumed to include parts of oil-shale deposits yielding more than 25 gallons of oil per ton of shale in deposits 25 feet or more thick that extend to limiting depths of 1,000 feet below surface. These limits are based mainly on recent pilot-scale mining and processing experiments of the U. S. Bureau of Mines and of commercial concerns in western Colorado. Both

Table 1 Order of magnitude of total stored energy in organic-rich shale of the United States and principal land areas of the world [Estimates and totals rounded]

Continent or country	Approximate area underlain by sedimentary rocks (millions of square miles)	Shale containing 10-65 per cent organic matter			Shale containing 5-10 per cent organic matter		
		Shale in deposits (trillions of short tons)	Minimum organic content (trillions of short tons)	Combustion energy content Q (10^{18} Btu)	Shale in deposits (trillions of short tons)	Minimum organic content (trillions of short tons)	Combustion energy content Q (10^{18} Btu)
United States	1.6	120	12	310	1,200	60	1,600
Africa	5.0	370	37	960	3,700	190	4,900
Asia	7.0	500	50	1,300	5,000	250	6,500
Australia	1.2	90	9	230	900	45	1,200
Europe	1.6	120	12	310	1,200	60	1,600
North America (including United States)	3.0	220	22	570	2,200	110	2,900
South America	2.4	180	18	470	1,800	90	2,300
World total	20	1,500	150	4,000±	15,000	750	20,000±

Table 2 Shale oil resources of the United States, in billions of barrels [ne, no estimate. Estimates and totals rounded]

Deposits	Known resources				Order of magnitude of possible extensions of known resources			Order of magnitude of undiscovered and unappraised resources			Order of magnitude of total resources		
	Recoverable under present conditions	Marginal and submarginal (oil equivalent in deposits)			Marginal and submarginal (oil equivalent in deposits)			(oil equivalent in deposits)			Oil equivalent in deposits		
Range in grade (oil yield, in gallons per ton of shale)	10–100	25–100	10–25	5–10	25–100	10–25	5–10	25–100	10–25	5–10	25–100	10–25	5–10
Green River Formation, Colorado, Utah, and Wyoming	80	520	1,400	2,000	600	1,400	2,000				1,200	2,800	4,000
Devonian and Mississippian shale, Central and Eastern United States	None	None	200	200	None	800	1,800					1,000	2,000
Marine shale, Alaska	Small	Small	Small	Small	250	200	Large				250	200	Large
Shale associated with coal	do	do	ne	ne	Small	Large	do	60	250	210	60	250	210
Other shale deposits	do	do	Small	ne	ne	ne	ne	500	22,000	134,000	500	22,000	134,000
Total	80	520	1,600	2,200	850	2,400	3,800	550	22,000	134,000	2,000	26,000	140,000

the thickness-grade-depth limits and amounts of recoverable oil might be changed greatly, however, by use of different recovery or extraction methods, or by different market conditions. In those foreign areas where oil shale industries are established or have recently operated on a sustained basis, deposits that have the grades and thicknesses of those already mined are considered recoverable. These can be roughly grouped as: (1) deposits yielding 25–100 gallons of oil per ton, in beds a few feet thick or more, extending to depths of 1,000 feet below surface and (2) some lower grade deposits yielding 10–25 gallons of oil per ton, in units 25 feet thick or more, which are minable by open-pit methods. About 50 percent of the oil shale in place is assumed to be minable under present conditions, although larger percentages could be recovered from parts of deposits minable by open-pit methods.

Marginal and Submarginal Resources

Except for the recoverable resources previously defined, oil-shale and other organic-rich shale deposits are considered uneconomic sources of oil or energy at present. They are classed as marginal and submarginal resources. The deposits are classified according to their organic content or oil yield. No attempt is made here to classify the deposits according to thickness, depth, or other factors that might affect commercial use.

Deposits that have not been assayed for oil yield are grouped into two categories according to organic content: deposits which contain 10 percent or more organic matter and deposits which contain 5–10 percent organic

matter. The organic and energy content of these deposits are inventoried in Table 1, and their estimated oil potential is shown in Tables 2 and 3.

Deposits that have been assayed for oil yield are subdivided into units that yield 25–100, 10–25, and 5–10 gallons per ton. These are inventoried in Tables 2 and 3 as known resources and their possible extensions.

Minimum thicknesses of shale resources included in the inventory vary with the deposit and opinions of different estimators, from about 20 inches (or 50 cm) to 25 feet. The principal known deposits generally lie at depths less than a few thousand feet, but in a few areas deposits as much as 10,000 feet below surface are included. A limiting depth of 20,000 feet, roughly the present limit of commercial drilling, is used in the inventory of undiscovered and incompletely appraised deposits.

Total Resources of Organic-Rich Shale

According to data taken principally from Trask and Patnode (1942), somewhat more than 5 percent of the sedimentary rocks in the United States is shale, which contains 5 percent organic matter or more, and somewhat more than 0.5 percent of the sedimentary rocks is shale containing 10 percent organic matter or more. The orders of magnitude of these organic-rich shale resources, their contained organic matter and estimated energy potential in the United States, and—by extrapolation according to area—other major lands of the world are shown in Table 1. They were estimated with the following assumptions. The land areas including terrains underlain by both ma-

Table 3 Shale oil resources of the world land areas, in billions of barrels [ne, no estimate. Estimates and totals rounded]

Continents	Known resources				Order of magnitude of possible extensions of known resources			Order of magnitude of undiscovered and unappraised resources			Order of magnitude of total resources		
	Recoverable under present conditions	Marginal and submarginal (oil equivalent in deposits)						(oil equivalent in deposits)			Oil equivalents in deposits		
Range in grade (oil yield, in gallons per ton of shale)	10–100	25–100	10–25	5–10	25–100	10–25	5–10	25–100	10–25	5–10	25–100	10–25	5–10
Africa	10	90	Small	Small	ne	ne	ne	4,000	80,000	450,000	4,000	80,000	450,000
Asia	20	70	14	ne	2	3,700	ne	5,400	106,000	586,000	5,500	110,000	590,000
Australia and New Zealand	Small	Small	1	ne	ne	ne	ne	1,000	20,000	100,000	1,000	20,000	100,000
Europe	30	40	6	ne	100	200	ne	1,200	26,000	150,000	1,400	26,000	140,000
North America	80	520	1,600	2,200	900	2,500	4,000	1,500	45,000	254,000	3,000	50,000	260,000
South America	50	Small	750	ne	ne	3,200	4,000	2,000	36,000	206,000	2,000	40,000	210,000
Total	190	720	2,400	2,200	1,000	9,600	8,000	15,000	313,000	1,740,000	17,000	325,000	1,750,000

rine and nonmarine sedimentary rocks were modified from summary data prepared by J. F. Pepper (written commun., 1962). The average thickness of sedimentary rocks extending to a maximum depth of 20,000 feet was assumed to be 1½ miles. About one-half the sedimentary rock is shale. A cubic mile of organic-rich shale constitutes about 10 billion tons. The average combustion energy of 1 ton of organic matter in shale is assumed to be 26 million Btu.

The estimates of tonnage and organic content are believed to be minimum amounts for the grades of shale considered. More nearly correct figures may be double the amounts shown, if Rubey's (1951) speculation of 25 quadrillion metric tons of reduced organic carbon, equivalent to about 35 quadrillion tons of organic matter, in sedimentary rocks of the earth is valid.

Shale Oil Resources

Although many organic-rich shale deposits are reported in the land areas of the world, information on quality, thickness, and extent of most deposits is inadequate for detailed appraisal of their energy, oil, or gas potentials. The reported appraised deposits shown in Fig. 1 are demonstrated to contain oil shale, and the principal available inventory of their resources is that of their oil potential which is summarized in Tables 2 and 3. Alternative resource potentials of combustion heat, or combustible gas obtainable from some of these deposits, is discussed but not inventoried in detail.

The orders of magnitude of the total oil potentials of organic-rich shale deposits of major land areas are derived from Table 1. The possible yield of oil shown as total resources in Tables 2 and 3 or gas (not tabulated) by processes known from laboratory experiments (Hubbard and Fester, 1959; Shultz, 1962) but not applied commercially is estimated to represent about half the contained energy, equivalent to about 2.38 barrels of light-oil product, or 13,000 cubic feet of 1,000 Btu gas per ton of organic matter. Energy of the remaining organic matter in the shale would presumably be sufficient for the conversion process. Shale that contains 5–10 percent organic matter is assumed to have a potential yield of 5–10 gallons of oil per ton and is included in total resources in Tables 2 and 3. Shale containing 10–65 percent organic matter is assumed to have a potential oil yield equivalent to the combined 10–25 and 25–100 gallon yields of shale shown in Tables 2 and 3. The estimate of the undiscovered and unappraised higher grade shale is speculative. It is based on the assumption that the shale oil resources in undiscovered deposits yielding more than 25 gallons per ton should be about one-twentieth of the resources in shale yielding 10–25 gallons per ton.

Oil Shale Deposits—United States

Known oil shale deposits in the United States are distributed in rocks ranging from Ordovician to late Tertiary in age. Resource estimates of the principal better known deposits are shown in Table 2 and their locations are shown on Fig. 2.

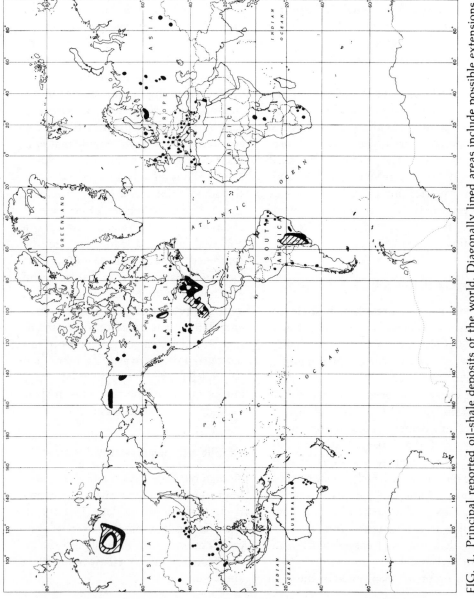

FIG. 1. Principal reported oil-shale deposits of the world. Diagonally lined areas include possible extensions of some major deposits.

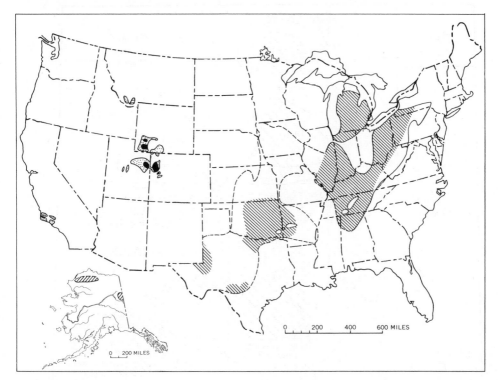

EXPLANATION

 Tertiary deposits. Green River Formation in Colorado, Utah, and Wyoming; Monterey Formation, California; middle Tertiary deposits in Montana. Black areas are known high-grade deposits.

 Mesozoic deposits
Marine shale in Alaska

 Permian deposits
Phosphoria Formation, Montana

 Devonian and Mississippian deposits (resource estimates included for hachured areas only).
Boundary dashed where concealed or where location is uncertain.

FIG. 2. Principal reported oil-shale deposits of the United States.

Green River Formation, Colorado, Utah, and Wyoming

The Green River Formation of Eocene age underlies about 16,000 square miles of several basin areas in Colorado, Utah, and Wyoming (Fig. 3) and contains the largest known higher grade oil-shale deposits in the United States. The regional extent and oil potential of these lake basin deposits are summarized by Winchester (1923), Bradley (1931), and Duncan (1958). The oil-shale resources of the more completely explored of these deposits in the Piceance Basin, Colo., are reported in more detail by Donnell (1961) and Stanfield, Smith, Smith, and Robb (1960). Oil-shale resources of parts of the Uinta Basin, Utah, are described by Cashion and Brown (1956), Cashion (1957, 1959, 1962, 1964), Stanfield, Rose, McAuley, and Tesch (1954), and

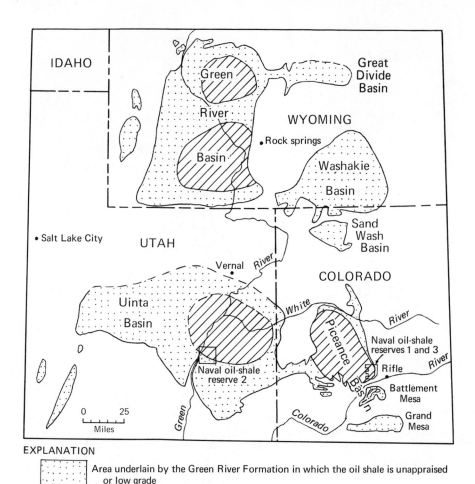

EXPLANATION

⬚ Area underlain by the Green River Formation in which the oil shale is unappraised
or low grade

▨ Area underlain by oil shale more than 10 feet thick, which yields 25 gallons or more
oil per ton of shale

FIG. 3. Distribution of oil shale in the Green River Formation, Colorado, Utah, and
Wyoming.

Stanfield, Smith, and Trudell (1964). Resources of parts of the Green River basin, Wyoming, are described by Culbertson (1964) and Stanfield, Rose, McAuley, and Tesch (1954).

The moisture and the ash-free organic matter of the richer oil shale of the Green River Formation yields about 16,000 Btu per pound. Between 75 and 80 percent of the potential energy is converted to energy in heavy shale oil, about 6 percent to energy in combustible gas, and the residue remains as coke or char in the shale when processed by the standard Fischer retort assay (Stanfield and others, 1951). The resource estimates that follow, however, include only the shale oil producible by the conventional retort assay. By different extraction methods other proportions of oil, combustible gas, and char can be produced. For example, by hydrogenolysis, about 65 percent of the gross energy potential of the rich shale can be converted to net energy in high-heat-value gas (Elliott and others, 1961; Shultz, 1962). About 100 cubic feet of fuel gas yielding 1,000 Btu per cubic foot reportedly could be produced by this alternative method for each gallon of oil producible by conventional retort methods. Light-oil products in substantial amounts are producible by hydrogenolysis under somewhat different conditions (Hubbard and Fester, 1959). For lack of systematic information these alternative energy or product potentials of the shale deposits of the Green River Formation are not treated in detail in this report.

Shale units that yield a few gallons to about 65 gallons of oil per ton are distributed throughout much of the Green River Formation, which ranges in thickness from a few hundred feet to about 7,000 feet. In general the central parts of the Piceance Basin and the Uinta Basin contain thick rich oil-shale sequences that grade to thinner and leaner oil shale at the basin margins. Somewhat thinner and generally lower grade oil shale in the Green River Basin and Washakie Basin, Wyoming, also show decrease in grade toward the basin margins.

Combined estimates of the shale oil resources of the Green River Formation are shown in Table 2. Although parts of the deposits have been explored in detail by core drilling, the oil potentials of most of the deposits are known mainly from assays of rotary drill cuttings. These cuttings supply a general indication of the grade and thickness of the deposits but probably also supply analytical data on the resource potential of higher grade shale that are conservative because of contamination of higher grade material by interbedded leaner shale or barren rock (Stanfield and others, 1964, p. 17). The estimates show the shale oil potential of units 10 feet thick or more yielding 25–65, 10–25, and 5–10 gallons per ton of shale. The estimates are somewhat different from some previous estimates by the U. S. Geological Survey, as resources within each grade range used in this report exclude resources of other grade categories. In the previous estimates the higher grade shale was included in each successively lower grade category, and cutoff values were not used. The major resources of current interest are parts of the deposits in which combined low-grade and high-grade oil shale, excluding very lean or barren rock units, range in thickness from a few hundred to 2,000 feet and average in oil yield from 15–30 gallons per ton.

Known parts of the deposits that yield 25–65 gallons of oil per ton contain about 450–500 billion barrels oil equivalent in the Piceance Basin, Colo., about 90 billion barrels in the Uinta Basin, Utah, and about 30 billion barrels in the Green River basin, Wyo., totaling about 600 billion barrels for the three basins. Approximately 160 billion barrels oil equivalent is in part of this higher grade shale averaging 30–35 gallons of oil per ton in units more than 25 feet thick and lying less than 1,000 feet below surface. Assuming that approximately half of this higher grade more accessible shale could be mined under present conditions, about 80 billion barrels of shale oil is herein considered recoverable by demonstrated mining and retorting methods.

Known oil-shale deposits that yield 10–25 gallons of oil per ton contain about 800 billion barrels oil equivalent in the Piceance Basin, Colo.; about 230 billion barrels in the Uinta Basin, Utah; and about 400 billion barrels in the combined Green River basin and Washakie Basin, Wyoming.

Known shale deposits that yield 5–10 gallons of oil per ton contain about 200 billion barrels oil equivalent in Colorado, 1,500 billion barrels in Utah, and approximately 300 billion barrels in Wyoming.

The possible extensions and possible upward revisions of the oil-shale resources of the Green River Formation are estimated to be about equal to the known resources. The larger undiscovered better grade resources are perhaps in the deeply buried parts of the formation in the Uinta Basin.

Other United States Shale Deposits
Black shale deposits of marine origin are widely distributed in Upper Devonian and lowest Mississippian formations between the Appalachian and Rocky Mountains (Conant and Swanson, 1961, pl. 14). Parts of these deposits included in this inventory underlie about 250,000 square miles of the region (diagonal-patterned area, Fig. 2), are distributed in units ranging in thickness from a few feet to about 800 feet, contain organic matter ranging from 5–25 percent of the shale, and yield as much as 7 million Btu per ton of shale by direct combustion.

Incompletely appraised or little-studied marine oil-shale deposits, which are mostly of Triassic and Jurassic age,

are reported in several areas in Alaska (Smith and Mertie, 1930; Miller and others, 1959).

Although the known oil-shale resources in Alaska are small, possible extensions are estimated to contain an order of magnitude of 250 billion barrels oil equivalent in deposits that yield more than 25 gallons per ton and perhaps more than 200 billion barrels in deposits that yield 10–25 gallons per ton. (See Table 2.) Deposits that yield 5–10 gallons per ton are presumed to be large.

Organic-rich shale is widely distributed in the coal fields of the United States in rocks ranging in age from Mississippian to Tertiary. The general distribution of the coal fields containing associated shale is shown on maps by Trumbull (1960) and Barnes (1961).

Some cannel-shale deposits in the United States were used in a small way to produce illuminating gas and oil in the middle 1800's, but they have not been used since. The small number of deposits that have been appraised in detail seem to be comparable in size and oil potential to many of the foreign cannel-shale deposits that have been mined in oil-short areas. Some of the United States deposits could be of commercial interest as sources for by-products in modern or future coal utilization.

Assuming that the shale in the northern Interior coal province is fairly representative, about 2 percent of the shale associated with coal in the United States yields 25–100 gallons of oil per ton and contains about 60 billion barrels oil equivalent; about 20 percent yields 10–25 gallons per ton and contains 250 billion barrels; and about 30 percent yields 5–10 gallons per ton and contains 210 billion barrels. Estimates of these unappraised and undiscovered resources are shown separately in Table 2.

Total Shale Oil Resources

The estimates of total shale oil resources of the United States shown in Table 2 are derived from data in Table 1. The difference between the total resources and the known shale oil resources plus extensions of known resources is shown as undiscovered and unappraised resources. A somewhat larger proportion of high-grade shale is estimated for the United States than for other world areas, for the reason that the deposits in the Green River Formation may be uniquely large.

References

Barnes, F. F., 1961, Coal fields of the United States, Sheet 2, Alaska: U. S. Geol. Survey Map.

Bradley, W. H., 1931, Origin and microfossils of the oil shale of the Green River Formation of Colorado and Utah: U. S. Geol. Survey Prof. Paper 168, 58 p.

Cadman, W. H., 1948, The oil shale deposits of the world and recent developments in their exploitation and utilization, reviewed to May 1947: Inst. Petroleum Jour., v. 34, no. 290, p. 109–132.

Cashion, W. B., Jr., 1957, Stratigraphic relations and oil shale of the Green River Formation in the eastern Uinta Basin [Utah], in Intermountain Assoc. Petroleum Geologists Guidebook, Eighth Ann. Field Conf., Geology of the Uinta Basin: p. 131–135.

——— 1959, Geology and oil-shale resources of Naval Oil-Shale Reserve No. 2, Uintah and Carbon Counties, Utah: U. S. Geol. Survey Bull. 1072-0, p. 753–793 [1960].

——— 1962, Potential oil-shale reserves of the Green River Formation in the south-eastern Uinta Basin, Utah and Colorado, in Short papers in the geologic and hydrologic sciences: U. S. Geol. Survey Prof. Paper 424-C, p. C22–C24.

——— 1964, Oil Shale, in U. S. Geol. Survey, Mineral and water resources of Utah: U. S. 88th Cong., 2d sess., Senate Comm. on Interior and Insular Affairs, Comm. print, p. 61–63.

Cashion, W. B., and Brown, J. H., Jr., 1956, Geology of the Bonanza-Dragon oil-shale area, Uintah County, Utah, and Rio Blanco County, Colorado: U. S. Geol. Survey Oil and Gas Inv. Map OM-153 [with text].

Conant, L. C., and Swanson, V. E., 1961, Chattanooga shale and related rocks of central Tennessee and nearby areas: U. S. Geol. Survey Prof. Paper 357, 91 p.

Crouse, C. S., 1925, An economic study of the black Devonian shales of Kentucky: Kentucky Geol. Survey, ser. 6, v. 21, p. 59–97.

Culbertson, W. B., 1964, Oil shale resources and stratigraphy of the Green River Formation in Wyoming: The Mountain Geologist, v. 1, no. 3, p. 18.

Donnell, J. R., 1961, Tertiary geology and oil-shale resources of the Piceance Creek basin between the Colorado and White Rivers, northwestern Colorado: U. S. Geol. Survey Bull. 1082-L, p. 835–891.

Duncan, D. C., 1958, Oil shale deposits in the United States: Indep. Petroleum Assoc. America Monthly, v. 29, no. 4, p. 22, 49–51.

Elliott, M. A., Linden, H. R., and Shultz, E. B., Jr., 1961, Production of low molecular weight hydrocarbons from solid fossil fuels: U. S. Patent Office, Patent 2,991,-164, 4 p. and 4 figs.

Feth, J. H., 1963, Tertiary lake deposits in western conterminous United States: Sci., v. 139, no. 3550, p. 107–110.

Fettke, C. R., 1923, Oil resources in coal and carbonaceous shales of Pennsylvania: Pennsylvania Geol. Survey, 4th ser., Bull. M2, 119 p.

Forsman, J. P., and Hunt, J. M., 1958, Insoluble organic matter (kerogen) in sedimentary rocks of marine origin, in Weeks, L. G., ed., Habitat of oil—a symposium: Tulsa, Okla., Am. Assoc. Petroleum Geologists, p. 747–778.

Gejrot, Claes, 1958, Svenska Skifferolje A B: Orebro, Sweden, 35 p.

Great Britain Mineral Resources Bureau, 1924, The mineral industries of the British Empire and foreign countries, petroleum and allied products (1913–1919): London, H M Stationery Office, 296 p.

Guthrie, B., and Thorne, H. M., 1954, Shale oil, in Encyclopedia of chemical technology: New York, The Intersci Encyclopedia, Inc., v. 12, p. 207–220.

Hoover, K. V., 1960, Devonian-Mississippian shale sequence in Ohio: Ohio Div. Geol. Survey Inf. Circ. 27, 154 p.

Hubbard, A. B., and Fester, J. I., 1959, A hydrogenolysis study of the kerogen in Colorado oil shale: U. S. Bur. Mines Rept. Inv. 5458, 26 p.

Hunt, J. M., and Jamieson, G. W., 1958, Oil and organic matter in source rocks of petroleum [repr.], in Weeks, L. G., ed., Habitat of oil—a symposium: Tulsa, Okla., Am. Assoc. Petroleum Geologists, p. 735–746.

Institute of Petroleum, 1938, Oil shale and cannel coal: London, 476 p.

——— 1951, Oil shale and cannel coal, v. 2: London, 832 p.

Jaffé, F. C., 1962, Oil shale, nomenclature, uses, reserves and production: Colorado School of Mines, Mineral Industries Bull., v. 5, no. 2, 11 p.

Lamar, J. E., Armon, W. J., and Simon, J. A., 1956, Illinois oil shales: Illinois Geol. Survey Circ. 208, 21 p.

McAuslan, E. A., 1959, In the Niobrara—oil may yield to special methods: Oil and Gas Jour., v. 57, no. 38, p. 158–166.

Miller, Don J., Payne, Thomas G., and Gryc, George, 1959, Geology of possible petroleum provinces in Alaska: U. S. Geol. Survey Bull. 1094, 131 p.

Parker, Albert, 1962, Survey of energy resources: London, World Power Conf., 68 p.

Prien, C. H., 1951, Oil shale and shale oil, in Oil shale and cannel coal: London, Inst. Petroleum, v. 2, p. 76–111.

Rubel, A. C., 1955, Shale oil—as a future energy resource: Mines Mag., Oct. 1955, p. 72–76.

Schopf, J. M., 1956, A definition of coal: Econ. Geology, v. 51, no. 6, p. 521–527.

Shultz, E. B., Jr., 1962, Methane, ethane and propane from American oil shales by hydrogasification. I. Green River Formation shale. II. Shales of the eastern United States and New Brunswick, in Part II of Am. Inst. Chem. Engineers, Symposium on hydrocarbons from oil shale, oil sand, and coal: Am. Inst. Chem. Engineers, 48th Ann. Meeting, Denver, Colo., 1962, Preprint 9, p. 44–57.

Smith, H. N., Smith, J. W., and Kommes, W. C., 1959, Petrographic examination and chemical analyses for several foreign oil shales: U. S. Bur. Mines Rept. Inv. 5504, 34 p.

Smith, J. W., and Stanfield, K. E., 1964, Oil yields of Devonian New Albany shales, Kentucky: Am. Assoc. Petroleum Geologists Bull., v. 48, no. 5, p. 712–714.

Smith, P. S., and Mertie, J. B., Jr., 1930, Geology and mineral resources of northwestern Alaska: U. S. Geol. Survey Bull. 815, 351 p.

Stanfield, K. E., and Frost, I. C., 1949, Method of assaying oil shale by a modified Fischer retort: U. S. Bur. Mines Rept. Inv. 4477, 13 p.

Stanfield, K. E., Frost, I. C., McAuley, W. S., and Smith, H. N., 1951, Properties of Colorado oil shale: U. S. Bur. Mines Rept. Inv. 4825, 27 p.

Stanfield, K. E., Rose, C. K., McAuley, W. S., and Tesch, W. J., Jr., 1954, Oil yields of sections of Green River oil shale in Colorado, Utah, and Wyoming, 1945–52: U. S. Bur. Mines Rept. Inv. 5081, 153 p.

Stanfield, K. E., Smith, J. W., Smith, H. N., and Robb, W. A., 1960, Oil yields of sections of Green River oil shale in Colorado, 1954–57: U. S. Bur. Mines Rept. Inv. 5614, 186 p.

Stanfield, K. E., Smith, J. W., and Trudell, L. G., 1964, Oil yields of sections of Green River oil shale in Utah, 1952–62: U. S. Bur. Mines Rept. Inv. 6420, 217 p.

Swanson, V. E., 1960, Oil yield and uranium content of black shales: U. S. Geol. Survey Prof. Paper 356-A, 44 p.

——— 1962, Geology and geochemistry of uranium in marine black shales, a review: U. S. Geol. Survey Prof. Paper 356-C, p. 67–112.

Thorne, H. M., Stanfield, K. E., Dinneen, G. U., and Murphy, W. I., 1962, Oil-shale technology in second symposium on the development of the petroleum resources of Asia and the far east: U. S. Dept. Interior, p. 211–236.

Trask, P. D., and Patnode, H. W., 1942, Source beds of petroleum: Tulsa, Okla., Am. Assoc. Petroleum Geologists, 566 p.

Trumbull, J. F. A., 1960, Coal fields of the United States, Sheet 1: U. S. Geol. Survey Map.

Twenhofel, W. H., 1950, Principles of sedimentation: New York, McGraw-Hill Book Co., 673 p.

U. S. Bureau of Mines, 1960, Oil shale, *in* Mineral facts and problems: U. S. Bur. Mines Bull. 585, p. 573–580.

U. S. Geological Survey, 1951, Fuel reserves of the United States: U. S. 82d Cong., 1st sess., Senate Comm. on Interior and Insular Affairs, Comm. print, 49 p.

Vine, J. D., 1962, Geology of coaly carbonaceous rocks: U. S. Geol. Survey Prof. Paper 365-D, p. 113–170.

Weeks, L. G., 1960, The next hundred years energy demand and sources of supply: Geotimes, v. 5, no. 1, p. 18–21, 51–55.

Winchester, D. E., 1918, Results of dry distillation of miscellaneous shale samples: U. S. Geol. Survey Bull. 691-B, p. 51–55.

———— 1923, Oil shale of the Rocky Mountain region: U. S. Geol. Survey Bull. 729, 204 p.

———— 1928, The oil possibilities of the oil shales of the United States: Federal Oil Conservation Board of the President of the United States, Rept. 2, Jan. 1928, app. 1, p. 13–14.

Environmental Impact

"The American Colossus was fiercely intent on appropriating and exploiting the riches of the richest of all continents—grasping with both hands, reaping where he had not sown, wasting what he thought would last forever."

Gifford Pinchot
Breaking New Ground

In Reading 27 Hubert Risser states, "The problem that confronts the mineral industry today is that of finding ways to comply with the requirements for environmental quality protection and still provide the nation with the minerals it requires at an acceptable cost." He explores the alternatives involved in reducing environmental effects and reviews current and proposed regulations which apply to mineral production, transportation, and utilization. It behooves industry to take the present concern for the environment seriously; and the consumer must be prepared to pay a fair share of the cost of environmental protection.

Man's exploitation of natural resources has led to a variety of environmental problems. The magnitude of surface mining and the problems which result from this form of exploitation are reviewed in Reading 28. Less than 1 per cent of the total land area of the United States has been disturbed by surface mining, but the effects go well beyond the mine site. Mining activity not only influences the quality of the land but it also has far-ranging impacts on air, water, and plant and animal life. Furthermore, surface mining affects some portion of every state and frequently conflicts with other demands for land use. Surface mining will increase greatly in future years. Technological advances will enable us to mine ore at greatly accelerated rates and also, if Alvin Weinberg is correct, to consider lower grade ores. In view of the fact that the rehabilitation of mine sites has been discouragingly slow, it is imperative that technological

Photo on page 300. Courtesy of U.S. Bureau of Mines, R. L. Williams.

advances be applied to rehabilitation as well as exploitation.

Subsurface mining activities can also have adverse effects on the environment. Underground mining of solid resources and the withdrawal of underground fluids—water, oil, and gas—can cause the subsidence or sinking of the land. Specific examples and case histories of subsidence are presented in Readings 29 and 30. These Readings document the magnitude of the problem in western United States and the economic and political impact of this phenomenon. Subsidence at Long Beach, California, for example, by 1962 had reached 29 feet and caused more than 100 million dollars in damages. The draining of peat bogs, the irrigation of certain soils, and the application of surface loads can also cause subsidence. In some instances subsidence can lead to catastrophic failures of dams or levees, and public agencies and private developers should be aware of the problem and of the methods for stopping or reducing subsidence.

Lewis Weeks points out in Reading 25 that the subsea petroleum resources of the world are vast, and we can anticipate that efforts to recover these resources will be greatly accelerated. The United States is rich in petroleum and natural gas accumulations both on land and offshore, but there are current production shortages and projected increases in need. The petroleum industry has therefore turned to offshore prospecting and exploitation as a natural extension of the development of numerous onshore prospects. During normal development of a prospective oil pool about 6½ miles southeast of Santa Barbara, California, a blowout occurred on January 28, 1969, during completion of the fifth well being drilled from Platform A on Federal Tract OCS P–0241. The well flowed uncontrolled until February 7 and spilled oil over a large part of the channel and adjacent beaches. The problem was compounded by moderate and steady seepage long after the well was brought under control.

The Santa Barbara incident cannot be looked upon as typical of offshore development activity. Of 9000 wells drilled on the Outer Continental Shelf only twenty-five have experienced blowouts. But the incident served to raise many questions about the adequacy of offshore drilling technology and regulations, and about our ability to cope with an oil spill. It also raised the question of the advisability of drilling in a hazardous geologic setting. The Santa Barbara Channel, located in an area of high seismicity, is subject to earthquakes, tsunamis, and seiches. Furthermore, oil reservoirs in the chan-

nel are often inadequately sealed, and it can be anticipated that weak traps will leak oil if their equilibrium is disturbed during drilling activity.

Harvey Molotch vividly describes the activities, emotions, frustrations, and confusion surrounding the blowout at Santa Barbara in Reading 31. It is obvious that the degree of sophistication which characterizes petroleum exploration and drilling did not characterize the industry's efforts to control the oil spill. The environmental, economic, social, legal, and political implications of this inadequacy are sweeping. The response to the problem of oil-spill control is reviewed in Reading 32. The problem of oil spillage goes beyond drilling and includes the transportation, refining, and marketing of oil. It appears that progress is being made in a broad range of areas through the cooperation of industry, government, and the public, but there remains a need for more extensive organization, coordinated laws, and more research.

27 Environmental Quality Control and Minerals*
Hubert E. Risser

During the past several years an increasing concern for the quality of our national environment has arisen. Within the last two years the volume of articles and speeches—of criticism, accusations, and demands—has crescendoed and shows no signs of subsiding.

Some persons, whether sincerely concerned or merely seeking attention, have gained national prominence by declaring that the nation will be doomed within the next year, 5 years, or 10

years. Other voices are more moderate, but nonetheless insistent that many of

* Presented at the Annual Meeting of the American Association of Petroleum Geologists, Houston, Texas, March 31, 1971.

Risser, H. E., 1971, "Environmental Quality Control and Minerals," *Environmental Geology Notes Number 49*, Illinois State Geological Survey. Reprinted with light editing by permission of the author and the Illinois State Geological Survey, Urbana, Illinois.
Mr. Risser is on the staff of the Illinois State Geological Survey.

the patterns of activity and material consumption within the United States must be altered, if not totally abandoned.

Most of the environmental effects that concern our nation today are not the result of deliberate intent or disregard. They are the by-product of activities aimed at very worthwhile goals. The farmer who applies nitrate or other fertilizer that can run off his field to add to pollution in streams and rivers is only trying to make his land more productive and obtain a larger crop yield. The housewife who uses phosphate detergent hopes to make her clothes cleaner. Those who mine by surface methods are attempting to produce materials at the lowest practicable cost.

As is true of many activities, efforts to correct or avoid the detrimental effects of mineral production will bring into play factors that are not anticipated or desired. Ultimately, the goal must be that of achieving the best balance possible.

Although various activities have come under criticism, it appears, at least to those of us who are connected in any way with minerals, that minerals have been a special target—not only the production of minerals but their transportation, processing, and utilization as well.

There are perhaps three principal reasons why so much attention has been focused on minerals.

1. By virtue of their manner of occurrence and their physical and chemical makeup, minerals are actually an integral part of the environment. Therefore, their production, movement, or utilization without modification of the environment would be entirely unrealistic.

2. The quantities involved are so huge and mineral production and consumption activities so widespread geographically that their effects are observable to everyone. As sources of energy, as metallic and non-metallic materials, and as plant foods, minerals are directly related to or involved in almost every form of industrial, economic, and recreational activity. Between 3 and 4 billion tons of solid fuels and minerals, 5 billion barrels of liquid fuels, and 22 trillion cubic feet of natural gas are consumed each year. Furthermore, the rate of use of some minerals has been doubling every 9 to 15 years.

3. Many mineral materials are so durable they remain as scrap long after the product has served its useful purpose. Reclamation may not be economic, but the production of new materials is criticized because old materials are so obviously available.

Minerals and the Environment

The problem that confronts the minerals industry today is that of finding ways to comply with the requirements for environmental quality protection and still provide the nation with the minerals it requires at an acceptable cost. The environmental components we most frequently think of are the atmosphere, the water, and the land, but recently increased public attention has been turned to plant and animal wildlife as well.

Let's examine for a moment the relation between the environment and mineral production and use. Any production of minerals will, without exception, involve financial costs and will result in some effects on the environment. The balance of these three factors is illustrated in Fig. 1, where mineral production on the one hand is accompanied by costs and environmental effects on the other. In some instances these effects may consist only of the void left by removal of the minerals. In other instances the effects may be detrimental, completely benign, or even beneficial. The nature and extent of the effects will vary in degree and character, depending on the type of mineral, the manner of its occurrence, the method of production used, and other factors. But its very removal will cause some modification of the environment.

If we accept the premise that any mineral production or use will inevitably carry with it some environmental effects and financial costs, a logical corollary appears to be that our steadily expanding demand for and use of minerals will, other things being equal, also result in an increase in the magnitude of these effects. Thus an increase

FIG. 1.

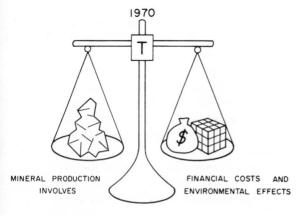

MINERAL PRODUCTION INVOLVES | FINANCIAL COSTS AND ENVIRONMENTAL EFFECTS

in the mineral output on the left side of the scale in Fig. 1 brings a parallel increase on the right side.

Although greater mineral output is accompanied by increases in both total costs and over-all environmental effects, from the public standpoint a significant difference exists between these factors that cannot be ignored by the mineral industry. Production expenditures quickly become identified as unit costs, and the cost of each unit to the consumer may not change significantly as total quantity produced increases. On the other hand, seldom, if ever, are the incremental environmental effects (unless expenditures are made to correct them) identified with, or allocated to, the additional units of material produced or energy consumed. Instead, within a given mining area the total cumulative environmental effects are observed in their entirety rather than as a series of discrete units.

To provide for the industrial growth of our nation and supply the demands of a growing population for material goods and energy, a steady increase in the use of minerals of all types has occurred. Expansions in the output of fuels and metals have tended to parallel each other, increasing on the average of about 3 percent per year.

The growth in use of nonmetallics, which consist primarily of construction and plant-food materials, has been considerably more rapid than that of metals. An especially significant aspect of this growth is the extremely large total quantity of minerals material involved. The combined output of the major construction minerals—crushed stone, sand, and gravel—currently amounts to about 1.8 billion tons per year and it is projected to reach 5.6 to

8.0 billion tons per year by 2000 (U. S. Bur. Mines, 1971, p. 22). Because most construction activity normally occurs in or near large centers of population and industrial activity, most production of construction materials is highly visible to a large segment of the public and is therefore subjected to increasing objections and regulations.

Reducing Environmental Effects

Once we recognize that environmental effects are inherent in the production and use of any mineral, we might ask what, if anything, can be done to reduce the undesirable or adverse effects. One obvious way would be to decrease the amount of mineral materials produced and consumed (Fig. 2). Through such a reduction, both the total environmental effects and the total (but not necessarily the unit) production expenditure would be reduced. But there has been as yet no indication that this alternative is acceptable to the American public. The consumption figures of a few mineral commodities (Fig. 3) gives evidence to the contrary. Not only has the production of minerals expanded to provide for popula-

tion growth, but it also has provided a dramatic increase in the average per capita consumption.

Consumption of electric power, most of which is generated by mineral fuels, has been doubling every 10 years, and in the 1970s it is expected to equal the total amount consumed during the past 70 years.

Another way to reduce environmental effects is through increased expenditures (Fig. 4). Increased costs may result from changes made in production procedures to protect the environment, from expenditures to restore the environment after production has occurred, or from expenses related to other types of action, such as installation of pollution-control devices.

In the past, the minerals industry's primary assignment has been to provide minerals to meet the nation's needs at the lowest possible cost. In at least some cases, environmental protection now is taking precedence over lowest cost as the prime objective. An added demand now is that these mineral materials be produced with a minimum of undesirable environmental disruption.

While some members of the public

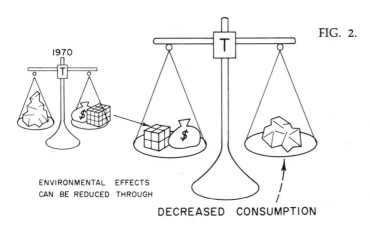

FIG. 2.

1970

ENVIRONMENTAL EFFECTS
CAN BE REDUCED THROUGH

DECREASED CONSUMPTION

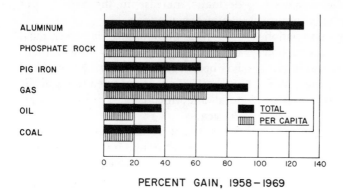

MINERAL CONSUMPTION GROWTH   FIG. 3.

ALUMINUM
PHOSPHATE ROCK
PIG IRON
GAS
OIL
COAL

TOTAL
PER CAPITA

0 20 40 60 80 100 120 140

PERCENT GAIN, 1958–1969

no doubt partially realize that increased costs will be involved in this shift of emphasis, it is doubtful that the general public fully recognizes the extent of these costs or the fact that these increased production costs must ultimately be borne by the consumer through increased prices if production is to continue.

As the effort toward environmental improvement progresses and the relative magnitudes of both the costs and benefits become more apparent, a greater public tendency to balance one against the other may develop. It may

be decided that, beyond a certain point, the incremental benefits do not justify the added costs. Nonetheless, there is a public mood today that reflects a strong conviction that the quality of the environment must be protected from further deterioration, and the official government attitude reflects that public mood. An effort to point out the magnitude of the costs involved in complying with new regulations is unlikely to receive much sympathetic attention today. Nor will the fact that a proposed regulation or procedure appears completely impractical or infeasi-

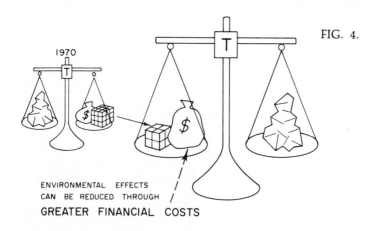

FIG. 4.

1970

ENVIRONMENTAL EFFECTS
CAN BE REDUCED THROUGH
GREATER FINANCIAL COSTS

ble necessarily mean that legislation requiring such procedure will not be enacted.

Still another way in which some environmental effects may be reduced is through improved technology in the production and use of minerals (Fig. 5). Such technological improvements may or may not result in increased costs. They may, in fact, bring the desired results at a reduced cost. But new technology does not just happen. Its development requires time, concerted effort, and increased investment.

Effects of Environmental Regulation

Some of the impact of environmental regulations is already apparent, and the effect of many others will be felt during the next few years. New regulations will be applied to production, transportation, and utilization of mineral materials. A brief review will serve to point out some of these.

Mineral Production

Increasingly stringent regulations controlling production techniques and reclamation procedures have recently been enacted. Some proposals have been made that would completely halt certain types of mineral production because of their effects on the environment. Already pits and quarries have been banned in some urban areas and strip mining has been prohibited in certain regions. Proposals have been introduced in Congress to halt all offshore drilling and both in Congress and in certain state legislatures to prohibit strip coal mining completely.

The banning of pits and quarries by zoning ordinances makes near-by short-haul resources unavailable and increases the transportation cost and, in turn, the delivered price of construction materials to builders within the metropolitan area.

The proposed banning of further offshore drilling would make inaccessible more than 9 percent of the nation's known oil reserves and almost 13 percent of the known gas reserves. In addition, it would remove from exploration large areas that offer some of the greatest potential for the future discoveries that will be required to meet our fuel needs. If the proposed ban on offshore drilling were extended to cur-

FIG. 5.

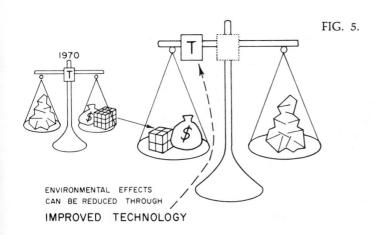

1970

ENVIRONMENTAL EFFECTS
CAN BE REDUCED THROUGH
IMPROVED TECHNOLOGY

rent production, a significant portion of the current oil and gas output would be halted.

The total prohibition of strip mining of coal would eliminate about one third of the current output in the United States. At present there would be no means of replacing, through underground mining, the approximately 200 million tons per year of strip coal that would be lost, and there would be other effects also. In 1969, underground mining costs were, on the average, about 40 percent higher than strip mining costs. In the same year, about 22,000 men produced almost 200 million tons of coal from strip mines. To produce the same amount of coal from underground mines would have required about 27,000 additional miners because underground miners have a lower average of productivity. The total coal mining labor force would thus need to be increased by 21.5 percent at a time when there is a shortage of mining manpower. Too, since underground mining recovers only about 50 percent of the coal in the ground, nearly twice as much coal resource would be exhausted in providing the same amount of output. Finally, the loss of lives in underground coal mining has historically been about 3½ times that for the same production by strip coal mining.

Complete banning of strip mining of all solid minerals other than coal would have even more impact, because 94 percent of the nation's production of nonfuel minerals comes from surface mining operations.

Transportation

The transportation of solid minerals has not, in general, resulted in major environmental problems, although the noise and traffic of trucks has been partly responsible for objections to pits and quarries in and near metropolitan areas.

Recently, much more attention has been directed to the effects of oil spillage, occasionally from ruptured pipelines but most frequently from waterborne shipments. Oil spillage is not a new problem. A publication issued in 1925 dealt with pollution of bathing beaches by oil spilled from ships along the east coast from Connecticut to Florida, parts of the Gulf Coast, and the Pacific Coast (U. S. Public Health Service, 1925).

As the water transportation of oil increases, problems of tanker spillage also are likely to increase. Our own increasing dependence on foreign sources will bring more of these shipments to our shores. The increased size of tankers should reduce the number of tankers required and perhaps the incidence of tanker accidents. On the other hand, as tanker size increases, any accidents that do occur are likely to have far greater effects. A tanker of 372,400 DWT (dead weight tons) capacity is reported currently under construction, and one of 477,000 DWT capacity is reportedly being planned (Industry Week, 1971). The cargoes of two ships of this size will exceed the reported 794,000 tons of combined capacity of 95 ships sunk by U-boats in World War II (Bachman, 1971). Some of these ships, with their cargoes still intact, are reported to remain on the ocean bottom off the east coast of the United States.

The oil transportation project currently receiving the greatest attention is the proposed Alyeska Pipeline from

Prudhoe Bay to Valdez, Alaska (Fig. 6). Construction is being delayed pending further study of potential environmental effects of the construction and operation of the pipeline and the designing of methods to control these effects. The greatest uncertainty relates to the impact of the passage of oil through the pipes at high temperatures in an Arctic environment. Anyone who has worked at construction in Arctic areas is aware of the problems that permafrost can bring, even for normal, small-scale excavations.

Nearly 500 oil pipeline leaks were reported to have occurred in the United States in 1968. Most of these resulted in only minor spillage, and only about one fifth involved spills of as high as 1,000 to 12,000 barrels (Carter, 1969). Because of the operating conditions that will prevail in Alaska and the large spillage likely to occur if the 48-inch pipeline should be ruptured, it is considered especially critical that pipeline breaks should be prevented.

Attention has also been called to the possibility of oil spills along the Canadian Pacific Coast from tankers moving between Valdez and the coastal parts of the western United States. To avoid this danger it has been proposed that, instead of crossing Alaska, the pipeline be constructed along an alternative route through Canada to the United States border (Wall Street Journal, 1971). Although the Canadian route would avoid some of the mountainous terrain of northern Alaska and the zone of high seismic activity in Alaska, a much longer pipeline would be needed.

Whatever the final outcome, the cost of the delays and of compliance with environmental regulations will add significantly to the cost of the oil when it is finally delivered in the United States.

Mineral Utilization

A third type of environmental quality regulation affecting minerals is directed at the consumer rather than the mineral-producing industry. These con-

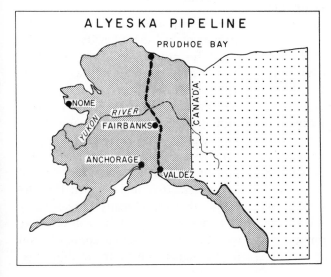

FIG. 6.

sumer-directed regulations may well have greater impact than those applying to mineral production activities, for already they are radically changing the patterns of mineral use.

One of the proposals would prohibit the use of tetraethyl lead in gasoline. Besides altering the refinery product, the prohibition of lead as a gasoline additive, if fully implemented, would immediately reduce the market for lead by about 20 percent and create a drastic impact on the producers of lead and associated minerals.

Recent discoveries of the transformation, through bacterial action, of metallic mercury to highly toxic methyl mercury have led to laws for control of spillage of mercury into lakes and other natural waters. The modification of processes has led to a reduction in the loss of mercury, which, in turn, has resulted in a significant decline in demand for that metal.

Perhaps the most dramatic and far-reaching impact has been that resulting from recently proposed and already established sulfur dioxide emission standards for fuels. The standards are such that much of the coal currently being produced and most of the reserves throughout the country cannot meet them without the use of emission control devices on combustion units. Unfortunately, such control devices have not yet proved effective on a commercial basis. In an effort to comply with the new air quality standards, fuel consumers attempted to procure natural gas as a substitute for coal. As present supplies of gas cannot even meet the growth in the traditional markets, the sudden additional demand for gas as a substitute fuel could not be met.

Unable to get either low-sulfur coal or natural gas, utilities and large industrial firms attempted to obtain low-sulfur residual fuel oil. Residual traditionally had been so low in value that only a minimum amount was produced by most refiners. Because there was so little low-sulfur residual to meet the sudden demand, it quickly became a premium product with a premium price.

Hopefully, within the next few years, satisfactory devices and techniques for the control of sulfur oxide emission will be available so that high-sulfur coal can be burned without violating air quality standards. In the future, coal will also be processed into sulfur-free synthetic pipeline gas to supplement the declining reserves of natural gas and into liquid fuel to supplement natural petroleum products. In the meantime, it will be necessary to use those fuels that are available, for in many instances there are no alternatives to either doing that or shutting down.

Conclusions

The widespread concern for the environment and the intensity of the demand for corrective action appear to be rather recent phenomena, but they do have a history extending back several decades. Expression of environmental concern has taken many forms, and some of the demands and regulations resulting from it are beyond the present technology and capability of the nation. It is to be hoped that demands that are patently unreasonable or impossible to comply with will give way to a more rational approach. But for the minerals industry to think that all of the present concern for the environment is merely a passing public fancy would be a serious mistake.

The mineral producers of this nation and the world, and the mineral consumers as well, are faced with a future in which mineral costs will increase as prices rise to cover the additional costs of environmental protection activities.

It is too early to measure accurately just what price increases will be required and what impact on demand these increases will ultimately have. The nation's industrial growth for two centuries has been assisted by the availability of low-cost energy and mineral materials.

Secretary of the Interior Rogers C. B. Morton was recently quoted as stating:

Now, because we have finally achieved the measure of concern for the environment that we should have summoned 30 years ago, these social costs are at last going to be charged to the proper accounts. Those who benefit from the production and consumption of energy will be asked to pay the full tab, and for the first time the user will have some feel for the true cost of the energy he consumes.[1]

Although the statement referred specifically to energy, it applies equally to all other mineral products.

The Secretary is correct in that the consumer ultimately will pay the full tab. But for the minerals industry to take this too literally and become complacent about allocation of environmental costs could be extremely hazardous. The public still has the option of paying the cost or doing without. There is at present no way of pinpointing the level at which the consumer will balk at paying increased prices.

It behooves the industry to pass along the necessary costs involved in protecting the environment and to identify these costs as such for the public. But it is also extremely important that the minerals industry continue to produce and provide its products at the lowest possible cost.

Notes

[1] (AGI Report, 1971.)

References

AGI Report, 1971, National Petroleum Council (March 4): The AGI Report, Geo-Times Newsletter, v. 4, no. 10, p. 1.

Bachman, W. A. [Sr. ed.], 1971, U-boat as a polluter: Oil and Gas Jour., v. 69, no. 2, p. 13.

Carter, L. J., 1969, North slope: Oil rush: Science, v. 166, no. 3901, p. 85–92.

Industry Week, 1971, Oil supertankers becoming more super: Industry Week, v. 168, no. 3, p. 26.

U. S. Bureau of Mines, 1971, Minerals yearbook 1969, Metals, minerals and fuels: U. S. Bur. Mines, Dept. Interior, Washington, D. C., v. 1, 2, 1194 p.

U. S. Public Health Service, 1925, Oil pollution at bathing beaches: Reprint no. 980 from the Public Health Reports, v. 39, no. 51, p. 3195–3208.

Wall Street Journal, 1971, Ruckelshaus says delay trans-Alaska pipeline, study Canadian route: March 15, 1971, p. 14.

28 Surface Mining, Its Nature, Extent, and Significance

U. S. Department of the Interior

Stated in the simplest terms, surface mining consists of nothing more than removing the topsoil, rock, and other strata that lie above mineral or fuel deposits to recover them. In practice, however, the process is considerably more complex.

When compared with underground methods, surface mining offers distinct advantages. It makes possible the recovery of deposits which, for physical reasons, cannot be mined underground; provides safer working conditions; usually results in a more complete recovery of the deposit; and, most significantly it is generally cheaper in terms of cost-per-unit of production. Surface mining is not applicable to all situations, however, because the ratio between the thickness of the overburden that must be moved in order to recover a given amount of product places a definite economic limitation upon the operator. While this ratio may vary widely among operations and commodities owing to differences in the characteristics of the overburden, types and capacities of the equipment used, and in value of the material being mined, it is nonetheless the factor that primarily determines whether a particular mining venture can survive in a competitive market.

"Surface Mining, Its Nature, Extent, and Significance," in Surface Mining and Our Environment, Strip and Surface Mine Study Policy Committee, U. S. Department of the Interior, 1967, 124 pp. Reprinted with light editing.

The procedure for surface mining usually consists of two steps: Prospecting, or "exploration,"—to discover, delineate, and "prove" the ore body—and the actual mining or recovery phase. Topography and the configuration of the deposit itself strongly influence both. Exploration techniques generally employed consist of either drilling to intersect deeper-lying ore bodies, or excavating shallow trenches or pits to expose the ore. Although drill sites or excavations associated with exploration are usually small, their large number constitutes a serious source of surface disturbance in some of the Western States. Surface methods employed to recover minerals and fuels are generally classified as (1) open pit mining (quarry, open cast); (2) strip mining (area, contour); (3) auger mining; (4) dredging; and (5) hydraulic mining.

Open pit mining is exemplified by quarries producing limestone, sandstone, marble, and granite; sand and gravel pits; and, large excavations opened to produce iron and copper. Usually, in open pit mining, the amount of overburden removed is proportionately small compared with the quantity of ore recovered. Another distinctive feature of open pit mining is the length of time that mining is conducted. In stone quarrying, and in open pit mining of iron ore and other metallics, large quantities of ore are obtained within a relatively small surface area because of the thickness of the deposits. Some open pits may be mined for many years—50 or more; in fact, a few have been in continuous operation for more than a century. However, since coal beds are comparatively thin—the United States average being about 5.1 feet for bituminous coal and lignite strip mined in 1960—the average surface coal mine has a relatively short life.

Area strip mining usually is practiced on relatively flat terrain. A trench, or "box cut," is made through the overburden to expose a portion of the deposit, which is then removed. The first cut may be extended to the limits of the property or the deposit. As each succeeding parallel cut is made, the spoil (overburden) is deposited in the cut just previously excavated. The final cut leaves an open trench as deep as the thickness of the overburden plus the ore recovered, bounded on one side by the last spoil bank and on the other by the undisturbed highwall. Frequently this final cut may be a mile or more from the starting point of the operation. Thus, area stripping, unless graded or leveled, usually resembles the ridges of a gigantic washboard. Coal and Florida phosphate account for the major part of the acreage disturbed by this method, although brown iron ore, some clays, and other commodities are mined in a similar manner.

Contour strip mining is most commonly practiced where deposits occur in rolling or mountainous country. Basically, this method consists of removing the overburden above the bed by starting at the outcrop and proceeding along the hillside. After the deposit is exposed and removed by this first cut, additional cuts are made until the ratio of overburden to product brings the operation to a halt. This type of mining creates a shelf, or "bench," on the hillside. On the inside it is bordered by the highwall, which may range from a few to perhaps more than 100 feet in height, and on the opposite, or outer, side by a rim below which there is frequently a precipitous downslope that has been covered by spoil material cast down the hillside. Unless controlled or stabilized, this spoil material can cause severe erosion and landslides. Contour mining is practiced widely in the coal fields of Appalachia and western phosphate mining regions because of the generally rugged topography. "Rim-cutting" and "benching" are terms that are sometimes used locally to identify workbenches, or ledges, prepared for contour or auger mining operations.

Anthracite strip mining in Pennsylvania is conducted on hillsides where the coal beds outcrop parallel with the mountain crests. Although most of the operations are conducted on natural slopes of less than 10 degrees, the beds themselves vary in pitch up to 90 degrees. Beds that are stripped are thicker than in the bituminous fields, most varying from 6 to 20 feet, and can be mined economically to much greater depths. Because of the angles at which the beds lie, the methods employed may not be correctly identified either as contour or area mining, but rather as a combination of both. In a few instances, the operations may resemble open pits and quarries, while others are long, deep narrow canyons.

Auger mining is usually associated with contour strip mining. In coal fields, it is most commonly practiced to recover additional tonnages after the coal-overburden ratio has become such as to render further contour mining uneconomical. Augers are also used to extract coal near the outcrop that could not be recovered safely by earlier underground mining efforts. As the name implies, augering is a method of producing coal by boring horizontally into the seam, much like the carpenter bores a hole in wood. The coal is extracted in the same manner that shavings are produced by the carpenter's bit. Cutting heads of some coal augers are as large as seven feet in diameter. By adding sections behind the cutting head, holes may be drilled in excess of 200 feet. As augering generally is conducted after the strip-mining phase has been completed, little land disturbance can be directly attributed to it. However, it may, to some extent, induce surface subsidence and disrupt water channels when underground workings are intersected.

Dredging operations utilize a suction apparatus or various mechanical devices, such as ladder or chain buckets, clamshells, and draglines mounted on floating barges. Dredges have been utilized extensively in placer gold mining. Tailing piles from gold dredging operations usually have a configuration that is similar to spoil piles left by area strip mining for coal. Dredging is also used in the recovery of sand and gravel from stream beds and low-lying lands. In the sand and gravel industry most of the material (volume) produced is marketed, but in dredging for the higher-priced minerals virtually all of the mined material consists of waste that is left at the mine site. Some valuable minerals also are recovered by dredging techniques from beach sands and sedimentary deposits on the continental shelf.

In *hydraulic mining* a powerful jet of water is employed to wash down or erode a bank of earth or gravel that either is the overburden or contains the desired ore. The ore-bearing material is fed into sluices or other concentrating devices where the desired product is separated from the tailings, or waste—by differences in specific gravity. Hydraulic mining was extensively used in the past to produce gold and other precious metals, but is practiced only on a limited scale today. As both hydraulic mining and dredging create sedimentation problems in streams, some States exercise strict controls over these techniques, either through mining or water-control regulations.

Regardless of the equipment used, the surface mining cycle usually consists of four steps: (1) Site preparation, clearing vegetation and other obstructions from the area to be mined, and constructing access roads and ancillary installations—including areas to be used for the disposal of spoil or waste; (2) removal and disposal of overburden; (3) excavation and loading of ore; and (4) transportation of the ore to a concentrator, processing plant, storage area, or directly to market.

Reclamation may not be considered by a majority as an integral component of the mining cycle. Experience here and abroad has demonstrated, however, that when reclamation of the land is integrated into both the pre-planning and operational stages, it can be done more effectively and at a lower cost than as a separate operation. This is particularly true because much of the machinery used in the mining operation can be easily used in reducing peaks of spoil piles, segregating toxic materials, and establishing controlled drainage from the site.

The rapid expansion of surface mining since World War II may be attributed primarily to the development of larger and more complex earth-moving equipment. Equipment used today includes bulldozers, loaders, scrapers, trucks up to 100-ton capacity, and a miscellany of other devices. A shovel is now working that can handle 185-cubic yards in one "bite," with a monster having a 200-cubic yard bucket on the engineers' drawing boards. Draglines of up to 85-cubic yard capacity are in operation and larger ones are being planned. Clamshells and wheel excavators are used where conditions permit. There are floating dredges, tower excavators, drag scrapers, and augers; and to move the overburden and ores beyond the reach of the basic excavating machines, tram or rail cars, conveyor belts, overhead cable buckets, and pipelines.

Extent

An estimated 3.2 million acres of land, 5,000 square miles, had been disturbed by surface mining in the United States prior to January 1, 1965. This total includes only the excavation, or pit, and areas required to dispose of waste or spoil from the mining operation alone. An additional 320,000 acres have been affected by mine access roads and exploration activities. About 95 percent of the acreage disturbed by surface mining is attributable to but seven commodities: Coal for approximately 41 percent of the total; sand and gravel, about 26 percent; stone, gold, clay, phosphate, and iron, together, about 28 percent; and, all others combined, 5 percent.

Table 1 Land disturbed by strip and surface mining in the United States, as of January 1, 1965, by mineral and type of mining[1] [Thousand acres]

Mineral	Strip Mining			Quarry-open pit			Dredge, hydraulic, and other methods	Grand total[2]
	Contour	Area	Total	Into hillside	Below ground level	Total		
Coal[3]	665	637	1,302					1,302
Sand and gravel	38	258	296	82	371	453	74	823
Stone	6	8	14	100	127	227		241
Gold		8	8	1	3	4	191	203
Clay	10	26	36	22	44	66	7	109
Phosphate	28	49	77	13	93	106		183
Iron	7	31	38	30	96	126		164
All Other	11	12	23	59	81	140		163
Total	765	1,029	1,794	307	815	1,122	272	3,188

[1] Data by method of mining estimated on basis of information obtained by random sampling survey.

[2] Data compiled from reports submitted by the States on U. S. Department of the Interior form 6-1385X, from Soil Conservation Service, U. S. Department of Agriculture, and estimates prepared by the study group.

[3] Includes anthracite, bituminous, and lignite.

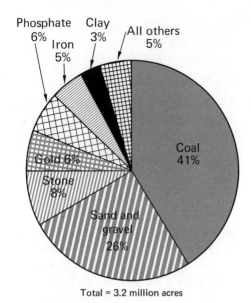

Phosphate 6%
Clay 3%
Iron 5%
All others 5%
Coal 41%
Gold 6%
Stone 8%
Sand and gravel 26%

Total = 3.2 million acres

FIG. 1. Percentage of land disturbed by surface mining of various commodities as of January 1, 1965.

Harmful off-site effects are also an important component of the surface mining picture. These effects include stream and water-impoundment pollution from erosion and acid mine water; isolation of areas by steep highwalls; and, the impairment of natural beauty by the creation of unsightly spoil banks, rubbish dumps, and abandoned equipment. All of these add appreciably to the total that must be considered as being adversely "affected" by surface mining.

Unreclaimed Acreage

The total acreage needing reclamation can only be approximated because definitions of two key words, "reclamation" and "adequacy," are a matter of individual judgment. Professionals in many scientific disciplines can agree on certain essential elements, but the many variables involved preclude a general agreement on a definition of "adequate reclamation" that would be applicable at any given time and for every geographic location. From a survey conducted by the Soil Conservation Service and data submitted by certain States it is concluded that probably only one-third of the total acreage disturbed by surface mining has been adequately reclaimed—either by natural forces or by man's own effort. Thus, approximately two-thirds of the acreage (about 2.0 million) still require some remedial attention.

Annual Increase in Disturbed Acreage

The annual increment to the total disturbed acreage is not known exactly, but can be calculated roughly. Based on data reported by producers to the U. S. Department of the Interior it is estimated that 153,000 acres of land were disturbed in 1964 by strip and surface mining. Sand and gravel accounted for 60,000 acres; coal, 46,000; stone, 21,000; clay and phosphate rock, each 9,000; and the remaining minerals accounted for 8,000 acres. This annual rate of disturbance is expected to increase in future years with an increased demand for minerals and solid fuels and a further diminution in the grade of mineral deposits available for exploitation. Indicative of this trend is the fact that surface mining production of all metals and non-metals increased from 2.5 billion net tons of crude ore (including waste) in 1960 to 3.0 billion in 1965. Strip-mine production of coal (anthracite, bituminous, and lignite) increased from 138 million net tons to 185 million over the same period.

Significance

The economic potential of any nation is founded primarily upon its soil, its waters, and its mineral deposits. Where these are deficient, the economic well-being of the nation will depend upon the ability of its people to import raw materials required to manufacture and compete successfully in world trade.

The United States is blessed with a wealth of natural resources, needing only to import a small portion of its total mineral requirements. Tens of thousands of firms are engaged in the production of semi- and finished goods. These industries are supported, in turn, by a wide variety of extractive and processing activities and services. The extractive industries are the primary source of metallic ores and non-metallic minerals and fuels—with agriculture and forestry contributing a wide range of products. Our population, with its varied skills, completes the design and confirms an old truth: Man creates nothing—it is only through his ability to produce crops, convert, process, and synthesize that his civilization flourishes.

The importance of surface mining to the extractive industries is easily measured. In 1965, for example, surface mining accounted for about four-fifths of the total ore and solid fuels produced. Economists recognize that the extractive mineral industries are primarily suppliers of basic materials, rather than producers of end products. Some appreciation of the extent to which other industries depend upon the mineral industries can be obtained through an examination of the Input-Output table prepared by the Office of Business Economics, U. S. Department of Commerce, which divides the national economy into 82 industrial sectors and shows the interchange of goods among them. Although the data are not current, the patterns have not changed appreciably. For example, the table indicates that 76 percent of all coal mined is used directly (almost entirely as an energy source) by 56 industries to produce other products. The remaining 24 percent represents exports, consumption by individual and public establishments, and intra-company transfers.

Although the relationship of coal to other industrial activities is quite clear, the influence of some other minerals is not always so direct and easily recognized. Examples of indirect, but equally important influences, can be found in iron and ferroalloy ore mining. Over 81 percent of all the iron and ferroalloy ore mined is consumed by the primary iron and steel industry. Yet, output of this industry is used as direct input for 55 of the 82 industrial categories. It is evident that the real value to our economy of the minerals and fuels obtained by surface mining can be measured only by adding to their prices as crude materials the "value added by manufacturing," a concept that entails an evaluation of their contribution to a finished product. But, the story does not end there. As a consumer, the minerals industry is also a substantial contributor to the economy. The products of 49 or more industries are needed to equip and maintain the coal, iron, ferroalloy mining industries, and petroleum and natural gas producers.

FIG. 2. Total acreage disturbed by surface mining as of January 1, 1965.

EXPLANATION

= 50,000 Acres

Table 2. Land disturbed by strip and surface mining in the United States as of January 1, 1965, by commodity and State [Acres]

State	Clay	Coal (bituminous, lignite and anthracite)	Stone	Sand and gravel	Gold	Phosphate rock	Iron ore	All other	Total
Alabama [1]	4,000	50,600	3,900	21,200	100		52,600	1,500	133,900
Alaska [2]		500		2,000	8,600				11,100
Arizona [1]	2,700		1,000	7,200	1,200			20,300	32,400
Arkansas [2]	600	10,100	900	2,600			100	8,100	22,400
California [2]	2,700	20	8,000	19,900	134,000		900	8,500	174,020
Colorado [1]	2,000	2,800	6,200	15,500	17,100		25	11,400	55,025
Connecticut [1]			100	16,100				100	16,300
Delaware [2]	200		200	5,200			100	10	5,710
Florida [1]	13,200		25,300	3,900		143,600		2,800	188,800
Georgia	e 1,300	e 300	e 6,800	e 1,200			e 100	e 12,000	[1] 21,700
Hawaii [2]								10	10
Idaho [2]	500		700	11,200	21,200	3,100	35	4,200	40,935
Illinois [2]	1,400	127,000	5,700	9,000					143,100
Indiana [2]	1,500	95,200	10,200	18,000				400	125,300
Iowa [1]	1,300	11,000	12,200	17,600			6	2,300	44,406
Kansas	[1] 1,100	[2] 45,600	[1] 7,500	[1] 5,100				[1] 1,200	59,500
Kentucky	[1,2] 2,400	[1,2] 119,200	[1] 3,900	[1] 1,700				[1] 500	127,700
Louisiana [1]	900		100	29,700			50		30,750
Maine [1]	400		4,400	28,200	12		100	1,700	34,812
Maryland	[1,2] 1,200	[2] 2,200	[1] 2,200	[1] 18,800			[1] 20	[1] 1,800	25,220
Massachusetts [1]	700		1,200	36,400			1,100	900	40,300

State									Total
Nevada [1]	100	1,600		5,500	5,600		600	19,500	32,900
New Hampshire [2]		100		8,000				200	8,300
New Jersey [2]	1,400	2,000		27,600			1,000	1,800	33,800
New Mexico [2]	13	1,200	100	400	40		100	4,600	6,453
New York [1]	1,700	12,500		42,200	5		700	600	57,705
North Carolina [1]	5,800	6,000	10	18,400	2,200	300	100	4,000	36,810
North Dakota	[1] 800	[2] 7,700	[2] 300	[1] 26,100			[1] 2,000		36,900
Ohio	[1] 10,200	[2] 212,800	[1] 21,000	[1] 28,100		1,000	1,600	2,000	276,700
Oklahoma [2]		23,500		[e] 2,500			1,400		27,400
Oregon [2]	100	300		1,300	6,300	10	1,400		9,410
Pennsylvania	[1] 10,400	[2] 302,400	[1] 24,400	[1] 23,800	[1] 2	[1] 8,800	[1] 400		370,202
Rhode Island [1]		20		3,600					3,620
South Carolina [1]	10,900	1,400		10,400	200	8,100	100	1,600	32,700
South Dakota	[2] 2,000	[2] 900		[e] 28,000				[2] 3,300	34,200
Tennessee [2]	2,700	29,300	4,400	18,400		27,000	5,300	13,800	100,900
Texas [1]	6,800	2,900	21,900	122,300		9,600	2,800		166,300
Utah [2]	600	200		2,200	10	500	2,000		5,510
Vermont		[2] 2,300		[1] 4,000				[2] 400	6,700
Virginia	[1][2] 1,100	[2] 29,800	[1] 4,300	[1] 13,100	[1] 600	[1] 100	[1][2] 7,700	[1][2] 4,100	60,800
Washington [2]	500	100	1,300	5,700	400	20		800	8,820
West Virginia [2]	300	192,000	2,800	300		100			195,500
Wisconsin [2]	100	9,000		26,400	5	49			35,554
Wyoming	[1][2] 3,500	[1][2] 1,000	[1][2] 300	[1][2] 200	[1][2] 800	[1][2] 300		[2] 4,300	10,400
Total	108,513	1,301,430	241,430	823,300	203,167	183,110	164,255	162,620	3,187,825

[e] Estimate.

[1] Data obtained from Soil Conservation Service, U. S. Department of Agriculture.

[2] Data compiled from reports submitted by the States on U. S. Department of the Interior form 6-1385X.

Impact on Environment

Environment is defined as "the surrounding conditions, influences, or forces which influence or modify." Within this context there are physical, biological, social, physiosocial, biosocial, and psychosocial factors. Thus, the all-inclusive term, "environment." encompasses almost every aspect of life and living. The environment is everchanging. Throughout geologic time the earth has been subjected to a continuing cycle of orogeny, erosion, transportation, and deposition. Natural land disturbances are neither new nor intrinsically bad; but, to these natural phenomena a new dimension has been added—man.

Surface mining frequently shocks the sensibilities, not so much by what is done as by the sheer magnitude of man's accomplishments. He literally has moved mountains, and some of his surface excavations are so vast as to resemble craters on the moon. Surface mining destroys the protective vegetative cover, and the soil and rock overlying the mineral deposit is frequently left in massive piles cast onto adjoining land. The result is a drastic reshaping of the surface, an alteration of normal surface and sub-surface drainage patterns. Square miles of land may be turned over to a depth of 100 feet or more and valleys rimmed by mile after mile of contour benches. Massive landslides have blocked streams and highways, waters have been polluted by acid and sediment, land areas isolated, and economic and esthetic values seriously impaired.

Our derelict acreage is made up of tens of thousands of separate patches. In some regions they are often close together. Where one acre in ten is laid waste, the whole landscape is disfigured. The face of the earth is riddled with abandoned mineral workings, packed with subsidence, gashed with quarries, littered with disused plant structures and piled high with stark and sterile banks of dross and debris,

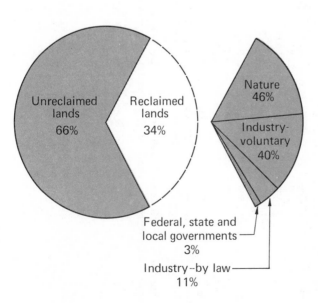

FIG. 3. Status of land disturbed by surface mining as of January 1, 1965.

Unreclaimed lands 66%

Reclaimed lands 34%

Nature 46%

Industry-voluntary 40%

Federal, state and local governments 3%

Industry--by law 11%

Table 3 Status of land disturbed by strip and surface mining in the United States as of January 1, 1965, by State (Thousand acres)

State	Land requiring reclamation [1]	Land not requiring reclamation [1]	Total land disturbed [2]	State	Land requiring reclamation [1]	Land not requiring reclamation [1]	Total land disturbed [2]
Alabama	83.0	50.9	133.9	Nebraska	16.8	12.1	28.9
Alaska	6.9	4.2	11.1	Nevada	20.4	12.5	32.9
Arizona	4.7	27.7	32.4	New Hampshire	5.1	3.2	8.3
Arkansas	16.6	5.8	22.4	New Jersey	21.0	12.8	33.8
California	107.9	66.1	174.0	New Mexico	2.0	4.5	6.5
Colorado	40.2	14.8	55.0	New York	50.2	7.5	57.7
Connecticut	10.1	6.2	16.3	North Carolina	22.8	14.0	36.8
Delaware	3.5	2.2	5.7	North Dakota	22.9	14.0	36.9
Florida	143.5	45.3	188.8	Ohio	171.6	105.1	276.7
Georgia	13.5	8.2	21.7	Oklahoma	22.2	5.2	27.4
Hawaii	(3)	(3)	(3)	Oregon	5.8	3.6	9.4
Idaho	30.7	10.3	41.0	Pennsylvania	229.5	140.7	370.2
Illinois	88.7	54.4	143.1	Rhode Island	2.2	1.4	3.6
Indiana	27.6	97.7	125.3	South Carolina	19.3	13.4	32.7
Iowa	35.5	8.9	44.4	South Dakota	25.3	8.9	34.2
Kansas	50.0	9.5	59.5	Tennessee	62.5	38.4	100.9
Kentucky	79.2	48.5	127.7	Texas	136.4	29.9	166.3
Louisiana	17.2	13.6	30.8	Utah	3.4	2.1	5.5
Maine	21.6	13.2	34.8	Vermont	4.2	2.5	6.7
Maryland	18.1	7.1	25.2	Virginia	37.7	23.1	60.8
Massachusetts	25.0	15.3	40.3	Washington	5.5	3.3	8.8
Michigan	26.6	10.3	36.9	West Virginia	111.4	84.1	195.5
Minnesota	71.5	43.9	115.4	Wisconsin	27.4	8.2	35.6
Mississippi	23.7	5.9	29.6	Wyoming	6.4	4.0	10.4
Missouri	43.7	15.4	59.1	Total	2040.6	1147.2	3187.8
Montana	19.6	7.3	26.9				

[1] Compiled from data supplied by Soil Conservation Service, U. S. Department of Agriculture.
[2] Data compiled from reports submitted by the States on U. S. Department of the Interior form 6-1385X, from Soil Conservation Service, U. S. Department of Agriculture, and estimates.
[3] Less than 100 acres.

Table 4 Land disturbed and production at strip and surface mines in the United States in 1964 for selected commodities, by ownership and geographic areas [1]

	Clay						Coal					
	Acres disturbed				Production		Acres disturbed				Production	
Geographic area	Private	Per cent	Public	Per cent	Thousand short tons	Per cent [2]	Private	Per cent	Public	Per cent	Thousand short tons	Per cent [2]
New England	37	100.0			290	64.0						
Middle Atlantic	386	99.5	2	0.5	2,136	41.1	5,246	94.0	334	6.0	15,365	45.3
South Atlantic	672	99.6	3	.4	8,413	56.8	3,888	95.7	173	4.3	7,992	38.9
East North Central	304	98.4	5	1.6	5,704	51.6	14,674	95.9	629	4.1	58,782	86.2
East South Central	238	99.2	2	.8	1,384	37.8	4,004	96.9	126	3.1	25,603	72.6
West North Central	458	99.8	1	.2	2,152	49.8	1,896	99.9	2	.1	4,913	92.9
West South Central	1,749	98.8	21	1.2	4,753	71.3	469	71.3	189	28.7	3,202	92.9
Mountain	487	64.2	272	35.8	1,873	84.1	534	91.0	53	9.0	6,352	93.9
Pacific	460	98.3	8	1.7	1,557	34.9	10	25.0	30	75.0	528	68.6
Total	4,791	93.8	314	6.2	28,262	53.4	30,721	95.2	1,536	4.8	122,737	70.3

	Stone						Sand and gravel					
	Acres disturbed				Production		Acres disturbed				Production	
Geographic area	Private	Per cent	Public	Per cent	Thousand short tons	Per cent [2]	Private	Per cent	Public	Per cent	Thousand short tons	Per cent [2]
New England	51	100.0			7,148	43.3	462	94.3	28	5.7	13,102	22.9
Middle Atlantic	556	99.3	4	0.7	46,721	49.5	692	98.4	11	1.6	23,910	32.7
South Atlantic	1,271	93.3	91	6.7	27,644	18.7	1,756	95.7	78	4.3	19,465	29.7
East North Central	954	98.1	18	1.9	69,380	45.8	3,035	94.7	170	5.3	104,792	57.2
East South Central	344	84.3	64	15.7	6,763	13.3	342	87.2	50	12.8	6,554	29.3
West North Central	1,588	98.3	27	1.7	51,915	65.7	4,218	93.3	305	6.7	36,290	32.1
West South Central	1,420	100.0			33,143	40.0	4,593	93.3	329	6.7	25,865	42.2
Mountain	319	67.4	154	32.6	9,060	37.4	2,519	72.3	967	27.7	42,813	41.5
Pacific	414	77.2	122	22.8	8,243	10.4	1,182	36.7	2,036	63.3	57,313	30.2
Total	6,917	93.5	480	6.5	260,017	35.8	18,799	82.5	3,974	17.5	330,104	38.0

[1] As reported voluntarily by producers on U. S. Department of the Interior forms 6-1386X and 6-1387X.

[2] Per cent of production reported and published in the U. S. Bureau of Mines Minerals Yearbook, 1964.

Note: Phosphate rock; land reported disturbed in 1964 totaled 2,450 acres, only 20 acres of which was publicly owned. Production reported, 20,740,000 net tons, or 28 per cent of the United States total. Of total land disturbed, 81 per cent was in the South Atlantic States; 15 per cent in the East South Central States; and, 4 per cent in the Mountain States.

and spoil and slag. Their very existence fosters slovenliness and vandalism, invites the squatter's shack and engenders a "derelict land mentality" that can never be eradicated until the mess itself has been cleared up. Dereliction, indeed, breeds a brutish insensibility, bordering on positive antagonism, to the life and loveliness of the natural landcape it has supplanted. It debases as well as disgraces our civilization. . .

Although the preceding paraphrased excerpts from "Derelict Land" were written to describe conditions in Great Britain, they are equally relevant to certain mining districts in the United States. To many individuals, natural beauty may exist only in a particular national monument, mountain, forest, park, lake, or well-remembered scenic view. However, this narrow concept is giving way to an awareness that natural beauty is everywhere and in everything.

There is no question that many surface-mining operations blight the landscape. Nearly 60 percent of the more than 690 surface mine sites examined could be observed from public-use. areas. Where the sites contrasted with greener suroundings, they could be considered unsightly, or even repellent. In arid, or desert, areas public concern is less evident because of the sparse population and the mine sites are somewhat similar in appearance to the surrounding areas.

It was found in the majority of cases (78 percent), that no abandoned structures or equipment had been left on the site of the operation; however, about one-third of the areas visited were being used illegally by the public to discard garbage, rubble, junked vehicles, and construction materials. Such misuse endangers public health and safety and destroys the appearance of an area. In addition mine fires, which cost the Nation millions of dollars annually, are often started by burning trash and other materials in abandoned coal strip pits.

As yet, only a small percentage (about 0.14 percent) of the total land area of the United States has been disturbed by surface mining. But the effects are evident in every State, varying from small prospecting trenches in the West to the widespread disturbances of Appalachia. Effects of such mining upon the environment also vary widely, depending upon the steepness of the terrain, amount of precipitation, temperature, chemical characteristics of the mineral, and method of mining.

Basic Disturbances

Surface mining affects the environment in three ways. To some degree, it influences the quality of our air, land, and water; and, through these, animal and plant life.

Air

Although air pollution is one of our more serious environmental problems, surface mining, per se, cannot be considered a major contributor. However, the dust and vibrations resulting from blasting and movement of equipment during mining operations can be annoying and, in densely populated areas, a public nuisance. Some abandoned surface mines and waste piles also may be a source of air-borne dust.

Land

Two factors that are essential to the establishment of vegetation on surface-mined areas are the physical and chemical characteristics of the spoil. The spoil material was considered suitable for agricultural use at only 25 percent of the sites observed during the random-sampling survey. Where excessive stoniness exists (at about 20 percent of the sites inspected) the possibility of getting a quick vigorous cover is hampered by the rapid run-off and lack of soil. Most of the remaining 55 percent might be receptive to tree or herbaceous type plantings if climatological conditions are favorable.

There were no serious erosion problems at about 60 percent of the areas examined primarily because some vegetation had been established and the slope of the land was relatively gentle before and after mining. Most of the remaining sites showed evidence of erosion in the form of gullies less than one-foot deep; but, at 10 percent of the sites gullies were found that exceeded this depth. Sediment deposits were found in 56 percent of the ponds and 52 percent of the streams on or adjacent to the sample sites.

Spoil bank materials which have a pH of 4.0 or less are lethal to most plants. A pH of 7.0 is neutral; values higher than 7.0 indicate alkalinity. Free acid may be leached enough in 3 to 5 years to permit planting, but the leaching process will not improve soil conditions if erosion is allowed to expose more sulfuritic minerals in the spoil. Although some plants achieve successful growth in spoil with a pH range under 5.0, most plants require a less acid environment for successful growth. Of the measurements taken on spoil banks, 1 percent showed a pH of less than 3.0 and 47 percent, a range between pH 3.0 and 5.0.

About 15 percent of the spoil banks are covered with vegetation sufficient to provide adequate site protection. Another 15 percent have fair to good cover which, with more time and some spot planting, should suffice to protect the areas and speed renewal of the soil. Twenty percent will require direct seeding, seedlings, and fertilization. About 30 percent of the sites inspected had little, or no, cover and will, therefore, require extensive treatment. On the remaining 20 percent of the sites examined, vegetation will be extremely difficult to grow because of excessive stoniness or toxic conditions. It was also observed that wide variations occur in the rate at which natural revegetation takes place because of differences in physical and chemical characteristics of the spoil, and proximity to seed sources.

It was assumed for the random-sampling survey that, generally, mined land had been used prior to mining for purposes similar to those on adjoining tracts, and that, if left untreated by man, the mining site would eventually regain the same types of cover. Field observations made during the survey showed this to be largely untrue, however, because only about one-half of the areas assumed to have been forested had returned to forest and land classified as idle had increased almost fourfold. Land which had been devoted to crops and human occupancy, of course, had not voluntarily returned to these uses. Curiously, most land assumed to have been grassland had returned to grass. Clearly then, in most cases, natural forces will need a strong assist from man if mined sites are to be brought back to their former uses.

When natural vegetation is removed

by exploration and mining activities, the area becomes virtually useless for wildlife because it becomes barren of food, nesting, and escape cover. Even in the most arid areas of the country, erosion eventually follows removal of vegetation, and the resulting silt and sediment may affect fish and wildlife habitat. Thus, except in a few limited areas of the Midwest, poorer soils and vegetative cover resulting from surface mining create less favorable wildlife habitat. However, the rough broken ground found at many sites does afford protection from hunters for some species.

Water

Although basic to human existence, water is perhaps America's most abused resource. The surface mining industries are not the major contributor to the degradation of our water supplies on a national basis, yet in many areas such as Appalachia, they are a significant source of pollution.

Chemical pollution of water by surface mines takes many forms. The polluted water may be too acid, too alkaline, or contain excessive concentrations of dissolved substances such as iron, manganese, and copper. High concentrations of dissolved minerals may make the water unsuitable for certain purposes, but not for others; for example, water unsuitable for domestic use because of chemical content may often be used by industry, and some forms of aquatic life may flourish in it.

Sulfur-bearing minerals are commonly associated with coal, and are a major cause of water pollution. When exposed to air and water, they oxidize to form sulfuric acid. This acid may enter streams in two ways: (1) Soluble acid salts formed on the exposed spoil surfaces enter into solution during periods of surface run-off, and (2) ground water, while moving to nearby streams, may be altered chemically as it percolates through spoil, or waste dumps.

Acid drainage is but one of several adverse chemical effects caused by surface mining. Even in minute concentrations, salts of metals such as zinc, lead, arsenic, copper, and aluminum are toxic to fish, wildlife, plants, and aquatic insects. Indirectly associated with acid drainage are the undesirable slimy red or yellow iron precipitates ("yellow boy") in streams that drain sulfide-bearing coal or metal deposits. Of the streams receiving direct run-off from surface mine sites, 31 percent of those examined contained noticeable quantities of precipitates. Water discoloration was recorded at 37 percent of the streams adjacent to the sites observed, suggesting chemical or physical pollution. The discoloration occured most frequently in connection with the mining of coal, clay, sand and gravel, peat, iron, stone, and phosphate rock.

Streams are also polluted by acid water from underground mines, preparation plants, and natural seepage from unworked coal and other pyritic material. Because of the intermingling of effluents from these sources, it is difficult, if not impossible, to determine the quantity of acid that comes from surface mining alone. Many authorities believe, however, that not more than 25 percent of the acid load created by coal mining can be attributed directly to surface operations. Many streams in the Appalachian region are affected to various degrees by acid drainage from both surface and underground mines.

Although acid conditions are associated with coal mining conducted elsewhere, the problems are not usually so severe because the topography is not as rugged, rainfall is less profuse, pyritic materials oxidize more slowly, and, in some cases, limestone formations act as a neutralizing agent. Where acidity is neutralized by alkaline water, or limestone, the concentration of certain dissolved substances still may remain high and the water may not be usable without treatment.

Acid mine drainage affects fish and wildlife in several ways. Acid changes the water quality of streams into which it is discharged and, although the concentration may not be lethal to fish or wildlife, it may bring about changes in their physical condition and rate of growth. However, acid may be present in such concentration as to be directly lethal to fish or tend to suppress or prevent reproduction of the most desirable species.

The Bureau of Sport Fisheries and Wildlife reported that in the United States some 5,800 miles of streams (about 57,000 acres) and 29,000 surface acres of impoundments and reservoirs, are seriously affected by surface coal mining operations. The Bureau reported that, in 1964, 97 percent of the acid mine pollution in streams and 93 percent in impoundments, resulted from coal mining operations. Similar data were obtained by a United States Geological Survey reconnaissance conducted in 1965, which disclosed that water quality at 194 of 318 sampling sites in Appalachia was measurably influenced by acid mine drainage. None of these data, however, reflect the percentage of damage that can be attributed to surface mining alone.

Access roads built of pyritic waste material may also be sources of acid water. In past years, some highway departments have hauled waste from the mines for road building purposes. This practice is not generally followed today, and is forbidden in some States; however, roads built of this material continue to acidify rainwater passing over them—despite long periods of leaching. In addition, some privately constructed mine-access roads are being built of pyritic material.

Roads opened on National Wildlife Refuges by prospectors frequently result in broken levees; interfere with controlled burning; increase human activity, which interferes with the nesting and breeding of birds and animals; and, restrict animal movements. The distance that each species, or even individual animals, will place between themselves and the disturbance varies greatly, but some species will leave an area entirely when their natural habitat is invaded by people and equipment.

Physical pollution is most serious in areas typified by high-intensity storms and steep slopes, particularly during and shortly after mining. In areas undisturbed by strip mining within the Appalachian region, the average annual sediment yield ranges from about 20 to 3,000 tons per square mile of watershed, depending upon land use. Research conducted in Kentucky indicated that yields from coal strip-mined lands can be as much as 1,000 times that of undisturbed forest. During a four-year period, the annual average from Kentucky spoil banks was 27,000 tons per square mile while it was estimated at only 25 tons per square mile from forested areas.

Erosion and sedimentation problems

from surface mining are less severe in arid regions; however, even in such areas, storms do occur during which large quantities of sediment are discharged from mine workings, spoil heaps, and access roads. At some idle surface mines in arid country, the effects of wind and water erosion are still evident on steep spoil banks that were abandoned many years ago.

One of the major causes of sedimentation problems is the failure to control surface run-off following rainstorms. In areas outside Appalachia, 86 percent of the surface-mined areas investigated were found to have adequate run-off control. Areas lacking sufficient control were confined almost exclusively to the surface mining of coal, phosphate, manganese, clay, and gold.

Some 7,000 miles of stream channels have had their normal storm-carrying capacity reduced according to the Bureau of Sport Fisheries and Wildlife. It was observed that the normal water-carrying capacity of about 4,500 miles of these streams had been moderately to severely affected. The remaining 2,500 miles had been affected only slightly (debris reducing channel by less than one-third of capacity). Sediment generally was not a significant problem on small streams located more than two miles from the sample site.

Substandard access and haulage roads, and others built in connection with prospecting activities, are a major source of sediment. Based on the sample data, 95 percent of these roads were less than 3 miles long, but the proximity of many to natural stream channels had considerably increased their potential for sedimentation damage. The roads were fairly passable in

the majority of cases; however, approximately 15 percent were eroded to a point that would make them difficult to traverse by ordinary vehicles.

Beneficial Effects of Surface Mining

When massive rocks are fragmented during surface mining, the resulting piles of material contain considerably more void space than existed in the fractures, partings, and pore spaces of the undisturbed rock. As a result, certain desirable hydrologic effects may occur. The danger of floods is diminished because a significant portion of the rainfall is trapped in depressions and behind the spoil banks where it sinks into the earth to augment groundwater supplies, rather than running off rapidly to nearby streams. Because water stored in the banks moves slowly, drainage will continue for a long time before the water level declines to that of adjacent streams. Thus, streams near surface-mined areas often maintain a longer sustained flow during dry weather than those draining undisturbed ground. This phenomenon was verified through field studies conducted in the Midwest by the Indiana University Water Research Center, but it occurs less frequently in most of Appalachia because of the rapid run-off.

In the Western United States, some surface mines have exposed groundwater sources and made water available where none existed before. This water has proved invaluable to livestock and wildlife. At some surface mining operations along mountainsides, the pits impound surface run-off from torrential rains, minimize the sediment load of streams draining the area, and effect considerable ground water recharge as well.

In California, piles of dredge tailings are quite permeable. However, because of their irregular conformation, they undoubtedly inhibit surface run-off to a greater degree than the original slopes, thus making some contribution to flood control and ground-water recharge. In Alaska, dredge mining for gold has destroyed the permafrost and the resulting tailings and mined area are considered premium property for residential and industrial development.

Many mine-access roads, when properly repaired and maintained, can be of considerable value since they may be used to promote the multiple-land-use potential of extensive areas. Accessibility for fire protection, recreation, and management activities, can mean the difference between use and isolation. For example, by improving fire protection, investments can be made more safely in growing timber, and hazards to human and wildlife considerably reduced. Where massive equipment was used in the mining process, the access roads were usually well constructed, and the cost of repairing and maintaining them would be low. By converting some of these roads to public use, tourism might also be encouraged because many of the sites examined (33 percent) were located in areas that afforded spectacular views of mountains, valleys, and lakes.

Surface mining has created many opportunities to develop recreational areas where none existed before. Water in the form of small ponds or lakes, and the spoil piles themselves, frequently provide a pleasant topographic change in areas of virtually flat land. Examples may be found in flat coastal areas and in such States as Kansas, Illinois, Indiana, Ohio, and California.

Related Problems

Although on-site and some off-site conditions associated with strip and surface mining are discussed, this report does not cover waste materials resulting from processing mineral ores and preparing solid fuels for market. Neither does it explore problems associated with waste brought to the surface from underground operations, mine fires, surface subsidence, acid drainage from underground mines, possible accumulations of spent oil shale, seepages of oil and brine, mining on the continental shelf, and conflicting land uses. However, some of these problems are discussed briefly in the following sections to alert the reader to their significance, and to outline some of the efforts being taken to resolve them.

Bureau of Mines Solid Waste Disposal Program

Under Public Law 89-272, the Solid Waste Disposal Act, the Secretary of the Interior has delegated responsibility to the Bureau of Mines for a study of problems associated with the disposal, or use, of solid wastes resulting from the extraction, processing, or utilization of mineral or fossil fuels. To discharge this responsibility, the Bureau has initiated two types of projects:

a. *Economic and resource-evaluation investigations aimed at identifying the causes of waste disposal problems in the mineral and fossil fuel industries; and*

b. *scientific and engineering research to develop methods of utilizing, or*

FIG. 4. Active operation adjacent to reclaimed areas—Sand and gravel. Photo by T. Hazlett, Courtesy of National Sand and Gravel Association.

otherwise disposing of, a variety of inorganic waste materials.

The economic and resource-evaluation studies are directed toward determining the magnitude, nature, and location of solid waste piles; identifying problems in terms of priority; appraising the effectiveness of current disposal practices, including costs and possible profits that might accrue from further beneficiation or treatment; and, estimating the quantity of waste that may accumulate from future operations. A series of case studies will be included that will attempt to evaluate specific waste piles from the standpoint of public health and safety (such as burning culm banks) and the extent to which they retard industrial or urban development. In addition to wastes that may still contain some mineral values, slag dumps and tailings will be investigated to determine whether they are potential sources of road materials and lightweight aggregates.

The current research program includes projects at Bureau research installations, grants-in-aid to universities and colleges, and one contract to private industry. Research by the Bureau includes projects designed to produce a clean steel scrap from automobile bodies; to develop technically- and economically-feasible methods of recovering and utilizing the metal content of red-mud residues of the alumina industry; to use auto scrap and non-magnetic taconite ores for the production of marketable magnetic iron oxide concentrates; to develop new or improved methods of salvaging metal from municipal wastes; and, to devise processes for the production of marketable products therefrom.

Grants-in-aid include studies on grass and other plants that might flourish on waste piles; use of mine and mill wastes in manufacturing bricks, lightweight block, structural clay products, or as aggregates for concrete; potential uses for spent oil shale; recovery of valuable products from mine dumps; and, removing contaminating metals from automobile scrap. The private contract is for the purpose of developing techniques to remove and recover copper from auto scrap melted in a cupola. Iron ingots suitable for use in iron or steel foundries will be produced and copper recovered from the slag, thus providing from auto scrap two metals which have well-established markets.

Mine Fires and Subsidence

A coal formation is a vast bed of combustible fuel. Mining makes oxygen available and all that is required to initiate combustion is a source of heat. One of the most common causes of coal mine or waste bank fires is the practice of burning trash or rubbish in strip pits or near the banks. Mine fires not only have a demoralizing effect upon a community, they pose a menace to public health and safety by emitting noxious gases and fumes, endanger surface lands and property, and destroy valuable resources. Of the more

than 200 mine fires located in the United States in 1964, many had been burning for years, a few for several decades. These fires, with nearly 500 waste bank fires, thus exert a considerable adverse effect upon the environment in certain areas. An insidious aspect of these types of fire is that, because of their proximity to each other, a mine fire may ignite a culm bank and vice versa.

Underground mining removes that part of the surface support supplied by the mineral extracted. Regardless of the type of mining and roof support used, subsidence usually occurs when the ore body, or coal seam, is relatively near the surface. Surface subsidence resulting from underground mining has caused loss of life and millions of dollars of damage to buildings, streets, water mains, and sewage lines in built-up areas. In addition, subsidences disrupt drainage patterns and permit surface water to infiltrate underground mine workings, thus frequently creating enormous underground impoundments in abandoned mines. Where the water is acid, its return to the surface, either by pumping or gravity flow, presents a serious pollution problem in the receiving streams.

Disposal of Spent Oil Shale

About one-half barrel of oil may be recovered from a ton of oil shale by a number of retorting processes. It is estimated that, for a 50,000 barrel-per-day operation, the disposal problem would involve 100,000 tons of spent shale per day. "High-grading" and unwise plant practices could waste large amounts of oil shale, resulting in enormous spoil piles of low-grade shale, and create stream and air pollution problems. Underground mining could induce surface subsidence that might adversely affect the recovery of minerals that lie above the oil shale deposits in some places.

Oil Seepage and Brines

Leaks in well casings and the disposal of brines and other wastes seriously contaminate fresh water supplies in many of the older oil fields. Leaks that allow brines to percolate downward to the ground water reservoir and the presence of permeable sands beneath some disposal pits are two of the major sources of contamination. Another major problem lies in locating oil wells which may be contaminating ground water. After they are found, the procedure is to clean and cement them from the bottom to seal off permeable formations. However, the problems mentioned require continued study.

Ocean Floor Mining

Ocean floor mining is emerging as a source of future mineral supply. Though in its infancy, commercial operations are being conducted for (1) shells off the coast of Iceland, in San Francisco Bay, and in the Gulf of Mexico; (2) tin off the coasts of Indonesia and Thailand; (3) diamonds off South-West Africa; (4) aragonite in Florida; and (5) iron sand in Ariaka Bay, Kyushu, Japan. Oil and sulfur have long been recovered from off-shore deposits, and gold dredging in off-shore areas of Alaska is being actively investigated. Effective disposal of the tailings (waste) without seriously impairing the utilization of other marine resources and creating objectionable on-shore waste piles appears to be the most important problem so far encountered.

Conflicting Mineral Land Use Problems

Surface mining often disturbs other resources. In many instances, timber is removed, wildlife habitat disrupted, natural streams diverted or contaminated, roads are built in undisturbed areas, and holes drilled. There is also the question of whether the initial mining operation will reduce our mineral-resource base by interfering with or precluding entirely the ultimate recovery of other underlying minerals. The demand for land to support both urban growth and mineral development (particularly sand and gravel) also creates serious social and political questions in densely-populated areas. In addition, when reclamation is contemplated, disagreements often occur as to the type of land use that will contribute most to society.

A nationwide study by the Bureau of Mines that is scheduled for completion in fiscal year 1967 is aimed at determining the effect of mineral extraction on land values. Although primary efforts will be directed toward urban centers and scenic and recreational areas, other locales will be included. The study will attempt to delineate problems of land rehabilitation and end-use following various types of mining such as strip, open pit, quarrying, and underground. Conditions under which mined-out land may enhance in value as well as some of the factors that lead to deterioration of value will also be determined. A special feature will deal with methods of handling future, or potential, land conflicts in order to maximize the utilization of the Nation's mineral resources and yet minimize the objectionable economic and sociologic after-effects of mining.

References

Hundreds of reports have been published on many aspects of surface mining and mined-land reclamation. The subject matter varies widely, ranging from technical details of a single problem in a small water-shed to in-depth studies of problems in areas the size of Appalachia. Because of the sheer volume and diversity of the subject matter covered by the literature, no attempt has been made to compile a comprehensive list of references. Rather, to assist those who might wish to delve further into pertinent writings, the following bibliographies are presented:

Berryhill, Louise R. Bibliography of the U. S. Geological Survey Publications Relating to Coal, 1882-1949. U. S. Geol. Survey Circ. 86, Jan. 1951, 52 pp.

Bituminous Coal Research, Inc., for the Coal Research Board, Commonwealth of Pennsylvania, Mine Drainage Abstracts. A Bibliography, 1910-63. 1964.

Bowden, Kenneth L. A Bibliography of Strip Mine Reclamation, 1953-60. Dept. of Conserv., The Univ. of Mich., 1961, 13 pp.

Funk, David T. A Revised Bibliography of Strip Mine Reclamation. U. S. Forest Service. Central States Forest Expt. Sta. Misc., Release 35, 20 pp.

Lorenz, Walter C. Progress in Controlling Acid Mine Water: A Literature Review. U. S. BuMines Inf. Circ. 8080, 1962, 40 pp.

Pacific Southwest Inter-Agency Committee. Annotated Bibliography on Water Quality in Pacific Southwest Inter-Agency Committee Area, 1950-63. Dec. 1965, 94 pp.

U. S. Department of Agriculture, Forest Service. Annotated List of Publications, Central States Forest Expt. Sta., Jan. 1965-Mar. 1966, 18 pp.

The following publications include comprehensive lists of references that are directly related to the subject matter indicated in the titles.

Averitt, Paul. Coal Reserves of the United States—A Progress Report, January 1, 1960. U. S. Geol. Survey Bull. 1136, 1961, 116 pp.

Bauer, Anthony M. Simultaneous Excavation and Rehabilitation of Sand and Gravel Sites. Nat. Sand and Grav. Assoc., Silver Spring, Md., 1965, 60 pp.

Biesecker, J. E., and J. R. George. Stream Quality in Appalachia as Related to Coal-Mine Drainage, 1965. U. S. Geol. Survey Circ. 526, 1966, 27 pp.

Brooks, David B. Strip Mine Reclamation and Economic Analysis. Natural Resources J. v. 6, No. 1, Jan. 1966, pp. 13–44.

Derelict Land, A study of industrial dereliction and how it may be redeemed. Civic Trust, 79 Buckingham Palace Road, London S. W. 1, 1964, 70 pp.

Federal Water Pollution Control Administration, Region VIII. Disposition and Control of Uranium Mill Tailings Piles in the Colorado River Basin. U. S. Dept. of H. E. W., Mar. 1966, 36 pp. and 28 p. Appendix.

Forest Service, Eastern Region and the Soil Conservation Society of America. Strip Mine Reclamation (a digest). U. S. Dept. Agr., Rev., 1964, 69 pp.

Johnson, Craig. Practical Operating Procedures for Progressive Rehabilitation of Sand and Gravel Sites. Nat. Sand and Grav. Assoc., Silver Spring, Md., 1966, 75 pp.

Kinney, Edward C. Extent of Acid Mine Pollution in the United States Affecting Fish and Wildlife. U. S. BuSport Fish. and Wildlife Circ. 191, 1964, 27 pp.

Ministry of Housing and Local Government, Her Majesty's Stationery Office. New Life for Dead Lands, Derelict Acres Reclaimed. Brown, Knight and Truscott, Ltd., London and Tonbridge. 1963, 30 pp.

Research Committee on the Coal Mine Spoil Revegetation in Pennsylvania. A guide for Revegetating Bituminous Strip-Mine Spoils in Pennsylvania. 1965, 46 pp.

The Council of State Governments. Proceedings of a Conference on Surface Mining, Roanoke, Virginia, April 1964. Surface Mining—Extent and Economic Importance, Impact on Natural Resources, and Proposals for Reclamation of Mined-Lands. 1964, 64 pp.

Udall, Stewart L. Study of Strip and Surface Mining in Appalachia. An Interim Report to the Appalachian Regional Commission. U. S. Dept. of the Int. June 1966, 78 pp.

29   Land Subsidence in Western United States*

Joseph F. Poland

Introduction

Volcanic eruptions, earthquakes, tsunamis, and landslides are instantaneous events that often have disastrous consequences. On the other hand, land subsidence due to man's activities, which I will be discussing in this paper, ordinarily is a relatively slow process that may continue for several decades. Subsidence may produce conditions or stresses that trigger some instantaneous event such as the failure of a dam or a levee, and public agencies should be aware of such potential hazards; but in many areas that have experienced appreciable subsidence, the problems created, although of considerable economic significance, are not hazards to human life.

Subsidence may occur from one or more of several causes, including withdrawal of fluids (oil, gas, or water), application of water to moisture-deficient deposits above the water table, drainage of peat lands, extraction of solids in mining operations, removal of solids by solution, application of surface loads, and tectonic movements (including earthquakes).

In western United States, the subsidences of appreciable magnitude and area have been caused chiefly by the withdrawal of fluids, but also by application of water to moisture-deficient deposits and drainage of peat lands. This paper, therefore, will be limited to a brief description of these three types of subsidence, the problems created, and remedial measures, actual or potential.

Subsidence of Organic Deposits Due to Drainage

The peat lands which underlie roughly 450 square miles of the Sacramento-San Joaquin Delta constitute one of the largest areas of organic deposits in western United States. These peat deposits are as much as 40 feet thick. Drainage of the Delta islands for agricultural use began shortly after 1850. The land surface of many of the islands, initially about at sea level, is now 10 to 15 feet below sea level. Protective levees have been raised as the island surfaces have subsided. Leveling by Weir shows that the surface of Mildred Island subsided 9.3 feet from 1922 to 1955 at an average rate of 0.28 foot per year. Weir (1950) concluded that the causes of the subsidence were (1) oxidation of the deposits dewatered by lowering the water table to permit cultivation (by aerobic bacteria primarily, and probably the major cause), (2) compaction by tillage machinery,

* Publication authorized by the Director, U. S. Geological Survey.

Poland, J. F., 1969, "Land Subsidence in Western United States," in *Geologic Hazards and Public Problems*, May 27-28, 1969, Conference Proceedings, Olson, R. A. and Wallace, M. W., eds. U. S. Govt. Printing Office, pp. 77–96. Lightly edited by permission of the author. The paper was originally read before the conference and illustrated with slides.
Mr. Poland is a research hydrologist with the Ground Water Branch of the U. S. Geological Survey, Sacramento, California.

(3) shrinkage by drying, (4) burning, and (5) wind erosion.

The lower the island surfaces sink below the water surface in the Delta channels, the greater the stress on the protecting levees. This past winter, a levee reach on Sherman Island failed and the island was flooded. Although the water is being pumped out of Sherman Island, the levee-maintenance problem will increase in the Delta as continued drainage for cultivation lowers the island surfaces farther.

Subsidence Due to Application of Water (Hydrocompaction)

Locally, along the west and south borders of the San Joaquin Valley, moisture-deficient alluvial-fan deposits above the water table have subsided 5 to 15 feet after the application of water (Lofgren, 1960). These deposits are composed chiefly of mudflows and water-laid deposits and have higher clay content than the non-subsiding deposits, according to Bull (1964), who concluded that the compaction by the overburden load occurred as the clay bond supporting the voids was weakened by wetting.

This near-surface subsidence, or hydrocompaction, has been a serious problem, resulting in sunken irrigation ditches and undulating fields and has damaged canals, roads, pipelines, and transmission towers. It is particularly serious in construction and maintenance of large canals. As a preventive measure, deposits of this type along about 20 miles of the San Luis section of the California Aqueduct and along about 50 miles of the Aqueduct in Kern County were precompacted by prolonged wetting, prior to canal construction. The estimated cost of this operation was $25 million.

According to Lofgren (1969), moisture deficient alluvial deposits that compact on wetting also have been reported in Wyoming, Montana, Washington, and Arizona, where subsidence of as much as 6 feet after wetting has created problems in engineering structures. Also, moisture-deficient loessial deposits as much as 100 feet thick covering extensive areas in the Missouri River basin have caused problems in the construction of dams, canals, and irrigation structures. Precompaction by wetting has been the usual solution, once this property of the sediments is recognized.

Subsidence Due to Withdrawal of Fluids

Subsidence due to withdrawal of fluids is by far the most common type of man-made regional subsidence. It may occur over oil and gas fields or over intensively exploited ground-water reservoirs. In either case, the cause is the same. The withdrawal of water reduces the fluid pressure in the aquifers and increases the effective stress (grain-to-grain load) borne by the aquifer skeleton. In ground-water reservoirs, the increase in effective stress in the permeable aquifers is immediate and is equal to the decrease in fluid pressure. The aquifers respond chiefly as elastic bodies. The compaction is immediate, but usually is small and mostly recoverable if fluid pressures are restored.

On the other hand, in the confining clays or the clayey interbeds, which have low hydraulic conductivity and high compressibility, the vertical escape of water and adjustment of pore pressure is slow and time-dependent. In these fine-grained beds, the stress applied by the head decline becomes effective only as rapidly as pore pressures decay toward equilibrium with pressures in adjacent aquifers. It is the time-dependent nature of the pore-pressure decay in these fine-grained beds that complicates the problem of predicting compaction or subsidence.

Intensive ground-water withdrawal and decline of head in heterogeneous confined aquifer systems in unconsolidated to semiconsolidated deposits of late Cenozoic age have produced the major areas of subsidence in western United States. Therefore, I will first review the dimensions and problems of subsidence due to ground-water withdrawal, and then comment briefly on subsidence of oil fields.

Subsidence Due to Ground-Water Withdrawal

In the Houston-Galveston area of the Texas Gulf Coast, 1 to 6 feet of subsidence has occurred over an area of about 1,500 square miles. This is due almost wholly to lowering of artesian head in the ground-water reservoir, although there are subsidiary depressions due to oil-field subsidence.

In south-central Arizona, subsidence of 1 to 3 feet has been defined by leveling in several areas where water levels have been lowered 150 to 250 feet. The maximum known subsidence in southern Arizona is in the Eloy-Casa Grande area where subsidence of 7.5 feet occurred between 1949 and 1967. The extent of the area is not defined.

At Las Vegas, Nevada, subsidence of 3 feet was indicated by leveling in 1963.

Figure 1 shows the principal areas

of subsidence in California. In the Sacramento-San Joaquin Delta, we have the organic deposits that I described earlier. The areas of subsidence due to ground-water withdrawal include the Santa Clara Valley, which is at the south end of San Francisco Bay, and where about 250 square miles have been affected and maximum subsidence by 1967 was 13 feet in San Jose. Then we have the large area in the San Joaquin Valley extending from about Los Banos on the west side south to Wasco on the east side, and the area at the south end which is referred to here as the Arvin-Maricopa area. The maximum subsidence in the San Joaquin Valley is on the west side and was about 26 feet in 1966. To the south, in southern California, the location of the Wilmington oil field is shown, and about 20 miles to the northwest of the Wilmington oil field is the Inglewood oil field in the Baldwin Hills (not shown).

There is one other area of subsidence that I might mention. That is Antelope Valley (Lancaster area in Fig. 1). It is just north of the San Gabriel Mountains and at least 160 square miles have been affected; subsidence in Lancaster is at least 3 feet.

Figure 2 shows the magnitude and extent of subsidence in the San Joaquin Valley but not for the same period of time in all areas, because the year span is determined by the available leveling control. The maximum subsidence is on the west side of the valley southeast of Los Banos.

As of 1963, subsidence exceeded 20 feet west of Fresno, and extensive areas had subsided 12 to 20 feet. On the east side, in the area between Tulare and Wasco, maximum subsidence was 12

FIG. 1. Areas of land subsidence in California. Major subsidence due to fluid withdrawal shown in black; subsidence in Delta caused by oxidation of peat.

feet by 1962; and that is the latest leveling control in that area. South of Bakersfield the maximum subsidence was 8 feet in 1965, which is the latest complete leveling in that area. The total area that is affected by more than one foot of subsidence exceeds 3,500 square miles or almost a third of the San Joaquin Valley. Each of the subsiding areas is underlain by a confined aquifer system in which the water level has been drawn down 200 feet or more —on the west side as much as 450 feet—by the intensive withdrawal. The dotted line is the position of the California Aqueduct which passes through the western and southern areas of subsidence.

The land subsidence in the Santa Clara Valley from 1960 to 1967 is shown in Fig. 3; it was nearly 4 feet in San Jose in the 7 years, and this happened to be the period of most rapid land subsidence in the Santa Clara Valley. The total subsidence has been about 13 feet in downtown San Jose. You will note that from 1960 to 1967 there was about 2 feet of subsidence at the south end of San Francisco Bay.

Figure 4 illustrates the change in altitude (subsidence) of a bench mark in downtown San Jose, where the elevation changed from 98 feet above sea level to about 85 feet above sea level from 1912 to 1967, representing a sub-

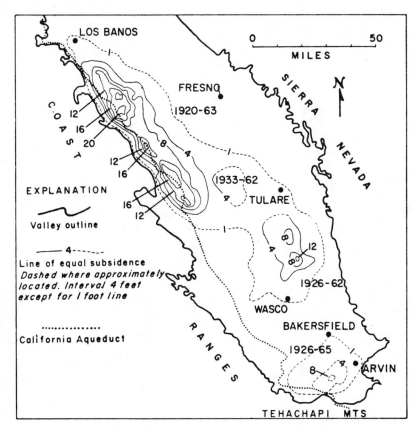

FIG. 2. Map showing the magnitude and areal extent of subsidence in southern San Joaquin Valley.

sidence of 13 feet. The hydrograph shows the fluctuation of water level in a nearby well. I call your attention to the fact that during a period of artesian-head recovery from 1936 to 1943, the subsidence stopped; it presumably began again about 1947 and reached its steepest rate of about 0.7 foot a year in the early 60's, due to the rapid decline in head from 1959 to 1963. The rate of subsidence in San Jose has decreased substantially in the past 2 years because there has been a winter water-level recovery of about 30 feet above levels of the middle 1960's.

Figure 5 shows the relation of the subsidence of 25 feet occurring in western Fresno County in the San Joaquin Valley between 1943 and 1966 and a decline of approximately 400 feet in the water level in nearby wells. This bench mark is at the locus of maximum subsidence in the San Joaquin Valley.

Subsidence can be measured by two methods: by repeated leveling of bench marks at the land surface, which is the common way of measuring it, and also is the only way to get full areal coverage, or, it can be measured at one site,

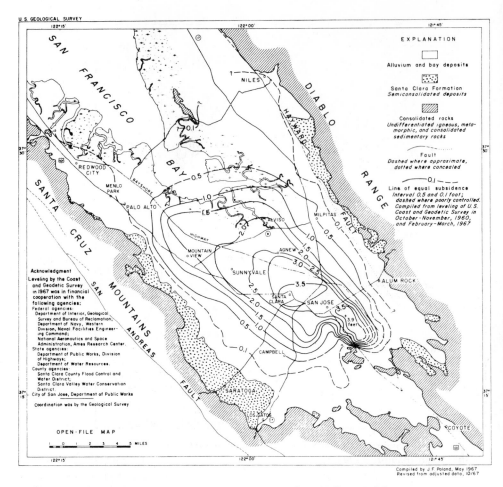

Compiled by J. F. Poland, May 1967
Revised from adjusted data, 10/67

FIG. 3. Land subsidence from 1960 to 1967, Santa Clara Valley, California.

by measuring compaction directly. Releveling is the basis for knowing how much subsidence has occurred in the San Joaquin Valley. The level net in the subsidence areas plus the ties to bedrock total about 1,500 miles of leveling. Considering that first-order leveling costs about $200 a mile and second-order leveling about $100 a mile, releveling that entire area requires a substantial amount of funds.

Subsidence can be measured at a single point by using what can be ele-

gantly called a bore-hole extensometer or can be referred to simply as a compaction recorder. Figure 6 is a simplified diagram of the type of compaction recorder operated in the San Joaquin and Santa Clara Valleys—consisting of an anchor connected to a stainless steel cable that passes over sheaves at the land surface and is, kept taut by a counterweight. The cable is connected to a recorder. If there is compaction between the land surface and the anchor, the cable moves up with respect

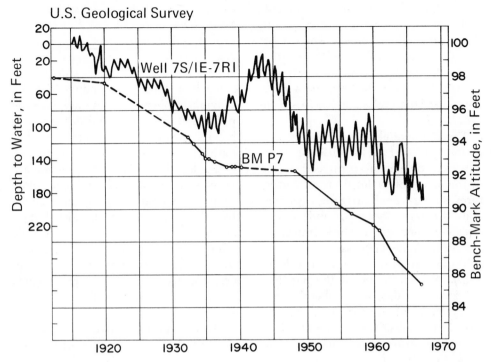

FIG. 4. Change in altitude at bench mark P7 in San Jose and change in artesian head in nearby well.

to the land surface and the magnitude can be recorded. The measured compaction equals land subsidence if the anchor is below the compacting interval.

Figure 7 illustrates a record obtained on the west-central side of Fresno County at Cantua Creek from 1958 to 1966 of compaction in three wells— one about 500 feet deep, another 700, and a third, 2,000 feet deep. At the time the recorders were installed, the 2,000-foot well was almost as deep as any of the water wells nearby. Measured compaction 1958 to 1966 in the 500-foot well was small, in the 700-foot well, about 2 feet, and in the 2,000-foot well, more than 8 feet. The straight line connecting the three dots

shows subsidence of a bench mark on the land surface as determined by leveling from distant stable bench marks and illustrates that the compaction measured in the 2,000-foot well was almost equal to the subsidence of the land surface during this period. This type of multiple-depth installation can be utilized to find the magnitude and rate of compaction between the depth intervals; it can be used also to determine at what depth compaction is occurring.

Problems Caused by Subsidence

If the subsiding area borders the ocean or a bay as in the Santa Clara Valley, levees have to be built and maintained to restrain flooding of lowlands. If yearly high tides happen to coincide with times of excessive stream runoff, levees may be overtopped. The Christmas floods of 1955 caused inundation of the town of Alviso at the south end of San Francisco Bay due to a combination of high tides and heavy stream runoff.

The differential change in elevation of the land surface in subsiding areas creates problems in construction and maintenance of water-transport structures, such as canals, irrigation systems, and drainage systems, and affects stream-channel grade. For example, the California Aqueduct passes through the subsiding areas on the west side of and at the south end of the San Joaquin Valley; also, a peripheral canal, when built, will be about at the east edge of the subsidence in the Delta.

The construction of the San Luis canal section of the aqueduct began in 1963. The map (Fig. 8) illustrates a problem that was faced in planning and construction of the canal in this subsidence area. The map shows subsidence in the 3 years ending in 1963. Obviously, then, planning involves the prediction of future subsidence, but beyond the physical characteristics that have to be considered, the economic and political aspects of the problem are very substantial. For example, how soon will Congress appropriate funds for the construction of distribution systems, and how soon will people who are going to utilize the canal stop pumping ground water and thereby decrease or stop subsidence? These kinds of questions complicate the problem of subsidence prediction.

Another problem that is common to the subsidence areas in the Santa Clara

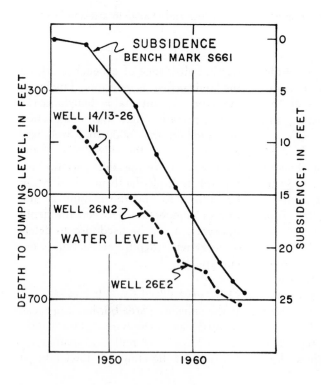

FIG. 5. Subsidence and artesian-head decline 10 miles southwest of Mendota.

and San Joaquin Valleys, and also in south-central Arizona, results from the fact that the compaction of the deposits develops compressive stresses on well casings. Many of the failures have been repaired by swaging out the ruptured casings and inserting liners. The costs of repair or replacement in central California probably have exceeded $10 million.

Subsidence of Oil Fields

Subsidence of a few feet has been noted in many oil fields and probably has occurred unnoticed in many more. The two oil fields in which subsidence has caused or contributed to major problems are the Wilmington and Inglewood oil fields in the Los Angeles coastal plain.

My comments on the Inglewood oil field in the Baldwin Hills area are summarized from a paper by Jansen, Dukleth, Gordon, James, and Shields (1967). These men were all members of the State Engineering Board of Inquiry that investigated the Baldwin Hills Dam failure. In December 1963, the Baldwin Hills Reservoir was destroyed by failure of its foundation. Extensive damage was done to neighboring communities. This reservoir is on the northeast flank of the Inglewood oil field. Subsidence had been observed in the vicinity for many years and was estimated by Jansen and others (1967) to have been 9.7 feet between 1917 and 1963 at a point approximately one-half mile westerly of the reservoir. They concluded that "the earth move-

FIG. 6. Compaction-recorder installation.

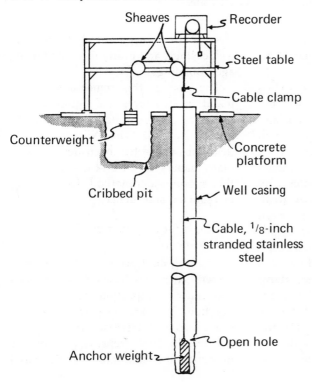

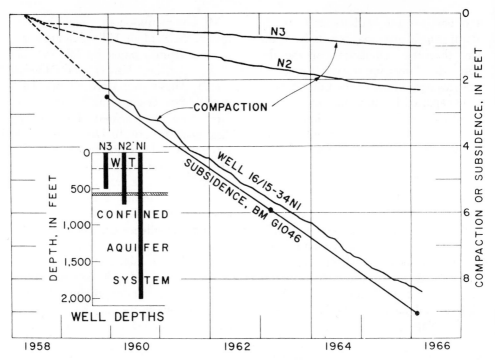

FIG. 7. Compaction and subsidence, Cantua Creek site.

ment which triggered the reservoir failure evidently was caused primarily by subsidence."

In the Los Angeles-Long Beach Harbor area, the Wilmington oil field experienced a costly and spectacular land subsidence beginning in 1937, which had reached 29 feet at the center by 1967. The area is intensively industrialized, and this is one reason why the remedial costs have been so great. Extensive remedial measures have been necessary to keep the sea from invading the subsiding lands and structures, because much of the subsiding area initially was only 5 to 10 feet above sea level. The remedial measures for restraining the sea have been chiefly massive levees, retaining walls, fill, and raising of structures. Horizontal as well as vertical movement developed

stresses that ruptured pipelines, oilwell casings, and utility lines, and damaged buildings.

The cost of this remedial work to maintain structures and equipment in operating condition had exceeded $100 million by 1962. The Wilmington oilfield subsidence has been described in many papers, so I won't discuss it further except under methods for stopping or reducing subsidence.

Methods for Stopping or Reducing Subsidence

Decreasing fluid pressure in a confined system increases grain-to-grain load and causes compaction; also, increasing fluid pressure decreases grain-to-grain load and decreases or stops subsidence. In 1958, repressuring of the oil zones at Wilmington began, based

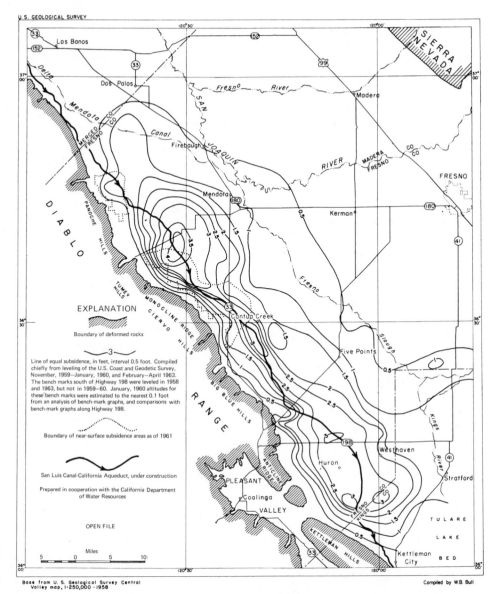

FIG. 8. Map showing land subsidence in the Los Banos-Kettleman City area, Calif., 1959–63.

on this premise and on the expectancy of increased oil recovery. The area stopped subsiding in 1958 immediately after injection began. It was essentially stable into 1961 and then rebounded about 0.5 foot by 1964. The maximum rebound of bench marks due to the repressuring as of the present time is on the order of 1.1 foot. Maps prepared by the Department of Oil Properties, City of Long Beach, indicate that by 1968 the subsidence had been stopped in most of the Wilmington oil field by the repressuring operation. I think this is an outstanding demonstration of subsidence control. And I think the people responsible deserve a great deal of credit for overcoming many problems—legal and otherwise—in controlling this subsidence.

Although no subsiding ground-water basins have been extensively repressured through wells, water imported to the Tulare-Wasco area in the southeastern part of the San Joaquin Valley through the Friant-Kern Canal since 1951 has reduced the pumping draft and caused substantial recovery of water level. Figure 9 shows that subsidence of bench marks near Delano, south of Tulare, decreased greatly after 1954, due to recovery of artesian head. Importation of water to the Santa Clara Valley is helping to raise the artesian head and decrease subsidence there, also. As a matter of record, water is or soon will be imported to all the major areas of subsidence due to

ground-water withdrawal in California, so that ten years from now subsidence rates in many of these areas probably will be reduced greatly.

References

Bull, W. B., 1964, Alluvial fans and near-surface subsidence in western Fresno County, Calif.: U. S. Geol. Survey Prof. Paper 437-A, p. A1–A71.

Jansen, R. B., Dukleth, G. W., Gordon, B. B., James, L. B., and Shields, C. E., 1967, Earth movement at Baldwin Hills Reservoir: Am. Soc. Civil Engineers Proc., Jour. Soil Mech. Found. Div., SM4, no. 5330, p. 551–575.

Lofgren, B. E., 1960, Near-surface land subsidence in western San Joaquin Valley, Calif.: Jour. Geophys. Research, v. 65, no. 3, p. 1053–1062.

—— 1969, Land subsidence due to the application of water: Geol. Soc. America, Rev. Eng. Geology 2, p. 271–303.

Weir, W. W., 1950, Subsidence of peat lands of the Sacramento-San Joaquin Delta, Calif.: Calif. Univ. Agr. Expt. Sta., Hilgardia, v. 20, no. 3, p. 37–56.

FIG. 9. Correlation of water-level fluctuations and subsidence near center of subsidence south of Tulare.

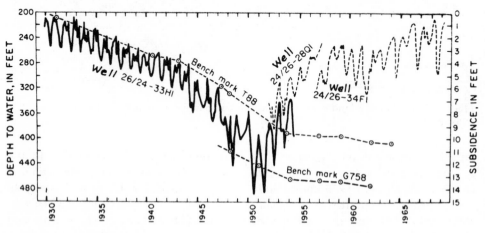

30 Long Beach Subsidence

M. N. Mayuga and D. R. Allen

Introduction

In many of the areas where land subsidence is a problem, the sinking can be directly related to man's use of the land and its resources. This is certainly true in all cases attributable to oil and gas withdrawals. The most dramatic and widely publicized case of subsidence is the Long Beach, California area which most authorities agree is directly related to the withdrawal of oil reservoir fluids. However, in southern California and probably world-wide, oil field subsidence affects a very small percent of the earth's surface when compared with compaction from other causes. Other notable cases of subsidence related to hydrocarbon withdrawals are Lake Maracaibo, Venezuela and Niigata, Japan.

The Long Beach subsidence problem has attracted world-wide attention because of its location in the center of a highly industrialized area and particularly because of its effect on the Port of Long Beach and the Long Beach Naval Shipyard (Fig. 1).

The subsiding area is located over the crest of the underground structure of the Wilmington Oil Field. Vertical movement has now reached 29 feet at the center of the elliptical shaped bowl. Horizontal movements of nearly 10

Mayuga, M. N. and Allen, D. R., 1966, "Long Beach Subsidence," in *Engineering Geology in Southern California*, R. Lung and R. Proctor, eds., pp. 281–85. Reprinted by permission of the senior author and the Association of Engineering Geologists, Arcadia, California. Dr. Mayuga is Assistant Director, City of Long Beach, Department of Oil Properties.

feet have been measured. These movements have caused extensive damage to wharves, pipelines, buildings, streets and bridges, necessitating costly repairs and surface filling.

Small amounts of regional subsidence related to ground water withdrawals or other causes were noted in the area as long ago as 1928. A significant amount of subsidence did not occur until after the oil field development began in 1938 and 1939. The first major elevation changes were recorded in 1940 and 1941 when 1.3 feet of subsidence occurred at the easterly end of Terminal Island. The Navy was dewatering a nearby area for a large graving dock when the accelerated subsidence was noticed. Levels indicated the rate of subsidence to be higher in the vicinity of the dewatering operation and it was assumed by many of the geologists and engineers examining the problem that subsidence would stop when these operations were completed. However, by July, 1945 United States Coast and Geodetic survey levels indicated the easterly end of Terminal Island had subsided over 4 feet. The threat to inundation was very real because of the low harbor elevations. Extensive diking, filling and land raising operations were undertaken throughout the harbor area. Remedial operations included the raising and replacement of wharves, bridges and approaches, oil wells and buildings of all types. Repair and maintenance costs including those of the City of Long Beach, the United States Naval

Within the figure:
SIGNAL HILL
LONG BEACH
TERMINAL ISLAND
PIER A
PIER
PIER
TOTAL SUBSIDEN
1928 TO 1968

FIG. 1.

Causation

Shipyard and various private industries may total nearly $100 million.

Many authorities, including geologists, engineers, soil experts and mathematicians were called in to study the subsidence problem as to causation, probably ultimate subsidence and possible methods for arrestment. Some of the earliest studies related the rapidly developing subsidence bowl to the oil field outline. Early predictions of the ultimate subsidence ranged from about 7 to 12 feet at the bowl center. During this period the rate of subsidence increased so fast that predictions were exceeded in a very short time. By 1951 the annual rate of subsidence was over 2 feet per year at the center of the bowl (Fig. 2). Estimates of total subsidence made during the time from 1950 to 1956 ranged as high as 70 feet although most authorities predicted from 30 to 45 feet.

Some of the postulated causes of subsidence were:

1. Lowering of hydraulic head due to ground water withdrawals.
2. Oil reservoir compaction due to fluid withdrawals.
3. Compaction of shales and silts in the oil.
4. Surface loading by buildings.
5. Vibrations due to land usage.
6. Tectonic movements.
7. A lack of structural rigidity in the oil field itself.
8. Movements along the known faults in the field.
9. A lack of preconsolidation in the sediments.

Area leveling indicated some regional

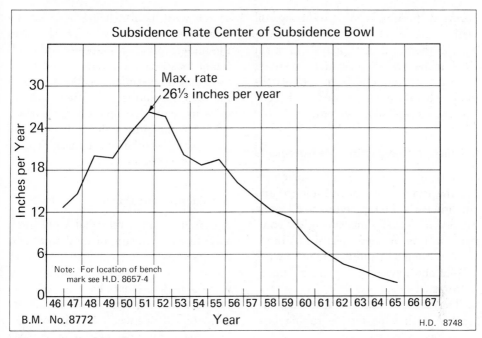

Subsidence Rate Center of Subsidence Bowl

FIG. 2.

subsidence which could be a combination of tectonic movement and ground water withdrawals. The subsidence actually occurring was of a magnitude far greater than could be attributed to these causes.

Most authorities agreed that withdrawal of fluids from the oil zones and the consequent lowering of pressure caused a compaction to take place in the oil sands and the interfingered silts and shales. The relative amounts contributed to the subsidence problem by the shales and the sands are still in question.

Mechanics of Movement

As the elliptical bowl-shaped depression developed along the oil field axis, the center settled more or less uniformly. Areas along the edge of the

bowl were consequently stretched with surface movements recorded as high as 9 or 10 feet toward the center of subsidence. This bending of the sediments left the center of the bowl in compression and the sides in tension with the amount of tension decreasing away from the bowl center. Enormous damages were suffered by buildings, pipe lines, railroad tracks, etc. that were not designed to take compressive and tensional stresses. These stresses were relieved several times over the years by sudden horizontal slippages along clays and soft shales about 1,550 to 1,750 feet below the surface. These depths are about one-half way between the surface and approximate center of compaction. The small earthquakes generated by these movements are recognizable to seismologists by their particular pattern. When these movements occurred hundreds of producing oil wells were severed or severely damaged at the point of slippage. As much as 9 inches of displacement resulted from one earthquake. Five such earthquakes have been recorded with continuing "creep" also evident.

Subsurface Compaction Measurements

Because of the controversy surrounding the exact cause of subsidence and the intervals being compacted, some method of actually measuring the compaction was needed. Many methods were examined including the following:

1. Old and new well log measurement comparisons.
2. The use of a buried dead-man anchor with a protective tubing projecting to the surface.
3. Wire line depth measurement of casing joints.

The method that proved feasible was developed primarily by Mr. Jan Law, petroleum consultant for the City of Long Beach, in conjunction with the Lane Wells Electric Logging Company. This method, commonly called "collar counting," involves a very precise location of collar joints and comparisons of the joint lengths with those measured prior to placing the casing in the well. Any compaction occurring between the surface and the bottom of a well must be reflected in a shortening of casing lengths opposite the compacting interval. By the use of this method many wells were surveyed and found to have shortenings of over one foot per 40 feet in many of the joints penetrating the oil zones.

Compaction measurements are still being made by the City of Long Beach using the collar count technique. Research work is also being done on the location of radioactive bullets shot into the underground formations. Although bullet locations have not proved to be as accurate as collar locations, this is the only technique that offers a direct measurement of formation compaction that is completely independent of the well casing or other mechanical devices mounted in the hole.

Subsidence Arrestment

Although surface remedial work such as diking and raising of land areas and repairs to wharves, oil wells and other facilities kept the area in operation, it was obvious to most observers that the ultimate answer had to be an arrestment of subsidence. The solution recommended by most petroleum experts was to repressure the oil reservoirs by water injection. This would be a very expensive undertaking and the economics were questioned by many people because of the relatively viscous crudes present in the field. In addition to the engineering and economic problems to be resolved, there were complex legal problems caused by many diverse mineral ownerships. A special legislation was passed in 1958 by the California State Legislature to permit and enforce, if necessary, the unitization of various properties for water injection operations. These problems were resolved and most of the Long Beach Harbor area is now being water flooded voluntarily. Approximately 700,000 barrels per day are currently being injected in the Wilmington Oil Field and it is expected that the daily injection rate will exceed one million barrels per day within the next few years.

Subsidence has now been stopped over a large portion of the field and the area affected has been reduced from 20 square miles to 4 square miles near the center of the bowl. A small amount of surface rebound has occurred in the areas of heaviest injection (Fig. 3). The center of the subsidence bowl is still subsiding at about two-tenths of a foot per year but it is hoped that this will also be stopped in the near future.

Subsidence Monitoring

The City of Long Beach now maintains constant surveillance of bench mark elevations with some 900 bench marks run on a quarterly basis. Reservoir pressures are closely watched in the developed portion of the field. In the Long Beach Unit area (East Wilmington) currently being developed, a pres-

sure maintenance and monitoring program was established prior to drilling. Tidal gauges are being installed on the drilling islands off Long Beach as an aid in detecting subsidence. Certain wells will be logged on a yearly basis to detect any changes in casing joint lengths which should reflect any compaction occurring in the reservoirs.

References

Berbower, R. F. and Parent, C. F., Subsidence Effects in the Long Beach Harbor District: Presented at A. S. T. M. meeting, Los Angeles, California, October 1962.

Gilluly, James and U. S. Grant, 1949, Subsidence in the Long Beach Harbor area, California: Geol. Soc. America Bull., vol. 60, p. 461–529.

Grant, U. S., 1954, Subsidence of the Wilmington Oil Field, California: Calif. Div. Mines and Geology, Bull. 170, Chapt. 10, p. 19–24.

FIG. 3.

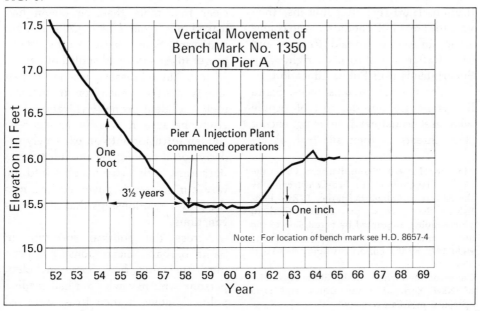

Grant, U. S. and Sheppard, W. E., 1939, Some recent changes in elevation in the Los Angeles basin of southern California, and their possible significance, Bull. Seism. Soc. Am., vol. 29, p. 299–326.

Harris, F. R. and Harlow, E. H., 1948, Subsidence of the Terminal Island-Long Beach area, California: Trans. ASCE, vol. 113, p. 375–403.

Hoffmaster, B. N., Subsidence, its effects and remedies: Long Beach Harbor Department, Long Beach California.

Various private reports on file, Department of Oil properties, Harbor Administration Building, Long Beach, California.

31   Santa Barbara: Oil in the Velvet Playground

Harvey Molotch

Santa Barbara seems worlds apart both from the sprawling Los Angeles metropolis a hundred miles further south on the coast highway and from the avant-garde San Francisco Bay Area to the north. It has always been calm, clean and orderly. Of the city's 70,000 residents, a large number are upper and upper-middle class. They are people who have a wide choice of places in the world to live, but they have chosen Santa Barbara because of its ideal climate, gentle beauty and sophistication. Hard-rock Republicans, they vote for any GOP candidate who comes along, including Ronald Reagan and Max Rafferty, California's right-wing Superintendent of Public Education.

Under normal circumstances, Santa Barbarans are not the sort of people who are accustomed to experiencing stark threats to their survival, or ar-

Molotch, H., 1970, "Santa Barbara: Oil in the Velvet Playground," in *Eco-Catastrophe* by the Editors of *Ramparts*, Harper & Row Publishers, New York, pp. 84–105 (without photographs). Reprinted by permission of the author and the editors of *Ramparts*. Copyright 1970 by the Editors of Ramparts Magazine, Inc.

Professor Molotch is at the State University of New York at Stony Brook and is a specialist in urban ecology.

bitrary, contemptuous handling of their wishes. They are an unlikely group to be forced to confront brutal realities about how the "normal channels" in America can become hopelessly clogged and unresponsive. Yet this is exactly what happened when the Union Oil Company's well erupted in the Santa Barbara Channel, causing an unparalleled ecological disaster, the effects of which are still washing up on the local beaches.

In the ensuing months it became clear that more than petroleum had leaked out from Union Oil's drilling platform. Some basic truths about power in America had spilled out along with it. The oil disaster was more than simply another omen for an increasingly "accident-prone" civilization. Precisely because it was an accident—a sudden intrusion into an extremely orderly social process—it provided Santa Barbarans with sharp insights into the way our society is governed and into the power relationships that dictate its functions.

Across the political spectrum in Santa Barbara, the response has been much the same: fury. Some, including persons who never before had made a political move in their lives, were led from petition campaigns to the picket line and demonstrations, to the sit-down, and even to the sail-in. The position they finally came to occupy shows that radicalism is not, as experts like Bruno Bettelheim have implied, a subtle form of mental imbalance caused by rapid technological change or by the increasing impersonality of the modern world; radicals are not "immature," "undisciplined" or "anti-intellectual." Quite the contrary. They are persons who live in conditions where injustice is apparent, and who have access to more complete information about their plight than the average man, giving them a perspective that allows them to become angry in a socially meaningful way. In short, radicals are persons who make the most rational (and moral) response, given the social and political circumstances. Thus, as recent sociological studies have shown, radical movements like SDS draw their memberships disproportionately from the most intelligent and informed members of their constituent populations.

Optimistic Indignation: Government by the People

For over fifteen years, Santa Barbara's political leaders attempted to prevent the despoilation of their coastline by oil drilling in adjacent federal waters. Although they were unsuccessful in blocking the leasing of *federal* waters beyond the three-mile limit, they were able to establish a sanctuary within *state* waters (thus foregoing the extraordinary revenues which leases in such areas bring to adjacent localities). It was therefore a great irony that the one city which had voluntarily ex-changed revenue for a pure environment should find itself faced, in January of 1969, with a massive eruption which was ultimately to cover the entire city coastline with a thick coat of crude oil. The air was soured for many hundreds of feet inland, and tourism—the traditional economic base of the region—was severely threatened. After ten days, the runaway well was brought under control, only to erupt again in February. This fissure was closed in March, but was followed by a sustained "seepage" of oil—a leakage which continues today to pollute the sea, the air and the famed local beaches. The oil companies had paid a record $603 million for their lease rights, and neither they nor the federal government bore any significant legal responsibility toward the localities which those lease rights might endanger.

The response of Santa Barbarans to this pollution of their near-perfect environment was immediate. A community organization called "GOO" (Get Oil Out!) was established under the leadership of a former state senator and a local corporate executive. GOO took a strong stand against any and all oil activity in the Channel and circulated a petition to that effect which eventually gained 110,000 signatures and was sent to President Nixon. The stodgy Santa Barbara News-Press (oldest daily newspaper in Southern California, its masthead proclaims) inaugurated a series of editorials, unique in their uncompromising stridency and indicative of the angry mood of the community. "The people of the Santa Barbara area can never be repaid for the hurt that has been done to them and their environment," said a front-page editorial. "They are angry—and this is not the time for them to lose their anger. This is the time for them to fight for action that will guarantee absolutely and permanently that there will be no recurrence of the nightmare of the last two weeks. . . ."

The same theme emerged in the hundreds of letters published by the News-Press in the weeks that followed and in the positions taken by virtually every local civic and government body. Rallies were held at the beach, and GOO petitions were circulated at local shopping centers and sent to sympathizers around the country. Local artists, playwrights, advertising men, retired executives and academic specialists from the local campus of the University of California executed special projects appropriate to their areas of expertise.

A GOO strategy emerged for an attack on two fronts. Local indignation, producing the petition to the President and thousands of letters to key members of Congress and the executive, would lead to appropriate legislation. Legal action against the oil companies and the federal government would have the double effect of recouping some of the financial losses certain to be suffered by the local tourist and fishing industries while at the same time serving notice that drilling in the Channel would become a much less profitable operation. Legislation to ban drilling was introduced by Senator Alan Cranston in the U. S. Senate and Representative Charles Teague in the House of Representatives. Joint suits for $1 billion in damages were filed against the oil companies and the federal government by the city and county of

Santa Barbara (later joined by the State of California).

All of these activities—petitions, rallies, court action and legislative lobbying—expressed their proponents' basic faith in "the system." There was a muckraking tone to the Santa Barbara protest: the profit-mad executives of Union Oil were ruining the coastline, but once national and state leaders became aware of what was going on and were provided with the "facts" of the case, justice would be done.

Indeed, there was good reason for hope. The quick and enthusiastic responses of the right-wing Teague and the liberal Cranston represented a consensus of men otherwise polar opposites in their political behavior. But from other important quarters there was silence. Santa Barbara's representatives in the state legislature either said nothing or (in later stages) offered only minimal support. Most disappointing of all to Santa Barbarans, Governor Ronald Reagan withheld support for proposals which would end the drilling.

As subsequent events unfolded, the seemingly inexplicable silence of most of the democratically-elected representatives began to fall into place as part of a more general pattern. Santa Barbarans began to see American democracy as a very complicated affair— not simply a system in which governmental officials carry out the desires of their constituents once those desires become known. Instead, increasing recognition came to be given to the "all-powerful Oil lobby"; to legislators "in the pockets of Oil"; to academicians "bought" by Oil and to regulatory agencies that lobby for those they are supposed to regulate. In other words,

Santa Barbarans became increasingly ideological, increasingly sociological and, in the words of some observers, increasingly "radical." Writing from his lodgings in the Santa Barbara Biltmore, the city's most exclusive residence hotel, an irate citizen penned these words in a letter published in the local paper: "We the People can protest and protest and it means nothing because the industrial and military junta are the country. They tell us, the People, what is good for the oil companies is good for the People. To that I say, Like Hell! . . . Profit is their language and the proof of all this is their history."

Disillusionment: Government by Oil

From the start, Secretary of Interior Walter Hickel was regarded with suspicion, and his publicized associations with Alaskan oil interests did little to improve his image in Santa Barbara. When he called a halt to drilling immediately after the initial eruption, some Santa Barbarans began to believe that he would back them up. But even the most optimistic were quite soon forced to recognize that government policy would indeed confirm their worst fears. For, only one day later, Secretary Hickel ordered a resumption of drilling and production—even as the oil continued to gush into the Channel.

Within 48 hours Hickel reversed his position and ordered another halt to the drilling. But this time his action was seen as a direct response to the massive nationwide media play then being given to the Santa Barbara plight and to the citizens' mass outcry just then beginning to reach Washington. Santa Barbarans were further disenchanted with Hickel and the executive branch both because the Interior Department failed to back any legislation to halt drilling and because it consistently attempted to downplay the entire affair—minimizing the extent of the damages and hinting at possible "compromises" which were seen locally as near-total capitulation to the oil companies.

One question on which government officials systematically erred on the side of Oil was that of the *volume* of oil spilling into the Channel. The U. S. Geological Survey (administered by the Department of the Interior), when queried by reporters, produced estimates which Santa Barbarans could only view as incredible. Located in Santa Barbara is a technological establishment among the most sophisticated in the country—the General Research Corporation, a research and development firm with experience in marine technology. Several officials of the corporation made their own study of the oil outflow and announced findings of pollution volume at a minimum of *tenfold* that of the government's estimate. The methods which General Research used to prepare its estimates were made public. The Geological Survey and the oil interests, however, continued to blithely issue their own lower figures, refusing to provide any substantiating arguments.

Another point of contention was the effect of the oil on the beaches. The oil companies, through various public relations officials, constantly minimized the actual amount of damage and maximized the effect of Union Oil's cleanup activities; and the Department of the Interior seemed determined to support Union Oil's claims. Thus Hickel referred at a press conference to the "recent" oil spill, providing the impression that the oil spill was over at a time when freshly erupting oil was continuing to stain local beaches. When President Nixon appeared locally to "inspect" the damage to beaches, Interior arranged for him to land his helicopter on a city beach which had been thoroughly cleaned in the days just before, thus sparing him a close-up of much of the rest of the county shoreline, which continued to be covered with a thick coat of crude oil. (The beach visited by Nixon has been oil-stained on many occasions subsequent to the President's departure.) Secret servicemen kept the placards and shouts of several hundred demonstrators at a safe distance from the President.

The damage to the "ecological chain," while still of unknown proportions, was treated in a similarly deceptive way. A great many birds died from oil which they had ingested while trying to preen their oil-soaked feathers—a process Santa Barbarans saw in abundant examples. In what local and national authorities called a hopeless task, two bird-cleaning centers were established (with help from oil company money) to cleanse feathers and otherwise minister to injured wildfowl. Spokesmen from both Oil and the federal government then adopted these centers as sources of "data" on the extent of damage to the bird life. Thus, the number of birds killed by oil pollution was computed on the basis of the number of fatalities at the wildfowl centers. It was a preposterous method and was recognized as such. Clearly, the dying birds in the area were provided with inefficient means of propelling themselves to these designated centers.

At least those birds in the hands of local ornithologists could be confirmed as dead, and this fact could not be disputed by either Oil or Interior. This was not so, however, with species whose corpses are more difficult to produce on command. Several official observers at the Channel Islands, a national wildlife preserve containing one of the country's largest colonies of sea animals, reported sighting unusually large numbers of dead sea lion pups on the oil-stained shores of one of the islands. Statement and counter-statement followed, with Oil's defenders (including the Department of the Navy) arguing that the animals were not dead at all, but only appeared inert because they were sleeping. In a similar case, the dramatic beaching in Northern California of an unusually large number of dead whales—whales which had just completed their migration through the Santa Barbara Channel—was acknowledged, but held not to be caused by oil pollution.

In the end, it was not simply the Interior Department, its U. S. Geological Survey and the President who either supported or tacitly accepted Oil's public relations tactics. The regulatory agencies at both national and state levels, by action, inaction and implication, effectively defended Oil at virtually every turn. In a letter to complaining citizens, for instance, N. B. Livermore Jr. of the Resources Agency of California referred to the continuing oil spill as "minor seepage" with "no major long term effect on the marine ecology." The letter adopted the perspective of Interior and Oil, even though the state was in no way being held culpable for the spill. This tendency was so blatant that it led the State Deputy Attorney General Charles O'Brien, to charge the state conservation boards with "industry domination." Thomas Gaines, a Union Oil executive, actually sits on the state agency board most directly connected with the control of pollution in Channel waters.

Understandably enough, Secretary Hickel's announcement that the Interior Department was generating new "tough" regulations to control offshore drilling was met with considerable skepticism. The Santa Barbara County Board of Supervisors was invited to "review" these new regulations and refused to do so in the belief that such participation would be used to provide a false impression of democratic responsiveness.

In previous years when they were fighting against the leasing of the Channel, the Supervisors had been assured of technological safeguards; now, as the emergency continued, they could witness for themselves the absence of any method for ending the leakage in the Channel. They also had heard the testimony of Donald Solanas, a regional supervisor of Interior's U. S. Geological Survey, who said about the Union platform eruption: "I could have had an engineer on that platform 24 hours a day, seven days a week and he couldn't have prevented the accident." His explanation of the cause of the "accident"? "Mother earth broke down on us." Given these facts, Santa Barbarans saw Interior's proposed regulations— and the invitation to the County to participate in making them—as only a ruse to preface a resumption of drilling. Their suspicions were confirmed

when the Interior Department announced a selective resumption of drilling "to relieve pressures." The new "tough" regulations were themselves seriously flawed by the fact that most of their provisions specified measures (such as buoyant booms around platforms, use of chemical dispersants, etc.) which had proven almost totally useless in the current emergency.

The new regulations did specify that oil companies would henceforth be financially responsible for damages resulting from pollution mishaps. Several of the oil companies have now entered suit (supported by the ACLU) against the federal government, complaining that the arbitrary changing of lease conditions deprives them of rights of due process.

Irritations with Interior were paralleled by frustrations encountered in dealing with the congressional committee which had the responsibility of holding hearings on ameliorative legislation. A delegation of Santa Barbarans was scheduled to testify in Washington on the Cranston bill to ban drilling. From the questions which congressmen asked them, and the manner in which they were "handled," the delegates could only conclude that the committee was "in the pockets of Oil." As one of the returning delegates put it, the presentation bespoke of "total futility."

At this writing, six months after their introduction, both the Cranston and Teague bills, though significantly softened, lie buried in committee with little prospect of surfacing.

Disillusionment: Power Is Knowledge

The American dream is a dream of progress, of the efficacy of know-how and technology; science is seen as both servant and savior. From the start, part of the shock of the oil spill was that such a thing could happen in a country having such a sophisticated technology. The much overworked phrase "If we can send a man to the moon . . ." took on special meaning in Santa Barbara. When, in years previous, Santa Barbara's elected officials had attempted to halt the original sale of leases, "assurances" were given by Interior that such an "accident" could not occur, given the highly developed state of the industry. Not only did it occur, but the original gusher of oil spewed forth completely out of control for ten days, and the continual "seepage" which followed it remains uncontrolled to the present moment—seven months later. That the government would embark upon so massive a drilling program with such unsophisticated technology was shocking indeed.

Further, not only was the technology inadequate and the plans for stopping a leak, should one occur, nonexistent, but the area in which the drilling took place was known from the outset to be extremely hazardous. That is, drilling was occurring on an ocean bottom known for its extraordinary geological circumstances—porous sand lacking a bedrock "ceiling" capable of restraining uncontrollably seeping oil. Thus, the continuing leakage through the sands at various points above the oil reservoir cannot be stopped, and this could have been predicted from the data known to all parties involved.

Another peculiarity of the Channel that had been known to the experts is the fact that it is located in the heart of earthquake activity in a region which is among the most earthquake prone in the country. Santa Barbarans are now asking what might occur during an earthquake; if pipes on the ocean floor and casings through the ocean bottom should be sheared, the damage done by the Channel's thousands of potential producing wells would devastate the entire coast of Southern California. The striking contrast between the sophistication of the means used to locate and extract oil and the primitiveness of the means to control and clean its spillage became extremely clear in Santa Barbara.

Recurrent attempts have been made to ameliorate the continuing seep by placing floating booms around an area of leakage and then sending workboats to skim off the leakage from within the demarcated area. Chemical dispersants of various kinds have also been tried. But the oil bounces over the booms in the choppy waters, the workboats suck up only a drop in the bucket, and the dispersants are effective only when used in quantities which constitute a graver pollution threat than the oil they are designed to eliminate. Cement is poured into suspected fissures in an attempt to seal them up. Oil on the beaches is periodically cleaned by dumping straw over the sands and then raking it up along with the oil which it has absorbed. The common sight of men throwing straw on miles of beaches, within view of complex drilling rigs capable of exploiting resources thousands of feet below the ocean's surface, became a clear symbol to Santa Barbarans. They gradually began to see the oil disaster as the product of a system that promotes research and development in areas which lead to strategic profitability—without regard for social utility.

This kind of subordination of science to profit came out more directly in the workings of the Presidential committee of "distinguished" scientists and engineers (the DuBridge Panel) which was to recommend means of eliminating the seepage under Platform A. When the panel was appointed, hopes were raised that at last the scientific establishment of the nation would come forth with a technologically sophisticated solution to the problem. Instead, the panel—after a two-day session and after hearing no testimony from anyone not connected with either Oil or the Interior Department—recommended the "solution" of drilling an additional 50 wells under Platform A in order to pump the area dry as quickly as possible. One member of the panel estimated that the process would take from 10 to 20 years. Despite an immediate local clamor, Interior refused to make public the data or the reasoning behind the recommendations. The information on Channel geological conditions had been provided by the oil companies (the Geological Survey routinely depends upon the oil industry for the data upon which it makes its "regulatory" decisions). The data, being private property, thus could not be released—or so the government claimed. In this way both parties are neatly protected, while Santa Barbara's local experts remain thwarted by the counter-arguments of Oil/Interior that "if you had the information we have, you would agree with us."

Science played a similarly partisan role in other areas of the fight that Santa Barbarans were waging against the oil companies. The Chief Deputy Attorney General of California, for example, complained that the oil industry "is preventing oil drilling experts from aiding the Attorney General's office in its lawsuits over the Santa Barbara oil spill." Noting that his office had been unable to get assistance from petroleum experts at California universities, The Deputy Attorney General stated: "The university experts all seem to be working on grants from the oil industry. There is an atmosphere of fear. The experts are afraid that if they assist us in our case on behalf of the people of California, they will lose their oil industry grants."

At the Santa Barbara campus of the University, there is little oil money in evidence and few, if any, faculty members have entered into proprietory research arrangements with Oil. Petroleum geology and engineering is simply not a local specialty. Yet it is a fact that oil interests did contact several Santa Barbara faculty members with offers of funds for studies on the ecological effects of the oil spill, with publication rights stipulated by Oil. It is also the case that the Federal Water Pollution Control Administration explicitly requested a U. C. Santa Barbara botanist to withhold the findings of his study, funded by that agency, on the ecological effects of the spill.

Most of these revelations received no publicity outside of Santa Barbara. The Attorney's allegation, however, did become something of a state-wide issue when a professor at the Berkeley campus, in his attempt to refute the charge, actually confirmed it. Wilbur H. Somerton, professor of petroleum engineering, indicated he could not testify against Oil "because my work depends on good relations with the petroleum industry. My interest is serving the petroleum industry. I view my obligation to the community as supplying it with well-trained petroleum engineers. We train the industry's engineers and they help us."

Santa Barbara's leaders were incredulous about the whole affair. The question—one which is asked more often by the down-trodden sectors of the society than by the privileged—was posed: "Whose university is this, anyway?" A local executive and GOO leader asked, "If the truth isn't in the universities, where is it?" A conservative member of the state legislature, in a move reminiscent of SDS demands, went so far as to demand an end to all faculty "moonlighting" for industry. In Santa Barbara, the only place where all of this publicity was appearing, there was thus an opportunity for insight into the linkages between knowledge, the university, government and oil—and into the resultant non-neutrality of science. The backgrounds of many members of the DuBridge Panel were linked publicly to the oil industry. DuBridge himself, as a past president of Cal Tech, served under a board of trustees which included the president of Union Oil and which accepted substantial Union Oil donations.

While "academic truth" was being called into question, some truths not usually dwelt on by Oil's experts were gaining public attention. In another of its front-page editorials, the News-Press set forth a number of revealing facts about the oil industry. The combination of output restrictions, extraordinary tax write-off privileges for drilling expenses, the import quota, and the 27½ per cent depletion allowance creates an artificially high price for U. S. oil—a price almost double the world market price for a comparable product

delivered to comparable U. S. destinations. The combination of available incentives creates a situation where some oil companies pay no taxes whatsoever during extraordinarily profitable years. In the years 1962–1966, Standard Oil of New Jersey paid less than four per cent of its profits in taxes. Standard of California less than three per cent, and 22 of the other largest oil companies paid slightly more than six per cent. It was pointed out again and again to Santa Barbarans that it was this system of subsidy which made the relatively high cost deep-sea exploration and drilling in the Channel profitable in the first place. Thus the citizens of Santa Barbara, as federal taxpayers and fleeced consumers, were subsidizing their own eco-catastrophe.

The Mechanisms of Deception

The way in which federal officials and the oil industry frustrated the democratic process and thwarted popular dissent in Santa Barbara is hardly unfamiliar. But the upper-middle-class nature of the community, and the sharp features of an event which was a sudden disruption of normality, make it an ideal case for illustrating some of the techniques by which the powers that be maintain the status quo.

The first of these has been described by Daniel Boorstin as the technique of the "pseudo-event." A pseudo-event occurs when men arrange conditions to simulate a particular kind of event so that certain prearranged consequences follow as though the actual event had taken place. Several pseudo-events took place in Santa Barbara. From the outset, it was obvious that national actions concerning oil were aimed at freezing out any local participation in decisions affecting the Channel. Thus, when the federal government first called for bids on a Channel lease in 1968, local officials were not even informed. Further, local officials were not notified by any government agency in the case of the original oil spill, nor (except after the spill was already widely known) in the case of any of the previous or subsequent more "minor" spills. The thrust of the federal government's colonialist attitude toward the local community was contained in an Interior Department engineer's memo released by Senator Cranston's office. Written to the Assistant Secretary of the Interior to explain the policy of refusing to hold public hearings prior to drilling, it said: "We preferred not to stir up the natives any more than possible."

The Santa Barbara County Board of Supervisors turned down the call for "participation" in drawing up new "tougher" drilling regulations precisely because they knew the government had no intention of creating "safe" drilling regulations. They refused to utilize "normal channels," refusing thereby to take part in the pseudo-event and thus to let the consequences (in this case the appearance of democratic decision-making and local assent) of a non-event occur.

There were other attempts to stage pseudo-events. Nixon's "inspection" of the Santa Barbara beachfront was an obvious one. Another series of such events were the congressional hearings set up by legislators who were, in the words of a well-to-do lady leader of GOO, "kept men." The locals were allowed to blow off steam at the hearings, but their arguments, however cogent, failed to bring about legislation appropriate to the pollution crisis. Many Santa Barbarans had a similar impression of the court hearings regarding the various legal maneuvers against oil drilling.

Another technique for diffusing and minimizing popular protest evidenced in the Santa Barbara affair might be called the "creeping event." A creeping event is, in a sense, the opposite of a psudo-event. It occurs when something *is* actually taking place, but when the manifestations of the event are arranged to occur at an inconspicuously gradual and piecemeal pace, thus avoiding some of the consequences which would follow from the event if it were immediately perceived to be occurring.

The major creeping event in Santa Barbara was the piecemeal resumption of production and drilling after Hickel's second moratorium. Authorization to resume *production* at different specific groups of wells occurred on various dates throughout February and early March. Authorization to resume *drilling* of various groups of new wells was announced by Interior on dates from April 1 through August. Each resumption was announced as a particular safety precaution to relieve pressures, until finally on the most recent resumption date, the word "deplete" was used for the first time in explaining the granting of permission to drill. There is thus no *specific* point in time at which production and drilling were reauthorized for the Channel—and full resumption still has not been officially authorized.

A creeping event has the consequence of diffusing resistance by withholding what journalists call a "time peg" on which to hang the story. By the time it becomes quite clear that "something *is* going on," the sponsors of the creeping event (and the aggrieved themselves) can ask why there should be any protest "now" when there was none before, in the face of the very same kind of provocation. In this way, the aggrieved has resort only to frustration and the gnawing feeling that events are sweeping by him.

A third way of minimizing legitimate protest is by use of the alleged "neutrality" of science and the knowledge producers. I have discussed the "experts" and the University. After learning of the collusion between government and Oil and the use of secret science as a prop to that collusion, Santa Barbarans found themselves in the unenviable position of having to demonstrate that science and knowledge were not, in fact, neutral arbiters. They had to prove, *by themselves*, that continued drilling was not safe; that the "experts" who said it was safe were the hirelings, directly or indirectly, of oil interests; and that the report of the DuBridge Panel recommending massive drilling was a fraudulent document. They had to show that the university petroleum geologists themselves were in league with the oil companies and that information unfavorable to the oil interests was systematically withheld by virtue of the very structure of the knowledge industry. This is no small task. It is a long and complicated story, and one which pits lay persons (and a few academic renegades) against an entire profession and the patrons of that profession. An illustration of the difficulties involved may be drawn from very recent history. Seventeen Santa Barbara plaintiffs, represented by the ACLU, sought a temporary injunction against additional Channel drilling at least until the in-

formation utilized by the DuBridge Panel was made public and a hearing could be held. The injunction was not granted, and in the end the presiding federal judge ruled in favor of what he termed the "expert opinions" available to the Secretary of the Interior. Due to limited time for rebuttal, the disorienting confusions of courtroom procedures, and also perhaps the desire not to offend the Court, the ACLU lawyer could not make his subtle, complex and highly controversial case that the "experts" were partisans and that their scientific "findings" followed from that partisanship.

A fourth obstacle was placed in the way of dissenters by the communications media. Just as the courtroom setting was not amenable to a full reproduction of the facts supporting the ACLU case, so the media in general— due to restrictions of time and style— prevented a full airing of the details of the case. A more cynical analysis of the media's inability to make known the Santa Barbara "problem" in its full fidelity might hinge on an allegation that the media were constrained by fear of "pressures" from Oil and its allies. Metromedia, for example, sent to Santa Barbara a team which spent several days documenting, interviewing and filming for an hour-long program—only to suddenly drop the project entirely due to what is reported by locals in touch with the network to have been "pressures" from Oil. Even without such blatant interventions, however, the full reproduction of the Santa Barbara "news" would remain problematic.

News media are notorious for the anecdotal nature of their reporting; even so-called "think pieces" rarely go beyond a stringing together of proximate events. There are no analyses of the "mobilization of bias" or linkages of men's actions with their pecuniary interests. Science and learning are assumed to be neutral; regulatory agencies are assumed to function as "watchdogs" for the public. Information contradicting these assumptions is treated as an exotic exception.

The complexity of the situations to be reported and the wealth of details needed to support such analyses require more time and effort than journalists have at their command. Their recitation would produce long stories not consistent with space limitations and make-up preferences of newspapers, or with analogous requirements within the other media. A full telling of the story would tax the reader/viewer and would risk boring him. The rather extensive media coverage of the oil spill centered on a few dramatic moments in its history (e.g., the initial gusher of oil) and a few simple-to-tell "human interest" stories such as the pathetic deaths of the sea birds struggling along the oil-covered sands. With increasing temporal and geographical distance from the initial spill, national coverage became increasingly rare and sloppy. Interior Department statements on the state of the "crisis" were reported without local rejoinders as the newsmen who might have gathered them began leaving the scene. While the Santa Barbara spill received extraordinarily extensive national coverage relative to other controversial events, this coverage nevertheless failed to adequately inform the American public about a situation which Santa Barbarans knew from first-hand experience.

Finally, perhaps the most pernicious technique of all because of the damage it does to the social conscience, is the routinization of evil. Pollution of the Santa Barbara Channel is now routine; the issue is not whether or not the Channel is polluted, but *how much* it is polluted. A recent oil slick discovered off a Phillips Oil platform in the Channel was dismissed by an oil company official as a "routine" drilling by-product which was not viewed as "obnoxious." That about half of the oil currently seeping into the Channel is allegedly being recovered is taken as an improvement sufficient to preclude the "outrage" that a big national story would require.

Similarly, the pollution of the moral environment becomes routine; it is accepted as natural that politicians are "on the take," "in the pockets of Oil." The depletion allowance remains a question of percentages (20 per cent of 27½ per cent), rather than a focus for questioning the very legitimacy of such special benefits. "Compromises" emerge, such as the 24 per cent depletion allowance and the new "tough" drilling regulations, which are already being hailed as "victories" for the reformers. Like the oil spill itself, the depletion allowance debate becomes buried in its own disorienting detail, in its pseudo-events and in the triviality of the "solutions" which ultimately come to be considered as the "real" options. Evil is both banal and complicated, and each of these attributes contributes to its durability.

The Mechanisms of Change

What the citizens of Santa Barbara learned through their experience was that the parties competing to shape decision-making on oil in Santa Barbara do not have equal access to the means of "mobilizing bias." The Oil/ Government combine had, from the start, an extraordinary number of advantages. Lacking ready access to media, the ability to stage events at will, and a well-integrated system of arrangements for achieving their goals (at least in comparison to their adversaries), Santa Barbara's citizens have met with repeated frustrations.

Their response to their relative powerlessness has been analogous to that of other groups and individuals who, from a similar vantage point, come to see the system up close. They become willing to expand their repertoire of means of influence as their cynicism and bitterness increase. Letter writing gives way to demonstrations, demonstrations to civil disobedience. People refuse to participate in "democratic procedures" which are a part of the opposition's event-management strategy. Confrontation politics arises as a means of countering official events with "events" of one's own, thus providing the media with stories which can be simply and energetically told.

Thus, in Santa Barbara, rallies were held at local beaches; congressmen and state and national officials were greeted by demonstrations. (Fred Hartley of Union Oil inadvertently landed his plane in the middle of one such demonstration, causing a rather ugly name-calling scene to ensue.) A "sail-in" was held one Sunday with a flotilla of local pleasure boats forming a circle around Platform A, each craft bearing large anti-Oil banners. City hall meetings were packed with citizens reciting demands for immediate and forceful local action.

A City Council election held during the crisis resulted in a landslide for the Council's bitterest critic and the defeat of a veteran councilman suspected of having "oil interests." In a rare action, the News-Press condemned the local Chamber of Commerce for accepting oil money for a fraudulent tourist advertising campaign which touted Santa Barbara (including its beaches) as completely restored to its former beauty.

One possible grand strategy for Santa Barbara was outlined by a local public relations man and GOO worker, who said, "We've got to run the oil men out. The city owns the wharf and the harbor that the company has to use. The city has got to deny its facilities to oil traffic, service boats, cranes and the like. If the city contravenes some federal navigation laws [which such actions would unquestionably involve], to hell with it. The only hope to save Santa Barbara is to awaken the nation to the ravishment. That will take public officials who are willing to block oil traffic with their bodies and with police hoses, if necessary. Then federal marshals or federal troops would have to come in. This would pull in the national news media."

This scenario has thus far not occurred in Santa Barbara, although the continued use of the wharf by the oil industries has led to certain militant actions. A picket was maintained at the wharf for two weeks to protest the conversion of the pier from a recreation and tourist facility into an industrial plant for the use of the oil companies. A boycott of other wharf businesses (e.g., two restaurants) was urged. The picket line was led by white, middle-class adults—one of whom was a local businessman who, two years earlier, was a close runner-up in the Santa Barbara mayoralty race.

Prior to the picketing, a dramatic Easter Sunday confrontation (involving approximately 500 persons) took place between demonstrators and city police. Just as a wharf rally was breaking up, an oil service truck began driving up the pier to make a delivery of casing supplies for oil drilling. There was a spontaneous sit-down in front of the truck. For the first time since the Ku Klux Klan folded in the '30s, a group of (heavily) middle-class Santa Barbarans was publicly taking the law into its own hands. After much lengthy discussion between police, the truck driver and the demonstrators, the truck was ordered away and the demonstrators remained to rejoice over their victory. The following day's News-Press editorial, while not supportive of such tactics, was quite sympathetic, which was noteworthy given the paper's long-standing bitter opposition to similar tactics when exercised by dissident Northern blacks or student radicals.

A companion demonstration on the water failed to materialize. A group of Santa Barbarans was to sail to the Union platform and "take it," but choppy seas precluded a landing, and the would-be conquerors returned to port in failure.

It would be difficult to predict what forms Santa Barbara's resistance will take in the future. A veteran News-Press reporter who covered the important oil stories has publicly stated that if the government fails to eliminate both the pollution and its causes, "there will, at best, be civil disobedience in Santa Barbara and at worst, violence." In fact, talk of "blowing up" the ugly platforms has been recurrent—and it is heard in all social circles.

But just as this kind of talk is not entirely serious, it is difficult to know the degree to which the other militant statements are meaningful. Despite frequent observations about the "radicalization" of Santa Barbara, it is difficult to determine the extent to which the authentic grievances against Oil have been generalized into a radical analysis of American society. Certainly an sds membership campaign among Santa Barbara adults would be a dismal failure. But that is too severe a test. People, particularly basically contented people, change their world-view very slowly, if at all. Most Santa Barbarans still go about their comfortable lives in the ways they always have; they may even help Ronald Reagan win another term in the state house. But I do conclude that large numbers of persons have been moved, and that they have been moved in the direction of the radical left. They have gained insights into the structure of power in America not possessed by similarly situated persons in other parts of the country. It can be a revealing shock to experience an event first-hand and then to hear it described, and distorted, by the press and the government. People extrapolate from such experiences to the possibility that official descriptions of other events may be similarly biased and misleading. And when these questions arise, deeper ones follow. As a consequence some Santa Barbarans, especially those with the most interest in and information about the oil spill, while still surrounded by comfort and certainty, have nevertheless come to view power in America more intellectually, more analytically, more sociologically—more radically—than they did before.

32   Oil-Spill Control: A Hard Fight but Industry Is Slowly Winning

GOOD PROGRESS! That's the best way to describe a changing tide for the better in the nation's battle to prevent and control pollution of its coastal and inland waters from oil spills.

Gains made during the past year have been painfully slow, but they're steady and definite and carry an optimistic sign for solid achievements in the future. The result is almost a certainty because of the cooperation given to getting the oil-spill hazard in hand by industry, governmental agencies, and the public.

Despite feelings of frustration that persist in dealing with oil spills, oilmen can count these developments as progress:

Dimensions of the problem are being fixed—where spills are most likely to occur and why, how severe and what is the impact, the outlook for greater mishaps—all are being pinpointed.

Authority for enforcement, for counteraction against a spill, and for responsibility for damages also are being fixed by new laws, regulations and industry practice.

Contingency plans for quick action by all levels of government, by industry groups and by individual companies are being completed.

Cooperative organizations for immediate response to contain and clean up a spill have been formed covering single harbors, coastal regions, individual plant areas. They are taking several forms: Industry-wide effort in an area; community-wide with industry, governmental agencies, the public cooperating; and subscription plan with a contractor undertaking to supply equipment, materials, and key manpower.

A variety of new and improved equipment, chemicals, and other materials has been developed to help prevent, control, and clean up spills.

More experience and technical knowhow in selective use of equipment and materials is adding to capability against spills. Each spill is a different fight, requiring differing tools and approaches, but the overall capability for handling them is expected now to grow rapidly.

Research has been stepped up into effects of pollution, into ways to prevent spills, and into developing equipment to clean them up.

In summary, the state of the art is this: There'll always be oil spills of some sort. The industry and Government are well along in gaining capability for handling spills in protected waters. They still are hampered in combatting major spills in rough seas, although this capability will be increased greatly within the next 2 or 3 years.

Problem a Big One

Potential for oil spills on both inland and coastal waters admittedly is tremendous and will continue to grow as petroleum demand expands and indus-

"Oil-Spill Control: A Hard Fight but Industry Is Slowly Winning," *Oil and Gas Journal*, vol. 69, no. 34, pp. 69–87, 1971. Abridged and reprinted by permission of the publisher. Copyright 1971 by the Petroleum Publishing Company, Tulsa, Oklahoma.

try facilities to handle this business grow larger in size and numbers.

Prospects for U. S. oil demand is one measure of the scope of the problem. The Bureau of Mines projects domestic demand to grow at an annual rate of 4% from 14.7 million b/d in 1970 to 23.6 million b/d by 1985. An increasing volume of this will be supplied from domestic offshore fields and by foreign oil moved by tankers, all possible sources of pollution.

A recent study, made by the Dillingham Corp. for the American Petroleum Institute, showed that 75% of past major oil spills were associated with vessels. This also undoubtedly is true for small spills in such protected waters as harbors and bays where oil is transferred or ships of all kinds are refueled and disposal made of their wastes.

Other activities of the oil industry also offer potential for oil spills but they are more easily controlled. These include:

Offshore drilling and production—the National Petroleum Council in its latest report explains that spills in this area result from uncontrollable natural causes, equipment failure, or human error. The potential, however, can be substantially reduced by sound practices, regulations, and supervision.

The industry has drilled an estimated 14,000 offshore wells through 1970. Of the 9,000 wells drilled on the Outer Continental Shelf, only 25 experienced blowouts. And only three produced spills sufficient to pose any serious pollution threat.

Pipelines—no oil spills of relative consequence, according to the NPC study, have been associated with off-

FIG. 1.

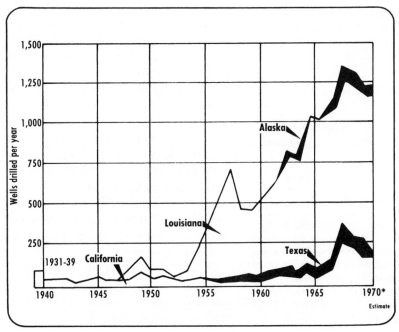

shore pipelines, the safest known method of transportation.

Refining—the industry has taken positive steps for many years to reduce potential water pollution from its processing activities. All the nation's refineries have waste-water treating systems designed to handle various types of liquid and solid wastes. Even more advanced waste-water treatment processes are being developed and put into operation at many plants. These should almost eliminate refining as a water polluter.

Marketing—as long as good housekeeping practices are followed, marketing operations pose little potential for water pollution. Potential pollution in this area arises from improper disposal of used lubricating oils and other wastes. Industry efforts to assure proper disposal have relegated this as a minor pollutant source.

This rundown of the pollution potential explains why the nation's efforts to prevent, control, and clean up oil spills of necessity is centering around marine transport.

Table 1 How U. S. Oil moves

| Transportation | per cent of product | |
	Domestic crude*	Refined products†
Pipelines	82.33	30.92
Tankers, barges	16.25	26.14
Rail tank cars	} 1.42	2.46
Trucks		40.48

* Based on 1969 refinery receipts. Source: U. S. Bureau of Mines, "Crude Petroleum, Petroleum Products, and Natural Gas Liquids, 1969," Mineral Industry Surveys (Annual Petroleum Statement, Dec. 15, 1970).
† Source: Association of Oil Pipe Lines, "Shifts in Petroleum Transportation, Table 3," Press Release (Apr. 8).

Profile of a Spill

The Dillingham study did more than indict vessels as the chief culprit for major oil spills. It gave the industry an idea of what to expect in a typical spill situation.

From its research on spills of more than 2,000 bbl, this profile emerged: The source is likely to be a tanker. Crude or residual fuel oils are likely to be involved. Size of the spill probably will be more than 5,000 bbl. The spill probably will occur within a few miles of shore and last for more than 5 days. Shoreline threatened will be at least partially recreational with a reasonable chance that only light coastal contamination will occur. It also is fairly likely that the spill will occur within 25 miles of a port suitable for staging control action and more likely not more than 50 miles from such a port.

Dillingham also used statistical data to outline coastal regions where spills are most likely to occur, those with large tanker traffic in heavy oils. These include the northeastern section from Virginia to Maine, and Central and West Gulf Coast regions from Alabama to Texas. Regions with lesser potential for spills include the Florida Straits, the major Pacific Coast ports, and the Panama Canal Zone.

The report showed that 15 of the 19 major spills in U. S. waters were in or near these areas. This evidence will furnish a guideline for government and industry concentration of preventive and control efforts.

A final feature of the Dillingham study was a report to pollution fighters on how such factors as waves, wind, tides, temperatures, and visibility will

Table 2 Tanker fleet grows

Oceangoing vessels of 2,000 gross tons and over			
	Number of ships	Total dwt	Average dwt
U. S. FLEET			
Present	365	8,797,900	24,100
Ordered†	22	1,458,000	66,300
WORLD FLEET			
Present	3,893	146,029,100	37,500
Ordered†	570	59,328,000	104,100

* Analysis of World Tank Ship Fleet, Dec. 31, 1969 (Philadelphia, Sun Oil Co., corporate development group, Aug. 1970).
† On order or under construction as of Dec. 31, 1969.

affect their ability to control a slick. These constraints were outlined:

Little effective control action is possible from smaller vessels in wave heights above 6 ft. And containment booms or oil-recovery devices are not useful in wave heights above 3 ft.

Wind data should be maintained to predict the approximate wind direction of a drifting oil slick and the onshore area most likely to be affected. Successful containment is unlikely where surface currents of 1 knot or better are setting the oil against a floating boom.

The effects of tides may significantly complicate shoreline protection and cleanup. Changing tides will distribute oil over a band on the beach marked by the high and low waterlines.

Temperatures above 60° F. appear to be necessary for successful use of dispersants. Low air or water temperatures increase the viscosity of the oil, thus increasing the tendency of the heavier fractions to persist.

Poor visibility because of fog, rain, or snow may have the most significant effect by restricting vessel operations and by limiting observation of drifting oil slicks.

Any Hope?

Given these environmental hardships, what chance is there to overcome oil spills?

The National Petroleum Council in its report to the Secretary of Interior summarized the status of oil-spill control measures with a degree of hope.

Mechanical methods naturally have limitations. Currently available booms can easily be positioned and are effective for containing spills in protected harbors and calm inland waters but are ineffective in rough open seas, the report said. The same is true of recovery devices. Air barriers have been found effective at terminals and in some offshore operations.

Next to containment and mechanical recovery, the council reports, the sorption of oil and removal of sorbent from the water surface is the most desirable method of oil-spill control. The sorption materials, however, still present logistical problems of both dispersal and collection which are not adequately met by present equipment.

Attacking oil slicks with chemicals, by combustion or by bacteria also has been proved possible in particular cases but with limitations. Materials for sinking oil have been available for years but run into objections from regulatory agencies responsible for fish and game. Chemical dispersants are available and effective in a variety of forms, but their use frequently is restricted because of fear of toxicity to marine life especially in enclosed or shallow waters. Destroying slicks by combustion has been attempted with limited success.

In beach cleanup, operations can be complicated by use of detergents and dispersants at sea or on a sandy beach. Greater success was achieved in both the Torrey Canyon and Santa Barbara incidents with straw mulch to collect oil at sea and on beaches, followed by removal and disposal of the oil-soaked straw.

In summarizing its report, the council observed that the oil and gas industries "are well aware of the environmental problems" and added, "real progress has been made in defining these problems and developing solutions to them."

Industry Capability

This same awareness and progress were apparent at the recent Washington conference sponsored by the API, the federal Environmental Protection Agency, and the U. S. Coast Guard. Developments in every phase of the spill problem were obvious.

Since most spills are the result of human error and two-thirds of the incidents occur in port or harbor areas during routine transfer operations, the industry is placing heavy emphasis on prevention methods. The theory is that

it's much simpler and less expensive to stop a spill than clean it up.

It is reported that instruments have been developed to prevent tank overfilling during loading. One of the best spill-prevention approaches is to upgrade the knowledge and operating practices of tanker personnel. Shipboard pollution-control indoctrination programs have been designed. They are presented on board during passage and cover all aspects of ship operations at sea and in ports which have pollution potential.

The defense against pollution from offshore drilling and production lies in planning and investment. A sound safety-in-depth or fail safe approach should become standard procedure in offshore drilling and production. Spill prevention can be achieved only by considerable planning and investment in well procedures and equipment before a foot of hole is drilled.

Advances are being made in another area of pollution, the discharge of oily ballast and tank cleanings.

Developments in tracing spills to their source or detecting unreported slicks at sea before they reach shore also are being made.

Cleanup Problems

One conclusion is becoming generally accepted by pollution fighters. Each oil spill is different, requiring different techniques and equipment. This means that industry and federal agencies must be prepared with a variety of methods and tools.

What About Chemicals?

A government researcher urges caution in the use of chemicals as sorbents, sinkants, dispersers, or detergents in oil-spill cleanup operations.

The massive use of highly toxic detergents during the Torrey Canyon incident set off a controversy which exists today over use of chemicals. The uproar has caused scientists to examine the toxicity of these chemicals to marine life. Other potential problems, such as the rate of degradation and ultimate oxygen demand of the chemicals which have lethal effects on marine life, also have arisen.

Government regulations are designed to allow controlled application of chemicals to treat oil spills. Their use may be needed to eliminate a hazard of human life, to protect segments of an endangered marine species, or prevent further environmental damage.

New Industry

An amazing array of equipment, materials, and new processes recently has been introduced in the oil-spill field by companies which virtually have formed a new industry.

A few companies are marketing integrated systems that will contain and remove oil spills in a variety of different circumstances. Others offer products or equipment dealing only with a single phase of the problem.

What's Needed

The nation and the oil industry have come far in attacking the oil-spill problem but need more widespread organization, more coordinated laws, and much research before the problem is in hand.

The API in late 1969 prepared and distributed to the industry a model contingency plan dealing with oil spills. The API, in addition, has urged member companies to form harbor cooperatives for pooling equipment and materials for use when a spill occurs beyond the capabilities of the individual company. By early 1970 there were 42 such cooperatives formed and 35 more under development.

The U. S. Coast Guard, with the support of the oil industry and other governmental agencies, is developing strong capability in the area of airborne equipment for fast deployment to spills at sea. This will be available within a few years along the nation's coasts.

Legal experts, meanwhile, complain that environmental laws and regulations in many instances have not evolved in an orderly manner and tend to add confusion to the control scene. Contributing to the confusion have been:

State legislatures which acted precipitously without insuring coordination with federal and local regulations.

Earlier laws which have been stretched by courts to apply to polluters setting precedents difficult to reconcile with later laws.

Large number of enforcement agencies at all levels.

Lack of adequate technical data on the precise harmful effects of various pollutants, resulting in poorly based regulations.

In the area of research needs, the National Petroleum Council recently observed that "considerable effort is underway" but much more is needed.

In addition to research on containment and recovery of oil at sea, specific areas for research include:

Methods of off-loading tankers at sea in an emergency.

Methods of identifying oils as to sources of pollution.

Definition and classification of oil-spill treating agents to provide guidance and safeguards in their use.

Advanced techniques for rapid and efficient beach and shoreline cleanup, restoration, and disposal of the oil.

Development of improved material specifications, testing procedures and instrumentation.

The fate and behavior of oil on water and its true effect on the marine environment.

In every instance of need pointed out by NPC, development work already is well advanced or has been initiated under sponsorship of the API or a governmental agency. The nation is well on the way to developing the capability to reduce the number of oil spills and minimize their impact on the environment.

Supplementary Readings

(Anonymous), University of California, Santa Barbara, Santa Barbara, California, 1970, *Santa Barbara Oil Pollution, 1969*, Department of Interior, Federal Water Pollution Control Administration.

(Anonymous), Electric Power and the Environment—a report sponsored by the Energy Policy Staff, Office of Science and Technology, U. S. Government Printing Office, 1970, 71 pp.

Barnett, H., 1967, The Myth of Our Vanishing Resources, *Trans-Action*, v. 4, pp. 6–10.

Brooks, D. B., 1966, Strip Mine Reclamation and Economic Analysis, *Natural Resources Jour.*, v. 6, pp. 13–44.

Brown, T. L., 1971, *Energy and the Environment*, C. E. Merrill, Columbus, Ohio, 141 pp.

Cloud, P. E., Jr., 1968, Realities of Mineral Distribution, *Texas Quarterly*, v. 11, n. 2, pp. 103–26.

Cloud, P. E., Chr., Committee on Resources and Man, 1969, *Resources and Man: A Study and Recommendations*, W. H. Freeman and Company, San Francisco, Calif., 259 pp.

Flawn, P. T., 1966, Mineral Resources—Geology, Engineering, Economics, Politics, Law, Rand McNally & Co., 406 pp.

Flawn, P. T., 1970, *Environmental Geology: Conservation, Land-Use Planning and Resource Management*, (chap. 4), Harper & Row, New York, 313 pp.

Hill, A. and McCloskey, M., 1971, Mineral King: Wilderness versus Mass Recreation in the Sierra, in *Patient Earth* by J. Harte and R. H. Socolow, Holt, Rinehart, Winston, pp. 165–80.

Hubbert, M. King, 1971, The Energy Resources of the Earth, *Sci. Amer.*, v. 224, n. 3, p. 61–70.

Katz, Milton, 1971, Decision-Making in the Production of Power, *Sci. Amer.*, v. 225, n. 3, p. 191–200.

Legget, R. F., 1968, Consequences of Man's Alteration of Natural Systems, *Texas Quarterly*, v. 11, n. 2, pp. 24–35.

Leopold, L. B., Clarke, F. E., Hanshaw, B. B., and Balsley, J. R., 1971, A Procedure for Evaluating Environmental Impact, *U. S. Geol. Survey Circ. 645*, 13 pp.

McKelvey, V. E., Tracey, J. I., Jr., Stoertz, G. E., and Vedder, J. G., 1969, Subsea Mineral Resources and Problems Related to Their Development, *U. S. Geol. Survey Circ. 619*, 26 pp.

Meiners, R. G., 1964, Strip Mining Legislation, *Natural Resources Jour.*, v. 3, pp. 442–69.

Nace, R. L., 1967, Are We Running Out of Water?, *U. S. Geol. Survey Circ. 536*, 7 pp.

Park, C. F. and Freeman, M. C., 1968, *Affluence in Jeopardy: Minerals & the Political Economy*, Freeman-Cooper, 368 pp.

Pecora, W. T., 1968, Searching Out Resource Limits, *Texas Quarterly*, v. 11, n. 2, pp. 148–54.

Price, C. A., 1971, The Helium Conservation Program of the Department of the Interior, in *Patient Earth*, J. Harte and R. H. Socolow, pp. 70–83.

Schlee, J., 1968, Sand and Gravel on the Continental Shelf off the Northeastern United States, *U. S. Geol. Survey Circ. 602*, 9 pp.

Starr, Chauncey, 1971, Energy and Power, *Sci. Amer.*, v. 255, n. 3, p. 36–49.

Walsh, J., 1965, Strip Mining: Kentucky Begins to Close the Reclamation Gap, *Science*, v. 150, pp. 36–39.

Weeden, R. B. and Klein, D. R., 1971, Wildlife and Oil: A Survey of Critical Issues in Alaska, *The Polar Record*, v. 15, n. 97, pp. 479–494.

Wenk, Edward, Jr., 1969, The Physical Resources of the Ocean, *Sci. Amer.*, v. 221, n. 3, p. 166–67.

White, Donald, 1965, Geothermal Energy, *U. S. Geol. Survey Circ. 519*, 17 pp.

Yerkes, R. F., Wagner, H. C., and Yenne, K. A., 1969, Petroleum Development in the Region of the Santa Barbara Channel Region, California, *U. S. Geol. Survey Prof. Paper 679-B*, pp. 13–27.

Aerial view of New Orleans, Louisiana. Courtesy of ESSA, U. S. Department of Commerce.

III. Urban Geology

"Urbanization—the concentration of people in urban areas and the consequent expansion of these areas—is a characteristic of our time. It has brought with it a host of new or aggravated problems that often make new demands on our natural resources and our physical environment."

E. L. Hendricks
Water in the Urban Environment

For many people, today's world is an urban world. Approximately 70 per cent of the United States population lives in urban areas. Furthermore, it is anticipated that most of our future population increase will be absorbed by cities. The implications of population growth and settlement patterns in terms of demands on the physical environment are overwhelming. It has, therefore, become necessary to anticipate and recognize the resultant problems and to plan intelligently to cope with them. Urban geology—a field of applied geology—can contribute significantly to the solution of many problems associated with urbanization.

Some of the urban land-use problems are related to natural geologic hazards inherent in the environment. Volcanism is a potential threat to Seattle (Reading 3). Earthquake activity presents problems for San Francisco and Los Angeles (Reading 7). Venice is plagued by subsidence and sea level changes (Reading 12) and Anchorage by quick clay deposits (Reading 15). Floods are a hazard in the Chicago metropolitan area (Reading 21). The poorly planned exploitation of mineral resources has had a negative impact on such urban areas as Long Beach (Reading 30). These aspects of urban geology have been dealt with in Parts One and Two. Part Three will concentrate on problems associated with: (1) water as a resource vital to the urban setting; (2) the disposal of waste material—a product of urbanization; and (3) conflicts in land-use decisions near urban areas.

John T. McGill introduces the subject of urban geology in Reading 33. He reviews the role of the geologist in identifying and solving a variety of urban problems and stresses the need to develop an adequate base of information through a program of detailed geologic mapping. He describes the need for geologic information as urgent and as one which geologists should meet if they are to fulfill their obligations as scientists, educators, and good citizens.

Water is a vital resource and represents a critical problem in many urban areas. The outlook, in terms of the quantity of water available, is explored in Reading 34. It appears that, although water resources are generally sufficient to meet the needs of most cities, shortages result from overtaxed collection, storage, and distribution systems as population growth outstrips development. "Crisis planning," unilateral developments, and apathy have characterized previous approaches to the problem of shortages. Future development of water resources must consider regional demands and resources. Co-ordinated long-range planning among hydrologists, economists, engineers, and local governments is necessary. Several case histories illustrating water problems in the urban environment are presented in Readings 34 and 35. The response of the hydrologic system on Long Island, New York, to population trends and attendant changes in the use and disposal of water are impressively documented in Reading 36. This Reading also calls attention to salt water incursion—a common problem in coastal urban communities relying on ground water.

Human modifications of natural flow systems are intensified by the urbanization process. Many of these modifications produce inconveniences, annoyances, and even property damage and thus constitute a nuisance. Sediment problems are some of the inevitable results of urbanization. Harold Guy reviews the extent of the problems and some possible solutions in Reading 36. It is evident that sedimentation can lead to a deterioration of the total environment, and so the recognition and solution of sediment problems become socially and economically important.

Solid wastes are accumulating at the rate of more than 1400 million pounds per day in the United States. The per capita production of waste is highest in urbanized areas where diverse industrial wastes are added to the garbage and rubbish generated by individuals. The disposal of this material is one of the most serious problems confronting many municipalities. Safe disposal sites are at a premium in many areas, and indiscriminate disposal can lead to serious health and environmental problems. What are the principal methods of solid-waste disposal? What are the critical elements of the geologic environment which govern the suitability of a disposal site? What are the hydrologic implications of solid-waste disposal? These questions and others are considered by William Schneider in Reading 37.

In addition to solid wastes, urbanized areas generate large volumes of exotic liquid wastes. These wastes may be disposed of by underground injection, surface irrigation, or septic tanks. Each of these methods has inherent advantages and dangers. The subsurface disposal of liquid waste at the Rocky Mountain Arsenal well near Denver, for example, led to the development of earthquake swarms (Reading 8) and revealed our limited understanding of safe injection pressures. In other cases subsurface disposal has interfered with natural zones of ground water circulation and has proved to be a health hazard.

The advantages and disadvantages of irrigation are reviewed in Reading 38. Although this method has the potential for disposing of large volumes of both municipal and industrial wastes while at the same time recharging the ground water system, the danger of contaminating ground water cannot be overemphasized.

In areas where the rate of urban development has outpaced the installation of city sewer lines, septic tank systems have been installed to handle liquid wastes. In some areas local soils cannot properly absorb the septic tank effluent, and disposal becomes unsafe or the system fails to operate efficiently. The relationship among soil conditions, septic tank design, and the disposal of septic tank effluent is outlined in Reading 39.

As our urban population has increased, use of the land has been intensified. This has frequently forced us to compare the advantages and disadvantages of one land use with another. The basis for intelligent land-use decisions includes geologic, ecologic, economic, social, and esthetic considerations. Hubert Risser and Robert Major discuss the conflicts between urban expansion and industrial mineral producers in Reading 40. William C. Ackermann in Reading 41 reviews a controversy in land use surrounding the proposed damming of the Sangamon River. This is a classic example of widely divergent social values and is not unlike the controversy facing Venice (Reading 12). When the economic and social needs of a community indicate the desirability of damming a stream, it is imperative that these needs be met only if geologic considerations indicate the availability of a safe dam site. Thomas Clements (Reading 42) cites the St. Francis dam as an example where the dam site was selected in response to economic and social need without considering geologic suitability. The failure of the St. Francis dam in 1928 led to a law that requires the geologic investigation of all dam sites in California. As John McGill points out in Reading 33, the enactment of this law marked the real beginning of urban geology in California.

33   Growing Importance of Urban Geology*
John T. McGill

Urban geology is much too broad a subject to cover comprehensively or in any satisfactory detail in a short presentation. It has been with us for many years, yet possesses a timeliness and an

* Adapted from a talk presented at the 75th Annual Meeting of the Geological Society of America, New York, N. Y., November 18, 1963.

McGill, J. T., 1964, "Growing Importance of Urban Geology," U. S. G. S. Circ. 487, 4 pp. Reprinted by permission of the author.
Mr. McGill is on the staff of the U. S. Geological Survey, Denver, Colorado.

urgency that is regrettably little appreciated. The purpose of this brief paper, therefore, is to alert the geological profession, and others, to the present and future significance of what has been until recently a relatively minor field of applied geology. I hope to increase not only your awareness, but your concern, for concern is surely warranted.

Urban Growth and Its Implications

Urban geology is growing in importance in the United States primarily because urban areas are growing. Urban areas are growing because the population of the nation is increasing and also because proportionally more people are congregating in urban areas. The critical factors are the phenomenal rate, magnitude, and changing pattern of urban population growth that have developed in recent decades. The trends are well documented in the census records.

For more than a hundred years, the urban population has grown more rapidly than the rural, until today approximately 70 percent of our inhabitants live in urban areas. From 1950 to 1960, the total population of the United States grew from nearly 151 million to over 179 million, an increase of well over 28 million, or 19 percent. In the same period, the urban population grew from nearly 96½ million to over 125 million, an increase of nearly 29 million, or 30 percent. All the nation's massive population increase during this 10-year interval occurred in urban areas.

A notable feature of current urban growth is that it is predominantly metropolitan, and furthermore is concentrated in the very largest metropolitan areas. Of the total population increase for the United States from 1950 to 1960, over 84 percent occurred in the 212 Standard Metropolitan Statistical Areas, each of which contains at least one city of 50,000 inhabitants or more. But within these metropolitan areas the growth rate was very uneven. The population of the central cities increased by about 9 percent, while that of the suburban fringes grew by a spectacular 48 percent. Expressed another way, and perhaps more meaningfully, roughly two-thirds of the entire population growth of the United States since 1950 has been taking place in the suburbs. There is no reason to expect any slowing down in the foreseeable future; indeed, acceleration is much more likely.

If the data on population growth and trends seem surprising, the implications are almost overwhelming. The rapidity and the changing pattern of urban growth have given rise to unprecedented problems of city and regional planning in the course of suburban development and urban renewal and redevelopment. The planning problems are noteworthy for their magnitude, diversity, and complexity, but it will suffice here to mention only a few of the areas of greatest difficulty, by way of illustration. Transportation and traffic probably constitute the foremost problem in most growing cities. Also high on the list is the expansion of the various basic city services and utilities, especially water supply, sewerage and sewage disposal, and drainage, including flood control. An immediate concern in the suburbs is the acquisition of appropriate sites for schools and other essential public facilities and for recreational purposes well in advance of local population growth.

Clearly most problems of physical planning are, or soon become, problems of engineering. Therefore the physical planning process necessarily is based to a large degree on engineering principles and practices. Many city planners are, in fact, civil engineers. Since 1923, early in the history of modern city planning, the American Society of Civil Engineers has sponsored a technical division on city planning. Planners, because of their overlap of interests, are coming to realize what civil engineers have been learning slowly and for a much longer time—the value of geologic information.

A major phase of master planning is the evaluation of the advantages and disadvantages of one use of land as compared to another use, so as to make planning and zoning possible for the conservation and maximum beneficial use of land, our most fundamental natural resource. Sooner or later we all pay, directly or indirectly, for unintelligent use of land. So we all have a stake in land-use planning. To a signficant degree it is the characteristics of the earth materials underlying its surface that determine how land can be most effectively and safely used. Correlation of the requirements for potential use with pertinent geologic considerations will help assure that land use will not conflict with the limitations imposed by natural conditions. This is especially true when the easily developed sites are depleted and suburban expansion is forced into marginal or hilly areas, where new and more imposing difficulties are encountered. Factors other than geology commonly dictate a given use for land, but this may then make knowledge and consideration of the geology even more important.

Problems of urban land use that are related to geology ultimately involve every aspect of civil engineering through their effect upon the design, construction, and maintenance of specific engineering works. Certain of these problems, such as earthquakes and some landslides, occur as natural geologic hazards inherent in the environment. Other problems, such as instability of cuts and ground-water pollution, pose actual or potential threats because of unwise or poorly planned activities of man. Still others may have more to do

with the economics of land use or development than with its safety; problems of difficult excavation or lack of nearby sources of earth material suitable for fill are examples.

The importance of geology to planning and to civil engineering obviously is very great, and is by no means limited to urban areas. On the other hand, it is essential to point out that not all applied urban geology is engineering geology. Sand and gravel and other raw materials of construction are a concern of engineering geologists, but the economic geology of any mineral resource occurring within an urban area may have a critical bearing on local land-use planning and development. Accessibility to valuable mineral lands or their preservation for future use often can be assured through judicious zoning and other regulations.

The Los Angeles Area—An Outstanding Example

Man Versus Nature

The Los Angeles area provides an outstanding and instructive example of the growing importance of urban geology. As on the national scene, the importance is the result of the activities of man impinging on the natural environment, but in this megalopolis of southern California both elements are notoriously unpredictable.

Population growth in the Los Angeles area has been truly explosive, and the explosion largely uncontained, as any traveler arriving there by air can easily judge for himself. From 1950 to 1960, the population of the City of Los Angeles grew from nearly 2 million to almost 2½ million, an increase of about 25 percent. Despite the city's vast geographic extent, which is well publicized, the spread of residential subdivisions has been so rapid that now only hilly and mountainous terrain remains as the last large area of relatively undeveloped land. Some 60 percent of the city, or roughly 250 square miles, consists of this hillside area, as it is called in the municipal code. It is perhaps 10 percent built upon, with over 60,000 homes, at least 40,000 of them constructed in the last 10 years. City officials contend there is room in the hills for 2 million people, which also happens to be the population increase anticipated for the city within the next 25 years or so. The story of growth is similar for the entire County of Los Angeles, where about 40 percent of the people of California live. The County's 1960 population of over 6 million was exceeded by that of only 8 States.

The natural setting of the Los Angeles area is characterized by rugged topography, complex and highly variable geology, and a semi-arid climate in which the rainfall is concentrated in a few winter months. This is a combination that resulted in increasingly serious and widespread engineering problems as urban growth accelerated after World War II and thousands of new cuts scarred the hills. Problems of landslides, other slope instabilities, floods, and debris flows have tended to dominate, but the total list is long and the consequences of neglect are extremely costly.

The crisis came with the heavy rains of early 1952, and this crisis turned into a major disaster largely because land developers had generally disregarded things geological. Within months the City of Los Angeles had enacted the nation's first comprehensive grading ordinance and taken other steps to remedy the situation and prevent its recurrence. The County of Los Angeles and other cities and counties within the metropolitan area have since followed suit. Grading and subdivision regulations specify the requirements for rigorous engineering geology and soil engineering investigations, and the regulations are diligently enforced. The relatively minor damage from storms in recent years is proof of how well the controls are paying off.

Urban Engineering Geology

The history of urban engineering geology in southern California has been brief but eventful. It had its real beginnings after the St. Francis dam failure of 1928, which led to a State law making compulsory the geologic investigation of all dam sites. Engineering geology played an important role in the planning and construction of the Metropolitan Water District's famed Colorado River Aqueduct during the 1930's. The local profession grew steadily but very slowly until the late 1940's, when the population increase, and hence new construction, began to assume massive proportions.

Employment of engineering geologists in all types of urban investigations in the Los Angeles area was rather impressive by 1953, even before the full effect of hillside development controls was felt, but there has been a 3-fold increase in the last 10 years, from about 50 to about 150 geologists, including some part-timers. A brief summary of present employment in the Los Angeles area is pertinent because it is the most convincing way of showing the extent to which engineering geology is now being used. Keep in mind that the following figures are all for this one urban area. The summary does not include the many men trained as geologists who are now working essentially as engineers, even though their geologic background commonly was a valuable prerequisite for employment. Nor does it include the numerous engineering geologists headquartered in Los Angeles who are not engaged in local urban investigations to any appreciable degree.

Government geologists total about 70. This is more than double the number 10 years ago, chiefly because of increases in State and county organizations. At the Federal level, the largest group consists of some 11 geologists of the Corps of Engineers district office working mainly on major flood control projects, harbor development, and other civilian applications. The Geological Survey is represented by 5 members of the Engineering Geology Branch, carrying out 3 projects of detailed areal mapping, much of which is being done at the request of and in cooperation with the County of Los Angeles.

The largest of three State agency staffs is that of the Department of Water Resources, with 17 engineering geologists engaged in local studies of ground-water basin geology and development, waste disposal, salt-water encroachment and contamination, and related matters. Nine engineering geologists of the Division of Highways are responsible for all local investigations of bridge foundations for the extensive freeway and State highway systems, as well as for many route surveys and materials investigations. Two geologists

of the Division of Mines and Geology, which is the State's geological survey, have been doing detailed areal mapping under a cooperative agreement with the County.

The County of Los Angeles, which has a civil service payroll of more than 40,000 persons, employs engineering geologists in two of its biggest departments. Ten geologists work for the Flood Control District on a wide variety of projects about equally divided between the District's two integrated programs of flood control and water conservation. Their principal effort currently is with salt-water encroachment barrier projects. The Engineering Geology Section of the County Engineer's Department came into existence only 4 years ago, and now has a staff of 5 professionals who are nearly swamped with responsibilities in all geologic aspects of hillside development control and major capital projects. These geologists, in addition, serve as advisers for most other County departments, including the Road Department and the Regional Planning Commission.

Within the City of Los Angeles, several geologists are employed by the Public Works Department, mostly on hillside investigations, and three geologists work for the Dams and Foundations Section of the Water and Power Department, which is the largest municipally owned utility in the United States. Recently a geologist position was established within the Department of Building and Safety in order to provide needed assistance in control over grading on private property.

The Metropolitan Water District of Southern California, a public corporation, employs only 1 or 2 geologists at present, though it has had a larger staff in the past during periods of major construction programs.

The field of private utilities is of minor importance locally, with 3 engineering geologists working for the Southern California Edison Company.

The greatest number of geologists is in the field of private geological and engineering firms and consultants, for this field has had a tremendous growth, chiefly because of the necessity or requirement for detailed geologic mapping in connection with hillside residential developments. In 1953, perhaps 4 full-time engineering geologists were in private employ. Today there are about 28 in engineering geology firms plus another 20 or so working for soil and foundation engineering companies. Noteworthy is an engineering geology firm that started in 1959 with 2 partners, now has 12 geologists, and recently added a soil engineering group in a reversal of the usual procedure. Part-time engineering geology consultants have increased slightly in number in the past decade, to about 20, but they now handle much more work. More than one college faculty member has enough business to keep full-time assistants occupied.

Lessons To Be Learned

The importance of the Los Angeles experience to geologists, engineers, planners, and indeed to the public, is that it illustrates the sort of thing that can happen and already is beginning to happen elsewhere, though on a lesser scale and with variations because of differing local conditions. Other urban communities would do well to take note and hopefully avoid some of the more violent growing pains in the acquisi-

tion and application of geologic information. In particular, the experience suggests an ideal sequence of mapping investigations to best meet the needs for geologic data in an expanding urban area.

First, and an absolute essential, is modern general-purpose mapping of quadrangles or other large areas, such as is undertaken by Federal and State surveys. Where possible, this should precede urban development so that the maps can serve as guides for land planning and zoning, and provide background for more-detailed local studies. The mapping of suburban fringe areas before the central city generally will meet greater needs first and take advantage of better exposures. The 7½-minute, 1:24,000-scale (i.e., 1 inch equals 2,000 feet) topographic maps are becoming the standard base for urban planning activities throughout the country, and thus are also the most appropriate base for general geologic mapping of urban areas. However, in some urban areas geologic complexities may make desirable initial large-scale mapping on an enlarged base.

The most useful general-purpose maps for urban development are those that emphasize geologic processes and characteristics of geologic materials that are significant to land use and civil engineering. But even where such emphasis is lacking, valuable guidance can be derived from interpretations of the basic geologic data.

The second stage in the mapping sequence consists of larger scale and commonly special-purpose mapping of selected areas. Both the County and the City of Los Angeles have recognized the need for maps at a scale of about 1 inch equals 400 feet in areas where landslides are prevalent and where no geologic maps were available at scales larger than 1:24,000. As part of the cooperative program between the County and the State Division of Mines and Geology, the broad coastal peninsula of Palos Verdes Hills recently was mapped at a scale of 1 inch equals 200 feet, with subsequent compilation at 1 inch equals 400 feet. This is an area of approximately 26 square miles. The assembled field maps, properly fitted together, would measure about 8 by 12 feet! Geologists of the City of Los Angeles have embarked on an ambitious program of mapping some 80 square miles of hilly and mountainous terrain on new photogrammetric base maps at a scale of 1 inch equals 400 feet. Such activities are by no means limited to governmental surveys. Private engineering geology firms have done extensive mapping at comparable scales for private developments covering up to tens of thousands of acres.

The third stage in the mapping sequence, and the one involving by far the greatest number of geologists, consists of extremely detailed investigations, chiefly for individual hillside subdivisions or specific engineering projects. A common scale for tentative tract maps is 1 inch equals 100 feet, and for final grading plans 1 inch equals 40 feet. Most such mapping is for private development and is done by geologists in engineering and consulting firms.

Meeting the National Need for Urban Geologic Information

The population figures for the United States show that urban growth, with its Pandora's box of planning and en-

gineering problems, is not peculiar to Los Angeles. It is a nationwide phenomenon. And so also the need for urban geologic information, both basic and specialized, is nationwide. Much can and should be done to take full advantage of such geologic data as are already available in published and unpublished form, but for most urban areas these will afford at best no more than an interim and partial solution.

New York was the first and still is about the only large city in the nation with anywhere near adequate engineering geology information. Most metropolitan areas of the United States desperately need new, detailed mapping, and this can only be achieved through a greatly magnified engineering geology effort involving municipal, county, and State agencies and private firms, as well as our universities and colleges. The master key to real progress belongs to the local governments. They can provide the greatest stimulus for urban geologic investigations, and they are in the best position to insure that the results are applied for the maximum benefit of their citizens. Cities and counties can use the geological information not only in the formulation of long-range policies and plans, but in the day to day applications that are possible with continuity of local operation.

The recent history of the geological profession in Los Angeles and in a number of other cities fosters optimism about the future job outlook for well-trained engineering geologists interested in urban work. The major emphasis must always be on quality rather than quantity, however, because this is work that deserves and demands the best talents. Many of our academic institutions would do well to reexamine their curricula with a view to improving the capabilities of their graduates for this field of specialization.

The U. S. Geological Survey has been mapping cities for many years as part of its national mapping responsibility. The 1902 folio of the New York metropolitan area was a notable early effort. Most of the older maps, however, are no longer adequate to meet modern requirements for more detailed, specialized, and up-to-date information. In its limited program of urban geology studies, the Geological Survey hopes to encourage by example the greater use of engineering geology in urban areas, and to educate public agencies and private concerns in the needs and applications of this field to the end that they will develop their own capabilities.

Mapping and related research by the Geological Survey in urban areas is intended to provide general background for more detailed site investigations. Individual projects tend to emphasize different aspects of the geology, depending on the local situation. Studies by the Engineering Geology Branch are currently underway in the following metropolitan areas: Boston, Mass.; Washington, D. C.; Great Falls, Mont.; Rapid City, S. D.; Omaha-Council Bluffs, Nebr.-Iowa; Salt Lake City, Utah; Denver and Pueblo, Colo.; Seattle, Wash.; and San Francisco-Oakland, San Mateo-Palo Alto, and Los Angeles, Calif. Studies have been completed in recent years in Anchorage, Alaska; Knoxville, Tenn.; and Portland, Oreg., and the reports have been published.

The problems of urban growth are a tremendous challenge. Planners and engineers need all the help they can get to meet the challenge most effectively. It is time geologists fully appreciated that a fundamental part of this help must come from their own ranks. The challenge to the geological profession is actually the more urgent because much of the geologist's work should be completed before that of the planners and engineers begins. In short, this is a time of opportunity but also a time for responsibility. We have an obligation as scientists, as educators, and as good citizens to see that the benefits of geologic information are brought to bear as widely and fully as possible in the solution of problems of urban growth.

34 Water for the Cities—the Outlook*

William J. Schneider and Andrew M. Spieker

* This paper was presented at a symposium on "Geology and the urbanization process," at a meeting of the Northeastern Section of the Geological Society of America, Albany, N. Y., March 14, 1969.

Schneider, W. J. and Spieker, A. M., 1969, "Water for the Cities—the Outlook," *U. S. Geol. Survey Circ. 601-A*, 6 pp.
The authors are affiliated with the United States Geological Survey.

The Problem

If water is used as a criterion of evaluation, we are indeed an affluent society. All economic levels of our society use it extravagantly. This is especially true of the urban dweller and his suburban neighbor who are accustomed to an almost unlimited supply at the turn of a faucet handle. Our society in 1965 used more than 150 bgd (billion gallons per day) of water to meet its needs and satiate its desires, exclusive of rural and agricultural uses. In addition to this direct use, the social impact of water resources is increasing demands for its consideration for fish and wildlife conservation, recreation, and aesthetics. Because water is neither created nor destroyed in sufficient quantity to alter significantly its total amount on earth, our supply is essentially limited. But is this supply sufficient? Are we running out of water? To answer this, though, we must also consider a related question: Why do our cities now face water problems?

The United States is rapidly becoming an urbanized society. According to Bureau of Census figures, about 130 million people—two out of every three persons—lived in metropolitan areas in 1965. Between 1960 and 1965, this urban population increased by more than 11 million people—an increase of over 9 percent. To meet the demands for this urban population, municipal water systems are supplying more than 24 billion gallons of water per day.

If population predictions can be relied upon and existing water-use practices are continued, during the next decade and a half the United States will be called upon to provide more than twice this amount of water to meet the demands of the metropolitan areas. Population predictions estimate that by the year 2000, about 280 million people will live in metropolitan areas—about 85 percent of the population of the United States. Supplying water for this urban growth will be a major challenge to the urban planner, the engineer, and the geologist.

Lewis Mumford (1956, p. 395) sums up the urban water demand as follows:

"Already, New York and Philadelphia . . . find themselves competing for the same water supply, as Los Angeles competes with the whole state of Arizona. Thus, though modern technology has escaped from the limitations of a purely local supply of water, the massing of population makes demands that even apart from excessive costs (which rise steadily as distance increases), put a definite limit to the possibilities of further urbanization. Water shortages may indeed limit the present distribution long before food shortages bring population growth to an end."

Mumford may be overly pessimistic in his outlook, though. Hydrologic data indicate that enough water is generally available for man's needs, but not always where and when he needs it or at a cost he considers reasonable. According to the Water Resources Council's First National Assessment (1968), water demands for all uses totaled 270 bgd in 1965, with a consumptive use of 78 bgd. Projected requirements for the year 2020 show total demands will be at 1,368 bgd and consumptive use, at 157 bgd. This current demand is less than 7 percent of the average of 4,200 bgd precipitation that falls on the conterminous United States, and the projected demand is less than 33 percent of the present average. However, seasonal and spatial variability in precipitation make these figures misleading; the history of water supplies for urban areas has been a constant cycle of shortage and development. A look at the history of municipal supply for two major cities and at the regional effect of the recent Northeast drought will illustrate this point.

Miami, Fla.

Miami, Fla., derives its water supplies from ground water in the Biscayne aquifer—a highly permeable water-bearing limestone that underlies much of southern Florida. The first wells were drilled into the Biscayne aquifer in 1896 to supply water for the newly constructed Royal Palm Hotel and for the Miami Hotel, heralding the start of massive urbanization of the area. In 1900, the local water system served a population of 1,680; by 1925 the population had increased to 30,200. New wells, added in 1907 to the existing location at Spring Garden, supplied municipal water at rates that lowered the water table until salt water encroached on the well field and forced its abandonment in the early 1920's, only 2 years after pumps were added to obtain the necessary flow.

In 1925, the Spring Garden well field was abandoned, and new wells were drilled in the Hialeah-Miami Springs area. However, increased demand for water coupled with the need to lower water levels for flood protection caused salt-water intrusion at this site, and stringent remedial measures have been necessary to insure protection of this source. Only through concerted efforts at preventing overdrainage and controlling water levels through construction of salt-water barriers in drainage canals has further contamination of Miami's water supply been averted.

Despite present conservation measures, increased water use by an expanding population will undoubtedly cause further problems in water availability, in salt-water intrusion, and in pollution. Population estimates by the Dade County Development Department, for example, predict an increase for the Miami area from 1 million people in 1960 to 4 million people in 1995. Daily water use is also expected to rise, from 145 gallons per person in 1960 to 220 gallons per person in 1995. The per capita increase results from a projected expansion in industrial water use. The total increase in water use will require 1.4 bgd as compared with the present use of 230 mgd (million gallons per day).

To supply this 1.4-bgd requirement in the future, Kohout and Hartwell (1967) estimate that the entire amount of rainfall over a 500-square-mile area would need to be collected. They point out, however, that total rainfall is never available for man's use; in the Everglades, almost 80 percent of the rainfall is consumed by evapotranspiration. Therefore, if the remaining 20 percent—$10\frac{1}{2}$ inches per year—were diverted to the Miami well fields, it would require an area of 2,800 square miles to supply Dade County alone in 1995. This is an area as large as the entire Everglades from Lake Okeechobee to Cape Sable.

The Miami case is an excellent example of a large metropolitan water system where careful planning has averted shortages and assured an adequate supply to meet future demands. The increased demands will probably be met by water management practices such as reduction of fresh-water discharge to the ocean via canals, by backpumping excess water to inland storage reservoirs, and by reuse of water. Water is a reusable resource, and advanced technology and enlightened water management should insure a continuing supply of fresh water in southern Florida.

New York City

The history of the New York City water-supply system presents a somewhat different situation. Whereas Miami has an abundant supply locally available, New York has had to go to great lengths—literally—to meet its demands.

In its early years, New York's water was supplied by shallow wells and small reservoirs, all privately owned. None of these sources was satisfactory, and epidemics were frequent. By the 1820's it was clear that a public supply was needed, but there were no adequate reservoir sites nearby. New York's population was then approaching 300,000. A proposal to build a 37-mile aqueduct to a reservoir site near Croton was first considered preposterous but gradually became accepted as a necessity. A cholera outbreak in 1832 killed 3,500 people and dramatized the necessity of a new supply, which was authorized in 1834. A disastrous fire in 1835 further demonstrated the desperate need and construction was accelerated. The system was completed in 1842.

At that time the Croton Reservoir was no doubt regarded as the ultimate answer to New York's water needs. Within 20 years, however, it had to be enlarged. Several new reservoirs and a larger aqueduct were needed before the turn of the century. By then, all satisfactory sites in the Croton watershed had been exhausted, and the demand was fast catching up with the available supply. Clearly, new sources of supply would have to be sought.

The Catskill Mountains, about 120

miles from New York, were chosen for the new reservoir sites. Construction began in 1907, and the system was completed in two stages: the Ashokan Reservoir was completed in 1917 and the Schoharie Reservoir, in 1928. Although addition of the Catskill system more than doubled the previous supply, the new supply was barely able to keep up with the rapidly increasing demand. By the late 1920's another water crisis was in sight.

This time alternatives were considered. The Hudson River was ruled out because of its allegedly inferior quality. New Yorkers insist on drinking pure mountain water. The Adirondacks were eliminated because of the excessive distance. In 1928, then, it was decided to expand the Catskill system and to develop new reservoirs in the headwaters of the Delaware River basin. The Delaware River is an interstate stream, so the consent of New Jersey and Pennsylvania was needed to divert water from this basin. The issue was resolved after considerable litigation in 1931 by a decree of the U. S. Supreme Court that allowed New York to divert no more than 440 mgd from the Delaware River basin. First the depression, then World War II delayed construction. The first operational phase of the expansion consisted of an emergency diversion from Rondout Creek to the new Delaware aqueduct from 1944 to 1951.

In the meantime, yet another crisis occurred. The postwar urbanization explosion strained the Croton and Catskill systems almost to their limit. Average pumpage exceeded 1 bgd. Abundant rainfall deferred the day of reckoning until 1949, when reservoir levels dropped to the danger point.

Stringent water conservation measures were enforced, and for the first time the Hudson River was tapped at Chelsea as an emergency source of supply.

Rondout Reservoir, an expansion of the Catskill system, became operational late in 1950 and the diversion from the Hudson was discontinued. Neversink and Pepacton Reservoirs, with their diversion appurtenances, began being used in 1953, but full use of the Delaware system was not achieved until 1955.

History repeats itself. The crisis of 1949 and the forecasts of the even greater population explosion to come made the water planners all too painfully aware that even the Delaware River basin supply system under construction would only temporarily satisfy the city's needs. An additional source would be needed. Thus, planning began for a new reservoir in the Delaware River basin. In 1954 the Supreme Court authorized New York to increase its diversion and in 1955 construction started on the Cannonsville Reservoir. Planners estimated that, with this new addition, the system would have total capacity of 1,800 mgd, sufficient to meet demands through 1980.

The record breaking drought of 1961–66 occurred, however, before the Cannonsville Reservoir was completed. At one time the existing reservoirs were drawn down to 26 percent of capacity (near the minimum safe drawdown for which the system was designed). The most stringent water-use controls in the city's history were put into effect, and the Chelsea pumping station on the Hudson River was rebuilt. By 1967 abundant rainfall eased the crisis, and the situation returned to "normal." But if history can be taken

as any guide, it will not be too long before New York is again faced with a water crisis. Indeed, planning has already started on alternative means of meeting expanded needs.

The history of the New York water system has been one of continuing crisis in order to satisfy the demands of the population explosion. Yet part of the water demand might be regarded as unnecessary or artificial. Wasteful and inefficient use of water is encouraged by the absence of metering and unrealistic pricing. While the elaborate network of reservoirs and aqueducts has been built at great cost, the Hudson River, which might supply New York's needs many times over, has, like many other rivers, been allowed to degenerate in quality. The State's Pure Water Program improvements show promise of effecting some regeneration. Planning decisions must be sensitive to economics, politics, and public attitudes. The citizens of New York have become conditioned to drinking "mountain water," and any change in established practices of water supply would require a massive campaign of public information and education.

Northeast Drought of 1961–66

The recent drought in the Northeastern United States points out the regional impact of natural catastrophic events on water for urban areas. In September 1961 precipitation and water levels throughout the northeastern part of the United States fell below normal. Although unheralded at the time, it marked the beginning of a drought— the largest, longest, and most severe in the history of the Northeast United States.

For over 5 years the drought persisted over a 13-state area extending from Maine to North Carolina, an area of more than 400,000 square miles. Each year since 1962 there was a reduction in yields of crops and pasture lands and an increasing threat and occurrences of forest fires. The effects on public water supplies increased with the duration and intensity of the drought. The effect was cumulative from year to year as reserves were depleted and streamflow and groundwater levels dropped to record lows. During the early part of the drought, the effects were largely absorbed by the built in resiliency and planned reserves of the water supply systems. By the summer of 1965, though, about one public water system out of every eight found its reserves at critically low levels.

Drought-related water shortages and problems in 1965 were severe enough to warrant emergency actions by federal, state, and local agencies. In Maine, 21 supply systems restricted water use; more than 50 towns and cities in Massachusetts imposed restrictions; 14 systems in New York faced water shortages; and northern New Jersey, with its interconnected water companies, was also seriously affected. At one time, storage in the New York City reservoir system was reduced to 124 billion gallons, only 26 percent of maximum capacity, and the chloride concentration in the Delaware River at the Philadelphia water intake at Torresdale reached over 50 mg/l (milligrams per liter), with the 250 mg/l isochlor located only 8 miles downstream. At the height of the drought, the water-use habits of more than 20 million people were directly and drastically affected.

Only concerted efforts at all levels enabled the region to continue to supply the water needs. Stringent conservation measures such as bans on use of water for air conditioning, car washing, and lawn sprinkling were enacted. A "water bank" was established in the New York City reservoir system to retain the 200 mgd which normally would be released for flow augmentation in the Delaware River and permit greater flexibility in management of that system. Emergency actions were taken to rehabilitate the Torresdale water intake for Philadelphia.

Many wells in the region, both individual and public supplies, "went dry" and had to be deepened, redeveloped, or replaced with wells of greater capacity. Here again, these well failures usually did not reflect insufficient sources of supply, but rather inadequately planned or constructed wells.

Despite the critical water shortages, it should be emphasized that never during the drought was there an overall shortage of water in the region. During the entire emergency there was only one outright failure of a city water-supply—that of Lancaster, Pa. The shortage was rather one of facilities for its collection, treatment, storage, and delivery to points of need. The execution of carefully prepared long-range plans can without doubt meet all water requirements of the Northeast for many years.

Outlook

The experiences of Miami, New York, and the Northeast region point out the universal problem of municipal water supply: population growth has tended to outstrip development. In the past, many municipal water systems have operated on marginal conditions. Because of the massive investments involved water utilities seldom manage to keep far enough ahead of our burgeoning population.

These marginal operating conditions suddenly become critical when faced with catastrophic events such as salt-water contamination of a well field or a series of near-dry reservoirs resulting from drought. This situation points more to lack of planning and development rather than to actual water shortages. Water is available for the cities, but the cities must plan effectively and in coordinated fashion if the requirements of all are to be met.

Predicted demands for municipal water are expected to increase from 23.7 bgd in 1965 to 74.3 bgd in 2020, an increase of 213 percent (Water Resources Council, 1968, p. 4–1–4). This demand will strain our ability to meet water requirements for the cities, but the job can and must be done.

Planning will play a major role in insuring adequate water for the cities. Regional planning must supersede local-interest planning as cities are ever increasingly forced to expand their sources of supply. As these sources of supply overlap, jurisdictional disputes will undoubtedly develop. Regional planning must replace uncoordinated unilateral development if chaos is to be avoided.

Moreover, the water-resources planners of the future will have to use considerably more imagination than has been evident in some of the plans of the past and the present if the job is to be done. Management of both the resource and its use may be necessary as the demand approaches the available supply. All alternative sources of supply should be considered in order to arrive at an optimal plan. For example, ground water could be used to supplement a surface reservoir or vice versa. The conjunctive use of surface and ground water should be considered; in many situations this may be the most efficient solution to the water-supply problem. Research is needed in advanced techniques of treatment that could convert marginal or unsatisfactory sources into usable supplies. Desalination, as it becomes economically viable, must be considered as an alternative.

The management of water use could be fully as important as the management of water supplies. It has already been demonstrated that water use can be substantially reduced by judicious management. Industrial water systems can be designed so that most of the water is reused. Saline water could be used in some instances for cooling, which accounts for a large part of industrial water use.

Water-use management need not be confined to industry, however. Municipal supplies can be made more efficient by systematic detection and repair of leaks in water mains. Modern plumbing fixtures generally use less water than outmoded ones. In this regard, building codes can require such fixtures in new construction. Water of less than drinking-water quality could be used for some domestic purposes such as lawn watering and air conditioning. Realistic pricing would exert a strong influence on water-use habits. Public education and information campaigns might be necessary to gain widespread public acceptance of such changes in traditional water-use practices.

The outlook for water for the cities then, can be regarded as cautiously optimistic. Though the population explosion of the next half century will strain existing systems, the water demands for our cities can be met. To meet these demands, however, coordinated comprehensive planning that gives adequate consideration to all viable alternatives must replace the crisis planning that has characterized much of the water-resources development of the past.

References

Kohout, F. A., and Hartwell, J. H., 1967, Hydrologic effects of Area B Flood Control on urbanization of Dade County, Florida: Florida Geol. Survey Rept. Inv. 47, 61 p.

Martin, R. C., 1960, Water for New York: Syracuse, N. Y., Syracuse University Press, 264 p.

Mumford, Lewis, 1956, The natural history of urbanization, in Thomas, W. L., ed., Man's role in changing the face of the Earth: Chicago, Ill., Univ. of Chicago Press, p. 382–398.

U. S. Water Resources Council, 1968, The nation's water resources—the first national assessment of the Water Resources Council: Washington, D. C., U. S. Govt. Printing Office, 410 p.

35 The Changing Pattern of Ground-Water Development on Long Island, New York

R. C. Heath, B. L. Foxworthy, and Philip Cohen

Introduction

Even before the severe drought that is now (1965) affecting the Northeastern United States, Long Island was well known among water specialists for its underground-water resource, mainly as a result of both the magnitude of the ground-water resource and the unique aspects of man's utilization of that resource. The current drought has focused increased attention upon the vast amount of ground water in storage on

Heath, R. C., Foxworthy, B. L., and Cohen, Philip, 1966, "The Changing Pattern of Ground-Water Development on Long Island, New York," U. S. Geol. Survey Circ. 524, 10 pp.
The authors are on the staff of the United States Geological Survey.

Long Island and upon the large quantity of water being pumped from the system. In 1963, for example, an average of about 380 mgd (million gallons per day) was pumped from Long Island wells; these wells tap a fresh ground-water reservoir that has an estimated storage capacity of 10 to 20 trillion gallons. Nearly all the water pumped was for domestic and industrial use, and this pumpage probably represents one of the largest such uses of a single well-defined ground-water reservoir anywhere in the world.

The history of ground-water development on Long Island has been thoroughly documented, largely as a result of studies made by the U. S. Geological Survey in cooperation with the New York State Water Resources Commission and Nassau and Suffolk Counties. The water development has followed a general pattern which, although somewhat related to population density and local waste-disposal practices, has been controlled largely by the response of the hydrologic system to stresses that man has imposed upon the system. The purpose of this report is to summarize the highlights of the historical pattern of ground-water development on Long Island and to consider briefly the insight that the history of development affords regarding the future development and conservation of Long Island's most valuable natural resource.

Geologic Environment

Long Island (Fig. 1) has a land area of about 1,400 square miles and is geographically a large detached segment of the Atlantic Coastal Plain. The island is underlain by crystalline bedrock, the uppermost surface of which ranges in altitude from about sea level at the northwest corner of the island to about 2,000 feet below sea level in the southeastern part of Suffolk County (Fig. 2).

The bedrock is overlain by a wedge-shaped mass of unconsolidated sedimentary deposits that attain a maximum thickness of about 2,000 feet. These deposits constitute the ground-water reservoir of Long Island and can be divided into six major stratigraphic units, which differ in their geologic ages, mineral composition, and hydraulic properties. These units are, from oldest to youngest, (1) Lloyd Sand Member of the Raritan Formation, (2) clay member of the Raritan Formation, (3) Magothy Formation, (4) Jameco Gravel, (5) Gardiners Clay, and (6) glacial deposits. (Suter and others, 1949). The first three units listed are of Cretaceous age, and the last three are of Pleistocene age.

The Lloyd Sand Member of the Raritan Formation has a maximum thickness of about 300 feet and consists mainly of fine to coarse sand and some gravel and interbedded clay. It forms

FIG. 1. Long Island and vicinity.

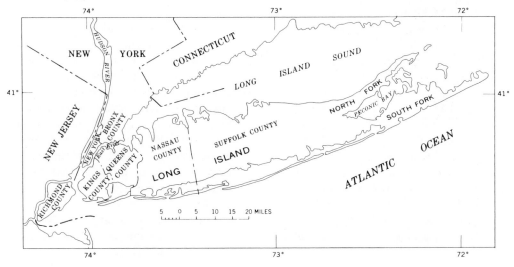

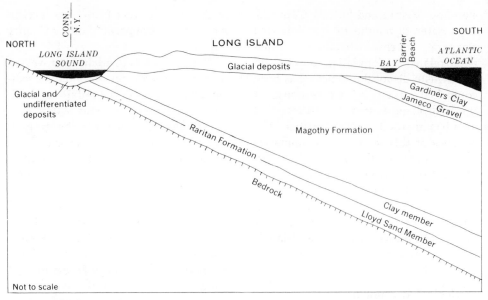

FIG. 2. Diagrammatic section showing general relationships of the major rock units of the ground-water reservoir in Nassau County.

the basal water-bearing unit of the ground-water reservoir. The clay member of the Raritan Formation is composed mainly of clay but locally contains considerable sand; it also has a maximum thickness of about 300 feet. Hydraulically, the clay member is a leaky confining layer for the Lloyd Sand Member—retarding, but not preventing, vertical leakage of water to and from the Lloyd.

The Magothy Formation on Long Island is partly correlative with the Magothy formation in New Jersey. It consists of complexly interbedded layers of sand, silt, and clay and some gravel in the lower part. The complexity of the interbedding and the character of fossils it contains suggest that the formation was mainly laid down under continental (flood-plain) conditions. The Magothy Formation is the thickest unit of the ground-water res-

ervoir on Long Island, attaining a maximum thickness of about 1,000 feet. Its horizontal permeability differs widely from place to place and is considerably higher than its vertical permeability. It commonly yields more than 1,000 gpm (gallons per minute) per well. Water in the formation is largely under artesian conditions.

Near the north and south shores of the island, the Magothy Formation locally is overlain by the Jameco Gravel. The maximum thickness of the Jameco is about 200 feet. It consists mainly of medium to coarse sand, but locally contains abundant gravel and some silt and clay. The Jameco Gravel is moderately to highly permeable and yields as much as 1,500 gpm per well. Water in the formation occurs under artesian conditions.

The Gardiners Clay is mainly restricted in extent to two moderately narrow bands that parallel the north and south shores, and it is commonly underlain by either the Jameco Gravel or the Magothy Formation.

The surface of Long Island is composed mostly of material deposited either directly by Pleistocene continental ice sheets or by melt water derived from the ice sheets. These glacial deposits consist mainly of sand and gravel outwash in the central and southern parts of the island, and mixed till and outwash atop and between the hills in the northern part of the island. The glacial outwash deposits are highly permeable and therefore permit moderately rapid infiltration of precipitation.

Hydrologic System

The four major water-bearing units of the ground-water reservoir of Long Island are the glacial deposits, Jameco Gravel, Magothy Formation, and Lloyd Sand Member of the Raritan Formation (Fig. 2). These four units contain

mostly fresh ground water; however, locally they contain salty ground water or they are hydraulically connected with salty water of the ocean, sound, or bays. Under natural conditions recharge to the ground-water reservoir resulted entirely from the infiltration of precipitaton, which is estimated to have averaged roughly 1 mgd per square mile (Swarzenski, 1963, p. 35). Most of the ground water moved laterally through the glacial deposits and discharged into streams or into bodies of salt water bordering the island without first reaching deeper water-bearing zones. Most of the remainder of the ground water moved downward through the glacial deposits into the Jameco Gravel or Magothy Formation, and from there part flowed laterally to the ocean and the remainder flowed downward through the clay member of the Raritan Formation into the Lloyd Sand Member. (See Fig. 4.)

Estimates of ground-water discharge under natural conditions can be developed by extrapolation of data listed by

FIG. 3. Generalized contours on the water table (the upper surface of the ground-water reservoir) in 1961.

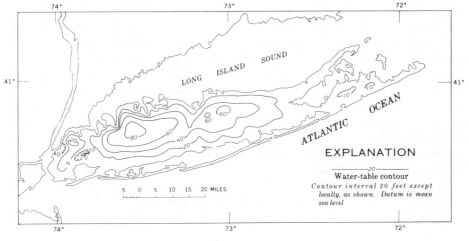

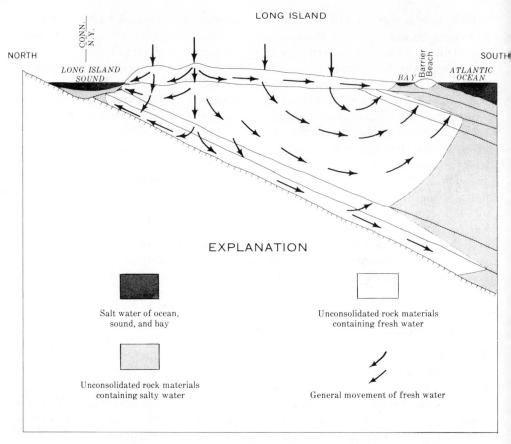

FIG. 4. Diagrammatic section showing predevelopment (phase 1) generalized ground-water conditions. Contacts between rock units are as shown in Fig. 2.

Pluhowski and Kantrowitz (1964, p. 38–55) for the Babylon-Islip area, a large and reasonably representative part of Long Island. Those data suggest that about 90 percent of the total recharge ultimately discharged from the glacial deposits (mainly by seepage to streams), and about 10 percent discharged by subsurface outflow from the Magothy Formation, the Jameco Gravel, and the Lloyd Sand.

The water table on Long Island (Fig. 3) and also the piezometric (pressure) surfaces of the underlying artesian aquifers (which have about the same general shape as the water table) form elongate mounds following roughly the configuration of the land surface. Two prominent highs characterize the water table—one centered in Nassau County and one centered in Suffolk County. Northwestern Queens County also has a small high in the water table. Other notable features are the cones of depression that extend below sea level in Kings and Queens Counties; these cones are in areas of past or current local overdevelopment of ground water.

Changes in Ground-Water Development with Time

Phase 1—Predevelopment Conditions

Ground-water development on Long Island has progressed and is progressing through several distinct phases. Under natural or predevelopment conditions (Fig. 4), the hydrologic system was in overall equilibrium and long-term average ground-water recharge and discharge were equal. The general positions of the subsurface interfaces between fresh and salty water in each of the previously described geologic units were stable, reflecting the overall hydrologic balance. The interfaces were virtually at the coasts in the glacial deposits and were off-shore in the underlying units.

Phase 2

In the initial stage of development (Fig. 5), which began with the arrival of the first European settlers, virtually every house had a shallow well draw-

FIG. 5. Diagrammatic section showing generalized ground-water conditions during phase 2 of ground-water development (shallow supply wells and waste disposal through cesspools). Contacts between rock units are shown in Fig. 2.

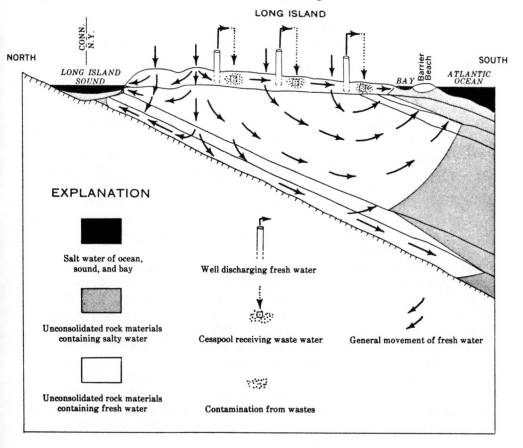

LONG ISLAND

NORTH

CONN.
N.Y.

LONG ISLAND
SOUND

SOUTH

Barrier
Beach

BAY

ATLANTIC
OCEAN

EXPLANATION

Salt water of ocean,
sound, and bay

Well discharging fresh water

Unconsolidated rock materials
containing salty water

Cesspool receiving waste water

General movement of fresh water

Unconsolidated rock materials
containing fresh water

Contamination from wastes

ing water from the glacial deposits and a cesspool returning waste water to the same deposits. As the population increased, individual wells were abandoned and public-supply wells were installed in the glacial deposits. The individual cesspools, however, were retained and little water was lost from the system during use. Although a considerable amount of ground water was being withdrawn, practically all of it was returned to the same aquifer from which it was removed. In general, therefore, the system remained in balance, and the positions of the interfaces between fresh and salt water remained practically unchanged. However, this cycle of ground-water development and waste-water disposal resulted in the pollution of the shallow ground water in the vicinity of the cesspools.

Phase 3

In time, as the cesspool pollution spread, some shallow public-supply wells had to be abandoned and these were replaced with deeper public-supply wells, most of which tapped the Jameco Gravel and the Magothy Formation. Supply wells were also constructed in the deeper units at places where the glacial deposits contained water with objectionable amounts of dissolved iron or other troublesome natural constituents. Most of the water withdrawn from the deeper units was returned to the shallower glacial deposits by means of cesspools, and subsequently discharged to the sea by subsurface outflow or by seepage to streams (Fig. 6).

As a result of the withdrawal of water from the Magothy Formation and the Jameco Gravel, and the concurrent

decrease in hydraulic heads in these units, the downward movement of ground water from the overlying glacial deposits locally was increased. However, the increased downward movement only partially compensated for the withdrawals of water from the Magothy and Jameco deposits. Locally, a hydraulic imbalance developed in the Magothy and Jameco deposits and caused a decrease in the amount of fresh ground water in storage and a landward movement of salty water.

Phase 4

The next major phase in the development of ground water on Long Island (Fig. 7) was the introduction of large-scale sewer systems—notably in that portion of Long Island that is part of New York City (Kings and Queens Counties). Most of the pumped ground water that previously had been returned to the ground-water reservoir by means of cesspools was thereafter discharged to the sea through the sewers. Whereas the net draft on the ground-water system during the preceding phases of development was negligible, virtually all the ground water diverted to sewers during phase 4 represented a permanent loss from the system. The newly imposed stress on the ground-water system locally resulted in a rapid landward encroachment of salty water into the previously fresh ground-water reservoir. The most dramatic example occurred during the 1930's in Kings County (the Borough of Brooklyn), which by that time had been completely sewered for many years. In 1936, decreased natural recharge owing to urbanization and increased ground-water withdrawals, which during the previous few years

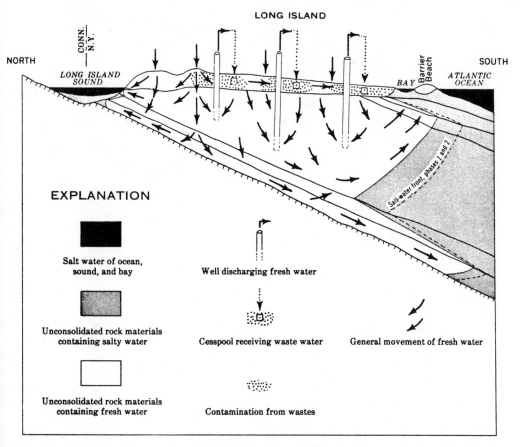

EXPLANATION

Salt water of ocean, sound, and bay

Well discharging fresh water

Unconsolidated rock materials containing salty water

Cesspool receiving waste water

General movement of fresh water

Unconsolidated rock materials containing fresh water

Contamination from wastes

FIG. 6. Diagrammatic section showing generalized ground-water conditions during phase 3 of ground-water development (deep supply wells and waste disposal through cesspools). Contacts between rock units are as shown in Fig. 2.

averaged more than 75 mgd, caused ground-water levels in Brooklyn locally to decline to as much as 35 feet below sea level (Lusczynski, 1952, pls. 1 and 2). This local overdevelopment caused contamination of large parts of the ground-water reservoir in that area from sea-water encroachment.

In 1947 virtually all pumping for public supply in Kings County was discontinued and the Borough was thereafter supplied with water from the New York City municipal-supply system, which utilizes surface-water

reservoirs in upstate New York. A notable exception was ground-water withdrawal for air-conditioning use. Such usage was permitted, however, only under the condition that the water was returned to the ground-water reservoir by means of injection wells (locally referred to as "diffusion' wells).

Present Areal Differences in Ground-Water Development

The present pattern of ground-water development on Long Island affords an

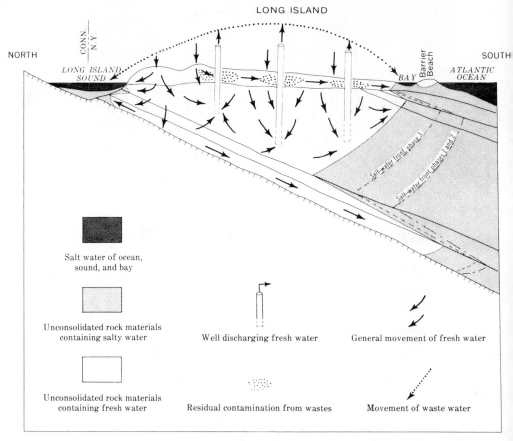

FIG. 7. Diagrammatic section showing generalized ground-water conditions during phase 4 of ground-water development (deep supply wells and waste disposal through sewers to adjacent salt-water bodies). Contacts between rock units are as shown in Fig. 2.

excellent opportunity to observe and evaluate the historic trend of that development, because all the major phases of development described herein, except the predevelopment phase, can be observed now in different subareas of the island (Fig. 8). Moreover, once the transitory status of present development in each subarea is recognized in relation to the pattern of historical trends, it becomes possible to predict and perhaps forestall some of the undesirable aspects of those trends.

Subarea A (Fig. 8) includes roughly

the eastern two-thirds of Suffolk County. Except for several small communities, the subarea is largely rural and has the lowest population density on Long Island. On the whole, the subarea can be characterized as being in phase 2 of ground-water development (Fig. 5)—that is, most of the wells in the subarea tap the shallow glacial deposits and supply water to single-family dwellings. The bulk of this water is returned to the glacial deposits through individually owned cesspools, and in overall aspect the ground-water system is still in hydraulic balance.

Subarea B, in central Suffolk County, is experiencing the impact of the sub-urban expansion associated with the entire New York City metropolitan area. Farms and woodlands are giving way to housing developments, and

FIG. 8. Water-development subareas in 1965.

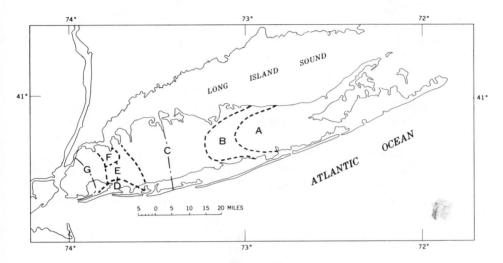

EXPLANATION

Subarea	Characteristics
A	Phase 2 of development. Pumpage mainly from shallow privately owned wells. Waste water returned to shallow glacial deposits through cesspools; local contamination of glacial deposits by cesspool effluent. System virtually in balance; positions of salt-water fronts unchanged.
B	Transition between phase 2 and 3. Pumpage from privately owned and public-supply wells. Waste water returned to shallow glacial deposits by way of cesspools; areas of cesspool-effluent contamination spreading. System virtually in balance.
C	Phase 3 of development. Pumpage mainly from deep public-supply wells; waste water returned to shallow glacial deposits by way of cesspools. System locally out of balance, causing local salt-water intrusion.
D	Phase 4 of development. Pumpage almost entirely from deep public-supply wells; waste water discharged to the sea by way of sewers. System out of balance; salty water actively moving landward.
E	Phase 4 of development. Pumpage almost entirely from deep public-supply wells; waste water discharged to the sea by way of sewers. System out of balance; may be subject to salt-water intrusion in the future.
F	Very little ground-water development. Water supply derived from New York City municipal-supply system; waste water discharged to the sea by way of sewers. System in balance.
G	Very little ground-water development. Water supply derived from New York City municipal-supply system; waste water discharged to the sea by way of sewers. Large areas contain salty ground water owing to former intensive ground-water development and related salt-water intrusion.

most of the pumpage in the subarea is now from large-capacity public-supply wells that tap the glacial deposits. However, most of the sewage disposal is still through individually owned cesspools. Thus, the area is in a transition between phase 2 and phase 3 of development. Cesspool pollution still is not widespread, but is substantial enough to be of concern to local government agencies. Accordingly, plans are currently (1965) being made to construct sewers in the area and to gradually replace the wells that tap the glacial deposits with wells that will tap the Magothy Formation.

Subarea C includes the westernmost part of Suffolk County and the eastern two-thirds of Nassau County. Mainly because it is closer to New York City, this subarea was subjected to intensive suburban development earlier than was subarea B. Therefore, the population density and, accordingly, the water requirements in subarea C are substantially greater than in subarea B. Virtually the entire water supply for subarea C is obtained from large-capacity public-supply wells. The part of the subarea that is in western Suffolk County obtains most of its water supply from public-supply wells, of which about half tap the glacial deposits and most of the remainder tap the Magothy Formation. In the part of the subarea that is in Nassau County, most of the public-supply wells tap the Magothy Formation.

Except for a few communities along the coast, most of subarea C is not sewered; practically all the domestic sewage is disposed of through individually owned cesspools. Thus, on the whole the subarea is in phase 3 of development (Fig. 6). The system locally

is out of balance owing to this development; however, substantial widespread salt-water encroachment has not yet occurred. Plans are being made to install sewers throughout the subarea.

Subareas D and E, which include parts of western Nassau and southeastern Queens Counties, are moderately to highly urbanized and are almost completely sewered. Practically the entire water supply for these subareas is derived from wells tapping the Magothy Formation, Jameco Gravel, and the Lloyd Sand Member of the Raritan Formation. Thus, these subareas are mainly in phase 4 of development and are characterized by a hydrologic imbalance (Fig. 7). The imbalance, which is accentuated because more than 70 mgd of water derived from the ground-water reservoir of these subareas currently is being discharged to the sea by way of sewage-treatment plants, is most clearly manifested in subarea D, where salty water is moving landward (Lusczynski and Swarzenski, 1960; Perlmutter and Geraghty, 1963). If the present trend continues, subarea D (the area of active salt-water encroachment) probably will expand at the expense of subarea E.

Subarea F, in northeastern Queens County, receives nearly its entire water supply from the New York City municipal-supply system. The subarea is sewered; however, because groundwater pumpage is negligible, the ground-water system is largely in balance.

Subarea G is the most highly urbanized and receives virtually all its water from the New York City municipal system. The entire subarea is sewered. As previously noted, large areas in

Kings County were invaded by salty water because of substantial overdevelopment and the resulting decline in ground-water levels. Similarly, salty water had invaded the ground-water reservoir in parts of western Queens County. Water levels in Kings County have recovered appreciably since the mid 1940's, when the consumptive ground-water uses were drastically reduced. Presumably, the salty water is retreating seaward and is being diluted by recharge derived from precipitation, but precise data regarding these changes are lacking.

Conclusion

Ground water probably will continue to be the major source of water for most of Long Island (except for Kings and Queens Counties) for at least the next several decades. Moreover, if the present trends continue, the ground-water resources of the island probably will continue to be depleted—perhaps at an accelerated rate. The historic trends of ground-water development and the present status of development strongly suggest that such depletion will in time cause salt-water contamination of larger and larger parts of the ground-water reservoir. Moreover, the areas in which such contamination occurs, in addition to extending inward from the coasts, probably will also extend farther and farther eastward as the population continues to expand in that direction.

Several alternative methods of conserving and augmenting the ground-water resources of Long Island are currently being considered. These include, among others, desalting of sea water with the use of atomic energy, artificial recharge, and the reclamation of water from sewage. The consequences of such possible meaures are highly significant inasmuch as the future well-being of several million people is at stake. However, even with the most promising of conservation methods, wise management will be required to gain the fullest use from the available fresh-water supply while also preventing undue hardships resulting from local overdevelopment of the ground-water reservoir. Fully effective management requires:

1. Recognition of the unity of the hydrologic system of Long Island.

2. The best obtainable scientific information about the system and how it functions.

3. Sound evaluation of the various alternative methods of water development and conservation, guided by available scientific information—including the hydrologic consequences of the historic and present-day changing pattern of ground-water development on Long Island.

References

Lusczynski, N. J., 1952. The recovery of ground-water levels in Brooklyn, New York from 1947 to 1950: U. S. Geol. Survey Circ. 167, 29 p.

Lusczynski, N. J, and Swarzenski, W. V., 1960, Position of the salt-water body in the Magothy(?) Formation in the Cedarhurst-Woodmere area of southwestern Nassau County: N. Y. Econ. Geology, v. 55, no. 8, p. 1739–1750.

Perlmutter, N. M., and Geraghty, J. J., 1963, Geology and ground-water conditions in southern Nassau and southeastern Queens Counties, Long Island, New York: U. S. Geol. Survey Water-Supply Paper 1613-A, 205 p.

Pluhowski, E. J., and Kantrowitz, I. H., 1964, Hydrology of the Babylon-Islip area, Suffolk County, Long Island, New York: U. S. Geol. Survey Water-Supply Paper 1768, 119 p.

Suter, Russell, de Laguna, Wallace, and Perlmutter, N. M., 1949, Mapping of geologic formations and aquifers on Long Island, New York: New York State Power and Control Comm. Bull. GW-18, 212 p.

Swarzenski, W. V., 1963, Hydrology of northwestern Nassau and northeastern Queens Counties, Long Island, New York: U. S. Geol. Survey Water-Supply Paper 1657, 90 p.

36   Sediment Problems in Urban Areas
Harold P. Guy

Introduction

A recognition of and solution to sediment problems in urban areas is necessary if society is to have an acceptable living environment. Soil erosion and sediment deposition in urban areas are as much an environmental blight as badly paved and littered streets, dilapidated buildings, billboard clutter, inept land use, and air, water, and noise pollution. In addition, sediment has many direct and indirect effects on streams that may be either part of or very remote from the urban environment. Sediment, for example, is widely recognized as a pollutant of streams and other water bodies.

One obstacle to a scientific recognition and an engineering solution to sediment-related environmental problems is that such problems are bound in conflicting and generally undefinable political and institutional restraints. Also, some of the difficulty may involve the fact that the scientist or en-

Guy, H. P., 1970, "Sediment Problems in Urban Areas," *U. S. Geol. Survey Cir. 601-E*, 8 pp. Lightly edited by permission of the author.
Mr. Guy is on the staff of the United States Geological Survey.

gineer, because of his relatively narrow field of investigation, cannot always completely envision the less desirable effects of his work and communicate alternative solutions to the public. For example, the highway and motor-vehicle engineers have learned how to provide the means by which one can transport himself from one point to another with such great efficiency that a person's employment in this country is now commonly more than 5 miles from his residence. However, providing such efficient personal transport has created numerous serious environmental problems. Obstacles to recognition of and action to control sediment problems in and around urban areas are akin to other environmental problems with respect to the many scientific, engineering, economic, and social aspects.

Problem Extent

In a study of sediment problems in urban areas, it is necessary to remember that sediment movement and deposition was a part of· the natural environment before the intervention of civilization. Like flooding, the sediment problems become important only when man is affected. Sometimes the problems result from natural conditions, but usually they result when the natural circumstances are altered to effect such a different kind of environment that previous small unnoticed problems are greatly magnified. Severe sediment problems occur, for example, when covering vegetation is removed in construction areas, when the flow regime in channels is altered by realinement or by increased or decreased flow, or when fill, buildings, or bridges obstruct the natural flowway.

The average sediment yield from the landscape and the condition of the stream channels tend to change with the advancing forms of man's land-use activity, as indicated by Table 1. As in many other situations involving intensive use of resources and rapid growth, one can expect that sediment problems will be most serious during the urban construction period (E). This is not to say that problems are not likely to occur during the stable period (G) because physical and esthetic values or quality standards with respect to both

water and property are expected to increase with time. For example, a stream carrying an average suspended-sediment concentration of 200 mg/l (milligrams per liter) after 2 years into the stable period may be more acceptable than 100 mg/l after 20 years into the stable period.

It is impossible to isolate sediment problems completely from the many interrelated problems associated with urban development, especially with respect to water (Anderson, 1968; Leopold, 1968). However, the sediment problems can usually be classed into groups related to land and channel erosion, stream transport, and deposition processes (Guy, 1967), regardless of the land-use phases mentioned in Table 1. Land erosion, including the sheet, rill, and gully forms, is likely to be most severe during the urban construction period (E), though it may be present to some degree regardless of land use. Channel erosion is most severe during the stabilization period (F), especially when channels have been realined, waterways have been constricted, and (or) the amount and

Table 1 Effect of land-use sequence on relative sediment yield and channel stability [Modified from Wolman (1967)]

Land use	Sediment yield	Channel stability
A. Natural forest or grassland.	Low	Relatively stable with some bank erosion.
B. Heavily grazed areas.	Low to moderate	Somewhat less stable than A.
C. Cropping	Moderate to heavy	Some aggradation and increased bank erosion.
D. Retirement of land from cropping.	Low to moderate	Increasing stability.
E. Urban construction.	Very heavy	Rapid aggradation and some bank erosion.
F. Stabilization	Moderate	Degradation and severe bank erosion.
G. Stable urban	Low to moderate	Relatively stable.

intensity of runoff have been increased because of imperviousness and "improved" drainage. Sediment transport problems are usually associated with the pollution of water by sediment from either or both the esthetic or physical utilization viewpoints. Transport problems also occur in regard to coarse sediment when the transport capacity in a stream section does not match the input supply of the coarse sediment—hence, aggradation or degradation. The sorting and differential transport of sediment result in deposition problems ranging from the fan deposits at the base of graded banks to deposits in reservoirs and estuaries.

The following is a list of some of the urban sediment erosion, transport, and deposition problems:

1. Public health may be affected in a number of ways. Efforts to control mosquito breeding have been ineffective because sediment has filled drainage channels. Also harmful bacteria, toxic chemicals, and radionuclides tend to be absorbed onto sediment particles. The absorbed substances may not be harmful in their original residence but become hazardous when transported into a water supply or deposited and perhaps concentrated at a new location.

2. Sheet, rill, and gully erosion and associated deposition may cause undesirable changes in graded areas typical of urban construction sites. Figure 1, from Wolman and Schick (1967, p. 455), shows the effect of

FIG. 1. Effect of construction intensity and drainage area on sediment yield (from Wolman and Schick, 1967, p. 455). Most of the data are from the Baltimore and Washington, D. C., metropolitan areas. The term "dilution" refers to drainage from relatively stable nonconstruction areas.

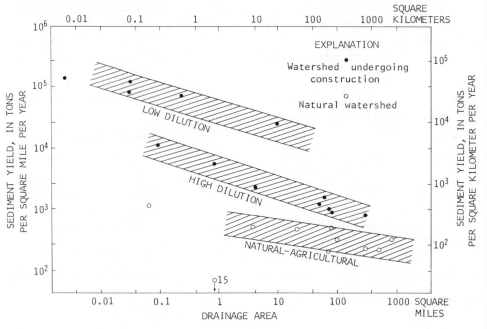

the intensity of construction and drainage-basin size on sediment yield. Erosion and subsequent deposition in cut-and-fill areas can easily exceed 1 cubic yard for each 100 square feet.

3. Dispersion of soil particles by raindrop impact seals the land surface and thereby reduces infiltration, increases stream runoff, and decreases groundwater recharge.

4. Deposition of coarse sediments may reduce the flow capacity or completely plug natural and man-made channels as well as close drains.

5. Floodwater damage is increased manyfold in homes, stores, and factories because of sediment. Evaporation can erase many of the effects of a "pure water" flood, but it cannot do so when the flow contains suspended sediment.

6. Streams and other bodies of water are damaged esthetically by unsightly deposits as well as by fine sediment in suspension. Though stream esthetics are considered much more inclusive than recreation alone, Brown (1948, p. 79) has estimated that recreation losses in the Meramec River basin near St. Louis, Mo., in 1940 amounted to 49,090 person-days as a result of above-normal flows (but less than floodflows) of high turbidity.

7. Water-treatment costs for domestic and industrial uses are increased. Reduction of Potomac River sediment turbidity to optimum could produce an annual savings of $25,000 per year (1963 values) for Washington, D. C. (Wolman, 1964, p. 68).

8. Erosion and (or) deposition in channels, estuaries, and other water bodies may cause bridge or culvert failure as well as serious ecological changes by alteration of species composition and population density (Peters, 1967).

9. Impoundments for municipal water storage are often built upstream from cities. The release of clear water from such impoundments can create serious degradation and bank erosion in downstream areas where picnic and other recreational facilities are planned.

10. Reservoir storage and channel conveyance for water supply are lost. Wolman (1964, p. 63) indicated that the alternative cost per acre-foot of storage lost to sediment in water storage and recreation reservoirs in Maryland ranges from less than $100 to over $78,000.

11. Maintenance costs are increased for streets, highways, and other public-use areas.

12. As implied in the introduction, perhaps the most serious urban sediment problem is the general deterioration of the total environment—a condition usually not recognized by the public.

As with many hydrologic problems, most urban sediment problems have visual impact for relatively short periods of time because they are rainstorm related (Guy, 1964). Also, because these problems are usually rooted within the urban or urbanizing area, they are limited to relatively small areas of the country. However, because of the intense capital investment in and human use of urban areas, the recognition of and solution to sediment problems become socially and economically very important.

Sediment damage is apparent when a storm-drain inlet becomes clogged, rill erosion cuts a graded area, a traffic accident occurs because of a wet fine-sediment deposit on a street, a swimming area must be closed because of turbid water, a water-treatment plant cannot clarify water, or a recreation lake is filled with sediment (Guy and Ferguson, 1962). Because sediment is often part of a complex environmental problem (Ferguson and Guy, 1970), many other sediment problems go unnoticed even though they may be economically significant. A study of air pollution in Chicago showed that dust-fall amounts ranged from 21 to 61 tons per square mile per month at 20 stations during 1966 (American Public Works Association, 1969, p. 25). The Chicago study also showed that street-litter sweepings consisted of more than 70 percent dirt and rock by weight—the remainder was classified as metal, paper, vegetation, wood, and glass. Higher percentages of dirt occurred in the litter after rainstorms, even in a business area that was 100 percent built up.

A sound sediment-measurement program in and adjacent to urban areas will help people to recognize what the problems are, where they occur, and when to expect them. Such a sediment-measurement program should document erosion sources and amounts, concentration in runoff, stream-channel changes, and the location and amounts of deposition. The measurement program, though mostly a documentation of the nature of conditions, will provide the basis upon which research needs (Guy, 1967) can be evaluated.

There are many laws concerning problems of sedimentation (Busby, 1962, 1967). In general the cases make it eminently clear that downstream owners can recover damages if changes and costs are well documented. In States where the civil law rule applies, a higher land is entitled to have flow discharge across the property of a lower landowner as it does in nature. Sometimes, however, a "reasonableness of use" rule is applied (*Sainato* v. *Potter*, 159 A. 2d 632, 222, Md. 263) where strict application of the civil law rule would result in hardship to either party. In considering aspects of sedimentation law, the following quotation from the decision in *Neubauer* v. *Overlea Realty Co.* (142 Md. 87, 98, 120 A. 69, 73) is of additional interest,

It is no answer to a complaint of nuisance that a great many others are committing similar acts of nuisance upon a stream. Each and every one is, liable to a separate action, and to be restrained.

Roalman (1969) described "a bounty on water polluters" based on the Harbor Act of June 29, 1888 (25 Stat. 209), as amended on June 7, 1924 (S. 1942), whereby any private citizen can bring action against almost any water polluter. Though it has been little used for the past 80 years, it provides for a stiff fine and a jail sentence for the polluter, and it specifically directs that a bounty be paid to the citizen who proves his case—literally a bounty law on water polluters.

Some Aspects of Problem Solution

Of the many facets of sediment problems in urban areas, the foremost are recognition and evaluation. Recognition would be easier if specific data on the cost of the many kinds of sediment problems in urban areas were available. The costs of sediment problems are rarely computed, and then they are generally estimated, even under the relatively less dynamic and more familiar rural conditions. Moore and Smith (1968) showed that "rural erosion and sediment" problems in the United States cause more than a $1-billion loss each year, $800 million of which occurs from erosion of cropland. Brown (1948) reported that annual damage from sediment deposition alone in rural areas amounts to $175 million. This in itself is 1.7 times the average annual flood damages for the 20-year period 1925–44. In the accounting of flood damages, sediment deposition was apparently not considered a flood cost.

The economic aspects of sedimentation in all its forms from erosion to deposition have been discussed recently by Maddock (1969). His section with regard to municipalities consists of only two paragraphs, as follows:

The economic problems associated with the control of turbidity in municipal and industrial water supplies are well known. Equally or perhaps more important, however, every community has its water courses. As the community grows, it seems inevitable that there will be a decision of some kind that will modify the behavior of these streams. Discharges are diminished or increased, stream channels are straightened or confined, and sediment loads are modified. These modifications generally result in problems that are solved at relatively high expense. The expense for one modification is not very great, but there are so many modifications that the aggregate costs are large.

The writer has discussed this phase of the erosion and sediment problem with engineers whose practice is largely in the municipal engineering field. Almost without exception, they all say that the control of natural drainage is one of the most irritating and aggravating problems they have to deal with. Many high-cost drainage projects result from an inability to cope with what appear to be relatively simple problems. Thus an alluvial channel must be transformed into a pipe or a lined channel because its slope is too steep for the amount of water it is expected to carry. Straightening alluvial channels seems to be a minor adjustment but it inevitably leads to more serious problems. A realization that most natural channels respond to the movement of both water and sediment would do much to prevent obvious mistakes.

Evaluation of the sediment problem is also complicated because sediment measurements are rather expensive and because sediment erosion, movement, and deposition are occurring in a highly dynamic and complicated environment. For example, in a drainage basin undergoing residential development (Guy, 1965), the area denuded of vegetative cover and subject to intensive erosion is continually changing. The process is complicated by the fact that storms occur as somewhat random events. The environment, too, is complicated by the fact that subsoils of varied erodibility are exposed to varying degrees with time and that man-made drainage may concentrate the magnitude and location of channel flow. During stabilization after urban construction (Table 1, F), channel instability is marked by serious degradation and severe bank erosion as a result of increased flows of relatively low sediment concentration from impervious areas.

As already mentioned, heavy loads of sediment are moved into channels below construction areas; the fine particles move through rapidly and the coarser particles tend to fill the channel system. In regard to the period of returning stability after development, Dawdy (1967, p. 242) stated,

the slug of coarse sediment produced during construction may well travel through a channel system as a discrete mass or wave, causing geomorphic changes. These, in turn, change the hydraulics of the channel, cause bank erosion, and may alter the ecology of the stream. No data nor studies of the impact of urban sediment on downstream ecology are available, however. If a channel system is steep enough and discharge is sufficiently great to transport the contributed sediment, the geomorphic and hydraulic effects may be short lived, and the impact of the sediment and of its associated problems is transferred downstream to a major river, a lake or reservoir, an estuary, or the ocean.

With our advanced state of technology, solutions to the physical urban sediment problem are usually available even though the problem may occur under a dynamic and complicated environment. Such solutions may seem economically and socially expensive, but in the light of our high standard of living the expense will prove to be relatively low. Because of the importance of sediment control, it is to be hoped that implementation will not be fraught with institutional difficulty.

In many situations, a program to obtain sediment knowledge is justified in order to wisely choose a suitable solution among many alternatives. A complete sediment-evaluation program may, in reality, be a complete systems study of input-storage-output components. For example, where the problem involves a stream channel, it is essential to know the sources of the inflowing sediment, the degree and extent of transport in the stream, and the nature of the deposit, in terms of time and space, at the estuary or other body of water.

Several steps needed to achieve control of urban sediment have been outlined by Guy and others (1963). These are:

1. Public-program adjustments, including a specific policy toward potential problems, planning and zoning, local ordinances, and assistance to insure proper judicial interpretation.

2. Erosion-control measures, including the proper use of vegetation for both temporary and permanent control, diversions and bench terraces, stabilization structures, storm drainage systems, storage of excess rainfall on lots, floodwater retarding structures, and the provision of "blue-green areas," usually parks, along streams and in headwater areas having critical runoff.

3. Adequate education of both the general public and urban officials is essential. Such education in turn requires adequate sediment information, without which neither 1 nor 2 can be effectively accomplished.

Attempts to control some of the sediment problems in the Los Angeles area have involved the construction of numerous "debris" basins on small streams draining steep foothill areas. Sediment yields of as much as 124,000 cubic yards per square mile per year have been noted to occur as long as 5 years after the accidental burning of the vegetal cover (Tatum, 1965, p. 891). The primary purpose of these debris basins is to prevent heavy sediment loads from clogging drains and streams in developed urban areas. Bank erosion and other sediment problems are reduced in the Los Angeles area by stabilization of banks and sometimes streambeds in an attempt to increase the flow capacity through urban areas.

A good example of an institution attempting to control sediment in urban development, and thus to eliminate or reduce many sediment problems, is Montgomery County, Md. It was the first county (July 1965) to adopt a "Sediment Control Program" that requires approval of subdivision development plans by the Department of Public Works, which in turn is in consultation with the Soil Conservation Service. If the developers' plan for erosion and sediment control seems inadequate, then the Soil Conservation Service is asked to recommend suitable measures. Sometimes the measures may include only revision in timing and location of construction activity. In October 1966, the Fairfax (Va.) Board of Supervisors adopted a set of subdivision land-erosion-control measures similar to those of Montgomery County.

Sediment control is also being effected as a result of Executive Order 11258 issued in 1966 through the authority of the Water Quality Act of 1965. This order requires a review of all Federal and federally aided operations where there is a significant potential for reduction of water pollution by sediment. The reviewers may prescribe suitable remedial practices as necessary. This should prove particularly significant in view of sediment problems in connection with urban and suburban highway construction (Vice, Guy, and Ferguson, 1969).

Conclusions

Much of the disturbed soil in urban construction areas erodes and becomes sediment in streams; the sediment damages water-control works and aquatic habitat, degrades water quality, increases flood damages, and lowers the environmental attractiveness. During the process of stabilization of an area after construction, streams tend to erode their beds and banks as a result of increased runoff. All such sediment, whether from construction erosion or from channel erosion, is transported by streams and often deposited somewhere downstream at a location previously assigned to the movement or storage of water.

Documentation of erosion sources and amounts, of sediment concentration in runoff, of stream-channel changes, and of the location and amounts of deposition together with an economic analysis of sediment damages and a pertinent research program will provide the knowledge needed to find the best solutions to a wide variety of existing and future urban sediment problems. Aside from the knowledge needed for better design of systems, documentation of sediment conditions will provide baseline information from which damages, both on site and downstream, can be evaluated. Defense against damage claims often rests upon attempts to demonstrate that the claimant had no knowledge of preexisting conditions, that the source of damages was not discernable, or that conditions had always been so.

Increasing numbers of communities will likely attempt to alleviate their many sediment problems because of the adverse effects of such problems on the local environment. The public sentiment needed to support such programs to control sediment is built from a series of events that restrict, offend, or otherwise concern people.

References

American Public Works Association, 1969, Water pollution aspects of urban runoff: Federal Water Pollution Control Adm., Pub. WP-20-15, 272 p.

Anderson, D. G., 1968, Effects of urban development on floods in northern Virginia: U. S. Geol. Survey open-file report, 26 p.

Brown, C. B., 1948, Perspective on sedimentation—purpose of conference: Federal Inter-Agency Sedimentation Conf., Denver, Colo., 1947, Proc., U. S. Bur. Reclamation, p. 307.

Busby, C. E., 1962, Some legal aspects of sedimentation: Am. Soc. Civil Engineers Trans., v. 127, pt. I, p. 1007–1044.

——— 1967, Aspects of American sedimentation law: Jour. Soil and Water Conserv., v. 22, no. 3, p. 107–109.

Dawdy, D. R., 1967, Knowledge of sedimentation in urban environments: Am. Soc. Civil Engineers Proc., v. 93, no. HY6, p. 235–245.

Ferguson, G. E., and Guy, H. P., 1970, Sedimentation as an environmental problem: Jour. Soil and Water Conserv. (In press.)

Guy, H. P., 1964, An analysis of some storm-period variables affecting stream sediment transport: U. S. Geol. Survey Prof. Paper 462-E, 46 p.

——— 1965, Residential construction and sedimentation at Kensington, Md.: Federal Inter-Agency Sedimentation Conf., Jackson, Miss., 1963, Proc., U. S. Dept. Agriculture Misc. Pub. 970, p. 30–37.

——— 1967, Research needs regarding sediment and urbanization: Am. Soc. Civil Engineers Proc, v. 93, no. HY6, p. 247–254.

Guy, H. P., and Ferguson, G. E., 1962, Sediment in small reservoirs due to urbanization: Am. Soc. Civil Engineers, Proc., v. 88, no. HY2, p. 27–37.

Guy, H. P., and others, 1963, A program for sediment control in the Washington Metropolitan Region: Washington, D. C., Interstate Comm. Potomac River Basin, May, 48 p.

Leopold, L. B., 1968, Hydrology for urban land planning—a guidebook on the hydrologic effects of urban land use: U. S. Geol. Survey Circ. 554, 18 p.

Maddock, Thomas, Jr., 1969, Economic aspects of sedimentation: Am. Soc. Civil Engineers Proc., v. 95, no. HY1, p. 191–207.

Moore, W. R., and Smith, C. E., 1968, Erosion control in relation to watershed management: Am. Soc. Civil Engineers Proc., v. 94, no. IR3, p. 321–331.

Peters, J. C., 1967, Effects on a trout stream of sediment from agricultural practices: Jour. Wildlife Management, v. 31, no. 4, p. 805–812.

37   Hydrologic Implications of Solid-Waste Disposal

William J. Schneider

Schneider, W. J., 1970, "Hydrologic Implications of Solid-Waste Disposal," *U. S. Geol. Survey Circ. 601-F*, 10 pp. Reprinted by permission of the author.

Mr. Schneider is on the staff of the United States Geological Survey.

Introduction

The disposal of solid-waste material—principally garbage and rubbish—is primarily an urban problem. However, unlike liquid waste disposal of sewage and industrial effluents, the problem has received only limited recognition. It is common practice in many metropolitan areas to overlook or ignore the consequences of waste-disposal programs. The full scope of the problem, though, cannot be ignored.

The urban population of the United States is now producing an estimated 1,400 million pounds of solid wastes each day. Disposal of these wastes is a major problem of all cities. In many instances, seemingly endless streams of trucks and railroad cars haul these wastes long distances—as much as hundreds of miles—to disposal sites. Based on a volume estimate of 5.7 cubic yards per ton of waste, this refuse is sufficient to cover more than 400 acres of land per day to a depth of 10 feet. Local governments spend an estimated $3 billion each year on collection and disposal, a sum exceeded in local budgets only by expenditures for schools and roads.

The disposal of these solid wastes poses many problems to local government agencies. Unfortunately, the problem is handled by many governments on the basis of expediency without due regard to environmental considerations. Garbage and rubbish are collected, hauled minimum distances commensurate with public acceptance, and dumped. Occasionally, the waste is either burned or mixed with soil to provide landfill. As long as the procedure removes the refuse and as long as the disposal site is not a health hazard and does not offend esthetic values too greatly, the operation is considered successful. Overlooked or even ignored is the effect of the disposal on the total environment, including the water resources of the area. Although the disposal of solid wastes can create many serious health, esthetic, and environmental problems, only the hydrologic implications—the effect upon water resources—are considered in this report.

Types of Solid Wastes

Our urban society generates many types of solid wastes. Each may exert a different influence on the water resources of an area. In order to understand the effect of each type, it is necessary to identify the various types as to the principal constituents. Table 1 lists the various categories and sources of refuse material primarily generated by urban activities. Not included are wastes from industries and processing plants; hazardous, pathological, or radioactive wastes from institutions and industries; solids and sludge from sewage-treatment plants; and other special types of solid wastes. These items usually pose special handling problems and are usually not a part of normal municipal solid-waste-disposal programs. The following descriptions of the categories of solid wastes are abbreviated from descriptions by the American Public Works Association (1966).

Waste refers to useless, unused, unwanted, or discarded materials including solids, liquids, and gases.

Refuse refers to solid wastes which can be classified in several different ways. One of the most useful classifications is based on the kinds of material: garbage, rubbish, ashes, street refuse, dead animals, abandoned automobiles, industrial wastes, demolition wastes, construction wastes, sewage solids, and hazardous and special wastes.

Table 1 Classification of refuse materials [Adapted from American Public Works Association (1966)]

Kind of refuse	Composition	Source
Garbage	Wastes from preparation, cooking, and serving of food; market wastes; wastes from handling, storage, and sale of produce.	Households, restaurants, institutions, stores, and markets.
Rubbish	Combustible: paper, cartons, boxes, barrels, wood, excelsior, tree branches, yard trimmings, wood furniture, bedding, and dunnage. Noncombustible: metals, tin cans, metal furniture, dirt, glass, crockery, and minerals.	Do.
Ashes	Residue from fires used for cooking and heating and from onsite incineration.	Do.
Trash from streets	Sweepings, dirt, leaves, catch-basin dirt, and contents of litter receptacles.	Streets, sidewalks, alleys, vacant lots.
Dead animals	Cats, dogs, horses, and cows	Do.
Abandoned vehicles	Unwanted cars and trucks left on public property	Do.
Demolition wastes	Lumber, pipes, brick, masonry, and other construction materials from razed buildings and other structures.	Demolition sites to be used for new buildings, renewal projects, and expressways.
Construction wastes	Scrap lumber, pipe, and other construction materials	New construction and remodeling.

Garbage is the animal and vegetable waste resulting from the handling, preparation, and cooking of foods. It is composed largely of putrescible organic matter and its natural moisture. It originates primarily in home kitchens, stores, markets, restaurants, and other places where food is stored, prepared, or served.

Rubbish consists of both combustible and noncombustible solid wastes from homes, stores, and institutions. Combustible rubbish is the organic component of refuse and consists of a wide variety of matter that includes paper, rags, cartons, boxes, wood, furniture, bedding, rubber, plastics, leather, tree branches, and lawn trimmings. Noncombustible rubbish is the inorganic component of refuse and consists of tin cans, heavy metal, mineral matter, glass, crockery, metal furniture, and similar materials.

Ashes are the residue from wood, coke, coal, and other combustible materials burned in homes, stores, institutions, and other establishments for heating, cooking, and disposing of other combustible materials.

Street refuse is material picked up by manual and mechanical sweeping of streets and sidewalks and is the debris from the public litter receptacles. It includes paper, dirt, leaves, and other similar materials.

Dead animals are those that die naturally or from disease or are accidentally killed. Not included in this category are condemned animals or parts of animals from slaughterhouses which are normally considered as industrial waste matter.

Abandoned vehicles include passenger automobiles, trucks, and trailers that are no longer useful and have been left on city streets and in other public places.

Methods of Solid-Waste Disposal

The disposal of these solid wastes generated by our urban environment is generally accomplished by one or more of six methods. All are currently in use to one degree or another in various parts of the United States. To a large extent, the method of waste disposal in any particular area depends upon local conditions and, to some extent, upon public attitude. In many areas several methods are employed. Each has its unique relation to the water resources of the area. The six general methods of solid waste disposal are:
1. Open dumps.
2. Sanitary landfill.
3. Incineration.
4. Onsite disposal.
5. Feeding of garbage to swine.
6. Composting.

Open Dumps

Open dumps are by far the oldest and most prevalent method of disposing of solid wastes. In a recent survey, 371 cities out of 1,118 surveyed stated that this method was emphasized within their jurisdictions. In many cases, the dump sites are located indiscriminately wherever land can be obtained for this purpose. Practices at open dumps differ. In some dumps, the refuse is periodically leveled and compacted; in other dumps the refuse is piled as high as equipment will permit. At some sites, the solid wastes are ignited and allowed to burn to reduce volume. In general, though, little effort is expended to prevent the nuisance and health hazards that frequently accompany open dumps.

Sanitary Landfill

As early as 1904, garbage was buried to provide landfill. Although in subsequent years, the practice was used by many cities, the technique of sanitary landfill as we know it today did not emerge until the late 1930's. By 1945, almost 100 cities were using the practice, and by 1960 more than 1,400 cities were disposing of their solid wastes by this method.

Sanitary landfill consists of alternate layers of compacted refuse and soil. Each day the refuse is deposited, compacted, and covered with a layer of soil. Two types of sanitary landfill are common: area landfill on essentially flat land sites, and depression landfill in natural or manmade ravines, gulleys, or pits. Depth of the landfill depends largely on local conditions, types of equipment, availability of land, and other such factors, but it commonly ranges from about 7 feet to as much as 40 feet as practiced by New York City.

In normal operation, the refuse is deposited and compacted and covered with a minimum of 6 inches of compacted soil at the end of each working period or more frequently, depending upon the depth of refuse compacted. Normally about a 1:4 cover ratio is satisfactory; that is, 1 foot of soil cover for each 4-foot layer of compacted refuse. Ratios as high as 1:8, however, have been used. The final cover is at least 2 feet of compacted soil to prevent the problems associated with open dumps.

Incineration

Incineration is the process of reducing combustible wastes to inert residue by burning at high temperatures of about 1,700° to 1,800°F. At these temperatures all combustible materials are consumed, leaving a residue of ash and noncombustibles having a volume of 5 to 25 percent of the original volume.

Although incineration greatly reduces the volume and changes the material to inorganic matter, the problem of disposal is still present. Much of the residue is hauled to disposal sites or is used for landfill, although the land required for disposal of the residue is about one-third to one-half of that required for sanitary landfill. Some cities require that combustible materials be separated from noncombustibles prior to collection, while others use magnetic devices to extract ferrous metal for salvage.

The combination of urban growth, increasing per-capita output of refuse, and the rising costs of land for sanitary landfills has stimulated the use of incineration for solid-waste disposal. Today, there are an estimated 600 central-incinerator plants in the United States with a total capacity of about 150,000 tons per day.

Onsite Disposal

With the increasing rate of production of solid wastes in the urban environment, there is a growing trend toward handling this waste in the home, apartment, and institution. Onsite disposal has become increasingly popular during the past decade as a way of minimizing the waste problem at its source. Most widely used devices for onsite disposal are incinerators and garbage grinders.

Onsite incineration is used widely in apartment houses and institutions. The incinerators do, however, require constant attention to insure proper operation and complete combustion. Domestic incinerators for use in individual homes are not a major factor in solid-waste disposal, nor are they likely to be a major factor in the near future. Maintenance and operating problems are usually considerable.

Garbage grinders, on the other hand, are becoming increasingly prevalent in homes for disposal of kitchen food wastes. It is estimated that more than a million grinders are now in home use. The grinders are installed in the waste pipe from the kitchen sink; food wastes are simply scraped into the grinder, the grinder is started, and the water turned on. The garbage is ground and flushed into the sanitary-sewer system. In some local communities, garbage grinders have been installed in every residence as required by local ordinance.

Swine Feed

The feeding of garbage to swine has been an accepted way of disposing of the garbage part of solid wastes from urban areas for quite some time. Even as late as 1960, this method was employed in 110 American cities out of 1,118 cities surveyed on their solid-waste-disposal practices. In addition to the municipal practices of using garbage for swine feed, many cities and municipalities permit private haulers to service restaurants and institutions to collect garbage for swine feed. The feeding of raw garbage led to a widespread virus disease in the middle 1950's, which affected more than 400,000 swine. As a result, all States now require that garbage be cooked before feeding to destroy contaminating bacteria and viruses. However, according to the American Public Works Association (1966), more than 10,000 tons of food wastes—about 25 percent of the total quantity of garbage produced—is still used daily in the United States as swine feed.

Composting

Composting is the biochemical decomposition of organic materials to a humuslike material. As practiced for solid-waste disposal, it is the rapid but partial decomposition of the moist, solid-organic matter by aerobic organisms under controlled conditions. The end product is useful as a soil conditioner and fertilizer. The process is normally carried out in mechanical digesters.

Although popular in Europe and Asia where intensive farming creates a demand for the compost, the method is not used widely in the United States at this time. Composting of solid-organic wastes is not practiced on a full-scale basis in any large city today. Although there are several pilot plants in operation, it does not seem likely that composting will be a major method of solid-waste disposal.

The selection of one or more of these methods of solid-waste disposal by a municipality depends largely on the character of the municipality. Geographic location, climate, standard of living, population distribution, and public attitudes play important roles in the selection. In general, the natural resources and environmental factors have been given only small recognition

in this selection. Only recently has there been a considerable upsurge of scientific interest in the effects of solid-waste disposal on our water resources.

Hydrologic Implications

Types of Pollution

The disposition of solid wastes in open areas carries with it an inherent potential for pollution of water resources, regardless of the manner of disposal or the composition of the waste material. Of the six principal methods of solid-waste disposal, only swine feeding and composting offer no direct possibility of pollution of water resources from the waste material itself. Quite the contrary: properly composted garbage is a soil conditioner that improves the permeability of the soil and may actually assist in improving the quality of water that percolates through it. Although the cooked garbage that is fed to swine does not directly contribute to pollution of water resources, the manure from the feedlots may cause serious problems if not managed properly.

The type of pollution that may arise is directly related to the type of refuse and the manner of disposal. Leachates from open dumps and sanitary landfill usually contain both biological and chemical constituents. Organic matter, decomposing under aerobic conditions, produces carbon dioxide which combines with the leaching water to form carbonic acid. This, in turn, acts upon metals in the refuse and upon calcareous materials in the soil and rocks, resulting in increasing hardness of the water. Under aerobic conditions, bacterial action decomposes organic refuse, releasing ammonia, which is ultimately oxidized to form nitrate. In both land-fills and open dumps, where decomposition is accomplished by bacterial action, the leachate has a high biochemical oxygen demand (BOD).

Table 2 indicates the magnitude of the constituents leached from solid wastes under various conditions. These data were compiled by Hughes (1967) from various sources.

Relation to Hydrologic Regimen

That part of the hydrologic regimen associated with pollution from solid-waste disposal begins with precipitation reaching the land surface and ends

with the water reaching streams from either overland or subsurface flow. The manner in which this precipitation moves through this part of the cycle determines whether or not the water resource will become polluted.

Precipitation on the refuse-disposal site will either infiltrate the refuse or run off as overland flow. In open dumps, there is little likelihood of direct runoff unless the refuse is highly compacted. In sanitary landfills, the rate of infiltration is governed by the permeability and infiltration capacity of the soil used as cover for the refuse. A part of the water entering the refuse

Table 2 Percentages of materials leached from refuse and ash, based on weight of refuse as received [Adapted from Hughes (1967)]

Material leached	Percentage leached under given conditions*					
	1	2	3	4	5	6
Permanganate value 30 min	0.039					
Do 4 hr	.060	0.037				
Chloride	.105	.127		0.11	0.087	
Ammonia nitrogen	.055	.037		.036		
Biochemical oxygen demand	.515	.249		1.27		
Organic carbon	.285	.163				
Sulfate	.130	.084		.011	.22	0.30
Sulfide	.011					
Albumin nitrogen	.005					
Alkalinity (as $CaCO_3$)				0.39	0.042	
Calcium				.08	.021	2.57
Magnesium				.015	.014	.24
Sodium			0.260	.075	.078	.29
Potassium			.135	.09	.049	.38
Total iron				.01		
Inorganic phosphate				.0007		
Nitrate					.0025	
Organic nitrogen	.0075	.0072		.016		

* Conditions of leaching:
1. Analyses of leachate from domestic refuse deposited in standing water.
2. Analyses of leachate from domestic refuse deposited in unsaturated environment and leached only by natural precipitation.
3. Material leached in laboratory before and after ignition.
4. Domestic refuse leached by water in a test bin.
5. Leaching of incinerator ash in a test bin by water.
6. Leaching of incinerator ash in a test bin by acid.

percolates downward to the soil zone and eventually to the water table. If the water table is above the bottom of the refuse deposit, the percolating water travels only vertically through the refuse to the water table. During the vertical-percolation process the water leaches both organic and inorganic constituents from the refuse.

Upon reaching the water table, the leachate becomes part of and moves with the ground-water flow system. As part of this flow system, the leachate may move laterally in the direction of the water-table slope to a point of discharge at the land surface. In general, the slope of the water table is in the same direction as the slope of the land. The generalized movement of leachate in this part of the hydrologic cycle is shown in Fig. 1.

There are several well-documented cases of pollution caused by leachates from solid-waste-disposal sites, especially those compiled by the California

Water Pollution Control Board (1961). Most of these studies, however, were able to determine only that the pollution originated from solid-waste-disposal sites; few, if any, data on the gross magnitude of the pollution and its fate in the hydrologic cycle are available.

One well-documented case is that of pollution from about 650,000 cubic yards of refuse deposited in a garbage dump near Krefield, Germany, over a 15-year period in the early 1900's. High salt concentrations and hardness were detected in ground water about a mile downgradient from the site within 10 years of operation. Concentrations up to 260 mg/l (milligrams per liter) of chloride and a hardness of 900 mg/l were measured—an increase of more than sixfold in chloride concentration and fourfold in hardness. The pattern of pumping of wells in the area precludes detailed understanding of the course of the pollution in the ground

FIG. 1. Generalized movement of leachate through the land phase of the hydrologic cycle.

water, but wells near the dumping site were still contaminated 18 years later.

In Schirrhof, Germany, ashes and refuse dumped into an empty pit extending below the water table resulted in contamination of wells about 2,000 feet downstream. The contamination occurred 15 years after the dump was covered; measures of hardness up to 1,150 mg/l were recorded as compared with 200 mg/l prior to the contamination.

In Surrey County, England, household refuse dumped into gravel pits polluted the ground water in the vicinity. Refuse was dumped directly into the 20-foot-deep pits where water depth averaged about 12 feet. Maximum rate of dumping was about 100,000 tons per year over a 6-year period, and this occurred during the latter part of the period of use (1954–60). Limited observations on water quality extending less than a year after the closing of the pits showed chloride concentrations ranging from 800 mg/l at the dump site, through 290 mg/l in downgradient adjacent gravel pits, to 70 mg/l in pits 3,500 feet away. Organic and bacterial pollution were detected within half a mile of the dumping sites, but not beyond. Because of the limited study period and the slow travel of the pollutants, the maximum extent of pollution was not determined.

More recently, a study was made of the ground-water quality associated with four sanitary landfill sites in northeastern Illinois (Hughes and others, 1969). At the DuPage County site, total solids of more than 12,500 mg/l and chloride contents of more than 2,250 mg/l were measured in samples collected about 20 feet below land surface under the fill. These were by far the highest concentrations measured at any of the four sites. In general, total solids ranged from 2,000–3,000 mg/l under the fill to as low as 223 mg/l adjacent to the fill.

Hydrologic Controls

The movement of leachate from a waste-disposal site is governed by the physical environment. Where the wastes are above the water table, both chemical and biological contaminants in the leachate move vertically through the zone of aeration at a rate dependent in part upon the properties of the soils. The chemical contaminants, being in solution, generally tend to travel faster than biological contaminants. Sandy or silty soils especially retard particulate biological contaminants and often filter them from the percolating leachate. The chemical contaminants, however, may be carried by the leachate water to the water table where they enter the ground-water flow system and move according to the hydraulics of that system. Thus, the potential for pollution in the hydrologic system depends upon the mobility of the contaminant, its accessibility to the ground-water reservoir, and the hydraulic characteristics of that reservoir.

The character and strength of the leachate are dependent in part upon the length of time that infiltrated water is in contact with the refuse and the amount of infiltrated water. Thus, in areas of high rainfall the pollution potential is greater than in less humid areas. In semiarid areas there may be little or no pollution potential because all infiltrated water is either absorbed by the refuse or is held as soil moisture and is ultimately evaporated. In areas of shallow water table, where refuse is in constant contact with the ground water, leaching is a continual process producing maximum potential for ground-water pollution.

The ability of the leachate to seep from the refuse to the ground-water reservoir is another factor in the degree of pollution of an aquifer. Permeable soils permit rapid movement; although some filtering of biological contamination may take place, the chemical contamination is generally free to move rapidly under the influence of gravity to the water table. Less permeable soils, such as clays, retard the movement of the leachate, and often restrict the leachate to the local vicinity of the refuse. Under such conditions, pollution is frequently limited to the local shallow ground-water reservoir and contamination of deeper lying aquifers is negligible.

Leachate that does reach the water table and enters an aquifer is then subject to the hydraulic characteristics of the aquifer. Because the configuration of the water table generally reflects the configuration of the land surface, the leachate flows downgradient under the influence of gravity from upland areas to stream valleys, where it discharges as base flow to the stream systems. The rate of flow is dependent upon the permeability of the rock material of the aquifer and on the slope of the water table. In flat areas or areas of gentle relief, minor local topographic variations may have no effect on the configuration of the water table, and movement of ground water may be uniform over large areas.

In some places dipping confined aquifers crop out in upland areas and thus are exposed to recharge. Contaminants entering the aquifer in these areas move downgradient into the confined parts of the aquifer. Although there is usually some minor leakage to confining beds above and below the aquifer, the contaminants in general will be confined to the particular aquifer, and water-supply wells tapping that aquifer will thus be subject to contamination to the extent that the contaminants are able to move from the outcrop to the wells.

Optimum conditions for pollution of the ground-water reservoir exist where the water table is at or near land surface, subjecting the solid waste to continual direct contact with the water. Such conditions commonly exist where abandoned quarries that penetrate the ground-water reservoir are used as refuse-disposal sites. The continual contact of the water with the refuse produces a strong leachate highly contaminated both biologically and chemically. Under hydrogeologic conditions of permeable materials and steep hydraulic gradients, the leachate may move rapidly through the ground-water system and pollute extensive areas. The hydrologic effects of solid-waste disposal in four geologic environments are shown in Fig. 2.

Figure 2A illustrates a waste-disposal site in a permeable environment. The waste is shown in contact with the ground water in a permeable sand-and-gravel aquifer underlain by confining beds of relatively impermeable shale. In this case, the potential for pollution is high because conditions of both high infiltration and direct contact between wastes and ground water exist. Because of the permeability of the aquifer, the contaminants move downgradient with the water in the aquifer and are diffused and diluted during this move-

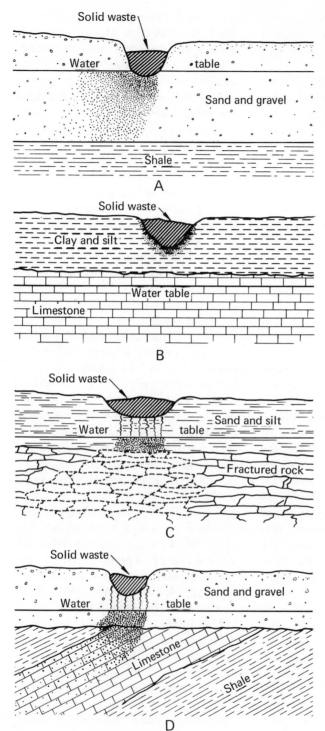

FIG. 2. Effects on ground-water resources of solid-waste disposal at a site (*A*) in a permeable environment, (*B*) in a relatively impermeable environment, (*C*) underlain by a fractured-rock aquifer, and (*D*) underlain by a dipping-rock aquifer. Leachate shown by dots.

ment. In areas where the water table is below the bottom of the waste material, the degree of contamination is lessened because the wastes are no longer in direct contact with the ground water. In this case, leachate from the wastes moves vertically through the zone of aeration to the water table. It then enters the ground water and moves downgradient as in the case of a shallow water table.

Figure 2B illustrates a waste-disposal site in a relatively impermeable environment. In humid areas, the water table may be near land surface, and the disposed waste may or may not be in direct contact with the ground water. In the illustration, ground water is shown confined to the underlying limestone aquifer. The relative impermeability of the overburden prevents significant infiltration of the rainfall; consequently there is only minor leaching of contaminants from the wastes. Pollution is confined locally to the vicinity of the waste-disposal site; movement in all directions is inhibited by the inability of the water to move through the tight soils. If significant amounts of rainfall penetrate the wastes, a local perched water table may develop in the vicinity of the fill, and that water will likely be highly contaminated, both chemically and bacteriologically.

Figure 2C illustrates a waste-disposal site above a fractured-rock aquifer. The position of the water table in the overburden relative to the waste-disposal site is dependent upon the amount of infiltration and the geometry of the ground-water flow system. The water table shown here is below the body of waste. In this case, the potential for pollution is not high because of limited vertical movement of the leachate to the water table. However, the contaminants that reach the fractured-rock zone may move more readily in the general direction of the ground-water flow. Dispersion of the contaminants is limited because the flow is confined to the fracture zones. A thin, highly permeable overburden with a shallow water table (similar to that shown in Fig. 2A) overlying the fractured rock would provide an ideal condition for widespread ground-water pollution.

Figure 2D illustrates a waste-disposal site in a geologic setting in which dipping aquifers are overlain by permeable sands and gravels. In this illustration, the waste-disposal site is shown directly above a permeable limestone aquifer. Here leachate from the landfill travels through the sand and enters the limestone aquifer as recharge. Again, the strength of the leachate depends in part upon whether the water table is in direct contact with the waste. Leachate will move downgradient with the ground-water flow in both the sands and gravels and the limestone, as shown in the illustration. If the waste-disposal site were located above the less permeable shale, most of the leachate would move downgradient through the sand and gravel, with very little penetrating the relatively impermeable shale as recharge. However, in its downgradient movement, it would enter any other permeable formations as recharge.

A high pollution potential exists also where waste-disposal sites are located on flood plains adjacent to streams. Water-table levels generally are near land surface in flood-plain areas, especially during the usual period of high water in winter and spring throughout much of the humid areas of the United States. In such environments the water may have contact with the refuse for extended periods, giving rise to concentrated leachate. The contaminated water moves through the flood-plain deposits and discharges into the stream during low-flow periods when the bulk of the streamflow is from ground-water discharge. The degree of pollution of the stream depends upon the concentration of the leachate, the amount of leachate entering the stream, and the available streamflow for dilution.

Hydrologic Considerations in Site Selection

It is obvious that our current national policy of pollution abatement and protection of our natural environment requires full consideration of the water resources in selection of sites for solid-waste disposal. To date, with few exceptions, these considerations have been on a local scale, dealing primarily with the hydrological characteristics of the immediate site.

The American Society of Civil Engineers in a manual on sanitary landfill (American Society of Civil Engineers, 1959) discussed site selection from a hydrologic standpoint as follows:

In choosing a site for the location of a sanitary landfill, consideration must be given to underground and surface water supplies. The danger of polluting water supplies should not be overlooked.

The report states further that:

Sufficient surface drainage should be provided to assure minimum runoff to and into the fill. Also, surface drainage should prevent quantities of water from causing erosion or washing of the fill . . .

Although some apprehension has been expressed about the underground water supply pollution of sanitary landfills, there has been little, if any, experience to indicate that a properly located sanitary landfill will give rise to underground pollution problems. It is axiomatic, of course, that when a waste material is disposed of on land, the proximity of water supplies, both underground and surface, should be considered . . . Also, special attention should be given areas having rock strata near the surface of the ground. For example, limestone strata may have solution channels or crevices through which pollution contamination may travel. Sanitary landfills should not be located on rock strata without studying the hazards involved. In any case, refuse must not be placed in mines or similar places where resulting seepage or leachate may be carried to water-bearing strata or wells . . . In summary, under certain geological conditions, there is a real potential danger of chemical and bacteriological pollution of ground water by sanitary landfills. Therefore, it is necessary that competent engineering advice be sought in determining the location of a sanitary landfill.

Consideration of hydrology in site selection is required by law in several States. Section 19–13–B24a of the Connecticut Public Health Code requires that:

No refuse shall be deposited in such manner that refuse or leaching from it shall cause or contribute to pollution or contamination of any ground or surface water on neighboring properties. No refuse shall be deposited within 50 feet of the high water mark of a watercourse or on land where it may be carried into an adjacent watercourse by surface or storm water except in accordance with Section 25–24 of the General Statutes which require approval of the Water Resources Commission.

The rules and regulations of the Illinois Department of Public Health require that:

The surface contour of the area shall be such that surface runoff will not flow into or through the operational or completed fill area. Grading, diking, terracing, diversion ditches, or tilling may be approved when practical. Areas having high ground water tables may be restricted to landfill operations which will maintain a safe vertical distance between deposited refuse and the maximum water table elevation. Any operation which proposes to deposit refuse within or near the maximum water table elevation shall include corrective or preventive measures which will prevent contamination of the ground-water stratum. Monitoring facilities may be required.

Other States have similar regulations.

A common denominator in these sets of recommendations is the general concern for the onsite pollutional aspect. This is characteristic of most current approaches, especially from the engineering and legislative viewpoints. Another characteristic is the restrictive approach to the problem. Hydrologic conditions are documented under which disposal of solid wastes is either discouraged or prohibited. In general, the pollutional problem is treated more in local than in regional context. These are, of course, important considerations and should be followed in any site selection. In fact, even stronger guidelines are desirable, to the extent of requiring detailed knowledge of the extent and movement of potential pollution at any site before the site is activated.

The water resource, however, must be considered also as a regional resource, not just a localized factor. As such, it should be considered in a regional concept in its relation to solid-waste disposal. This, of course, requires that adequate regional information on the water resource is available. Given such information, the planner can weigh all available alternatives and insure that the final site selection is compatible with comprehensive regional planning goals and environmental protection. The Northwestern Illinois Planning Commission followed this comprehensive approach in developing its recommendations on refuse-disposal needs and practices in northeastern Illinois (Sheaffer and others, 1963).

It is, of course, quite possible that, in the comprehensive approach, some otherwise optimum sites for solid-waste disposal may be only marginally acceptable from a hydrologic viewpoint. Under such conditions detailed information on the hydrology should be obtained and detailed evaluations made of the impact of the potential waste disposal before the site is put into use; the actual impact should then be monitored during and after use. In general, although such studies are desirable for all solid-waste-disposal sites, they are essential where geologic, hydrologic, or other data indicate a possibility of undesirable pollutional effects.

The problem of solid-waste disposal is one of the most serious problems of urban areas. The ever-increasing emphasis on protection and preservation of natural resources through regional planning is evident today. The implementation of these commitments and goals can insure adequate protection of vital water resources from pollution by disposal of solid wastes.

References

American Public Works Association, 1966, Municipal refuse disposal: Chicago, Ill., Public Adm. Service, 528 p.

American Society of Civil Engineers, Committee on Sanitary Landfill Practices, 1959, Sanitary landfill: Am. Soc. Civil Engineers Eng. Practices Manual 39, 61 p.

Anderson, J. R., and Dornbush, J. N., 1967, Influence of sanitary landfill on ground water quality: Am. Water Works Assoc. Jour., April 1967, p. 457–470.

California Water Pollution Control Board, 1961, Effects of refuse dumps on ground water quality: California Water Pollution Control Board Pub. 24, 107 p.

Hughes, G. M., 1967, Selection of refuse disposal sites in northeastern Illinois: Illinois Geol. Sur. Environmental Geology Note 17, 18 p.

Hughes, G. M., Landon, R. A., and Farvolden, R. N., 1969, Hydrogeology of solid waste disposal sites in northeastern Illinois: Washington, D. C., U. S. Public Health Service, 137 p.

Sheaffer, J. R., von Boehm, B., and Hackett, J. E., 1963, Refuse disposal needs and practices in northeastern Illinois: Chicago, Ill., Northeastern Illinois Metropolitan Area Planning Comm. Tech. Rept. 3, 72 p.

38 Hydrogeologic Considerations in Liquid Waste Disposal

S. M. Born and D. A. Stephenson

Municipal wastes have been disposed of by irrigation on sewage farms for almost a century, but the idea of disposing of industrial wastes by irrigation has evolved primarily since World War II.

The earliest irrigation disposal method was ridge-and-furrow irrigation, a process by which wastes are transported to furrowed plots of land

Born, S. M. and Stephenson, D., 1969, "Hydrogeologic Considerations in Liquid Waste Disposal," Jour. Soil and Water Conservation, vol. 24, no. 2. Reprinted by permission of the authors and the Soil Conservation Society of America. Copyright 1969 by S. C. S. A.

Dr. Born is Project Leader, Environmental Resources Unit, University of Wisconsin Extension, Madison, Wisconsin. Dr. Stephenson is Associate Professor of Geology, University of Wisconsin, Madison, Wisconsin and chairman of the Water Resources Management Program at the university.

and allowed to infiltrate the soil. But ridge-and-furrow irrigation has several serious shortcomings. A comparatively large amount of reasonably level land is required for the disposal site, and the site requires clearing and preparation prior to the application of waste water. The ridge-and-furrow method is also prone to flooding, which creates odors and may damage crops. In recent years, pressing demands for more intensive use of land have further diminished the popularity of the system for disposal of industrial wastes. It is still used locally, however, for disposal of stabilized municipal wastes.

An improved technique for wastewater irrigation was developed in 1947 and was first used by a canning company in Hanover, Pennsylvania.[3] Effluent water was applied to the land by sprinklers, giving rise to the name "spray irrigation." Waste water is thus disposed of by infiltration and evaporation.

Spray-irrigation disposal systems have numerous advantages: (1) The possibility of creating odor nuisances is minimized since the waste water is aerated during the application process, and oxygen-deficient conditions resulting from ponding and surface flooding at the irrigation site can be avoided due to the mobility of the sprinkler system. (2) No special land preparation may be necessary, and sloping areas and woodlands can be irrigated. (3) Spray-irrigated land can be farmed. (4) The spray system is readily expanded to accommodate increased volumes of effluent, and the distribution system can be salvaged.

The method is not without its disadvantages. Unfavorable sites or poor management practices can lead to surface runoff from spray-irrigation areas. This runoff may be of sufficient magnitude to condemn the method. Wind can transport both sprayed effluent and odor to unwanted places. Some waste water cannot be sprayed without extensive pre-treatment, such as sedimentation with or without flocculants, cooling, and screening. Clogging of sprinkler nozzles by solids in the effluent or by precipitated chemicals can decrease disposal efficiency. Where practicable, however, spray irrigation is a satisfactory means of disposing of liquid wastes on land.

Spray-irrigation disposal systems vary widely in design, cost, and capacity. Choice of a system is largely controlled by the physical characteristics of the site. One efficient system, located at Seabrook Farms in New Jersey, disposes of 5 to 10 million gallons of process water daily on 84 wooded acres of loamy sand.[3] Total cost of the Seabrook installation was about $150,000.

Waste disposal by irrigation has benefits other than the immediate one of protecting surface-water quality. In some cases, nutrient-charged waste water can be used to fertilize cultivated lands. A team of scientists and engineers at Pennsylvania State University recently demonstrated that the application of treated sewage effluent to croplands increased hay yields 300 percent, corn yields 50 percent, corn silage yields 36 to 103 percent, and oat yields 17 to 51 percent.[4] Concentrations of various nutrients originally in the effluent were essentially removed from the plot. The crop functioned as a "living filter."

Augmentation of groundwater recharge by treated effluent water is another important potential benefit of irrigation with waste water. Regions long dependent on groundwater supplies are experiencing an overdraft on these reserves. The overdraft is expressed in terms of a declining water table, increased water cost, local water quality deterioration, and even a water shortage. Recharge by irrigation with waste water can provide a partial answer to this problem of depleted groundwater supplies. In the Pennsylvania State University experiment, 60 to 80 percent of the applied effluent entered the groundwater reservoir relatively free of nutrients. However, the potential danger of contaminating groundwater cannot be overemphasized.

The ideal approach to irrigation disposal of liquid wastes is to derive secondary benefits from the operation and simultaneously guard against endangering the quality of groundwater supplies. Careful selection of the disposal site and wise management of the irrigation installation maximizes the chance of achieving both of these goals. Fortunately, nature has provided a remarkable purification system of its own. Removal of solids and nutrients from effluent water is accomplished by the microbial population in the soil and by the soil and rock medium itself through adsorption by clays, ion exchange, precipitation, and filtration. Man can supplement the natural purification of irrigated waste water by renovation techniques such as the cropping practice mentioned previously.

Pollution from irrigated areas can be controlled by adequate preliminary evaluation of the proposed site with due consideration given to the geologic and hydrogeologic environments. These physical environments should be influential factors in the design of a waste-disposal system.

Determining Flow Systems

Definition of a groundwater flow system allows an operator of a plant producing liquid wastes to select the optimum disposal site available on his land and further permits him to know in which direction effluent waters will travel in the ground, at what rate they travel, and where they will surface. In general, the flow system of interest for irrigation purposes is a local (shallow) system; however, in some geologic environments, the local system is only a small element of a larger regional system where the flow path of the effluent is governed by a deeper flow pattern.

Until recently, surface-water bodies have been studied as entities separate from groundwater; now these systems are recognized as being interconnected and are studied as such. Groundwater is derived from surface water by infiltration through the soil and includes all water within the saturated zone below a water table. Thus, the upper limit of this zone of saturation defines the water table, which is a subdued replica of surface topography. A water table is high under uplands, and slopes toward lowlands. Where the land surface intersects the water table, a surface body of water is present.

Water in the ground ultimately returns to the surface and becomes run-off in the lowlands. Movement in a groundwater flow system is along flow paths from areas of high potential (upland or recharge zone) to areas of lower potential (lowland or discharge zone). Potential is water elevation expressed as feet above sea level. Lines connecting points of equal potential are called equipotential lines.

In a recharge zone, the groundwater gradient is downward from the water table; in a discharge zone, it is up toward the water table (Fig. 1). Evidence of a groundwater discharge zone is commonly a wetland area or marsh in humid regions and a playa or "alkali flat" in arid zones. Water may be present perennially in a discharge area because of the upward movement of groundwater. Irrigation, therefore, must be undertaken with caution in a discharge area because infiltration is at a minimum and the effluents remain on or near the surface.

The pattern of groundwater flow from a recharge to a discharge area constitutes a dynamic flow system.[5] A flow system is controlled by topog-

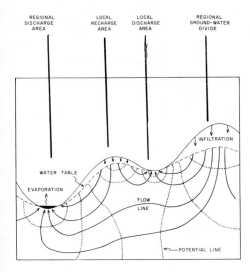

FIG. 1. Idealized groundwater flow system, homogenous soil conditions.

raphy but modified in flow direction and flow rate by the soil-rock conditions prevailing along individual flow paths. Groundwater flow systems can be defined in the field with empirical geologic and hydrogeologic techniques.

Each geographic area has unique rock-soil-water relationships since geology, topography, and climate vary regionally. On a gross pattern, however, it is likely that conclusions regarding flow systems for one area can be extrapolated to areas of similar or like environments. A mapped system has numerous applications with respect to water quality and quantity problems, including more efficient use of land for developmental, waste-disposal, and water supply purposes.

Effluent Infiltration and Movement

The ability of water to permeate the surface (infiltration capacity) is the critical element in efficient irrigation

disposal operations. Successful disposal of waste water, especially by spray or ridge-and-furrow irrigation, allows the effluent to infiltrate the ground and undergo natural purification (particularly clarification) while percolating through the geologic medium prior to being discharged from the area. This minimizes malodorous effects and the possibility of surface water contamination at the discharge point.

Infiltration capacity is controlled by a number of variables.[7] Topographic relief controls the disposition of surface runoff and, therefore, to a large degree, the amount of water available for infiltration at a given location. As noted previously, topography further controls groundwater gradients and, hence, how the flow system operates at any specified point. Infiltration in discharge areas of humid and subhumid regions is sometimes limited by a prevailing upward gradient and saturation of the soil due to a frequent vertical proximity of the water table and ground surface. In recharge portions of the flow system, the limiting factor controlling water intake is geological, that is, the nature of the surface material (Fig. 2).

Infiltration is also influenced by rock type and the rock's weathering history which determine the nature and extent of pore space, the depth to impermeable zones, and the texture of the ground surface. Rates of infiltration are further reduced by mechanical compaction (by livestock, man, machines, and rain) and by pore clogging resulting from the erosion of natural materials and the in-wash of organic materials and solids in many industrial effluents. Surface runoff, which increases the chance of direct surface-

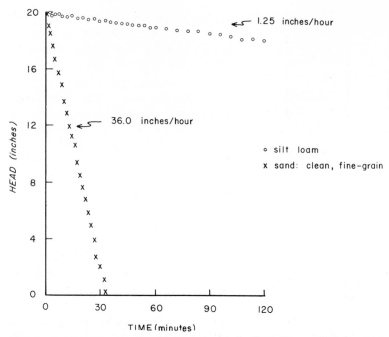

FIG. 2. Infiltration rate curves for two markedly different geologic materials (data from infiltration ring studies in northern Wisconsin by the authors).

water pollution, is one by-product of reduced infiltration.

Another influence on infiltration is the soil's state of saturation. Water is removed naturally from the soil profile by evaporation through the air-soil interface and by transpiration through vegetation. This removal produces a soil moisture deficiency which benefits the infiltration of effluent disposed of by irrigation. A dry soil will generally absorb at least twice as much water as a wet one. This fact explains the sometimes rapid decline in infiltration capacity that occurs under continued irrigation.

Having long-term records of rainfall and climate available is desirable so that pre-irrigation soil moisture conditions can be anticipated; such records are maintained by the U. S. Weather Bureau. A disposal site must be able to accommodate a volume of waste water over and above the natural "background" of precipitation. This consideration is especially important in designing a spray-irrigation system for a humid region.

In many operations, generation of waste water is almost continuous. Variations in precipitation and soil moisture—and, therefore, infiltration capacity—must be provided for in the system, either by creating temporary holding capacity and thereby reducing discharge during periods of rainfall, or by utilizing sufficient acreage to cope with precipitation and liquid-waste disposal simultaneously.

Once effluent infiltrates the ground, it eventually enters a groundwater flow system. Velocity of water within the saturated zone is controlled by permeability and gradient (Darcy's Law). The permeability of a material is defined as "the ability of a soil or rock to transmit fluids." Permeability in rocks and soils is controlled by the nature of the interconnected open space, either as pores between the grains, or fractures, or solution cavities.

Permeability of soil or rock samples collected in the field can be routinely measured in a laboratory with an instrument known as a permeameter. However, laboratory testing may not be accurate because the natural packing of the sample material is difficult to duplicate in the testing apparatus, and a small sample may not be representative of field conditions where discontinuities in the soil or rock medium frequently occur. Where accurate data are mandatory, pumping tests of wells must be conducted. The groundwater gradient can be determined in the field by monitoring groundwater levels in a group of sand-point observation wells.

Calculating the velocity of effluent movement in the ground permits disposal-site operators to predict the length of time required for decay of groundwater mounds built up during irrigation. In a sprinkler rotation system, such predictions enable scheduling of "rest periods" for different parts of the site. Knowing the velocity and direction of groundwater flow also enables the operator to predict where and when effluent which has entered the ground will discharge. By monitoring groundwater quality along its flow path, the operator can ensure that waste water is renovated and that contaminated water is not entering surface water at the point of discharge. In view of the present outcry over polluted water and the strong legislative response by state and federal governments, such information may prove valuable should the concerned industry become involved in pollution litigation.

Evaluating a Disposal Site

A thorough knowledge of geologic conditions is necessary where waste water is to be disposed of by irrigation. Of particular importance is the geology of unconsolidated, surficial deposits. The thickness, nature and distribution of these deposits define the effectiveness of filtration of effluent water, the adsorptive capacity of soil types present for the removal of specific constituents in the effluent, and the location of impermeable horizons which impede downward movement of the waste water. The amount of pore space in the geologic medium above the water table permits the geologist to calculate the storage capacity of the unsaturated portion of the soil profile. This potential storage volume, together with the rates of infiltration and ground-water movement, limits the application of effluent on the disposal site.

Infiltration rates can be determined in situ with an infiltrometer.[2] Reasonable estimates of infiltration and permeability can also be determined by comparing textural properties of sediments at the site (grain size, shape, amount of clay and silt) with known hydraulic characteristics for given sediment types. Where relatively crude data are acceptable, such information can be derived by microscopic inspection of samples, thereby saving the cost of laboratory permeameter tests or expensive well pumping tests.

Occurrence of bedrock valleys of

glacial or alluvial origin may permit the location of a satisfactory disposal site in otherwise unacceptable terrain. The existence of such valleys has been documented in geological studies of many areas. Relatively simple geophysical surveys can be used to define them where they are likely to be present.[1]

Zones of increased weathering, solution, and high permeability commonly are localized along fractures in geologic materials. Permeability along bedrock fractures is often many times greater than in adjacent, unfractured bedrock; velocity of groundwater movement is fast; and very little filtration may occur. Therefore, fractured bedrock, particularly limestone and dolomite, near the surface of a disposal site may provide "avenues of pollution" for downward-moving waste water. Fracture patterns oftentimes can be identified by field investigations and mapped on aerial photographs. The disposal site can then be positioned to minimize the danger of largely unfiltered, contaminated water being discharged from the area by these routes.

It was noted earlier that flow systems exist that are larger than local systems, in which case the discharge area is not necessarily the lowland adjacent to an upland recharge area. Instead, downward-moving water may follow a deeper flow system along fractures or solution channels and travel many miles along an unfiltered path to a regional discharge area[6] (Fig. 1). The source of pollutants at such a discharge point may be more difficult to locate, but the resulting pollution is of no less concern. Carbonate and volcanic terrains are especially susceptible to rapid travel of effluents. Regional geologic studies can be used to define

such areas and prevent their use for disposal sites.

Preliminary Studies Imperative

National concern over the deteriorating quality of our surface water resources has resulted in federal and state laws for regulating the disposal of polluting effluents. Many small industries have been affected and, of necessity, have considered land disposal of process waters. A common method adopted by these industries has been disposal of effluent onto an irrigation plot. This practice can and does degrade both surface water and groundwater at irrigation sites where inadequate technical consideration has been given to location and maintenance.

Giving adequate consideration to geologic and hydrogeologic factors in selecting and operating disposal sites for liquid wastes minimizes the pollution potential. Costs associated with preliminary investigations can be high; but weighed against the consequence of inadequate planning, these costs may never be cheaper and should be an inherent part of any budget for an irrigation disposal facility.

Notes

[1] Drescher, William J. 1956. *Ground water in Wisconsin.* Inf. Circ. No. 3. Wisc. Geol. Surv., Madison, Wisc. 37 pp.

[2] Johnson, A. I. 1963. *A field method for measurement of infiltration.* Water-Supply Paper 1544-F. U. S. Geol. Surv., Washington, D. C. 27 pp.

[3] Lawton, G. W., L. E. Engelbart, G. A. Rohlich, and N. Porges. 1960. *Effectiveness of spray irrigation as a method for the disposal of dairy plant waste.* Res. Rept. No. 6. Wisc. Agr. Exp. Sta., Madison, Wisc. 59 pp.

[4] Parizek, R. R., L. T. Kardos, W. E. Sopper, E. A. Myers, D. E. Davis, M. A. Farrell,

and J. B. Nesbitt. 1967. *Waste water renovation and conservation.* Study No. 23. Penn. State Univ., University Park, Penn. 71 pp.

[5] Toth, J. 1962. *A theory of ground water motion in small drainage basins in Central Alberta, Canada.* J. Geophys. Res. 67(11): 4375–4387.

[6] Winograd, I. J. 1962. *Interbasin movement of ground water at the Nevada Test Site.* Prof. Paper 450-C. U. S. Geol. Surv., Washington, D. C. pp. C108–C111.

[7] Wisler, C. O., and E. F. Brater. 1959. *Hydrology.* John Wiley and Sons, New York, N. Y.

39   Disposal of Septic Tank Effluent in Soils

John M. Cain and M. T. Beatty

Before World War II, septic tank systems were used mainly on farms and for widely separated residences in largely rural areas. During the postwar building boom, septic tanks were employed in many subdivisions as areas beyond city sewage disposal facilities were rapidly developed. At present, it is estimated by Bendixen[3] that 25 percent of the nation's population depends on waste disposal through soil absorption.

The septic tank used today for individual homes is essentially the same in form as that used in the early 1920's.[10] Now, as then, all private liquid waste disposal systems do not operate perfectly. McGauhey and Winneberger[11] found that as many as one-third of the septic tank systems in a single subdivision failed during the first 3 or 4 years

Cain, J. M. and Beatty, M. T., 1965, "Disposal of Septic Tank Effluent in Soils," *Jour. Soil and Water Conservation,* vol. 20, no. 3, pp. 101–5. Reprinted by permission of the authors and the Soil Conservation Society of America. Copyright 1965 by S. C. S. A.
John Cain is on the staff of the Wisconsin Department of Natural Resources, Madison, Wisconsin. Dr. Beatty is Professor of Soil Science at the University of Wisconsin and Chairman, Environmental Resources Unit, University Wisconsin-Extension, Madison, Wisconsin.

of use. In one case, wholesale failure of septic tank systems in an entire subdivision meant that all of the more than 1,000 homes in the subdivision had to be repossessed, then refinanced and resold after the septic tank systems had been rebuilt.

Functions of a Septic Tank

In its simplest form, a septic tank is a water-tight container with an inlet and an outlet. The function of the septic tank[20] is to condition the sewage so that it may be more readily percolated into the subsoil. Biological decomposition of solids by anaerobic bacteria takes place in the septic tank; part of the solids are retained in the tank. Contrary to popular belief, the septic tank does not remove a large proportion of harmful microorganisms from the waste.

Effluent from the septic tank is discharged into the soil by means of a seepage pit, seepage bed, or seepage trench. The rate at which the soil absorbs the effluent is critical to the operation of the sewage disposal system. If the effluent is not absorbed rapidly enough, it may back up into the drains in the home and eventually it may rise to the surface of the ground over the seepage area. If the effluent drains through the soil too rapidly, it may travel unfiltered into wells or surface-water supplies and contaminate them with various types of disease-bearing organisms.

Soil Permeability

The approach to design of sewage effluent absorption systems has been based on an estimate of soil permeability. The first attempt at quantitative evaluation of soil permeability in relation to septic tank effluent was made by Ryon[18] in 1928. From 50 septic tank systems that were operating at full capacity or had overflowed, he collected information on the amount of effluent applied per square foot of bottom area of the seepage system. He also conducted percolation tests at each sewage disposal system site. First, he saturated the soil around a 1-foot square hole about 18 inches deep with water. Then, after placing 6 inches of water in the hole, he recorded the time required for the water level to drop 1 inch. On the basis of information obtained in this study, he developed a relationship among percolation rate, water use, and bottom area of the seepage system. Thereafter, this relationship was used for septic tank system design purposes.

Ryon's work was widely accepted and served as the standard for evaluation by most agencies responsible for control of sewage disposal practices. The same type of percolation test, with some modifications, is given as the standard in the *Manual of Septic Tank Practice*.[20] The results of this test are reported in terms of the number of minutes it takes the water level to drop 1 inch in the hole. The lower the value

in minutes per inch, the greater the permeability of the soil.

Another method of measuring soil permeability involves taking an undisturbed soil core and in the laboratory determining the rate of water movement through it under a one-half inch head of water. The rates measured by this method are called the hydraulic conductivity of the soil and are expressed in terms of the number of inches of water that move through the soil core per hour. The higher the value in inches per hour, the greater the permeability of the soil.

A third method of estimating soil permeability is outlined by O'Neal.[14] With this method an attempt is made to relate soil characteristics observable in the field to measured hydraulic conductivity. O'Neal found that though permeability could not be estimated on the basis of any one characteristic, soil structure is the most important single characteristic influencing it. Other observable soil characteristics that affect permeability are soil texture, the relation between horizontal and vertical axes of aggregates, the amount of overlap of aggregates, mottling, size and number of visible pores, and direction of easiest natural fracture.

Devereux, Steele, and Turner[8] reported on the use of O'Neal's system on the soils of Virginia. In most cases, predictions of permeability based on carefully written field descriptions correlated closely with the results of laboratory tests. Devereux and his co-workers conclude, "It is believed that this technique can be developed sufficiently for all interested technicians to make reasonably accurate field estimates." At least, the technician can arrive at an estimate that is as useful and as meaningful as the results of a percolation test.

One reason that it is difficult to measure soil permeability accurately is that the percolation rate changes with time. Christiansen,[6] Allison,[1] Sillanpaa,[19] and Muckel,[12] working with various kinds of soil under both field and laboratory conditions, found that during a prolonged testing period the permeability varies in three distinct phases. Phase one is a period of initial decrease in percolation rate, phase two a period of increase in rate, and phase three a period of gradual but steady decrease in rate (Fig. 1).

The initial decrease in percolation rate probably is due to swelling of soil particles and dispersion of soil aggregates. The increase in rate during phase two is attributed to an increase in the amount of pore space available for water movement, which occurs as a result of the dissolving of entrapped air. The gradual reduction in permeability during phase three, which is the aspect of this soil property important insofar as septic tank operation is concerned, is due to (a) mechanical disintegration of soil aggregates, (b) clogging of soil pores by biological material, and (c) dispersion of soil aggregates by microorganisms.

Allison[1] demonstrated that the reduction in percolation rate did not take place in a sterile system during a 70-day test. He concluded that the rate reduction that normally occurs is due to microbial action and that the clogging material probably consists of microbial cells, slimes, and polysaccharides.

The changes of permeability with time suggest a number of limitations to the usefulness of the percolation test. Among them are the following:

1. Data from the tests are not applicable if there is a fluctuating water table near the soil surface or if there are abnormal situations such as root channels, large soil cracks, or small animal burrows in the test area.

2. The test cannot be performed on frozen ground and is not reliable when run on dry soil.

3. There is considerable variation in the techniques used in performing the test; often, it may be run improperly.

4. There is no valid reason for assuming that the percolation rate from a carefully prepared test hole will be

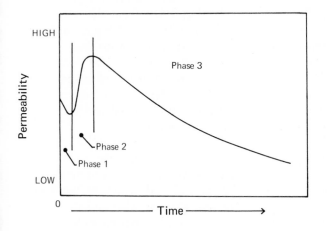

FIG. 1. The effect of prolonged submergence on permeability of soil.

the same as that from an absorption area constructed on the same soil with heavy machinery.

5. It is quite likely that there may be no relationship between the ability of the soil to accept water for a short period of time and its ability to accept sewage effluent for a long period. The research on soil clogging shows that a number of factors other than initial soil permeability affect clogging and the ultimate percolation rate.

Soil Clogging

Since soil permeability gradually decreases with time, even when distilled water is used, it appears logical that this decrease would proceed at an increasingly rapid rate when the soil receives septic tank effluent, which contains suspended solids, a variety of chemicals, and a large and varied microbial population. The possibility that soil pores may be clogged by septic tank effluent has been mentioned by several workers, but very little quantitative research has been done in this area until recently.

For discussion purposes, soil clogging can be divided into three types—physical, chemical, and biological—although they actually are interrelated. Physical clogging occurs when solid material carried in the effluent is deposited in the pores of the soil. As the pores are filled, the percolation rate is lowered until the absorptive surface becomes sealed. Orlob and Butler[15] and Orlob and Krone[16] found that organic matter generally is deposited near the absorbing surface of the soil; for example, on the wall of a seepage trench. The coarser the soil, the deeper the organic matter will penetrate. In fine-textured soil, most of the organic matter is de-

posited within one-half inch of the absorbing surface. Bendixen and his co-workers[4] report that the rate of clogging is proportional to the amount of suspended solids in the effluent.

Since soil clogging is due in part to suspended solids in the effluent, it seems that serious consideration should be given to septic tank design that will reduce the solids content. Baumann and Babbitt[2] studied the operation of six different septic tanks; they found considerable variation in the quality of effluent, both from day to day for any one septic tank and in the average between septic tanks. During an 8-month test period, 85 percent of the suspended solids were removed by the best tank and only 68.2 percent were removed by the poorest tank.

Baumann and Babbitt point out that at certain times gas bubbles cause turbulence in the septic tank and this results in abnormally large amounts of solids being carried out in the effluent. Effluent collected during these periods of "sludge unloading" showed a greater clogging tendency than normal effluent in sand filter tests. Certain of the septic tanks were equipped with a gas baffle, which is a slanted plate mounted below the outlet to divert the gas bubbles and solids away from the outlet. The three septic tanks with gas baffles did not exhibit sludge unloading.

This type of evidence accentuates the importance of sound sanitation ordinances, strictly enforced to insure that properly designed septic tank systems are installed.

Soil clogging also may be caused by chemicals that are able to alter the composition of the soil and break down the natural soil structure. Sodium is one ion that can cause soil structure to break down, but not enough presently is known about its effects in septic tank absorption fields to permit soil scientists to make a definitive assessment.

Biological materials seem to be the most important cause of soil clogging. The exact nature of the clogging material is not known, but McGauhey and Winneberger[11] have found deposits of ferrous sulfide where effluent is absorbed into the soil and they believe this is an important clogging material. The insoluble ferrous sulfide precipitate is probably a result of anaerobic bacteria acting on organically bound iron and sulfur. Under aerobic conditions, the ferrous sulfide is oxidized to the soluble sulfate form. Allison[1] indicates that clogging is probably due to products of microbial growth. Although it is desirable to know more about the exact nature of the clogging material, the important fact is that clogging takes place mainly under anaerobic conditions.

Research by a number of workers indicates that when clogged soil is allowed to dry, permeability is partially restored. During this resting period under aerobic conditions, the clogging material is oxidized and in some cases the microbial activity may result in better soil aggregation and increased permeability.

One of the most promising areas for research in improved septic tank system design appears to be that of devising some type of field rotation in the absorptive phase. In 1924, Hardenbergh[10] prepared a diagram for a distribution box with stop blocks so effluent could be directed into or away from three separate sections of a tile drain field. The dosing chamber and automatic dosing siphon, which have been given consideration in the past,

apparently are being overlooked at present. Use of paired tile lines, seepage beds, or pits seems to be worth further study and may provide a method for making marginal soils safer for septic tank systems and for prolonging the useful life of systems on suitable soils.

The necessity for aerobic conditions to minimize soil clogging makes it imperative that the depth to water table in the soil be evaluated. Below the water table, anaerobic conditions exist. Above the water table is a capillary fringe where the soil is nearly saturated. In most soils, the depth to water table fluctuates during the year. If the water table is at or near the level of the absorption system for even part of the year it can cause soil clogging to start. Once started, soil clogging can be self perpetuating, since the effluent will pond in the trench, bed, or pit and maintain anaerobic conditions even after the water table drops.

Defects in Septic Tank Systems

Not all failures of septic tank systems are due to soil factors; many can be traced to faulty design and improper construction practices. Numerous faulty septic tank systems are installed because builders are unaware of the importance of certain construction features, enforcement of local health and building codes is difficult, and prospective buyers do not recognize the importance and the value of a well-designed and correctly installed system.

McGauhey and Winneberger[11] cite examples of septic tank failure caused by the practice of laying tile directly on the soil and then covering it with only a thin layer of gravel. Coulter, Bendixen, and Edwards[7] were able to relate septic tank system failure to amount of water used. In a survey of seepage beds in Knox County, Tennessee, they found that as water use increased the percentage of systems failing increased. Bendixen and his co-workers[4] found that homes with food waste grinders should have increased septic tank capacity and increased absorption areas to take care of the additional load.

If a septic tank is not cleaned out when it should be, sludge and scum may flow into the absorption area and cause clogging of the soil.

One factor that has not been evaluated quantitatively is the damage done to soil structure by construction machinery. Heavy machinery may smear the sidewalls and compact the bottom of trenches if the soil is wet during construction. If this happens, a seepage system may never attain its full absorptive capacity.

Ground Water Contamination

Fear that effluent from septic tanks may contaminate ground water has been expressed frequently. However, very little information on this subject has been available until recently. When septic tanks were widely scattered, distance and the opportunity for effluent dilution prevented contamination of water supplies from becoming a widespread or serious problem. But awareness of the potential pollution problem has increased with the use of septic tanks in crowded subdivisions and the widespread use of household detergents not easily decomposed by microorganisms.

Woodward, Kilpatrick, and Johnson[22] surveyed 63,000 wells in 39 communities in Minnesota; they found that 13,800, or 21.8 percent, of them contained measurable quantities of synthetic detergents. Campenni[5] tested half of the wells in a 50 home subdivision in Rhode Island; he found that all but one contained synethtic detergents.

Nichols and Koepp[13] tested 2,167 samples from privately owned wells in Wisconsin. They reported that 32.1 percent of the samples contained measurable amounts of detergents. Even more important, 20.3 percent of the samples that contained synthetic detergent were unsafe for human use from a bacteriological standpoint; only 9.2 percent of the samples without synthetic detergent were unsafe. This study indicates that there may be some relation between the presence of synthetic detergents in wells and bacteriological contamination of them.

Not a great deal of precise information is available on the ability of different kinds of soils to filter septic tank effluent or on the exact processes that take place during filtration. Robeck and his co-workers[17] found that synthetic detergents and other organic compounds are adsorbed by the soil particles and are decomposed by microorganisms. They indicate that the greatest degree of purification occurs near the point where the effluent is absorbed and that it is important to maintain an aerobic environment for proper microbial decomposition. They conclude that the best soil for filtering is one that will accept effluent at a reasonably rapid rate, has an ample adsorption surface, and has permeability characteristics that allow adequate time for microbial decomposition.

The main attempts to prevent well water contamination by septic tank effluent have been directed toward establishment of minimum lot size requirements and minimum spacings between septic tanks, wells, and lot boundaries. The studies by Flynn, Andreoli, and Guerrara,[9] Vogt,[21] and Campenni,[5] seem to indicate that this alone is not the answer. Although adequate spacing is desirable and in many cases may help prevent contamination, spacing regulations by themselves will not prevent ground water contamination; consideration must also be given to soil, ground water, and geologic conditions.

General Summary of Problems

Most of the problems associated with septic tank use can be grouped into three general categories. The first category involves problems related to the use of septic tanks on small lots in crowded subdivisions. Under such conditions, there often is either an inadequate area for disposal of effluent or contamination of ground water supplies. Not infrequently, the houses in attractive subdivisions with private wells and septic tanks must be connected to public sewer and water facilities soon after the subdivision is completed. This means that roads must be torn up, lawns disturbed, and additional expense incurred by all the homeowners. Problems of this type can be avoided by good community planning.

Many areas have restricted use of septic tanks to homes on lots that are considerably larger than conventional city lots. The objective of this restriction is to provide space for a new seepage system if the original one fails and to assure that distances between sewage disposal systems and wells are great enough to prevent ground water contamination. However, these large lots also introduce many new problems, for they result in such a low population density that it may never be economical to connect the homes on them to the municipal sewer and water facilities. Also, other community facilities, such as utilities, police and fire protection, roads and transportation, and other services, will be unduly expensive throughout the life of the community. All communities should consider carefully how much of this type of urban sprawl they can afford, both in terms of the best use of available land resources and the continuing cost of community services.

The second category involves problems resulting from failure of septic tank systems due to faulty design and construction. Such problems can be caused by septic tanks or absorptive areas of inadequate size or by other defects in design and construction. Problems of this type can be controlled by the strict enforcement of good sanitation ordinances.

The third type of problem has to do with the installation of septic tank systems in soils not suited to use for waste disposal. This can result in the development of an ill smelling, unhealthful bog if the soil is so impermeable that the effluent rises to the surface of the lawn. Conversely, the soil may be so permeable that it accepts effluent too rapidly to provide sufficient filtration; this results in the contamination of ground water.

All of the aforementioned problems stem from lack of adequate control over the installation of septic tank systems. To be adequate, control must involve both the mechanical aspects of a system—size, shape, and type of construction—and the conditions under which septic tank systems are permitted. Control in the first instance is accomplished by sanitation ordinances and in the second by both sanitation ordinances and sound land use planning and zoning.

An especially useful tool to assist community leaders, planners, and sanitarians in better planning and control is the soil survey report, including maps, prepared by soil scientists.

Using Soil Survey Information

With a soil map and the related interpretive information on the soils, it is possible to delineate areas where septic tank systems cannot be used successfully. These areas include poorly drained soils, very fine textured soils, rock outcrops, very steep slopes, and flood plains. Also easily outlined on soils maps are areas where the use of a septic tank system is limited; such areas include somewhat poorly drained soils, slowly permeable soils, and highly variable soils. If a community decides that it is necessary to allow some areas to develop with septic tanks, the areas with soils suited for such development can be selected readily with the help of a soil map. These areas include soils that are permeable, have a deep water table, and have demonstrated an ability to function well for effluent disposal purposes.

The soil map is useful for describing soil conditions over large areas, but small inclusions of different soils may not be shown on the map. Where a large investment is planned, such as a septic tank seepage field, it is advisable to make an on-site evaluation. Such an on-site investigation can be performed by someone trained in the techniques used by soil scientists. This approach is unique, for it makes possible interpretations based on observable morphological characteristics of the soil at the site and also on the relationship of this soil to others with similar morphology that have been studied elsewhere. The findings from field and laboratory studies that have been performed on similar soils can then be related to the soil at the site. The use of soil survey information can contribute much to sound community planning, land use control, and development of regulations for land use applicable to each local situation.

Notes

[1] Allison, L. E. 1947. *Effect of microorganisms on permeability of soil under prolonged submergence.* Soil Sci. 63: 439–450.
[2] Baumann, E. R., and H. E. Babbitt. 1953. *An investigation of the performance of six small septic tanks.* Bul. No. 409. Engineering Experiment Station, University of Illinois, Urbana. 75 pp.
[3] Bendixen, T. W. 1962. *Field percolation tests for sanitary engineering application.* Special Tech. Publ. No. 322. American Society for Testing and Materials, Philadelphia, Pa. pp. 3–6.
[4] Bendixen, T. W., M. Berk, J. P. Sheehy, and S. R. Weibel. 1952. *Studies on household sewage disposal systems, part II.* U. S. Govt. Printing Office, Washington, D. C. 94 pp.
[5] Campenni, L. G. 1961. *Synthetic detergents in ground waters, part 2.* Water and Sewage Works 108: 210–213.
[6] Christiansen, J. E. 1944. *Effect of entrapped air upon the permeability of soils.* Soil Sci. 58: 355–365.
[7] Coulter, J. B., T. W. Bendixen, and A. B. Edwards. 1960. *Study of seepage beds.* Robert A. Taft Sanitary Engineering Center, U. S. Public Health Service, Columbus, Ohio. 62 pp.
[8] Devereux, R. E., F. Steele, and W. L. Tur-

ner. 1950. *Permeability and land classification for soil and water conservation.* Soil Sci. Soc. Am. Proc. 15: 420–423.

[9] Flynn, J. M., A. Andreoli, and A. A. Guerrara. 1958. *Study of synthetic detergents in ground water.* J. Am. Water Works Assoc. 50: 1551–1562.

[10] Hardenbergh, W. A. 1924. *Home sewage disposal.* J. B. Lippincott Co., Philadelphia, Pa. 66 pp.

[11] McGauhey, P. H., and J. H. Winneberger. 1963. *Summary report on causes and prevention of failure of septic tank percolation systems.* Report No. 63-5. Sanitary Engineering Research Laboratory, University of California, Berkeley. 66 pp.

[12] Muckel, D. C. 1953. *Research in water spreading.* Trans. Am. Soc. Civil Eng. 118: 209–219.

[13] Nichols, M. S., and E. Koepp. 1961. *Synthetic detergents as a criterion of Wisconsin ground water pollution.* J. Am. Water Works Assoc. 53: 303–306.

[14] O'Neal, A. M. 1949. *Some characteristics significant in evaluating permeability.* Soil Sci. 67: 403–409.

[15] Orlob, G. T., and R. G. Butler. 1955. *An investigation of sewage spreading on five California soils.* Sanitary Engineering Research Laboratory, University of California, Berkeley. 53 pp.

[16] Orlob, G. T., and R. B. Krone. 1956. *Movement of coliform bacteria through porous media: final report.* Sanitary Engineering Research Laboratory, University of California, Berkeley. 42 pp.

[17] Robeck, G. G., J. M. Cohen, W. T. Sayers, and H. L. Woodward. 1963. *Degradation of ABS and other organics in unsaturated soils.* Water Pollution Control Federation J. 35: 1225–1236.

[18] Ryon, H. 1928. *Notes on the design of sewage disposal works, with special reference to small installations.* Published by the author, Albany, N. Y.

[19] Sillanpaa, M. 1956. *Studies on the hydraulic conductivity of soils and its measurement.* Published by the author, Helsinki, Finland. 109 pp.

[20] United States Department of Health, Education and Welfare. 1960. *Manual of septic tank practice.* Public Health Service Publ. No. 526. U. S. Govt. Printing Office, Washington, D. C. 93 pp.

[21] Vogt, J. E. 1961. *Infectious hepatitis epidemic at Posen, Michigan.* J. Am. Water Works Assoc. 53: 1238–1242.

[22] Woodward, F. L., F. J. Kilpatrick, and P. B. Johnson. 1961. *Experiences with ground water contamination in unsewered areas in Minnesota.* Am. J. Public Health 51: 1130–1136.

40 Urban Expansion—An Opportunity and a Challenge to Industrial Mineral Producers

H. E. Risser and R. L. Major

Introduction

In the years since World War II, the industrial minerals industry has been faced with the greatest opportunities and the greatest challenges in its history. Furthermore, both the opportunities and the challenges promise to ·become even greater in the coming decades.

The opportunities stem primarily from the increased demand resulting from a rapidly growing population and from an even more rapid growth in per

Risser, H. E. and Major, R. L., 1967, "Urban Expansion—An Opportunity and a Challenge to Industrial Mineral Producers," *Environmental Geology Notes Number 16*, Illinois State Geological Survey, pp. 1–19. Abridged by permission of the authors and reprinted by permission of the Illinois State Geological Survey, Urbana, Illinois.

The authors are on the staff of the Illinois Geological Survey.

capita consumption of mineral products. Urbanization is leading to a greater concentration of population, which provides larger, more concentrated market outlets. These, in turn, bring the opportunity for bigger units, which can operate at greater efficiency and economy of scale. Delivery to such markets may also permit the use of unit trains or other large-tonnage, low-cost transportation.

While the opportunities are fairly apparent, it also is clear that numerous challenges must be met and obstacles overcome in order to take fullest advantage of these opportunities.

The challenge of greater demand will require the development of an industry composed of operating units with sufficient size, resources, and financial strength to enable it to produce on the large scale necessary to supply that demand.

New sources of raw materials will be needed to replace those that are being rapidly depleted. Some sources are being rendered uneconomic because of various operational restrictions. Many of the potential reserves are being covered as a result of urbanization or are being made unavailable by restrictive zoning ordinances.

Population Trends

In the 25 years from 1940 to 1965, the U. S. population increased almost 50 percent, from 132 million to 194 million people. The projections for 1975 indicate a population of 214 to 227 million (U. S. Bur. Census, 1966, pp. 5–6).

The population growth has not been equal for all areas, however. The total increase in the United States between 1950 and 1960 was 19 percent, but in Florida it was 78.7 percent, in California, 48.5 percent, and in Pennsylvania only 7.8 percent (U. S. Bur. Census, 1966, p. 13).

Along with increased population, there has been a notable trend towards increased urbanization. In 1910, 46 percent of the U. S. population was classified as urban. By 1960, urban population had increased to 70 percent (U. S. Bur. Census, 1966, p. 15). Today, an estimated 70 percent of the population is concentrated on about one percent of the land area (Abrams, 1965, p. 151).

Figure 1 shows that in California, which has a population of 18.6 million, 70 percent of the people live on 8 percent of the land. Los Angeles County alone, with less than 3 percent of the state's area, accounts for almost 40 percent of the population. Figure 2 shows the extreme concentration of population in the New York City area. In 1960 the five boroughs of the city, shown in black, contained 7.8 million people in an area of only 299 square miles. The metropolitan New York area (black and dotted area) constitutes only 4.5 percent of the state's area but contains more than 60 percent of the population. Figure 3 shows the relationship between the population in the Detroit metropolitan area and that of the state of Michigan. The three-county metropolitan region makes up only 3.5 percent of the state's land area but contains almost half of the population.

Locational Factors

Production of industrial minerals, especially those used for construction purposes, tends to be concentrated in or

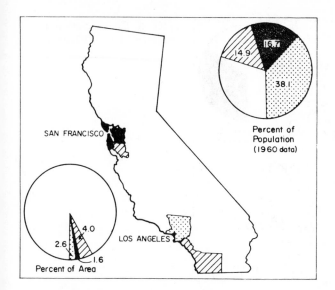

FIG. 1. Concentration of population in California.

SAN FRANCISCO

LOS ANGELES

4.0

2.6

1.6

Percent of Area

16.7

14.9

38.1

Percent of
Population
(1960 data)

near the urban centers. Other factors, such as geology, availability of low-cost transportation, and the ratio of unit value to unit transportation costs, modify this tendency.

Figure 4 shows the 10 most populous states and the percentage of domestic production of various major industrial

minerals mined in them. These 10 states constitute only 21 percent of the land area of the United States, but they contain 55 percent of the population. As a group they consistently produce a greater share of the minerals listed than the proportion of land area they occupy, which seems to corrobo-

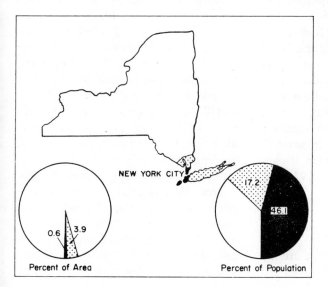

FIG. 2. Concentration of population in New York state.

NEW YORK CITY

0.6

3.9

Percent of Area

17.2

46.1

Percent of Population

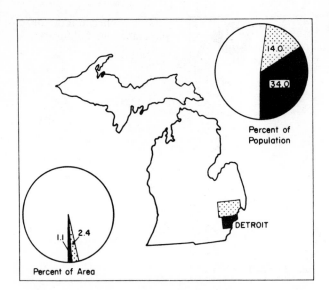

FIG. 3. Concentration of population in Michigan.

rate the thesis that industrial minerals production tends to be concentrated near population centers.

Low-cost, high-volume, widely occurring minerals tend to have a high "place value"; that is, the location of the deposit with respect to the point of consumption is extremely important in determining which deposits are economical and which will be utilized. On the other hand, minerals of more limited geologic occurrence and higher unit value may be profitable to mine despite their distance from market and thus have a relatively low place value. Some examples of mineral commodities with high place value are sand, gravel, crushed stone, pumice, lime, common clays, and gypsum, which, in general, are produced as near the point of consumption as possible (Ladoo, 1959, pp. 304–305).

Mineral Aggregates Industry

Because sand, gravel, and stone are the principal industrial minerals from the standpoint of tonnage, geographic distribution, and land area involved, we will concentrate primarily on these commodities. Sand, gravel, and stone production in the United States was 10 times greater than the combined production of all other industrial minerals in 1964.

Despite their low unit values of $1.00 to $1.50 per ton, the total 1964 value of the United States production of sand, gravel, and stone was estimated at $2.03 billion (U. S. Bur. Mines, 1965b, p. 4). For comparison, this dollar value is equal to 44 percent of the value of production for *all* nonmetallic minerals, to 9.9 percent of the value of total domestic production of all minerals including fuels, and to 90 percent of the value of production for all metallic minerals produced in 1964.

From 1940 to 1965, cumulative stone production in the United States amounted to 10.1 billion tons. Sand and gravel production during the same period was 12.9 billion tons—enough to cover the entire state of Rhode Island to a depth of about 7 feet—while strip coal production was 2.95 billion tons, and phosphate rock production was only 317 million tons (U. S. Bur. Mines, 1941–1966).

Figure 5 compares the 1940 to 1965 growth in production of sand and gravel and stone with the growth in United States population. Projections of future growth to 1975 also are shown. The projected growth rate of sand and gravel production between 1964 and 1975 is 6.8 percent per annum and for crushed stone 6.9 percent per annum (U. S. Bur. Mines, 1965a, p. 13).

Table 1 shows the concentration of production of mineral aggregates in seven metropolitan areas. Not only do these areas account for a large percentage of their states' total production, but also the absolute amounts they produce are quite sizable. For example, in 1964 the production of sand and

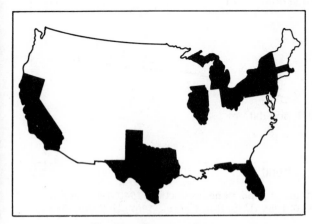

FIG. 4. Area, population, and industrial mineral production of the 10 most populous states as a percentage of the U. S. total.

Ten Most Populous States
(1960 data)

	Per cent of United States Total
AREA (including Alaska and Hawaii)	21
POPULATION	55
TONNAGE PRODUCED, 1964:	
Sand and Gravel	42
Clays	44
Cement	44*
Stone	46
Gypsum	48
Frasch Sulphur	53
Asbestos	54
Flurospar	59
Lime	60*
Salt	68
Phosphate Rock	75

*Minimum figures; data is partially concealed.

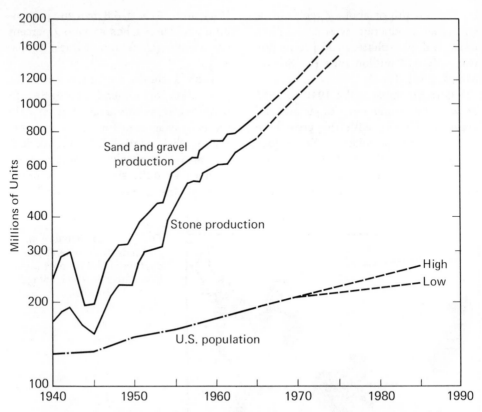

FIG. 5. Rates of growth for sand, gravel, and stone production, 1940–1975, and for total United States population, 1940–1985 (U. S. Bur. Census, 1967; U. S. Bur. Mines, 1965a).

gravel from the Los Angeles metropolitan area was 39 million tons, an amount which exceeded the individual state production of sand and gravel in all states but New York, Michigan, and California for the same year (U. S. Bur. Mines, 1965a, pp. 922–923).

Case History: Chicago Metropolitan Area

The discussion to this point has dealt with the broad, nationwide picture. The Chicago metropolitan area provides a much more detailed example of these problems.

Illinois is a major industrial minerals producer; in 1964 it ranked sixth in sand and gravel production with 35 million tons and third in total stone production with 43 million tons. Figure 6 shows the relationship between population, urban areas, and the production of sand, gravel, and stone in the state. The eight metropolitan areas shown make up only 21 percent of the state's area but contain 78 percent of the population. The northeastern Illinois region (Chicago metropolitan area), shown in black, occupies only 7 percent of the area but contains 62 percent of the population. In 1964 this region produced 38 percent of the stone, 39 percent of the sand, and 51 percent of the gravel for the state.

The six counties of the area—Cook, DuPage, Lake, Kane, McHenry, and Will—cover 3714 square miles. In 1965, 6.7 million people resided there, compared to 4.5 million in 1940. A population of 9.3 million is projected for 1990 (N. Ill. Plan. Comm., 1965, p. 12). The area is presently being urbanized at the rate of 10,000 acres or 15.6 square miles per year (N. Ill. Plan. Comm., 1965, p. 14). The greatest demand is for land for residential building. In northeastern Illinois there is not only a concentration of population and

mineral production, but there is also a combination of nearly all the pressures and problems that confront mineral industries in other urban areas.

This region has been blessed with abundant resources of stone, sand, and gravel. However, years of production have been gradually depleting the resources at the earliest worked, and perhaps best, production sites. In the future new sites must be selected in locations outside the existing built-up areas, where the greatest problems of conflicting land use occur. Here mineral producers must compete with agriculture, expanding industry, real estate developers, highway builders, and park

Table 1 Examples of extreme concentration of industrial mineral production in or adjacent to urban areas in the United States*

Commodity	Geographical area	Percent of state area	1964 tonnage (million)	Percent of state tonnage
Stone (Crushed & broken)	Cook County (Chicago), Ill.	1.7	12.2	31.6
Limestone (Crushed & broken)	Dade County (Miami), Fla.	3.7	10.2	32.3
Stone (All types)	St. Louis County, Mo.	0.7	5.2	16.5
Sand and gravel	Chicago Metropolitan Area (Cook, Will, Kane, DuPage, McHenry, and Lake Counties)	6.6	12.6	41.6
Sand and gravel	Los Angeles County	2.6	26.2	23.2
Sand and gravel	Los Angeles Metropolitan Area (Los Angeles, Orange, and San Diego Counties)	8.2	39.2	34.7
Sand and gravel	Detroit Metropolitan Area (Livingston, Washtenaw, Oakland, Macomb, and Wayne Counties)	5.7	18.7	36.0
Sand and gravel	Suburban Long Island (Nassau and Suffolk Counties)	2.5	10.6	27.0
Sand and gravel	Denver Metropolitan Area (Adams, Denver, Arapahoe, Boulder, and Jefferson Counties)	3.5	6.3	30.1

* Source: U. S. Bureau of Mines and U. S. Bureau of the Census

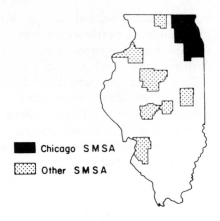

FIG. 6. Relation between land area, population, and mineral production in Standard Metropolitan Statistical Areas (SMSA) of Illinois.

■ Chicago SMSA

▧ Other SMSA

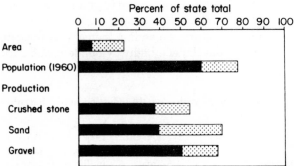

and recreation agencies for the decreasing amount of available land.

Stone Resources and Operations

Figure 7 shows the production of stone in northeastern Illinois from 1942 to 1965 by geographic region. The Chicago metropolitan area is shown in dotted and lined patterns, while the black area indicates the outer tier of counties surrounding the metropolitan region. This fringe area is included because part of the growing demand for mineral aggregates within the metropolitan region will probably be met by quarries located in this outlying area. Cook County, shown in dotted pattern, has, to date, continued to supply the bulk of stone production despite increasing demands. Although the great-

est increase in production has occurred in Cook County, both other areas shown have more than doubled their tonnage of stone during the past 25 years.

Figure 8 shows the bedrock geology (Suter et al., 1959, p. 23) and the locations of major stone quarries operating in the northeastern Illinois area. These quarries accounted for more than 99 percent of the reported production in the six-county area in 1965. The major quarries, with one exception, produce from the Silurian rocks, which are predominately dolomites.

One of the principal factors determining the location of a quarry is the thickness of the stone. For high-tonnage operations, producers generally are interested in quarrying the thickest

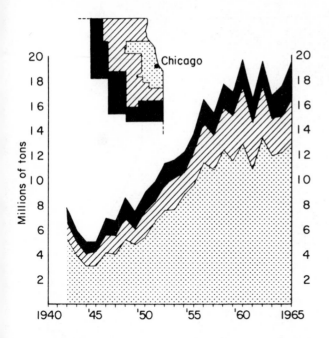

FIG. 7. Stone production in northeastern Illinois, 1942–1965. Dotted and lined patterns indicate the Chicago metropolitan area; outlying fringe area is shown in black.

deposits available. The stone, of course, must be of sufficient quality to meet specifications. Present quarry operations are concentrated in the thicker deposits in the southeastern quarter of the region.

In Fig. 9, the areas in which the thickness of overburden is 50 feet or less are shown by the dotted pattern (Suter et al., 1959, p. 18). The presence of thick overburden helps explain the absence of operations in the northern half of the region. This map indicates beds of thick rock are present at shallow depths in southern Cook County for potential production in the future. Unfortunately, other factors tend to restrict their use.

Figure 10 shows the pattern of urbanization for the area and the relation between pits and quarries and urban areas. The "urbanized areas" include all incorporated cities, towns, and villages, all parks, and all government in-

stallations. The map shows that much of the thick, shallow stone deposits in Cook County are no longer available for mining by open pit methods because they have been built over by the city of Chicago and its suburbs, which presents serious restrictions to future development of the quarrying industry.

As the present quarries are worked out, future production must come from new and more distant sites, or possibly from underground operations. Underground mining beneath large cities presents its own problems, too involved to deal with here. The maps indicate that moving to outlying sites generally would mean quarrying thinner stone and removing possibly thicker overburden. Stone up to 100 feet is sufficiently thick to provide good quarrying conditions. Such thickness would, nevertheless, represent quite a change from the 200- to 400-foot stone commonly quarried in northeastern Illinois

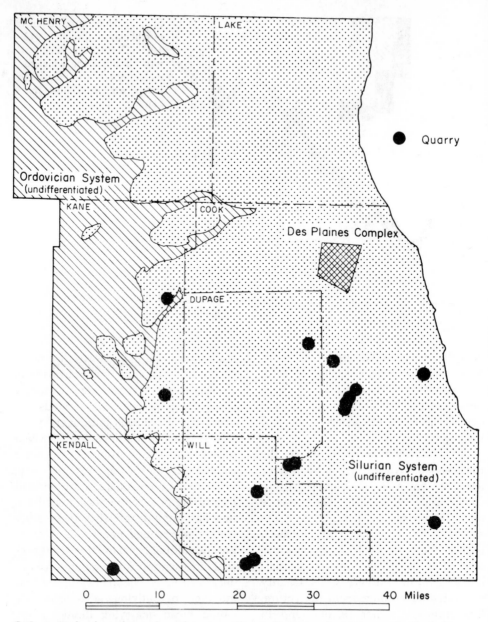

FIG. 8. Bedrock geology of northeastern Illinois (Suter et al., 1959, p. 23). Black dots indicate the locations of major quarries reported operating in 1965.

and would require larger areas to produce a given amount of stone.

It appears likely that the greatest possibilities in the long-term future expansion of the stone industry of the Chicago area will be to the south and west into northern Will County. Such a shift will greatly increase the hauling distance to metropolitan consuming centers. For example, should the stone

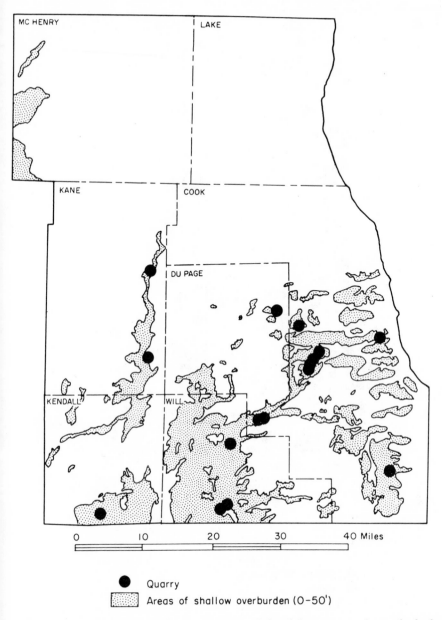

●   Quarry

░░   Areas of shallow overburden (0-50')

FIG. 9. Areas where the thickness of unconsolidated deposits overlying the bedrock are 50 feet or less (Suter et al., 1959, p. 18).

that presently comes from within Cook County become unavailable because the present quarries were closed and stone from Will County used to replace it, the hauling distance would be more than doubled. At 5 cents per ton-mile, this would add at least $1.00 per ton to the delivered cost of aggregate in the inner city. Average hauling distances and costs will be lessened to

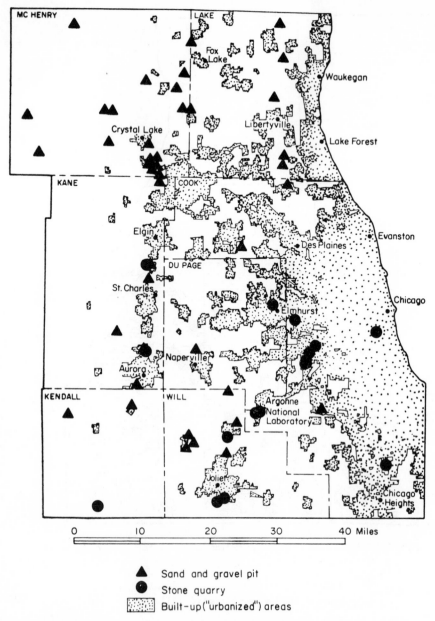

MC HENRY

LAKE

Fox
Lake

Waukegan

Crystal Lake

Libertyville

Lake Forest

KANE

COOK

Elgin

Des Plaines

Evanston

DU PAGE

St. Charles

Elmhurst

Chicago

Naperville

Aurora

KENDALL

WILL

Argonne
National
Laboratory

Joliet

Chicago
Heights

| 0 | 10 | 20 | 30 | 40 Miles |

▲   Sand and gravel pit

●   Stone quarry

▨   Built-up ("urbanized") areas

FIG. 10. Urbanized areas in relation to sand and gravel pits and stone quarries in northeastern Illinois.

some degree as urbanization and construction activities move toward the outlying quarries.

Zoning Restrictions

At the present time, one of the most serious challenges to the mineral producers in urban areas is the growing amount of regulation by local government through zoning ordinances. The courts have upheld the right of zoning boards to prohibit the opening of a new quarry or pit and to close down an existing mineral operation if it is ruled to be a nuisance. *Rock Products* magazine recently polled hundreds of producers across the U. S. and revealed actual cases of pits and quarries having been closed down by community action and of plants forced to relocate because of local pressures (Stearn, 1966, pp. 77–78). In addition to the usual zoning regulations, many communities have passed ordinances that place restrictions of an operational nature on producers. These ordinances relate to the permitted hours of operation, dust control, noise level, blasting vibrations, screening, use of minor residential streets for haulage, and many more features of operations.

Future Planning

Advance planning for multiple or sequential land use, with land rehabilitation and optimum final land use in mind, can be of great assistance in helping stone, sand, and gravel producers to retain their present operating rights or to gain new rights in the face of threats from more stringent zoning ordinances. The industry is becoming increasingly aware of the need to edu-

cate the public about the proper and useful role of the industrial minerals producer, not only in the community's economy, but also in the wise sequential use of land in the community. Some excellent public relations and educational programs of this type are already being carried out by trade associations and individual companies.

Projections indicate that a cumulative production of 13.5 billion tons of sand and gravel and 11.4 billion tons of stone will be required to meet the market demands in the U. S. within the next decade. This is the great challenge. But to benefit from this huge demand, producers must be willing and able to face up to the associated problems.

References

Abrams, Charles, 1965, The use of land in cities: Scientific American, v. 213, no. 3, p. 150–156, 160.

Ekblaw, George E., and Lamar, J. E., 1964, Sand and gravel resources of northeastern Illinois: Illinois Geol. Survey Circ. 359, 8 p.

Ladoo, R. B., 1959, Marketing of industrial minerals: Economics of the mineral industries: Am. Inst. Min. Met. Engr., p. 298–311.

Northeastern Illinois Planning Commission, 1965, Problems, goals, and choices: Ann. Rept. pt. III, N. I. P. C., Chicago, 40 p.

Stearn, Enid W., 1966, A saner look at zoning regulations: Rock Products, July 1966, p. 76–79, 112.

Suter, Max, Bergstrom, R. E., Smith, H. F., Emrich, G. H., Walton, W. C., and Larson, T. E., 1959, Preliminary report on ground-water resources of the Chicago region, Illinois: Coop. Ground-Water Rept. 1, Illinois State Water Survey and Illinois Geol. Survey, 89 p.

U. S. Bureau of the Census, 1966, Statistical abstract of the United States, 1966, 87th ed.: U. S. Govt. Printing Office, Washington, D. C., 1039 p.

U. S. Bureau of Mines, 1965a, 1964 Minerals yearbook, v. I: U. S. Bur. Mines, Dept. of Interior, Washington, D. C., 1258 p.

U. S. Bureau of Mines, 1965b, 1964 Minerals

yearbook, v. III: U. S. Bur. Mines, Dept. of Interior, Washington, D. C., 1152 p.

U. S. Bureau of Mines, 1941–1966, Minerals yearbooks for the years 1940–1965: U. S. Bur. Mines, Dept. of Interior, Washington, D. C.

41 The Oakley Project— A Controversy in Land Use

William C. Ackermann

This paper will recount and comment upon the proposed Oakley Dam, around which has developed a classic example of controversy in land use and widely divergent social values. The issues have created two polarized groups of advocates with a bewildered public in the middle.

I will first describe the general location and illustrate the lands that are in contention, then recount the actions of the principal parties to the controversy, interspersing some personal views of this interesting fight.

The broad setting for this drama is the Sangamon River, which flows for about 150 miles westward across the generally flat countryside of central Illinois to its mouth in the Illinois River.

Oakley Dam Site

The Oakley Dam site is in east-central Illinois and is proposed as a flood con-

Ackermann, W. C., 1971, "The Oakley Project—A Controversy in Land Use," in *Environmental Geology Notes Number 46*, Illinois State Geological Survey, arranged by R. E. Bergstrom, pp. 33–39. Reprinted by permission of the author and the Illinois State Geological Survey, Urbana, Illinois.

Dr. Ackermann is Chief, Illinois State Water Survey, Urbana, Illinois.

trol structure with added features for water supply and recreation.

Oakley Dam might have remained a relatively obscure engineering work but for its potential impact upon the Robert Allerton Park, which is located along the Sangamon at the headwaters of the proposed Oakley Reservoir. This park is highly prized by conservationists, and it is they who have organized and led opposition to the project.

Although the organized opposition has attacked every facet of the Oakley project, including its purposes and the upstream and downstream effects, their many and unrelenting forays have all been concerned with killing a project which it is feared will injure the park lands. Since that is the case, we should start by taking a look at Allerton Park.

Allerton Park Area

Allerton Park, located a few miles west of Monticello, is a magnificent estate that is owned by the University of Illinois. It was conveyed to the University in 1946 by the late Robert Allerton along with other farm lands, the income from which would assist in maintaining the property.

The property includes a stately mansion that the University now uses as a conference center. The building is surrounded by formal and informal gardens of great beauty.

Allerton Park contains about 1,500 acres of land, and one of the important points to keep in mind is that this tract is in part upland area on which the mansion, the gardens, and the statuary are located. No variation of reservoir proposals would directly affect this *developed* part of the park. The bottom land along the Sangamon River, an area of some 600 acres within the park, *is* directly involved with possible flooding from Oakley reservoir.

The bottom lands contain trees and underbrush of great variety. This bottom floods every year, usually for extended periods, and the existing flora and fauna have adapted to this regimen. It is this land that the conservationists believe to be a unique, natural area of great value as a link with our past and an irreplaceable resource for ecological research. Opposing interests have termed this bottom land a worthless tract, infested by snakes and mosquitoes.

I will not burden you with many statistics, but one of the numbers to bear in mind is the elevation of the floodplain here at the Allerton estate, which is about 630 feet above sea level.

Principal Parties in Oakley Controversy

Corps of Engineers

Having looked briefly at the area that principally gives rise to the controversy, we should now begin to introduce the parties to the action. I will start with the Corps of Engineers,

which proposes a dam downstream from the park. The basic purpose for this is flood control, to which have been added water supply and recreation, and, for a time, it also was intended to contain storage for low-flow dilution of treated wastes. The conservation pool, containing a reserve for sediment accumulation, was originally set at elevation 621, well below the level of the Allerton bottoms. Flood levels, however, would be deep over the bottom and extend well up on the second banks.

The Oakley project has a long history. It was first conceived in 1939 and was considered feasible for building by the Corps in 1947, but this original version of the project was defeated by farmers whose lands would be inundated or whose agricultural drainage would be affected.

The present project was authorized by Congress in 1962 as part of the Illinois River Basin plan and was to cost about 30 million dollars.

The authorized project accumulated a series of added features and changes, which at one point raised the conservation pool from 621 to 640, and this is what really activated the conservationists. I find it interesting to recount the changes which raised the proposed pool level. First, there was an addition of storage for water supply for the city of Decatur in the amount of 11,000 acre-feet. This is, of course, a perfectly legitimate action under federal law in which the city of Decatur agrees to pay its proportional share of the added cost. Second, an anlysis by the Public Health Service, also provided for in the law, found that conditions downstream from Decatur would result in zero dissolved oxygen in the water; so 48,000 acre-feet of reservoir storage was added for low-flow dilution of treated wastes.

Refined topographic maps of the reservoir area revealed less volume than was previously anticipated, so the pool was raised to maintain the equivalent storage. In line with changed federal policy, the economic life of the project was extended from 50 to 100 years, and this required doubling the anticipated sediment pool. The situation was aggravated by adoption of a higher assumed rate of sediment accumulation, so that with both increases the sediment pool grew from 4,500 to 12,000 acre-feet. The assumptions on economic life also resulted in increased storage to guarantee the water supply.

A revised estimate of the historic flood led to increasing flood storage from 132,500 to 168,700 acre-feet to control the flood of record. Finally, the Illinois Sanitary Water Board raised its stream water quality standards from 4 to 5 parts per million of dissolved oxygen, and this required still more storage for added dilution water.

Usually one can count upon changes being somewhat offsetting, but these were all in the direction of requiring a higher pool level. The cost of the project, including rising construction rates, escalated from 30 to 70 million dollars. All of these changes were doubtless a matter of embarrassment to the Corps and to those interested in having the project go forward. To the opponents it was sufficient basis for attacking the credibility of the Corps.

University of Illinois

We have spoken of Allerton Park and have briefly summarized a progression of events related to the proposed Oak-

ley Dam and its sponsor, the Corps of Engineers. We should also speak of the University of Illinois, which owns the park, and may be thought of as the second party in the dispute.

The Allerton estate was conveyed to the university to be used, maintained, preserved, operated, improved, and developed for educational and research purposes, as a forest, wild and plant life reserve, as an example of landscape gardening, and as a public park.

The university seems to have wished to avoid becoming involved as a party in a public controversy and has maintained a low profile. Originally the university reacted to the Oakley proposal by saying that it would not stand in the way of a broader public interest. Later, in 1968, it engaged the Harza consulting engineering firm to review the project. Their report recommended consideration of a series of alternatives, and this proved useful in bringing about reconsiderations by state, federal, and public interest groups through a widened array of possible compromises and solutions. Although the university, with major interests at stake, has maintained a low key, I am sure they take very seriously their public trust regarding the estate.

City of Decatur

A third party to the Oakley controversy is the city of Decatur, which has consistently been in strong support of the project. To enhance progress in the undertaking, that city has consistently agreed to proposed changes—whether they were for an enlarged or a reduced project.

Decatur is downstream from the proposed Oakley Dam and has an urgent

water supply problem. Its Lake Decatur is upstream from the city and
just downstream from Oakley. Lake
Decatur was created in 1923, was raised
in 1956, and is now about 35 percent
filled with sediment. Although Decatur
has other alternatives for augmenting
its water supplies, it has supported the
Oakley project, including added water
supply storage. I think that Decatur
welcomed the prospect of a major
recreational facility, which would be a
feature of a new lake, and the benefits
of area and regional development, as
well as the water supply feature. While
the controversy has raged, Decatur has
watched its water demand rise ever
closer to the shrinking capacity of its
existing reservoir.

Meanwhile the Corps received a
Congressional request to restudy the
Oakley project, and in March of 1969
issued a report that included 14 alternate solutions, which were presented in
public hearings. In this way the public and agencies were given an opportunity to consider choices. This is a
major departure from past procedures,
not only with the Corps, but other
agencies as well, when alternatives
were only considered internally and
one plan adopted and presented for
approval or rejection.

The alternatives studied by the Corps
were prompted by suggestions of the
Harza report and involved various com-
binations of measures, including a sub-
impoundment on a reservoir tributary
named Friend's Creek, which would
absorb a part of the main reservoir
storage and would also absorb much of
the pool fluctuation. They considered
levees through the Allerton bottom,
land exchange for research, alternative
ground-water supplies for Decatur,

water-shed treatment to reduce sediment, and advanced waste treatment at
Decatur to reduce or eliminate the need
for dilution water.

Division of Waterways of the
Illinois Department of Public Works
and Buildings

At this point we introduce the fourth
major party to the Oakley controversy,
which is the Division of Waterways of
the Illinois Department of Public Works
and Buildings. That agency had been
involved throughout the saga, but in
early 1970 they came forward with a
so-called "modified project," which was
effective in bringing together the principal parties and also substantially
represents the present version of the
project. This modified project set the
joint-use pool at elevation 623, which
you will recall is well below the flood-
plain level of about 630 at Allerton
Park. The modified project incorporated the Friend's Creek sub-impound-
ment and enlarged the water supply
storage. It proposed that the state take
over the responsibility of water supply
storage, giving Decatur a first option
on its use. Flood control storage was
reduced. A major innovation was the
treatment proposed for the 100 miles
of downstream channel. Only a portion of this would be protected from
flooding, with other land remaining in
a green belt subject to periodic flooding but with recreational value. Reservoir storage was provided so that the
downstream reach could be left as a
natural flowing stream instead of an
efficient but unnatural conveyance
channel. The State of Illinois, the university, and the city of Decatur all
signed an agreement supporting the

plan. The conservationists also seemed to agree, but when the plan was processed through the Corps and emerged with slight changes, the conservationists again erupted.

The Committee on Allerton Park

The fifth and final party to the Allerton controversy is the band of conservationists — ecologists-naturalists — who banded together in 1967 in "The Committee on Allerton Park." They have been extremely vocal and effective in representing the antidam point of view. One of the local newspapers was a powerful ally and maintained a steady barrage of one-sided and often inaccurate arguments. Other allies have been the conservation clubs and various high U. S. officials. For example, Justice Douglas was walked through the park, and Senator Proxmire of Wisconsin was quoted as having said, "The project is a pork barrel boondoggle of the most blatant kind." Other weapons were petitions, of which a third version is now being circulated. One of these petitions gathered 85,000 signatures.

The battle cry "Save Allerton Park" implies that the park would be destroyed, which even in the earlier, high-pool proposal was an exaggeration and is hardly true with respect to the current version. The dogma of the conservationists is that Allerton Park is a unique, natural preserve and an ecological link with the past. That the Allerton bottoms are a wild oasis in the nearly unbroken miles of flat Illinois corn land is a fact, but in my judgment the conservationists, who set themselves up as the scientific high priests of ecology, either deliberately or innocently are promoting a deception

or maintaining an illusion. The Allerton bottoms are not natural, virgin land or a living fossil of the past. The Sangamon River has a small channel for a drainage area of about 800 square miles, because 100 years ago, and for thousands of years before that, the upstream drainage area was largely swamp and marsh. This retained a great deal of runoff and released it slowly, so that a small channel was all that was required. Since about 1920 this land has been drained and is now among the most productive agricultural lands in the world, with most of the cultivated area in corn and soybeans. The effect on runoff has been dramatic. Floods are much greater, and the bottoms are covered with flood water every year—often for long periods. The sediment load from erosion is also great, and the river is using this sediment to attempt to achieve a new equilibrium with the changed watershed environment. With each flood a thin film of silt is deposited on the floodplain, while stream velocities are sufficient to keep the channel scoured. By this means, over some period of years which I have not calculated, the channel is being enlarged by the process of building up the adjacent floodplain. If left to its own devices, the river system will some day create a channel adequate to contain the increased annual floods that result from man's activities. In the meantime, however, and when viewed with some time perspective, the river and overbank are in a highly dynamic state. The vegetation which is there consists of species that can adapt to this harsh environment. But natural, in any historical sense, it is not.

Yet, the conservationists have a right to seek to protect this flooding bottom land, even if it is not what they say it is, and they have been dedicated and ingenious in their cause. When the plan was to build a high dam, which would indeed have permanently flooded the bottom, they emphasized the extent of flooding and implied that the entire park would be under water. They said it was an expensive catch basin for silt, and that the park would be a mudflat. They claimed that multipurpose reservoirs have been proved defective (which is contrary to widely held views), that the benefits of the project were exaggerated, that storage for low-flow dilution was to flush Decatur's raw sewage (which of course isn't true), and that Decatur has other alternative sources for water supply (which is true). They charged that the project is greatly changed from the one which Congress authorized in 1962 and therefore requires re-authorization, but that the Corps has circumvented this because the project will not survive the higher interest rates now being applied (which may be true).

Now that the Committee on Allerton Park has been largely successful in reducing the height of the dam and keeping the permanent pool out of the park, they are still fighting to kill the project, but with a new set of arguments. They say the lake will be too polluted for water-based recreation, that it will be shallow and warm with oozing, stinking mudflats, a tangled mass of water weeds, which will die and create a stench.

Summary

And so the controversy goes on. It has been a fascinating struggle to observe and yet a costly and frustrating way for society to work its will. One might regret the public's dependence upon an advocate system that gives rise to exaggerated and questionable arguments.

The Corps of Engineers has been made a villain for following its established procedures at a time when social values were changing faster than they could adapt to them. We might hope that out of this and similar other contests will come a system of weighing the environmental impacts as projects are being studied, and there is good reason to believe that this will be so in the near future.

As to the final fate of the Oakley project, one set of rumors has it that the Corps has quietly shelved the whole embarrassing business. Another rumor has it that the project has been cleared by the President's Offices of Management and Budget and Council on Environmental Quality. The newspapers say that if the project is in the President's budget, the Commitee on Allerton Park will go to court with a lawsuit against the Corps. The end is not yet in sight.

42   St. Francis Dam Failure of 1928

Thomas Clements

The failure of the St. Francis Dam near Saugus, California, in 1928, did more to focus public attention on the need for geologic advice in the location of dam sites than any other one event of the present century. Thus, in spite of the great loss of life and property that it entailed, it proved a blessing in one sense, and doubtless has brought about the saving of many lives since.

The St. Francis Dam site is located in San Francisquito Canyon about nine miles from the town of Saugus, and 45 miles northwesterly from Los Angeles. Construction on the dam started in April, 1924 and was completed on May 4, 1926. It was a solid, concrete, gravity type dam, arched on a radius of 500 feet to the upstream face. The height was 205 feet from the bottom of the maximum section to the crest of the spillway lip, and the main section was 700 feet long on the center of the curved crest. In addition a wing wall extended the westerly end 500 feet along the crest of a narrow ridge, and beyond a high point on this ridge a low concrete wall continued another 200 feet. The capacity of the reservoir formed by the dam was 38,000 acre-feet.

The rocks into which the easterly end of the dam was notched are schists

of probably Proterozoic age (Pelona Schist), with the planes of schistosity parallelling the canyon wall. Although recent and ancient landslide scars in the canyon indicated that the rock was unstable, the wing of the dam was carried up the natural inclined plane of the rock, without steps and with no cut-off wall.

The rocks forming the westerly abutment were red, land-laid sedimentary breccia (fanglomerate), sandstone, and siltstone of probable Oligocene age (Sespe Formation). These rocks formed rather bold ridges, suggesting that they were somewhat resistant to erosion under the semi-arid conditions that existed locally. However, when dropped into water the rocks disintegrated rapidly, a test that was not tried until after failure of the dam, although the results could be observed all along the shoreline on the westerly side of the lake at any time after water started accumulating.

The contact between these two entirely different rock types came under the main section of the dam about one-third of the way up the westerly side of the canyon from the bottom of the channel. The presence of approximately five feet of gouge, and of several feet of sheared and brecciated rock on both sides of the contact as well as drag folds that occur in the red beds at another outcrop, indicate that the contact is a fault. It was crossed not only by the excavation for the dam itself, but also by a work road on the westerly side of the canyon. Furthermore, the presence of a fault in the

Clements, T., 1966, "St. Francis Dam Failure of 1928," in *Engineering Geology in Southern California*, R. Lung and R. Proctor, eds., pp. 89–91 (without figures). Reprinted by permission of the author and the Association of Engineering Geologists, Arcadia, California.
Mr. Clements is a consulting geologist in Los Angeles, California.

canyon was shown on the Fault Map of California, published by the Seismological Society of America in 1922. Nevertheless, the fault nature of the contact either was not recognized or was ignored by the persons responsible for the location and construction of the dam. Needless to say, competent geological advice was not sought.

Storage of water behind the dam began on March 1, 1926, but did not begin to approach capacity until 1927. The water level reached three feet below the spillway in May of that year, but was maintained at that height for only 17 days, after which it was lowered to about 20 feet below the spillway. In the early part of 1928 the storage was gradually increased until the water level reached to about 0.25 foot below the spillway. This was on March 5, 1928, and the water surface remained at that level until March 12, when the dam failed.

The writer was a graduate student at the California Institute of Technology at the time of the failure of the dam, and for some time had been mapping the southeast portion of the old Tejon Quadrangle, in which the site is located. He had mapped a fault across a ridge and up San Francisquito Canyon, but when he found that it passed under the St. Francis dam he began to doubt his own competence, for he thought that surely no one would build a dam across so large and obvious a fault.

He was seeking further evidence in the canyon below the dam the day before it failed. It was raining and he decided not to camp that night at his favorite spot under a large cottonwood tree. Instead he drove around and went up Charley Canyon, the next canyon to the west, where the small Model T

got stuck in the mud. After finally extricating it, he gave up in disgust and returned to Los Angeles. That night the dam gave way.

Failure of the dam could have occurred from any one of three causes: (1) slipping of the schists on the easterly side of the canyon along the planes of schistosity; (2) slumping of the fanglomerate and associated rocks on the westerly side of the canyon as the result of their becoming soaked with water, or (3) seeping of water under pressure along the fault and the washing out of the gouge. When failure occurred, chunks of the westerly section were carried more than a mile down-stream, most of the easterly section collapsed almost in place, and the center section remained standing.

The evidence suggests that failure occurred as the result of seepage along the fault plane until finally the soft gouge was washed out. The stream of water pouring through quickly enlarged the opening by attack on the weak, water-soaked fanglomerate. The entire westerly abutment then gave way causing collapse of the westerly section of the dam, pieces of which were carried far down stream by the sudden rush of water.

As the water gushed from the now enlarged opening it swirled across the canyon and undercut the schist of the easterly abutment. With the removal of the support of the base the schist slid down into the canyon carrying the easterly section of the dam with it. Although later surveys seem to indicate that the central section of the dam was moved slightly, it remained standing.

The many inquiries that followed the disaster brought out no evidence that either the construction or the design of the dam was faulty. Although suggestions were made that the structure had been dynamited or that movement on the fault had caused the failure, these were discarded for lack of evidence. The consensus of opinion of all competent engineers and geologists was that the dam failed because of adverse geological conditions at the site which either were unrecognized or ignored. As a result, more than 500 persons lost their lives and more than $10,000,000 worth of damage was done to property.

References

Committee Report for the State, 1928, Causes leading to the failure of the St. Francis Dam: Calif. State Printing Office, Sacramento. (Excellent before and after photos).

Forbes, Hyde, 1928, Geological foundations at the St. Francis dam site: Eng. News-Record, vol. 100, p. 596–597.

Hill, L. C., H. W. Evans and F. H. Fowler, 1929, Essential facts concerning the failure of St. Francis Dam: Report of the ASCE Committee, Am. Soc. Civil Engrs. Trans., vol. 94.

Longwell, C. R., 1928, Lessons from the St. Francis Dam: Science, vol. 68.

Outland, C. F., 1963, Man-made Disaster, the story of St. Francis Dam (Western Land and Water Studies, Series No. 3) Glendale, Calif. A. H. Clark, 249 p. (Excellent discussion and bibliography; well illustrated).

Ransome, F. L., 1928, Geology of the St. Francis Dam site: Econ. Geol., vol. 23.

Supplementary Readings

Anderson, P. W. and McCall, J. E., 1968, Urbanization's Effect on Sediment Yield in New Jersey, *Jour. Soil and Water Conservation*, v. 23, pp. 142–44.

Bergstrom, R. E., 1968, Disposal of Waste: Scientific and Administrative Considerations, *Environ. Geol. Notes No. 20*, Ill. State Geol. Survey, Urbana, Ill., 12 pp.

Durfor, C. N. and Becker, E., 1964, Public Water Supplies of the 100 Largest Cities in the United States, 1962, *U. S. Geol. Survey Water-Supply Paper 1812*, 364 pp.

Flawn, P. T., 1965, Geology and Urban Development, *Baylor Univ. Geol. Studies, Bull. 8: 5–7.*

Hackett, J. E., 1968, Geologic Factors in Community Development at Illinois, *Ill. State Geol. Survey, Environ. Geol. Notes, No. 22*, 16 pp.

Harte, J. and Socolow, R. H., 1971, The Everglades: Wilderness versus Rampant Land Development in South Florida, in *Patient Earth* by J. Harte and R. H. Socolow, Holt, Rinehart, Winston, pp. 181–202.

Leopold, L. B., 1968, Hydrology for Urban Land Planning—A Guidebook on the Hydrologic Effects of Urban Land Use, *U. S. Geol. Survey Circ. 554*, 18 pp.

McGauhey, P. H., 1968, Earth's Tolerance for Wastes, *Texas Quarterly*, v. 11, n. 2., pp. 36–42.

McGuinness, C. L., 1969, Scientific or Rule-of-Thumb Techniques of Ground-Water Management—Which Will Prevail? *U. S. Geol. Survey Circ. 608*, 8 pp.

Piper, A. M., 1969, Disposal of Liquid Wastes by Injection Underground—Neither Myth nor Millennium, *U. S. Geol. Survey Circ. 631*, 15 pp.

Pluhowski, E. J., 1970 Urbanization and Its Effect on the Temperature of the Streams on Long Island, New York, *U. S. Geol. Survey Prof. Paper 627-D*, 110 pp.

Rickert, D. A. and Spieker, A. M., 1971, Real-Estate Lakes, *U. S. Geol. Survey Circ. 601-G*, 19 pp.

Seaburn, G. E., 1969, Effects of Urban Development on Direct Runoff to East Meadow Brook, Nassau County, Long Island, New York, *U. S. Geol. Survey Prof. Paper 627-B*, 14 pp.

Seaburn, G. E., 1970, Preliminary Results of

Hydrologic Studies at Two Recharge Basins on Long Island, New York, *U. S. Geol. Survey Prof. Paper 627-C*, 17 pp.

Smith, W. C., 1966, Geologic Factors in Dam and Reservoir Planning, *Ill. Geol. Survey, Env. Geol. Note 13*, 10 pp.

Spieker, A. M., 1970, Water in Urban Planning, Salt Creek Basin, Illinois, *U. S. Geol. Survey Water-Supply Paper 2002*, 147 pp.

Thomas, W. L. Jr., ed., 1956, *Man's Role in Changing the Face of the Earth*, Univ. Chicago Press, 1193 pp.

Thomas, H. E. and Schneider, W. J., 1970, Water as an Urban Resource and Nui-sance, *U. S. Geol. Survey Circ. 601-D*, 9 pp.

Walker, W., 1969, Illinois Ground Water Pollution, *Jour. Amer. Water Works Assoc.*, v. 61, pp. 31–40.

Wayne, W. J., 1969, Urban Geology—A Need and a Challenge, *Proceedings Indiana Academy of Science for 1968*, v. 78, pp. 49–64.

Williams, F. E., 1967, Urbanization and the Mineral Aggregate Industry, Tucson, Ariz. Area, *U. S. Bureau of Mines Information Circ. 8318*, U. S. Dept. Int. 23 pp.

Appendix A: Geologic Time Scale

RELATIVE GEOLOGIC TIME			*ATOMIC TIME
ERA	PERIOD	EPOCH	
Cenozoic	Quaternary	Holocene	
		Pleistocene	—2-3—
	Neogene	Pliocene	—12—
		Miocene	—26—
	Tertiary Paleogene	Oligocene	—37-38—
		Eocene	—53-54—
		Paleocene	—65—
Mesozoic	Cretaceous	Late Early	—136—
	Jurassic	Late Middle Early	—190-195—
	Triassic	Late Middle Early	—225—
Paleozoic	Permian	Late Early	—280—
	Carboniferous — Pennsylvanian	Late Middle Early	
	Carboniferous — Mississippian	Late Early	—345—
	Devonian	Late Middle Early	—395—
	Silurian	Late Middle Early	—430-440—
	Ordovician	Late Middle Early	—500—
	Cambrian	Late Middle Early	—570—
Precambrian			3,600 +

* Estimated ages of time boundaries (millions of years)
From *Geology* by W. C. Putnam, 2nd ed., revised by A. Bassett, Oxford University Press, 1971.

Appendix B:
Glossary

A A LAVA A lava flow characterized by a rough clinkery surface.

ABUTMENT A supporting structure.

ACCELOGRAPH An instrument for recording the acceleration in velocity of earthquake vibrations.

ADIT A tunnel or passage way by which a mine is entered.

AEROBIC CONDITION Characterized by presence of free oxygen.

AGGRADATION The general building up of the land by depositional processes.

ALLUVIAL (ALLUVIUM) Pertains to material deposited by moving water. The deposits may assume a fan shape where a mountain stream enters a flat plain (alluvial fan).

ANAEROBIC CONDITION Characterized by absence of air or free oxygen.

ANASTOMOSING Branching or interlacing with a braided appearance.

ANDESITIC BASALT A fine-grained extrusive igneous rock composed of plagioclase feldspars and ferromagnesian silicates.

ANTHRACITE COAL = "hard coal" A hard, black, lustrous coal containing a high percentage of fixed carbon and a low percentage of volatile matter.

AQUIFER A water bearing rock formation.

AQUITARD A rock formation which retards the flow of water.

ARTESIAN HEAD The level to which water from a well will rise when confined in a standing pipe.

ARTESIAN WELL A well in which water rises above the top of the aquifer. In some cases the well may flow without the aid of pumping.

AUGER MINING A method of extracting ore by boring horizontally into a seam much like a carpenter bores a hole in wood.

BASALT A fine-grained, extrusive, basic igneous rock.

BASALTIC SPATTER Agglutinated clots of primary magmatic ejecta which is erupted in a fluid or plastic condition. It may be produced by the frothing of erupting magma in lava fountains.

BENCH MARK A mark on a fixed object indicating a particular elevation.

BIOSPHERE Zone at and adjacent to the earth's surface including all living organisms.

BITUMINOUS Refers to a rock which yields bitumen or oil by thermal decomposition of the contained organic matter.

BITUMINOUS COAL = "soft coal" A coal which is high in carbonaceous matter and having between 15 per cent and 50 per cent volatile matter.

BOD (biochemical oxygen demand) The oxygen used in meeting the metabolic needs of aquatic aerobic microorganisms. A high BOD correlates with accelerated eutrophication.

BOMB, VOLCANIC Detached mass of lava or solid fragment ejected from a volcano. They range from 32 mm to several meters in length.

BOUGUER GRAVITY ANOMALY The gravity value after a correction has been made for the altitude of the station and the rock between the station and sea level.

BRACKISH WATER Water with a

salinity intermediate between that of fresh water and sea water.

BRECCIA   A rock made up of angular fragments. It may be produced by sedimentary, volcanic, or tectonic processes.

BREEDER REACTOR   A nuclear reactor capable of producing fissionable fuel as well as consuming it, especially one that creates more than it consumes.

BURNER REACTOR   See converter reactor.

CALDERA   A large semicircular volcanic depression commonly found at the summit of a volcano.

CANNEL SHALE   An oil shale that burns with a bright flame.

CARBONACEOUS SHALE   An organic-rich shale containing coaly material, graphitic material, or other carbonaceous matter that is presumed to be predominantly nonvolatile.

CINDER CONE   A conical structure composed of volcanic ash and cinders.

CIRCUM-PACIFIC BELT   A belt of modern earthquake and volcanic activity which includes the margins of the Pacific Ocean basin.

CLARKE   The average abundance of an element in the earth's crust.

CONTINENTAL SHELF   The gently sloping zone bordering a continent and extending from low tide to the depth where there is a marked increase in the slope of the ocean bottom. The greatest average depth is 600' (100 fathoms).

CONVERTER REACTOR   (1) A nuclear reactor that produces some fissionable material, but less than it consumes. (2) A reactor that produces a fissionable material different from the fuel burned, regardless of the ratio.

CREEP   (1) Gravitational creep is the slow downslope movement of soil or other surficial material. (2) Tectonic creep is slight, apparently continuous movement along a fault.

CREST-STAGE   Refers to the highest point of a flood.

CULM BANK   Refuse coal screenings often piled in heaps or banks.

CULVERT   A pipelike structure serving as a conduit for water.

CURIE POINT   The temperature below which a substance ceases to be paramagnetic.

DDT   (dichloro diphenyl trichloroethane)   An insecticide. One of several chlorinated hydrocarbons.

DEGRADATION   The general lowering of the land by erosional processes.

DEPLETION ALLOWANCE   A proportion of income derived from mineral production that is not subject to income tax.

DESALINATION   Any process capable of converting saline water to potable water.

DETRITAL   Relates to deposits formed of minerals and rock fragments transported to the place of deposition.

DIASTROPHISM   The process by which the earth's crust is deformed. Includes folding, faulting, warping, and mountain building.

DIP   The angle at which a rock surface departs from a horizontal plane.

DUNITE   An ultrabasic igneous rock

composed almost entirely of olivine.

EARTHQUAKE Natural vibrations or tremors which are generated by the rupturing of rocks.

EFFLUENT Anything that flows forth; a stream flowing out of another, a lava flow discharged from a volcanic fissure, discharge from sewage treatment facilities, etc.

EJECTA Solid material thrown out of a volcano. It includes volcanic ash, lapilli, and bombs.

ELASTIC DEFORMATION A nonpermanent deformation which returns to its original shape after the load is released. Elastic energy is released during return to original shape and this may produce tremors.

ELECTROLYTE A conducting medium involving the flow of current and movement of matter.

ELECTROLYTIC HYDROGEN Hydrogen derived from water through the application of high current electrodes.

EN ECHELON Offset but parallel structural features.

EPICENTER The point on the earth's surface directly above the point of origin of an earthquake.

EPITHERMAL Refers to those ore deposits formed from ascending hot solutions at shallow depths.

ESCARPMENT The steep face of a ridge.

EUSTATIC Refers to worldwide and simultaneous changes in sea level.

EUTROPHICATION A process whereby natural bodies of water rich in plant nutrients and organisms become deficient in oxygen.

EVAPORITE Chemically precipitated material resulting from evaporation of the solvent.

EVAPOTRANSPIRATION The sum of evaporation from wetted surfaces and of transpiration by vegetation.

FANGLOMERATE Alluvial fan deposits which have been cemented into solid rock.

FAULT SCARP A cliff formed by a fault. It is the topographic expression of vertical displacement within the crust of the earth.

FLOOD-PLAIN The area bordering a stream which becomes flooded when the stream overflows its channel.

FOCUS The point of origin of an earthquake.

FUMAROLE A hot spring or geyser which emits gaseous vapor.

GABBRO A coarse-grained, basic, intrusive igneous rock.

GEODETIC STATION A station which is used to record changes in the shape and dimensions of the earth.

GEODIMETER An electronic-optical instrument that measures distance on the basis of the velocity of light.

GNEISS A textural term which refers to coarse-grained, banded metamorphic rocks.

GOUGE A layer of soft material occurring along the wall of a fault.

GRABEN A down faulted block. May be bounded by upthrown blocks (horsts).

GROUND WATER Water located beneath the surface and within the zone of saturation.

GROUT A fine mortar for finishing surfaces.

HORST An up faulted block. May be bounded by downthrown blocks (grabens).

HYDROCARBON Organic compounds containing only carbon and hydrogen. Commonly found in petroleum, natural gas, and coal.

HYDROGENATION The decomposition of hydrocarbons at high temperatures and pressures with the addition of hydrogen to the molecules formed.

HYDROGENOLYSIS A chemical reaction in which hydrogen plays a role similar to that of water.

HYDROGRAPH A chart which records the changing level of water in a stream, reservoir, or well.

HYDROLOGIC Relates to the properties, occurrence, and movement of water.

HYDROLOGIC CYCLE The complete cycle of phenomena through which water passes from the atmosphere to the earth and back to the atmosphere.

HYDROSPHERE The aqueous portion of the earth. Includes the waters of the oceans, lakes, streams, ground water, and atmospheric water.

HYDROSTATIC PRESSURE Relates to pressures exerted by liquids.

HYPOCENTER (1) The region where an earthquake is initiated. (2) The point on the earth's surface directly below the center of a nuclear bomb explosion.

IMPERMEABLE Impervious to the natural movement of fluids.

INFRARED SENSING Detection of invisible radiation of greater wavelength than that of red light. Infrared rays can be detected by use of special film.

IONOSPHERE The uppermost ionized layer of the earth's atmosphere.

ISOSTACY A condition of balance or equilibrium in large areas of the earth's crust.

JUVENILE MAGMATIC MATERIAL Molten silicate material brought to the surface for the first time.

KINEMATIC PROCESSES Includes processes dealing with aspects of motion apart from considerations of mass and force.

LAPILLI Pea-sized volcanic ejecta. Accretionary lapilli experience a natural increase in size through the addition of extraneous material.

LASER INTERFEROMETER An instrument for measuring wavelengths of light and very small distances.

LAVA Molten material derived from a volcanic eruption or a rock which solidifies from such molten material.

LEACHATE The liquid material which has filtered through deposits of solid waste.

LEVELING The process of establishing the elevations of different points on the surface of the earth by use of the surveyor's level.

LITHOSPHERE The solid or rocky portion of the earth.

LITHOSTATIC PRESSURE Pressure

related to the weight of overlying rocks.

LOESS Refers to homogeneous deposits of silt deposited primarily by wind.

MAGMA A naturally occurring silicate melt.

MALTHUSIAN Refers to the doctrine of Malthus which states that population tends to increase at a faster rate than its means of subsistence.

MANTLE (1) The layer of the earth between the crust and the core. (2) Loose, unconsolidated surficial deposits overlying bedrock (=Regolith).

MARL A calcareous clay, silt, or fine-grained sand.

MASS MOVEMENT Movement of earth materials as a unit or *en masse*.

MERCALLI SCALE A scale of earthquake intensity ranging from I to XII. Based on observable effects at a given place (compare with Richter scale).

MUDFLOW A flowage of a mixture of rock, soil, and water.

NUCLEAR REACTOR A device in which a fission chain reaction can be initiated, maintained, and controlled.

OIL-SHALE Any part of an organic-rich shale deposit that yields at least 10 gallons (3.8 per cent) of oil per short ton of shale by conventional methods of destructive distillation is considered to be an oil shale.

OLIVENE A green, silicate mineral commonly found in basic or ultrabasic igneous rocks.

ORE A "mineral" deposit which can be mined at a profit. Includes metals, fossil fuels, and nonmetalliferous deposits.

ORGANIC-RICH SHALE A fine-textured sedimentary rock containing 5 per cent to 65 per cent indigenous organic matter.

OVERBURDEN (1) Material overlying an ore deposit (= spoil). (2) Unconsolidated materials overlying bedrock.

PAHOEHOE Lava flow characterized by a smooth, ropy surface.

PEAT Partly decayed plant matter found in bogs or swamps. May be used as a fuel or soil conditioner.

PEGMATITE Very coarse-grained igneous rocks usually found as dikes associated with a large mass of intrusive igneous rock. Some pegmatites may contain a variety of rare minerals.

PERMAFROST Permanently frozen ground.

PERMEABILITY The ability of a rock to transmit fluids. Effective porosity.

PESTICIDE Any chemical used for killing noxious organisms.

PHENOCRYST A large crystal set in a fine-grained matrix.

PHREATOMAGMATIC ERUPTION A sudden and violent volcanic eruption produced when ascending magma comes into contact with ground water or waters in a crater lake.

PIEZOMETRIC SURFACE The surface to which water from a given aquifer will rise under its full head.

POROSITY The percentage of void space in a rock.

PORPHYRITIC A textural term for igneous rocks which contain larger crystals (phenocrysts) set in a finer matrix. A copper porphyry would contain disseminated copper minerals in a large body of porphyritic rock.

PRORATION A legal restriction of oil production to some specified fraction of potential production.

PROTORE Low-grade mineral deposits which can be concentrated by natural surface processes to become ore.

PUMICE A light-colored volcanic froth which is cellular in texture.

QUICK CLAY Deposits of clay or soil which quickly change from a solid to a liquid state when suddenly jarred.

RESONANCE Amplification by reinforcing vibrations.

RICHTER SCALE A scale of earthquake magnitude based on the logarithm (base 10) of the amplitudes of the deflections created by earthquake waves and recorded by a seismograph. (See Mercalli scale.)

RIFT-VALLEY A graben or elongated valley formed by down faulting.

RIGHT-LATERAL MOVEMENT A fault with movement parallel to strike and right-handed separation. A reference point on the side opposite the observer appears to have moved toward the right of the observer.

ROCK FLOUR Finely ground rock fragments produced by glacial abrasion.

SAG POND Ponds formed by the uneven settling of the ground.

SANITARY LANDFILL A disposal area for solid wastes consisting of alternate layers of compacted refuse and soil.

SCARP A cliff or steep slope which may be produced by a fault in the earth's crust.

SCHIST A textural term referring to coarse-grained metamorphic rocks displaying a foliated structure.

SEICHE A periodic oscillation of a body of water.

SEISMIC ACTIVITY Pertains to earth vibrations or disturbances produced by earthquakes.

SEISMIC SEA WAVES See tsunami.

SEISMIC TREMORS Earth vibrations.

SEISMOGRAPH An instrument for recording earth vibrations (syn. seismometer).

SEPTIC TANK A tank receiving solid and liquid wastes. The wastes are temporarily retained and decomposed by anaerobic bacteria.

SERPENTINE A silicate mineral associated with metamorphic rocks.

SHEARING STRENGTH The internal resistance offered to tangential stress.

SINKHOLE A topographic depression developed by the solution of limestone, rock salt, or gypsum bedrock.

SORB—To take up and hold either by adsorption or absorption.

SPOIL See overburden.

STRAIN Changes in the geometry of a body which result from applied forces.

STRATIFICATION The structure produced by a series of sedimentary layers or beds (strata).

STRESS Forces that act to change the geometry of a body. Forces may be compressional, tensional, or tortional.

STRIKE The bearing or direction of the line of intersection of an inclined stratum and a horizontal plane.

STRIKE-SLIP FAULT A fault in which movement or slip is parallel to the strike of the fault.

SUBSIDENCE A sinking or settling of a large part of the earth's crust.

TAILINGS (1) Those portions of washed ore that are regarded as too poor to be treated further. (2) The sand, gravel, and cobbles which pass through the sluices in hydraulic mining.

TALUS DEBRIS Unconsolidated rock fragments which form a slope at the base of a steep surface.

TECTONIC Refers to deformation of the earth's crust through warping, folding, or faulting.

TECTONIC CREEP Slight, apparently continuous movement along a fault.

TENSILE STRENGTH A measure of the ability of materials to resist forces tending to pull them apart.

TERRACE Relatively flat, horizontal, or gently inclined surfaces which are bounded by steeper slopes. May be produced by stream or wave activity.

TILL Unstratified and unsorted sediments deposited by glacial ice.

TILTMETER An instrument used to detect changes in the slope of the ground surface. Measures horizontal displacement and can be used to indicate impending volcanic or earthquake activity.

TRANSFORM FAULT A fault displaying a change in structural style, e.g., strike-slip to ridgelike structures.

TSUNAMI A large ocean wave produced by earthquake activity. Also referred to as a tidal wave or seismic seawave.

VESICULAR A textural term indicating the presence of many small cavities in a rock.

VISCO-ELASTIC Materials exhibiting viscous and elastic properties.

WATER TABLE The surface marking the boundary between the zone of saturation and the zone of aeration. It approximates the surface topography.

WAVE LENGTH The horizontal distance between two similar points on two successive waves.

ZONE OF AERATION The zone in which the pore spaces in permeable materials are not filled (except temporarily) with water.